Leith's Cookery Course

Leith's Cookery Course

PRUDENCE LEITH
and
CAROLINE WALDEGRAVE

BOOK CLUB ASSOCIATES · LONDON

This edition published 1981 by
Book Club Associates
By arrangement with André Deutsch Ltd.
First published by André Deutsch 1980
Copyright © Leith's Farm Ltd 1979
Filmset in Monophoto Times by
Northumberland Press Ltd, Gateshead, Tyne and Wear
and printed in Great Britain by
Richard Clay (The Chaucer Press) Ltd, Bungay, Suffolk
Colour printing by Fakenham Press Limited,
Fakenham, Norfolk

ISBN 233 97153 X

This is a one-volume edited version
of the three-volume *Leith's Cookery Course*
published by Fontana Paperbacks

To Rayne and William

CONTENTS

ACKNOWLEDGEMENTS

We would like to thank, first and foremost, the staff and students of Leith's School of Food and Wine for testing, re-testing and perfecting the recipes, with special thanks to Sally Procter.

We also pay grateful tribute to most of the good cookery writers of today, especially to Rosemary Hume, Elizabeth David, Jane Grigson, Delia Smith, Katie Stewart, Robin Howe and Margaret Costa, whose recipes we have unashamedly pinched for use in the School, and used for inspiration and reference for this book.

For painstaking work in compiling the book, and for constant good temper, we would like to thank Polly Tyrer, Seemah Joshua, Margaret Cain and June Avis; and for recipe ideas and general helpfulness Jean Reynaud and Chef Max Markarian of Leith's Restaurant, and the staff of Leith's Good Food (Caterers).

In addition our thanks are due to Colin Cullimore, CBE, Managing Director of J. H. Dewhurst Ltd, for his help on the meat chapters, and to the White Fish Authority and the Herring Industry Board for helping on the fish chapters.

P.L.
C.W.

Note: Purists will complain about the hotch-potch of English and French culinary terms used in these books. We are unrepentant: French words are now so much part of the cook's vocabulary that they cannot be substituted. 'Sauté potatoes', for example, is precise and unambiguous. 'Fried potatoes' could mean chips, 'pommes sautées' could mean apples, and 'pommes de terre sautées' is too long and pompous. French words, we contend, are part of the international language of the kitchen.

P.L
C.W.

INTRODUCTION

Once the basic cooking methods have been mastered, advanced cookery is much like simple cookery: the techniques and ingredients are merely used in ever more interesting combinations. Someone who can make shortcrust pastry, custard, choux paste and caramel, and can whip cream, can also make that amazing pyramid of a French wedding cake, Gateau St Honoré. However, many keen enthusiasts, having realized this, start too soon to be 'creative', wrongly imagining that if one glass of sherry in a dish is good, four must be four times better; that if a recipe calls for a pinch of fresh thyme, two tablespoons of dried herbs must be an improvement.

My advice, especially to beginners, is to stick like a limpet to the recipe, and not hesitate to weigh and measure quantities. After a while you begin to tell by the look, texture or taste if the quantities are right; but I've been cooking all my grown-up life and I still weigh the beef to work out the roasting time, look up quantities for unfamiliar cakes, measure every ingredient for choux pastry.

When planning a menu, the rule is to keep it simple. If the main course needs last-minute work, choose a starter and pudding that can be done in advance. Try to balance the texture, colour and taste of the meal: avoid three white courses (vichyssoise, chicken with rice, and syllabub, for example); avoid cream or alcohol in all the courses; try to include something crisp and crunchy if the main part of the meal is soft and smooth. Serve vegetables that provide contrast in colour and texture – not cabbage with sprouts, for example.

The sight of food should make the mouth water, and induce feelings of positive greed and hunger. I think this is best achieved not by cutting radishes into roses or tomatoes into waterlilies, but by presenting food simply and freshly, with perhaps a sprig of

11

watercress to set off the colour, or surrounded by simple fried croutons, or dusted with finely chopped herbs.

This does not mean that food should ever be sloppily served, or presented in a way which suggests anything other than care and calm organization. The cherished vision of great chefs gripped with rage and hurling knives is a myth. By and large, knife-hurlers make bad chefs, and the qualities required to earn a reputation for culinary genius are more mundane: a quiet temperament, a logical mind, a love of order – and of food. Another pre-requisite is clear information and a set of interesting, reliable recipes that whet the appetite and challenge the cook to attempt new dishes. I hope that this is what *Leith's Cookery Course* provides.

P.L.

1
All about Cooking

CONVERSION TABLES

The tables below are approximate, and do not conform in all respects to the official conversions, but we have found them convenient for cooking.

WEIGHTS

Imperial	Metric
$\frac{1}{4}$oz	$7\frac{1}{2}$–8g
$\frac{1}{2}$oz	15g
$\frac{3}{4}$oz	20g
1oz	30g
2oz	55g
3oz	85g
4oz ($\frac{1}{4}$lb)	110g
5oz	140g
6oz	170g
7oz	200g
8oz ($\frac{1}{2}$lb)	225g
9oz	255g
10oz	285g
11oz	310g
12oz ($\frac{3}{4}$lb)	340g
13oz	370g
14oz	400g
15oz	425g
16oz (1lb)	450g

Imperial	Metric
1¼lb	560g
1½lb	675g
2lb	900g
3lb	1·35 kilos
4lb	1·8 kilos
5lb	2·3 kilos
6lb	2·7 kilos
7lb	3·2 kilos
8lb	3·6 kilos
9lb	4·0 kilos
10lb	4·5 kilos

LIQUID MEASURES

	ml	fl.oz
1¾ pints	1000 (1 litre)	35
1 pint	570	20
¾ pint	425	15
½ pint	290	10
⅓ pint	190	6·6
¼ pint (1 gill)	150	5
	56	2
2 scant tablespoons	28	1
1 teaspoon	5	

WINE QUANTITIES

	ml	fl.oz
Average wine bottle	730	25¾
1 glass wine	100	3½
1 glass port or sherry	70	2½
1 glass liqueur	45	1½

14

LENGTHS

Imperial	Metric
½in	1cm
1in	2½cm
2in	5cm
6in	15cm
12in	30cm

APPROXIMATE AMERICAN/EUROPEAN CONVERSIONS

Commodity	USA	Metric	Imperial
Flour	1 cup	140g	5oz
Caster and granulated sugar	1 cup	225g	8oz
Caster and granulated sugar	2 level tablespoons	30g	1oz
Brown sugar	1 cup	170g	6oz
Butter/margarine/lard	1 cup	225g	8oz
Sultanas/raisins	1 cup	200g	7oz
Currants	1 cup	140g	5oz
Ground almonds	1 cup	110g	4oz
Golden syrup	1 cup	340g	12oz
Uncooked rice	1 cup	200g	7oz

Note: In American recipes, when quantities are stated as spoons, 'level' spoons are meant. English recipes (and those in this book) call for rounded spoons except where stated otherwise. This means that 2 American tablespoons equal 1 English tablespoon.

USEFUL MEASUREMENTS

1 American cup	225ml/8 fl.oz
1 egg	56ml/2 fl.oz
1 egg white	28ml/1 fl.oz
1 rounded tablespoon flour	30g/1oz
1 rounded tablespoon cornflour	30g/1oz
1 rounded tablespoon sugar	30g/1oz
2 rounded tablespoons breadcrumbs	30g/1oz
2 level teaspoons gelatine	8g/$\frac{1}{4}$oz

30g/1oz granular (packet) aspic sets 570ml (1 pint) liquid. 15g/$\frac{1}{2}$oz powdered gelatine, or 4 leaves, will set 570ml (1 pint) liquid. (However, in hot weather, or if the liquid is very acid, like lemon juice, or if the jelly contains solid pieces of fruit or meat and is to be turned out of the dish or mould, 20g/$\frac{3}{4}$oz should be used.)

OVEN TEMPERATURES

C	F	Gas mark
70	150	$\frac{1}{4}$
80	175	$\frac{1}{4}$
100	200	$\frac{1}{2}$
110	225	$\frac{1}{2}$
130	250	1
140	275	1
150	300	2
170	325	3
180	350	4
190	375	5
200	400	6
220	425	7
230	450	8
240	475	8
250	500	9
270	525	9
290	550	9

GLOSSARY OF COOKING TERMS

Abats: French for offal (hearts, livers, brains, tripe etc.). Americans call them 'variety meats'.

Bain-marie: A baking tin half-filled with hot water in which terrines, custards etc. stand while cooking. The food is protected from direct fierce heat and cooks in a gentle, steamy atmosphere. Also a large container which will hold a number of pans standing in hot water, used to keep soups, sauces etc. hot without further cooking.

Bard: To tie bacon or pork fat over a joint of meat, game bird or poultry, to be roasted. This helps to prevent the flesh from drying out.

Baste: To spoon over liquid (sometimes stock, sometimes fat) during cooking to prevent drying out.

Beignets: Fritters.

Beurre manié: Butter and flour in equal quantities worked together to a soft paste, and used as a liaison or thickening for liquids. Small pieces are whisked into boiling liquid. As the butter melts it disperses the flour evenly through the liquid, so thickening it without causing lumps.

Beurre noisette: Browned butter – see *Noisette* (a).

Bisque: Shellfish soup, smooth and thickened.

Blanch: Originally, to whiten by boiling, e.g. briefly to boil sweet-breads or brains to remove traces of blood, or to boil almonds to make the brown skin easy to remove, leaving the nuts white. Now commonly used to mean parboiling (as in blanching vegetables when they are parboiled prior to freezing, or pre-cooked so that they have only to be reheated before serving).

17

Bouchées: Small puff pastry cases like miniature vol-au-vents.

Bouillon: Broth or uncleared stock.

Bouquet garni: Parsley stalks, small bay leaf, fresh thyme, celery stalk, sometimes with a blade of mace, tied together with string and used to flavour stews etc. Removed before serving.

Braise: To bake or stew slowly on a bed of vegetables in a covered pan.

Canapé: A small bread or biscuit base, sometimes fried, spread or covered with savoury paste, egg etc., used for cocktail titbits or as an accompaniment to meat dishes. Sometimes used to denote the base only, as in *champignons sur canapé.*

Caramel: Sugar cooked to a toffee.

Chateaubriand: Roast fillet steak, for two people or more.

Clarified butter: Butter that has been separated from milk particles and other impurities which cause it to look cloudy when melted, and to burn easily when heated. It is usually clarified by first heating until foaming, then skimming; or (which is easier) straining through a double thickness of muslin, a coffee filter paper, or 2 J-cloths.

Court bouillon: Liquid used for cooking fish (see page 306).

Crêpes: Thin French pancakes.

Croquettes: Paste of mashed potato and possibly poultry, fish or meat, formed into small balls or patties, coated in egg and bread-crumbs and deep fried.

Croûte: Literally crust. Sometimes a pastry case, as in fillet of beef *en croûte,* sometimes toasted or fried bread, as in Scotch woodcock or scrambled eggs on toast.

Croutons: Small evenly sized cubes of fried bread used as a soup garnish, and occasionally in other dishes.

Dariole: Small castle-shaped mould used for moulding rice salads and sometimes for cooking cake mixtures.

Déglacer: To loosen and liquefy the fat, sediment and browned juices stuck at the bottom of a frying pan or saucepan by adding liquid (usually stock, water or wine) and stirring while boiling.

Deglaze: See *Déglacer.*

Dégorger: To extract the juices from meat, fish or vegetables, generally by salting then soaking or washing. Usually done to remove indigestible or strong-tasting juices.

Dépouiller: To skim off the scum from a sauce or stock: a splash of cold stock is added to the boiling liquid. This helps to bring scum and fat to the surface, which can then be more easily skimmed.

Dropping consistency: The consistency where a mixture will drop reluctantly from a spoon, neither pouring off nor obstinately adhering.

Duxelle: Finely chopped raw mushrooms, sometimes with chopped shallots or chopped ham, often used as a stuffing.

Eggwash: Beaten raw egg, sometimes with salt, used for glazing pastry to give it a shine when baked.

Entrecôte: Sirloin steak.

Entrée: Traditionally a dish served before the main course, but usually served as a main course today.

Entremets: Dessert or sweet course, excluding pastry sweets.

Escalope: A thin slice of meat, sometimes beaten out flat to make it thinner and larger.

Farce: Stuffing.

Fécule: Farinaceous thickening, usually arrowroot or cornflour.

Flamber: To set alcohol alight. Usually to burn off the alcohol, but frequently simply for dramatic effect. (Past tense flambé or flambée.) English: to flame.

Flame: See *Flamber.*

Fleurons: Crescents of puff pastry, generally used to garnish fish or poultry.

19

Fold: To mix with a gentle lifting motion, rather than to stir vigorously. The aim is to avoid beating out air while mixing.

Frappé: Iced, or set in a bed of crushed ice.

Fricassé: White stew made with cooked or raw poultry, meat or rabbit and a velouté sauce, sometimes thickened with cream and egg yolks.

Fumet: Strong flavoured liquor used for flavouring sauces. Usually the liquid in which fish has been poached, or the liquid that has run from fish during baking. Sometimes used of meat or truffle-flavoured liquors.

Glace de viande: Reduced brown stock, very strong in flavour, used for adding body and colour to sauces.

Glaze: To cover with a thin layer of shiny jellied meat juices (for roast turkey), melted jam (for fruit flans) or syrup (for rum baba).

God's gravy: Jus de viande or roasting juices, unthickened, served as sauce.

Gratiner: To brown under a grill after the surface of the dish has been sprinkled with breadcrumbs and butter and, sometimes, cheese. Dishes finished like this are sometimes called *gratinée* or *au gratin.*

Hard ball: Term used in sugar boiling. As *soft ball* (see below), but further heated and reduced until the sugar forms hard balls.

Hors d'oeuvre: Usually simply means the first course. Sometimes used to denote a variety or selection of many savoury titbits served with drinks, or as a mixed first course (*hors d'oeuvres variés*).

Infuse: To steep or heat gently to extract flavour, as when infusing milk with onion slices.

Julienne: Vegetables or citrus rind cut in thin matchstick shapes or very fine shreds.

Jus or jus de viande: God's gravy, i.e. juices that occur naturally in cooking, not a made-up sauce. Also juice.

Jus lié: Thickened gravy.

Knock down or *knock back:* To punch or knead out the air in risen dough so that it resumes its pre-risen bulk.

Knock up: To separate slightly the layers of raw puff pastry with the blade of a knife to facilitate rising during cooking.

Lard: To thread strips of bacon fat (or sometimes anchovy) through meat to give it flavour, and in the case of fat, to make up any deficiency in very lean meat.

Lardons: Small strips or cubes of pork fat or bacon generally used as a garnish.

Leavening or *leavening agent:* Ingredient used to make mixtures rise during cooking, e.g. yeast, baking powder, whisked egg whites.

Liaison: Ingredients for binding together and thickening sauce, soup or other liquid, e.g. roux, beurre manié, egg yolk and cream, blood.

Macedoine: Small diced mixed vegetables, usually containing some root vegetables. Sometimes used of fruit meaning a fruit salad.

Macerate: To soak food in a syrup or liquid to allow flavours to mix.

Mandolin: Frame of metal or wood with adjustable blades set in it for finely slicing cucumbers, potatoes etc.

Marinade (verb): To soak meat, fish or vegetables before cooking in acidulated liquid containing flavourings and herbs. This gives flavour and tenderizes the meat.

Marinade (noun): The liquid described above. Usually contains oil, onion, bay leaf and vinegar or wine.

Marmite: French word for a covered earthenware soup container in which the soup is both cooked and served.

Médallions: Small rounds of meat, evenly cut. Also small round biscuits. Occasionally used of vegetables if cut in flat round discs.

21

Mirepoix: The bed of braising vegetables described under Braise.

Moule-à-manqué: French cake tin with sloping sides. The resulting cake has a wider base than top, and is about 3cm/1½in high.

Napper: To coat, mask or cover, e.g. éclairs *nappées* with hot chocolate sauce.

Needleshreds: Fine, evenly cut shreds of citrus rind (French *julienne*) generally used as a garnish.

Noisette (a): Literally 'nut'. Usually means nut-brown as in beurre noisette, i.e. butter browned over heat to a nut colour. Also hazelnut.

Noisette (b): Boneless rack of lamb rolled and tied, cut into neat rounds.

Panade or *Panada:* Very thick mixture used as a base for soufflés or fish cakes etc., usually made from milk and flour.

Papillote: A wrapping of paper in which fish or meat is cooked to contain the aroma and flavour. The dish is brought to the table still wrapped up. Foil is sometimes used, but as it does not puff up dramatically, it is less satisfactory.

Parboil: To half-boil or partially soften by boiling.

Parisienne (usually *pommes Parisiennes*): Potato (sometimes with other ingredients) scooped into small balls with a melon baller and, usually, fried.

Pass: To strain or push through a sieve.

Pâte: The basic mixture or paste, often used of uncooked pastry, dough, uncooked meringue etc.

Pâté: A savoury paste or liver, pork, game etc.

Pâtisserie: Sweet cakes and pastries. Or cake shop.

Paupiette: Beef (or pork or veal) olive, i.e. a thin layer of meat, spread with a soft farce, rolled up, tied with string and cooked slowly.

Poussin: Baby chicken.

Praline: Almonds cooked in sugar until the mixture caramelizes, cooled and crushed to a powder. Used for flavouring desserts and ice cream.

Prove: To put dough or yeasted mixture to rise before baking.

Purée: Liquidized, sieved or finely mashed fruit or vegetables.

Quenelles: A fine minced fish or meat mixture formed into small portions and poached. Served in a sauce, or as a garnish to other dishes.

Ragout: A stew.

Rechauffée: A reheated dish made with previously cooked food.

Reduce: To reduce the amount of liquid by rapid boiling, causing evaporation and a consequent strengthening of flavour in the remaining liquid.

Refresh: To hold boiled green vegetables under a cold tap, or to dunk them immediately in cold water to prevent their further cooking in their own steam, and to set the colour.

Relax or *rest:* Of pastry: to set aside in a cool place to allow the gluten (which will have expanded during rolling) to contract. This lessens the danger of shrinking in the oven.
Of batters: to set aside to allow the starch cells to swell, giving a lighter result when cooked.

Render: To melt solid fat (e.g. beef, pork) slowly in oven.

Roux: A basic liaison or thickening for a sauce or soup. Melted butter to which flour has been added.

Rouille: Garlic and oil emulsion used as flavouring.

Salamander: A hot oven or grill used for browning or glazing the tops of cooked dishes, or a hot iron or poker for branding the top with lines or a criss-cross pattern.

Salmis: A game stew sometimes made with cooked game, or partially roasted game.

Sauter: Method of frying in a deep-frying pan or sautoir. The food is continually tossed or shaken so that it browns quickly and evenly.

23

Sautoir: Deep-frying pan with a lid used for recipes that require fast frying and then slower cooking (with the lid on).

Scald: Of milk: to heat until on the point of boiling, when some movement can be seen at the edges of the pan but there is no over-all bubbling.
Of muslin, cloths etc.: to dunk in clean boiling water, generally to sterilize.

Seal or *seize:* To brown meat rapidly (usually in fat), forming a dryish skin to trap juices inside.

To season: Of food: to flavour, generally with salt and pepper.
Of iron frying pans, girdles etc.: to prepare new equipment for use by placing over high heat, generally coated with oil and sprinkled with salt. This prevents subsequent rusting and sticking.

Slake: To mix flour, arrowroot, cornflour or custard powder to a thin paste with a small quantity of cold water.

Soft Ball: The term used to describe sugar syrup reduced by boiling to sufficient thickness to form soft balls when dropped into cold water and rubbed between finger and thumb.

Suprême: Choice piece of poultry (usually from the breast).

Sweat: To cook gently (usually in butter or oil, but sometimes in the food's own juices) without frying or browning.

Tammy: A fine muslin cloth through which sauces are sometimes forced. After this treatment they look beautifully smooth and shiny. Tammy cloths have recently been replaced by blenders or liquidizers which give much the same effect.

Tammy strainer: A fine mesh strainer, conical in shape, used to produce the effect described under *Tammy*.

To the thread: Of sugar boiling. Term used to denote degree of thickness achieved when reducing syrup, i.e. the syrup will form threads if tested between finger and thumb. Short thread: about 1cm/½in; long thread: 5cm/2in or more.

Timbale: A dish which has been cooked in a castle-shaped mould, or a dish served piled up high.

Tournedos: Fillet steak. Usually refers to a one-portion piece of grilled fillet.

To turn vegetables: To shape carrots or turnips to a small olive shape. To cut mushrooms into a decorative spiral pattern.

To turn olives: To remove the olive stone with a spiral cutting movement.

Velouté: See under Sauces, pages 63 and 312.

Vol-au-vent: A large pastry case made from puff pastry with high raised sides and a deep hollow centre into which is put chicken, fish etc.

Well: A hollow or dip made in a pile or bowlful of flour, exposing the table top or bottom of the bowl, into which other ingredients are placed prior to mixing.

Zest: The thin coloured skin of an orange or lemon, used to give flavour. It is very thinly pared without any of the bitter white pith.

CLASSIC GARNISHES

Anglaise: Braised vegetables such as carrots, turnips and quartered celery hearts (used to garnish boiled salted beef).

Aurore: A flame-coloured sauce obtained by adding fresh tomato purée to a bechamel sauce; used for eggs, vegetables and fish. Means 'dawn'.

Bolognaise: A rich sauce made from chicken livers or minced beef flavoured with mushrooms and tomatoes. Usually served with pasta.

Bonne femme: To cook in a simple way. Usually, of chicken, sautéed and served with white wine gravy, bacon cubes, button onions and garnished with croquette potatoes. Of soup, simple purée of vegetables with stock. Of fish, white wine sauce, usually with mushrooms; and served with buttered mashed potatoes.

Boulangère: Potatoes and onions sliced and cooked in the oven in stock. Often served with mutton.

Bouquetière: Groups of very small carrots, turnips, French beans, cauliflower florets, button onions, asparagus tips etc. Sometimes served with a thin demi-glaçe or gravy. Usually accompanies beef or lamb entrées.

Bourgeoise: Fried diced bacon, glazed carrots and button onions. Sometimes red wine is used in the sauce. Used for beef and liver dishes.

Bourguignonne: Button mushrooms and small onions in a sauce made with red wine (Burgundy). Used for beef and egg dishes.

Bretonne: Haricot beans whole or in a purée. Sometimes a purée of root vegetables. Usually served with a gigot (leg) of lamb.

Chasseur: Sautéed mushrooms added to a sauté of chicken or veal.

Clamart: Garnish of artichoke hearts filled with buttered petits pois. Sometimes a purée of peas, or simply buttered peas.

Doria: A garnish of cucumber, usually fried in butter.

DuBarry: Denotes the use of cauliflower: potage DuBarry is cauliflower soup. Also, cooked cauliflower florets masked with Mornay sauce and browned under the grill, used for meat entrées.

Flamande: Red cabbage and glazed small onions used with pork and beef.

Florentine: Spinach in purée, or leaf spinach. Also a sixteenth-century name for a pie.

Indienne: Flavoured with curry.

Joinville: Slices of truffle, crayfish tails and mushrooms with a lobster sauce, used for fish dishes.

Lyonnaise: Denotes the use of onions as garnish – the onions are frequently sliced and fried.

Meunière: Of fish, lightly dusted with flour, then fried and served with beurre noisette and lemon juice; also frequently (but not classically) chopped parsley.

Milanese: With a tomato sauce, sometimes including shredded ham, tongue and mushrooms. Frequently served with pasta.

Minute: Food quickly cooked, either fried or grilled. Usually applied to a thin entrecôte steak.

Mornay: With a cheese sauce.

Nantua: With a lobster sauce.

Napolitana: A tomato sauce and Parmesan cheese (for pasta). May also mean a three-coloured ice cream.

Nicoise: Name given to many dishes consisting of ingredients common in the South of France, e.g. tomatoes, olives, garlic, fish, olive oil.

Normande: Garnish of mussels, shrimps, oysters and mushrooms. Or creamy sauce containing cider or calvados, and sometimes apples.

Parmentier: Denotes the use of potato as a base or garnish.

Paysanne: Literally, peasant. Usually denotes the use of carrots and turnips sliced across in rounds.

Portuguaise: Denotes the use of tomatoes or tomato purée.

Princesse: Denotes the use of asparagus (usually on breast of chicken).

Printanière: Early spring vegetables cooked and used as a garnish, usually in separate groups.

Provençale: Denotes the use of garlic, and sometimes tomatoes and/or olives.

St Germain: Denotes the use of peas, sometimes with pommes Parisienne. Also the name of a cream of pea soup.

Soubise: Onion purée, frequently mixed with a béchamel sauce.

Vichy: Garnish of small glazed carrots.

TRADITIONAL BRITISH
ACCOMPANIMENTS

Roast lamb: Mint sauce or redcurrant jelly, onion sauce or gravy.

Roast beef: Horseradish, very thin gravy, Yorkshire pudding, mustard.

Roast chicken: Bacon rolls, sausages, bread sauce, gravy.

Roast turkey: Cranberry sauce, bread sauce, sausages, bacon, stuffings, gravy, sprouts or chestnuts.

Ham: Cumberland sauce or parsley sauce, mustard.

Game: Game chips, fried breadcrumbs, bread sauce, redcurrant jelly, unthickened 'God's gravy'.

Roast pork and goose: Apple sauce or gooseberry sauce, gravy.

METHODS OF COOKING

The tougher the food, or the larger its volume, the slower it must be cooked.

The quick methods of cooking – frying, deep frying (the quickest) and grilling – are suitable therefore for small pieces of tender meat, whereas the slower methods – braising, stewing etc. – are best for tough ones.

GRILLING

Brushing the grilling meat with butter or oil is done for two reasons – to stop it sticking to the pan or grill and to give flavour. The speed with which the food is cooked is the essential factor in keeping it moist. An outside cooked surface is quickly formed, which prevents the juices inside the meat running out. If the grill is not hot enough, the outer seal will not be formed and the inner juices will escape, giving a dried-up result. With practice it is possible to tell by pressure of the fingers if the food is cooked, but if you don't trust your 'feel' you will have to cut one piece open and look.

Heat

The grill must be really hot. Always pre-heat the grill well in advance.

Preparation of the food

The meat or fish should be brushed with oil or butter and seasoned with pepper. Never season foods for grilling with salt as this draws out the juices and renders the meat dry and tough.

Distance from the heat

The grill pan should be held at about 7·5cm/3in from the grill itself so that the meat can be 'sealed' immediately. The pan can be lowered for any further cooking that may be necessary. Thick pieces of meat are cooked further away from the heat for longer. Thin pieces are cooked close to the heat, faster.

Turning the food over

This should be done with a pair of tongs or with two spoons but not with a fork, which would pierce the meat and allow the juices to run out.

Serving

Grilled foods should be served at once. They dry out and toughen if kept hot.

FRYING

(*a*) SHALLOW FRYING

The principle of shallow frying is similar to that of grilling (see above). The essential difference is that whereas in grilling the fat drops off the meat, in frying it stays in the pan and can sometimes be served with the dish. Fat used for shallow frying should never be more than half the depth of the food.

1. Never add too many pieces of food to a frying pan at once as this reduces the temperature of the fat and the food will stew rather than fry.
2. Always fry first the side of the chop, steak, fish etc. which is to be uppermost; being fried in clean fat generally makes it look better.

(*b*) DEEP FRYING

Most foods to be deep fried are given a protective coating of beaten egg, or a batter or egg and breadcrumbs. This is done for five reasons:

1. The frying fat is at an extremely high temperature (about 185 C/360 F), which would burn the outside of some foods before the middle was cooked. The insulating coating allows the food inside to cook evenly.

   Some foods, such as potato crisps, do not need any coating because they are in and out of the hot fat too fast to burn. All they have to do is brown and then they are done. Other unprotected foods (such as the larger potato chips) are generally given a first frying at a non-burning lower temperature to ensure that the insides are cooked before the foods are browned in the very hot fat.

2. The heat of the fat would make uncooked moist food (like fish fillets or pineapple rings) splutter and splash dangerously, and the hot fat would bubble over the edge of the pan, possibly causing a fire.
3. As the fat is to be used again it must be prevented from absorbing the taste and smell of foods, especially of fish. The neutral egg batter or egg and crumb layer in contact with the fat is tasteless and odourless.
4. Many foods, such as cheese or cooking apple, become liquid on being cooked. The crisp batter then becomes a container for the runny inside.
5. The crisp coating provides a pleasing contrast with the moist food inside, which is the chief attraction of deep-fried food.

After use the fat should be cooled, then strained through muslin to remove food particles. When it has become at all dark it should be replaced, rather than topped up.

Fats suitable for deep frying are almost-tasteless vegetable oils and lard as these can be heated without burning to the required 170–185 C/330–360 F. The lower temperature (which will produce a gentle fizzing if a piece of bread is dropped in) is suitable for the first frying of potato chips and for deep-fried choux pastry dishes such as beignets soufflés.

The higher temperature (when tested with a piece of bread the fat will fizz vigorously and the bread will begin to brown) is suitable for rissoles, croquettes, fruit fritters and the second frying of potatoes.

Deep-frying technique

When cooking a large amount of food in a fryer, fry only a small amount at a time – little enough not to lower the temperature of the fat significantly. If the fat has cooled too much, the batter or outer layer of the food will not instantly form an impervious crisp crust, but will become soggy and allow the fat to enter the food, producing a greasy unattractive dish. Once the food is cooked, lift it immediately out of the fat and drain it on absorbent paper. Crumpled brown paper, kitchen paper, or even dry-inked newspaper will do.

If you cannot serve the food immediately (which would be best) do not cover it with a lid. If you do, steam trapped inside will make the food soggy. Spread the cooked food in one layer only (if piled up the bottom pieces will become soggy) on a hot dish and put it in the warm oven, with the door ajar to allow free circulation of air.

Add a sprinkling of salt to the food (if savoury) or caster sugar (if sweet) just before serving.

Safety precautions when deep frying

Because of the great heat of the liquid fat the deep fryer is potentially the most dangerous object in the kitchen. The following points should be observed for safety's sake:

1. The fat or oil should not be too deep. When a basket of food is lowered into hot fat it will bubble up briefly, and if it should spill over (especially on to a naked gas flame beneath) fire could result.

2. Make sure that food is properly coated in batter or egg and breadcrumbs, or is really dry. Dry off potato chips in a tea-towel before frying. Wet food causes the fat to splash and splutter.

3. If the fat rises up dangerously, remove the food immediately and cool the fat slightly (or remove some of the food from the basket) before trying again.

4. Never go away and leave a heating fryer. Deep fat or oil does not boil; it simply explodes into flame. But if you are in the room, before it reaches that stage you will have seen and smelt it smoking.

5. Never attempt to move over-hot or burning fat. The danger is that you will spill it on your arm, or on to the flame beneath. Just turn off the source of heat and leave it where it is. Have the lid of the pan close at hand so that if the fat does catch fire, you can quench the flames calmly by shutting off their oxygen supply with the lid. Failing that, drop a thick woollen (not nylon) blanket or coat over the whole burning pot. Better a singed blanket than a burnt kitchen!

6. If the fat is obviously too hot, but not on fire, it will cool without danger if you turn off its source of heat. The cooling process can be hurried by putting a raw potato (dry) or a

large piece of bread into the fat. This will cool the fat as it browns.

BROILING

Broiling is an American word usually used to mean grilling, but sometimes roasting.

ROASTING

Roasting is the most satisfactory way of cooking large pieces of fairly tender, or very tender, meat. The extremely fast frying, grilling or deep frying would char the outside while the middle is still raw. However the same principles apply, i.e. the meat is first 'sealed' (the outer surface is cooked very fast either in a frying pan or in a very hot oven) so that the juices of the meat are locked in. The temperature is then lowered (or the meat is put into a cooler oven) until the required degree of roasting has been reached. With a small piece of meat it is not necessary to lower the oven temperature as the cooking time will be short, so the outside cannot over-cook.

The roasting meat is generally basted during cooking. Melted fat (perhaps butter) and/or juices or stock are regularly ladled over the roasting meat. This is done to add flavour and to keep the outer skin from drying to a very hard and inedible layer.

When meat was roasted on a turning spit the dripping fat was caught in a tray beneath the turning meat, and spooned back over the top of it. Spit roasting is considered better than oven roasting simply because as the meat turns, the fat runs automatically over the surface, even without the help of the additional basting. With oven roasting, the top of the meat is bound to be dryer than the bottom as the juices run down both inside and outside the meat. For this reason it is a good idea to start roasting a turkey or chicken upside down in the roasting pan to enable some of the juices to run into the breast, before turning it right side up to brown.

Roasting in a bag, in foil, or in a clay brick pot, are all attempts

33

to keep the meat moist. They share the disadvantage that, because the meat is cooked in a closed steamy atmosphere, they do not have a crisp brown skin. But the oven is kept clean.

BAKING

Baking differs from modern roasting only in that with roasting, fat is generally basted over the food whereas baked food is left undisturbed. But they both entail putting food into a hot closed oven to cook. Baking, because of the perfectly controlled, all-over even heat, is most suitable for cakes and breads, where exact temperatures are vital. It is also an excellent method for the slow cooking of tough meats, which are usually baked in a closed container and therefore in a moist and steamy atmosphere. For breads, cakes etc. see pages 37–54.

STEAMING

There are two principal methods of steaming: for quickly cooked foods, such as fish, chicken or vegetables, the food is placed in the top of a two-tier steamer and cooked in the direct steam from the boiling water below. This method is frequently used for invalid cookery as no fat or sauce needs to be added to the food, and fatless food is easy to digest. It is a good method of cooking floury potatoes which might break up if boiled. Care should be taken not to overcook food as it may become tasteless with prolonged steaming. The steaming water should be saved for stock. If a two-tier steamer is not available one can be improvised by placing the food in a metal strainer (perhaps loosely lined with foil), and suspending this in a saucepan over boiling water. It may, however, be necessary to cover the saucepan and its lid with a layer of foil to prevent the steam from escaping under the lid which now will not fit properly on account of the strainer.

Foods that require prolonged gentle cooking, such as suet puddings and meat puddings, are steamed but the food itself does not come in contact with the moist steam. The pudding basin containing the food is placed in a large saucepan of boiling water, the water coming to within 5cm/2in of the rim of the pudding basin. The pudding must be carefully wrapped to prevent water getting into it and making it soggy. It is generally covered with a double layer of greaseproof paper which has a folded pleat down the centre, and tied firmly with string. The pleat is to allow the food inside to expand during cooking (even a Christmas pudding will rise slightly) without bursting through its coverings. The whole is then wrapped in foil. A folded cloth or double strip of foil laid under the basin but projecting up the sides of the saucepan will make lifting the pudding out of the boiling water easier. If the cloth used for this purpose is large it can be loosely tied over the top of the basin. It is vital that a well-fitting lid to the saucepan is used: if the steam is allowed to escape too freely the pudding will not cook in the specified time.

The water should be kept boiling vigorously throughout the process, and it is a good plan to have a kettle of steaming water handy to replenish the saucepan as and when necessary. The saucepan should be large enough for steam to surround the pudding easily.

Very large steamers with upper compartments large enough to take a pudding basin are available, but they are cumbersome items for the average kitchen, and a saucepan with a good lid works very well.

STEWING

Stewing is the perfect slow-cooking method for foods in a liquid. If there is any danger of the food breaking up with the agitation of the bubbling water or syrup (as with slices of apple) it is best to stew in the oven where the temperature can be fixed so low that it hardly moves the liquid. Stew pans are always covered to keep in the steam.

STEWING FRUIT

Fruit should never be boiled. It should be very gently poached in a sugar syrup (see page 618). The amount and thickness of the syrup depends on the fruit to be poached. Very juicy fruit (plums, cherries, raspberries, rhubarb) should be cooked in a small quantity of thick syrup while drier fruits (apples and pears) should be poached in a thinner syrup.

It is important to make a syrup rather than simply to put sugar, water and fruit together in a pan. The danger of the latter method is overcooking the fruit before the sugar is dissolved. Besides, heating undissolved sugar often leads to crystallized lumps.

When stewing whole fruits that are liable to discolour, there are several important rules to follow:

1. Peel the fruit with a stainless steel knife.
2. Dunk it, as soon as it is peeled, into the sugar syrup.
3. Allow the sugar syrup to boil once right up over the fruit, before turning down the heat to poach it gently.
4. Poach the fruit for at least 15 minutes in the syrup. This is to allow the sugar syrup (which will prevent discoloration) to penetrate the outer layer of fruit.

POT ROASTING

Pot roasting is not really roasting at all. But the resulting meat has the browned look of a roast. The meat is first browned by frying in the same deep pot that it will stew in. It is then covered and left to stew (in or out of the oven) in its own juice. This is done at a very low temperature. Great care must be taken not to allow the meat to catch at the bottom.

BRAISING

Braised foods (e.g. beef olives) are cooked on a bed of chopped-up root vegetables. Little or no liquid is added and the contents cook slowly in their own juices. The braising vegetables give flavour and moisture to the meat, but may be discarded before the meat is served, or used later in soup. Sometimes they are sieved and used for sauce.

BOILING

True boiling is a method of cooking rarely used except for the quick cooking of fresh vegetables, for rice and pasta, and for boiling puddings in a pudding bowl. It is also used for jam making, when a good rolling boil is essential.

Boiling often entails a considerable loss of nutritive value, as many nutrients are thrown away with the cooking water. The word 'boiled' is often incorrectly applied to dishes like boiled egg custard (which if it was really boiled would be curdled) and boiled salmon, which should be poached, not boiled.

POACHING

For food to be poached it must be submerged, or partly submerged, in a flavoured liquid (e.g. syrup for poached pears, or chicken stock for poached chicken), and it should be cooked so that the liquid barely moves. If it bubbles in only one part of the pan, it is simmering, and if it bubbles everywhere, it is boiling. Truly poached chicken or fish has a juiciness and tenderness not found in boiled food. If the food is cooled in the poaching liquid, so much the better. (Removing it allows it to dry out.) But the poaching pan should be stood in cold water so that the contents cool fast. This is to avoid the danger of food (kept too long in a warm steamy atmosphere) going bad.

BAKING BREADS, CAKES, PASTRIES ETC.

When wheat flour and water are mixed together and cooked, a primitive type of bread – a flat, hard biscuit – is produced.

37

Examples of this are the unleavened bread of the Israelites, the damper of the Australians and the flapjacks of prospectors and pioneers of America.

Wheat flour has a remarkable ingredient. This is the protein gluten, which, when wet, will stretch and expand, allowing the dough to be kneaded and pulled into a most elastic substance. The strands of dough can stretch without breaking even when expanding gas trapped inside caused the dough to puff up. This means that, provided we can get the dough to rise, the gluten will hold it in its puffed-up shape until it solidifies during baking. This makes a much lighter, less brittle bread and makes possible a hundred different recipes for breads, cakes and puddings which all depend on trapped gas for their lightness and open texture.

RAISING AGENTS

But how to get the gas into the mixture? And what gas will it be?

Air

There are several mechanical methods of incorporating air into a basic mixture, all of which depend on agitating the ingredients, rather like stirring up a bubble bath. These methods include sifting flour, creaming fat and sugar together until light and mousse-like, beating (as for batters) and whisking (as for egg whites). In all these, air is the raising agent.

Steam

Steam is also a raising agent. Some mixtures will rise, even though no effort has been made to beat air into them. These usually contain a high proportion of liquid, like Yorkshire pudding batter or choux pastry. What happens is that, because they are baked in a hot oven, the liquid ingredients quickly reach boiling point, and begin to convert to steam. As the steam rises it takes with it the dough or batter, and puffs it up, and while it is in this puffed-up state, the heat of the oven hardens the dry ingredients of the mixture and the dough becomes solidified with the steam trapped inside. The texture of such a mixture is generally very open and uneven, with large pockets of air.

Bicarbonate of soda

This is another effective raising agent. It is a substance which, when mixed with liquid and heated, will give off half its substance as the gas carbon dioxide (CO_2) which will puff up the mixture as it forms. But the residue of the 'bicarb' will remain in the cooked mixture as carbonate of soda. Unfortunately this carbonate of soda has an unpleasant taste and smell, and a yellow colour. This method of raising is therefore suitable for strong-tasting foods such as gingerbread, chocolate cake, and cakes flavoured with treacle, when the taste of the carbonate of soda will be masked.

The carbon dioxide trapped in the bread or cake will gradually escape and be replaced by air.

The addition of an acid substance (vinegar, sour milk, cream of tartar, tartaric acid, yoghurt, even marmalade or jam) speeds up the liberation of the carbon dioxide from the bicarbonate of soda, and is often included for this reason.

Bicarbonate of soda has a weakening effect on gluten, preventing it from forming a hard, bread-like crust. This makes it suitable for scones and cakes, when yeast (which does not so affect the gluten) would produce too crisp a crust.

A disadvantage of bicarbonate of soda is that it destroys many of the vitamins present in flour.

Baking powder

This is a mixture of bicarbonate of soda and acid powder – and also a filler to absorb any dampness in the air which might allow the two active ingredients to get going before they are thoroughly wet in a dough or cake mixture. A 'delayed reaction' baking powder is available in America which needs heat as well as moisture to start it off, but it is not widely known in Britain.

Self-raising flour

This is a flour (generally 'weak', i.e. low in gluten) already containing a raising agent (usually baking powder).

Yeast

Yeast, when activated, also produces carbon dioxide which will puff up the dough, but yeast cookery is complex enough to need a section of its own. See page 43.

CAKES

(See section on raising agents, page 38.)

THE FOUR BASIC METHODS

Rubbing-in method

The first stage of this method is similar to that for shortcrust pastry (see page 50): the fat is rubbed into the flour with the fingers. The remaining dry ingredients (sugar, peel etc.) are then added, and finally eggs and/or milk are added to give a sloppy 'dropping consistency' mixture.

This method is used in making rock buns and plain fruit cakes.

Melting method

The water, milk, syrup and the fat and any other liquid ingredients are heated together. They are then cooled and poured into a bowl containing all the sieved dry ingredients, usually including bi-carbonate of soda and/or baking powder. The mixture is stirred, not beaten, until it resembles a thick batter.

This method produces very moist cakes, e.g. gingerbread.

Creaming method

The butter or margarine is creamed with a wooden spoon until it is smooth and very light in colour. The sugar is then added by degrees and beaten in the same way until the mixture is pale and fluffy. The eggs are then added, also by degrees, and finally the sifted flour is folded into the mixture, with as little mixing and stirring as possible. Adding the egg slowly, with much beating, and perhaps a spoonful of flour between each addition, is said to help prevent curdling.

This method is used for Victoria sandwich cakes, Dundee and Madeira cakes. Butter gives a better flavour, but margarine is easier to cream.

Whisking method

The simplest whisked cake is a fatless sponge. The sugar and eggs are whisked together until light and thick, and then the flour is folded in. A Genoise 'commune' has just-runny butter folded into it with the flour. The richer Genoise 'fine' cake has a greater proportion of butter to flour, and the eggs are separated. The yolks and sugar are whisked, the butter and flour folded in, and lastly the whisked egg whites.

But in all the whisked cakes the whisked-in air is the raising agent, and throughout the process, every effort is made to keep in as much air as possible.

The sugar and eggs (or yolks only) are whisked in a bowl set over a pan of near-simmering water. It is important that the base of the bowl does not touch the surface of the water as the heat at the bottom of the bowl would then be too great and the eggs would scramble. The gentle heat helps to melt the sugar and speeds up the whisking process. The mixture has been sufficiently whisked when it is very pale in colour, and leaves a ribbon-like trail on the surface when the whisk is lifted. When the flour is folded in, great care should be taken to fold rather than stir or beat, as the aim is to incorporate the flour without losing any of the beaten-in air. The correct movement is more of lifting the mixture and cutting into it, than stirring.

Butter, which should be just runny but not hot, should be poured round the edge of the bowl. If it is poured on top of the whisked cake mixture, it will push out some of the air. Folding in should be gentle and not over-done.

The cakes are cooked when the impression left by a finger on the surface of the cake will disappear. The sponge will be slightly springy. Cakes should be cooled for a few minutes in the tin, then turned out on to a cake rack.

Whisked sponges are used for many gateaux and composite cakes. They are sometimes simply filled with jam or cream, or eaten plain, perhaps dusted with icing sugar.

41

PREPARING A CAKE TIN

All tins should be greased before use. This is to prevent the cake mixture sticking or burning at the edges or bottom. Lard or oil are the most suitable fats. If using oil, always turn the tin upside down after greasing to allow any excess oil to drain away. Use a paint brush to get a thin layer.

Buns

The tins need no preparation other than greasing.

Cakes made by melting or creaming methods

Grease the tin, then line the base with greaseproof paper, cut exactly to size, and brush out with more melted lard or oil.

Cakes made by whisking method

As above, but dust with caster sugar and flour after lining and greasing.

Fruit cakes

Grease tin, then line sides and base with greaseproof paper as follows:-
1. Cut two pieces of greaseproof paper to fit the base of the cake tin.
2. Cut another piece long enough to go right round the sides of the tin and to overlap slightly. It should be 1cm/½in deeper than the height of the cake tin.
3. Fold one long edge of this strip over 1cm/½in all along its length.
4. Cut 1cm/½in snips at right angles to the edge and about 1cm/½in apart, all the way along the folded side. The snips should just reach the fold.
5. Grease the tin, place one of the paper bases in the bottom and grease again.
6. Fit the long strip inside the cake tin with the folded cut edge

42

on the bottom (the flanges will overlap slightly), and the main uncut part lining the sides of the tin. Press well into the corners.

7. Grease again and lay the second base on top of the first.
8. Brush out with more melted lard and dust with flour.

COOKING WITH YEAST

Yeast baking, one of the most addictive and satisfying forms of cookery, needs a book to itself. One of the best is *Beard on Bread* by James Beard. Another is Elizabeth David's *English Bread and Yeast Cookery*.

WHEAT FLOUR

Wheat flour (rather than cornflour, potato flour, rice flour, rye flour etc.) is most commonly used because of its high gluten content. Gluten is the protein that allows the dough to become elastic. The more gluten in the flour, the more it will be able to rise, the strands of dough stretching without breaking as the loaf fills with gas.

White flour

Made from ears of wheat that have had their outer casing of bran and inner centre of wheatgerm removed, white flour is very fine and can be bought bleached or unbleached. Obviously the more refining and processing that the flour goes through, the less flavour and vitamins it will have. For this reason white flours generally have some of the B vitamins returned to them before packaging.

Strong flour

This flour is made from hard wheat. The best hard wheat comes from North America and has an exceptionally high gluten content. This makes it highly suitable for use in bread-making, giving a well-risen light loaf. It is the flour most commonly used by professional bakers.

Plain household flour

This is a general all-purpose flour suitable for cakes and breads but more often used for the former as it does not have the high gluten content of strong flour. It is generally made from soft wheat of the kind grown in Europe. Bread produced with household flour will not have quite the lightness of that produced with strong flour.

Self-raising flour

Usually 'weak' i.e. made from soft wheat, this is flour to which a raising agent (generally baking powder) has been added. It is not used in yeast cookery.

Wholemeal flour (or wholewheat flour)

This is flour milled from the whole grain, including bran and wheatgerm. As most of the B vitamins in wheat reside in the wheatgerm, and bran provides roughage for the digestive system, bread made from wholewheat is much better for you. But it undoubtedly produces a heavier loaf, and because of the presence of wheatgerm, the bread does not keep as well as the white variety. A mixture of wholewheat and white flour is a good compromise.

Stoneground flour

Produced by the ancient method of milling between stone rollers, this flour is said to be a less 'messed about' and processed flour than that made by modern milling methods. It is certainly a slightly coarser, heavier flour, and, even in the white version, is heavier than factory milled flour. It needs more yeast to make it rise.

Brown flour

This is brown but not necessarily because of the inclusion of wheatgerm and bran. It may simply be dyed flour, so look for the word 'wholewheat' or 'wholemeal' on the packet. Dyed brown flour is lighter than wholewheat and usually sold as 'wheatmeal'.

Bran

Bran can be bought on its own in health food shops, to give a coarseness and colour to the bread, but provides neither flavour nor nutrition. It does provide roughage for the digestive system, however.

To conclude: strong, unbleached white flour is best for white loaves and a mixture of this and wholewheat flour is best for brown bread.

LEAVENING

Raising agents other than yeast have been discussed previously, but yeast is the most usual agent for bread.

Yeast is a one-celled plant of the fungus family. Its main advantage from a cook's point of view is that, given the right humid conditions, it can reproduce amazingly fast, giving off carbon dioxide (CO_2) gas as it does so. If yeast cells are incorporated into a mixture for baking, the carbon dioxide produced as the organisms grow will puff up the dough or batter, giving a light and aerated result. Yeast can be bought in two forms:

Compressed or fresh yeast

This is generally considered the most satisfactory kind of yeast, less likely to produce a loaf smelling and tasting beery or over-yeasty. But it is becoming very difficult to obtain, especially in small quantities. However, if you buy a pound at a time it can be frozen successfully. Freeze it in small pieces so that you can thaw them as you need them. Use as soon as the yeast has defrosted. Fresh yeast will keep in the refrigerator wrapped in plastic for a fortnight or so.

Dried yeast (often called 'active' dried yeast)

This is bought in granular form. You need half, or less than half, the weight specified for fresh yeast. It will keep fresh for six months in a cool dry place. To avoid the 'beery' taste referred to earlier, under- rather than over-estimate the amount of yeast needed, and allow rising and proving to take a good long time.

OTHER INGREDIENTS

Sugar (or molasses)

Generally included in a bread recipe to give the yeast something to feed on while busily multiplying. It does, of course, also add a touch of sweetness to the dough, but this is incidental.

Fat

Some breads call for fat, usually butter, which gives a richness to the bread, and a good flavour.

Liquid

Water is usually called for, but sometimes other liquids, such as beer or milk, are used. Milk gives a golden coloured crust.

MIXING AND SPONGING

The basic aim while preparing the dough for the oven is to create the right conditions for the yeast to grow, and the maximum elasticity in the bread to contain the gas released by the yeast. In the first stage – mixing and sponging – we are creating the incubating conditions for the yeast:

The ingredients and bowl should be warm: not so hot that the yeast cells will be killed, and not so cold that they will be discouraged from multiplying. The yeast is usually creamed with a little sugar (upon which it feeds) and mixed with a spoonful of warm (i.e. about 40°C/100°F) liquid. When the yeast looks frothy you know it is on its way. This is called 'sponging'. It is done to check that the yeast cells are alive before mixing in all the flour.

If nothing happens (although you have the yeast in a warm kitchen) in 15 minutes, the yeast is probably dead, and there is nothing for it but to begin again with fresh yeast.

Some recipes require the yeast mixture and all the liquid to be beaten to a batter with a small proportion of the flour, and then 'sponged'. The rest of the flour is then added, and the mixing completed.

KNEADING

Once the dough is mixed it should be kneaded. This is to distribute the yeast cells evenly and to promote the elasticity of the dough. The length of time for kneading varies according to the type of flour and the skill of the kneader, but 10 minutes should do it. The dough should be elastic and satiny-smooth.

Kneading techniques vary, the most common method being to push the lump of dough down and away with the heel of one hand, then to pull it back with the fingers, slap it on the tabletop and repeat the process, turning the dough slightly with each movement.

RISING

The dough is now formed into a ball and put into a warm, lightly oiled bowl. It is a good idea to roll the ball of dough over in the greasy bowl to coat it on all sides. This will prevent hardening and cracking. Cover the bowl with a piece of oiled polythene or a damp cloth. Put the bowl in a warm (about 32°C/90°F) draught-free place and leave it alone for at least one hour. The slower the dough rises the better. Over-risen bread has a coarse texture and beery smell. When it has doubled in bulk, remove it.

KNOCKING DOWN (or knocking back)

This is exactly what the name implies: the air is punched out of the risen dough and it is knocked back to its original size. Then it is kneaded again and shaped (into a round, oblong, plaited or what-have-you loaf) and put into the loaf tin or on to a baking sheet. Again, cover it with oiled polythene.

PROVING

This is the second rising of the dough. It is done when the loaf has doubled in bulk and looks the size and shape you hope the finished bread will be. This rising can be done in a slightly warmer place, for a shorter time – say at 40°C/100°F for 20 minutes. This is because as the dough has now had further kneading it is even more elastic and will rise more easily – rather as a balloon is easier to blow up the second time you do it.

BAKING

The bread will, inevitably, continue to rise for a short time when put in the oven. This is partly due to the rising steam, and partly to the continued growth of the yeast as more warmth is applied. But once the temperature of the dough reaches 60°C/140°F the yeast will be killed and the heat of the oven will cook the dough into a rigid shape. This final rising in the oven is called 'oven spring' and usually causes the top crust to be pushed up away from the body of the loaf, causing larger holes just under the crust. There is nothing wrong with it, but obviously too much oven-spring would have the crust separated entirely from the loaf. Some breads, such as rye bread (which develops a hard and un-yielding crust) is docked half way through baking. This means simply that the top crust is sliced off to allow the gases to escape, and a new crust forms.

To avoid too much oven-spring, bread is baked at a fairly high temperature so that yeast is killed as quickly as possible. Too cool an oven will not kill the yeast cells quickly and they will continue to grow, giving an over-risen, unevenly textured loaf.

The loaf is done when it sounds hollow when tapped. Tap the top first, and if satisfied that it sounds hollow, turn the loaf out (your hand covered with a cloth) and tap the underside. If it feels heavy and solid return it to the oven. Test again in six or seven minutes.

COOLING

Large breads should be cooled out of their tins to allow the steam to escape, thus further lightening the bread. After two hours a loaf will slice easily. If the bread is to be stored in a bread tin or plastic bag (in a refrigerator or freezer) it should be stone-cold before storing. A lukewarm loaf, put into an airtight place, will go soggy, if not mouldy.

GLAZING

Coating the top of the loaf, towards the end of cooking, will give different effects according to the glaze used:

Brushing with *water* ensures a crisp crust.
Milk gives a good pale gold colour and a crisp crust.
Egg yolks and cream produce a dark golden top.
Melted *butter* gives a softer crust.
Melted *apricot jam* gives a sweet sticky shine to sweeter breads.

PASTRIES

In almost all cases 'short' (i.e. crisp, crumbly, but neither brittle nor hard) pastry is the aim. The degree of shortness of pastry comes from the amount and type of fat incorporated in it, and the way in which the paste (uncooked pastry) is handled.

Fats

Butter gives a crisp and short crust, with very good flavour.
Margarine gives a result similar to butter, slightly less rich.
Lard gives a soft, very short but rather tasteless pastry.
Cooking fat gives a crisper crust than lard, also short, but also lacking in flavour.
Suet is only used in suet crust pastry. It produces a soft, rather heavy pastry. To combat this doughiness a raising agent is usually added to the flour.

Flours

Plain household flour is the flour most commonly used, but wholemeal flour and self-raising are used sometimes. Wholemeal flour produces a delicious nutty-flavoured crust, but is inclined to be heavy. For this reason it is sometimes used in conjunction (half and half) with white flour. Self-raising flour produces a thicker, softer, more cakey crust. It is sometimes used to lighten what might be a heavyish pastry (e.g. cheese pastry or suet crust).

Water

As a general rule, the less of this the better. Any child who has mixed flour and water to make a paste knows that the baked result is not unlike concrete. But some crispness and firmness is desirable and the inclusion of a little water ensures this.

Pastry is made in so many different ways that it is difficult to give general rules for success. So to take the broad categories one by one:

SHORTCRUST PASTRY

In this method of pastry-making fat is rubbed into the flour with the fingertips, and then any other ingredients (egg yolks, liquid etc.) are added.

Keep everything as cool as possible: if the fat is allowed to melt, the finished pastry may be tough. Cut the fat, which should be cool and firm rather than softened, into tiny pieces using a small knife and floured fingers (the flouring prevents the fat from sticking to your warm fingers and starting to melt). Add *chilled* water. Roll on a cold surface. Handle the pastry as little as possible.

When rubbing in the fat, handle it lightly so that it doesn't stick to your fingers. Keep your hands well floured to facilitate this. Pick up a few small pieces of fat, and plenty of flour between the fingertips and thumb of each hand. Hold your hands a good 23cm/9in above the bowl and gently and quickly rub the fat pieces into the flour, squashing the fat lightly as you do so. Then immediately drop the lot, from that height, into the bowl (dropping from a height both aerates and cools the mixture). Do not mash each lump of fat – the less thoroughly you do the rubbing in, the better. Keep shaking the bowl so that the big unrubbed pieces of fat come to the top. When the mixture looks like very coarse (by no means 'fine', as many recipes will say) breadcrumbs, stop.

Add only enough liquid to get the pastry to hold together. Rich pastries (with a high proportion of fat) need little if any water added. Although rather moist pastry is easier to handle and roll out, the resulting crust is tough and may well shrink out of shape as the water evaporates in the oven. The drier and more difficult-to-handle pastry will give a crisp 'short' crust.

Do not add too much flour during rolling as the proportion of flour to other ingredients will be altered and the pastry may become heavy.

Allow the pastry to 'relax' in a cool place before baking. This period (10 minutes will do) allows the gluten in the flour to contract, making the pastry less elastic. This will produce a lighter pastry, less likely to shrink.

Always wrap or cover pastry left to relax – especially if there is more rolling to come. The dry atmosphere of a refrigerator dries out the outside of pastry, causing it to crack and flake and making it difficult to handle.

SUET CRUST

The method for suet crust is similar to that for shortcrust, but the suet is generally chopped or shredded into the flour. As self-raising flour (or plain flour and baking powder) is used in order to produce a less doughy pastry, it is important to cook the pastry as soon as possible after making, so that the raising agent is working as the pastry cooks, rather than already spent before the pastry starts to cook. (The raising agent causes the dough to puff up and rise slightly and as the paste hardens during cooking the air will be trapped, and the pastry be light and slightly cakey.)

FLAKY PASTRY (and Puff Pastries)

The first stage in making these pastries is similar to the method used for shortcrust pastry, although the consistency is softer and less 'short'. After this more fat, either in a solid block or small pieces, is incorporated into the paste, which is then rolled, folded and re-rolled several times. This quickly creates layers of pastry which, when baked, will rise in light thin leaves. Pastry folded in three (and rolled out) six times will have 729 layers.

The whole aim at this stage is to create the layers without allowing the fat to melt. This requires quick short strokes with the rolling pin rather than steady long ones. The short strokes allow the bubbles of air in the pastry to move about without being forced out, while the fat is gradually and evenly incorporated in the paste. If there is any danger of the fat breaking through the pastry or becoming warm and sticky, wrap the paste and chill it, then proceed. It sounds a complicated business, but is a lot easier done than said.

Pastry rises evenly to a crisp crust in a damp atmosphere, and for this reason pastries like these, that are expected to rise in the oven, are generally baked at a high temperature in an oven with a roasting tin full of water at the bottom of it, or on a wet baking sheet.

PÂTE SUCRÉE, ALMOND PASTRY AND PÂTE A PÂTÉ

These pastries and others like them are made by working the egg yolks and fat, and sometimes sugar, together, using the fingertips, until soft and creamy, and then gradually incorporating the flour until a soft, very rich paste is achieved.

The butter and sugar should not be creamed together as for a cake, as this produces too spongy a result.

Use only the fingertips of one hand. Succumbing to the temptation to use both hands, or the whole hand, leads to sticky pastry. The warmth of the fingertips is important for softening the fat, but once that is done the mixing and kneading should be as light and quick as possible. Because of the high proportion of fat, no water is added. A buttery rich pastry results, rather like shortcake. If the pastry is sticky it may need chilling before rolling or pressing to shape. Very soft pastry can be more easily rolled between two sheets of greaseproof paper.

This pastry can be made in a machine, as can many pastries, but it is vital to under- rather than over-mix.

When the pastry is biscuit-coloured and cooked it will still be soft. Do not worry, it will crisp up as it cools. Slide it off the baking sheet (using a palette knife) when cool.

HOT WATER CRUST

For this pastry water and fat are heated together and mixed into the flour.

Because of the high proportion of water, this pastry is

inclined to be hard. Also, as the fat used is generally lard, it can be lacking in flavour, so add a good pinch of salt. Do not allow the water to boil before the fat has melted. If the water reduces by boiling, the proportion of water to flour will not be correct.

Mix the water and melted fat into the flour quickly and keep the pastry in a warm bowl, covered with a hot damp cloth. This prevents the fat becoming set and the pastry flaking and drying out so that it is unmanageable.

CHOUX PASTRY

This pastry, containing eggs and butter, is easy to make but strict adherence to the recipe (pages 652–3) is vital. The following points are particularly important:

1. Measure the ingredients exactly.
2. Do not allow the water to boil until the butter has melted, but when it has, bring it immediately to a full rolling boil.
3. Have the flour ready in a bowl so that the minute your rolling boil is achieved, you can tip the flour in, all in one go.
4. Do not over-beat. Once the mixture is leaving the sides of the pan, stop.
5. Cool before adding the egg – too much heat would scramble the eggs.
6. Do not beat in more egg than is necessary to achieve a dropping consistency. If the mixture is too stiff, the pastry will be stodgy. If it is too sloppy it will rise unevenly into shapeless lumps.
7. Bake on a wet baking sheet – the steam helps the paste to rise.
8. Bake until it is a good even brown, otherwise the inside of the pastry will be uncooked.
9. If the pastry is to be served cold, split the buns/rings, or poke holes in them with a skewer to allow the steam inside to escape. If the steam remains trapped the pastry will be soggy and a little heavy.
10. Serve the pastry on the day it is made, or store frozen. It will not keep well in a tin.

STRUDEL PASTRY

Unlike almost every other pastry, this one benefits from very heavy handling. It is in fact beaten and stretched, thumped and kneaded. This is all to allow the gluten to expand and promote elasticity in the dough. The paste is rolled and stretched on a cloth (the bigger the better) until it is so thin that you should be able to read fine print through it. Keep the paste covered and moist when not in use. When rolled out, brush with butter or oil to prevent cracking and drying.

SOUFFLÉS

Soufflé means 'puffed up', and that is what soufflés are. A true soufflé is hot and, because whisked egg white (containing a lot of air) is incorporated in the mixture, it is very light and puffs up as the air inside expands and rises. Cold soufflés, which are not true soufflés since they do not puff up, are so called because they have a texture similar to the true hot soufflé as they too contain whisked egg white (full of air). They are in fact light mousses. The setting agent (usually gelatine) traps the air in the mixture by firmly setting the solid ingredients. But the mixture does not rise at all. A hot soufflé, having no setting agent, will not stay indefinitely puffed up, but the ingredients of the soufflé will solidify somewhat in cooking, so trapping the risen air temporarily.

HOT SOUFFLÉS

General opinion, and myth fostered by cookery writers and teachers, is enough to make the inexperienced cook too nervous to attempt a hot soufflé. This is nonsense. Soufflés are extremely easy to make, seldom go wrong, can be very inexpensive, are quick to prepare and perfectly delicious. The base can be prepared well in advance, the whites being whisked and folded in whenever required.

In Leith's Restaurant we use a good trick, stolen from the Café Royal: the soufflé mixture is made, the egg whites folded in and the mixture turned into a soufflé dish. It is then immediately and very rapidly frozen. When a soufflé is ordered by a customer it is simply taken from the deep-freeze and immediately (without any thawing) baked. The baking time needed is generally one quarter as long again as the unfrozen soufflé requires. This takes the worry out of last-minute mixing and folding, and ensures that every soufflé is as it should be, having been carefully and exactly made in the peace of the morning.

The soufflé base for a savoury soufflé is generally a thick béchamel sauce (called a panade) mixed with the desired flavouring – grated cheese, flaked fish, purée of spinach or what have you. A sweet hot soufflé is often made with a white sauce panade (plus the puréed apricots, rhubarb etc.) but a crème pâtissière or a thick custard made with milk, arrowroot and butter may be used. The richest and most delicious sweet soufflé base is undoubtedly the crème pâtissière, but it is inclined to sink rather more quickly than the others.

All hot soufflés will finally sink, but if they are properly made they will not do so as soon as they are taken from the oven. Indeed, if the soufflé is not immediately required it can sit in a turned-off oven for ten minutes without coming to harm, and there will still be time to take it from the oven, dust it with icing sugar or grated Parmesan, wrap a napkin around it and carry it to the dining room at a leisurely pace, *and serve it*, before it looks any the worse for wear.

If you were to make a soufflé simply by mixing some sort of good tasting farinaceous mixture with whisked egg whites, pouring it into a dish and baking it, you would probably get a perfectly good result. But having mastered such simple methods it is useful to know how the perfect, well and evenly risen, crisp-on-the-outside-and-moist-in-the-middle soufflé is achieved.

The following notes then are for the perfectionist, or for when something has gone wrong.

The base

When the base is made, and still warm, it should have a soft, not-quite-runny consistency. The too-solid base will not fold easily into the egg whites, and the too-runny one will not be held by the egg whites and will not rise as well. If the base has been made in advance and is cold, it should be gently warmed before the whites are added. Do not add more liquid to it as this will spoil the proportions.

The egg whites

Most recipes call for slightly more egg whites than egg yolks. This is because the aim is to achieve more bulk of whites than bulk of base. Obviously the more whites, the more the mixture will rise, but *too* many will make the rising too sudden and uneven, and the mixture will sink rapidly as there will not be enough solid ingredients to hold the risen mixture in place. It will also taste insipid. Too few whites will produce a poorly risen soufflé. The whites should be whisked at the last minute (they re-liquefy if left standing, and cannot be re-whisked satisfactorily). They should be whisked until the mixture, when the whisk is lifted, will stand in 'medium peaks' (i.e. the peaks will flop over slightly at the top, and not stay rigidly in place). If the whites are over-whisked and dry-looking they will be difficult to fold into the mixture. If they are underwhisked and still slightly runny they will not cause the soufflé to rise enough. In order to fold them in easily, it is a good idea first to mix in one table-spoon, which will loosen the base, then fold in the rest. The egg whites should be folded in to the base with a large metal spoon, held close to the bowl, not at the end of the handle. This makes it easier to lift and turn the mixture, getting the whites well distributed without bashing out all the carefully incorporated air. In order to dispel any large pockets of air that may be trapped in the mixture, cut through the mixture several times with a knife, once it is in the soufflé dish. Also give the dish a sharp crack on the table to 'settle' it evenly. Both these actions are to ensure even (as opposed to lop-sided) rising.

Note: It is true that whites steadily whisked by hand in a copper or metal bowl, with a balloon whisk, contain the most air at the end of the process, but machines are here to stay, and we have found machine-whisked whites perfectly satisfactory.

The soufflé dish

The ideal dish is a fine fireproof china one with straight sides up which the soufflé will easily rise. China is a good conductor of heat, and as it is thin the heat will penetrate quickly. But soufflés can be made in pie dishes or even bread or cake tins. The essential rule is to brush the sides lightly with melted butter so that the rising soufflé will not stick to the dry surface but will glide up smoothly. Another advantage of thin china is that it will not hold the heat like earthenware, and so the soufflé will not continue to cook once taken from the oven.

When preparing the soufflé dish a double band of greaseproof paper can be tied round the top of the dish to hold the rising soufflé in place. It is removed before serving and gives an evenly risen soufflé. But it is not necessary – unless the heat is uneven the soufflé will not fall over the edge. Too high a band of paper will prevent the heat from penetrating. About 2·5cm/1in is ideal. The inside of the paper, like the dish, must be brushed with butter.

The oven

It is vital that the oven be pre-heated completely. Uneven heat will produce a lop-sided result. Remove the shelves above the middle shelf so that the soufflé does not rise through them! To give the soufflé 'bottom heat' and extra 'lift', put a baking sheet into the oven on the middle shelf when heating it. Then the dish can be placed on this already hot surface. Do not open the oven door until the cooking time is up, or at least not until there is only five minutes to go – the blast of cold air could cause premature collapse. Obey the oven temperature instruction religiously. A moderately hot oven is ideal; too fierce a heat will cause a top crust to form before the soufflé has risen. The crust will then effectively prevent the mixture from rising. Too low a temperature will discourage rising and the soufflé will be stodgy and heavy.

To test if the soufflé is cooked

Open the door a crack and look at it. It should be well risen and a good brown. If it is not, shut the door carefully. The ideal soufflé is a little moist, not completely dry in the middle. With practice it is possible to tell if a soufflé is done by giving the dish a slight shove. If the mixture wobbles alarmingly it is still too raw, but if it only wobbles slightly and seems firm, it is done.

If there is a danger of the soufflé overcooking (perhaps because your lunch guests are notoriously unreliable about arriving on time) make a sauce (mornay sauce for a cheese soufflé, tomato sauce for a spinach soufflé etc.). Then if the soufflé is on the dry side, it won't matter.

COLD SOUFFLÉS

For these soufflés a band or collar of greaseproof paper (which should be lightly oiled, not buttered) is a good idea, as the resulting soufflé will then look even more like a hot one since the mixture will come above the rim of the dish. But it is not essential: the soufflé will taste as good without it.

Cold soufflés are a little trickier than hot ones as the timing of the actions and the temperature of the mixtures is very important.

The base

This is either made simply by beating egg yolks and sugar together, and adding the flavouring purée, melted chocolate or fruit juice; or it may be a thick custard; or a panade (thick white sauce); or it may consist of milk thickened with arrowroot. The base, if made in advance, should not be chilled, as too cold a mixture will cause the gelatine, when it is stirred in, to set in strings before it is thoroughly incorporated.

The cream

It should be fresh and half-whipped. Stiffly whipped cream will not easily be folded into the mixture; underwhipped cream makes the mixture too liquid, and less likely to set well.

The gelatine

This should be first soaked in liquid. Put the liquid (usually a few tablespoons) into a small saucepan and sprinkle on the gelatine powder. Leave undisturbed for at least 10 minutes to 'sponge': the gelatine will absorb the liquid and look solid and spongy. Then warm it over very gentle heat, resisting the temptation to stir, until the gelatine is clear and runny, but not very hot. If it boils it will go stringy and unusable. Weigh the gelatine or measure it accurately (7g/¼oz to ½ litre/¾ pint mixture). Too much and the soufflé will be rubbery, too little and it will be sloppy. The base must be briskly stirred when the gelatine is added, or it will set in strings or lumps.

Note: Gelatine leaves are very much easier to use than dry powder, but they are difficult to obtain. The above remarks assume powder is used. Gelatine leaves are simply melted in the liquid, the 'sponging' process being unnecessary.

Egg whites

As with hot soufflés the number of egg whites usually exceeds the yolks called for. They must be whisked just before folding in, until stiff but by no means dry. One spoonful may be thoroughly stirred in to loosen the base if the base is obviously stiffer than the whites, but it should not be necessary if the base is of the right consistency.

To sum up: the base, fruit purée (or melted chocolate etc.) and the egg whites should, as far as possible, have the same soft consistency. If there is an unavoidable difference in consistency add the thinner to the thicker one. The gelatine should be warm, clear and runny when added. The base should be at room temperature, not icy-cold or hot.

Once set, cold soufflés are usually decorated with whipped cream, nuts and/or fruit.

STOCKS

Good strong natural stocks are behind almost every good sauce or casserole. Stock-cubes are often over-salty and 'packet-flavoured', so should be used guardedly.

Brown stock is used in brown sauces and soups, and is of a stronger flavour than white stock. The secrets of a good brown stock are very thorough, even browning of the ingredients by frying, very slow cooking, and constant skimming.

Stocks should be simmered rather than boiled, and skimming off scum and fat is vital. A stock containing a lot of fat, boiled vigorously, will have an unattractive smell and a greasy, rather muddy taste, even if the fat is subsequently removed.

Salt should not be added to basic stocks as the stock may be used for cooking salted foods, which would then become over-salty. Add salt if necessary when using the stock.

Brown and white stock can be simmered with advantage for many hours, but fish bones become bitter with more than 30 minutes' cooking. Brown and white stocks can be kept on the go for weeks, as long as they are strained and religiously brought to the boil every day. The straining is to discard all the bones and vegetables that have given up their flavour. The boiling is to prevent fermenting – a disaster more likely to happen to chicken stocks than any other.

Stocks can be reduced by boiling to a very strong, almost thick consistency and frozen in small quantities (e.g. in an ice tray). They can then be used as needed with the addition of water to bring them back to the original strength.

Strong stocks should set like a jelly. Pigs' trotters or veal bones added to the stock will ensure setting.

Strong jellied stocks can be kept refrigerated for seven to ten days. If to be kept longer they should be reboiled.

SAVOURY SAUCES

Larousse defines a sauce as a 'liquid seasoning for food'. A sauce is normally thickened to prevent it running right off the food. There are four basic thickening agents:

Roux

Butter and flour are cooked together before the liquid is added. There are three degrees to which a roux can be cooked:

White: The butter and flour are merely mixed over a gentle heat without browning.
Blond: The roux is allowed to cook to a biscuit colour.
Brown: The roux is cooked until the butter and flour are distinctly brown.

These act as the base for three classic sauces mères (mother sauces) from which there are many derivatives or daughter sauces. See the sauce table.

Cornflour or arrowroot (fécule)

These are 'slaked' (mixed to a paste with cold water, stock or milk), added to hot liquid and allowed to boil for one or two minutes.

Beurre manié

Equal quantities of butter and flour are kneaded to a smooth paste and whisked into a boiling liquid. As the butter melts the flour is evenly distributed throughout the sauce, thickening the liquid without allowing lumps to form.

Egg yolks

These are used in two ways to thicken sauces. Oil or butter beaten into egg yolk will form an emulsion, as in mayonnaise and hollandaise sauces. Egg yolk can also be mixed with cream (or other liquid) to form a liaison. This is then added to a sauce or to milk, and the whole heated without boiling – enough to thicken the yolks without scrambling them. This is the method of thickening used in English custard and in blanquette de veau.

Most classic sauces are derived from basic mother sauces. The following table gives examples of classic daughter sauces and briefly explains how the mother sauce is made. After the table there follows a list of miscellaneous, but nonetheless classic, sauces that do not exactly fit into the mother/daughter pattern.

MOTHER	DAUGHTER	USES
WHITE SAUCE		
Seasoned milk thickened with a white roux.	*Anchovy:* with added anchovy essence.	Fish
Used for vegetables and as a binding for croquettes etc.	*Béchamel:* flavoured with bay leaf, onion, peppercorns.	Eggs, fish, chicken
	Cardinale: béchamel mixed with fish stock and flavoured with truffle essence, lobster butter, cayenne.	Fish
	Crème: with added cream.	Eggs, veal
	Egg: with added chopped, hardboiled eggs.	Fish
	Mornay: with added grated cheese.	Fish, eggs, cauliflower
	Soubise: with added cooked, chopped onion.	Mutton, eggs, fish, cauliflower

MOTHER	DAUGHTER	USES

BLOND SAUCE (Velouté)

White stock thickened with a blond roux.	*Aurore:* with added tomato purée.	Eggs, fish, meat, vegetables
Used for eggs, fish, vegetables and white meat.	*Poulette:* with added mushroom essence, lemon juice and chopped parsley.	Carrots, broad and French beans, boiled potatoes, calf's head, veal
	Suprême: made with chicken stock and cream, flavoured with mushroom peelings. Sometimes finished with an egg and cream liaison.	Chicken, vol-au-vents
	Mushroom: sauce suprême, with added mushrooms. Sometimes finished with an egg yolk and cream liaison.	Chicken, sweetbreads

BROWN SAUCES

Sauce espagnole
(also called easy demi-glace sauce)

A mirepoix of vegetables is cooked in fat until coloured. Flour is added and cooked until brown and sandy in texture. Brown stock is added with tomatoes and mushroom peelings.	*Chasseur:* espagnole with mushrooms, tomato and white wine, chopped parsley.	Grills, entrées, roasts, rabbit, chicken
Used for red meats and game.	*Robert:* chopped onions sweated in butter with added vinegar, white wine and pepper, reduced by half and added to espagnole. Flavoured with mustard.	Pork, kidneys, tongue, ham

MOTHER	DAUGHTER	USES

Sauce demi-glace

This is a more sophisticated brown sauce, made by simmering equal quantities of espagnole sauce with jellied bone stock. The sauce is then reduced by gentle boiling to half quantity, and is repeatedly skimmed. A good demi-glace looks like a rich syrupy gravy, when hot semi-clear in appearance and setting to a jelly when cold.

Madeira: espagnole or demi-glace with Madeira.

Veal, tongue

Bordelaise: demi-glace with reduced wine, shallots and thyme.

Grilled steaks

Poivrade: parsley stalks, thyme, crushed pepper corns and bay leaves cooked with a mirepoix which is then marinaded in wine or vinegar and reduced by half. Added to demi-glace and cooked 30 minutes, then strained.

Game

Used for red meats and game.

Diane: poivrade with cream.

Grilled steaks

Reforme: equal quantities of poivrade and demi-glace, garnished with julienne of egg whites, gherkins, truffles and tongue.

Lamb

Perigueux: demi-glace with truffles or truffle essence.

Red meat, game

Note: All the brown daughter sauces can be made with either espagnole or demi-glace but the richer ones (madeira, bordelaise, poivrade, diane, reforme and perigueux) should classically by made with a proper demi-glace.

MOTHER	DAUGHTER	USES

BUTTER SAUCE
(Beurre à l'Anglaise)

MOTHER	DAUGHTER	USES
White roux plus boiling water with added butter beaten in, flavoured with lemon juice.	*Bâtarde:* with added egg yolk.	Cauliflower, veal, eggs etc.
	Câpre (caper): with added capers.	Boiled turbot, cod, mutton
Used for vegetables and fish.	*Fennel:* with added blanched chopped Florence fennel.	Fish

EMULSIONS

Hollandaise sauce

MOTHER	DAUGHTER	USES
This is an emulsion made with egg yolks and butter, flavoured with vinegar, peppercorns and salt.	*Béarnaise:* reduction of chopped shallots, pepper, tarragon, added to hollandaise, served with chopped tarragon and chervil.	Grilled steaks
Used for asparagus, broccoli, eggs etc.	*Choron:* béarnaise with added tomato purée.	Grills, fish and asparagus
	Mousseline: with added whipped cream.	Asparagus, sole, sea kale
	Moutarde: with added mustard.	Herrings, mackerel, poached fish

Mayonnaise

MOTHER	DAUGHTER	USES
An emulsion of egg yolk and oil, seasoned with vinegar, pepper and salt.	*Aioli:* crushed garlic (and sometimes mashed potato) beaten into the emulsion of egg yolk and oil.	Soups, especially provençal fish soups
Served cold with cold salads and cold fish, poultry or meat.		Raw vegetables

65

MOTHER	DAUGHTER	USES
	Remoulade: with added mustard and sometimes capers, parsley, gherkins, chervil, tarragon and anchovy essence.	Celeriac, celery, salads and herrings
	Tartare: with added chopped hardboiled eggs, capers, gherkins and onions.	Fried fish and shellfish
	Andalouse: with added tomato purée and chopped sweet red peppers.	Salads, chicken and fish

MISCELLANEOUS

CRANBERRY

Cranberries, sugar and water, poached and sieved.

APPLE

Cooking apple, butter and sugar, cooked together to a thick purée and sieved.

BIGARADE

Duck gravy, orange juice and butter, thickened with arrowroot.

BREAD

Milk flavoured with bay leaf, onions and cloves and thickened with breadcrumbs. Seasoned with pepper and salt and enriched with added butter.

CUMBERLAND

Redcurrant jelly and port simmered together and flavoured with orange juice, lemon juice, mustard, cayenne, ginger and chopped cooked shallots. Served cold.

MINT

Vinegar, sugar, salt, pepper, chopped mint, sometimes mixed with small amount of boiling water.

TOMATO

Mirepoix, stock, tomato purée and fresh tomatoes, cooked for 30 minutes and sieved.

VINAIGRETTE

French dressing.

SOUPS

The word soup covers almost anything from a hefty peasant meal, thick with cereals or root vegetables, to a delicate clear consommé meant only to wake up the appetite for greater things to come.

BROTHS

Broths (or bouillons) are well-flavoured stocks which are served unthickened and unclarified. They are made from the liquor in which meat (and sometimes vegetables) has been cooked. Very little is done to the basic stock – it may be further seasoned with pepper and salt, or watered down if too strong, or reduced by rapid boiling if not strong enough. Broths are frequently garnished with a small handful of cooked rice, barley or small pasta such as vermicelli, or with small pieces of root vegetables cut into dice, or with chopped fresh parsley, or finely chopped leek.

CLEAR SOUPS

Clear soups (or consommés) are similar in taste to broths, but they have been cleared by the addition of egg whites and crushed egg shell to the stock, which is then filtered through the cooked egg-white mass, and through muslin. There is generally a good meat base (chicken, veal or beef) to a consommé, and if it is to be served chilled, a veal bone or extra gelatine is added to the stock to ensure a jelly-like set.

Many consommés take their names from their garnishes: julienne strips of vegetables (consommé Julienne), miniature choux pastry profiteroles (consommé aux profiteroles). Consommé is sometimes served with a dash of sherry in it – too often with too much sherry, to the ruin of an otherwise good soup. Cheese straws are frequently handed separately when consommé is served – a good idea as the crispness and tang of the cheese straws contrasts well with the silken, almost sticky, soup.

Chilled consommés form the base of many iced first courses, topped with sour cream and mock caviar for example, or with a curry-flavoured spoonful of cream cheese in each coup.

CREAM SOUPS

The word cream in this context does not necessarily mean that there is cream in the soup, only that the soup has been liquidized, beaten or mashed to a 'cream'. The simplest form of the cream soup is the vegetable purée, which is simply a liquidized mixture of vegetable and cooking stock. Cauliflower and parsnip soup, for example, may consist of a few roast parsnips left over from yesterday's lunch, the remains of a cauliflower in white sauce, a pint of chicken stock (perhaps made from a stock cube) and an onion, finely chopped and gently cooked in butter. All these ingredients liquidized together would give a delicious, though not grand, soup.

Cream soups are usually thickened with flour, however, or by the addition of some floury ingredient, such as potato. If potato or other starchy food (such as lentils or sweetcorn) is to provide the thickening, these are simply cooked in the soup, and the whole sieved or liquidized before serving. If flour is to be used, it is first mixed with butter (about 30g/1oz of each for 570ml/1 pint of liquid) and then dropped in small blobs into the hot soup, while it is stirred. The melting butter evenly distributes the flour, so preventing lumps forming. This flour-and-butter paste is called beurre manié (kneaded butter).

A similar, and more common way of thickening soups is the roux method. Here the butter is melted in the saucepan, the flour is then stirred into it, the liquid added, and the whole stirred until boiling. If the recipe calls for, say, onions to be gently 'sweated' in butter at the beginning of the process, this is done and the flour is then added to the onion/butter mixture before the liquid.

With both the beurre manié and the roux methods, it is essential that the soup be allowed to boil or simmer for at least 1 minute to thoroughly cook the flour, and to allow it to thicken the liquid.

The most difficult method of thickening soups and sauces is the egg and cream liaison, but it gives by far the richest and most velvety result. Egg yolks (usually two to 570ml/1 pint of soup) are mixed with half a cup or so of cream. Hot soup is then poured into the cup, mixed well, and the whole then poured back into the soup, while the soup is stirred. But on no account must the soup be allowed to approach boiling point, or the egg yolks will scramble into a curdled mess. Just enough heat is needed to thicken the yolks without cooking them completely.

Tapioca, sago, cornflour or arrowroot will thicken soup too, but give it a glassy, unattractive look.

BISQUES

There are soups made from shellfish, and, usually, fish stocks. The shells of the shellfish are boiled in the stock to give colour and flavour to the bisque. They are smooth cream soups, slightly thickened with an egg and cream liaison and often highly seasoned.

CHOWDERS

Chowders are thick soups, containing plenty of solid ingredients, which are not creamed to a smooth consistency. Clam chowder has whole clams in it; corn chowder, whole kernels of corn etc. The biblical 'mess of potage' would today be a chowder, a meal on its own.

69

GARNISHES FOR SOUP

In classic haute cuisine there are written rules about which garnish is permissible with what soup, but nowadays such pedantry seems irrelevant. The question to settle is, 'Will the garnish *do* anything for the soup?' If the answer is no, it is not worth the fiddling about. Just serve crisp hot toast.

Spicy garnishes, with a crisp texture (such as cayenne-flavoured croutons) are just right with a smooth bland soup. Very rich garnishes, such as cheese squares, are good with an acid, light soup, such as a thin tomato broth.

Some suggested garnishes:

For thin broths and clear soups

Tiny, deep-fried profiteroles made with cheese choux pastry.
Tiny, baked profiteroles sprinkled with cayenne before cooking.
Tiny, shell-shaped noodles or vermicelli.
Pulses – cooked rice or barley.
Cooked diced carrot, turnip and celery.
Squares (croutons) of fried bread or toast.
Squares of bread covered thickly with cheese and toasted.
Finely shredded raw lettuce leaf, spinach leaf or sprig of water-
   cress (added at the last minute).
Finely shredded leek or cabbage (allowed to cook in the soup
   for one minute).
Cooked fine slices of Chinese dried mushroom.
Small slivers of peeled raw tomato.

For thick soups

Whole fresh small cooked peas in a pea soup.
Small squares of ham in a pulse (e.g. lentil or split pea) soup.
A thick paste of creamed cheese, flavoured with chopped fresh
   onion and curry paste, for cucumber soup, watercress soup,
   or chicken soup, especially if the soups are served chilled.
Small slices of fried apple for curry soup.
Sour cream for borscht (beetroot soup).
Slices of mushroom for chicken soup.

Chopped fresh basil and/or oregano for tomato soup.

Sour damsons or fresh plums cooked in red wine for potato soup.

Red caviar (salmon roe) or mock caviar (lumpfish roe) for fish soups.

Cucumber slices for all cold soups.

Swirl of cream on all thickened soups.

Liquor – dash of port in potato soup, sherry in tomato soup, brandy in seafood bisque.

VEGETABLES

Vegetables in Britain are served as an accompaniment to a main meat course. It is worth considering them, however, as first courses on their own, or as main courses if served in sufficient variety, or with, for example, a cheese sauce. For a salad or starter they may be served raw or cooked, with a dressing.

Bouquetière de légumes

A collection (or *bouquetière*) of freshly and simply cooked, well presented vegetables is a rare pleasure. Care should be taken, however, that each vegetable is carefully prepared and garnished with an appropriate herb and/or brushed with melted butter. Choose vegetables that are of contrasting flavour and colour, and arrange them on a heated platter so that, for example, green peas and green broccoli are separated by the red of tomatoes or carrots, and that white vegetables (like new potatoes and salsify) are not placed side by side. See the notes overleaf for cooking methods, and the following table for cooking times etc. for specific vegetables.

FRESH GREEN VEGETABLES

Blanching and refreshing

This method of cooking vegetables is commonly used in restaurants where some advance preparation is vital. It is worth doing when coping with a large selection of vegetables.

Boil the vegetables separately: bring the water to a good boil and drop in the vegetables. Use enough water only barely to cover them and add one teaspoon of salt for each pint of water. Do not cover the pan. Boil as rapidly as you dare (delicate vegetables like broccoli can break up if *too* rapidly boiled). As soon as they are tender, but not yet totally soft, drain them and rinse in cold water to prevent further cooking and to set the colour. This is called *refreshing*. Just before serving toss the vegetables separately in melted butter over a good heat.

Note I: As the cooking liquid contains much of the vitamins and minerals it should, if possible, be preserved and used for soups or sauces.

Note II: The word 'blanching' as used above is confusing since it used to mean to whiten (*blanche* = white in French) by rapid boiling, e.g. to blanch almonds would be to boil them to enable the cook to peel the brown skins off, leaving them white. Here, however, it simply means to boil until very nearly cooked. The cooking is finished in the re-heating process.

Boiling

Follow the same procedure as above. Drain the vegetables (without refreshing) and dish up. Brush with melted butter.

Sweating or half-steaming

There is no doubt that from a nutritional point of view this is a better way of cooking green vegetables as no minerals or vitamins are lost with the cooking water. This method, however, does not always produce a very attractive green colour, and cannot successfully be done in advance.

72

Put the prepared vegetables in a heavy saucepan with a tablespoon of butter or margarine (or, if preferred, water). Cover tightly with a lid. Cook very slowly. Shake the pan frequently until the vegetables are tender. Add salt and dish up.

Steaming

Steaming (in a proper steamer) is an excellent method of cooking root vegetables, but is less successful with green ones as their bright colour is sometimes lost. Nutritionally superior to boiling.

Stir frying

This cooking method (much beloved of Chinese cooks) is excellent for green vegetables. It preserves vitamins and minerals, and the vegetables remain bright in colour. The disadvantage is that you must stand over the cooking vegetables all the time.

Slice the vegetables as finely as you can, put in a large deep-sided frying pan (the Chinese wok is perfect) with a splash of oil. Toss the vegetables in the hot oil over a fierce heat. Shake the pan, and stir and turn the vegetables continually until they are just tender. Sprinkle with salt and serve.

FRESH NON-GREEN VEGETABLES

Boiling

Put the vegetables into cold salted water and bring slowly to the boil. Cook until completely tender. With the possible exception of carrots (which are good *al dente* or with a bit of bite to them), root vegetables should be cooked until soft right through. Drain and brush with melted butter. Unlike green vegetables, root vegetables are generally cooked in a covered saucepan, as their colour is unaffected by slower cooking in a closed pan, but they can be boiled rapidly as are green vegetables. Care should be taken to prevent potatoes breaking up.

Refreshing (see page 72)

This is sometimes advisable for carrots as this sets the bright colour, but is not necessary.

Sweating or half-steaming

Slice the vegetables fairly thickly. Cook them slowly in a covered saucepan with plenty of butter or oil. They will absorb more fat than green vegetables. Very good for mushrooms.

Steaming

Excellent for all root vegetables, particularly for large potatoes which might otherwise break up while boiling.

DRIED PULSES

Dried peas and beans (lentils, split peas, chick peas, green peas, black-eyed peas, haricot beans, lima beans, butter beans, brown beans, red kidney beans etc.) are generally cheaper than their fresh or tinned equivalents, are easy to cook and very nutritious. They should be bought from grocers with a good turnover, and as a rule small butter beans are better than large ones, small chick peas better than large etc.

Most pulses need soaking until softened and swollen before cooking. Soaking can take as much as 12 hours (e.g. butter beans) or as little as 20 minutes (e.g. lentils). Do not soak for more than 12 hours in case the beans start germinating or fermenting. If there is no time for preliminary soaking, unsoaked pulses may be cooked either in a pressure cooker or very slowly; but remember that enough water must be used to allow the beans first to swell and then to cook. Preliminary soaking is less hazardous.

To cook the pulses, simply cover them with fresh cold salted water, bring to the boil and simmer until tender. (Boiling the vegetables without salt is said to produce better results but we have not found this to be so.) Boiling times vary according to the age and size of the pulses (last season's pulses will cook faster than three-year-old ones). Small lentils may take as little as 15 minutes and large haricot beans or chick peas can take as long as 2 hours.

Vegetable	Preparation	Suggested method of cooking	Approx. cooking time	Suggested garnish
Artichoke, Jerusalem	Wash and peel.	Steam, sweat or boil.	30–40 min	Melted butter, black pepper and squeeze lemon juice.
Asparagus	Wash, remove hard ends and peel tough outer skin if necessary. Tie in bundles.	Steam or boil in unsalted water. Stems will cook slower than heads so stand bundles upright with heads above water level (where they will cook slowly in the steam while the stems cook fast in the boiling water).	10–15 min	Hollandaise sauce or melted butter (seasoned with salt, pepper and lemon juice) handed separately.
Beans, broad	Shell. (If very young they are good boiled whole.)	Boil in salted water. Remove outer skins after cooking if tough.	7–10 min	Melted butter and fried bacon bits, or white sauce, or fried chopped walnuts.
Beans, French	Wash, top and tail. String if necessary.	Boil in salted water.	8–12 min	Melted butter, fried almonds.
Beans, runner	String if necessary. Wash. Cut into 5cm/2in lengths.	Boil in salted water.	7–10 min	Melted butter, chopped fresh thyme.

Vegetable	Preparation	Suggested method of cooking	Approx. cooking time	Suggested garnish
Beetroot, young	Wash but do not peel.	Boil in salted water. Then peel.	1–2 hrs	White sauce. *Or* butter (melted) with raw onion, chopped.
Broccoli	Wash. Remove tough leaves or stalks.	Boil in salted water.	8–15 min	Melted butter *or* hollandaise sauce.
Broccoli, sprouting	Wash. Remove hard stalks.	Boil in salted water.	6–10 min	Melted butter *or* hollandaise sauce.
Brussels sprouts	Trim off outer tough leaves. Trim stalks. If large make a deep cup in base to promote quicker cooking.	Boil in salted water.	6–12 min	Melted butter, pinch nutmeg *or* caraway seeds.
Cabbage, Chinese	Wash. Slice coarsely.	Stir fry, sweat or boil very briefly.	4–6 min	Melted butter, squeeze of lemon. Black pepper.
Cabbage, red	Shred finely.	Stew gently (covered) in heavy pan with butter, chopped onions, chopped apples, sultanas, salt, pepper, sugar and a little vinegar. Turn frequently.	2–3 hrs or until very mushy	Serve as it is.

Vegetable	Preparation	Method	Time	Serving
Cabbage, spring	Wash. Shred very finely.	Stir fry, or boil in salted water.	*Stir fry:* 10 min *Boil:* 5–7 min	Melted butter and caraway seeds.
Carrots	Peel and slice or cut into sticks.	Boil in salted water with pinch of sugar.	8–10 min	Melted butter, and chopped mint.
	Or peel and grate coarsely. Do not salt.	Stir fry in butter.	2 min	Salt, pepper, pinch of sugar.
Cauliflower	Wash. Break into florets. Remove large stalks.	Boil in salted water.	12 min	Browned butter (beurre noisette) or white sauce or mornay sauce.
Celery	Wash and cut in 5cm/2in pieces.	Boil in salted water.	15–20 min	White sauce or chopped dill and melted butter.
Courgettes	Peel strips of skin lengthwise from the courgette, leaving half the skin on. This looks pretty and stripey.	Boil in salted water, or sweat in butter.	*Boil:* 4–6 min *Sweat:* 5–10 min	Melted butter or Béchamel sauce.
	Or grate coarsely, including skin. Do not salt.	Stir fry in butter	35 sec	Salt and pepper

Vegetable	Preparation	Suggested method of cooking	Approx. cooking time	Suggested garnish
Endive	Wipe dry. Leave whole.	Steam, or bake in oven, covered, in water with lemon, chopped tarragon and thyme.	*Steam:* 20–30 min *Bake:* 1–1½ hrs	*Steamed:* white sauce. *Baked:* melted butter, chopped parsley.
Kale, curly	Wash. Remove hard stalks.	Put in covered saucepan with no extra water. Shake over moderate heat. Drain very well.	6–10 min	Melted butter, pinch of nutmeg and squeeze of lemon.
Leeks	Wash. Remove outer leaves and tough dark green part. Split if large.	Boil in salted water in roasting tin or frying pan. Lift out with a fish slice.	10–15 min	Melted butter and black pepper *or* white sauce
Mange-tout	Wash, top and tail.	Stir fry, sweat or boil.	5–6 min	Melted butter only.
Marrow	Wash and peel if tough-skinned. Cut into 5cm/2in chunks.	Bake covered in moderate oven with a coating of melted butter. Or steam.	30 min	Browned butter (beurre noisette) and chopped parsley *or* white sauce.
Mushrooms	Do not peel unless very old and tough. Wipe and trim off any ragged stalks. Quarter if large.	Sweat in butter with squeeze of lemon juice. Or grill, brushed with butter.	4–8 min	Melted butter, black pepper and lemon juice. *Or* a little double cream *or* soured cream.

Onions	Peel.	Boil, steam or bake. If to be baked, peel after cooking.	*Boil:* 15–30 min *Steam:* 20–40 min *Bake:* 1–1½ hrs	*Boiled:* toss in butter plus pinch of sugar until pale brown. *Steamed:* white sauce. *Baked:* melted butter.
Parsnips	Peel, and cut up if large.	Boil in salted water. Or boil and mash. Or roast with butter.	*Boil:* 20–30 min *Roast:* 1–2 hrs	Melted butter, black pepper. Nothing if roasted.
Peas	Hull.	Boil in salted water with a good pinch of sugar and a sprig of mint.	5–20 min	Melted butter. Chopped mint.
Potatoes	Peel for steamed or boiled (except new). Scrub and rub with salt for baked. Blanch 5 min then scratch all over with fork for roast.	Steam, boil, sweat, bake or roast. See also deep-frying, potatoes (pages 31–3, 243–244, 228).	*Roast:* 1–1½ hrs *Other methods:* up to 30 min	Melted butter and chopped parsley *or* mint; *or* dill for boiled and steamed.
Pumpkin	Wash and peel. Cut into 5cm/2in chunks.	Roast: with butter and lemon juice. Steam or sweat: in butter.	*Steam or sweat:* 30 min *Roast:* 1–2 hrs	Melted butter and chopped parsley. Nothing if roasted.

Vegetable	Preparation	Suggested method of cooking	Approx. cooking time	Suggested garnish
Salsify (white-skinned)	Wash and cut into 5cm/2in lengths.	Boil. Peel after cooking.	15–20 min	Beurre noisette (browned butter).
Scorzonera (black-skinned salsify-like root)	Wash, peel and cut into 5cm/2in lengths.	Boil, steam or sweat.	15–20 min	Beurre noisette (browned butter).
Sea Kale	Wash and remove any tough stem.	Boil in salted water or steam.	10–20 min	Hollandaise sauce, *or* melted butter (seasoned with salt, pepper and lemon juice) handed separately.
Shallots	Peel.	Boil in salted water. Steam, sweat or roast with butter.	15–30 min More for roasting	*Steamed:* white sauce. *Boiled:* browned butter (beurre noisette).
Spinach	Wash well. Pull away stalks.	Put into covered saucepan *without any water.* Shake over moderate heat. Drain and squeeze dry.	4 min	Melted butter, grated nutmeg *or* crushed fried garlic.

Swedes	Peel thickly. Slice.	20–30 min	*Mashed:* plenty of butter, salt and pepper. *Whole:* melted butter *and* or chopped parsley.
	Sweat or steam. Mash if very wet and shake over heat to dry.		
Sweetcorn	Remove the outside leaves and thread-like fibres.	5–6 min (longer if old)	Melted butter and freshly ground black pepper.
	Boil in salted water.		
Tomatoes	Wash. Split in half.	*Grill:* 5 min *Bake:* 12–15 min in moderate oven.	Chopped basil or parsley and black pepper.
	Grill or bake (boiled tomatoes are very dreary) sprinkled with butter and chopped onion and/or garlic.		
Turnips	Peel thickly. Slice thickly.	20–30 min	Melted butter and lemon juice.
	Sweat or steam. Mash if very wet and shake over heat to dry.		

HERBS AND SPICES

Many herbs (aromatic green plants used for flavouring) can be home-grown. Most spices have to be bought as they are the seeds, roots, berries or bark of plants grown in tropical climates.

Buying and storing

As far as possible always use fresh rather than dried herbs. They freeze well and taste infinitely better than their dried counterpart.

Dried herbs and spices lose flavour fairly rapidly and so it is essential to buy in small quantities to ensure as quick a turnover as possible. Always keep them in air-tight containers in a cool, dry place – not near the oven or sink.

Most fresh green herbs keep well for a few days in a plastic bag in the refrigerator.

FISH

The word 'fish' is used to include freshwater and sea fish, but not shellfish (see pages 104–11).

Freshwater fish are divided into coarse fish, fished mainly for sport with rod and line and generally thrown back live into the rivers, and game fish, which are caught both for sport and commercially. Recently, freshwater fish farms have been set up. Many freshwater fish, such as bass, sturgeon, sea trout and salmon spend most of their adult lives in the sea, swimming back up the rivers to spawn, but they are still classified as freshwater fish despite the fact that most of them are caught by trawl in the sea. Coarse river fish, such as roach, gudgeon and tench are not sold commercially and are seldom eaten except by anglers' families.

Most of our fish come from the sea. As the fishing industry

'modernizes' it is increasingly difficult to get locally caught fish, and in some villages and towns not ten miles from the sea the only fish available is in frozen packets – perhaps a choice of fish fingers, kipper fillets or cod steaks. For the cook this is sad. Fish is a valuable source of protein, vitamin D (in oily fish), calcium and phosphorus (especially found in the edible bones of whitebait, sardines etc.), iodine, fluorine and some of the B vitamins.

Fish contains very little fat. Even oily fish seldom has more than 20 per cent fat content. (A mutton chop will contain 50 per cent fat or more.) This means that fish is easily digestible, and contains fewer calories than its equivalent weight in meat. Fish flesh is so composed (with little connective tissue and little fat) that over-vigorous or over-long cooking will cause dryness and disintegration. For this reason fish is generally grilled or fried fast, or poached gently in barely moving liquid. It cooks a great deal quicker than meat.

Fish, unlike meat, does not improve on keeping. Some *aficionados* say that salmon is best eaten three days after catching, but we feel this is a rationalization of the fact that it used to take three days to bring a salmon down from Scotland to London. Likewise there are some fish chefs and restaurateurs who say that sole is better for a day or two in the chiller, as the flesh is then firmer. But what is undisputed is that any fish (including salmon or sole) eaten within a few hours of catching is remarkably good. Fish as fresh as that should be served as plainly as possible, perhaps with nothing but melted butter and a wedge of lemon.

Fish are either round when seen in section (like a salmon) or flat (like a sole), and are so described.

PREPARATION FOR COOKING

Removing the scales

Large fish have dry scales which should be removed before cooking. To do this, scrape a large knife the wrong way along the fish (from tail to head). This can be a messy business as the scales tend to fly about. But, unless you are buying fish from a wholesale market, the fishmonger will do it for you.

Gutting and cleaning

The fishmonger will probably clean the fish, but if you are to do it yourself you will need a very sharp knife. (Fish skin blunts knives faster than anything else.) If the fish is to be stuffed or filleted it does not matter how big a slit you make to remove the entrails. If it is to be left whole, the shorter the slit the better. Start just below the head and slit through the soft belly skin. After pulling out the innards wash the fish under cold water. If it is large, and of the round type, make sure all the dark blood along the spinal column is removed.

Now carefully cut away the gills. Take care not to cut off the head if you want to serve the fish whole. If you do not, cut off head and tail now. To remove the fins cut the skin round them, take a good grip (if you salt your fingers well it will stop them slipping) and yank sharply towards the head. This will pull the fin bones out with the fin.

Skinning and filleting flat fish

Fish skin is easier to remove after cooking when it comes away easily. But sometimes the fish must be skinned before cooking. Most whole fish are not skinned or filleted before grilling, but sole are skinned on at least the dark side, and sometimes on both sides. To do this make a crosswise slit through the skin at the tail, and push a finger in. You will now be able to run the finger round the edge of the fish loosening the skin. When you have done this on both edges, take a firm grip of the skin at the tail end (salt your fingers to prevent slipping) with one hand, and with the other hold the fish down. Give a quick strong yank, peeling the skin back towards the head. If necessary, do the same to the other side.

Flat fish are generally filleted into four half-fillets. To do this, lay the fish on a board with the tail towards you. Cut through the flesh to the backbone along the length of the fish. Then, with a sharp pliable knife, cut the left-hand fillet away from the bone, keeping the blade almost flat against the bones of the fish. Then swivel the fish round so the head is towards you and cut away the second fillet in the same way. Turn the fish over and repeat the process on the other side. (If you are left-handed, tackle the right-hand fillet first.)

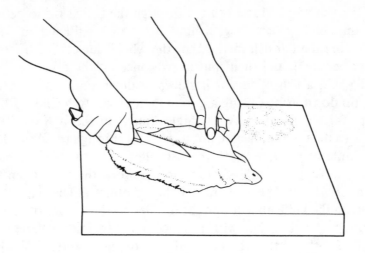

Filleting and skinning round fish

Round fish are filleted before skinning. If they are to be cooked whole, they are cooked with the skin, but this may be carefully peeled off after cooking (e.g. a whole poached salmon). To fillet a round fish lay it on a board and cut through the flesh down to the backbone from the head to the tail. Insert a sharp pliable knife between the flesh and the bones, and slice the fillet away

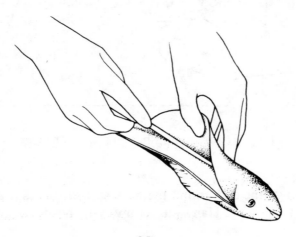

from the bones, working with short strokes from the backbone and from the head end. Remember to keep the knife as flat as possible, and to keep it against the bones. When the fillet is almost off the fish you will need to cut through the belly skin to detach it completely. Very large round fish can be filleted in four, following the flat fish method, or the whole side can be lifted as described here, and then split in two once off the fish.

To skin a fish fillet, put it skin side down on a board. Hold the tip down firmly, using a good pinch of salt to help get a firm grip. With a sharp, heavy, straight knife, cut through the flesh, close to the tip, taking care not to go right through the skin. Hold the knife at rightangles to the fish fillet, with the blade almost upright. With a gentle sawing motion work the flesh from the skin, *pushing* the fillet off rather than cutting it. The reason for keeping the knife almost upright is to lessen the danger of cutting through the skin, but with practice it is possible to flatten the knife slightly, so that the sharp edge is foremost, and simply slide it forward, without the sawing motion.

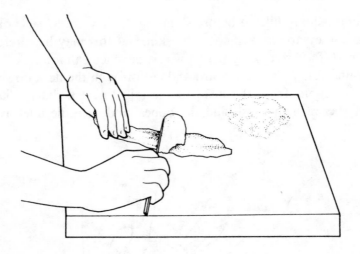

See also page 97 for boning herring and other small fish.

Skinning eel
Cut through the skin round the neck and slit the skin down the length of the body. Hang the eel up by its head – a stout hook

through the eyes is best. Using a cloth to get a good grip, pull hard to peel off the skin from neck to tail.

Stuffing fish

Round fish are more suitable for stuffing whole than flat fish, as there is more space in the body cavity after gutting. Stuffings usually contain breadcrumbs, which swell during cooking, so care should be taken not to overfill the fish. Fish fillets can be sand-wiched with stuffing, or rolled up round the mixture. Well-flavoured expensive fish is less often stuffed than the more tasteless varieties, which need the additional flavour of an aromatic filling.

Slicing smoked salmon

Place the side of salmon, skin side down, on a board. Run the tips of the fingers of one hand over the surface of the flesh to locate the ends of the small bones. Pull the bones out with tweezers or pliers. Now slice the flesh in horizontal paper-thin slices, using a long, sharp ham knife. The slices should be long and wide. It is customary to remove the central narrow stripe of brownish flesh, but this is not strictly necessary – it tastes excellent.

If the whole side is not to be sliced, place a piece of plastic wrap on the cut surface of the remaining salmon to prevent drying out.

FRESHWATER FISH

Bass

Name given to many fish, both sea and freshwater. Freshwater bass is in season mid-June to mid-March. Can weigh up to 3·4 kilos/8lb, is sold whole, and has a pale pink, firm, delicately-flavoured flesh. Delicious cooked any way, but the plainer methods are probably best – poached, fried or grilled. Both black and white bass are available, though neither are abundant.

Bream

Sometimes a disappointing fish, lacking flavour and having rather too soft flesh. But good plainly cooked, if very freshly caught, or baked with a herby stuffing to give it bite. In season mid-June to mid-March. Weighs up to 4·5 kilos/10lb but smaller fish (1·35 kilos/3lb) are the norm.

Carp

Usually sold between 1·35 kilos/3lb and 3·4 kilos/8lb but can reach enormous size. Considered a festive fish in parts of Europe (rather like our Christmas Turkey), it is usually sold whole. Coarse texture, not very interesting taste, but good baked with stuffing, or fried in butter with plenty of lemon. In season mid-June to mid-March.

Char

A member of the salmon family, but small – 450g/1lb to 900g/2lb in weight. The flesh resembles that of trout, and recipes for trout will do well for char.

Eel

Usually caught weighing 225g/$\frac{1}{2}$lb–900g/2lb. The very small eels are unsatisfactory as they are too bony, and the very large ones (90cm/3ft long and more) have a coarse texture and taste. A 675g/1$\frac{1}{2}$lb–900g/2lb eel is best, traditionally eaten cold in a savoury eel jelly, or in pies. But eating habits change, and today they are more often sold smoked, or for use in fish soups or stews. Good coated in egg and breadcrumbs and fried. In season all the year round, best in autumn.

Grilse

This is young salmon which, having spent a year feeding at sea, returns to its native river to spawn. It is paler in colour, more delicate in flavour than older salmon and weighs up to 3·2 kilos/7lb or so.

Pike

Young pike (weighing up to 1·8 kilos/4lb) are best for flavour, but all pike make good quenelles, fish stocks and stews. This is because they contain a high proportion of gelatine. Pike is often added to salmon quenelle mixture to give tackiness and flavour. But they can be cooked in any other way, having good flavour and white flesh. In season mid-June to March.

Salmon

The king of fish, not only in flavour (which is superbly rich) but regrettably in price too. It has an oily, bright pinkish-red flesh ideal for plain poaching, grilling, steaming and frying. (See also under smoked fish.) Fish can reach 9 kilos/20lb or so, but are best at about 3·4 kilos/8lb. The first salmon of the season (which starts in February) are truly unsurpassed in flavour and delicacy. Towards the end of the season (October/November) the taste is sometimes slightly muddy. Canadian salmon sold in Britain is good, but not on a par with Scotch. Salmon steaks cut from the 'middle cut' are the most expensive to buy, but the tail steaks, though less uniform in shape, are even richer in taste. See also Grilse.

Sea trout

Often called salmon trout by fishmongers because of its similarity in looks and colour (pale pink to reddish when raw) to salmon. In fact salmon trout are simply river trout (brown trout, rainbow trout or speckled trout), but because they have spent a season or more in the sea, living on a diet largely composed of crustaceans, their flesh takes on a pink colour and fine flavour akin to that of salmon. It costs rather less than salmon, but is often more difficult to buy. The fish, when really fresh, are perhaps preferable even to salmon, being less rich and solid. They are smaller fish, seldom reaching more than 1·8 kilos/4lb. In season March to August and, like salmon, are best at the beginning of the season. Best cooked whole in the oven or poached. But they can be fried or grilled in fillets.

Smelt

Sometimes classed as a freshwater fish as it is caught in river
estuaries as well as in coastal seas. (See under sea fish.)

Trout

Brown river trout and speckled trout are less widely available,
and less popular, than Rainbow trout, but this is illogical as they
are equally good. Both have firm, white-tending-to-pinkish flesh
and are generally sold between 200g/7oz and 340g/¾lb in weight,
but they may grow much larger. They are generally cooked whole,
either fried or poached 'au bleu' (i.e. killed, gutted and dropped
instantly into boiling liquid).

The fishing season is from March to September, but due to
fish-farming and freezing rainbow trout are now available all the
year round. However, it must be admitted that a line-caught trout,
fresh from the river, is a finer thing than an artificially fattened
one from a farm, unless the farmer goes to the trouble and
expense of feeding his fish on the sort of diet they would find
in rivers. Slightly pinkish flesh is common in line-caught fish and
is usually an indication of fine flavour.

SEA FISH

FLAT WHITE FISH

(The term 'white' refers to the colour of the flesh, not the skin.)

Brill

An underrated fish, perhaps because its flesh is not as pure-
white as some. But it has an excellent flavour. The texture is not
as firm as that of turbot, which the fish resembles. Brill seldom
grows larger than 3·4 kilos/8lb. It is served poached, grilled or
fried, usually in flat pieces of fillet.

Dover sole

The undisputed king of white fish, it has a price to match.
Very firm white flesh. The fish comes, not from Dover, but from
the North Sea. It can weigh up to 900g/2lb, and is best grilled
or fried on the bone, or in a delicate sauce. 170g/6oz soles are
called slip soles. A 340g/¾lb sole is the usual weight for a main
course. The skin on one side is brownish grey, on the other pearly
white.

Lemon sole

So often considered the 'poor man's Dover sole' (it is less firm
and flavoursome), it is a delicious fish in its own right. One side
is white, the other lightish brown – paler and less grey than the
Dover. It is also more rounded in shape, with a pointed nose.
Weighs between 225g/½lb and 900g/2lb. The flesh is very white
and delicate. Excellent grilled or fried. The fillets are good stuffed
and baked in milk. Best in autumn or winter.

Plaice

Similar in shape (though often very much larger, reaching perhaps
2·3 kilos/5lb) to the lemon sole or witch. It has a brownish-grey
side, spotted with orange. The other side is white. The flesh,
delicious when very fresh, has the disadvantage of being soft rather
than firm. Cooked in every possible way, plaice, next to cod, is
Britain's most popular fish. It is best plainly grilled or fried. Or
the fillets may be stuffed and baked, and served with a cheese
sauce. At its best from June to January.

Turbot

An excellent, and expensive, fish of very firm texture and pure
white flesh. One of the few fish large enough and firm enough
to be cut into cubes and grilled on a skewer. The larger turbot
(weighing up to 20 kilos/45lb) are cut across in steaks, the smaller
ones (900g/2lb–1·35 kilos/3lb) cooked whole to serve two or three
people. Any method of cooking is good. A fish popular with
restaurant chefs due to their good size, flavour that does not

disappear if the fish is kept for a day or two, and versatility. Best between July and March.

Witch

Used to be called Torbay sole, but this is now illegal. Very like lemon sole, though seldom larger than 675g/1½lb. Cooked similarly, and best in autumn or winter. The skin is pale grey on one side, white on the other.

ROUND WHITE FISH

Cod

Britain's most popular fish, most of it ending up in frozen packets or fish fingers and the like. Good firm white flesh, freezes almost perfectly. The flesh has large creamy flakes, and few bones, but not much taste. Its very non-fishiness may account for its popular appeal, and of course the fact that it is comparatively plentiful. Needs good seasoning, a cheesy sauce, or a crisp batter to counteract slight dullness. Available all the year round.

Conger eel

The sea eel, stronger in flavour than the small freshwater one, can be up to 9 kilos/20lb in weight. In season from March to October. Used in pies or fish soups, or jellied with parsley. It has a strong and pervading taste, greatly liked by many people but detested by others. Baby eels caught in shoals and cooked like whitebait are excellent but rare.

Dabs

Small plaice-like fish, best served whole, plainly grilled.

Dogfish (flake, huss)

Once also called rock-salmon but this is outlawed now. Only good when very fresh – it develops an unattractive ammonia-like smell when stale. A cheapish fish, very common in fish-and-chip shops, it can be good if fresh and freshly cooked, but has a bad reputation from misuse. Deep frying in batter is best, as the rather soft and oily flesh needs the contrast of crisp batter. There are several varieties of dogfish, some spotted, and all long, round and looking slightly like baby sharks.

Grey mullet

Used to be a cheap and despised fish, but largely due to the Chinese restaurant trade wisely buying up all available stocks for baking whole, it is more popular, and consequently more difficult to buy today. It needs, more than most fish, to be really fresh to be good, quickly becoming dreary and tasteless if stale. Even when fresh it is helped by careful cooking such as baking whole, either stuffed, or sprinkled liberally with lemon, fennel or dill. The fish is generally sold weighing between 340g/¾lb and 1·35 kilos/3lb.

Haddock

Similar in shape to cod, but smaller. But haddock is an infinitely superior and unhappily more expensive fish, with a firmer, more flavoursome flesh. Good cooked almost any way, but a whole small haddock baked in the oven is one of life's big treats. Larger fish are sold in steaks for grilling or frying. Makes the best fish pie.

Hake

Similar in shape to cod and haddock, weighing up to 4·5 kilos/ 10lb. Can be rather dry if carelessly cooked, but has a good flavour. Cook as cod.

Halibut

A large flattish fish of excellent white firm flesh, and rich good flavour. Steaks are sold from the larger fish (they can weigh as much as 18 kilos/40lb) and the smaller halibut (known as chicken halibut) weighing as little as 900g/2lb are sold whole. Excellent grilled or fried plainly, baked, steamed, or poached. Needs no seasoning other than salt, pepper and a squeeze of lemon.

Huss – see Dogfish

John Dory

Sometimes called St Peter's fish, because like haddock (which is also known as St Peter's fish) it carries the 'finger-and-thumb' mark on each flank. Legend has it that when St Peter caught the fish, it groaned so loudly he tossed it back into the sea, leaving his imprint on it. It is also, confusingly, known as golden haddock. But there the resemblance ends. John Dory has such an ugly head fishmongers usually remove it before sale. It has a firm, almost lobster-like or nutty-flavoured flesh. Best grilled, fried or plainly baked. The fish can weigh up to 5·4 kilo/12lb but are frequently small enough for two portions. Unfortunately rare.

Ling (not to be confused with the freshwater grayling, which is a smaller game fish, rare and good to eat)

A large fish with almost nothing to recommend it, except perhaps for use in soups or stocks. The deceptively beautiful flesh (large, lean, almost boneless) becomes, even with the most careful of cooking, dry, shreddy, and totally tasteless. Too dry and lacking in gelatine for quenelles, too boring for grilling, too large for baking stuffed and whole, ling is best simply not bought.

Redfish (Norway haddock, ocean perch, soldier: sometimes incorrectly, and illegally, labelled 'bream' on the fish slab)

Has a not-too-tasty, firm pink flesh. Best when very fresh. 2·7 kilo/6lb fish are probably the best, and are excellent baked whole, perhaps with a lemony stuffing.

Sea bass (French *bar*). Also sometimes called *loup de mer* which is confusing as this correctly means catfish. The confusion deepens because some varieites of catfish are nicknamed dogfish, and there are many dogfish, some of them totally unrelated to each other, and so on almost indefinitely.

A scarce, totally delicious Mediterranean fish, usually weighing between 340g/¾lb and 1·35 kilos/3lb. Best baked or grilled whole with a sprig or two of fennel. It is shaped like a small salmon, with grey skin, and firm white delicate flesh.

Sea bream (French *daurade* or *dorade*)

Comes in many colours and sizes, the best being the golden dorade. One-portion size fish are good rolled in flour or cornmeal and fried in butter. The larger fish are good grilled or baked. Sea bream can be pink (like redfish, which, before the Trades Description Act, were often passed off as bream) but they are not as good as the golden. They are tastier than redfish, however. As usual freshness is all.

Skate

Now an expensive fish, skate used to be one of the cheapest available. The best skates are those weighing less than 1·35 kilos/ 3lb – larger ones tend to be tough and coarse-textured. The skin of skate is slimy when fresh and the flesh should be faintly pink. Best in the winter. Only the side pieces of the pectoral fins or wings are eaten. Sold in pieces, or (particularly in France) whole if small enough. The flesh (found between and over the cartilaginous ribs of the fin) is soft and of good flavour. Best served fried, with browned butter, or in a caper sauce.

Smelt

A curious small fish smelling, when just caught, of cucumber. They are cooked whole, having been gutted through the gills – to do this grip the gills and pull firmly, and the entrails will come out too. Wipe the fish with a damp cloth (do not wash) and grill or deep fry. Sometimes several smelts (enough for a portion) are grilled or fried on a wooden skewer. They are strung through the eye sockets, and served on the skewer.

Snapper or *schnapper*

Not often available in Britain but deserves a mention simply because it tastes so good. Cooks travelling in Australia or America should not miss the opportunity of at least eating, if not cooking it. There are various varieties, the most famous of which is the North American (eastern seaboard) red snapper. It is about 60cm/2ft long, and usually served as grilled steaks. The flesh is white, with large creamy flakes, sometimes compared to sea bass or lobster meat. The grey snapper is softer-fleshed but just as good. It grows slightly larger than the red.

Whiting

A small fish of the cod family, it is sold whole, and sometimes fried with its tail pulled through a hole made in its head, to look as though biting its tail. We have no idea why such a strange tradition should exist, but it is common in France as well as in Britain. Whiting has little flavour, and must be eaten very fresh if it is to have any taste at all. Because of its boniness (and subsequently gelatinous flesh) it is excellent for quenelles. Often used to bind less tacky fish in quenelle making – lobster quenelles would certainly be made with either whiting, pike, or similar 'sticky' fish added to the mixture.

OILY FISH

Although most fish contain very little oil (apart from in the liver), there are some varieties which contain more than most.

Anchovies

Tiny (10cm/4in–13cm/5in long), very strongly flavoured members of the herring family. Usually sold salted in tins. Used as flavouring or garnishing, and to make sauces or pastes.

Brisling

Baby sprats (see sprats) – even smaller and eaten whole like whitebait, or with mustard sauce.

Herrings

A very nutritious fish, particularly popular in the North, and once cheap and plentiful. Today it is more expensive, and less easily available fresh, a large proportion of the catch being sold for kippering. Average weight 170g/6oz. They should be shiny, feel fairly stiff, and not smell over-strong. The chief disadvantage of herrings is their boniness. But they can be boned, or almost boned, before cooking: split them open completely and lay, skin side up, on a board. With the heel of your hand press down firmly on the backbone of the fish. This will loosen it. Turn it over, cut through the backbone near the head and pull it out with, hopefully, all the side bones attached to it. (This is a good method of dealing with any small fish, such as trout, if it is to be baked stuffed.)

Herrings are used for pickling raw (rollmops), cooking in a mild pickle (soused herring), and for simple grilling, baking and frying.

Mackerel

A beautiful shiny fish with colourful green and black markings and a pearly white belly. Weighs 285g/10oz to 900g/2lb, and has a distinctive, delicious taste when fresh. Almost tasteless, and soggy in texture, if kept more than a day or two.

Generally fried or baked. Good with a mustard sauce, or a sharp one like gooseberry, to counteract the richness and slight oiliness. In season throughout the year, but availability is patchy, and the fish are not at their best during the late autumn or winter.

Pilchards

Pilchards are adult sardines and are delicious, though strong, when fresh. They are cooked like herring. Unfortunately they are generally canned, in sweetish tomato sauce, and are, in the opinion of the authors, perfectly disgusting.

Red mullet

Small, bony, rather dry and firm red-skinned fish of the Mediterranean. Wonderful flavour when fresh, and generally cooked with the liver left in the fish – giving it a strong distinctive flavour. Almost always grilled or fried, and served with plenty of melted butter. Often very expensive. Two red mullet are served per person if of average size (about 170g/6oz).

Sardines

Young pilchards, about 10cm/4in long, absolutely delicious when freshly caught and grilled. Available (and very good) frozen. Most frequently they are tinned in oil, which is good, but bears little resemblance to the fresh fish.

Sprats

Related to the herring, sprats are about 10cm/4in long. They are sometimes cooked ungutted, but they may be cleaned if preferred. Usually served deep-fried with a mustard sauce, or grilled and served with mustard butter. In season from October to March.

Tunny (tuna)

An enormous fish, seldom, unhappily, available fresh in Britain, but good packed in oil in cans. Its flavour is sometimes compared to chicken, and certainly it has a most un-fishy firm flesh. Pinkish in colour. When fresh it is delicious plainly grilled or fried; or braised on a bed of Mediterranean vegetables (tomatoes, peppers, aubergines and courgettes). Found in warm seas only.

Whitebait

These are baby herring or sprats, caught in shoals and eaten ungutted, and whole, head and tail included. They are delicious deep-fried after being dipped in milk and shaken in flour, or in a very light batter. 110g/$\frac{1}{4}$lb of raw whitebait makes a good first course, served with brown bread and butter, half a lemon and salt, pepper and paprika.

SMOKED FISH

Most fish can be smoked. Small metal kits are available for smoking two or three small items – say a couple of trout or half a spring chicken. But most smoked fish is cured commercially, and sold ready to eat, or ready to cook.

Commercially smoked fish is first salted by immersion in brine. It is then hung up in the smoke of wood fires (originally simple pits were dug in the bottom of which smouldered a wood fire, and over which were suspended sides of fish, whole herring or what-have-you). The duration of the brining process and the length of time spent in the smoke determine the final colour and flavour of the fish. Refrigeration has meant that milder cures and less smoking are necessary. Smoking is now done for the flavour, where once it was a practical means of preserving fish.

Partly because the light smoking given today would produce a pallid-coloured fish, and partly because manufacturers regard bright colour as essential for 'plate appeal' for the housewife, many fish are coloured by immersion in food dye before smoking. There is also a chemical dipping process which simulates the flavour and colour of smoked fish, but it is illegal to sell fish as 'smoked' if it has not in fact been at least briefly hung in smoke. There is, however, a small 'connoisseur's market' for undyed smoked fish.

'Cold' smoking flavours but does not cook the fish, which is cooked before serving. 'Hot' smoked items are generally served without further cooking.

Bloaters

Made from longshore herring (or herring caught close enough to the shore to be landed while fresh: most herring destined for the kipper industry is salted on board the trawler). They are then only very lightly brined and cold-smoked. They do not keep well. Traditionally they are smoked ungutted, giving them a gamey flavour. Like kippers, bloaters are usually cooked before eating, though the fillets may be marinated and eaten raw.

Buckling

These are Baltic herring, imported already brined, and smoked in London. They, in contrast with the kipper or bloater, are hot-smoked at 100 C/212 F and can be eaten without further cooking. When fresh they are moist and delicious, milder in flavour than cold-smoked kipper, and make a good substitute for the more expensive smoked trout. Remove the tough skins before serving. They are bonier, and consequently more troublesome to eat, than trout.

Smoked cod

Cod fillet commercially available is dyed artificially, before light smoking. It lacks the flavour and firm texture of smoked haddock, being inclined to cook into dry shreds. It is used as a substitute for haddock.

Smoked eel

Both freshwater and sea eels are smoked, the commonest being the larger saltwater variety. They have a good rich taste, and are best eaten with a salad or bread, and plenty of lemon juice. Smaller eels are served in fillets, larger ones sometimes cut across in thick pieces.

Smoked haddock

Commonly sold by the pound, cut from large fillets. It is almost invariably dyed to a bright yellow hue. Today, with modern means of refrigeration, it is unnecessary to salt fish heavily to make it keep, and most smoked haddock is mild in flavour. Usually poached or grilled for breakfast or supper, or used in kedgeree. It makes good soup (in a creamy thickened fish stock) but few cooks realize this. The best smoked haddock are the famous Arbroath smokies, which once gutted and cleaned, are smoked closed; and those from Findon (known as finnan haddies) which are split and boned, and smoked opened out flat. Arbroath smokies' skin is almost black, finnans are pale translucent yellow. Sometimes Arbroath smokies are smoked ungutted, and occasionally whiting is used instead of young haddock.

Glasgow pales are small haddock, opened out and boned like finnans. All smoked haddock is cooked before eating.

Kippers

These are smoked herring. They are fairly strongly brined, and cold-smoked (at under 29°C/85°F). They are best poached in milk if very salty, or plainly grilled if not. The best kippers are from Craster in Northumberland and Loch Fyne in Scotland. Kipper fillets, sold packeted and frozen, are useful if boned flesh (for a pâté or mousse) is needed. Although kippers are generally cooked before serving, they can be marinated in oil and lemon juice for a few days, and served raw with toast or a salad.

Smoked mackerel

Mackerel can be either cold- or hot-smoked, the hot-smoked having a much more smoky flavour. Hot-smoked mackerel can be eaten without further cooking; cold-smoked mackerel is generally grilled and served with a mustard sauce. Smoked mackerel has very soft and moist flesh, and having bigger bones than many small fish it is easy to fillet for use in salads or pâtés. It does not keep well, and care should be taken to see it is absolutely fresh when bought. The skin should be dry to the touch and the smell light and pleasant.

Smoked salmon

Sides of smoked salmon are very lightly brined and smoked in coolish smoke for a maximum of 12 hours. Smoked salmon is eaten raw, with brown bread and butter. Less good smoked salmon (from Norway or Canada) has a rather reddish hue, and lacks the soft moistness and delicate pink colour of the best Scotch. But it is excellent for mousses or pâtés.

For carving, see page 87.

Smoked trout

Smoked trout are hot-smoked, and eaten without further cooking, usually served with brown bread and butter and horseradish sauce. The tough jacket of smoked skin is removed before serving, but the head and tail are usually left on. They make good, though expensive, pâté.

SALT FISH

All smoked fish are, to a greater or lesser degree, salted in brine before smoking. Indeed the cheaper varieties of 'smoked' fish may not be smoked at all, but simply brined and dyed. But some fish is dry-salted and sold without further treatment. The most common example is salt cod, beloved of the Portuguese, and once popular in Britain. But as salting is no longer necessary as a means of preservation, salt fish is becoming more difficult to find. Ling, a dreary fish when eaten fresh, profits from being salted, and there are few foods more delicious than Brandade de Morue made from salt cod. Salt fish needs 12 hours' soaking before cooking, if bought straight from the salt, but many fishmongers sell it ready-soaked. ,

FISH ROES

The roes of fish are very often a great delicacy. Some of them, such as cod roes, are sold boiled. They can be coated in egg and breadcrumbs and fried, served cold, or used in fish stuffings.

Caviar. Lightly salted sturgeon roes, of course, are the real thing, and the most famous varieties are Sevruga and Beluga. Beluga caviar is recognizable by its large, grey-black, translucent grains: Sevruga is smaller and darker. Both should be moist, oily and sweet-smelling. Once a jar is opened it should be kept refrigerated, and anyway eaten within two or three days.

Caviar is usually served (to the horror of connoisseurs who like it in large quantities on plain bread with no butter, lemon or anything else) with chopped egg yolk, chopped egg white, chopped parsley, finely chopped onion, pepper and lemon juice, the diner being offered all these condiments and hot toast and butter. It may be that all these bits and pieces 'stretch' the caviar, the most expensive food in the world, a little further. But, with or without the garnishes, caviar tastes wonderful. The cheaper, very salty pressed caviar is made from true sturgeon roes, but of damaged grains, or from less acclaimed fish than the Beluga or Sevruga.

Red caviar. Salmon roe, salted and sold in jars. Very good.

Mock caviar. Lump fish roe. Salty black small grains in jars. Adequate for cocktail party canapés.

102

Salted smoked soft roe of red mullet or cod is the main ingredient for taramasalata, and is sometimes eaten simply spread on bread or toast. Soft unsalted *herring roes*, sold canned or fresh, are delicious fried and served on toast as a first course or savoury.

Roes found in the fish you buy should not be discarded. Soft roes (the male fish's milt) are generally preferred by connoisseurs for their creamy soft texture, but the hard roe (female fish eggs) can be eaten too. Roes may be cooked and served with the fish, sieved and added to the sauce, or put in the stuffing. At the very least they should be frozen and kept for the next time you make fish stock.

COOKING TIMES FOR FISH

SMALL FISH

Small fish, or pieces of fish, are cooked according to their weight and thickness, but in any event the ultimate test of 'doneness' is how they look and feel. Whole small fish will have opaque eyes, the skin will peel easily, and the flesh will feel firm, and lift easily into flakes. A small brown trout, for example, dropped into hot poaching liquid, will take about six minutes; if fried it will need six minutes a side.

LARGE FISH

Large fish, poached or baked whole, are more difficult to test. The following is a rough guide of cooking times, after which the flesh should feel firm when pressed, and a skewer should glide easily into the thickest part of the flesh.

Poached

Eight minutes to the pound, timed from the minute the liquid reaches simmering point.

103

Baked

Assuming the oven is set at 180 C/350 F, gas mark 4, allow ten minutes for the fish to heat through (15 minutes if it is more than 2·3 kilos/5lb), then calculate 8 minutes to the pound. If it is stuffed weigh after stuffing.

SHELLFISH

The word *seafood* might be better than *shellfish* if we are categorizing those sea- or freshwater animals that are not scaled fish. However, the word seafood is unsatisfactory too, as fish are obviously food from the sea, and yet in culinary terms they are excluded when using the term.

To deal with real shellfish (i.e. those with shells) first: they fall into two broad categories – crustaceans and molluscs. The crustaceans all have legs, and move about, and some of them (like lobsters) have a jointed shell. Others (like crabs) do not, but they do get about on their legs.

Molluscs, on the other hand, do not usually move voluntarily. Indeed some bivalves (i.e. those with a hinged double shell, like oysters and mussels) stay on the same rock most of their lives. However, the bivalve cockles can leap short distances, and move with the tide in thousands. Most molluscs have an impenetrable protective shell, either of the hinged bivalve type, or a single conical shell like a limpet, or perhaps, for the slightly more mobile mollusc, a snail-like shell, such as found on the whelk or winkle. The exception to this general rule is the octopus family (which includes squid or ink-fish). They do not have a hard shell, and they swim, but nevertheless are molluscs. Oursins (those prickly black-brown molluscs beloved of the French who eat them raw, chilled like oysters) rely on their spines for protection. They are seldom available in Britain.

The clam (bivalve mollusc)

The most common clams in America are the soft shell (or long neck) clam, and the hard shell (or round) clam. Neither is frequently available in Britain, though the round clam is more often seen on the Continent. All clams are sandy and must be washed in several waters before cooking. After washing they are soaked in salty water to which a handful of oatmeal is added. (The clams ingest the oatmeal and excrete the dark matter from their intestines. This whitens them, improving their appearance. It is also said to cause the clam to open its shell, so allowing the sand to wash out.) They are then rinsed in fresh water and scrubbed well. Any that will not close tightly when tapped on the sink-edge must be discarded. Any that float or have damaged shells should be discarded too.

Long neck (or soft shell) clams are generally steamed in their shells – they will open during cooking – or are opened like oysters and eaten raw. To open a soft shell clam to eat raw run a sharp knife along the join of top and bottom shell, working over a basin so that none of the juices will be lost, and lift the top shell up. Cut the meat from the bottom shell, and slit the skin of the 'neck'. Pull the skin off and discard it. Serve with slices of lime or lemon and brown bread and butter.

The hard shell (or round) clams are generally steamed or used in chowders, or fried. The same washing, scrubbing and feeding with oatmeal procedure is necessary. If the clams have not been soaked in water with oatmeal, they must be opened before cooking (by cutting the muscle at the hinge with a short sharp knife and prising the shells apart) and the stomach opened up and cleaned.

Cockles (bivalve mollusc)

These are tiny shellfish with white fluted shells, similar in shape to a clam and found, like clams, on the beach, especially at low tide. Cockles are usually sold in Britain ready cooked, either plainly boiled or pickled. The old cockle stalls are disappearing fast, and cockles are proving uneconomic to harvest.

Crabs (crustacean)

Most crabs are edible but the small ones are too fiddly to bother with and the very large ones are sometimes almost hollow, coarse and dry in texture. The best are medium size (about 900g/2lb weight). They are brownish-pink before cooking, going bright orange when boiled. They are sold frozen cooked, freshly cooked and live. They undoubtedly have the best flavour if freshly cooked. The female or 'hen' crab is considered superior to the male crab because its roe imparts a distinctive 'crab flavour' to the flesh. Crabs are frequently plunged live into boiling water or court bouillon, where they die very quickly, but they may be killed by piercing the brain (found on the soft underside of the crab) before cooking. After cooking the legs are pulled off, the underside of the crab opened up, and the stomach sac, any green matter, and the lungs (spongy finger-like objects) are discarded. The soft brown meat is stronger in flavour and is generally mashed with lemon juice, or incorporated into a sauce, before serving. The meat in the claws and legs is very good, and the diner is generally served with these ready cracked to make extracting the flesh easier.

Crawfish (crustacean)

This is a saltwater crustacean, also known as the spiny lobster or rock lobster. It has no claws, but a very rough spiny back. Known as langouste in France, it is considered inferior to lobster, but of a good delicate flavour. They are available fresh or frozen in Britain, and are distinctly better if fresh. Generally between 225g/½lb and 1½ kilos/3lb in weight.

Crayfish (crustacean)

The crayfish is the most delicious and delicate of freshwater creatures. Generally weighing less than 450g/1lb they are rarely available live, except from tanks in smart restaurants. The tails containing most of the meat are available frozen raw, and are very good. Live crayfish are gutted by twisting off the middle tail fin, which takes the intestine with it, after which they are boiled in a court bouillon.

Lobster (crustacean)

Lobsters are blue-black when alive, turning bright red when boiled. They are best bought live, and will keep for a few hours in the warmest part of the refrigerator. If they are to be eaten cold, or in some sauce or pie, they are usually boiled. They can be dropped live into the boiling liquid (and contrary to legend they will *not* scream), or they can be killed first by being pierced through the clearly defined cross on the back of the head which indicates the nerve centre.

Many chefs claim that the tenderest and juiciest cold lobster is obtained by placing the lobster in cold court bouillon and bringing the liquid up to simmering point very slowly. This is inhumane if the lobster is dropped into fresh cold water, as it will live for a while until the heat overcomes it. But the method is not cruel provided the water or court bouillon has been previously well boiled, which eliminates the oxygen. The lobster is then put into the cold liquid, *and left for 30 minutes.* The lack of oxygen gently renders the lobster unconscious, and of course it then feels nothing when put over the heat.

For grilled lobster dishes, and for many other hot dishes such as lobster thermidor the animal is killed, then split in half down the back. The stomach sac, spongy gills and intestine – thread-like dark membrane running down the body – are removed and then the lobster is grilled or cooked in pan or oven. The meat of the lobster claws is much richer, more solid and of a different texture to the body meat, which is white (with a pinkish skin) when cooked. The claws must be cracked before serving to enable the diner to get at the flesh inside. The leg flesh is similar to that of the body. The flesh near the head (actually the liver) is often mistakenly thrown away by inexperienced cooks, as it has a soft grey-green look. But it is quite delicious and should be mixed with the sauce, or eaten as it is. The eggs (coral) of the 'hen' lobster are used, when available, to flavour sauces or lobster butter, and are perhaps the best-tasting part of a lobster.

Mussels (bivalve mollusc)

Mussels are seldom longer than a thumb and have blue-black shells. Like all seafood they must be bought absolutely fresh. Any that will not shut when tapped on the sink, or that float, or have damaged shells must be discarded. They are well washed in water, scrubbed hard, and their 'beards' (seaweed-like tentacles) are removed. They are generally cooked in a covered pan with very little liquid. They will open within a few minutes, and once open are cooked. The 'rubber band' of muscle surrounding the flesh may be gently pulled off and discarded.

Octopus (cephalopod mollusc)

The octopus (which can grow to 60cm/2ft long) consists of a large 'head' with two protruding eyes, and eight tentacles carrying suckers along their length. The body cavity contains a dark brown ink which the animal can squirt out to form a protective screen while it makes its escape from predators. It also has the ability to change colour like a chameleon.

   To prepare the octopus for eating the ink and intestines are washed out, the outer membrane-like skin is peeled off and the eyes are removed. The flesh is then cut into strips and simmered until tender. It will be tender either if eaten after barely five minutes in the simmering liquid, or immediately after deep frying, or if it is left to cook slowly for a prolonged time (about 40 minutes) when it will have gone through the stages of initial tenderness, subsequent rubbery toughness, to tenderness again – rather like a steak which must be eaten quickly grilled, or after prolonged stewing, but not after 25 minutes cooking, when it would be very tough and dry.

Oysters (bivalve mollusc)

English oysters are said to be the best in the world; they are certainly extremely expensive. They are normally eaten raw, having simply been prised open with an oyster knife: to do this wrap a tea-towel around your left hand, place the oyster on your left palm, flat side up. Slip a short, strong, wide-bladed knife under the hinge and push it into the oyster. Holding the oyster pressed tightly with the left-hand fingers, jerk up the knife in your right hand, and prize the two shells apart. Pull the oyster from its shell, but put it back on one of them to serve. Serve the oysters lying in their shells on a bed of crushed ice, and hand salt, pepper, lemon juice and Tabasco sauce separately. Traditionally garnished with seaweed and served with champagne or Chablis.

Shrimps or *prawns* (crustacean)

Incorrectly called prawns, saltwater shrimps are also known as *crevettes* in France and as *gambaretti* in Italy. The commonest variety is greyish before cooking, orangy-pink and bright afterwards. The much-prized brown shrimp is pale brown when live, deep reddish-brown when boiled. It is used, cooked and packed in well-seasoned clarified butter for potted shrimps, as well as eaten plainly boiled. Prawns are bought either whole or shelled in the cooked state, and whole only (never shelled) when raw. If bought frozen they will almost certainly be cooked and shelled. They may be frozen in a solid block, or individually, when they are packed in a 'free flow' pack. As a general rule the free flow prawns are more expensive, but of better quality, than the solid packs. Cooked or raw unshelled prawns are sold by the pint as well as by weight.

To shell a cooked prawn the legs and roe (if any) under the body are pinched off, the head is broken off and the shell peeled away from the body. If the prawns are to be used whole for garnish, the legs and any roe are removed but the head and shell are left intact.

Prawn (*Dublin bay*) (crustacean)

This is similar to the small prawn, but much larger, rarer and more expensive. It can be bought fresh or frozen, both raw or cooked. Similar to the French *langoustine*, and the Italian *scampi*, it is best bought raw in its shell, but is acceptable raw, shelled and frozen. It has a very tender, juicy flesh, white when cooked, although the shell becomes bright pink. True Dublin Bays are not common today, and have been largely replaced by the boiled and frozen Pacific Prawn.

Scallops (bivalve mollusc)

Scallops are generally prepared for cooking by the fishmonger, who should be asked to supply the shells as well as the fish. The scallop (or Coquille St Jacques) has a shallow and deep shell and the deep one is used as a serving dish. Frozen scallops are sold without shells. The shells, if well scrubbed, can be used again and again. Scallops require extremely careful handling and cooking, as over-cooking, too high a heat, or too much delay before serving can make them dry and unappetizing. After cooking the tough muscle, found opposite the red roe (or coral), should be removed.

Squid (cephalopod mollusc)

The squid is much smaller than the octopus and has ten tentacles. It has a long sac-like body containing a transparent shell which must be removed when the animal is cleaned. In all other respects it is like the octopus, though considerably smaller (up to 25cm/10in long).

Whelks and *winkles* (molluscs with snail-like shells)

Both whelks and winkles are normally sold cooked. Whelks are the larger creature and are eaten much like snails, or served in vinegar, ready shelled. Winkles are smaller and a large winkle picker (or pin) is needed to remove the 'cap' or scale at the entrance to get at the winkle, which is then pulled out with the pin.

SEASONS FOR SEAFOOD

Clam	All year round, best in autumn.
Cockles	All year round, best September to April.
Crab	All year round, best May to October.
Crawfish	April to September.
Lobster	All year round, best April to August.
Mussels	September to March.

Octopus and Squid	All year round, but scarce.
Oysters	September to April.
Prawns	All year round.
Dublin Bay Prawns (scampi)	All year round, best May to November.
Scallops	September to March.
Shrimps	All year round.
Whelks	All year round, best September to February.
Winkles	All year round, best October to May.

MEAT

(For rabbit, hare and venison see also pages 159–62.)

The younger the animal, and the less exercise it has taken, the tenderer will be its meat; but its flavour will be less pronounced. A week-old calf will be tender as margarine, and about as flavourless. An ox that has pulled a cart all its long life will be quite the reverse – good on flavour, but tough as old boots. A relatively young, and therefore tender animal will have white or pale fat, rather than yellow, the meat will be less dark, and the bones more pliable than in an older, tougher animal. So rump steak with a bright red hue and white fat may well be tenderer than the dark flesh and yellow fat of older meat, but it will probably lose on flavour what it gains on texture.

Because tenderness is today rated highly, the most expensive cuts of meat are those from the parts of the animal's body that have had little or no exercise. For example, the leg, neck and shoulder cuts of beef are tougher (and therefore cheaper) than those from rump or loin.

But apart from the age of the animal, there are other factors that affect tenderness. Meat must not be cooked while the muscle fibres are taut due to *rigor mortis* which can last, depending on the temperature in which the carcass is stored, for a day or two. The state of the animal prior to slaughter can also affect the

111

tenderness of the meat – if it is relaxed and peaceable the meat is likely to be more tender. Injections of certain enzymes (proteins that produce changes in the meat without themselves being changed) given to the animal before slaughter will produce the same result artificially.

But the most crucial factor affecting tenderness is the length of time it is stored before cooking. Meat hung in temperatures of 2 C/35 F will, due to enzyme activity, become increasingly tender. Temperatures should not be higher than this, because although the enzyme activity would be greater, the risk of spoilage due to bacterial action would become high. For beef 7 days is the minimum hanging time, 3 weeks or a month being desirable. However, with the commercial demands for quick turnover, the weight-loss during storage and the expense of storing, good hanging is rare these days.

Some enzyme activity continues if the meat is frozen, and the formation, and subsequent melting, of ice-crystals (which, in expanding, bruise the fibres of the meat) means that freezing meat can be said to tenderize it. However the inevitable loss of juices from the meat (and subsequent risk of dryness after cooking) is a disadvantage that outweighs the minimal tenderizing effect.

Hanging is most important in beef, as the animals are comparatively old, perhaps 2 or 3 years, when killed. It is less important for carcasses of young animals such as calves and lambs, as their meat is comparatively tender anyway.

Because, inevitably, some bacterial action (as well as enzyme action) must take place during hanging, the flavour of well-hung meat is stronger, or gamier, than that of under-hung meat. The colour will also deepen and become duller with hanging. But the prime reason for hanging meat is to tenderize it, rather than to increase or change its flavour. This is not so with game, including venison, which is hung as much to produce a gamey flavour as to tenderize the meat.

The last, and probably most important, factor that affects the ultimate tenderness of meat is the method of cooking. Half-cooked or rare meat will be tender simply because its fibres have not been changed by heat, and will still retain the softness of raw meat. But as the heat penetrates the whole piece of meat the fibres of meat set rigidly and the juices cease to run. Once the whole piece of meat is heated thoroughly, all the softness of raw meat is lost, and the meat is at its toughest. This explains the natural reluctance of chefs to serve well-done steaks – it is almost impossible to produce a *tender* well-done grilled steak.

But, paradoxically, further cooking (though not fast grilling or frying) will tenderize that tough steak. This is seen in cooking methods such as braising and stewing, when long slow cooking gradually softens the flesh. A joint from an older animal, which has done much muscular work during its lifetime, and is coarse-grained and fibrous, can be made particularly tender by prolonged gentle cooking. This is because much of the connective tissue present in such a joint, if subjected to a steady temperature of, say, 100°C/200°F, will convert to gelatine, producing a soft, almost sticky tenderness.

Joints with finer graining and little connective tissue, such as rump or sirloin, will never become gelatinous, and are consequently seldom cooked other than by roasting or grilling, when their inherent tenderness (from a life of inaction!) is relied on. But they will never be as tender as the slow-cooked shin or oxtail, which can be cut with a spoon.

It does not matter that few people have any idea which part of the animal their meat comes from. But it is useful to know, if not how to do the butcher's job, at least which cuts are likely to be tender, expensive, good for stewing, or not worth having, and what to look for in a piece of meat.

ROASTING MEAT

1. Weigh the joint and establish length of cooking time (see page 114).
2. Pre-heat the oven (electric ovens take much longer to heat up than gas ovens).
3. Prepare the joint for roasting (see page 125).
4. Heat some dripping in a roasting pan and if the meat is lean, brown the joint over direct heat so that it is well coloured. This helps to seal in the juices. Pork and lamb rarely need this but many cuts of beef do.

5. Place the joint in the pan, on a grid if you have one available, as this aids the circulation of hot air; roast for the time calculated.
6. Lean meat needs basting every 20–25 minutes, fatty meats need not be basted.

ROASTING TIMES

Obviously a long thin piece of meat weighing 2·3 kilos/5lb will take less time to cook than a fat round piece of the same weight, so that the times below are meant only as a guide. The essential point is that meat must reach an internal temperature of 60°C/ 140 F to be rare, 70 C/150 F to be medium pink and 80 C/170 F to be well done. A meat thermometer stuck into the thickest part of the meat, and left there during cooking, eliminates guesswork.

Beef

Beef is generally roasted in the hottest of ovens for 20 minutes to seal the meat (or it may be fried all over in fat before being transferred to the oven). Whatever the method, count the cooking time *after* the sealing has been done, and allow 15 minutes to the pound for rare meat, 20 minutes for medium and 25 for well done, roasting the meat in a pre-heated oven set at 190 C/375 F, gas mark 5.

Lamb

Put the lamb into the hottest of ovens, seal for 20 minutes, then allow 20 minutes to the pound at 190 C/375 F, gas mark 5. This will produce very slightly pink lamb. If lamb without a trace of pinkness is wanted allow an extra 20 minutes after the calculated time is up.

Pork

Pork must be well cooked. Allow 40 minutes to the pound at 170°C/325°F, gas mark 3. Sealing is not necessary. If crackling is required roast at 200°C/400°F, gasmark 6 for 25 minutes to the pound, plus 25 minutes over.

Veal

Seal in hot fat over direct heat. Or roast for 20 minutes at maximum temperature. Then allow 25 minutes to the pound at 180 C/350 F, gas mark 4.

BEEF

BEEF CUTS

For roasting: sirloin, wing rib, rump, fillet

For pot roasting: topside, silverside, brisket, thick flank

For stewing, braising and boiling, and for salting and boiling: chuck, shin, brisket, flank, neck, topside, silverside

For grilling and frying: fillet, rump and sirloin. But the names for steaks can be confusing:

Rump steaks (rumsteak or bifsteak in French)
These are thick (about 2cm/$\frac{3}{4}$in) slices cut across the grain of the rump, and then, if for individual servings, cut into smaller neat pieces.

Fillet steak
It comes in various guises. Cut across into neat thick (2$\frac{1}{2}$cm/1in) slices it is a tournedos. A neat piece for two or three people, weighing perhaps 225g/$\frac{1}{2}$lb cut from the thick end (but with all the coarser meat trimmed from it) can be grilled, spitted or roasted as a chateaubriand. Medallions are thin neat slices cut across the fillet.

Sirloin steak
The name sirloin covers steak from the upper side of the true sirloin, wing rib and fore rib. The French *entrecôte* means only the true tender sirloin, which is cut in individual steaks or as T-bone steaks (on the rib, with the sirloin on one side of the

BEEF

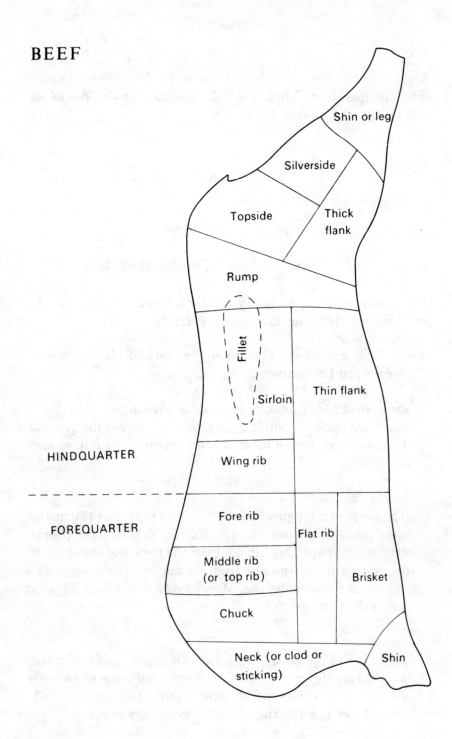

Shin or leg

Silverside

Topside

Thick flank

Rump

Fillet

Thin flank

Sirloin

HINDQUARTER

Wing rib

FOREQUARTER

Fore rib

Flat rib

Middle rib (or top rib)

Brisket

Chuck

Neck (or clod or sticking)

Shin

T and the fillet or undercut on the other). French *côte de boeuf* or our rib of beef are thick steaks on the rib bone, from the slightly less tender wing rib or fore rib. Porterhouse is a double-size T-bone, or double-size wing rib.

For pies: chuck, brisket, thick flank, shin (foreleg), shin or leg (hind leg)

Approximate times for cooking steaks

Steaks are grilled according to taste:

Blue	Dark on the outside but almost raw (hot but not cooked) in the middle.
Rare	Dark on the outside but red inside with plenty of red juices running freely.
Medium rare	As rare, but with very little free-flowing juices. Paler centre.
Medium	Pink in the centre but the juices set.
Well done	The centre pale beige but the steak still juicy.

	Total cooking time per side	
	Grilled	Fried
Fillet – 2½cm/1in thick		
Blue	2	1½
Rare	2½	2
Medium rare	3	2½
Medium	3½	3
Well done	5	4½
Sirloin – 2½cm/1in thick		
Blue	2½	2
Rare	3	2½
Medium rare	3½	3
Medium	4	3½
Well done	5½	4½

	Total cooking time per side	
	Grilled	Fried
Sirloin – 5cm/2in thick		
Blue	3	2½
Rare	3½	3
Medium rare	4	3½
Medium	5	4
Well done	7	6

Rump

As sirloin, but allow up to 50 per cent longer.

VEAL

The cuts of veal, and their names, more closely resemble those of a lamb or sheep than those of grown-up beef.

As veal is more tender than beef, more of the animal is suitable for quick cooking (roasting, frying). But as there is little fat on a calf, care must be taken to moisten the meat frequently during cooking to prevent dryness. Because of the absence of fat, veal is seldom grilled.

Dutch veal is milk-fed and expensive. It has a pale pink colour and the best cuts are exceptionally tender. But the taste is mild to the point of insipidity, and needs good seasoning, usually plenty of lemon, pepper or a good sauce. English veal is cheaper, has more flavour, and generally has a slightly more reddish hue. This is because the animals are killed older than their Dutch fellows, and are generally, though not always, grass-fed. But veal should never look bloody or really red.

VEAL CUTS

For roasting: leg, loin, best end, breast

For braising and stewing: leg, shoulder, neck end, scrag, breast,

For frying (and possibly grilling if frequently basted): cushion (fillet), loin chops, best end cutlets, rump, round (buttock)

118

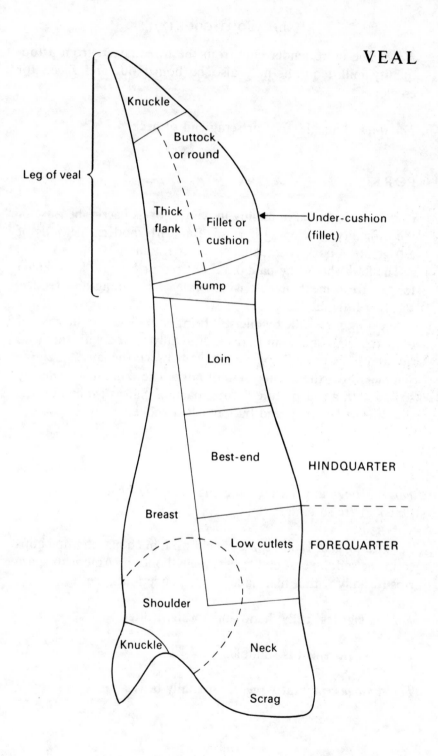

VEAL

Knuckle

Buttock or round

Leg of veal

Thick flank

Fillet or cushion

Under-cushion (fillet)

Rump

Loin

Best-end

HINDQUARTER

Breast

Low cutlets

FOREQUARTER

Shoulder

Knuckle

Neck

Scrag

Note: The more tender cuts from the forequarter, from a top-quality milk-fed calf, may also be boned out and sliced for escalopes.

For stock: knuckle, foot or scrag end of neck

PORK

Pork used to be eaten mainly in winter, or as bacon, because of the difficulty of keeping it fresh. But with modern methods of refrigeration pork is eaten all the year round.

The flesh should be pale pink, not red or bloody. Pork killed for the fresh meat market is generally very young and tender, carrying little fat.

Suckling pigs, killed while still being milk-fed, may be roasted or barbecued whole, and are traditionally served with the head on, and with an apple or an orange between the jaws.

Crackling is the roasted skin of pork. The skin must be deeply scored with a sharp knife before roasting. Salt is rubbed on the skin, making it crisp and bubbly when cooked.

PORK CUTS

For roasting: any part of the pig (bar the head, trotters and knuckle) are suitable.

For grilling and frying: spare rib chops, loin chops, chump chops from the saddle, best end cutlets, belly bones or American spare ribs (usually with a marinade), fillet (tenderloin), trotters

For boiling: leg, belly, hand and spring, trotters

For pies: any meat is suitable.

For sausages: any fatty piece, especially belly.

PORK

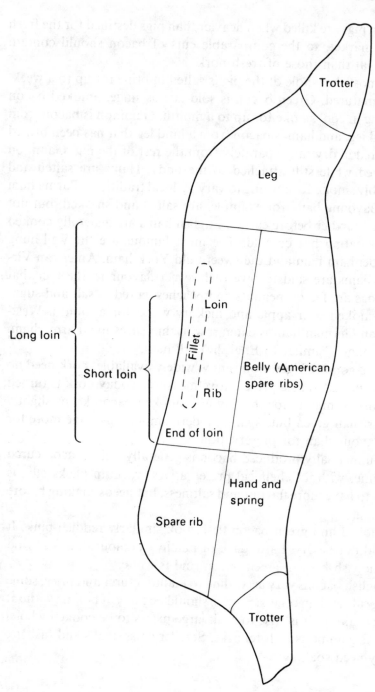

Trotter

Leg

Long loin

Short loin

Loin

Fillet

Rib

End of loin

Belly (American spare ribs)

Hand and spring

Spare rib

Trotter

BACON

Bacon pigs are killed when heavier than pigs destined for the fresh pork market, so the comparable cuts of bacon should contain more fat than those of fresh pork.

Almost the whole of the pig is salted in brine for up to a week, then matured. Green bacon is sold at this stage. Smoked bacon is hung in cool smoke for up to a month. Gammon is bacon from a hind leg, and ham is bacon from a hind leg that has been brined or cured in dry salt separately from the rest of the pig. Gammon is cured while still attached to the body. Hams are salted and possibly smoked according to varying local traditions. Parma ham and Bayonne ham, for example, are salted and smoked, but not cooked further before eating. English hams are generally cooked before eating hot or cold. The most famous are the well-hung Braddenham ham and the sweet mild York ham. American Virginia hams are said to owe their sweet flavour to the fact that the hogs are fed on peanuts and peaches, cured in salt and sugar and smoked over apple and hickory wood for a month. Westphalian German ham is eaten raw in thin slices like Parma ham. Paris ham is similar to English York ham.

Since good refrigeration is now widely available, pork need no longer be salted as a preservative measure. Today pork is turned into bacon mainly for the flavour. Smoked bacon keeps slightly longer than green but, again, modern smoking is done more for the flavour than for preservation.

Commercially produced bacon is generally mild. Bacon cured at home, without chemical preservatives, vacuum packs etc., is likely to have more flavour and saltiness, but needs soaking before cooking.

Smoked and green bacon flesh look similarly reddish-pink. It should not be dry, hard, dark or patchy in colour. Smoked rind is yellowish-brown; green bacon rind is white.

English bacons vary according to manufacturer and price, some being saltier than others. So care should be taken if boiling without prior soaking. It is wise to soak large pieces to be cooked whole, such as gammons or forehocks. Smaller cuts, steaks and rashers, rarely need soaking.

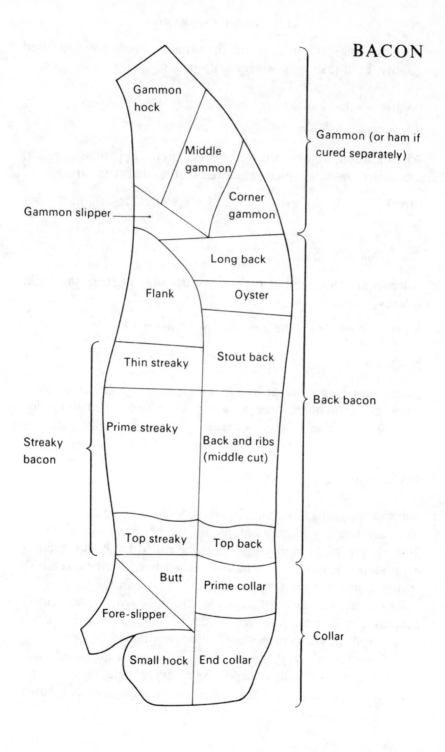

BACON

Gammon hock

Middle gammon

Corner gammon

Gammon slipper

Gammon (or ham if cured separately)

Long back

Flank

Oyster

Thin streaky

Stout back

Prime streaky

Back and ribs (middle cut)

Streaky bacon

Back bacon

Top streaky

Top back

Butt

Prime collar

Fore-slipper

Small hock

End collar

Collar

Danish pigs are all cured in the same manner, giving a good quality, mild-tasting, not-very-salty bacon.

BACON CUTS

For boiling or stewing

All cuts are suitable but the lean pieces (forehock, gammon, collar) are sometimes casseroled or stewed whole, tied with string.

Streaky and Flank are used diced for soups, or to add flavour to stews.

For frying or grilling

All cuts are suitable but rashers are usually cut from the back, streaky or collar.

Steaks are cut from the gammon or prime back.

For baking (usually boiled first)

Large lean pieces are generally used (whole gammon or ham, whole gammon hock, large piece of back, whole boned and rolled forehock or either of the collars).

LAMB AND MUTTON

Animals weighing more than 36 kilos/79·5lb are graded as mutton. Real mutton is seldom available in butcher shops since all the animals are killed young enough to be called lamb. But there is a difference between the small sweet joints of the new season's spring lamb, and the larger lambs killed later in the year.

Really baby lambs, killed while still milk fed, are extremely expensive, with very pale, tender flesh. A leg from such a lamb would feed only two or perhaps three people.

British lamb is very fine in flavour, but good imported New Zealand lamb is usually cheaper. As a general rule New Zealand lamb joints come from smaller animals than the full-grown English lambs, but it should be remembered that three grades of New Zealand lamb are imported into Britain, ranging from excellent to very tough. All New Zealand lamb comes into the country frozen, so it stands to reason that some lambs have been more recently killed than others. The best time to buy New Zealand lamb is from Christmas to the summer.

Lamb should be brownish-pink rather than grey in colour, but not bloody. Because the animal is killed young almost all the cuts are tender enough for grilling, frying or roasting, but the fattier, cheaper cuts are used for casseroles and stews too.

LAMB AND MUTTON CUTS

For roasting: Saddle or loin, best end of neck (rack of lamb), shoulder, leg, breast

For braising: chump chops, loin, leg

For grilling and frying: best end cutlets, loin chops, chump chops, steaks from fillet end of leg

For boiling and stewing: knuckle, scrag and middle neck, breast, leg

BUTCHERY

Most cuts of meat are available ready prepared from the shop or market. But it is useful to know how to bone and tie certain French and English cuts that a busy butcher may be unwilling to tackle.

Boning

Boning is easier than most people imagine. A short sharp knife is essential. Tunnel boning (where the bone, say from a leg, is extracted from the hole from which it protrudes, without opening out the meat) is more difficult than open boning, when the flesh is split along the bone, the bone worked out and the meat rolled up and tied or sewn. But, whether tunnel boning or open boning,

125

LAMB

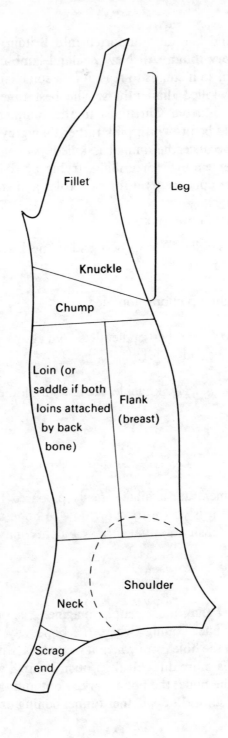

Fillet

Leg

Knuckle

Chump

Loin (or
saddle if both
loins attached
by back
bone)

Flank
(breast)

Shoulder

Neck

Scrag
end

the essential is to work slowly and carefully, keeping the knife as close to the bones as possible, and scraping the meat off the bone rather than cutting it. Any meat extracted inadvertently with the bone can be scraped off and put back into the joint. With most bones it is possible, when tunnel boning, to work from both ends – for example, a leg of mutton can be worked on where the knuckle bone sticks out of the thin end, and the leg bone out of the fillet end.

But in most cases it is simpler to cut neatly through the flesh, along the length of the bone, from the side nearest to the bone, and work the bone out all along its length. After all, some sewing or tying is necessary at the ends of the joints even if tunnel boned, and it is simpler to sew up the length of the joint.

For safety reasons trainee butchers are taught to use the knife in such a way that should it slip it will not hurt them. This means never pulling the knife directly towards the body. In addition the knife is held firmly like a dagger when working, with the point of the knife down (see drawing). But the safest precaution that cooks can take is to see that their knives are sharp. Blunt knives need more pressure to wield, and are therefore more inclined to slip.

Rolling and tying

Once a joint, such as a loin, is boned, remove most of the fat and lay it, meat side up, on the board. Season it or spread sparingly with stuffing. Roll it up from the thick end and use short pieces of thin cotton (not nylon) string to tie round the meat at 3cm/1½in intervals. These can easily be cut off when serving, or the carver can slice between them when cutting the meat into thick slices.

Sewing up whole joints after stuffing

Use a larding needle or large darning or upholstery needle. Some of these are curved slightly which makes the job easier. Use thin old-fashioned white string, not nylon which will melt under heat. Leave a good few inches of string at the beginning and end, but do not tie elaborate knots which are difficult to undo when dishing the meat. Not-too-tight simple largish stitches are best – the whole length of string can be pulled out in one movement when dishing.

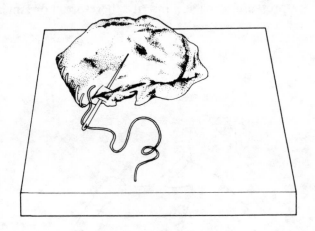

Larding

Some very lean or potentially tough meat is larded before roasting. This promotes tenderness and adds flavour. Most commonly used

COCKTAIL BITS

PEARS WITH STILTON AND POPPYSEED DRESSING

MOULES MARINIÈRES

BONED CHICKEN À LA CUISINE MINCEUR

for slow-roasted dishes like boeuf à la mode or roast veal. A special larding needle is used.

To lard a joint: cut the larding fat (usually rindless back pork fat) into thin strips and put one of them into the tunnel of the needle, clamping down the hinge to hold it in place. The fat should extend a few inches out of the needle. Thread through the meat, twisting the needle gently to prevent the fat pulling off. Once threaded through the meat, release the clamp, and trim the two ends of fat close to the meat. Repeat this all over the lean meat at 2½cm/1in intervals.

BEEF

Steaks for grilling or frying

Cut across the grain of the meat, if possible into thickish slices. Trim neatly, and cut rump slices into two or three individual steaks.

Minute steaks

Cut large thin steaks. Put them between two sheets of paper or polythene and bat gently with a cook's mallet or rolling pin to flatten the meat.

Tournedos steaks

Cut 2cm/1in slices across the trimmed fillet.

For stewing

Remove the gristle, but not *all* the fat (it will add moisture and flavour). Cut into 2½cm/1in cubes, or larger. Too-small pieces are difficult to seal, and may become shreddy and dry during cooking.

For stroganoff

Cut into small strips across the grain of the meat – about the thickness of a pencil.

For roasting

If the meat has no fat on it, tie a piece of pork fat, or fatty bacon, round it. Tie up as described on page 128.

LAMB

Saddle

This consists of both loins of the lamb, left attached at the back-bone, in the same way as a baron of beef.

First remove the skin: with a small sharp knife lift a corner of the skin, hold this firmly with a tea-towel (to get a good grip) and tug sharply to peel off. Trim off any very large pieces of fat from the edges of the saddle, but leave the back fat. Tuck the flaps under the saddle. Cut out the kidneys but keep them (they can be brushed with butter and attached to the end of the saddle with wooden skewers 30 minutes before the end of the roasting time). Using a sharp knife score the back fat all over in a fine criss-cross pattern.

The pelvic or aitch bone, protruding slightly from one end of the saddle, can be removed, or left in place and covered with a ham frill when the saddle is served.

French trimmed best end cutlets (and how to chine)

Skin the best end: lift a corner of the skin from the neck end with a small knife, hold it firmly (using a cloth to get a good grip) and peel it off.

Chine if the butcher has not already done so. This means to saw carefully through the chine bone (or spine) just where it meets the rib bones. Take care not to saw right through into the eye of the meat. Now remove the chine bone completely. Chop off the cutlet bones so that the length of the remaining bones is not more than twice the length of the eye of the meat. Remove the half-moon shaped piece of flexible cartilege found buried between the layers of fat and meat at the thinner end of the best end. This is the tip of the shoulder blade. It is simple to work out with a knife and your fingers.

If thin small cutlets are required cut between each bone as evenly

130

as possible, splitting the rack into six or seven small cutlets. If fatter cutlets are required carefully ease out every other rib bone. Then cut between the remaining bones into thick cutlets. Now trim the fat from the thick end of each cutlet, and scrape the rib bones free of any flesh or skin.

Noisettes

These are boneless cutlets, tied into a neat round shape with string. They are made from the loin or best end. Skin the meat: lift a corner of the skin with a small knife, holding it firmly (using a cloth to get a good grip), and pull it off.

Chine the meat (see page 130). Now remove first the chine bone and then all the rib bones, easing them out with a short sharp knife.

Trim off any excess fat from the meat and roll it up tightly, starting at the meaty thick side and working towards the thin flap. Tie the roll neatly with separate pieces of string placed at 3cm/1½in intervals. Trim the ragged ends of the roll to neaten them. Now slice the roll into pieces, cutting accurately between each string. The average English best end will give four good noisettes. The string from each noisette is removed after cooking.

Crown roast

Two racks (best ends) are needed. For a larger roast use three. The rack is prepared similarly to one destined for cutlets (see above) but the rib bones are left slightly longer, and the rack is not split into cutlets. But it is skinned, chined, the shoulder cartilege is removed, excess fat is cut off and the top inch of the bones are scraped in the same way.

Bend each best end into a semi-circle, with the fatty side of the ribs inside. To facilitate this it may be necessary to cut through the sinew between each cutlet, from the thick end for about 2cm/1in. But take care not to cut into the fleshy eye of the meat. Sew the ends of the racks together to make a circle, with the meaty part forming the base of the crown. Tie a piece of string round the 'waist' of the crown. Traditionally, stuffed; but this can result in undercooked inside fat.

Guard of honour

Prepare two best end racks exactly as for the crown roast. Score the fat in a criss-cross pattern. Hold the two best ends, one in each hand, facing each other with the meaty part of the racks on the board, and the fatty sides on the outside. Jiggle them so the rib bones interlock and cross at the top. Sew or tie the bases together at intervals. Stuff the arch if required.

To score crackling

It is vital that crackling should be scored evenly and thoroughly, each cut (which should penetrate the skin and a little of the fat below it) being even and complete. Unscored crackling is tough and difficult to carve. Make the cuts not more than 1cm/½in apart all over the skin. Score the crackling after boning but before rolling and tying the joint.

PORK AND BACON

Chops

Chops are trimmed of rind, and the fat snipped or cut across (from the outside towards the meat). This is because as the fat shrinks during cooking it tends to curl the chops out of shape.

Gammon steaks or bacon chops

Snip the surrounding fat as described above. Bacon chops (really thick rashers from the prime back) are sometimes cooked with the rind left on. But the snipping is still essential to prevent curling.

American or Chinese spare ribs

These are made from belly of pork (not English spare rib). They can be cut before or after cooking. Simply cut between each belly bone, splitting the meat into long bones.

CARVING MEAT

The most important factor in good carving is a really sharp knife, a fork with a safety guard, and a board or flat plate unencumbered by vegetables and garnishes. Common sense usually dictates how joints are to be tackled. Meat off the bone is simple – just cut in slices of whatever thickness you prefer, *across the grain* of the meat. Pork, beef and veal are traditionally carved in thinner slices than lamb.

Legs

The legs of pork, lamb, bacon (gammon, or ham), veal and venison are carved similarly. Put the leg meaty side up on the board or plate and grasp the knuckle bone with one hand, or pierce the joint firmly with a carving fork. Cut a small shallow V or scoop out of the middle of the top of the meat. Carve slices of meat from both sides of the V. Then turn the leg over and take long horizontal slices from the other side.

133

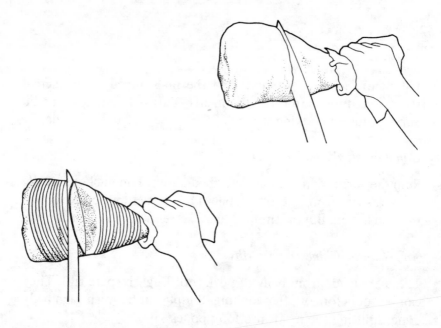

Legs can also be cut in diagonal slices from the knuckle end. This is more common with hams, but both methods are used for all legs.

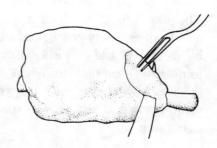

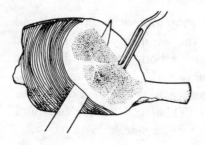

Loins

Loins and best ends of pork, veal and lamb are cut straight down between the bones if the joint is simply chined but not boned. If boned, the meat is cut similarly, but in thinner slices (about ¾cm/¼in thick). Beef strip loin (boned sirloin) is cut in the same way, thinly in Britain, thickly in America.

Sirloin of beef on the bone is tackled from the top and bottom, the slices cut as thinly as possible on the top, the undercut or fillet slices being carved more thickly. Each diner should be given a slice or two from both top and bottom.

Saddle of lamb

The chump end of the saddle is cut in thin slices across the grain of the meat, at rightangles to the backbone. But the main part of the saddle, lying each side of the backbone is cut in thin strips or narrow slices down the length of the saddle.

Under the rib cage, close to the backbone is found the tender thin mignon fillet. It is awkward to turn the saddle over and carve this, but it is the most delicious meat and should not be wasted.

Crown roast and *guard of honour*

Remove string and split into cutlets.

OFFAL AND ODDMENTS

Although in the West we are tucking into more and more meat, we have become squeamish about offal. In America the very word offal is thought so unattractive that it is called 'variety meats'. But such things as liver and kidney, and even intestines (for chitterlings) and blood (for black pudding) used to be part of our everyday diet. Most offal is highly nutritious, and some of it is comparatively cheap. It must be eaten very fresh.

LIVER

Liver should not have a strong smell when fresh, and should not be dry and wrinkled or discoloured. It may however be bloody.

The fine outer membrane should be peeled off before slicing for cooking, and any tubes or sinews removed.

Calves' liver

Should be pale milky brown in colour. It has a fine even texture and excellent delicate flavour. It is expensive. Dutch liver is considered better than English. Usually grilled or fried.

Lambs' liver

Is the next most expensive of the livers. It is reddish-brown, darker than calves'. It has a good flavour, is tender, and is generally fried.

Pigs' liver

Cheaper than lambs' liver. Dark brown and close textured, it is rather strong in flavour. It can be fried, but is usually made into pâtés or terrines.

Ox liver

Dark bluish-brown in colour, very strong in flavour, and tough. The cheapest of the livers. Needs soaking or blanching to reduce the flavour. Used, with other ingredients, for stews. Can be braised.

KIDNEY

Kidneys are sold either in their suet or loose. They keep, if they must be kept, better in the suet than out. They should smell mild and pleasant, be smooth and clean-looking, not have discoloured dark patches on them, and feel soft to the touch. The fine membrane enclosing them should, if possible, be removed, especially from lambs' or pigs' kidney. The core of sinew and gristle is removed before cooking.

Veal (calves') kidneys

These are the most expensive kidneys. They are pale milky brown, with creamy white suet, and are shaped rather like a bunch of grapes. They are very tender and delicate in flavour. Usually

136

sautéed, fried or grilled but may be barded with fat and roasted, or left in their suet and roasted. Also used for puddings, pies and stews. Generally in very short supply.

Lambs' kidneys

These are medium brown, sometimes faintly bluish, firm-textured and egg-shaped. Usually split in half, cored, and used for grilling, frying or in sauté dishes. Good taste, neither too strong nor insipid.

Pigs' kidneys

Pale brown, similar in texture to lambs', but slightly longer. Not sold in suet. Stronger flavour than lambs', used for stews and casseroles, and sometimes for frying or grilling.

Ox kidneys

The largest kidney, shaped as veal kidney, but much darker, almost bluish-red in colour. Strong flavour, tough in texture, suitable only for long slow cooking, e.g. in pies and puddings.

TONGUE

Pigs' tongues are sold in the head, and calves' tongues are very rarely available. Ox and lambs' tongues can be bought, however.

Ox tongue

Should feel soft to the touch, though it might have a rough and pigmented skin. It is sold whole, fresh or salted. It is usually boiled, skinned and served either hot or cold. Tongue is sometimes pressed while hot into a mould to give it a round shape when cold. The thicker, fattier part of the tongue is very soft, the tip leaner and tougher.

Lambs' tongues

Small and generally sold by the pound. They are usually pale pink in colour, but the roughish skin may be pigmented light or dark grey. Usually skinned after cooking. Lambs' tongues are very delicate in flavour, and extremely tender. Sometimes pressed and served cold in their jelly, or used for hot sauté dishes.

HEADS AND BRAINS

Calves' heads

Sometimes available if specially ordered. They are used mainly for boiling and serving hot. Salted, they are used for brawn.

Calves' brains

The most delicate and expensive. They are soaked and blanched to remove all traces of blood before cooking, and skinned of membrane and sinew after blanching. Excellent fried plainly or in a crumb coating. Almost creamy texture when cooked.

Pigs' heads

Used for brawn, fresh or salted, and can be used for sausages. The cheeks of certain long-faced breeds of pig are lightly salted, and sold as Bath Chaps. They are rather fatty, but of good flavour, usually eaten crumbed and fried, or cold like ham. A pig's head is sometimes used on banqueting tables as a stand-in for the now unavailable boar's head. Pigs' brains are sold in the heads.

Sheep's heads

Can be boiled or stewed for use in broths and pie fillings, but are seldom available, and involve a lot of labour for very little meat.

Sheep's brains

Less fine and delicate than calves', but more readily available. Treated in exactly the same way.

Ox cheek

Sold for brawns and stews.

138

SWEETBREADS

Each animal has a pair of thymus glands in the throat, and another pair (called heartbreads) in the body. The heartbreads are considered the best. Pigs' sweetbreads are not sold.

Calves' sweetbreads

The most expensive and delicate, but hard to come by. They have a soft texture, not as creamy as brains, but good. They are treated like brains, or sautéed and used in savoury mixtures.

Ox breads

Less tender than calves' but have an excellent flavour. They are sometimes available in provincial and country butcher shops, and are usually cheap.

Lambs' sweetbreads

The next best thing to calves', but they lack the extreme delicacy of taste and texture.

HEART

Heart is highly nutritious, but needs slow cooking to tenderize it. It is also very lean, and needs a sauce or plenty of basting to keep it moist. Hearts must be cleaned of all sinew and the tubes removed before cooking.

Ox heart

Large, very tough, strong-flavoured, coarse and muscular and bluish-red. It is generally used with other ingredients chopped or minced – perhaps for a filling or pie.

Lambs' hearts

The smallest and most tender of the hearts. But stuffing to add flavour, slow cooking and careful basting are still necessary to moisten and tenderize the naturally lean and tough flesh.

PLUCK

The pluck is the name given to the lights (lungs), liver, pancreas and spleen. Lights are today generally sold for pet food. The liver is sold separately. Sheep's pluck is minced for haggis.

FEET AND TROTTERS

Calves' feet

Seldom sold to the public. Good for stock and calf's foot jelly due to the high concentration of gelatine present in it.

Pigs' trotters are high in gelatine, good for setting stocks, and brawn. Can be boned, stuffed, braised, served hot with mustard sauce, or hot or cold with vinaigrette.

Sheep's trotters and ox feet are not sold.

Cow heel is treated before sale, and looks and tastes, similar to tripe. It consists of the whole foot and heel of the animal.

TRIPE

Tripe can come from all cud-chewing animals, being the first and second stomachs, but in practice only ox tripe is sold. The first stomach (blanket tripe) is smooth, the second honeycombed. Tripe is sold parboiled, but needs further long boiling to tenderize it. It is wise to ask the butcher how much more boiling it will need.

Grey, slimy, flabby, strong-smelling tripe should be avoided. It should be thick, firm and very white. Tripe can be stewed, boiled or deep fried. A very specialist taste, with its addicts and its detesters.

OXTAIL

Sold skinned and, usually, jointed. Choose fat large tails with plenty of meat on them. Cow tails, which are skinny and rather tasteless, are sometimes passed off as oxtail. The meat should be dark and lean, the fat creamy white and firm.

Oxtail is high in gelatine content, so cooks to a tender, almost sticky stew. Good for soups. Very rich in flavour.

MARROW BONES

Marrow bones are from the thigh and shoulder bones of beef. They are sawn across in short cylinders by the butcher. They are boiled whole and served in a napkin, the diner extracting the soft rich marrow and eating it on toast. Marrow is also used as a flavouring in other dishes, such as entrecôte à la bordelaise, where it moistens and flavours the steak.

BLOOD

Pigs' blood is used in the making of black pudding. It is mixed with fat, and stuffed into intestines like a sausage.

POULTRY AND GAME BIRDS

Domesticated birds lead an unenergetic but well-fed life. The resulting flesh from such creatures is naturally very tender (they get less exercise than their wild cousins and are almost always killed young) but it lacks the pronounced taste of wild birds feeding in woods and on moors. Bone meal or broilers' pellets can hardly be expected to produce the flavour of wild heather and grasses.

If a bird has not been plucked, and still has its head, it is easy to tell whether it is young or old. Young birds, be they chickens, ducks, pheasants or turkeys will have pliable beaks and smooth legs, the scales not coarse, and barely overlapping. The spurs of the male birds will be little more than knobs, and the breastbone, when pushed down with the heel of the hand will 'give' a bit. In addition, the webbing on ducks, geese and waterfowl will tear easily. If the bird has been freshly killed the eyes will be clear, there will be no loss of feathers, and the quill feathers will come out comparatively easily when pulled.

HANGING

Hanging of birds (i.e. suspending them in cool fresh air out of the reach of flies – usually in a larder) is done for three reasons: *a.* to allow the toughening effects of *rigor mortis* to disappear; *b.* to allow enzyme activity to tenderize the meat; and *c.* to improve the flavour.

No bird *need* be hung longer than 24 hours, when it will still be extremely fresh, but game birds are often hung for up to two weeks, by which time they have a markedly high gamey flavour, beloved of some, hated by others. Recently the trend has been to eat game birds hung for between four days and a week. Chickens are usually hung for 24 hours, ducks for one or two days, turkeys for three or four.

Traditionally small birds, such as pheasant and grouse, are hung by a piece of string round their necks, and large birds, such as geese and turkeys, by their feet. In fact all birds can be suspended by the feet, the only reason for hanging game birds by the neck being to increase their gameyness by preventing the bleeding from the beak that results if birds are hung head-down. Some sportsmen do not consider their game sufficiently high until the neck parts and the bird falls. Birds hung overlong of course will finally go bad – a bluish-green tinge will be seen on the skin when the feathers are plucked and the smell will be very unpleasant.

Hanging is always done before the bird is eviscerated. Once gutted, birds must be cooked and eaten. Birds that are to hang for more than a day or two are not plucked when freshly killed. This is because if the bird is to hang for any length of time the exposed skin of a plucked bird would dry out. But they may be hung plucked for short periods.

PLUCKING

Some birds are easier to pluck than others, ducks being notoriously tedious. All birds are easier to pluck if still warm when tackled. Work away from draughts, as the feathers fly about, and pluck straight into a dustbin. Tug the feathers, working from the tail to the head, pulling against the way the feathers grow. If the bird is very young indeed, pull downwards towards the tail to avoid tearing the flesh.

Once plucked, the bird should be singed. This can be done with a burning taper, or directly over a gas flame, but care should be taken to singe only the down and small feathers, and not to blacken the flesh. The bird should then be rubbed in a clean tea-towel to remove any remaining stubble. It is now ready for drawing.

CLEANING AND DRAWING

Surprisingly, birds keep better, when hanging, with their insides intact. Once eviscerated they must be cooked within a day or two. So when you are ready to cook the bird, take it down, and proceed as follows.

1. Pluck it if you have not already done so.
2. Cut round the feet, at the drumstick joint, but do not cut right through the tendons. Pull the legs off the bird, drawing the tendons out with them. (If the bird is small this is easy enough – just bend the foot back until it snaps, and pull, perhaps over the edge of a table. Turkeys are more difficult: snap the feet at the drumstick joint by bending them over the end of the table, then hang the bird up by the feet from a stout hook, and pull on the bird. The feet, plus tendons will be left on the hook, the turkey in your arms.) All too often birds are sold with the tendons in the legs, making the drumsticks tough when cooked.
3. Now the head and neck. Lay the bird, breast side down, on a board. Make a slit through the neck skin from the body to the head. Cut off the head and throw it away. Pull back the split neck skin, leaving it attached to the body of the bird (it will come in useful to close the gap if you are stuffing the bird). Cut the neck off as close to the body as you can.
4. Put a finger into the neck hole, to the side of the stump of neck left in the bird, and move the finger right round, loosening the innards from the neck. If you do not do this

143

you will find them difficult to pull out from the other end.

5. With a sharp knife slit the bird open from the vent to the parson's (or pope's) nose, making a hole large enough to get your hand in. Put your hand in, working it so the back of your hand is up against the arch of the breastbone, and carefully loosen the entrails from the sides of the body cavity, all the way round. Pull them out, taking care not to break the gall bladder, the contents of which would embitter any flesh they touch. The first time you do this it is unlikely that you will get everything out in one motion, so check that the lungs and kidneys come too. Have another go if necessary. Once the bird is empty, wipe any traces of blood off with a damp clean cloth. (Covering the gutting hand with a cloth helps extract the intestines intact.)

GIBLETS ETC.

The neck and feet go into the stockpot. So can the heart and the cleaned gizzard. To clean the gizzard, carefully cut the outside wall along the natural seam so that you can peel it away from the inner bag of grit. Throw the grit bag away, with the intestines, and the gall bladder (be careful not to pierce or break this).

Do not put the liver in the stockpot. It may make the stock bitter. It may be fried and served with the dish, or fried, chopped and added to the sauce, or kept frozen until enough poultry liver has been collected to make pâté. But if the liver is to be used, carefully cut away the discoloured portion of it where it lay against the gall bladder (it will be bitter) and trim off any membranes.

TRUSSING

Trussing is done to keep the bird in a compact neat shape. To truss the bird (usually done after stuffing) sew it up as shown in the following drawings. We feel, however, that trussing large birds is largely unnecessary as the bird is to be carved up anyway, and trussing serves to prevent the inside thigh being cooked by the time the breast is ready. Small birds, especially game birds where underdone thighs are desirable, are trussed, but their feet are left

144

on. Their feet may simply be tied together for neatness sake, and the pinions skewered under the bird. Or they may be trussed in any number of ways, one of which is described below. This is also suitable for large birds such as turkeys and chickens.

Arrange the bird so that the neck flap is folded over the neck hole, and the pinions turned under and tucked in tight. They will, if folded correctly, hold the neck flap in place, but if the bird is well stuffed the neck flap may have to be skewered or sewn in place. Press the legs down and into the bird to force the breast into a plumped up position.

Thread a long trussing needle with thin string and push it through the wing joint, right through the body and out of the other wing joint. Then push it through the body again, this time

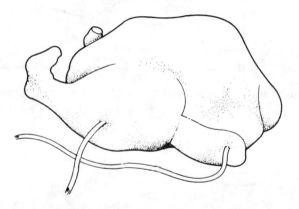

through the thighs. You should now be back on the side you started. Tie the two ends together in a bow to make later removal quick. Then thread a shorter piece of string through the thin end of the two drumsticks, and tie them together, winding the string round the parson's nose at the same time to close the vent. (Sometimes a small slit is cut in the skin just below the end of the breastbone, and the parson's nose is pushed through it.)

JOINTING

Small birds such as quail are invariably cooked whole, perhaps stuffed, and perhaps boned (see boning, pages 148–9). But medium-

145

sized ones, like chickens and guinea fowl, are often cut into two, four, six or eight pieces.

To split a bird in half simply use a sharp knife to cut right through flesh and bone, just on one side of the breastbone, open

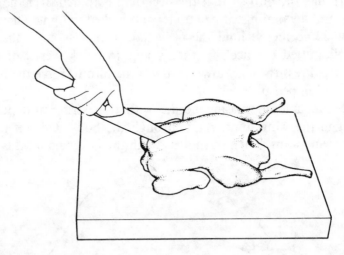

out the bird and cut through the other side, immediately next to the backbone. Then cut the backbone away from the half to which it remains attached.

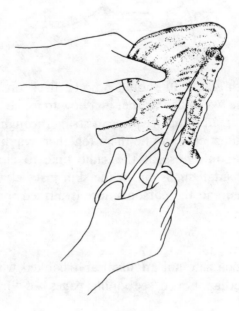

The knobbly end of the drumsticks, and the fleshless tips to the pinions can be cut off before or after cooking. In birds brought whole to the table they are left on.

To joint a bird into four, first pull out any trussing strings, then pull the leg away from the body. With a sharp knife cut through the skin joining the leg to the body, pull the leg away further and cut through more skin to free the leg. Bend the leg outwards and back, forcing the bone to come out of its socket close to the body. Turn the bird over, feel along the backbone to find the oyster (a soft pocket of flesh at the side of the backbone, near the middle). With the tip of the knife, cut this away from the carcass at the side nearest the backbone and farthest

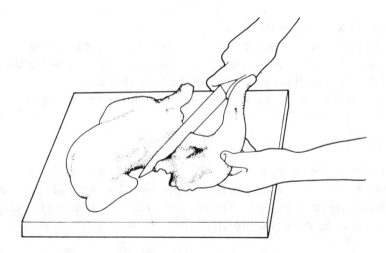

from the leg. Then turn the bird over again, and cut through the flesh (the knife going between the end of the thigh bone and the carcass) to take off the leg, bringing the oyster with it.

Then, using poultry shears or a heavy knife, split the carcass along the breastbone (see page 148). Then cut through the ribs on each side, to take off the fleshy portion of the breast, and with it the wing. Trim the joints neatly to remove scraps of untidy skin.

For six joints, proceed as above but split the legs into thigh portions and drumsticks. The exact join of the bones can be easily felt with a finger if the leg is laid on the board, skin side down.

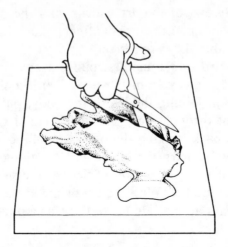

Cut between the bones.

For eight joints, proceed as above and then cut each wing, with a piece of breast attached to it, from the main breast portion. Make the cut almost parallel to the breastbone.

Keep the scraps, backbone, pinions etc. for the stockpot.

BARDING

Poultry liable to dry out during cooking is often barded: lay fatty bacon or rindless back pork fat strips over the body of the bird, and secure or tie in place. The barding is removed during cooking to allow the breast to brown.

BONING AND STUFFING

A short flexible knife is essential. The main point to remember is to keep the boning knife as close to the bone as possible, scraping and easing the flesh away carefully.

Turn the bird breast side down and cut through the skin, along the backbone, from the parson's nose to the neck. Work the skin and flesh away from the bones, peeling back the flesh as you go, gradually exposing the rib cage. When you get to the legs and wings, cut through the tendons close against the carcass at the joints. This will mean the wings and legs stay attached to the skin – not to the carcass. Continue working round the bird, taking special care when boning the breast where the skin and bone are very close.

If the wings and legs are to be boned too, chop off the wing pinions and the knuckle-end of the drumsticks. Working from the thicker end of the joints ease the bones out, scraping the flesh from them carefully. It may be necessary, especially with big birds, to work from the drumstick or the wing tip ends as well, but most of the work should be done from the body side.

Cut off any excess fat, especially from near the parson's nose. When all the bones are out scrape off any flesh still adhering to them and add it to the stuffing.

When stuffing the bird the stuffing is laid down the middle and the sides brought up to enclose it. The bird must then be sewn up if it is to be roasted, and sewn up and/or wrapped in muslin if it is to be poached.

CHICKEN AND BOILING FOWL

A chicken that has run about a bit, pecked at the ground, and perhaps been fed some corn and scraps, will have more flavour than a deep-litter broiler. In addition, if the commercially-reared broiler is frozen as soon as it is killed, it will have had little or no time to 'hang' or mature, and the taste will be delicate in the extreme. But worse can happen. If the bird is fed on fish-meal right up to the day of its death, the smell and taste of the flesh can be distinctly fishy.

Unfortunately, intensively reared chickens are all most of us can obtain. Our only hope is to buy, if we can get them, fresh rather than frozen chickens, and buy them from a reputable dealer who ensures that his poultry has been taken off fish-meal at least a week or so before slaughter, and fed a bit of corn.

Boiling fowls are rare today. The long slow cooking they require has made them almost unsaleable. But they can be had, especially from kosher butchers who sell them for their high proportion of fat (used extensively where the non-kosher cook would use butter), and their good strong taste for that Jewish culinary corner-stone, chicken noodle soup.

Butchers sell their chickens plucked and drawn and they are almost certain to be tender. The skin should feel dry to the touch, but soft, and there should be no strong unpleasant odour.

Most chickens in Britain are white-skinned, but they can be yellow. Boiling fowls will be larger and have plenty of fat around the vent.

Capons

These are de-sexed cockerels who, losing interest in sex, eat voraciously, and are very plump and tender. They have pale livers. They weigh between 2·7 kilos/6lb and 4·6 kilos/10lb, and can be cooked in all ways used for chicken or turkey.

DUCK

Most ducks sold today are really ducklings – seven to nine weeks old. A 1·8 kilos/4lb duck will feed only two people, in spite of its size. This is because there is little meat on the carcass, a great proportion of the weight coming from the fat, which runs from it during cooking. Because of its fattiness duck is roasted without additional fat, and indeed 290ml/$\frac{1}{2}$ pint of liquid fat can be extracted from an average duck.

Old ducks can be very tough. For this reason it is not wise to buy duckling frozen, unless from a reputable supplier, because it is impossible to tell, in a rigidly frozen duck, whether its backbone is pliable, and of course it has no telltale feet or bill.

The skin of a fresh duck should be dry, soft and smooth. It should not be slimy, and there should be no strong smell. The flesh is dark, very fine and rich in flavour, and more tender on the breast than leg.

GOOSE

A 4·6 kilos/10lb goose will feed five or six people. It is less fatty than the duck, and should be basted during cooking. Fresh young goose has a clean white skin, soft and dry to the touch.

Geese are large and have very short legs, which makes trussing them difficult, but as they are very compact, nicely shaped birds, trussing is even more unnecessary than usual.

Goose can be tough. Buy only from a good dealer, specifying a young tender bird. The flesh is rich, and a little heavy. Excellent for casseroles, cassoulet (hot-pot of haricot beans, salt pork and goose or mutton), and preserved or potted goose (French *confit d'oie*).

TURKEY

Turkeys used to have a reputation for being tough, dry and tasteless but today's turkeys are fattened fast and killed young, so are generally moist and tender. Hens are considered better than turkey-cocks, having plumper breasts, and less weight of bone.

The breast flesh is very white, inclined to be dry if over-cooked and the legs are dark meat, of good flavour but marginally tougher.

Fresh turkeys, as opposed to frozen ones, cost more but generally repay the expense with more pronounced flavour. Frozen turkeys, though perhaps lacking something in flavour, are seldom tough as only young birds are frozen.

Fresh turkeys should have a snow-white firm flesh, dry soft skin and a thin layer of fat over the back. They can weigh anything from 4·6 kilos/10lb to 9·9 kilos/22lb, and are usually served roasted whole and carved at table. Left-over meat is good in fricassées. Turkey breasts can now be bought separately, and they are cooked in any way suitable for chicken or veal.

Many cooks, tackling a fresh turkey for the first time are dismayed at the bloodiness, and comparatively 'high' smell of the neck and giblets. This is nothing to worry about. When the giblets and neck are removed (to be used for stock) and the bird well wiped inside and out with a damp clean cloth, the bird will be found to have a distinct, but by no means bad, smell. Of course if the smell makes you reel with digust, a second opinion should be sought – it is possible, though unlikely, that decomposition has begun.

GUINEA FOWL

Classed as a game bird, but in fact reared commercially, the guinea fowl is about the size of a chicken, and has beautiful grey feathers, spotted with white. The flesh is tender, with a taste somewhere between pheasant and chicken. Being rather dry if roasted in the English way, it is usually covered with a piece of fat or streaky bacon. A smallish fowl is usually served for two people.

QUAIL

Quail are small birds and for a good-sized portion two are served. One will do if it is a fat one, and has been boned and stuffed with a veal or poultry forcemeat. Most of today's quail come from farms, and are almost always plump and tender. They have the most delicate soft flesh, more flavour than a chicken, but less gameyness than their cousins the partridge.

Quail are often considered a fiddle to eat but, as long as finger-bowls are provided, this is not so. The flesh is so tender it comes off the breast easily, and the legs can be tackled in the fingers. Quails, like most white-fleshed birds, are served cooked through – not rare. When quails are boned the legs are usually left intact, so that the object still resembles a bird – without its legs such a small thing might look like a dumpling.

Quails must be eaten really fresh – preferably 24 hours after being killed. They are almost always bought plucked and cleaned, but should you need to pluck them yourself, do it as soon as they are killed.

GROUSE

In season 12 August to 10 December. Best early in season.

The prince of game birds. The best grouse is shot in Scotland, and has russet feathers. The hen is considered superior to the cock. It can be hung as long as a fortnight, when the gamey flavour and pronounced smell will be almost overpowering – but beloved of some *cognoscenti*. Today more grouse are eaten fresh and indeed to eat one on the evening of 13 August, 24 hours after the opening of the gaming season on the Glorious Twelfth is many a gourmet's aim. Indeed many are sold in London on the Twelfth, having been shot at dawn.

A fat hen grouse may serve two people, but grouse lovers prefer to have the bird to themselves. The flesh of a young bird is pink and tender on the breast, browner, and slightly tougher, on the legs. It is roasted, like steak, to the diner's preference, some liking it rare, some well-done. It has a full but not fatty flavour when fresh, tasting strong and gamey if well-hung.

Usually bought in brace (i.e. a pair, one cock, one hen) but can of course be bought singly. Older birds are casseroled, stewed, or used in pies.

Capercaillie and ptarmigan are species of grouse.

PHEASANT

In season 1 October to 1 February. Best from November to January.

The cock pheasant is a glorious bird, with brilliant green neck and long speckled tail feathers. The body, like the hen all-over, is mottled brown, but varies considerably from variety to variety. But the hen is plumper, tenderer and tastes better.

Pheasants may be eaten fresh (but benefit from at least three days' hanging, lest they taste as insipid as chicken) or really well hung. They are served underdone if required. The breast flesh is pale brown, the leg flesh darker.

Slightly larger than the grouse, a pheasant is served for two people, and if large and casseroled may serve three. Older birds are generally casseroled or used in pies, the young ones roasted in much the same way as grouse, the breast kept moist by a covering of pork fat.

Cock pheasant tail feathers are traditionally used to adorn a platter of roast birds.

153

PARTRIDGE

In season 1 September to 1 February. Best in October.

Smaller than grouse or pheasant, larger than quail, the common grey British partridge is thought by some to be finer in texture and taste than the much-marketed French red-leg. But the red-legged partridge is found in parts of Britain anyway, and most game-dealers make no distinction.

In feather, the partridge is small, round, and orangey in colour. Young birds of six months and under are *Perdreau* on a French menu, older birds *Perdrix*. Plucked young birds should have pale skin and fat breasts. They weigh up to 400g/14oz. They are roasted much as grouse or pheasant, but are not often served very under-done, though they may be. They may be fresh or well hung. In general young birds for plain roasting are less high than older birds, which may weigh 450g/1lb or more, for casseroling or pies.

A partridge is too small to serve two, and a hearty eater may indeed eat two by himself.

WILD DUCK, TEAL AND WIDGEON

Seasons vary according to variety, starting in August, ending in March.

The variety of wild duck is legion, ranging from largish mallard to the tiny teal. All are truly delicious, with rich well-flavoured flesh, even when eaten very fresh – which they should anyway be.

Wild duck are tricky to pluck. Sometimes they are painted with, or dipped in, melted paraffin wax which, when it dries and hardens, can be removed, bringing the feathers with it.

Unlike the domestic duck wild duck does not carry very much fat and needs to be barded and basted frequently if roasted. The flesh may have a distinctly fishy flavour and this can be par-ticularly, but never completely camouflaged by filling the cavity with sliced orange, by marinating in wine, or by parboiling in salty water before roasting. Some duck, notably widgeon, develop from their marshy feeding grounds a faintly muddy taste.

Although the French sometimes eat wild duck, and indeed domestic duck, underdone, this is not common in Britain.

PIGEON AND SQUAB

In season all the year as they are a real pest to farmers, and are classified vermin. They are generally much cheaper than other birds. But there is little flesh on them, and the best plan is to strip the breast of feathers, ease it away from the carcass, and discard the rest.

Squab (or fledgling pigeons) are killed at about four weeks old, and are fat and tender. In France they are farmed, but this is rare in England.

Pigeon breasts consist of dark lean flavoursome meat, which can, according to the age of the bird from which they were taken, be fried, grilled on a skewer, or casseroled. Whole squabs can also be cooked on a skewer. The average diner would need three pigeon breasts, or two whole squabs. Pigeon is a good cheap addition to game pie.

As mature pigeons are amazingly tough, care should be taken in ascertaining from the supplier that the pigeons in question are young. It is difficult to tell by the look of them.

SNIPE

In season August to January.

A small bird with a long bill which is sometimes pushed into the body of the bird, like a skewer, drawing the head through the legs, before roasting. Traditionally hung four days, then roasted ungutted, and served on a crouton. Can be served, two or three at a time, drawn and grilled on a skewer.

WOODCOCK

In season October to January, but best in November and December.

155

Resembles the snipe but is slightly larger. It is also roasted undrawn, and then served split in two, on toast as a savoury or starter.

CARVING POULTRY

Most small birds are served whole, the diner doing the best he can with his table knife and fork, and perhaps fingers if a finger-bowl is supplied.

But the breast of larger birds may be carved in slices, and some of both the breast meat, and of the dark leg meat or perhaps the whole drumstick, thigh or wing joint being offered. Large birds are carved as shown in the diagrams. Duck breast, however, is usually carved in long thin fillets, more or less parallel with the backbone.

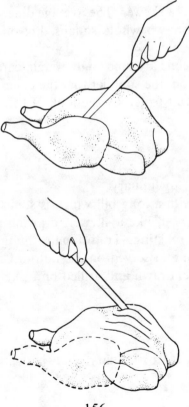

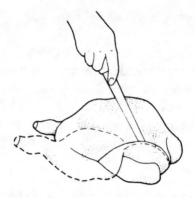

ROASTING TIMES

FOR POULTRY

White poultry, which is cooked usually through, not left pink, is done when the leg joint will wobble freely, not lifting the whole bird with it, and when the juices run clear, not pink, when the thigh is pierced with a skewer. To calculate cooking times, weigh after stuffing.

Chicken

With the oven set to 220 C/425 F, gas mark 7, allow 15 minutes to the pound. If the juices still run out pink when the flesh is pierced allow a further 15 minutes.

Turkey

Large turkeys should be slow-roasted but smaller birds (under 5·4 kilos/12lb) may be cooked at a higher temperature. Allow 10 minutes to the pound for small birds at 200 C/400 F, gas mark 6.

For larger turkeys use a cooler oven (180 C/350 F, gas mark 4) and allow 15 minutes to the pound, or an even cooler one (170 C/ 325 F, gas mark 3) and allow 25 minutes to the pound. Keep the breast covered to prevent burning, removing the covering (bacon, foil or what have you) for the last 45 minutes.

Thawing and cooking times for turkeys

Although the thawing time in this table can be relied on absolutely, the cooking times are dependent on an accurate oven. For safety's sake, plan the timing so that, if all goes right, the bird will be ready 1 hour before dinner. This will give you leeway if necessary. When the bird is cooked, open the oven door to cool the oven, then put the turkey on a serving dish and put it back in the oven to keep warm.

Thawing in a warm room (over 18 C/65 F) or under warm water is not recommended, as warmth will encourage the growth of micro-organisms, which might result in food poisoning.

Weight of bird when ready for the oven, regardless of whether it is boned stuffed or empty	Thawing time at room temperature 18 C/65 F	Thawing time in refrigerator 5 C/40 F	Cooking time at 180 C/ 350 F, gas mark 4	Cooking time at 170 C/ 325 F, gas mark 3
	hours	hours	hours	hours
4– 5 kilos/ 8–10lb	20	65	$2\frac{1}{4}$–$2\frac{3}{4}$	4 –$4\frac{1}{2}$
5– 6 kilos/11–13lb	24	70	3 –$3\frac{1}{2}$	5 –$5\frac{1}{2}$
6– 7 kilos/14–16lb	30	75	$3\frac{3}{4}$–$4\frac{1}{4}$	$5\frac{1}{4}$–$6\frac{1}{4}$
8– 9 kilos/17–20lb	40	80	$4\frac{3}{4}$–$5\frac{1}{4}$	$6\frac{1}{2}$–$7\frac{1}{2}$
9–11 kilos/21–24lb	48	96	$5\frac{1}{2}$–$6\frac{1}{2}$	8 –9

FOR GAME BIRDS

	C	F	Gas mark	Minutes
Pigeon	200	400	6	25–35
Grouse	190	375	5	25–35
Guinea Fowl	190	375	5	60–80
Partridge	190	375	5	20–25
Pheasant	190	375	5	45–60
Snipe	190	375	5	10–12
Wild Duck	200	400	6	30–35
Woodcock	190	375	5	20–30
Quail	180	350	4	20
Teal	210	425	7	20

OTHER GAME
(VENISON, RABBIT, HARE)

In France wild boar is still occasionally sold. The famous banquet showpiece, boar's head, today is a pig's head, cooked and covered in a heavy dark aspic. (The true wild boar has a long snout and cheeks with something to eat on them but the decorated centre-piece of the Mayor's banquet table today is not eaten – which is perhaps just as well.) But we are concerned only with the game easily available to the British non-sportsman – rabbit, hare and venison.

RABBIT

In season all year.

Most rabbits on the butcher's slab have been reared in farms. They are almost certain to be young and tender with pale delicate flesh very like chicken. Wild rabbits come tough, tender, tasty and inedible, depending on their age and what they have been eating. A rabbit from a cornfield is bound to be good, one from the garlic farm revolting.

Young rabbits have smooth sharp claws, older beasts rough hard ones. Young rabbits have small even white teeth, older rabbits look like Peter Rabbit. Young ones have delicate soft ears, easy to tear, older animals dry tough ones.

Wild rabbits are smaller than tame ones, and carry less fat. Rabbits must be eaten fresh. They are paunched (gutted) as soon as they are brought in, and hung for 24 hours by the legs. The skin is left on to keep the flesh moist.

To paunch a rabbit simply split the skin of the abdomen the length of the belly. The stomach and entrails practically fall out, and are easily removed. Look at the liver – if it is blotchy and unhealthy looking, throw away the rabbit. Make sure the inside

159

of the rabbit is quite clean, taking extra care near the tail and head, and wipe with a clean damp cloth.

To skin the rabbit first cut off the head and the feet. Work the skin off the body. With practice it will come off like a vest. Traditionally the head was left on but the eyes and ears removed. But the sight of a rabbit's head is more than squeamish townees, if not countryfolk, can take. Indeed, if the tastes of the people for whom the rabbit is intended are not known it is wise to joint (or 'unlace' as it once was called) the rabbit before taking it to table.

Rabbits are cooked in any way suitable for chicken – roasted, casseroled, grilled with mustard etc. They are jointed in the same way as hare, see below.

HARE

In season all year.

Much of what is written above about rabbits is true of hares: the age or otherwise of the animal is told the same way. In addition, young hares (or leverets) have a hardly noticeable hare-lip – this becoming deeper and more pronounced the older the animal. The paunching and skinning instructions apply. But there are major differences.

Hare has a much more pronounced and gamey flavour than rabbit, and this tendency is traditionally accentuated by five or six days hanging head down, *unpaunched*. The blood dripping from the mouth is caught and used as a liaison to thicken the sauce of, say, a jugged hare.

Only young hare is suitable for roasting and, because of a tendency to dry flesh, must be covered in a layer of pork fat and well basted. The saddle is the prime cut, the saddle and hind-quarters being used for roasts, the legs and belly for stews etc. The whole hare, in pieces, goes into a jugged hare.

JOINTING RABBITS AND HARES

Put the animal belly down on a board with the hind legs towards you. Cut round each hind leg in a curve, turn over and ease

160

MAKING AN OMELETTE

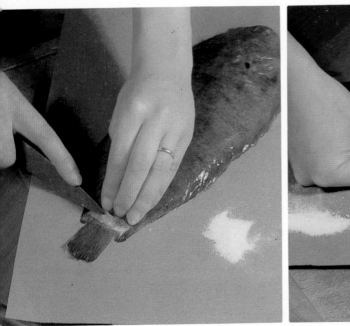

FILLETING SOLE. (1) Cut through the skin at tail. (2) Work finger or thumb round edge to loosen skin.

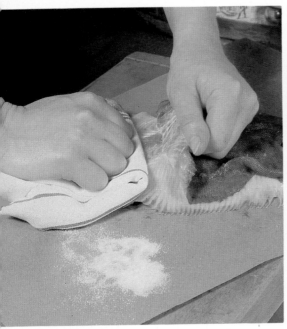
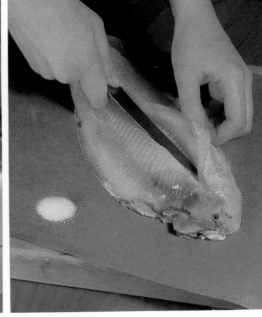

(3) Using cloth and salted fingers to prevent slipping, pull back skin. Repeat on other side.
(4) Use flexible knife flat against bones to lift each fillet

PAIN DE POISSON

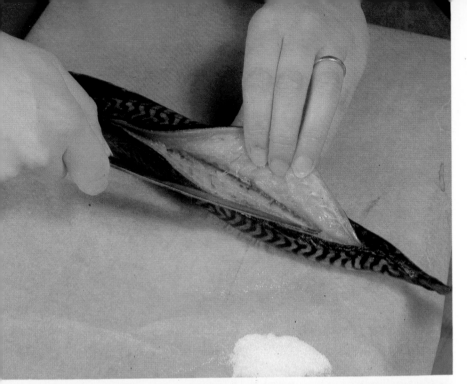

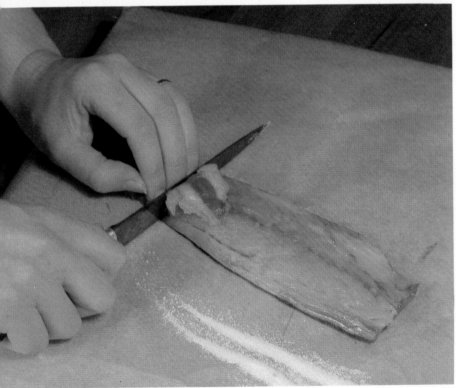

FILLETING MACKEREL. (1) Using flexible knife, cut along backbone to lift whole side of fish. (2) Using salted fingers to grip tail, ease flesh from skin with heavy knife

the legs out and away from the body to expose the ball and socket joint. Cut through the ligaments and remove the legs.

Twist the pelvis off the body and discard it (it is said to give too strong a flavour). Run the knife round under the shoulder blades and take them off, with the front legs. Now cut the back and saddle across in three or four even-sized pieces. With a large rabbit or hare, split the back piece or pieces in two along the backbones if they are over-large.

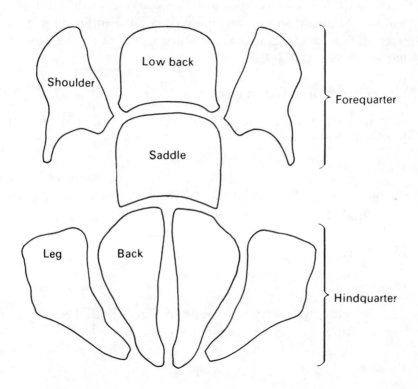

VENISON

Bucks are in season from June to September, does from October to December.

Venison (deer meat) is available frozen all the year round, and fresh only in the open season. The prime cuts for roasting are haunch, loin and saddle. The other, less tender, cuts are used for stewing or pies. Small collops or slices from the fillet can be treated as steaks, or fried à la crème.

Because venison is lean, and inclined to dryness, it is barded with fat, perhaps larded too, and basted well when roasted. It is frequently marinaded in wine and oil, both to tenderize it and to accentuate the flavour. Fresh venison has very little game flavour, tasting more like beef, but the longer it is hung, or marinaded, the more pronounced will be the taste.

When trimming a piece of venison for cooking, all the fat (there will not be much) should be removed, because although it may have a slight tenderizing and moisturising effect on the dish, it has an unpleasant taste.

ROASTING TIMES FOR GAME

Rabbit, hare and venison are lean meats and should be well barded before roasting.

Rabbit

Set the oven at 220 C/425 F, gas mark 7. Allow 15 minutes to the pound. Pierce the thigh with a skewer at the end of the cooking time, and if the juices run pink, not clear, give it another 15 minutes.

Hare.

Seal the meat by fast frying in fat over direct heat. Then roast, basting, for a total of 45–50 minutes for a young hare.

Venison

Seal in the hottest oven for 20 minutes, then roast at 170 C/325 F, gas mark 3, for 15 minutes to the pound for rare meat, 20 minutes for barely pink.

ICE CREAM

Note: On freezing, ice cream will lose a little colour, sweetness and taste, so this must be compensated for during preparation.

METHODS OF MAKING

HAND-OPERATED CHURN

This is a wooden or heavy plastic bucket with a tightly covered metal container which fits inside. There are paddles reaching into the centre of the container. These are churned by a handle at the side of the bucket. The space between the churn and the bucket is packed with freezing salt and ice. Do not let any of the salt get into the ice cream as this will ruin the taste.

1. Put the churn into the bucket.
2. Surround the metal container with chopped ice and rock salt (1 part salt to 3 parts ice) and pack it in tightly. (The salt first melts some of the ice, resulting in chips of ice suspended in a saline solution. This prevents the ice settling into a solid igloo round the churn. Then, paradoxically, this saline solution is cooled by the remaining ice to *below* water-freezing point, brine having a lower freezing point than water. Now the ice-chips, surrounded by the below $-0\,^{\circ}C$ solution, cannot readily melt and the mixture, thus stabilized, rapidly freezes the ice cream.)
3. Pour in the ice cream mixture taking care not to fill the container more than three-quarters full.
4. Insert the paddles and cover the metal churn with a piece of greaseproof paper. Fix the lid on over the paper. Assemble the rest of the machine.

5. Churn steadily, refilling the bucket with ice as it melts.
6. When the handle becomes difficult to turn the ice cream is set.
7. Remove the lid, scrape the paddles clean and replace the lid.
8. If the ice cream is for the day it is made, it should be kept in the refrigerator for one hour before serving.
9. If the ice cream is for a later date, pile it into a suitable container and keep it in the deep freeze until 1 hour before serving, when it should be put into the refrigerator to 'ripen'.

ELECTRIC ICE CREAM BUCKET

Pack the machine as for a hand churn and then set it in operation. When the hum of the motor becomes a high-pitched whine the ice cream is set.

ELECTRIC TRAY FREEZER (or sorbetière)

This is a rectangular aluminium box with plastic paddles. It fits into the freezer compartment of a refrigerator. Set the freezer at its lowest temperature, i.e. the highest setting. Pour the mixture into the sorbetière, place on the lid and put into the freezer. Turn on the machine; when the hum of the motor becomes a high-pitched whine the ice cream is set. Turn off the machine, scrape down and remove the paddles, cover the ice cream and leave to 'ripen' in the refrigerator for 1 hour.

REFRIGERATOR-FREEZER

This method does not rely on an ice cream machine of any sort but on everyday kitchen equipment.

Make sure that the fork, rotary beater, spoon, bowl and ice tray to be used are well chilled and that the freezer is set to the highest setting (lowest temperature). Pour the mixture into a chilled tray, and put into the freezer. Whisk with a fork every 20 minutes until the mixture is half frozen, then tip into a chilled bowl and whisk with a rotary beater. Return to the freezer in the bowl and whisk again at 20-minute intervals until the ice cream has become completely frozen. If the ice cream is to be eaten at a later date, allow 40–60 minutes in the refrigerator before serving, to soften slightly.

Exceptions

If the ice cream mixture already contains a high proportion of trapped air (for example, if it is made with a meringue base) the occasional whisk during the freezing process is not necessary. In addition, if a good processor such as a Magimix is available the ice cream can be completely frozen without whisking, then broken up and whisked in the machine to a creamy airy consistency. It must then be returned to the freezer.

WATER ICES

Water ices are better made in an ice cream machine, because the absence of any fat means that large ice crystals form very easily. The addition of whipped egg whites or gelatine helps to prevent this. A *granita* is a water ice made without egg whites or gelatine, having a rather icy and grainy, not creamy, texture.

BOMBES

Bombes are iced desserts frozen in a special bombe mould or in a pudding basin and turned out before serving. They generally consist of an outside layer of ice cream or sorbet and a filling of a contrasting ice cream, sorbet or a cream mousse or meringue mixture. When cut into segments the slices have a pretty stripey appearance. The traditional bombe mould was completely round, but modern ones are often shaped like jelly moulds. A pudding basin works perfectly well.

Making bombes

1. To line a bombe mould with ice cream:
   (i) Chill the mould in the freezer.
   (ii) Soften the ice cream so that it can be spread.
   (iii) Line the bottom and sides of the mould with ice cream.
   (iv) Freeze until firm.

2. For the filling:
   (i) Chill the filling well.
   (ii) Pour or spoon into the mould.
3. Cover and freeze until firm, preferably overnight.
4. Place in the ordinary refrigerator one hour before serving.
5. To unmould:
   (i) Remove lid. Prick the mixture to release any vacuum.
   (ii) Invert a plate over the mould and turn mould and plate over together.
   (iii) Cover with a cloth wrung out in hot water and hold it there. When the cloth becomes cold, wring it out again in hot water and replace it over the bombe.
   (iv) Remove the cloth. The bombe case should now lift off easily.
   (v) If the ice cream has melted slightly, return the bombe to the freezer until firm.
6. Decorate with fruit, nuts or whipped cream, as appropriate.

Easy bombe filling

Flavour whipped cream as you like (e.g. with a liqueur or with finely chopped fruit or with ginger). Mix it with an equal quantity of broken meringues.

FREEZING

Freezing is a method of preserving food – not indefinitely, but for some weeks or months. Bacterial action, which causes spoilage, is prevented by keeping the food at extremely low temperatures. Some deterioration in the taste, texture and colour of the food will take place if food is kept frozen for longer than the recommended times.

Providing the simple instructions for freezing are followed religiously, some food can be successfully stored without loss of nutritional value or quality.

RAPID FREEZING

The quicker the freezing process the smaller will be the ice-crystals formed in the food. Large ice-crystals, resulting from slow freezing, damage the cell walls of the food, and when that food is thawed liquid will be lost, including some soluble nutrients. Meat, particularly, will lose moisture on thawing if too slowly frozen, and will be dry when cooked.

PACKING THE FREEZER

In order to facilitate rapid freezing, only small amounts of unfrozen food should be put into the freezer at one time. Large quantities of room-temperature food would raise the temperature in the freezer, and the freezing process would inevitably be slower. For the same reason food should not be packed in large parcels, and the parcels should be separated in the freezing compartment, allowing the air to circulate round them. Once they are frozen, however, they can be – and indeed should be for economy's sake – packed tightly together with as little space between them as possible. A full freezer costs less to run than a half-empty one. Most freezers contain a fast-freeze compartment for the actual freezing, and larger compartments for storage. The freezer should be set to its coldest setting at least 12 hours before the food to be frozen is put into it. This is essential for meats, less important for vegetables, but advisable anyway.

WRAPPING THE FOOD

Because the cold atmosphere of a freezer is very drying, and direct contact with the icy air causes 'freezer burn' (dry discoloured patches) on some foods, most foods need careful wrapping before freezing. Heavyweight polythene bags are the cheapest and best wrappers, because it is possible to see through them, and they take various shapes of food without too many air-spaces. But any

167

air-tight container will do. Foil is sometimes used, as are rigid plastic containers, old yoghurt cartons, bowls with lids etc. Whatever the container it must be robust enough to withstand a bit of bashing about in the freezer, and it must be possible to label it clearly. Freezer labels, or polythene bags with white labels on which it is possible to write with a Chinagraph pencil or 'freezer pen' are best. Once the food is packed into the container. as closely wrapped as possible, it should be labelled with the contents and the date, and frozen immediately.

Liquids can be poured into a polythene bag set in square containers and frozen. Once solid, the bag is lifted out of the outer container and stored thus. This means fewer kitchen containers are out of use because they are in the freezer, and liquids can be stored in space-saving rectangular shapes.

Liquids in plastic tubs or containers should be frozen with a $2\frac{1}{2}$cm/1 in gap between bowl and lid to allow for expansion.

Food should be used up in the right order – peas frozen last week should not be eaten before the batch frozen 2 months ago. To facilitate this a record or inventory of what is in the freezer should be kept on it, in it or near it, with additions and subtractions made each time food is put in or taken out.

OPEN FREEZING

Fruits and vegetables, if frozen in a mass, will emerge from the freezer in a solid block. This can be inconvenient for thawing in a hurry, or if only a small quantity of the food is needed. For this reason many foods are frozen on open trays so that each raspberry, pea, broad bean or sprig of cauliflower is individually frozen before packing into bags. The frozen produce will then be free-flowing and separate. Use this method for sausages, hamburgers, breadcrumbs, bread rolls etc. as well as for fruit and vegetables. Decorated cakes and puddings can be open-frozen then packed once the decoration is hard enough to withstand the tight wrapping around it.

MASS FREEZING

If the food to be frozen is not the type suitable for open freezing, make sure that the block is not too thick. This will make cooking and thawing easier and quicker. For example, meatballs in tomato sauce should be laid one deep in a plastic box, not piled one on top of each other; spinach should be in a flattish pack so it can be cooked from frozen (a thick block would mean overcooked outside leaves when the middle was still frozen).

Air should be excluded as far as possible. This is especially important with casseroles, where the chicken or meat should be completely coated or covered by the sauce. Otherwise the meat may become dry and shreddy.

THAWING

Thawing, if it is necessary before cooking, reheating or eating, should be as slow as possible. Rapid thawing leads to loss of moisture and subsequent dryness or tastelessness of the food. However it is sometimes imperative to thaw food in a hurry. To do this put it into an air-tight polythene bag and dunk it in cold, not hot, water. Hot water tends to cook the outside of the food, and anyway encourages bacterial activity which would cause the food to go bad if not immediately completely cooked.

Meat should be completely thawed, and should be at room temperature before it is cooked. Half frozen or very cold meat becomes tough on cooking. This does not apply to meatballs or sausages where the meat is minced. For thawing turkeys, see the table on page 158.

RE-FREEZING FROZEN FOOD

Freezing does not kill bacteria present in food, it simply inhibits growth. So when food is out of the freezer the bacteria in it will multiply normally. When put back, the now considerably increased population of bacteria will cease breeding, to start afresh when the food is brought back into the warmth. For this reason frozen food manufacturers caution purchasers not to re-freeze the product once thawed. They are justly nervous that if the food is in and out of the freezer, the food could contain germs in dangerous concentrations, and the cook will still regard the product as perfectly fresh, because it has just emerged from the freezer. The foods most likely to cause illness are commercial ice cream and seafood, as both deteriorate rapidly. But this is not to say that no food should *ever* be re-frozen. It is a matter of common sense. Say, for example, a loaf of bread is freshly made, then frozen: a week later it is thawed. Similarly liver pâté is freshly made, frozen, then thawed in the same way. Sandwiches are then made using the bread and the pâté, and frozen. The total time that either bread or pâté would have had to deteriorate would have been the time they remained unfrozen – perhaps a few hours; so they would be perfectly good to eat when next thawed. But if that pâté had been in the refrigerator for a week before being frozen, then at room temperature for a day before being used for sandwiches, then out in a sunny garden for half a morning before being eaten, the bacteria present would have had plenty of breeding time to do their dirty work.

The main thing to remember is to keep food as cold as you can between freezings, and put it back as quickly as possible. For example if stuffing a frozen turkey for Christmas two weeks before the day the following procedure should be followed:

1. Thaw the turkey in the refrigerator or cool larder, not at room temperature.
2. Get the freshly made stuffing well chilled before tackling the turkey.
3. Bone and stuff the turkey in a cool place, working as rapidly as possible.
4. Freeze it again immediately.
5. Thaw again in the refrigerator, not in the room.
6. Roast in a hottish oven (this will kill any bacteria present, whereas a cool oven would encourage breeding, spoiling the food before the increased heat killed the organisms).

To sum up, it is vital to know how fresh the food in your freezer is. It will come out as fresh, or as stale or as bad as it went in.

FOODS THAT CANNOT BE FROZEN SUCCESSFULLY

Although most food will be prevented from going bad if kept at freezing point, some foods cannot be successfully frozen as the texture is ruined by freezing. This is particularly true of foods with a high water content. However, some of these may be frozen if wanted for soups or purées, in which case they should normally be frozen in purée form. Examples are *bananas, cucumbers, lettuce* and *watercress*.

Emulsions such as *mayonnaise* or *hollandaise* sauce do not freeze successfully as they separate when thawed.

Yoghurt, milk and cream can be frozen but will not be totally smooth when thawed. Double cream freezes better if whipped first. Storage time: 4 months.

Eggs cannot be frozen in the shell, but both whites and yolks freeze well, either lightly beaten together or separated. Storage time: 9 months.

Jelly, both savoury and sweet, loses its texture if frozen, and would have to be reboiled and allowed to set again after thawing if required jellied.

Strawberries keep their colour and flavour well, but become soft on thawing.

Melon is too watery to remain crisp when thawed. Best frozen in balls in syrup. But even this is not totally satisfactory.

Tomatoes emerge mushy when thawed, but are good for soups and sauces. One bonus of freezing tomatoes whole is that they peel well if run, still frozen, under the hot tap. They can, of course, be frozen as purée or juice.

Fats, or foods with a high fat content, as a rule freeze less success-fully than those without. They have a tendency to develop a slightly rancid flavour if stored for more than three months.

FOODS THAT FREEZE SUCCESSFULLY

Most foods freeze well if some care is taken with wrapping etc. But some foods freeze so well that no-one would know that they had been frozen. Baked or raw *pastries*, *breads*, *bread or biscuit doughs*, *cakes* and *sandwiches* containing not-too-wet fillings, are good examples.

As a general rule raw food (or briefly blanched food, see veget-ables, pages 173–4) keeps better and longer than cooked food. But cooked food, especially if well covered in a sauce, or under a potato or pastry crust, keeps well. There is a snag: soups and sauces thickened with flour sometimes thaw to a too-thin con-sistency. This can be overcome by using special thickening agents designed for frozen food, but as the liquid will usually re-thicken on heating anyway it does not seem worth it.

Vegetables freeze well if they are to be eaten cooked. They cannot be frozen if intended to be eaten raw. In order to prevent enzyme activity green vegetables are briefly boiled, then rapidly cooled, before freezing. They may be frozen without this 'blanch-ing' but their storage time would be much less, and it is foolish to lose food through lazy freezing. Only the best vegetables, very fresh, should be used. They should be washed, or picked over, or otherwise prepared as if for immediate cooking. A large sauce-pan of water is brought to a rapid boil, and the vegetables (not more than a pound or so at a time) lowered into it. Accurate timing of the blanching process is important. The minutes are counted from the time the water reboils. As soon as the time is up, the vegetables are lifted out, and *immediately* cooled in a sink full of cold water, if possible. Once stone cold, the vegetables are lifted out, drained well, patted dry if necessary, and frozen. The same blanching water can be used for several batches of veget-ables. Some vegetables (onions, mushrooms, potatoes) may be cooked completely in butter or blanched in oil instead of water. They are allowed to cool normally before freezing.

VEGETABLES

Where a choice of times is given the shorter time is for smaller vegetables, longer time for larger ones.

Vegetable		Blanching time in minutes	Storage time in months
Asparagus	Do not tie in bunches.	3–4	12
Artichoke (globe)	Remove stalks and outer tough leaves.	7	6
Artichoke (Jerusalem)	Freeze cooked into a purée.	—	6
Beans, broad	Sort by size.	3	12
Beans, French or runner	French: trim ends. Runner: slice thickly.	2–3 $1\frac{1}{2}$–2	12 6
Beetroot	Freeze completely cooked and skinned. Slice if large.	—	6
Broccoli	Trim stalks.	$2\frac{1}{2}$–4	12
Brussels sprouts	Choose small, firm sprouts. Remove outer leaves.	4–6	12
Cabbage	Shred. (As cabbage is available all year freezing is not usual.)	$1\frac{1}{2}$	6
Carrots	Choose small young ones with good colour. Scrape. Freeze whole.	5–6	12
Cauliflower	Break heads into sprigs.	3–4	6
Celery	Will be soft when thawed, but good for soups and stews.	3	
Corn on the cob	Remove husks and silks.	6–10	9
Courgettes	Use only very small ones. Do not peel.	1	12
Kale	Remove stalks.	1	6

Vegetable		Blanching time in minutes	Storage time in months
Leeks	Finely slice, chop in chunks or leave whole.	1–3	12
Mushrooms	Do not peel. Freeze unblanched for up to 1 month. For longer storage, cook in butter.	—	4
Onions	Store unblanched onions, sliced or chopped, for up to 3 months. Sliced or chopped onions can be blanched in water or oil. Button onions can be blanched whole.	1–3	5
Peas	Choose young, very fresh peas.	1–2	12
Potatoes	Chips – blanch in oil. Boiled or mashed: freeze cooked and cooled.	4	6
Root vegetables	Cut into chunks and blanch or cook completely.	3	12
Spinach	Move about in water to separate leaves.	1	12
Tomatoes	Do not blanch. Freeze whole, in slices or as juice or purée, cooked or raw.		

FRUITS (Storage time: 9 months)

Only freeze fruit in prime condition. Unripe, overripe or blemished fruit gives poor results. There are three methods used to freeze raw fruit. (Cooked fruit may also be frozen, whole or puréed.)

Open freezing

Suitable for most soft fruit such as raspberries and currants. Spread the fruit out on a baking sheet or tray and place in freezer uncovered. When hard pack into polythene bags or rigid container, with or without adding sugar.

Purée

Suitable for any fruits. Stew the fruit and mash, liquidize or sieve. Allow the purée to cool. Pack into containers, leaving head space, cover, label and freeze. Raw purée freezes well, too.

Dry sugar pack

Suitable for most fruit to be used in cooked puddings. Prepare the fruit, toss it in sugar and freeze, with any juices that may have run from it during preparation. Care should be taken to exclude air, which may cause discoloration of the fruit.

HERBS (Storage time: 3 months)

Herbs should be frozen dry in small polythene bags or packets, or chopped finely, put into ice-trays and just covered with water. The frozen cubes can be transferred to labelled bags.

MEAT AND FISH (Storage time: raw meat, 9 months; cooked meat, 4 months; raw fish, 5 months; cooked fish, 3 months)

Special care should be taken in wrapping to prevent freezer burn.

CAKES AND BREADS (Storage time: 12 months)
Both raw and cooked doughs and pastries freeze well.

DEFROSTING THE FREEZER

A tedious but necessary job. Follow the manufacturer's instructions to the letter. Keep the frozen food wrapped in newspaper or a blanket so it will not thaw, and transfer rapid-thawing foods like ice cream to the refrigerator, while you work. Work as fast as possible, melting the ice in the freezer by standing trays or bowls of hot water in it, scraping the ice carefully with a *blunt* instrument that will not damage the freezer. Use the opportunity to have a sort-out, and re-label foods if necessary.

Most freezers need defrosting once a year, and late spring, before the garden vegetables come flooding in, is a good time to do it.

CATERING QUANTITIES

Few people accurately weigh or measure quantities as a control-conscious chef must do. But when catering for large numbers it is useful to know the minimum quantities required to provide well without great waste.

As a general rule, the more people you are catering for the less food *per head* you need to provide, e.g. 250g/½lb of stewing beef per head is essential for 4 people, but 180g/6oz per head would feed 60 people.

POULTRY

Chicken and turkey: 450g/1lb weight per person, weighed when plucked and drawn

Duck: 3 kilos/6½lb bird for 3–4 people; 2 kilos/4½lb bird for 2 people

Goose: 3·4 kilos/8lb for 4 people; 6·9 kilos/15lb for 7 people

GAME

Pheasant: 1 bird for 2 people (roast); 1 bird for 3 people (casseroled)

Pigeon: 1 bird per person

Grouse: 1 young grouse per person (roast); 2 birds for 3 people (casseroled)

Quail: 2 small birds per person, *or* 1 large boned stuffed bird (served on a crouton)

Partridge: 1 bird per person

Venison: 170g/6oz lean meat per person (casseroled); 2 kilos/4½lb cut of haunch weighed on the bone, for 8–9 people (braised or roast); weighed off the bone, 170g/6oz per person (braised or roast)

Steaks: 170g/6oz per person

MEAT

Lamb or mutton

Casseroled: 225g/½lb per person (boneless, with fat trimmed away)
Roast leg: 1·35 kilos/3lb for 3–4 people; 2 kilos/4½lb for 4–5 people; 3 kilos/6½lb for 7–8 people
Roast shoulder: 2 kilos/4½lb shoulder for 5–6 people; 3 kilos/6½lb shoulder for 7–9 people

Roast breast: 450g/1lb breast for 2 people

(British lamb joints are frequently larger than New Zealand joints.)

Grilled best end cutlets: 3–4 per person
Grilled loin chops: 2 per person

Beef

Stewed: 225/½lb boneless trimmed meat per person
Roast (off the bone): if serving men only, 225g/½lb per person; if
serving men and women, 200g/7oz per person
Roast (on the bone): 340g/¾lb per person
Roast whole fillet: 2 kilos/4½lb piece for 10 people
Grilled steaks: 200–225g/7–8oz per person depending on appetite

Pork

Casseroled: 170g/6oz per person
Roast leg *or* loin (off the bone): 200g/7oz per person
Roast leg *or* loin (on the bone): 340g/¾lb per person
(2 average fillets will feed 3–4 people)
Grilled: one 170g/6oz chop or cutlet per person

Veal

Stews or pies: 225g/½lb pie veal per person
Fried: one 170g/6oz escalope per person

Minced meat

170g/6oz per person for shepherd's pie, hamburgers etc.
110g/¼lb per person for steak tartare
85g/3oz per person for lasagne, canneloni etc.
110g/¼lb per person for moussaka
55g/2oz per person for spaghetti

FISH

Whole large fish (e.g. sea bass, salmon, whole haddock), weighed
uncleaned, with head on: 340–450g/¾lb per person

Cutlets and steaks: 170g/6oz per person

Fillets (e.g. sole, lemon sole, plaice): 3 small fillets per person (total weight about 170g/6oz)

Whole small fish (e.g. trout, slip soles, small plaice, small mackerel, herring): 225–340g/½–¾lb weighed with heads for main course; 170g/6oz for starter

Fish off the bone (in fish pie, with sauce etc.): 170g/6oz per person

Shellfish

Prawns: 55–85g/2–3oz per person as a starter; 140g/5oz per person as a main course

Mixed shellfish: 55–85g/2–3oz per person as a starter; 140g/5oz per person as a main course

VEGETABLES

Weighed before preparation and cooking, and assuming three vegetables, including potatoes, served with a main course: 110g/4oz per person, except (per person):

French beans: 85g/3oz

Peas: 85g/3oz

Spinach: 340g/¾lb

Potatoes: 3 small (roast); 170g/½lb (mashed); 10–15 (Parisienne); 5 (chateau); 1 large or 2 small (baked), 110g/¼lb (new)

Rice

Plain, boiled or fried: 55g/2oz (weighed before cooking) *or* 1 breakfast cup (measured after cooking)

In risotto or pilaf: 1oz per person (weighed before cooking) for starter; 55g/2oz per person for main course

Note: As a general rule men eat more potatoes and less 'greens' than women!

179

MISCELLANEOUS

Brown bread and butter: 1–1½ slices (3 triangular pieces) per person

French bread: 1 large loaf for 15 people; 1 small loaf for 10 people

Cheese

After a meal if serving one blue-veined, one hard and one cream cheese: 225g/½lb piece of each for 8 people if serving one variety of cheese only: 85g/3oz per person up to 8 people; 55g/2oz per person for up to 20 people; 30g/1oz per person for over 20 people.

At a wine and cheese party: 110g/¼lb per person for up to 8 people; 85g/3oz per person for up to 20 people; 55g/2oz per person for over 20 people.

Inevitably, if catering for small numbers, there will be cheese left over but this is unavoidable if the host is not to look mean.

Biscuits

3 each for up to 10 people
2 each for up to 30 people
1 each for over 30 people

Butter

30g/1oz per person if bread is served with the meal
45g/1½oz per person if cheese is served as well

Cream

20ml/¾oz per person for coffee
50ml/1½oz per person for pudding or dessert

Milk

¼ litre/1 pint for 18–20 cups of tea

SALADS

Obviously, the more salads served, the less guests will eat of any one salad. Allow 1½ large portions of salad, in total, per head – e.g. if *only* one salad is served make sure there is enough for 1½ helpings each. Conversely if 100 guests are to choose from five different salads, allow a total of 150 portions – i.e. 30 portions of each salad.

Tomato salad

450g/1lb tomatoes, sliced, serves 5 people

Cole slaw

1 small cabbage, finely shredded, serves 10–12 people

Grated carrot salad

450g/1lb carrots, grated, serves 6 people

Potato salad

450g/1lb potatoes (weighed before cooking) serves 5 people

Green salad

Allow a loose handful of leaves for each person (i.e. a large Cos lettuce will serve 8, a large Webb's will serve 10, a Dutch hothouse 'butterhead' will serve 4)

COCKTAIL PARTIES

Allow 10 cocktail mouthfuls per head if served at a 'cocktail party'
14 cocktail mouthfuls per head if served at lunchtime when guests are unlikely to go on to a meal
4–5 cocktail mouthfuls with pre-lunch or pre-dinner drinks
8 cocktail mouthfuls, plus 4 miniature sweet cakes or pastries, per head for a wedding reception

Sliced bread

A large loaf, thinly sliced, generally has 18–20 slices

Butter

30g/1oz soft butter will cover 8 large bread slices

Sausages

450g/1lb = 32 cocktail sausages

COFFEE-MAKING

Machines and devices for making coffee are legion. But delicious coffee can be made, like tea, in a pot or jug.

5 heaped tablespoons coffee to each litre/$1\frac{3}{4}$ pints water (more or less according to taste)

1. Heat the coffee pot and a large jug. Spoon the coffee into the jug.
2. Boil the water, remove it from the heat and pour on to the coffee. (It should not be actually bubbling as it is poured. Just a fraction cooler than for tea.)
3. Give one brisk stir and allow to stand for 5 minutes.
4. Strain into the coffee pot.

For white coffee
Serve with cream or hot (but not boiled) milk

If reheating coffee: Take care not to allow coffee to boil as it will become grey, bitter and oily.
Storing: The flavour of coffee is volatile and quickly lost if left open to the air. It is best to buy no more than 1 week's supply

at a time; or to buy it vacuum packed. Always store coffee in an air-tight container. It will not keep well beyond 5 weeks once opened, even if re-sealed. But coffee freezes perfectly: freeze the beans or the freshly milled coffee in an air-tight plastic bag. If using a percolator there is no need to thaw the grounds, but frozen coffee grounds make the coffee too cool if using the jug method described above.

2
Soups, First Courses and Light Meals

———◆———

SOUPS

Gazpacho

Gazpacho was made long before liquidizers were invented, but we feel that the laborious chopping and sieving involved is not justified. This recipe therefore assumes that the cook has a blender or liquidizer.

900g/2lb fresh, very ripe tomatoes, peeled
450g/1lb tin Italian peeled tomatoes
1 large mild-tasting Spanish onion
2 red peppers
1 small cucumber
1 thick slice white bread, the crust cut off
1 egg yolk

2 large cloves garlic
6 tablespoons olive oil
1 tablespoon tarragon vinegar
1 tablespoon tomato purée
Freshly ground black pepper
Plenty of salt (preferably sea salt)

To serve:
1 large bowl croutons

1. Chop or dice finely a small amount of the tomato, onion, red pepper, and cucumber and put in separate small bowls for garnish.
2. Put the bread, egg yolk and garlic into the liquidizer. Turn it on and add the oil in a thin steady stream while the

184

machine is running. You should end up with a thick mayonnaise-like emulsion.

3. Add the vinegar and then gradually add all the soup ingredients (roughly chopped if necessary) a little at a time and blend until smooth. It will be necessary to remove the contents when the liquidizer is about half full, to prevent the machine from clogging.

4. Sieve the soup to remove the tomato seeds and check that you have included the tomato purée and sufficient pepper and salt.

Note: Gazpacho should be served icy-cold with the small bowls of chopped vegetables and fried croutons handed separately. Sometimes crushed ice is added to the soup at the last minute.

If the soup is preferred thinner dilute it with iced water or tomato juice.

Serves 6

Lebanese Cucumber and Yoghurt Soup

1 large cucumber, peeled
290ml/½ pint single cream
150g/5 fl.oz carton yoghurt

2 tablespoons tarragon vinegar
1 tablespoon chopped mint
Salt and pepper

1. Wash and grate the cucumber coarsely.
2. Stir in the rest of the ingredients and season to taste.
3. Chill for 2 hours before serving.

Note: This soup may be garnished with cold croutons; chopped chives; a spoonful of soured cream added just before serving; chopped gherkins; a few pink shrimps. It is also good flavoured with garlic.

Serves 4

Chilled Cream Cheese Soup

340g/12oz can jellied
consommé
170g/6oz mild cream cheese

1 teaspoon curry powder
Squeeze of lemon juice

1. Reserve 1 cupful of consommé for the top.
2. Liquidize the remaining consommé with the cheese, curry powder and a squeeze of lemon juice. Pour into cocotte dishes.
3. Chill until set.
4. Spoon over the remaining consommé (which should be cool, on the point of setting) and chill again until ready to serve.

Note: Some tinned consommé will not set. Test it by chilling for an hour. If the soup is still liquid, melt a teaspoon of powdered gelatine in the consommé and allow to cool. Consommé with 'serve hot' on the label is generally non-setting.

Serves 4

Creamy Vegetable Soup

225g/½lb leeks, well washed
30g/1oz butter
225g/½lb onions, very finely
sliced
1 small head celery, finely
sliced
1 large potato, peeled and
finely sliced

1 tablespoon flour
570ml/1 pint chicken stock
290ml/½ pint creamy milk
Salt, pepper and nutmeg
1½ tablespoons thin cream
1½ tablespoons port (optional,
but very good)

1. Finely slice the leeks, both white and green parts, discarding any tough outside leaves.
2. Melt the butter in a very large pan and gently cook the sliced onions, leeks, celery, and potatoes in it, stirring occasionally, until the whole mass is soft and cooked (about 20 minutes).

186

The vegetables should not be allowed to brown at all. Do this 'sweating' of vegetables with the saucepan lid on, as the juices run more easily in a steamy atmosphere and they are less likely to fry brown.

3. Stir in the flour, then add the stock.
4. Bring to the boil stirring, and boil for 1 minute.
5. Add the salt, pepper and nutmeg to taste.
6. Simmer gently for 20 minutes.
7. Liquidize the soup in an electric blender or pass through a vegetable mill.
8. Add the milk, reheat, and add the cream and port. Use white port if you would prefer the soup not to go faintly pink.

Serves 4

Iced Vichyssoise

55g/2oz butter
1 medium onion, chopped
The white part of 3 large *or* 5 small leeks, washed and chopped
110g/¼lb potatoes, peeled and sliced

Salt and pepper
860ml/1½ pints chicken stock
290ml/½ pint creamy milk
2 tablespoons cream
Chopped chives

1. Melt the butter in a heavy-bottomed pan and add the chopped onion and leek.
2. 'Sweat' the vegetables for 15 minutes or so, i.e. cook very slowly with a tightly-fitting lid or covered with a piece of greaseproof paper. The vegetables must soften without crisping or browning. It is possible to 'sweat' vegetables without a covering, but much more difficult as the steam escapes and they are inclined to fry.
3. When they are transparent and soft, add the potatoes, salt and pepper and the stock. Simmer until the potatoes are soft.
4. Liquidize the soup or push it through a vegetable mill.
5. Add the milk and cream.

6.   Check the seasoning. Chill.
7.   Add the chives just before serving, and perhaps a swirl more cream.

Note: The soup is good hot, too. Reheat without boiling.

Serves 4

Cold Cucumber Soup

2 cucumbers
290ml/$\frac{1}{2}$ pint water
Salt and freshly ground black pepper
30g/1oz flour
570ml/1 pint chicken stock

1 bay leaf
2 cloves
1 carton soured cream
1 tablespoon chopped fresh dill
Finely grated rind of 1 lemon

1.   Peel and slice the cucumber and cook in the water until tender. Liquidize or push through a sieve and add salt and pepper to taste.
2.   Mix the flour with 4 tablespoons of stock. Heat the remaining stock.
3.   Add a little of the hot stock to the flour/stock mixture and return this to the pan. Stir until the liquid boils and thickens.
4.   Add the cucumber purée, bay leaf and cloves. Bring slowly to the boil and simmer for 2 minutes. Strain into a bowl.
5.   Allow to cool. Stir in the soured cream, dill and grated lemon rind. Chill before serving.

Serves 4

Artichoke Soup

675g/1½lb Jerusalem artichokes
55g/2oz butter
1 onion, sliced
570ml/1 pint milk

570ml/1 pint water
Salt and freshly ground black
  pepper

1. Peel the artichokes and leave in a bowl of cold acidulated water (water with lemon juice or vinegar added) to prevent discoloration.
2. Melt the butter in a saucepan and gently cook the onion in it until soft but not coloured.
3. Slice the artichokes, dry well and add to the pan. Continue cooking, covered, for about 10 minutes, giving an occasional stir.
4. Add the milk and water, season well and simmer for a further 20 minutes.
5. Liquidize or push through a sieve. Check for seasoning – this soup needs plenty of salt and pepper.

Serves 4

Stilton Soup

1 medium onion
2 sticks celery
55g/2oz butter
45g/1½oz flour
75ml/2½ fl.oz white wine
1 litre/1¾ pints white stock
  (chicken *or* veal)

290ml/½ pint milk
225g/½lb Stilton cheese, grated
  or crumbled
2 tablespoons cream
Salt and pepper
Hot croutons

1. Finely chop the onion and celery and soften in the butter over gentle heat. Add the flour and cook for 1 minute.
2. Take off the heat and stir in the wine and stock. Return to the heat and bring slowly to the boil, stirring continuously until the soup thickens. Simmer for 25 minutes.

189

3. Add the milk and simmer for 2 minutes. Remove from the heat and whisk in the Stilton.
4. Add the cream and salt and pepper. If the soup is not to be served immediately keep it covered to prevent a skin forming. When reheating the soup, take care not to let it boil, lest it curdle.
5. Hand the hot croutons separately.

Note I: White port, well chilled, is delicious with this soup.

Note II: The soup can be served chilled. In this event streak the cream into the soup just before serving, giving it an attractive marbled appearance.

Serves 4

Mushroom Soup

55g/2oz butter
340g/¾lb flat black mushrooms
3 heaped tablespoons chopped fresh parsley
½ garlic clove, crushed
2 large slices bread, crusts removed

1 litre/1¾ pints good chicken stock
Pinch of ground nutmeg *or* mace
Salt and plenty of freshly ground black pepper
150ml/¼ pint cream

1. Melt the butter in a very large thick-bottomed saucepan.
2. Chop the mushrooms and add to the butter with most of the parsley. Cook gently, stirring, until soft and mushy. Add the garlic and the bread, broken into bits. Stir until the bread and mushrooms are well mixed, then add the stock, nutmeg or mace and salt and pepper to taste. Bring to simmering point and cook slowly for 10 minutes.
3. Liquidize the soup or put it through a vegetable mill. Return to the pan, add the rest of the chopped parsley and the cream, and reheat. If the soup is to be served cold, reheating is

190

unnecessary, but in this case the cream and parsley garnish should be added only when the soup is cold.

Serves 4

Iced Creamy Borscht

450g/1lb raw beetroot
570ml/1 pint water
Salt and freshly ground black
   pepper
30g/1oz butter
1 large onion, sliced
225g/½lb raw potatoes, peeled
   and sliced
425ml/¾ pint milk

1 chicken stock cube
1 teaspoon cumin seeds *or* ½
   teaspoon ground cumin
Juice of ½ lemon
190ml/⅓ pint cream
290ml/½ pint soured cream
1 tablespoon chopped fresh
   chives

1. Wash the beetroot but do not peel them. Boil them in the water with a good pinch of salt for 3 hours or until very tender. Do not throw away the water, but peel the beets, discarding the skins.
2. Melt the butter in a heavy saucepan and in it slowly fry the onion until just turning colour. Add the sliced potatoes and cook over gentle heat for a further 5 minutes.
3. Add the milk, cumin and chicken stock cube. Simmer slowly until the potato is cooked.
4. Put the beetroot and cooking liquid through a liquidizer, vegetable mill or sieve. Then liquidize or sieve the contents of the saucepan. Mix with the beetroot.
5. Add the lemon juice and plenty of pepper. Taste for seasoning, adding salt if needed. Stir in the cream.
6. Chill well. Serve the soup in individual soup plates or cups, with a good dollop of soured cream in each serving, and the top sprinkled with the chives.

Serves 6

Lentil Soup

340g/¾lb lentils
1 litre/2 pints ham stock, saved
  from a bacon joint; *or* if not
  available use 1 small bacon
  bone and water
1 bay leaf
55g/2oz onion

1 stock cube
1 parsley stalk
3–4 tablespoons cream
Chopped fresh mint
Croutons
Water

1. Wash the lentils and drain them. Boil, covered with the ham stock, for about 30 minutes. If no ham stock is available use cold water and add the bacon bone, bay leaf, sliced onion, stock cube and parsley stalk.
2. When the lentils are soft remove the bone etc. Liquidize or sieve the soup.
3. Return the soup to the pan with the cream and heat up. Serve with a little chopped mint and the hot croutons.

Note: The addition of cream gives a richer texture and a blander taste.

Serves 4

Corn Chowder

1 large potato
3 sticks celery
1 large onion
110g/¼lb streaky bacon,
  rindless
1 large green pepper
30g/1oz butter

1 bay leaf
30g/1oz flour
570ml/1 pint milk
4 ears corn on the cob
Salt and pepper
Chopped fresh parsley

1. Wash and peel the potato.
2. Cut it, and the celery, onion and streaky bacon into dice.

192

3. Remove the seeds from the pepper and dice the flesh.
4. Fry the bacon in the butter. When brown but not brittle add the diced vegetables and the bay leaf. Turn down the heat and cook slowly until the onion looks soft and transparent.
5. Draw the pan from the heat; mix in the flour and then the milk.
6. Return the pan to the heat and stir steadily until boiling.
7. Scrape the kernels from the cobs and add them to the soup. Scrape the cobs with a sharp knife to extract all the juice and add this too. Season with salt and pepper to taste. Simmer for 5 minutes or until the vegetables are soft but not broken.
8. Serve sprinkled with chopped parsley.

Serves 4

Provençale Fish Soup

3 tablespoons olive oil
2 onions, sliced
1 garlic clove, crushed
2 leeks, sliced
1 litre/2 pints water
Trimmings from the fish (head, skin, bones)
3 tomatoes, peeled and quartered
Bouquet garni (celery, parsley, bay leaf, sprig of thyme)

Pinch of saffron
Salt and freshly ground black pepper
10–12 live mussels
1 kilo/2lb white fish fillets (any Mediterranean fish *or* haddock *or* brill *or* plaice *or* cod)
Seasoned flour
1 tablespoon tomato purée

For the rouille (garlic paste):
1 green pepper
1 dry chilli pepper *or* a few drops of Tabasco
150ml/$\frac{1}{4}$ pint water
2 garlic cloves, crushed

1 canned pimento cap
3 tablespoons olive oil
1 tablespoon stale breadcrumbs

1. Start with the soup: heat the oil in a large pan. Add the onion, garlic and leeks and cook until soft but not coloured.

Add the water, fish trimmings, tomatoes, bouquet garni, saffron, salt and pepper. Cook uncovered over a moderate heat for 30 minutes but no longer.

2. Scrub the mussels well, removing their 'beards' and discarding any that do not shut when tapped on the sink edge.

3. Meanwhile prepare the rouille: simmer the pepper and chilli in a little water for 10 minutes. Drain and dry well. Grind the pepper, garlic, pimento and chilli in a pestle and mortar to a smooth paste or blend finely in a liquidizer. Beat in the olive oil drip by drip. Add enough breadcrumbs to make the sauce hold its shape, and add the Tabasco if the chilli was omitted. Taste and season with salt if necessary.

4. Strain the fish bouillon into a clean saucepan, pressing the fish trimmings and vegetables to extract all their juices.

5. Cut the fish fillet into bite-sized cubes and toss them in seasoned flour. Add to the bouillon with the tomato purée.

6. Simmer for 5 minutes and add the mussels. Simmer until all the shells have opened. Taste and season.

7. Pour the soup into a tureen and hand the rouille separately. (If the rouille is very thick and paste-like, a little of the hot soup can be added to thin it slightly.)

Serves 6–8

Prawn Bisque

900g/2lb unshelled raw prawns	Blade of mace
2 tablespoons oil	1·14 litres/2 pints well
110g/¼lb butter	flavoured fish stock
2 shallots, chopped	(page 304)
Juice of ½ lemon	45g/1½oz flour
3 tablespoons brandy	Salt and pepper
1 bay leaf	Tabasco sauce
1 parsley stalk	3 tablespoons cream

1. Wash the prawns, reserving any roe.

2. In a large heavy pan heat the oil, add 30g/1oz of the butter and fry the prawns for 2 minutes or until they begin to change

194

colour. Add the shallots, lemon juice and brandy and continue to cook for a further 2 minutes or until the prawns are a bright pink. Allow to cool until the prawns can be handled.

3. Shell the prawns, keeping the shells. Reserve the pan with its juices, and any roe from the prawns.

4. Simmer the prawn shells, bay leaf, parsley stalk and blade of mace in the stock for 30 minutes (this will help to give the bisque flavour and colour).

5. Meanwhile blend or pound together nearly all the prawns with about 45g/1½oz butter and any reserved roe. Keep the remaining prawns for garnish.

6. Melt the remaining butter (about 45g/1½oz). Add the flour and cook for 30 seconds. Strain in the stock and bring slowly to the boil stirring constantly. Simmer for 2 minutes, strain in the pan juices, and whisk in the prawn butter.

7. Season with salt, pepper and Tabasco. Add the cream and finally the reserved prawns.

Note: If there is no roe to be found a tablespoon of tomato purée whisked into the bisque will give it a better colour.

Serves 4

Lobster Bisque

1 live lobster (675g/1½lb)
2 tablespoons oil
110g/¼lb butter
2 shallots, chopped
Juice of ½ lemon
3 tablespoons brandy
1 bay leaf
1 parsley stalk

Blade of mace
1.14 litres/2 pints fish *or*
   vegetable stock
45g/1½oz flour
3 tablespoons cream
Salt and pepper
Pinch of cayenne pepper

1. Set the oven to 180°C/350°F, gas mark 4.

2. Kill the lobster by pushing a sharp knife through its nerve centre (marked by a well-defined cross on the back of the head).

195

3. Lay the lobster flat out and split it in half lengthwise. Remove and discard the little stomach sac from the head and the thread-like intestine. Remove the coral (if any) and reserve it.

4. In a large heavy saucepan, heat the oil with 30g/1oz of the butter. In it sauté the lobster, flesh side down, for 5 minutes. Add the shallot, lemon juice and brandy. Cover and place the pan in the oven for 15 minutes.

5. Remove all the meat from the lobster, adding the greenish creamy paste from the head. Reserve the pan with its juices, and the lobster shell.

6. Simmer the broken up shells, bay leaf, parsley stalk and blade of mace in the stock for 30 minutes (this will help to give the bisque flavour and colour).

7. Meanwhile blend or pound together all but a small chunk of the lobster meat with about 45g/1½oz butter and the coral. Cut the reserved meat into neat dice and set aside for garnish.

8. Strain the stock. Melt the remaining butter, add the flour and cook for 30 seconds. Add the stock and bring slowly to the boil, stirring all the time. Simmer for 2 minutes, add the pan juices and whisk in the lobster butter.

9. Add the cream and finally the lobster pieces. Taste and add salt or pepper if necessary. Serve sprinkled with a pinch of cayenne pepper.

Serves 4

Cock-a-Leekie Soup

This is an unthickened chicken broth, and it should have plenty of chicken and leeks in it. At the end of the cooking process there should be about 1 litre/1¾ pints of soup.

6 prunes	1 bay leaf
1·5 kilos/3lb chicken	Few parsley stalks
2 teaspoons salt	6 leeks
Freshly ground black pepper	Chopped parsley

1. Soak the prunes in cold water for 6 hours. Remove the stones.
2. Joint the chicken and place the pieces in a pan with enough water to cover them generously. Add salt and pepper, bay leaf, giblets (except the liver) and parsley. Bring to the boil and skim. Cover and simmer for about 45 minutes.
3. Meanwhile wash and trim the leeks and cut them into 2·5cm/ 1in lengths. Skim the fat from the soup, add the leeks and prunes and simmer for a further 45 minutes.
4. Remove the chicken, giblets, bay leaf and parsley stalks. Skin the chicken and cut the flesh into small neat dice. Add the diced chicken to the soup.
5. Check the seasoning and serve hot with a little chopped parsley sprinkled over at the last minute.

Note I: It is sometimes desirable to use the chicken breast for a dish on its own, and it seems a pity to put it in a soup. But of course it can be used. Alternatively, chicken portions (thighs and drumsticks) can be bought more cheaply than whole chickens, but this means no giblets. Best of all, use a boiling fowl, but remember this will need a total of 3 hours simmering, with the water being topped up as necessary.

Note II: If there is no time to soak the prunes they may be cooked whole in the soup and the stones removed afterwards.

Serves 6

French Onion Soup

450g/1lb onions
55g/2oz butter
$\frac{1}{2}$ garlic clove, crushed
1 tablespoon flour
1·4 litres/2$\frac{1}{2}$ pints good stock, preferably beef
55g/2oz Gruyère cheese, grated

$\frac{1}{2}$ teaspoon dry English mustard
Salt and freshly ground black pepper
4 slices French bread
1 tablespoon grated Parmesan cheese

197

1. Slice the onions. Melt the butter in a large heavy pan and in it *slowly* brown the onions and garlic: this should take at least 45 minutes and the onions should become meltingly soft and greatly reduced in quantity. They must also be evenly brown all over and transparent.
2. Stir in the flour and cook for 1 minute.
3. Add the stock and stir until boiling. Season with salt and pepper and simmer for 20–30 minutes.
4. Set the oven to 200°C/400°F, gas mark 6.
5. Mix the grated Gruyère with mustard, salt and pepper. Spread this on the bread slices and put them on the bottom of an earthenware tureen. Pour over the soup. The bread will rise to the top. Sprinkle with the Parmesan cheese. Put the soup (uncovered) in the oven until well browned and bubbling.

Serves 4–6

Beef Consommé

1¾ litres/3 pints very well flavoured beef bouillon (page 306)
Whites of 3 eggs plus shells

5 tablespoons sherry *or* Madeira

1. Place the bouillon and sherry in a large clean metal saucepan. Place over a gentle heat.
2. Place the crushed shells in a bowl, add the egg whites, and whisk until frothy. Pour into the bouillon. Whisk with a balloon whisk until the mixture boils and rises. Stop whisking immediately and take the pan off the heat. Allow the mixture to subside. Take care not to break the crust formed by the egg white.
3. Bring the consommé up to the boil again and then again allow to subside. Repeat this once more. (The egg white will trap the sediment in the stock and clear the soup.) Allow to cool for 10 minutes.
4. Fix a double layer of fine muslin over a clean basin and carefully strain the soup through it, taking care to hold the

egg white crust back. When all the liquid is through (or almost all of it) allow the egg white to slip into the muslin. Then strain the soup again – this time through both egg-white crust and cloth. Do not try to hurry the process by squeezing the cloth as this will produce murky soup: it must be allowed to drip through at its own pace. The consommé is now ready for serving.

Note: To serve the consommé *en gelée* (jellied) pour the liquid into a shallow pan or tray to cool and refrigerate until set. Chop roughly with a knife and spoon into ice-cold soup cups. Serve with a wedge of lemon and toast.

Serves 6

Garnishes for Consommé

Aux pointes d'asperges

Cooked asparagus tips. Place at the bottom of a hot tureen and pour the soup over.

A la Julienne

Mixed carrot, turnip, leek and celery cut into Julienne strips. Add to the consommé and cook until tender. Chopped chervil or parsley is sometimes added at the last minute.

Lady Curzon

Chill the consommé in ovenproof cups. Flavour 2 tablespoons double cream with curry powder, salt and pepper and pour over each consommé. Place under a hot grill to brown the top. Put into a warm oven to heat the soup.

Aux profiteroles

Choux pastry seasoned with Parmesan, mustard and cayenne, piped in pea-size pieces and baked until crisp. Place in the bottom of a hot tureen, pour the soup over and serve immediately before the profiteroles can become soggy.

Aux quenelles

Small chicken quenelles, poached in stock. Float these in the consommé and sprinkle with chopped chervil or parsley.

Aux vermicelli

Vermicelli cooked in stock until tender. Rinse well, place in a hot tureen and pour the soup over. (Other small-size pastas are also used.)

Consommé Royale

Consommé (page 198)   4 tablespoons cream
1 egg white   Salt and pepper

1. Mix the egg white with a fork and beat in the cream and seasoning.
2. Place in an ovenproof dish and stand in a pan of gently simmering water until set.
3. Cool, cut into neat strips and add to the comsommé just before serving.

Serves 6

EGG DISHES

Egg Mayonnaise

290ml/½ pint mayonnaise   1 small lettuce
  (page 316)   6 hardboiled eggs
Milk *or* water

For the garnish:
Strips of cucumber skin *or*   Paprika pepper
  chopped parsley

1. Thin the mayonnaise to coating consistency by adding milk or water.
2. Finely shred the lettuce and with it cover the base of a serving plate.
3. Cut the eggs in half lengthwise and arrange, cut side down, on the bed of lettuce. Carefully coat each egg with mayonnaise.
4. Decorate every other egg with a small diamond shape cut from cucumber skin or with a neat sprinkling of chopped parsley. Decorate the remaining eggs with paprika pepper.

Note: Thin strips of anchovy fillet in a criss-cross pattern, stoned black olives, rings of radish or watercress leaves all make suitable garnishes for egg mayonnaise.

Serves 4

Anchovy Eggs

10 anchovy fillets	3 teaspoons mayonnaise
A little milk	(page 316)
10 hardboiled eggs	Anchovy essence
30g/1oz butter	Freshly ground black pepper

1. Soak the anchovy fillets for half an hour in milk to remove some of the salt. Drain them.
2. Split the eggs lengthwise and remove the yolks.
3. Mash or sieve the yolks.
4. Beat the butter until very soft and stir in the mayonnaise and egg yolks. Season to taste with anchovy essence and pepper.
5. Using a teaspoon or forcing bag fitted with a fluted nozzle fill the egg-white hollows with this mixture.
6. Split the anchovy fillets in half lengthwise and lay each one diagonally across an egg.

Makes 20

Portuguese Eggs

4 hardboiled eggs
45g/1½oz butter
1 tablespoon, chopped fresh
  parsley
Salt and pepper
4 ripe tomatoes
1 clove, crushed garlic

290ml/½ pint coating
  consistency Béchamel sauce
  (page 308)
45g/1½oz strong Cheddar *or*
  Gruyère, grated
1 tablespoon dried crumbs

1. Set the oven to 200 C/400 F, gas mark 6. Light the grill.
2. Cut the eggs in half lengthwise and sieve or mash the yolks.
3. Cream half the butter well and beat in the yolks, parsley and seasoning. Taste.
4. Pile this mixture back into the egg whites and press together until they resemble hardboiled eggs.
5. Plunge the tomatoes into a pan of boiling water for 5 seconds. Skin and slice them, cutting across horizontally.
6. Fry the tomato slices briefly in a frying pan with the crushed garlic and remaining butter. When barely cooked lay them in a heat-proof dish.
7. Place the eggs on top of the tomatoes and coat with the Béchamel sauce. Dust with grated cheese and crumbs.
8. Bake in the oven for 10 minutes and then place under the grill to brown.

Serves 4

Scrambled Eggs on Anchovy Toast

1 slice of crustless buttered
  toast, spread with anchovy
  paste
2 eggs

1 tablespoon cream *or* creamy
  milk
Salt and freshly ground black
  pepper
1 teaspoon butter

1. Get the toast ready first. Put on a heated plate and keep warm.
2. In a bowl mix together the eggs, cream or milk, salt and pepper.
3. Melt the butter in a frying pan. Tip in the egg mixture and, using a fish slice, keep it constantly moving until thickened and creamy but still fairly wet.
4. Pile on to the prepared toast and serve immediately.

Note: This method makes scrambled eggs of a creamy texture, with large egg pieces. If you want the smoother scrambled eggs with small egg pieces, use a saucepan and a wooden spoon instead of the pan and fish slice. Go very slowly and be careful not to overcook the eggs or they will become grainy and watery.

Serves 1

Plain French Omelette
(using a 15cm/6in pan)

3 eggs
Salt and fresh ground black
  pepper
Pinch of grated Parmesan
  cheese (optional)

1 tablespoon cold water
15g/$\frac{1}{2}$oz butter

1. Break the eggs into a bowl and with a fork mix in the seasoning, Parmesan and water.
2. Melt the butter in a heavy frying pan and swirl it around so that the bottom and sides are coated. When foaming pour in the egg mixture.
3. Hold the frying pan handle in your left hand and move it gently back and forth over the heat. At the same time, with a wooden spoon, move the mixture slowly, scraping up large creamy flakes of egg mixture. As you do this some of the liquid egg from the middle of the omelette will run to the sides of the pan. Tilt the pan to help this process. Leave over the heat until the bottom has set and the top is creamy. Remove from the heat.

4. With a fork or palette knife fold the nearside edge of the omelette over to the centre and then flick the whole omelette over on to a warmed plate with the folded edges on the

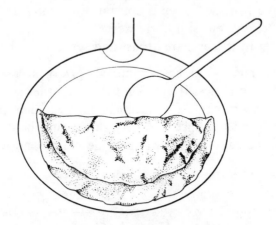

underside. Alternatively, fold the omelette in two and slide on to the plate.

Note: Grated cheese, fresh chopped herbs, fried mushrooms or other flavourings can be added to the basic omelette mixture.

Serves 1

Arnold Bennett Omelette

1 slice of onion	55g/2oz butter
1–2 slices carrot	15g/½oz flour
1 bay leaf	3 tablespoons cream
4 peppercorns	3 eggs, separated
150ml/¼ pint milk	1 tablespoon grated Parmesan
110g/¼lb smoked haddock	cheese
	Pepper

1. Put the onion, carrot, bay leaf, peppercorns and milk in a saucepan and heat slowly.

2. When the milk is well flavoured, add the haddock and poach gently for 10 minutes or until the fish is just cooked.
3. Take out the fish and flake it.
4. Melt half the butter in a small pan, add the flour and stir over heat for 1 minute.
5. Add 110ml/$\frac{1}{4}$ pint of the strained cooking milk. Stir until boiling.
6. Add 1 tablespoon of the cream and the flaked haddock. Set aside while making the omelette.
7. Beat the egg yolks with a tablespoon of cream. Season with pepper only (do not add salt as the haddock is salty).
8. Whisk the egg whites and fold into the yolks with the haddock and half the grated cheese.
9. Turn on the grill to a high heat.
10. Melt the remaining butter in an omelette pan over a good heat, tipping the pan so that the bottom and sides are coated. When the foaming begins to subside quickly pour in the egg mixture.
11. When the omelette is fairly firm, sprinkle on the remaining cheese, pour over the remaining tablespoon of cream and brown quickly under the pre-heated grill.
12. Slide on to a hot dish.

Serves 4

Tortilla

450g/1lb floury potatoes, peeled and finely sliced
1 small onion, finely sliced

Salt and freshly ground black pepper
4 eggs, beaten
Oil for frying

1. Heat about 1cm/$\frac{1}{2}$in of oil in a frying pan, add the potatoes and onions, season with salt and pepper and fry slowly until soft, but not coloured. Leave to cool and then add them to the beaten egg.

2. Tip all the oil, but for a thin film, out of the pan and pour in the egg mixture.
3. Cook the omelette over a moderate heat until it is set and then slip on to a plate. Turn it over and put it back into the frying pan with the uncooked side down.
4. Cook for a further minute and then turn out on to a serving plate – serve warm or cold, cut into wedges.

Note: Frying the potatoes from raw is the usual Spanish method. But if the potatoes are small and waxy a better result would be had by boiling them first, then slicing and frying. Unboiled potatoes can give a rather tough and bendable omelette rather than a light, soft one. Old floury potatoes need not be pre-boiled, however.

Serves 4

Tarragon Eggs

4 medium-sized eggs, preferably at room temperature	8 leaves fresh tarragon
	4 teaspoons single cream
	15g/½oz butter
Salt and pepper	

1. Heat up 4 cocotte dishes and brush out with butter. Stand them in a pan or roasting tin of hot water (a bain-marie).
2. Break an egg carefully into each dish and season with salt and pepper. Place two tarragon leaves on each egg and spoon over a little cream. Place a knob of butter on top.
3. Simmer gently on top of the cooker for 7–9 minutes with the bain-marie covered with a lid or foil. The whites should be set and the yolks runny.

Note: The eggs will continue cooking for a short time after removing from the heat so be very careful not to overcook. These eggs can also be baked in a moderate oven (180 C/350 F, gas mark 4), where they will take 12 minutes. They do not need to be covered if cooked this way, but it is still advisable to stand them in a bain-marie to prevent the edges drying out.

Serves 4

Baked Egg with Mushrooms

45g/1½oz butter
1 shallot, finely chopped
110g/¼lb mushrooms, finely
  chopped
2 teaspoons chopped fresh
  parsley

Salt and freshly ground white
  pepper
4 eggs
4 tablespoons cream *or* creamy
  milk

1. Set the oven to 180°C/350°F, gas mark 4. Butter 4 ramekin or cocotte dishes with 15g/½oz butter.
2. Melt half the remaining butter, add the shallot and cook until soft but not coloured.
3. Add the rest of the butter with the mushrooms. Toss over a gentle heat until the mushrooms are softened. Add the parsley and season well with salt and pepper.
4. Divide this mixture between the 4 cocotte dishes. Break an egg into each. Spoon a tablespoon of cream on to each egg and season with salt and pepper.
5. Stand the dishes in a bain-marie and bake in the oven for 10–12 minutes, until the whites are just set and the yolks still runny.

Note I: Traditionally served with fingers of hot toast.

Note II: The eggs may be cooked in the bain-marie over a gentle heat on the top of the cooker. But they must be covered with foil or a baking sheet. They will take only 7–8 minutes.

Serves 4

Lucullus Eggs

110g/¼lb mushrooms
1 small lettuce
30g/1oz butter
Salt and freshly ground black
    pepper

4 eggs
2 tablespoons double cream
1 tablespoon grated strong
    Cheddar cheese
Dried breadcrumbs

1. Set the oven to 180°C/350°F, gas mark 4.
2. Slice the mushrooms and chop the rinsed lettuce. Melt the butter in a saucepan and add the lettuce and mushroom. Cook gently until the mushroom is slightly softened. Season well and pour off all the liquid. Tip into an earthenware dish.
3. With the back of a large spoon make 4 small indentations in the lettuce mixture and into these break the eggs. Spoon over the cream and sprinkle the cheese and crumbs on top.
4. Bake in the oven for 12–15 minutes or until the egg white only is set and the cheese melted.

Serves 4

Oeufs Florentine

450g/1lb leaf spinach
15g/½oz melted butter
Salt and freshly ground black
    pepper
Good pinch of nutmeg

4 eggs, chilled
290ml/½ pint mornay sauce
    (page 309)
A little extra grated cheese
Browned crumbs

1. Remove the stalks of the spinach and wash thoroughly. Put into a pan *without water*. Add a sprinkling of salt, cover and cook gently, shaking the pan, for 5–7 minutes. It will reduce in quantity by about two-thirds. Drain very thoroughly by squeezing between two plates.
2. Chop finely and turn in the melted butter. Season with salt,

208

pepper and nutmeg. Place in the bottom of a fireproof dish.

3. Set the oven to 220 C/425 F, gas mark 7, and heat the grill.
4. Poach the eggs: three-quarters fill a large shallow pan with water, adding a tablespoon of vinegar for each pint of water. Bring to the boil, then lower the temperature to a fast simmer. Break an egg into a cup and slip it into the water. Immediately raise the temperature slightly so that the bubbles help to draw the white round the yolk. Poach for about 3 minutes, lift out with a perforated spoon.
5. Trim the whites neatly with a pair of scissors or a stainless steel knife and drain thoroughly on absorbent paper or a clean cloth.
6. Arrange the eggs on top of the spinach and coat with the cheese sauce. Sprinkle over the grated cheese and browned crumbs.
7. Brown the top under a hot grill.

Serves 4

Scotch Eggs

340g/$\frac{3}{4}$lb sausage-meat
Salt and pepper
4 hardboiled eggs, shelled
Flour
Oil for frying

Seasoned flour
Beaten egg
2 tablespoons dried
   breadcrumbs

1. Season the sausage-meat with salt and pepper. Divide it into four.
2. Roll the eggs in flour. Dip your hands in a little flour and mould the sausage-meat around each egg making sure they are completely and evenly covered.
3. Place at least 3·5cm/1$\frac{1}{2}$in of oil in a fryer and begin to heat it up slowly.
4. Dip the eggs in seasoned flour, brush with beaten egg and coat with breadcrumbs.
5. Place the prepared eggs into the wire basket from the fryer

and when the oil is hot enough to fizzle gently when a bread-crumb is added to it put in the eggs and fry for about 12 minutes.

6. Remove the basket and increase the temperature of the oil until a crumb will sizzle vigorously in it.
7. Return the eggs to the fryer and cook until the crumbs are golden brown (about 4–5 minutes). Drain well.

Note: Scotch eggs are cooked in two stages because the sausage-meat must cook completely. If fried in the cooler oil, the meat would be cooked, but the breadcrumbs soggy. If cooked in only the hotter oil, by the time the sausage-meat was cooked the breadcrumbs would be too dark.

Serves 4

Oeufs à la Villeroy

55g/2oz butter
2 small onions, finely chopped
340g/¾lb chopped mushrooms
55g/2oz flour
About 150ml/¼ pint stock
4 eggs

Oil for deep frying
Seasoned flour
1 egg, beaten
2 tablespoons dry breadcrumbs
Watercress *or* deep-fried
    parsley (page 787)

1. Melt the butter and add the onions. Cook gently until soft. Stir in the mushrooms, cook for a further minute and then stir in the flour. Cook for another minute, stirring, and add half the stock. Bring gradually up to the boil, stirring all the time. Add more stock if necessary to make a thick paste. Allow to cool, then refrigerate for 30 minutes.
2. Boil the eggs for 4–5 minutes and then plunge immediately into cold water. Shell them carefully.
3. Heat the fat in the fryer slowly.
4. Dry the eggs and with floured hands mould the very thick mushroom paste around each one so that they are completely

covered. Dip in seasoned flour. Roll in beaten egg and coat with breadcrumbs.

5. Put the eggs in the fryer basket and when the oil is hot enough to sizzle when a breadcrumb is dropped into it, lower them in and turn up the heat. Fry until the breadcrumbs are a golden brown (about 2 minutes). Drain well.

6. Serve with a sprig of watercress or fried parsley. The eggs, when cut open, should have runny yolks.

Serves 4

HORS D'OEUVRES AND SALAD FIRST COURSES

'Hors d'oeuvres' often means a selection of five or six 'starter' dishes of contrasting colours and textures arranged on individual plates or on one large platter. They can also be served as after-dinner savouries.

There are many commercially prepared foods which do very well as hors d'oeuvres (with perhaps a little 'doctoring'), for example:

Cold canned baked beans to which a little chopped onion and French dressing is added.

Best canned sardines in oil (preferably olive), with thin slices of raw onion.

Thin rolls of mortadella, salami or other cold meats.

Good-quality olives.

Good use can be made of leftover foods:

Strips of ham, cheese and green pepper in French dressing.

Cubes of beef, chopped tomatoes and black olives in a garlic and horseradish French dressing.

Cold flaked fish, mixed with mayonnaise and lemon juice.

Cooked cauliflower and hardboiled egg in a herb-flavoured French dressing

211

Simple salads can be colourful and delicious:
Cooked beetroot, chopped onion, soured cream topping.
Sweetcorn, chopped celery and almonds in French dressing.
Sliced tomatoes and mushrooms in garlicky French dressing.
Mixed shredded white cabbage and cos lettuce in herby French
dressing.

Recipes from page 200–261 are suitable for serving either as part
of a mixed hors d'oeuvre or as a first course on their own.

Stuffed Cream Cheese Tomatoes

4 tomatoes
110g/¼lb good cream cheese *or*
sieved cheese
1 tablespoon chopped fresh
mint
Squeeze of lemon
¼ garlic clove, crushed

Salt and freshly ground black
pepper
1 tablespoon chopped fresh
parsley
French dressing (page 319)
Sprigs of watercress

1. Dip the tomatoes in boiling water for 5 seconds. Peel them.
2. Slice a quarter of each tomato off at the rounded end. Scoop
    out the flesh and seeds. Discard the seeds and coarsely chop
    the flesh.
3. Mix a little of the flesh with the cream cheese, mint, lemon,
    garlic and the salt and pepper.
4. Fill the hollow tomatoes with this mixture and stick the tops
    back at a jaunty angle. Arrange on a plate.
5. Add the parsley to the dressing and shake or mix well. Spoon
    this over the tomatoes, and garnish with the well-washed
    watercress.
6. Serve with brown bread and butter.

Serves 2

Crudités

A selection of:

Celery

Green pepper

Cauliflower

Radishes

Button mushrooms

Spring onions

Carrots

Asparagus

Young turnips

Black olives

150ml/¼ pint mayonnaise (page 316)

1 garlic clove, crushed (optional)

1. Prepare the vegetables, making sure they are perfectly clean, and as far as possible evenly-sized:

    Celery: wash and cut into sticks.

    Pepper: wipe and cut into strips, discarding the seeds.

    Cauliflower: wash and break into small florets. Peel the stalks if tough.

    Radishes: wash and trim off the root and long leaves, but leave a little of the green stalk on each radish.

    Mushrooms: wash. Peel only if the skins are tough. Quarter if large.

    Spring onions: wash. Cut off most of the green part, and the beard (roots). Leave whole, or cut in half lengthwise if large.

    Carrots: peel and cut into sticks the same shape and size as the celery.

    Asparagus: peel the tough outer stalk and trim away the hard root ends.

    Turnip: peel and cut into strips. (Use young turnips only.)

    Black olives: stone with a cherry stoner if desired.

2. Mix the garlic (if using) with the mayonnaise. Spoon it into a small serving bowl.

3. Arrange the raw prepared vegetables and the olives in neat clumps on a tray or flat platter with the bowl of mayonnaise dip in the centre.

Stuffed Courgettes

170g/6oz frozen prawns
Lemon juice
Salt and pepper
4 medium courgettes
1 small onion
2 tomatoes
30g/1oz butter

1 teaspoon finely chopped fresh
  parsley
290ml/½ pint cheese (mornay)
  sauce (page 309)
A little grated cheese
A handful of browned crumbs

1. Defrost the prawns, preferably overnight, and season with lemon juice and salt.
2. Wash the courgettes and cut off the ends. Place them whole in a pan of boiling salted water and boil until barely tender. Cool in a colander under running cold water.
3. Split the courgettes lengthwise and, using a melon baller or spoon remove a 'channel' of flesh down the middle of each half courgette. Reserve the scooped-out flesh.
4. Drain the shells very well – otherwise the whole dish will become watery.
5. Heat the oven to 200 C/400 F, gas mark 6.
6. Chop the onion very finely.
7. Dip the tomatoes in boiling water for 5 seconds. Peel them, chop the flesh and discard the seeds.
8. Roughly chop the reserved courgette flesh.
9. Melt the butter in a frying pan and add the onion. Fry gently for 2 minutes. Add the tomatoes and courgette flesh and continue to cook without colouring until the ingredients are soft, allow to cool slightly.
10. Stir in the parsley and prawns and season well.
11. Place a spoonful of this mixture in each courgette shell and lay in a buttered ovenproof dish. Coat each courgette with a spoonful of cheese sauce and sprinkle over a little grated cheese and browned crumbs.
12. Heat up the grill.
13. Put the dish in the pre-heated oven for 15 minutes and then under the grill until delicately browned.

Serves 4

Stuffed Mushrooms

8 large flat mushrooms
1 shallot
1 garlic clove
55g/2oz butter
2 rashers of streaky rindless
  bacon, finely diced
85g/3oz chicken livers
1 tomato, skinned and finely
  chopped

½ teaspoon chopped fresh
  parsley
Dried white breadcrumbs
Salt and pepper
Oil for shallow frying
8 slices French bread
Chopped fresh parsley to
  garnish

1. Wipe the mushrooms and remove the stalks.
2. Chop the shallot and the mushroom stalks finely and crush the garlic.
3. Trim away and discard any discoloured parts of the livers and dice them finely.
4. Heat up the grill.
5. In a saucepan, melt half the butter and when foaming add the bacon and shallot. Fry gently until the shallot is soft.
6. Add the livers, increase the temperature, and fry rapidly until the livers start to brown.
7. Add the mushroom stalks and garlic. Cook for 1–2 minutes.
8. Add the tomato and parsley. Season.
9. Place the mushroom tops, smooth side down, on the grill pan, brush with the rest of the butter, and grill for 1 minute, turn over and grill for a further minute.
10. Fill the mushrooms with the stuffing and sprinkle over the breadcrumbs.
11. Heat the oil in a frying pan and fry the bread slices until a golden brown on each side. Drain well.
12. As the bread fries place the mushrooms back under the grill for a minue to reheat them.
13. Place the mushrooms on the rounds of fried bread and sprinkle with chopped parsley.

Serves 4

Aubergines Robert

2 aubergines
1 teaspoon chopped fresh
  chives

2 tablespoons French dressing
  (page 319)

1. Slice the aubergines and soak them in the dressing for 2 hours.
2. Heat the grill.
3. Grill the aubergines on both sides until pale brown. Sprinkle
    well with chives and more dressing and grill again for 1
    minute or until golden brown. Turn the slices over, sprinkle
    again with dressing and chives, and grill to a good brown.
4. Allow to cool. Chill well before serving.

Serves 4

Stuffed Vine Leaves (*dolmades*)

About 30 small young vine
  leaves
1 onion, finely chopped
2 tablespoons olive oil
225g/½lb cooked rice
Pinch of allspice
½ teaspoon chopped fresh
  mint

Salt and freshly ground black
  pepper
Chicken stock
Lemon juice
Plain yoghurt *or* tomato sauce
  (page 325)

1. Plunge the vine leaves into a pan of boiling salted water for
    10 seconds. Rinse under cold water and drain well. Lay the
    leaves, smooth side up, side by side on a tabletop or board.
2. Fry the onion in the oil until soft but not coloured. Mix
    together the onion (with its oil), the rice, allspice and mint.
    Season with salt and pepper.
3. Lay a teaspoon of rice on each leaf and roll up the leaf, tucking
    in the ends to make a small parcel. Squeeze the rolls in the

216

palm of your hand – this will ensure that the dolmades hold their shape and will not need tying up. Pack all the dolmades into a wide saucepan and add enough stock to half-cover them. Sprinkle over a tablespoon of lemon juice. Cover tightly, preferably with a small plate that fits inside the pan (which will prevent the dolmades moving during cooking) and a lid. Simmer for 1 hour.

4. Lift out the dolmades with a perforated spoon and arrange on a serving dish. Chill. Coat with yoghurt or tomato sauce.

Note: Dolmades may be served hot, with the yoghurt or sauce handed separately.

Serves 8

Three-Pea Salad

110g/¼lb brown lentils
110g/¼lb chick peas, soaked
  for 3 hours
110g/¼lb split green peas
150ml/¼ pint French dressing
  (page 319)

1 tablespoon chopped fresh
  parsley
1 teaspoon chopped fresh mint
1 teaspoon French mustard

1. Cook the lentils, chick peas and split green peas in separate pans of boiling water. The lentils and split peas will take anything from 30 to 75 minutes, and the chick peas up to 2 hours. Rinse them all under cold water and drain well.
2. Shake the dressing in a jar until well emulsified and divide equally between three cups. To one cup add the mint; to another, the parsley; and to the third, the mustard. Add a good pinch of salt to each. Toss the chick peas in the parsley vinaigrette, the split peas in the minty dressing and the lentils in the mustard one.
3. Arrange the piles of dressed peas on a serving dish or hors d'oeuvres tray.

Note: Other pulses, such as soya beans, red kidney beans and haricot beans, are good treated similarly.

Serves 8

Mushrooms à la Grecque

425ml/¾ pint water
2 tablespoons tomato purée
2 tablespoons olive oil
2 tablespoons white wine
2 shallots, finely chopped
1 garlic clove, crushed
6 coriander seeds
½ teaspoon dried *or* 1 teaspoon
  chopped fresh fennel

6 peppercorns
Small pinch of salt
450g/1lb button mushrooms
2 teaspoons chopped fresh
  parsley
Good squeeze of lemon juice

1. Place all the ingredients except the mushrooms and parsley in a saucepan and simmer gently for 15–20 minutes.
2. Add the mushrooms and simmer for 10 minutes. Remove the mushrooms.
3. Reduce the liquid by boiling to about 190ml/⅓ pint. Put the mushrooms back and allow to cool.
4. Check the seasoning and tip into a shallow bowl or dish. Sprinkle with chopped parsley.

Serves 4

Celeriac Remoulade

450g/1lb celeriac
150ml/¼ pint mayonnaise
  (page 316)
½ level teaspoon Dijon mustard

2 teaspoons finely chopped
  gherkin
2 teaspoons finely chopped
  fresh tarragon *or* chervil

2 teaspoons finely chopped   1 anchovy fillet, finely chopped
   capers

1. Mix together all the ingredients except the celeriac.
2. Peel the celeriac and grate it coarsely. Immediately mix with the sauce, before it has time to discolour.
3. Turn into a clean dish.

Note: Remoulade sauce is a mayonnaise with a predominantly mustard flavour. The other ingredients, though good, are not always present.

Serves 4

Tabouli

110g/¼lb cracked wheat   1 shallot
   (Burghul)   3 tablespoons olive oil
1 tomato   Salt and freshly ground black
½ cucumber   Pepper
5 leaves fresh mint   Lemon juice
Good handful of fresh parsley

1. Soak the wheat in cold water for 1 hour – it will expand greatly. Drain and wrap in a clean tea-towel. Squeeze out the moisture. Spread the wheat on a tray to dry further.
2. Dip the tomato in boiling water for 5 seconds. Peel it, cut in quarters and remove and discard the seeds. Chop the tomato flesh.
3. Chop the cucumber, skin and all, very finely. Or carefully cut it into very tiny dice.
4. Chop the mint leaves and the parsley very finely. Chop the shallot finely.
5. Mix all the ingredients together, adding salt, pepper and plenty of lemon juice to taste.

Serves 4

Avocado Pears Stuffed with Crab

2 ripe avocado pears
French dressing (page 319)
170g/6oz white crab meat
  (canned or frozen is fine)
1 dessert apple
Stick of celery, finely
  chopped

3 tablespoons mayonnaise
  (page 316)
1 tablespoon cream
1 teaspoon finely grated lemon
  rind
Salt and pepper

1. Split the avocados, remove the stones and immediately brush the cut surface with French dressing to prevent discolouring.
2. Sort through the crab meat to remove any pieces of inedible cartilage. Peel and chop the apple.
3. Mix crab, apple and celery with mayonnaise lightened by the addition of the cream and grated rind of lemon. Season with salt and pepper to taste and pile into the avocado halves.

Serves 4

Leeks Mimosa Vinaigrette

8 small leeks
2 hardboiled eggs

For the French dressing:
3 tablespoons oil
1 tablespoon vinegar
Salt and freshly ground black
  pepper

1 tablespoon chopped fresh
  parsley

Pinch of dry English mustard
Pinch of sugar (optional)

1. Cut off the roots of the leeks and all but 2½cm/1in of the green part. Split them from the green end towards the root end, cutting through to within 8cm/3in of the root end. This is to enable you to ruffle through the leaves as you hold them

220

under the cold tap to wash out the sand.

2. Cook the leeks in boiling salted water until just tender (about 6 minutes). Cool under running water and drain well.

3. Make the French dressing: put all the ingredients together in a screw-top jar and shake until well emulsified. Pour this over the leeks and leave to marinate for 2 hours.

4. Split the eggs in half and remove the yolks. Wash the whites and dry well. Chop them finely, using a stainless steel knife or push them through a nylon or stainless steel sieve. Sieve the egg yolks.

5. Arrange the leeks on a serving dish, pouring over the French dressing. Garnish with rows of chopped parsley, sieved egg yolk and chopped egg white.

Serves 4

Spinach Roulade

450g/1lb fresh spinach *or*
  170/6oz frozen leaf spinach
15g/½oz butter
Salt and freshly ground black
  pepper
4 eggs, separated
Pinch of nutmeg
Parmesan *or* strong Cheddar
  cheese, grated

For the filling:
15g/½oz butter
170g/6oz mushrooms, chopped
15g/½oz flour
190ml/⅓ pint milk
4 tablespoons cream
1 heaped tablespoon chopped
  fresh parsley
Salt and freshly ground black
  pepper

1. To prepare the spinach remove the stalks and wash thoroughly. Put into a pan without water. Add a sprinkling of salt. Cover and cook gently, shaking the pan occasionally for 5–7 minutes. The spinach will reduce in quantity by about two-thirds. Drain thoroughly by squeezing between two plates. Chop finely and push through a sieve. Beat in the butter.

221

.. Set the oven to 190°C/375°F, gas mark 5. Take a large
    roasting pan and cut a double layer of greaseproof paper
    slightly larger than the tin. Lay this in the tin. Don't worry
    if the ends stick up untidily around the sides. Brush the paper
    lightly with oil or melted butter.

3. To make the roulade gradually beat the egg yolks into the
    spinach and season with salt, pepper and nutmeg. Whisk the
    egg whites until stiff but not dry and fold them into the
    spinach. Pour this mixture into the prepared roasting tin,
    spread it flat and sprinkle with grated cheese. Bake for 10–12
    minutes or until it feels dry to the touch.

4. Melt the butter and gently cook the mushrooms in it. Remove
    the pan from the heat, add the flour and mix well. Return
    the pan to the heat and cook for half a minute. Add the
    milk and bring to the boil, stirring continually until you have
    a fairly thick creamy sauce. Add the cream and parsley and
    season well.

5. Sprinkle grated cheese on to a piece of greaseproof paper and
    place on a tea-towel. Turn the roulade out on to the paper and
    remove the original piece of paper. Spread the filling on to
    the roulade and roll it up as you would a Swiss roll, removing
    the paper as you go. Serve on a warmed dish either whole
    or in slices.

Serves 4

Spinach Mould

675g/1½lb fresh spinach
30g/1oz butter
100g/3½oz fresh white breadcrumbs
2 eggs, beaten

1 egg yolk
Pinch of ground nutmeg
Salt and freshly ground black
  pepper
345ml/12 fl.oz milk

1. Wash the spinach well and remove the tough stalks. Put, still
    wet, into a saucepan with a lid and holding the pan in one

hand and the lid on with the other shake and toss the spinach until it is soft and reduced in quantity.

2. Drain well and remove about 15 of the best and biggest leaves carefully. Drain these on absorbent paper.

3. Squeeze all the water from the remaining spinach, pressing it between two plates. Tip on to a board and chop very finely. Butter a 15cm/6in cake tin or soufflé dish and line it with the whole spinach leaves.

4. In a saucepan melt the butter, add the spinach and stir until very dry looking. Take off the heat and add the breadcrumbs, eggs, egg yolk, nutmeg and seasoning.

5. Heat the milk and stir it into the mixture.

6. Spoon the spinach mixture into the cake tin and cover with buttered foil or greaseproof paper.

7. Heat the oven to 180°C/350°F, gas mark 4. Stand the cake tin in a roasting pan full of boiling water. Transfer both roasting tin and spinach mould to the oven and bake for 45 minutes or until the mixture is firm.

8. Turn out on a hot serving dish.

Serves 4–6

Artichokes with Clarified Butter

4 artichokes   110g/4oz butter, clarified
                                        (page 784)

1. Wash the artichokes in salted water. Trim the sharp points of the leaves square with a pair of scissors or large knife. Cut away any of the very tough leaves and trim the stalk so that the artichoke will stand upright.

2. Plunge the artichokes into a pan of boiling salted water and cook for about 45 minutes or until a leaf can be easily pulled away from the whole. Drain well.

3. To serve, pull out the centre leaves and with a teaspoon carefully scrape out the fibrous 'choke' making sure that every

particle is removed. Serve with hot clarified melted butter, handed separately.

Note I: Clarified butter is not strictly necessary. Plain melted butter will do, but the crystal clear look of clarified butter is very pleasing.

Note II: It is a good idea to provide each guest with his own pot of melted butter to dip the artichoke leaves in, and an empty dish or plate for the debris, and a fingerbowl.

Note III: Artichokes are also delicious served cold with a French dressing, or with mayonnaise (pages 319, 316) which a stiffly beaten egg white has been added just before serving.

Serves 4

Tomato and Mozzarella Salad

55g/2oz tomatoes per person
55g/2oz mozzarella cheese per
person

Fresh basil
French dressing (page 319)
Black olives

1. Dip the tomatoes into boiling water for 5 seconds and skin. Slice them and the cheese.
2. Lay the tomato and cheese in alternating overlapping slices.
3. Chop the basil (about 3 leaves per person) finely and add to the dressing. Pour over the salad and sprinkle with a few olives.

Mushroom and Prawn Salad

170g/6oz prawns
Lemon juice
Freshly ground black pepper

170g/6oz button mushrooms,
sliced

For the French dressing:

3 tablespoons olive oil
1 tablespoon lemon juice
½ garlic clove, crushed

Salt and freshly ground black
  pepper
2 teaspoons chopped fresh mint

For the garnish:

1 teaspoon chopped fresh
  parsley

1. Sprinkle the frozen prawns liberally with lemon juice and black pepper and leave to defrost.
2. Mix together the ingredients for the French dressing and add the mushrooms. Leave to marinate for 6 hours.
3. Add the prawns, mix well and put into a clean serving dish. Garnish with the parsley.

Serves 4

MOUSSES AND SOUFFLÉS

Avocado Pear Mousse

15g/½oz gelatine
2 rashers rindless back bacon
About 10 walnut halves
2 ripe avocado pears
150ml/¼ pint mayonnaise (page
  316)
Lemon juice

1 teaspoon Worcestershire
  sauce
Salt and pepper
1 teaspoon onion juice
150ml/¼ pint double cream,
  whipped

1. In a small saucepan soak the gelatine in 3 tablespoons of cold water.
2. Grill the bacon until crisp but not brittle. Drain well and when cold chop finely. Chop the walnuts.
3. Peel the avocados and mash until smooth. Add the mayonnaise, lemon juice, Worcestershire sauce, salt and pepper, onion juice, walnuts and bacon.

225

4. Melt the gelatine over gentle heat and when dissolved stir into the avocado mixture. With a metal spoon fold in the cream.
5. Pour into an oiled mould and refrigerate until set.
6. Just before serving turn out on to a serving dish.

Note I: If the mousse is to be eaten from the dish in which it is set oiling is not necessary.

Note II: Avocado mixtures are inclined to discolour. This can be prevented by covering the mousse with a thin coating of seasoned cream cheese, soured cream or mayonnaise.

Serves 4

Tuna Fish Mousse

2 teaspoons gelatine
285g/10oz tinned tuna fish
150ml/¼ pint mayonnaise
  (page 316)
Salt and freshly ground black
  pepper
1 garlic clove, crushed

Lemon juice
1 tablespoon fresh chopped
  parsley
150ml/¼ pint double cream,
  whipped
Oil for greasing

For the garnish:
Slices of cucumber

Stoned black olives

1. In a small saucepan, soak the gelatine in 2 tablespoons water.
2. Oil a mould for the mousse and leave it to drain upside down.
3. Pour off the oil from the tuna fish and flake the fish with a fork. Mix to a pulp. Stir in the mayonnaise, seasoning, garlic, lemon juice and parsley.
4. Melt the gelatine over a gentle heat and when clear and runny stir into the mixture.
5. Fold in the cream. Pour into the mould. Refrigerate until set.
6. To turn out, invert a serving dish over the mould and then

turn both the dish and the mould over together. Give both
a sharp shake, and remove the mould.

7.   Decorate with slices of cucumber and stoned black olives.

Note: If the mousse is to stand for more than an hour after
decorating, the cucumber slices should be *degorgé*, i.e. salted,
allowed to stand for 30 minutes, rinsed well and patted dry. If
this is not done the salt in the mousse draws out the moisture
in the cucumber and the result looks wet and messy.

Serves 4

Egg Mousse with Anchovies

1 tablespoon water
2 teaspoons gelatine
6 hardboiled eggs
6 tablespoons mayonnaise
    (page 316)

2 teaspoons anchovy essence
3 tablespoons cream
Salt and pepper
Cayenne
Milk

For the garnish:
12 anchovy fillets
3 small gherkins

12 radishes
12 thin slices cucumber

1.   Put the water into a small heavy saucepan and sprinkle over
    the gelatine. Leave for 10 minutes. Soak the anchovy fillets in
    milk to extract some of the salt.
2.   Oil a soufflé dish or mould.
3.   Chop the eggs and mix them with the mayonnaise, anchovy
    essence and cream, and season with salt, pepper and cayenne.
4.   Dissolve the gelatine over gentle heat and when runny and
    clear add it to the mixture, stirring briskly.
5.   Pour into the mould or dish. Put in the refrigerator until
    set.
6.   Loosen the mousse round the edge, using fingers or thumb,
    and turn out on to a plate. Drain the anchovy fillets and
    split them lengthwise. Use them to lattice the top of the

227

mousse. Cut thin rings of radish and gherkin and place them in alternate diamond-shaped spaces of the lattice pattern. Decorate the sides of the mousse with thin rounds of cucumber. Trim the rest of the radishes, leaving a few leaves on each, and put them round the mousse.

Note: If this dish is made hours in advance the cucumber slices should be first salted and left to release their juices. They should then be rinsed and dried. If this is done they will not 'weep' when left on the sides of the mousse.

Serves 4

Haddock Mousse

450g/1lb haddock
150ml/¼ pint milk
2 slices onion
1 bay leaf
6 peppercorns
15g/½oz butter
15g/½oz flour
3 tablespoons water

8g/¼oz gelatine
2 hardboiled eggs
150ml/¼ pint double cream
150ml/¼ pint mayonnaise
  (page 316)
Salt and pepper
1 teaspoon anchovy essence

For the garnish:
Sliced hardboiled egg   Thin cucumber slices

1. Set the oven to 180°C/350°F, gas mark 4. Oil a 10cm/4in soufflé dish and stand upside down to drain off excess.
2. Place the haddock in an ovenproof dish. Pour over the milk and put in onion, bay leaf and peppercorns. Cover and poach in the oven for about 30 minutes.
3. Skin the haddock and strain the milk into a bowl.
4. Melt the butter and add the flour. Stir over a gentle heat for 1 minute. Take off the heat and add the milk the fish was cooked in. Return to the heat and stir continuously while gently bringing to the boil. You should now have a very thick white sauce. Cover to prevent a skin forming, and set aside to cool.

228

5. Pour the water into a small thick-bottomed pan and sprinkle over the gelatine. Set aside to 'sponge' for 10 minutes.
6. Meanwhile chop the hardboiled eggs. Flake the fish carefully, removing any bones.
7. Lightly whip the cream and mix with the mayonnaise. Add to the cooled sauce, the eggs and the fish. Season with salt, pepper and the anchovy essence.
8. Put the gelatine pan over a gentle heat until it is clear and warm. Using a large metal spoon stir the gelatine thoroughly into the fish mixture. Pour into the prepared soufflé dish. Cover and put in the refrigerator to set, preferably overnight.
9. To turn the mousse out wet a plate and place over the top of the dish. Turn dish and plate over together and give a sharp jerk downwards. The mousse should come out immediately. (Wetting the plate makes it easier to shift the mousse should it not turn out dead-centre.) Decorate with sliced hardboiled egg and cucumber.

Note: If the mousse is to be decorated some hours before serving the cucumber slices should be first salted, left for 30 minutes, rinsed well and patted dry. If this is not done the salt in the mousse will draw out the juice in the cucumber, giving a wet and unattractive appearance.

Serves 6

Cucumber Mousse

1 large cucumber *or* 1½ medium ones, peeled if preferred
110g/¼lb full-cream cream cheese
150ml/¼ pint double cream (whipped) *or* yoghurt *or* soured cream

Salt and freshly ground black pepper
Pinch of grated nutmeg
Juice of 1 lemon
15g/½oz gelatine
150ml/¼ pint chicken *or* vegetable stock

229

1. Grate the cucumbers, reserving about 2·5cm/1in to slice for decoration.
2. Oil a soufflé dish or mould.
3. Beat together the cream cheese and whipped cream, yoghurt or soured cream. Mix in the grated cucumber and season with salt, pepper and nutmeg. Add the lemon juice.
4. In a small pan soak the gelatine in the stock. When spongy warm over a very gentle heat until clear and add to the cucumber mixture, mixing gently but thoroughly.
5. Pour into the prepared mould and chill in the refrigerator until set.
6. To turn out, invert a plate over the mould and turn plate and mould over together. Give a sharp shake to dislodge the mousse. Decorate with slices of cucumber.

Note I: If an absolutely velvet-smooth texture is wanted, blend the cucumber with the yoghurt or cream in a liquidizer.

Note II: This mousse does not keep well. Eat within 24 hours.

Serves 4

Smoked Trout Mousse

2 large smoked trout
150ml/¼ pint double cream,
  lightly whipped
Squeeze of lemon juice

½ teaspoon horseradish cream
Freshly ground black pepper
4 slices smoked salmon
Buttered brown bread

1. Cut off the heads and tails of the fish. Skin the fish and remove the bones. Mince or pound the flesh and mix with the whipped cream, lemon juice, horseradish and pepper to taste.
2. Shape the mixture into a shallow mound, on a serving plate. Cover neatly with the slices of smoked salmon.
3. Serve with brown bread and butter.

Note: Individual mousses can be made by wrapping each portion of mousse in a slice of smoked salmon. Sometimes the heads and tails of the fish are placed at each end of the rolls to resemble whole fish.

Serves 3–4

Cheese Soufflé

55g/2oz butter
45g/1½ oz flour
290ml/½ pint milk
4 eggs, separated
85g/3oz grated strong Cheddar
  or Gruyère cheese

½ teaspoon made English
  mustard
Pinch of cayenne pepper
Salt and pepper

1. Set the oven to 200°C/400°F, gas mark 6. Melt a knob of the butter and brush out a 15cm/6in soufflé dish with it.
2. Melt the rest of the butter in a saucepan and stir in the flour. Add the milk and cook, stirring vigorously, for 1 minute. The mixture will get very thick and leave the sides of the pan. Take it off the heat.
3. Stir in the cheese, egg yolks, mustard, cayenne, salt and pepper.
4. Whisk the egg whites until stiff, but not dry-looking, and mix a spoonful into the mixture. Then fold in the rest and pour into the soufflé dish, which should be about two-thirds full. Cut through the mixture with a knife several times to ensure that there are no over-large pockets of air.
5. Bake for 25–30 minutes and serve straightaway. (Do not test to see if the soufflé is done for at least 20 minutes. Then open the oven just wide enough to get your hand in and give the soufflé a slight shove. If it wobbles alarmingly, cook a further 5 minutes.)

Serves 2

Cauliflower and Stilton Soufflé

1 medium cauliflower	55g/2oz Stilton, grated
150ml/¼ pint milk	3 eggs
15g/½oz butter	1 tablespoon grated Cheddar
15g/½oz flour	cheese
Salt and pepper	1 tablespoon dried
Nutmeg	breadcrumbs

1. Cut the cauliflower into florets and cook them in a pan of boiling salted water until just tender. Drain well and liquidize or sieve to a pulp with the milk.
2. Melt the butter, stir in the flour and cook, stirring, for 1 minute. Pour in the cauliflower purée. Stir until the sauce is boiling and has thickened. Taste and season very well.
3. Butter a 15cm/6in soufflé dish and set the oven to 180°C/350°F, gas mark 4.
4. Stir in the Stilton off the heat, returning the pan to the heat only if it does not melt, but being careful not to boil the mixture. Allow to cool slightly.
5. Separate the eggs and beat the yolks into the cauliflower mixture.
6. Whisk the whites until stiff but not dry and fold into the mixture. Pour into the buttered soufflé dish.
7. Sprinkle with cheese and crumbs. Bake for 20–25 minutes or until well risen, brown on top and fairly steady when given a slight shake. If it wobbles alarmingly, give it another 5 minutes.

Serves 4

Sorrel and Cheese Soufflé

110g/¼lb sorrel	Pinch of cayenne
340g/¾lb spinach	½ teaspoon mustard
55g/2oz butter	55g/2oz strong Cheddar *or*
Dried white breadcrumbs	Gruyère cheese

232

55g/2oz flour	4 eggs
290ml/½ pint milk	1 dessertspoon Parmesan
Salt and pepper	cheese

1. To prepare the sorrel and spinach, remove the stalks and wash the leaves very carefully. Place in a pan of boiling salted water for 2 minutes. Drain very well, squeezing water out through a colander or sieve or between two plates. Chop finely.
2. Set the oven to 200°C/400°F, gas mark 6. Lightly butter a 15cm/6in soufflé dish. Coat the sides lightly with breadcrumbs.
3. Melt the butter in a saucepan and stir in the flour. Add the milk and bring to the boil, stirring continuously, for 1 minute. Take the sauce off the heat, stir in the salt and pepper, cayenne, mustard, cheese, spinach and sorrel. Cool slightly.
4. Separate the eggs, adding the yolks to the sauce. Whisk the egg whites until stiff but not dry and mix a spoonful thoroughly into the sorrel mixture. Then gently fold in the rest.
5. Pour into the soufflé dish, which should not be more than two-thirds full. With a knife cut through the mixture several times to ensure that there are no large pockets of air. Sprinkle the top with Parmesan cheese.
6. Bake for 20–25 minutes or until the soufflé is still moist in the middle but crisp around the edges. (It should not wobble alarmingly when given a slight shove, nor be absolutely rigid.)

Serves 4

PÂTÉS AND TERRINES

Sardine and Lemon Pâté

110g/¼lb butter	Salt and freshly ground black
225g/½lb canned sardines	pepper

110g/¼lb cream cheese   1 egg white (optional)
½ teaspoon French mustard   6 black olives, stoned
Juice of ½ lemon

1. Beat the butter until soft and creamy.
2. Add the sardines with their oil and beat.
3. Add the cream cheese, mustard, lemon, salt and plenty of pepper and mix well. (Alternatively all the above ingredients can be beaten together in an electric machine.)
4. Whisk the egg white stiffly and fold into the mixture.
5. Pile onto a dish and garnish with black olives. Serve with hot toast.

Note: This pâté looks very festive and pretty served in scooped-out lemon halves with a sprig of mint decorating each stuffed lemon.

Serves 8

Kipper Pâté

340g/¾lb kipper fillets   Lemon juice
85g/3 oz softened butter   4 black olives *or* 4 slices
85g/3oz cream cheese   lemon
Freshly ground black pepper

1. Skin and mince the kipper fillets.
2. Beat the butter until very creamy (but do not melt it) and stir in the kippers and cream cheese.
3. Beat until completely incorporated.
4. Season well with black pepper and lemon juice.
5. Pile into a dish and garnish with slivers of black olive or slices of lemon.

Note: For a party this pâté can look very good spooned into scooped-out lemon halves and garnished with bay leaves.

Serves 6

Potted Turkey

225g/½lb smoked turkey
110g/¼lb butter, clarified, but
  cold

Pepper

1. Mince the turkey and pound it with three-quarters of the butter. Season with pepper.
2. Press the mixture tightly into small pots, making sure that there are no air spaces.
3. Melt the remaining butter, allow to cool until on the point of setting and pour over the pots. Leave to set. Store in a cool place. It will keep for two weeks, or more in a cold refrigerator.

Note: To clarify butter, heat until foaming, then strain through a piece of muslin or a J-cloth.

Serves 4

Chicken Liver Pâté

285g/10oz butter
1 large onion, very finely
  chopped
1 large garlic clove, crushed
450g/1lb chicken livers *or*
  225g/½lb duck livers and
  225g/½lb chicken livers

Salt and freshly ground black
  pepper
85g/3oz clarified butter (if the
  pâté is to be stored)

1. Melt half the butter in a large thick frying pan and gently fry the onion in it until soft and transparent.
2. Add the crushed garlic and continue cooking for a further minute.
3. Discard all the discoloured bits from the livers as they are very bitter.

235

4. Add the livers to the pan and cook, turning them to brown on all sides, for 8 minutes or so, when they should be firm and cooked.
5. Add salt and plenty of pepper.
6. Mince the mixture or liquidize it in an electric blender with the rest of the butter. Put it into an earthenware dish or pot.
7. If the pâté is to be kept for more than three days cover the top with a layer of clarified butter.

Serves 6

Taramasalata

Slice of white bread, crusts removed
1 large garlic clove, crushed
110g/¼lb bottled smoked cod's roe *or* 225g/½lb fresh smoked soft roe

About 150ml/¼ pint each salad oil and olive oil
Freshly ground black pepper
Juice of ½ lemon

1. Hold the bread slice under the tap to wet it. Squeeze dry and put it in a bowl with the cod's roe and the crushed garlic (if fresh roe is used the skin should be discarded first). With a wooden spoon or electric whisk, beat very well. Now add the oils very slowly, almost drop by drop (as with mayonnaise), beating all the time. The idea is to form a smooth emulsion, and adding the oil too fast will result in a rather oily, curdled mixture.
2. The amount of oil added is a matter of personal taste: the more you add, the paler and creamier the mixture becomes and the more delicate the flavour. Stop when you think the right balance of blandness and smoked-roe taste is achieved.
3. Add black pepper and lemon juice to taste.

Note: Taramasalata can be served as a spread for cocktail snacks, or with toast or fresh rolls. But it is best served as a starter with hot Greek bread (pitta).

Serves 6

Tuna Pâté in Lemon Shells

4 lemons of equal small size
225g/½lb boned tuna fish
170g/6oz butter
1 teaspoon anchovy essence
A little lemon juice

Salt and freshly ground black
    pepper
8 lemon leaves *or* nasturtium
    leaves *or* 8 thin slices
    cucumber

1. Cut the lemons in half and scoop out the flesh and membranes. Slice a little of the skin away at each end of the halves enabling them to stand upright on a dish.
2. Mash the tuna fish. Add the butter, mixing very well. Season with anchovy, lemon juice, salt and pepper.
3. Divide this mixture into eight and pile into the shells. Garnish with a leaf or cucumber slice.

Note: Young nasturtium leaves look very pretty as a garnish and are delicious and peppery to eat. This pâté is good served with hot buttered toast.

Serves 8

Smooth Duck Pâté with Aspic

This recipe must be started at least one day in advance.

1 large duck
1 onion
1 carrot
1 Stick of celery
6 peppercorns
2 bay leaves
Salt and freshly ground black
    pepper
1¼ litres/2 pints water

170g/6oz butter
3 tablespoons port
Ground mace
15g/½oz gelatine
1 egg white
2 egg shells
1 orange for garnish

To serve:
Hot toast

237

1. Take all the duck flesh off the bones. Put the bones, the onion, carrot, celery, peppercorns and bay leaves in a large saucepan. Season with salt. Add the water, bring to the boil and leave to simmer for at least 3 hours, without allowing the water to reduce to less than 290ml/½ pint.

2. Cut the duck flesh into 5cm/2in pieces. Melt 2 tablespoons of the butter and in it fry the duck, a few pieces at a time, until completely cooked (about 10 minutes). Add more butter and duck pieces as and when necessary.

3. Cut away and discard any discoloured parts from the liver. Melt more butter and fry the liver for 3 minutes.

4. Liquidize or pound together the cooked duck, liver and any remaining butter. Beat in the port and season with salt, pepper and ground mace. Spread flat in a dish, leave to cool and then put in the refrigerator overnight.

5. Strain the duck stock and refrigerate it overnight too.

6. Lift or skim any fat from the stock. Put the 290ml/½ pint stock into a large saucepan (making up the amount with water if necessary) and sprinkle on the gelatine. Put over a gentle heat.

7. Add the egg white to the crushed shells in a bowl and whisk until frothy. Pour into the warming stock and keep whisking steadily with a balloon whisk until the mixture boils and rises. Stop whisking immediately and draw the pan off the heat. Allow the mixture to subside. Take care not to break the crust formed by the egg white.

8. Bring the aspic, without whisking, to the boil again, and again allow to subside. Repeat this once more (the egg white will trap the sediment in the stock and clear the aspic). Allow to cool for 10 minutes.

9. Fix a double layer of fine muslin over a clean basin and carefully strain the aspic through it, taking care to hold the egg white crust back. When all the liquid is through (or almost all of it) allow the egg white to slip into the muslin. Then strain the aspic again – this time through both the crust and cloth. Do not try to hurry the process by squeezing the cloth or murky aspic will result. Leave to cool until nearly set.

10. Slice the whole orange thinly. Pour a little aspic on top of the duck pâté. Put into the refrigerator until nearly set. Arrange the slices of orange on top of this and return it to the refrigerator until set. Pour on more aspic just to cover the orange slices and return to the refrigerator. When this aspic is set pour over another layer and return to the refrigerator until set again.
11. Serve with plenty of hot toast.

Serves 4–6

Aubergine Salad

(*sometimes called aubergine caviar*)

3 small aubergines *or* 1 large
Oil
Slice of white bread, crusts removed
1 garlic clove, crushed to a cream with salt
1 shallot, finely chopped

1 tablespoon chopped fresh parsley
1 teaspoon chopped fresh, *or* ½ teaspoon dried, marjoram
Salt and pepper
4 tablespoons olive oil
Lemon juice to taste

1. Set oven to 190°C/375°F, gas mark 5.
2. Keeping the aubergines whole, brush them with oil. Bake them in the oven until soft (40–60 minutes). Alternatively grill all over until the skins are crinkled and black and the insides are soft. Allow to cool.
3. Peel them and put the flesh into a bowl.
4. Soak the bread in water and squeeze dry.
5. Pound the aubergine flesh with the garlic, shallot, bread, herbs, salt and pepper, or place these ingredients in a blender and liquidize until smooth.
6. Gradually beat in the olive oil and when the mixture is stiff stir in the lemon juice and check the seasoning.
7. Chill in the refrigerator for 2 hours before serving.

Serving suggestions:
a. With hot buttered toast.

b. Use to stuff scooped-out tomatoes.
c. Surround with a well-seasoned tomato salad.
d. Serve as a dip for crudités or biscuits.

Serves 4

Pork and Liver Terrine

Make the day before serving.

110g/¼lb pigs' liver, minced
225g/½lb rindless belly of pork,
  minced
2 shallots, finely chopped
1 garlic clove, crushed
2 teaspoons brandy
Pinch of allspice

Salt and freshly ground black
  pepper
225g/½lb streaky rindless
  bacon, in thin rashers
110g/¼lb chicken livers, cleaned
2 bay leaves

1. Set the oven to 170°C/325°F, gas mark 3.
2. Mix together the pigs' liver, belly pork, shallots, garlic, brandy and allspice. Season with salt and pepper.
3. Line a medium-sized terrine or loaf tin with the bacon.
4. Tip in half the prepared mixture and spread it flat.
5. Trim any discoloured parts from the chicken livers, then place an even layer of them over the mixture and top up with the other half of the mixture. Lay the bay leaves on the surface.
6. Cover with a piece of greased greaseproof paper. Stand in a roasting tin of hot water (bain-marie) and bake for 1½–2 hours. The mixture should feel fairly firm to the touch.
7. Remove from the roasting pan and place a weight on the terrine (a can of fruit in a second terrine will do) and leave overnight to cool and harden. Then refrigerate until needed, and turn out on to a plate to serve.

Note: Foil may be used to cover the baking terrine, but it must be well greased, or lined with a butter-wrapper or other paper.

If this is not done the foil corrodes into small holes while baking, and the top of the terrine is likely to be covered in metallic spots.

Serves 6

Hare Terrine

Begin preparations for this two days in advance. This recipe is sufficient for one 2 pint terrine.

For the marinade:
4 bay leaves
1 teaspoon salt
6 peppercorns
1 tablespoon redcurrant jelly
3 tablespoons brandy
8 juniper berries, crushed

1 hare
450g/1lb veal, minced
450g/1lb belly pork, minced
170g/6oz fresh white
  breadcrumbs
1 beaten egg
Salt and freshly ground black
  pepper
1 level tablespoon finely
  chopped fresh thyme or savory
340g/¾lb streaky bacon rashers

1. Mix together the ingredients for the marinade. Take about ½lb from the saddle of the hare. Cut into slices and leave in the marinade overnight.
2. The next day mince together any meat left on the hare with its cleaned liver, heart and kidney. Mix it together with the veal, belly of pork, crumbs and egg. Season very well and mix in the chopped herbs.
3. Cut the rind off the bacon and stretch the rashers on a board with the back of a knife. Line a 1 litre/2 pint terrine with slightly overlapping slices of bacon, allowing the ends to hang over the sides.
4. Put half the pork and veal mixture into the terrine. Arrange the slices of hare on top and pour over the marinade. Cover with the remaining pork and veal. Press down firmly and fold the bacon ends over the top. Cover with greaseproof paper and foil.
5. Set the oven to 190°C/375°F, gas mark 5. Place the terrine

241

in a roasting tin half-filled with hot water and bake for 1–1½ hours. It is cooked when it feels firm to the touch.

6. Remove from the oven and leave to cool for about 20 minutes. Cover with a clean piece of greaseproof paper and weigh it down with a 1 kilo/2lb weight. Leave overnight. Turn out and serve in slices.

Serves 8–10

Guacamole

2 ripe avocado pears	2 teaspoons olive oil
1 teaspoon onion juice	½ teaspoon ground coriander
Juice of ½ lemon	1 garlic clove, crushed
2 teaspoons tomato chutney	
Salt and freshly ground black pepper	Hot buttered toast

1. Peel the avocado pears and mash them with a fork.
2. Season with the onion juice, lemon juice, tomato chutney, oil, coriander, salt, pepper and garlic.
3. Serve with toast.

Serves 4

Note I: If the terrine cannot be satisfactorily pressed in the loaf tin, it may be turned out before pressing, but if this is done a less heavy weight should be used, for fear of breaking the terrine.

FRUIT FIRST COURSES

Pears with Stilton and Poppy Seed Dressing

110g/¼lb Stilton cheese   110g/¼lb cream cheese

4 ripe dessert pears, washed
  but not peeled
Squeeze of lemon juice
1 Small bunch of watercress,
  washed

For the dressing:
3 tablespoons oil
1 tablespoon lemon juice
1 level tablespoon poppy seeds
Salt and freshly ground black
  pepper

1. Put all the dressing ingredients together in a screw-top jar and shake until well emulsified. Taste and add more seasoning if necessary.
2. Beat together the Stilton and cream cheese until soft. Spoon into a forcing bag fitted with a plain large nozzle.
3. With an apple corer remove the centre of the pears. Sprinkle a little lemon juice into each hole and then pipe in the cheese mixture. Place in the refrigerator until ready to serve (at least 2 hours).
4. Slice each pear across into thin round slices. Spoon over the poppy seed dressing and garnish with watercress.

Serves 4

Pineapple Japonais

1 fresh pineapple

Caster sugar

For the dressing:
1 egg
3 tablespoons tarragon vinegar
2 tablespoons caster sugar

Pinch of salt
2 tablespoons lightly whipped
  cream

1. Slice the pineapple in half lengthwise, cutting through the fruit and the leaves. Using a grapefruit knife cut out the flesh in one piece from each pineapple half. Remove the woody core and discard it. Slice the flesh and return it upside down to the pineapple shell (i.e. rounded side up). Sprinkle with sugar and leave it to stand while preparing the dressing.
2. Beat the egg and add the vinegar and sugar with a pinch of

salt. Stand the bowl over a pan of simmering water and whisk continuously until thick. Allow to cool.

3. Stir in the cream and spoon the dressing over the pineapple.

Serves 4

PASTRY AND YEAST FIRST COURSES

Bacon Pasties

285g/10oz plain flour
Pinch of salt
70g/2½oz butter
70g/2½oz lard
225g/½lb uncooked gammon
  steak *or* lean bacon (soaked
  overnight)

1 very small onion
1 very small potato
Pinch of thyme
Freshly ground black pepper
Milk

1. Sift the flour and salt into a bowl. Rub in the fats and when the mixture resembles breadcrumbs mix in enough water to make a firm dough.
2. Set the oven to 200 C/400 F, gas mark 6.
3. Roll out the pastry on a floured board. Using a pastry cutter cut out six 15cm/6in circles. Place in the refrigerator to relax while you prepare the filling.
4. Cut off the rind of the gammon and dice the flesh. Chop the onion and dice the potato. Mix together and season with the thyme and pepper. Divide the mixture between the pastry rounds.
5. Brush the edges with cold water and bring them together over the filling so that the pasties look like closed purses. Using floured fingers and thumb crimp the edges to make a decorative pattern. Brush all over with a little milk.
6. Place on a baking sheet and bake for 45–50 minutes.

Serves 6

Quiche Lorraine

110g/¼lb flour–quantity rich shortcrust pastry (page 645)

For the filling:

½ small onion	1 egg
55g/2oz bacon	1 egg yolk
7·5g/¼oz butter	30g/1oz grated cheese (strong
5 tablespoons milk	Cheddar *or* Gruyère)
5 tablespoons single cream	Salt and pepper

1. Roll out the pastry and line a flan ring about 15cm/6in in diameter. Leave in the fridge for about 45 minutes to relax – this prevents shrinkage during cooking.
2. Set the oven to 190 C/375 F, gas mark 5.
3. Chop the onion finely and dice the bacon. Fry both gently in the butter. When cooked but not coloured, drain well.
4. Mix together the milk, cream and eggs. Add the onion, bacon and half the cheese. Season carefully with salt and pepper (the bacon and cheese are both salty, so be careful not to overseason).
5. Pour the mixture into the prepared flan ring and sprinkle over the remaining cheese. Place the flan in the middle of the heated oven and bake for about 20 minutes. Then turn down the oven to 150 C/300 F, gas mark 2 and cook for a further 15 minutes.
6. Remove the flan ring to allow the sides of the pastry to cook and take colour. Bake for a further 5 minutes until the filling is browned and set.
7. Serve hot or cold.

Note: If using a flan dish instead of a flan ring, the pastry case should be baked blind, i.e. before filling: line the raw pastry case with a piece of foil or a double sheet of greaseproof paper and fill it with dried lentils, beans, rice or even pebbles or pennies. This is to prevent the pastry bubbling up during cooking. When the pastry is half cooked (about 15 minutes) the 'blind beans' can be removed and the empty pastry case further dried out in the oven.

The beans can be re-used indefinitely.

Serves 4

Spinach Flan

110g/¼lb flour–quantity rich shortcrust pastry (page 645)

For the filling:

340g/¾lb spinach	1 egg
½ onion, finely chopped	1 egg yolk
15g/½oz butter	Salt and pepper
5 tablespoons milk	30g/1oz grated cheese (strong
5 tablespoons single cream	Cheddar *or* Gruyère)

1. Roll out the pastry and line a flan ring about 15cm/6in in diameter. Leave in the refrigerator for about 45 minutes to relax – this prevents shrinkage during cooking.
2. Set the oven to 200 C/400 F, gas mark 6.
3. Bake the pastry case blind for 10–15 minutes and remove from oven.
4. Reduce the heat to 170 C/325 F, gas mark 3.
5. Remove the stalks of the spinach, wash thoroughly and put into a pan *without water*. Add a sprinkling of salt. Cover and cook gently, shaking the pan, for 5–7 minutes. The spinach will reduce by about two-thirds. Drain very thoroughly by squeezing between two plates. Turn on to a board.
6. Chop the onion finely. Fry it gently in the butter. When cooked but not coloured drain well.
7. Mix together the milk, cream and eggs. Add the fried onion, spinach and half the cheese. Season carefully with salt and pepper (the cheese is salty, so be careful not to overseason).
8. Pour the mixture into the prepared flan case and sprinkle over the remaining cheese.
9. Place the flan in the middle of the prepared oven and bake for about 30–40 minutes.

10. Remove the flan ring to allow the sides of the pastry to cook evenly and colour. Bake for a further 5 minutes until the filling is brown and set.
11. Serve hot or cold.

Baking blind. See page 245

Serves 4 as a starter, 2 as a main course

Smoked Haddock and Mushroom Flan

225g/½lb smoked haddock
150ml/¼ pint milk
170g/6oz flour-quantity
   shortcrust pastry (page 645)
15g/½oz butter
1 small onion, chopped
55g/2oz button mushrooms, sliced

150ml/¼ pint cream
2 whole eggs
2 egg yolks
Salt and freshly ground black pepper
30g/1oz Gruyère *or* strong Cheddar cheese, grated

1. Set the oven to 150°C/300°F, gas mark 2.
2. Put the haddock and the milk into a roasting pan. Cover and bake for 15 minutes or until firm.
3. Set the oven to 200°C/400°F, gas mark 6.
4. Line a 20cm/8in flan ring with pastry. Bake blind for 15 minutes. Reduce the oven to 180°C/350°F, gas mark 4.
5. Melt the butter and gently cook the onion and mushrooms in it. Allow to cool.
6. Whisk the milk in which the haddock was cooked, the cream, eggs and egg yolks together. Season well.
7. Flake the smoked haddock, removing the bones and skin.
8. Place the onion, mushrooms and haddock at the bottom of the flan. Pour over the custard mixture. Sprinkle on the grated cheese.

9. Bake for about 25 minutes. Remove the flan ring and return to the oven for a further 5–10 minutes until the pastry case is firm and the custard lightly browned and set.

Baking blind. See page 245

Serves 4

Creamy Fish Flan with Burnt Hollandaise

170g/6oz flour-quantity
 shortcrust pastry (page 645)
1 small onion, finely chopped
30g/1oz butter
1 bay leaf
225g/½lb cooked flaked white
 fish
1 tablespoon chopped fresh
 parsley

30g/1oz flour
290ml/½ pint milk
Salt and freshly ground black
 pepper
1 egg
Squeeze of lemon juice
55g/2oz butter-quantity
 hollandaise sauce
 (page 320)

1. Set the oven to 190°C/375°F, gas mark 5. Line a 20cm/8in flan ring with pastry and bake blind.
2. Reduce the oven temperature to 180°C/350°F, gas mark 4.
3. Melt the butter, add the onion, and cook until soft but not coloured. Add the flour and bay leaf. Cook, stirring, for 1 minute. Draw off the heat, stir in the milk, and bring slowly to the boil, stirring continuously. Taste and season as necessary. Simmer for 2 minutes, remove the bay leaf and allow to cool.
4. Separate the egg and beat the yolk into the sauce. Stir in the flaked fish, parsley and lemon juice to taste. Whisk the egg white until stiff but not dry and fold into the mixture.
5. Pour into the pastry case. Bake until firm and set (about 25 minutes).
6. Heat up the grill 10 minutes before the flan is cooked.
7. Prepare the hollandaise sauce and spoon over the flan.

8.   Put the flan under the grill until the top is nicely browned. Serve at once.

Baking blind. See page 245

Serves 4 as a starter, 2 as a main course

Crayfish Flan

170g/6oz flour-quantity shortcrust pastry (page 645)
450g/1lb raw crayfish tails
290ml/½ pint milk
1 small onion, sliced
1 small carrot, sliced
1 stick celery, sliced

1 bay leaf
About 6 peppercorns
110g/¼lb mushrooms
55g/2oz butter
30g/1oz flour
1 tablespoon chopped fresh
   parsley

1.   Line a 20cm/8in flan ring with the pastry and bake blind until crisp and completely cooked. Keep warm.
2.   Remove the flesh from the crayfish shells. Crush the shells roughly.
3.   Place the milk, crayfish shells, onion, carrot, celery, bay leaf and peppercorns in a saucepan, bring gently to the boil and simmer for 10 minutes.
4.   Strain the milk, return it to the saucepan and add the crayfish. Poach for 3–4 minutes; do not boil. Strain and reserve the liquor.
5.   Chop the mushrooms finely.
6.   Heat half the butter in a pan and cook the mushrooms in it for 1 minute. Stir in the flour and cook for 30 seconds. Pour in the flavoured milk and stir while bringing to the boil. Add the remaining butter. Taste for seasoning.
7.   Cut the crayfish into chunks and add to the sauce. Reheat and pour into the flan. Serve at once.

Note: The flan case and the filling can be made the day before they are needed, but they should not be put together until just before heating for serving. If both pastry and filling are stone cold the flan can be filled and then heated. But do not pour hot filling into a cold pastry case because it will make the pastry soggy, and the flan will not be in the oven long enough to get crisp again.

Baking blind. See page 245

Serves 4–6

Blinis

225g/½lb buckwheat flour
45g/1½oz fresh yeast
2 teaspoons sugar
720ml/1¼ pints warm milk
225g/½lb plain flour

Salt
3 eggs
1 tablespoon melted butter
Lard for frying

1. Put the buckwheat flour into a warm dry mixing bowl.
2. Cream the yeast with the sugar and add half the milk. Mix well.
3. Pour the yeasty milk into the buckwheat flour and mix to a paste.
4. Cover the bowl with a sheet of greased polythene or a cloth and leave in a warm place to rise.
5. Sift the plain flour with a good pinch of salt into another basin. Make a hollow (or 'well') in the centre and drop in the 2 whole eggs and 1 egg yolk, reserving 1 egg white.
6. Gradually mix to a batter, bringing in the surrounding flour, and adding the melted butter and the rest of the milk. Beat well.
7. Beat this batter into the yeasty one, cover again with the greased polythene or cloth and leave in a warm place for 2 hours.
8. Just before cooking whip the remaining egg white and fold it in to the mixture.
9. Grease a girdle iron or heavy frying pan lightly with lard. Heat it gently over steady heat.

10. When the girdle is hot pour enough of the batter on to the surface to make a blini the size of a saucer. When bubbles rise, turn over and cook the other side to a light brown.
11. Keep the blinis warm in a cool oven.

To serve
Caviar: Butter the hot blini, place a spoonful of caviar (or Danish lumpfish roe) on top and surround with sour cream. Serve at once.
Smoked salmon: Butter the hot blini, spread liberally with sour cream and place a roll of smoked salmon on top. Serve at once.
Pickled herring: Mix herring fillets with sour cream. Butter the blini and top with the herring and sour cream mixture. Serve at once.

Note: If using dried yeast use half the amount called for, mix it with 3 tablespoons of the liquid (warmed to blood temperature) and a teaspoon of sugar. Leave until frothy, about 15 minutes, then proceed. If the yeast does not go frothy it is dead and unusable.

Serves 4

FISH FIRST COURSES

Marinated Kipper Fillets

8 kipper fillets
1 medium onion, sliced
2 bay leaves
Freshly ground black pepper

1 teaspoon mustard powder
150ml/¼ pint olive oil
1 teaspoon brown sugar
2 tablespoons lemon juice

To serve:
Lettuce
Lemon wedges

Onion rings
Brown bread and butter

1. Skin the kipper fillets.
2. In a small dish layer the fillets with the onion and bay leaves, grinding black pepper between the layers.

251

3. Place the mustard, olive oil, sugar and lemon juice in a jar with a lid and shake vigorously.
4. Pour over the fillets.
5. Cover the dish well with a lid or plastic film and leave refrigerated for at least two days, preferably a week.
6. Drain off most of the oil and discard the onion and bay leaves.
7. Serve on lettuce with lemon wedges and fresh onion rings. Hand brown bread and butter separately.

Serves 4

Marinated Fried Herrings

8 herrings
2 tablespoons flour seasoned
  with $\frac{1}{2}$ teaspoon each of salt
and pepper
Butter for frying

For the marinade:
6 tablespoons sugar
150ml/$\frac{1}{4}$ pint cider vinegar
150ml/$\frac{1}{4}$ pint wine vinegar
290ml/$\frac{1}{2}$ pint water
1 bay leaf
6 peppercorns
1 medium onion, cut into fine
  rings

1. Scrape away any scales from each fish and cut off the head and tail.
2. Make a long cut in the belly. Remove the entrails.
3. Split the fish right open and put them, skin side up, on a board or tabletop. Press down firmly with the heel of your hand. This will loosen the backbone. Turn over and remove the backbone and as many small bones as possible. Close the fish up again.
4. Dip the fish in seasoned flour.
5. Heat the butter in a frying pan and fry the fish on both sides until brown. Drain well and allow to cool.
6. Dissolve the sugar in the vinegar and water. Boil for 3 minutes. Add the bay leaf and peppercorns and allow to cool.
7. Place the herrings in a serving dish, pour over the marinade and add the onion rings. Keep for 24 hours before serving.

Serves 8

Moules Marinières

2 kilos/4lb mussels *or* 2 litres/
   4 pints
2 medium onions, chopped
2 shallots, chopped
2 garlic cloves, chopped
1 tablespoon chopped fresh
   parsley

150ml/¼ pint white wine
150ml/¼ pint water
45g/1½oz butter
Salt and freshly ground black
   pepper
Extra parsley to garnish

1. Clean the mussels by scrubbing them well under a running tap. Pull away the 'beard' (seaweed-like threads). Throw away any mussels which are cracked or which remain open when tapped.
2. Simmer the onion, shallot, garlic, parsley, water and wine together for 2 minutes. Add the mussels, put on the lid and leave to steam over a gentle heat until the shells open, shaking the pan occasionally. This should take about 5 minutes. Tip the mussels into a colander set over a bowl.
3. Throw away any mussels that have not opened. Pour the mussel liquid from the bowl into a saucepan. Place the saucepan over a low heat, whisk in the butter and check the seasoning.
4. Dish the mussels in a soup tureen or wide bowl, pour over the sauce and sprinkle with extra chopped parsley.

Note I: Moules marinières recipes vary from port to port in France. In Normandy cream is sometimes added to the sauce instead of, or as well as, butter. Sometimes the juice is thickened by the addition of beurre manié. Herbs other than parsley are frequently used in sophisticated restaurants. Sometimes one mussel shell from each mussel is removed and discarded after cooking, as is the 'rubber band' found round the mussel. The mussels are served in the remaining shells, neatly piled on a dish. But as the dish is essentially fisherman's fare the authors feel a good pile of unshelled glistening mussels, to be tackled by the diners, is more appropriate.

Note II: Extra soup plates or bowls should be provided to take the pile of discarded shells.

Serves 4

Baked Mussels Provençales

2 kilos/4lb mussels *or* 2 litres/
   4 pints
290ml/½ pint water
1 onion, chopped
Few sprigs fresh
   parsley
1 bay leaf
170g/6oz butter

2 small garlic cloves, crushed
1 shallot, finely chopped
3 tablespoons finely chopped
   fresh parsley
2 tablespoons grated Gruyère
   cheese
2 tablespoons dried browned
   crumbs

1. Scrub the mussels well, discarding any that are cracked or will not close when tapped.
2. In a large saucepan heat the water, onion, parsley and bay leaf. When simmering add the mussels and cover. Shake the pan occasionally until the mussels have opened. This should take about 2 minutes.
3. Strain through a colander, discarding any mussels which have not opened.
4. Completely open the shells, throwing away the top half. Remove the 'rubber band' around each mussel.
5. Heat the oven to 200°C/400°F, gas mark 6.
6. Cream the butter, stir in the garlic, shallot and parsley. Spread each mussel with the garlic butter and place on a flat ovenproof serving dish. Mix the cheese with the breadcrumbs and sprinkle the mixture over each shell.
7. Bake in the oven until hot and browned. This should take about 10 minutes.

Note: The water in which the mussels were stewed will make an excellent base for a fish sauce or soup so should not be thrown away.

Serves 4

Goujons with Tartare Sauce

85g/3oz white fish fillets per person
Oil for deep frying
Seasoned flour

Beaten egg
Dry white crumbs
Tartare sauce (page 318)
Lemon wedges

1. Cut the fish into finger-like strips, cutting across the grain of the fish or on the slant if possible.
2. Heat the oil until a crumb will sizzle vigorously in it.
3. Dip the fish into the seasoned flour, then into beaten egg and finally toss in the breadcrumbs. Twist each goujon slightly.
4. Fry a few goujons at a time until crisp and golden brown. Drain well on absorbent paper and sprinkle with salt. Serve with tartare sauce and lemon wedges.

Ceviche

225g/½lb fillet of monkfish *or* halibut, skinned and cut into thin slices *or* small strips *or* dice
1 onion, chopped
Juice of 2 lemons *or* 4 limes
1 tablespoon olive oil
Pinch cayenne pepper
2 fresh chillies, seeded and cut in strips (optional)

Salt and freshly ground black pepper
1 peeled tomato, chopped
½ small green pepper, seeded and chopped
Few slices avocado pear, cut small

1. Put the fish, onion, lemon juice, oil, cayenne pepper and chillies together and leave in a cool place for 6 hours, giving an occasional stir. (If the fish is really finely sliced, as little as 30 minutes will do; it is ready as soon as it looks 'cooked' – opaque white rather than glassy.)

2.   Season with salt and freshly ground black pepper. Add the chopped tomato, green pepper and avocado and mix well.

Note: Do not add salt until about to serve the Ceviche. It draws the juices from the fish, making the dish too wet.

Serves 2

Pain de Poisson

560g/1¼lb sole (filleted weight)
3 egg whites
Salt, freshly ground black
   pepper and cayenne
425ml/¾ pint double cream
3 eggs
170g/6oz fresh white breadcrumbs

4 level tablespoons chopped
   fresh parsley
2 level tablespoons chopped
   fresh tarragon and chives,
   mixed
Sprig of fresh tarragon
10 thin long rashers mild
   streaky rindless bacon

To serve:
Hollandaise sauce (page 320)

1.   Set the oven to 150°C/300°F, gas mark 2. Set aside four neat fillets of sole. Mince the remaining fillets twice or pound in a blender or mortar. When absolutely smooth beat in two egg whites.
2.   Season with salt, pepper and cayenne. Gradually beat in two-thirds of the cream. Cover and set aside.
3.   Meanwhile whisk the three whole eggs lightly and add the remaining cream to them. Stir this into the breadcrumbs with the chopped herbs. Season and mix well.
4.   Whisk the remaining egg white until frothy. Season the reserved fillets with salt and pepper.
5.   Lightly butter a loaf tin or terrine and put the tarragon sprigs on the bottom. Line the terrine with the rashers of bacon leaving the ends to be folded over the top of the terrine. Spread two-thirds of the fish mixture around the base and sides. Brush with a little of the frothy egg white and lay in two fillets of sole.

6. Brush with egg white and cover with half the herb and bread-crumb mixture. Brush with egg white, lay in the remaining two fillets of sole. Cover with remaining one-third of the fish mixture. Brush with egg white and cover with the remaining herb and breadcrumb mixture. Fold the bacon strips over the top of the terrine so that all the fish is covered.

7. Cover with damp greaseproof paper and foil and stand the terrine in a roasting tin of hot water. Bake for 1½–2 hours. To see if it is ready press a skewer into the centre of the pain de poisson, hold there for about 2 seconds and test its heat against the inside of your wrist – it should be hot. The top of the pain de poisson should feel firm to the touch.

8. To serve invert a dish over the terrine and turn the whole thing over. Give a gentle shake and remove the tin. Serve warm with Hollandaise sauce.

Note: Thin strips of barding fat may be used instead of the streaky bacon. Strong-tasting bacon should be soaked in cold water, then blanched in fresh water and cooled before use. Alternatively the bacon can be omitted, and the dish decorated with a few tarragon sprigs, after unmoulding.

Serves 6

Italian Seafood Salad

450g/1lb fresh squid
Few slices onion
Few parsley stalks
1 bay leaf
Salt
1 medium leek
1 medium carrot
55g/2oz white button
   mushrooms
55g/2oz cooked peeled prawns

For the dressing:
1 scant tablespoon olive oil
2 scant tablespoons other
   (milder) salad oil
1 teaspoon wine vinegar
1 teaspoon fresh lemon juice
Salt and freshly ground black
   pepper
1 small garlic clove, crushed
1 tablespoon finely chopped
   fresh parsley

1. Ask the fishmonger to gut and skin the squid. Alternatively tackle it yourself – it is rather messy, but quite easy: remove the entrails and the blood (ink) under cold running water – they will come out easily. Remove the clear plastic-like piece of cartilege that runs the length of the body on the inside. Cut off and throw away the head (it is the round middle bit with two large eyes). Scrape off the pinkish-purple outside skin – a fine membrane – from the body and the tentacles. Don't worry if you cannot get all the tentacles completely clear of it, Wash the body and tentacles to remove all traces of ink: you should now have a perfectly clean, white, empty squid.

2. Cut it into thin strips. Put them in a saucepan and just cover with water. Add the onion, parsley stalks, bay leaf and a pinch of salt. Simmer gently until the squid is tender. This can take up to 1 hour for strips cut from a large squid. Drain well.

3. Wash the leek and discard the tough outside leaves and the dark green part. Shred the rest finely and plunge it into boiling salted water for 2 minutes until just tender but still bright green. Rinse under running cold water to set the bright colour.

4. Peel the carrot. With a potato peeler shred it into long thin ribbons. Slice the mushrooms finely.

5. Combine the ingredients for the dressing in a screw-top jar and shake well.

6. When the squid is cool drain it (but keep the fish stock for some future soup or sauce – it is delicious) discard the onion, bay leaf and parsley stalks and put the squid into a bowl. Add prawns, mushrooms, carrot strips, cooked leek and dressing. Chill well before serving.

Note: Other seafood can be used too:
Frozen Cockles: less salty than those in brine. Fresh cockles must be left for an hour in salty water and turned often to rid them of sand before cooking as for mussels.
Mussels: scrub well under running water. Pull away the 'beard' and discard any that are broken or which will not close when tapped. Put in a heavy pan with a few spoons white wine, cover, and shake over heat for 5 minutes until the shells have opened.

Discard any which remain closed. Remove the mussels from the shells, and discard the 'rubber bands'.

Frozen cooked prawns: thaw slowly, season with lemon juice, salt and black pepper.

Frozen raw 'scampi': cook with the squid, allowing about 8 minutes. Do not boil.

Raw whole prawns: simmer for 8 minutes with the squid or in a separate pan. Shell carefully. If using whole for decoration remove the legs and any roe after cooking.

Serves 6

MISCELLANEOUS

Frogs' Legs

450g/1lb raw frogs' legs
55g/2oz butter
1 small garlic clove, crushed
1 tablespoon chopped fresh
  parsley
Lemon juice
Salt and freshly ground black
  pepper

For the marinade:
Olive oil
1 onion, sliced
1 parsley stalk
6 peppercorns
1 bay leaf

1. Split the pairs of frogs' legs and marinate them in a small cupful of olive oil with the other marinade ingredients for 2 hours or more. This is not essential but helps to improve the taste and texture of the meat. Drain the legs.
2. Melt the butter in a large sauté pan and when frothy add the frogs' legs and garlic. Sauté briskly for 5–10 minutes (they should fry to a very pale brown).
3. Add the parsley, lemon juice and seasoning. Serve with French bread to mop up the butter.

Note: Frogs' legs are normally sold frozen and are available at large fishmonger's.

Serves 4

Snails à la Bourguignonne

170g/6oz butter
Juice of ½ lemon
2 tablespoons chopped fresh
    parsley

6 garlic cloves
Salt
24 snails and 24 shells

1. Soften the butter very well and beat in the lemon juice and parsley. Crush the garlic with salt and beat this into the butter. Leave in a cool place.
2. Push a snail, tail first, into each shell with a teaspoon handle. Fill the remaining cavity of the shell with the garlic butter, scraping the top off neatly. Keep in the refrigerator until needed.
3. Set the oven to 200°C/400°F, gas mark 6. Place a snail, butter upwards in each indentation of snail dishes and cook in the oven for 8 minutes or until the butter has completely melted and starts to sizzle, but no longer. Overcooking snails toughens them.
4. Serve immediately with plenty of fresh French bread.

Note I: In the absence of snail dishes an ovenproof plate filled with dry rice or salt, into which you 'plant' the snails, will do.

Note II: Because preparing fresh snails is a specialized and long process, ready-to-use snails are bought in cans, even by the top French restaurants. Shells are bought separately and can be re-used. Small, but good English snails from the Mendip Hills are available.

Serves 4

Fried Gnocchi

570ml/1 pint milk
1 onion, sliced
1 clove
1 bay leaf
6 parsley stalks
110g/¼lb semolina
200g/7oz strong Cheddar
  cheese
2 tablespoons very fresh
  Parmesan cheese,
  grated

1 tablespoon chopped fresh
  parsley
Salt and freshly ground black
  pepper
Pinch of dried mustard
Pinch of cayenne
Beaten egg
Dried white breadcrumbs
Oil for deep frying

1. Infuse the milk with the onion, clove, bay leaf and parsley stalks over a very gentle heat for 7 minutes. Bring up to boiling point, then strain.
2. Sprinkle in the semolina, stirring steadily, and cook, still stirring, until the mixture is thick (about 1 minute). Draw the pan off the heat and add the cheeses, parsley, salt, pepper, mustard and cayenne. Spread this mixture into a neat round on a wet plate and leave to chill for 30 minutes.
3. Cut the gnocchi paste into eight equal wedges. Chill.
4. Heat the oil until a crumb will sizzle vigorously in it. Dip the gnocchi into beaten egg and coat with breadcrumbs.
5. Deep fry in hot oil until golden brown (about 2 minutes). Drain well on absorbent paper. Sprinkle with salt and serve.

Note: A thin tomato sauce (page 325) is good with fried gnocchi.

Serves 6

3
Vegetables, Rice and Salads

◆

BOILED

Boiled Rice

55g/2oz long-grain white rice   Slice of lemon
   for each person   1 tablespoon oil

1. Take a large saucepan and fill it with salted water (1 cup of rice will need at least 6 cups of water, but the exact quantities do not matter as long as there is plenty of water). Bring to a rolling boil.
2. Tip in the rice and stir until the water re-boils. Add the lemon slice and oil.
3. Boil for exactly 10 minutes and then test: the rice should be neither hard nor mushy, but firm to the bite (*al dente*). It may need 1 more minute.
4. Drain the rice in a colander or sieve, and swish plenty of hot water through it.
5. Stand the colander on the draining board. With the handle of a wooden spoon, make a few draining holes through the pile of rice to help the water and steam escape. Alternatively, every few minutes turn the mass of rice over with a spoon.

Note I: Rice may be rinsed, if for a salad, in cold water after cooking, but it will need longer to drain dry – if the water is hot it steams dry faster.

Cabbage with Caraway

450g/1lb white cabbage, finely sliced
30g/1oz butter
2 onions, sliced
1 level teaspoon caraway seeds
1 teaspoon vinegar *or* lemon juice
Salt and freshly ground black pepper

1. Put the cabbage into a pan of boiling water. Simmer until tender (about 5 minutes) and drain well.
2. While the cabbage cooks, melt the butter in a frying pan and add the sliced onion. Cook over a gentle heat until soft but not coloured.
3. Add the caraway seeds and lemon or vinegar and cook gently for 1 more minute.
4. Stir this into the drained cabbage and season well with salt and pepper.

Serves 4

Brussels Sprouts and Chestnuts

450g/1lb very small Brussels sprouts
225g/½lb fresh chestnuts
45g/1½oz butter
Salt, freshly ground black pepper and nutmeg

1. Wash and trim the sprouts, paring the stalk and removing the outside leaves if necessary.
2. Make a slit in the skin of each chestnut and put them into a pan of cold water. Bring to the boil and then take off the heat. Remove one or two nuts at a time and peel. The water must not boil again but can be reheated – the skins come off easily if the chestnuts are hot, but not too cooked.
3. Melt the butter in a frying pan, and slowly fry the chestnuts

263

(which will break up a little) until brown.

4. Bring a large pan of salted water to the boil, and tip in the sprouts. Boil fairly fast until they are just cooked, but not soggy: the flavour changes disastrously if boiled too long. Drain them well.

5. Mix the sprouts and chestnuts together gently, adding the butter from the frying pan. Season with salt, pepper and nutmeg.

Serves 4

Noodles with Red Peppers

1 medium red pepper, finely sliced
Salt and freshly ground black pepper

225g/½lb fettucine noodles
1 tablespoon olive oil

1. Boil the pepper in salted water for 2 minutes. Cool under running water to retain the colour and prevent the pepper from cooking further.
2. Cook the pasta in plenty of rapidly boiling salted water for about 6 minutes, until tender but not too soft. Drain and tip into a warmed serving dish.
3. Heat the oil, add the peppers and shake over the heat until sizzling. Mix with the pasta. Season with plenty of pepper.

Serves 4

Vichy Carrots

560g/1¼lb carrots
150ml/¼ pint water
2 teaspoons butter
½ teaspoon salt

1 teaspoon sugar
Freshly ground black pepper
2 teaspoons chopped mint and parsley, mixed

1. Peel the carrots and cut them into slices or even-sized barrel shapes; or if they are very young leave them whole.
2. Put everything except the pepper and herbs into a saucepan, and boil rapidly until the water has almost evaporated. Then turn down the heat and allow the carrots to brown slightly in the remaining butter and sugar.
3. Season with pepper and mix in the herbs.

Note I: It is important not to oversalt the water. When the water has evaporated the entire quantity of salt will remain with the carrots.

Note II: Vichy carrots, made classically, need careful watching lest they boil dry and burn. Ordinary boiled carrots may be tossed over the heat in butter and sugar until browned.

Serves 4

Boiled Brown Rice

55g/2oz brown rice per person   Salt

1. For each cup of rice use 2 cups of water. Put the water on to boil, add the rice and salt and cover with a well-fitting lid.
2. Lower the heat and cook very slowly until the water has been absorbed and the rice is cooked (about 45 minutes). Take care that the rice does not dry out and catch at the bottom of the pan.

STEAMED

Marrow with Garlic and Tomato

900g/2lbs marrow
30g/1oz butter
1 onion, finely chopped
1 garlic clove, crushed
2 tablespoons tomato purée

1 tablespoon white wine
1 teaspoon chopped fresh basil
Salt and freshly ground black
  pepper

1. Peel the marrow, cut it in half and remove the seeds. Cut the flesh into even-sized chunks (about 2·5cm/1in).
2. Put into a sieve over a pan of boiling water, or into a proper steamer, cover and steam for 30 minutes or until the marrow is completely tender.
3. Melt the butter, add the onion and garlic and cook gently until the onion is soft but not coloured. Add the steamed marrow, tomato purée, wine, basil, and season with salt and pepper.
4. Cover and cook (shaking the pan frequently to prevent sticking and burning) over a moderate heat for about 10 minutes.
5. Taste and season again if necessary. Serve hot or cold.

Note: Marrow is generally steamed because it holds a lot of water and when boiled is apt to be soggy.

Serves 6

ROAST

Roast Potatoes

900g/2lb potatoes
4 tablespoons dripping

1. Peel the potatoes and, if they are large, cut them into 5cm/2in pieces.
2. Bring them to the boil in salted water. Simmer for 5 minutes.
3. Drain them and, while still hot, scratch all over with a fork to roughen and slightly crumble the surface of each potato. (This produces deliciously crunchy potatoes that can be kept warm for up to two hours without coming to any harm. Potatoes roasted without this preliminary boiling and scratching tend to become tough and hard if not eaten straight away.)
4. Melt the fat in a roasting pan and add the potatoes, turning them so that they are coated all over.
5. Roast, basting occasionally, and turning the potatoes over at half-time. See note below.

Note: Potatoes can be roasted at almost any temperature, usually taking 1 hour in a hot oven, or 1½ hours in a medium one. They should be basted and turned over once or twice during cooking, and they are done when a skewer glides easily into them. Potatoes roasted in the same pan as the meat have the best flavour, but this is not always possible if the joint or bird is very large, or if liquid has been added to the pan.

Serves 4

Glazed Vegetables

450g/1lb large potatoes
450g/1lb carrots
450g/1lb turnips
12 button onions
1 tablespoon bacon *or* pork dripping
½ teaspoon sugar

Salt and freshly ground black pepper
110g/¼lb button mushrooms
55g/2oz butter
Juice of ½ lemon
1 tablespoon chopped fresh parsley

1. Wash and peel the potatoes, carrots and turnips. Using a melon scoop, scoop the flesh of the potato into balls. Dry

267

them in a clean cloth. Trim the carrots and turnips into small barrel shapes.

2. Peel the onions. (Dipping them into boiling water for 10 seconds makes this easier.)
3. Heat the oven to 200 C/400 F, gas mark 6.
4. Put the prepared vegetables in a roasting pan and baste with the dripping. Roast, shaking the pan occasionally and turning the vegetables over, for 25 minutes.
5. When the vegetables are tender, put the roasting pan over direct heat, add the sugar and shake the pan until browned to a good even colour. Season with salt and pepper. Keep warm.
6. Trim the mushroom stalks. Melt the butter over a good heat and toss the mushrooms into it. Shake the pan to make sure that every mushroom is coated with butter. When they are beginning to turn brown add the lemon juice and allow this to sizzle and evaporate a little. Add salt and pepper and the chopped parsley.
7. Serve the vegetables mixed together on a heated dish.

Note I: If these vegetables are to accompany a roast meat dish, the root vegetables can be cooked in the meat roasting tin. Add them about half an hour before the meat is due to come out.

Note II: The root vegetables can be 'pot roasted' instead of cooked in the oven. (This is a good idea if nothing else is being baked or roasted at the time, when it would be wasteful to heat the oven just for this dish.) In a heavy casserole or pan toss the vegetables in the fat. Cover with a lid, and turn the heat down low. Cook like this for 20 minutes or until the vegetables are tender, giving the pan a shake every now and then to prevent sticking. When they are cooked, brown them with the sugar, and fry the mushrooms etc. as described above.

Serves 6–8

Chateau Potatoes

675g/1½lb small even-sized
  potatoes
Oil *or* beef dripping

Salt and freshly ground black
  pepper

1. Wash and peel the potatoes. Trim each one into a barrel shape about 3·5cm/1½in long and 2cm/¾in wide.
2. Set the oven to 190 C/375 F, gas mark 5.
3. Heat a few spoons of oil or dripping in a sauté pan. Add the potatoes and brown gently on all sides (shaking the pan constantly) until they are just brown. Season with salt and pepper.
4. Cover the pan and place in the oven for about 45 minutes or until the potatoes are tender. (Alternatively, they can be cooked on the hob, but care must be taken so they do not burn: shake the pan frequently. Do not remove the lid as this allows the steam to escape, and the potatoes will fry rather than cook gently.)

Serves 4

BAKED

Baked Potato with Chives and Soured Cream

1 large potato, well scrubbed
Salt and pepper
2 tablespoons soured cream

1 teaspoon chopped chives

1. Prick the potatoes with a fork to eliminate any risk of their bursting in the oven.
2. Bake in a fairly hot oven (200 C/400 F, gas mark 6) for 1 hour or until a skewer glides easily through the largest potato.
3. Mix the remaining ingredients together and season with salt and pepper.

4. Split the potatoes without cutting them quite in half and fill with the soured cream mixture.
5. Serve immediately and hand the extra soured cream separately.

Note: There is some controversy about preparing potatoes for baking: oiling and wrapping them in foil gives a soft shiny skin, wetting them, with water, and sprinkling them with salt gives a dull very crisp skin.

Serves 1

Boulangère Potatoes

675g/1½lb potatoes, thinly
  sliced
55g/2oz butter
1 onion, thinly sliced

Salt and freshly ground black
  pepper
290ml/½ pint chicken stock

1. Heat the oven at 190 C/375 F, gas mark 5.
2. Butter a pie dish and arrange the potatoes in layers with the onion, adding a little salt and pepper as you go.
3. Arrange the top layer of potatoes in overlapping slices.
4. Dot with the rest of the butter and pour in the stock.
5. Bake in the oven for about 1 hour or until the potatoes are tender and the top browned.

Serves 4

Provençale Tomatoes

4 medium tomatoes
55g/2oz butter
1 onion, finely chopped

Salt and freshly ground black
  pepper
Pinch of nutmeg

270

½ garlic clove, crushed
4 tablespoons stale white
   breadcrumbs

2 teaspoons chopped fresh
   parsley
1 teaspoon chopped tarragon
Chopped parsley to garnish

1. Heat the oven to 200 C/400 F, gas mark 6.
2. Cut the tomatoes in half horizontally. Season well.
3. Melt half the butter and gently cook the onion in it until soft. Add the garlic and cook for 1 more minute.
4. Mix the breadcrumbs, seasoning, nutmeg, herbs, and onion mixture together with a fork.
5. Pile the breadcrumb mixture on to the tomatoes and place a knob of the remaining butter on each.
6. Put the tomatoes in an ovenproof dish and bake in the oven for about 20 minutes or until the breadcrumbs are golden.
7. Sprinkle with chopped parsley.

Serves 4

Pommes Anna

675g/1½lb potatoes
55g/2oz butter, clarified

Salt and pepper
Nutmeg

1. Heat the oven to 190 C/375 F, gas mark 5. Brush a small heavy frying pan with the butter.
2. Wash, peel and slice the potatoes very finely.
3. Arrange a neat layer of overlapping slices on the bottom of the frying pan. Brush the potatoes with the melted butter and season well with salt, pepper and nutmeg.
4. Continue to layer the potatoes, butter and seasoning until all the potatoes have been used. Finish with butter and seasoning.
5. Hold the pan over direct medium heat for two minutes to brown the bottom layer of potatoes.
6. Take off and cover with greased paper and a lid (or foil). Bake in the oven for about 45 minutes.

7. When the potatoes are tender, invert a serving plate over the pan and turn the potatoes out so that the neat first layer is now on top.

Serves 4

Nut Cutlets with Tomato Sauce

For the cutlets:

2 tablespoons milk
Thick slice of wholemeal bread, without crusts
30g/1oz butter
30g/1oz unskinned almonds
30g/1oz unskinned Brazil nuts
30g/1oz cashew nuts

30g/1oz hazelnuts
1 shallot, grated
1 carrot, grated
Salt and freshly ground black pepper
1 egg

For the coating:

Seasoned flour
Beaten egg

Dried white crumbs
Oil *or* butter for baking

To serve:
Tomato sauce (page 325)

For the garnish:
Watercress

1. To make the cutlets: boil the milk and pour it immediately over the bread. Add the butter and leave to soak.
2. Meanwhile grind all the nuts to a powder. This can be done in an electric blender, but care should be taken not to over-grind them – they would become too oily.
3. Set the oven to 190°C/375°F, gas mark 5. Oil a baking sheet.
4. Break up the bread with a fork; add the nuts, shallot and carrot. Season with salt and pepper. Beat in the egg. Shape the mixture into 8 flat rounds. Dip them in seasoned flour and brush with beaten egg. Coat each cutlet with crumbs and place on the oiled baking sheet. Sprinkle with oil or melted butter and bake for 25 minutes.
5. Coat each cutlet lightly with sauce before serving and garnish with watercress.

Serves 4

CREAMED

Bashed Neeps

675g/1½lb swedes
30–55g/1–2oz butter
Pinch of sugar

Salt and freshly ground black
pepper
Water

1. Peel and thinly slice the swedes.
2. Put the slices, with a good ounce of butter, in a thick-bottomed saucepan that has a good lid. Add a sprinkle of sugar, salt and pepper.
3. Pour in about 1cm/½in of water and put on the lid. Simmer *very gently* until the vegetable is soft right through (about 40 minutes), adding more water only if the pan is in danger of boiling dry.
4. Remove the lid and rapidly boil off the rest of the water, but do not let the swedes catch on the bottom.
5. Mash them patiently over a gentle heat until they look really smooth, dry and fluffy. Taste, adding extra butter, salt and pepper if necessary

Note: The Scots call a swede a neep (or turnip). Very confusing.

Serves 4

Celeriac Purée

2 medium potatoes
225g/½lb celeriac
290ml/½ pint milk

55g/2oz butter
Salt and white pepper

1. Wash and peel the potatoes and place them in a pan of cold salted water. Bring to the boil, cover and simmer until tender (about 25 minutes).

273

2. Meanwhile wash the celeriac, peel it and cut into chunks. Simmer slowly in the milk until tender (about 20–30 minutes).

3. Liquidize or mash the celeriac with its milk (which should by now be much reduced).

4. Drain the potatoes and mash them. Place the potatoes and celeriac together in a pan. Beat over a gentle heat adding the butter as you mix. Add salt and pepper to taste.

5. Pile into a serving dish and serve at once.

Serves 4

Purée Clamart

1 medium onion
45g/1½oz butter
Scant 150ml/¼ pint strong
  chicken stock

450g/1lb frozen *or* podded
  fresh peas
Salt and pepper
225g/½lb pommes purée
  (page 275)

1. Chop the onion finely and put it with the butter, stock and peas into a saucepan. Add a little salt and pepper. Cover the saucepan and simmer the ingredients together until the peas are tender. If the peas are fresh, or frozen in a solid block, it may be necessary to add a splash more stock during cooking as the cooking time will be longer.

2. Liquidize the peas with any remaining juice, or push through a sieve. Turn into a bowl.

3. Gradually beat the potato into the peas. The purée should be soft but able to hold its shape. Taste for seasoning and turn into a warm dish.

Serves 4

Pommes Mousseline

675g/1½lb potatoes
About 290ml/½ pint milk
55g/2oz butter

Salt and pepper
A little grated nutmeg

1. Peel the potatoes. Boil them in salted water until tender. Drain thoroughly.
2. Push the potatoes through a sieve or mouli. Return them to the dry saucepan.
3. Heat carefully, stirring to allow the potato to steam dry.
4. Push the mass of potato to one side of the pan. Put the exposed part of the pan over direct heat and pour in the milk. Tilt the pan to allow the milk to boil without burning the potato.
5. When the milk is boiling, or near it, beat it into the potato. Add the butter. Season with salt, pepper and nutmeg.

Note: The recipe is similar to that for pommes purée but gives a softer consistency.

Serves 4

Pommes Purée

675g/1½lb potatoes
150ml/¼ pint milk
45g/1½oz butter

A little grated nutmeg
Salt and pepper

Follow the instructions for pommes mousseline above.

Creamed Brussels Sprouts

290ml/½ pint very fresh double cream
900g/2lb Brussels sprouts, washed and trimmed

Salt and freshly ground black pepper
Grated nutmeg

1. Boil the cream in a small heavy saucepan until reduced in quantity by about half. It will thicken. Stir frequently during boiling to prevent burning. Keep warm.
2. Boil the sprouts in salted water until tender (about 8 minutes).

Drain well. Then finely chop or liquidize them.

3. Mix the cream with the sprouts, and add salt, pepper and nutmeg to taste.

Note: This dish may be prepared the day before serving. Allow sprouts and cream to cool before mixing. Reheat by tossing in a heavy frying pan over gentle heat, or in a shallow buttered dish in a hot oven or, best of all, rapidly in a microwave oven.

Serves 6

BRAISED

Petits Pois à la Française

225g/½lb peas, shelled (use frozen peas if fresh are not available)

1 large mild onion, finely sliced

1 small lettuce, shredded

150ml/¼ pint water

30g/1oz butter

Handful each of fresh mint and parsley

½ garlic clove, crushed (optional)

Salt, freshly ground black pepper

1 teaspoon sugar

1. Mix the peas, onion and lettuce in a heavy casserole. Add the water, butter, mint, parsley, garlic (if used), salt and pepper and sugar.
2. Cover tightly (a double seal of greaseproof paper put over the pan before the lid is pushed down makes a good seal).
3. Cook on a very gentle heat until the peas are tender, almost mushy (about 50 minutes), or, better still, bake in a slow oven 170 C/325 F, gas mark 3 for 1½–2 hours.

Note: The liquid may be thickened by the addition of beurre manié (see page 61) if preferred, but care should be taken not to mash the peas while stirring.

Serves 4

Vegetable Stew

110g/¼lb haricot beans
3 small onions
3 new potatoes
2 medium carrots, peeled
3 small tomatoes
¼ cauliflower
55g/2oz butter
2 leeks, washed and cut up
2 courgettes, cut in chunks

2 sticks celery, cut in chunks
290ml/½ pint vegetable stock
Salt and freshly ground black
  pepper
2 teaspoons flour
2 teaspoons chopped fresh
  parsley
2 teaspoons chopped fresh mint

To serve:
Brown rice (page 265)

1. Soak the haricot beans for 3 hours. Cook them in fresh
    boiling water until tender (about 1½–2 hours). Drain well.
2. Peel the onions and leave them whole. Wash the potatoes
    and the carrots, and cut them into even-sized chunks. Dip
    the tomatoes into boiling water for 5 seconds, peel them and
    cut them into quarters. Cut the cauliflower into florets.
3. Melt half the butter, add the onions and cook them slowly
    for 1 minute, then add the leeks, courgettes, carrots, celery
    and tomatoes. Pour on the stock and bring to the boil. Add
    the potatoes, season with salt and pepper and simmer for
    about 30 minutes. Add the cauliflower and beans and
    continue to simmer until all the vegetables are tender
    (about 15 minutes).
4. Mix the remaining butter and the flour to a paste (i.e. beurre
    manié). Slip a little at a time down the side of the pan and
    into the mixture, stirring gently. When all the beurre manié
    has been added you should have a smooth, slightly thickened
    sauce for the vegetables. Simmer the stew for 3 minutes to
    cook the flour. Add the parsley and mint. Taste and season
    as required. Serve with brown rice.

Serves 6

Braised Celery

1 head celery
15g/½oz butter
1 small onion, chopped
1 carrot, finely chopped
290ml/½ pint chicken stock

1 bay leaf
Salt and freshly ground black
  pepper
15g/½oz butter
15g/½oz flour

1. Heat the oven to 180°C/350°F, gas mark 4.
2. Wash and cut the celery into even-sized pieces, about 8cm/3in long. Remove any tough strings.
3. Melt the butter in a heavy roasting pan and cook the onions and carrots in it until soft but not coloured.
4. Add the celery, stock, bay leaf, salt and pepper and bring to the boil.
5. Cover with a lid or foil and bake in the oven until tender (about 1½ hours).
6. Mix the butter and the flour together to a smooth paste.
7. When the celery is tender place the roasting tin over direct heat. When the liquid boils stir in a little of the flour paste (beurre manié) to thicken the sauce. Do not add too much at a time. Stir until boiling.
8. Simmer for 2 minutes to cook the flour. Taste and adjust the seasoning if necessary.
9. Remove the bay leaf. Transfer celery and liquid to a warmed serving dish.

Serves 4

Marrow and Mushroom à la Cuisine Minceur

225g/½lb marrow
225g/½lb mushrooms
Lemon juice

Salt and freshly ground black
  pepper

278

1. Slice the marrows, skin and all, as finely as you can. Slice the mushrooms.
2. Drop the marrow slices into boiling water, bring back to the boil, and then immediately drain them.
3. Put them into a heavy saucepan with the mushroom slices and a good squeeze of lemon. Cover with a lid.
4. Cook over a low heat, shaking the pan occasionally until the vegetables are cooked but not mushy. Add plenty of pepper, and salt to taste. Serve at once.

Note I: The dish must be served at once or it will become rather wet, and lose its colour. If this does happen 'lift' it with a scattering of chopped parsley. It will taste good anyway.

Note II: The principle of the increasingly popular 'cuisine minceur' is to provide food with a subtle and delicious flavour without excessive use of butter, cream, egg yolk, flour or other high-carbohydrate or high-cholesterol ingredients. The acknowledged master of the art is Michel Guérard, a great chef by any standards, and now a propagandist for healthy eating.

Serves 4

Ratatouille

2 small aubergines
2 courgettes
Olive oil
1 large onion, sliced
1 garlic clove, crushed
1 medium green pepper, sliced
1 small red pepper, sliced

6 tomatoes, peeled, quartered and seeded
Salt and freshly ground black pepper
Crushed coriander
1 tablespoon chopped fresh basil (optional)

1. Wipe the aubergines and courgettes and cut into bite-sized chunks. Dégorge (sprinkle with salt and leave to drain for about 30 minutes). Rinse away the salt and dry the vegetables well.
2. Melt a little oil in a pan and add the onions and garlic. When

soft but not brown, add the aubergine and fry to a pale brown, adding more oil if necessary. Add the peppers and courgettes, cover and cook gently for 25 minutes.

3. Add the tomatoes, salt (if necessary), pepper and a pinch of crushed coriander. Cook, covered, for about 10 minutes.
4. Dish up and sprinkle with chopped basil. Serve hot or well chilled.

Note: A good catering trick if making large quantities of ratatouille: deep fry the aubergines, peppers and courgettes in hot, *very clean* deep oil. Drain them and put into the saucepan with the onions (gently fried in olive oil) and tomatoes. Cook, covered, for 10 minutes with the flavourings. Deep frying saves a lot of time, but the oil, though it need not be olive oil, *must* be clean.

Serves 4

Red Cabbage

1 small red cabbage
1 onion, sliced
30g/1oz butter
1 cooking apple, peeled and
  sliced
1 dessert apple, peeled and
  sliced

2 teaspoons brown sugar
2 teaspoons vinegar
Pinch of ground cloves
Salt and freshly ground black
  pepper

1. Shred the cabbage and discard the hard stalks. Rinse well.
2. Using a large pot, fry the onion in the butter until it begins to soften.
3. Add the drained but still wet cabbage, apples, sugar, vinegar and cloves, and season with salt and pepper.
4. Cover tightly and cook very slowly, mixing well and stirring every 15 minutes or so. Cook for 2 hours, or until the whole mass is soft and reduced in bulk. (During the cooking it may be necessary to add a little water.)
5. Taste and add more salt, pepper or sugar if necessary.

Serves 6

SERVED WITH A SAUCE

Vegetable Mornay

1 small cauliflower
Salt
225g/½lb shelled peas *or* 1 small
  packet frozen peas

450g/1lb carrots
3 tomatoes
570ml/1 pint mornay sauce
  (page 309)

1. Break the cauliflower into sprigs and cook them in boiling salted water until just tender, but not soft.
2. Boil the peas.
3. Peel and slice the carrots and boil in salted water until just tender.
4. Skin the tomatoes (plunge then into boiling water for 5 seconds to loosen the skins) and cut them in half.
5. Put all the vegetables into an ovenproof dish.
6. Heat the mornay sauce and pour it over the vegetables.
7. Heat the oven to 230 C/450 F, gas mark 8. Bake the vegetables until bubbling and brown on top.

Serves 6

Salsify (*or Scorzonera*) *in Mornay Sauce*

Salsify and scorzonera are classified as different vegetables but they taste very alike and are treated similarly, the only practical difference being that salsify is peeled before cooking and scorzonera afterwards. In fact both may be peeled before cooking but the flavour of scorzonera boiled in its skin is said to be superior.

8 roots salsify *or* scorzonera
Lemon juice (for salsify only)
290ml/½ pint mornay sauce
  (page 309)

Grated cheese
Dried breadcrumbs

If using salsify (which is white):

1. Wash, peel and cut each root into 3–4 pieces.
2. Place in a pan with a cupful of salted water with a little lemon juice and simmer, with a tightly closed lid, for 12–20 minutes. or until tender, topping up with water if necessary.
3. Drain well and arrange in a serving dish.
4. Coat with the hot mornay sauce, sprinkle with grated cheese and breadcrumbs and brown under the grill.

If using scorzonera (blackish in colour):

1. Wash and cut each root into 3–4 pieces.
2. Place unpeeled into a pan of boiling salted water and simmer until tender; about 15–20 minutes.
3. Drain well and peel off the skin.
4. Proceed as for salsify.

Serves 4

Beetroot in White Sauce with Spring Onions

2 cooked beetroots, sliced
6 spring onions
30g/1oz butter
20g/¾oz flour

290ml/½ pint milk
Freshly ground black pepper
Pinch of sugar
1 teaspoon wine vinegar

1. Put the beetroot in an ovenproof dish, cover and put in a warm oven to heat up.
2. Cut the spring onions into 2·5cm/1in sticks. Melt the butter, add the onions and cook till soft but not coloured.
3. Stir in the flour. Cook for 1 minute.
4. Draw the pan off the heat and add the milk.
5. Return to the heat and bring the sauce slowly to the boil, stirring continuously.
6. Add the seasonings, sugar and vinegar, and simmer for 2–3 minutes.
7. Pour over the beetroot and serve.

Serves 4

Cauliflower with Green Sauce

1 large cauliflower
425ml/$\frac{3}{4}$ pint green sauce
  (page 311)

1. Cut away and discard the outer leaves and very thick stalk of the cauliflower.
2. Break into florets. Drop these into boiling salted water and cook for 8 minutes or until the stalks are just tender.
3. Drain and put into a serving dish.
4. Cover with a creamy green sauce.

FRIED

Cooked Cucumber with Dill

2 cucumbers
Salt and pepper
30g/1oz butter

2 teaspoons chopped fresh dill
Squeeze of lemon juice

1. Peel the cucumbers and cut into 1cm/$\frac{1}{2}$ in cubes.
2. Drop them into boiling salted water and cook for 3 minutes.
3. Rinse under running cold water and drain well.
4. Melt the butter in a frying pan and when foaming add the cucumber and dill.
5. When the cucumber is beginning to turn a delicate brown season with pepper and lemon juice and shake over the heat.

Note: If cucumbers are cheap and plentiful it is worth shaping them into balls with a melon baller – wasteful but very pretty.

Serves 4

Sweetcorn Fritters

2 eggs
Salt and freshly ground black
pepper
225g/½lb cooked sweetcorn

1 teaspoon baking powder
15g/½oz fresh breadcrumbs
Oil for shallow frying

1. Separate the eggs. Mix the yolks with the seasoning and the sweetcorn.
2. Whisk the whites until stiff but not dry and fold them into the mixture.
3. Stir in the baking powder and add the breadcrumbs. Taste and add more salt and pepper if necessary.
4. Heat the oil in a frying pan and when hot add the batter in spoonfuls. Fry to a golden brown on both sides. Drain well.

Serves 4

Fried Rice

Salt and pepper
8 tablespoons polished rice
Oil

55g/2oz pine kernels
(optional)
2 spring onions

1. Bring a large saucepan full of salted water to the boil and tip in the rice. Stir, bring back to the boil, and cook for 10 minutes or until the rice is just tender.
2. Rinse plenty of hot water through the rice to remove the excess starch and drain well. While it is draining, occasionally turn it over with a spoon to allow trapped steam to escape.
3. Pour 3 tablespoons of oil into a frying pan and heat it. Put in the rice, now quite dry. Fry, turning all the time to brown evenly.
4. Add plenty of pepper, salt if necessary, and the pine kernels.
5. Chop the spring onions finely and stir them in.

Note: 'Easy cook' or polished rice is much easier to fry evenly.

Serves 4

Sauté Potatoes

675g/1½lb potatoes
2 tablespoons oil
45g/1½oz butter
Salt and freshly ground black
   pepper

1 tablespoon chopped fresh
   parsley *or* rosemary

1. Peel the potatoes and cook until just tender in boiling salted water. Drain and allow to dry. Cut into 2cm/1in irregular chunks.
2. Heat the oil in a large sauté or frying pan; add the butter and wait for the bubbles to disappear. Add all the potatoes at once.
3. Add the salt and pepper and shake the potatoes gently over the heat while they slowly fry to a pale brown. Turn them only occasionally or they will break up too much. But they should anyway be fairly dry and crumbly.
4. When delicately brown and crisp add the parsley or rosemary and tip into a warmed serving dish.

Serves 4

Pommes Parisienne

4 large potatoes
2 tablespoons oil

Knob of butter
Salt

1. Peel the potatoes and scoop into small balls with a melon baller. As you prepare the balls drop them into a bowl of

cold water (this prevents discolouring). Float a plate on top
to keep them submerged.

2. Heat the oil in a sauté pan and add the butter. Dry the potato
balls well and toss them in the pan until completely coated with
fat. Fry very slowly until they are browned and tender,
shaking the pan frequently to prevent them sticking.

3. Drain well, sprinkle with salt and serve immediately.

Note: Allow 15 Parisienne potatoes per head. The larger the
potatoes, the easier it is to scoop them into balls.

Serves 4

DEEP FRIED

Chips

675g/1½lb potatoes
Oil for frying
Salt

1. Peel and, as far as possible, cut the potatoes into 5cm × 1cm/
2in × ½in sticks. Keep them in a bowl of cold water until ready
for cooking. This will prevent any discoloration and remove
excess starch which tends to stick the chips together.

2. Heat the oil to a medium temperature (when a crouton of
bread is dropped in it should fizzle gently).

3. Dry the potatoes carefully and place a few at a time in the
chip basket (too many will stick together).

4. Fry for 7–8 minutes until soft. Remove from the fat.

5. Heat the oil until a crouton of bread will frizzle and brown
in 30 seconds.

6. Repeat the frying process in the hotter oil until the chips are
well browned and crisp.

7. Drain the chips on absorbent paper. Sprinkle with salt.
8. Serve immediately. Do not cover the chips or they will lose their crispness.

Note: Chips are cooked in two stages because if the fat is hot enough to crisp and brown the chips, the process is so quick that the middle of the potato will not be cooked. On the other hand, if the oil is cooler, although the chip will cook through, it will be soggy. The second frying, to create the crisp brown outside, should be done just before serving.

Serves 4

Game Chips

450g/1lb large potatoes
Oil for frying
Salt

1. Wash and peel the potatoes. If you want even-sized chips trim each potato into a cylinder shape.
2. Slice them very finely, preferably on a mandolin. Soak in cold water to remove the excess starch (this will prevent them from discoloring or sticking together).
3. Heat the oil until a crumb will sizzle vigorously in it.
4. Dry the chips very thoroughly on a tea towel.
5. Lower a basket of chips into the hot fat. They are cooked when they rise to the surface and are golden brown.
6. Drain on absorbent paper, sprinkle with salt and serve immediately.

Note: Commercial potato crisps, providing they are the plain variety and not 'cheese and bacon' or some such, will do very well as game chips. Simply heat them, uncovered, in a moderate oven.

Serves 4

Cauliflower Fritters

1 large cauliflower
Lemon juice
Freshly ground black pepper
Oil for deep frying

140ml/¼ pint fritter batter
 (page 660)
290ml/½ pint tomato sauce
 (page 325)

1. Cut the cauliflower into florets. Boil them in salted water for 3 minutes.
2. Drain the florets well. When dry sprinkle liberally with lemon juice and season with black pepper.
3. Heat the oil until a crumb will sizzle in it.
4. Dip each piece of cauliflower in the fritter batter and drop carefully into the hot fat.
5. The batter will puff up and when golden brown the cauliflower is ready. Drain well and serve immediately with tomato sauce.

Note: Although this dish makes a good vegetable accompaniment to plain meat dishes, it is delicious on its own as a lunch time dish, or as a starter for a more elaborate meal.

Serves 4

Matchstick Potatoes (*pommes allumettes*)

450g/1lb potatoes
Oil for deep frying

Salt

1. Wash and peel the potatoes. Cut them into tiny even matchsticks and soak in cold water for 15 minutes. This is to remove the excess starch and will prevent the potatoes from sticking together. Dry them thoroughly with a tea-towel.
2. Heat the oil until a crumb dropped in the fat sizzles vigorously. Fry the chips until golden brown and crisp (2–3

SALMON EN CROÛTE. Use teaspoon to cut scales in pastry

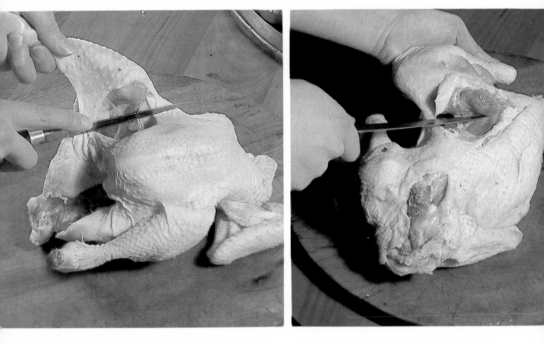

JOINTING CHICKEN. (1) Pull legs away from body. Cut through skin only. (2) Turn bird over. Remove legs, with 'oysters'.

(3) Split along breastbone. Open out. (4) Cut each side of backbone. Split breast/wing joints in half

CHICKEN
CHAUDFROID

TUNA PÂTÉ IN
LEMON SHELLS

 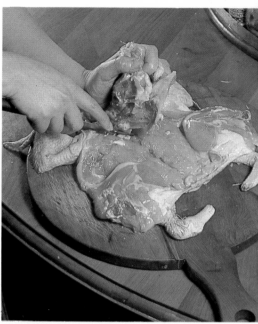

BONING CHICKEN. (1) Cut through skin to backbone. Ease away flesh, keeping knife close to bone. (2) Work round carcass, cutting and scraping against ribcage. Sever wing and leg tendons close to the body. Remove ribcage taking great care at breastbone.

 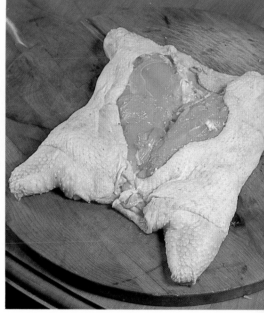

(3) and (4) To bone legs and wings, chop off wing pinions and knuckle ends of drumsticks. Working from thicker ends of joints, ease bones out

minutes). Drain on absorbent paper. Sprinkle with salt and serve at once.

Serves 4

Game Chip Baskets Filled with Chestnuts

See the notes on deep frying on pages 30–3.

675g/1½lb potatoes
Oil for deep frying
1 large can whole unsweetened chestnuts
Handful of raisins

Small bunch of white grapes, halved and pips removed
30g/1oz pinenuts
45g/1½oz butter

1. Peel the potatoes. Slice finely using a mandolin or a patterned cutter so that the finished basket will look like woven straw.
2. Dip a small wire strainer or sieve into the fat to get it well greased. Heat the fat until a crumb will sizzle vigorously in it.
3. Line the strainer with potato slices overlapping each other. Using a small ladle or a similar round-shaped object to prevent the chips floating away from the strainer as you cook them, deep fry the 'basket' until golden and crisp.
4. Drain well on absorbent paper.
5. Melt the butter and add the drained chestnuts, raisins, grapes and pinenuts. Fry until hot and beginning to brown.
6. Fill the baskets with this mixture just before serving.

Note: A gadget for making the baskets is available in shops selling to the catering trade, but the sieve-and-ladle method works perfectly well.

Serves 4

SALADS

Everything Green Salad

1 lettuce (any kind)   French dressing (page 319)

Choice of the following:

Green pepper	Watercress
Cucumber	Green beans
Fennel	Peas
Celery	1 teaspoon chopped fresh
Chicory	mint, parsley *or* chives
Spring onions	

1. Prepare the salad ingredients:
   Lettuce: Wash, drain and shake to allow to drip dry. Do not twist or wring the leaves together, which bruises them, but break each lettuce leaf individually and place in a salad bowl.
   Green pepper: Wash, cut off the top and remove the seeds. Slice finely.
   Cucumber: Peel or not, as desired. Slice finely.
   Fennel: Wash and shave into thin slices.
   Celery: Wash and chop together with a few young leaves.
   Chicory: Wipe with a damp cloth. Remove the tough core with a sharp knife and cut each head at an angle into 3 or 4 pieces.
   Spring onions: Wash and peel. Chop half the green stalks finely. Keep the white part with the rest of the salad.
   Watercress: Wash and pick over, discarding the thick stalks and any yellow leaves.
   Beans and peas: Cook in boiling salted water until just tender and cool under running cold water. Drain well and pat dry in a tea-towel.
2. Add the chopped herbs and the chopped spring onion tops (if used) to the dressing.
3. Mix the salad ingredients together and just before serving toss them in French dressing.

Frilly Bitter Salad

Any or all of the slightly bitter leaves: watercress; young kale; curly endive; young spinach; chicory; lamb's lettuce

For the dressing:

3 tablespoons salad oil
1 tablespoon olive oil
1 tablespoon red wine vinegar

1 teaspoon French mustard
Salt and pepper

1. Put the dressing ingredients into a screw-top jar and shake well.
2. Wash and dry the salad leaves, discarding any tough stalks.
3. Toss the salad in the dressing and tip into a clean bowl.

Caesar Salad

2 large garlic cloves
4 tablespoons olive oil
2 finely chopped anchovy
   fillets
2 tablespoons lemon juice
Dry English mustard

Freshly ground black pepper
1 egg
2 slices bread
1 cos lettuce
4 tablespoons Parmesan cheese

1. Crush the garlic and mix with the olive oil.
2. Strain off three-quarters of the olive oil (now flavoured with garlic) to make the dressing.
3. Add it to the anchovy fillets, lemon juice, mustard, pepper and raw egg and whisk well or blend in liquidizer.
4. Cut the crusts off the bread and cut the rest into small dice.
5. Pour the remaining oil and the garlic into a frying pan.
6. Heat slowly. When the garlic shreds begin to sizzle add the diced bread and fry, turning frequently with a fish slice or spoon, until the croutons are crisp and brown. With a per-

forated spoon lift out the croutons and drain and cool them on absorbent paper.

7. Toss the lettuce in the dressing.
8. Sprinkle over the croutons and cheese.

Serves 4

Tomato and Basil Salad

6 tomatoes   French dressing (page 319)
8–10 leaves of fresh basil

1. Dip the tomatoes in boiling water for 5 seconds and then skin them.
2. Chop the basil coarsely.
3. Slice the tomatoes horizontally and arrange them on a plate.
4. Mix the dressing and basil together and spoon over the tomatoes.
5. Chill for 1–2 hours before serving.

Serves 4

Carrot and Mint Salad

1 teaspoon caster sugar   French dressing (page 319)
Large pinch of cumin   2 tablespoons chopped fresh
  powder   mint
4 large carrots

1. Mix the sugar and cumin powder with the dressing.
2. Peel the carrots and grate coarsely. Put them straight into the French dressing.
3. Add the mint and toss the salad well. Taste and season with salt and pepper if necessary.

Serves 4

Chinese Cabbage and Apple Salad

450g/1lb Chinese cabbage
 (Chinese leaves)

2 dessert apples
Chopped parsley

For the dressing:
3 tablespoons oil
1 tablespoon vinegar

3 tablespoons chopped fresh
 mint
2 tablespoons soured cream

1. Mix all the ingredients for the dressing together in a screw-top jar and shake until well emulsified.
2. Shred the cabbage finely and slice the apples but do not peel them.
3. Toss the cabbage and apple in the dressing.
4. Tip into a wooden salad bowl and sprinkle with plenty of chopped parsley.

Serves 4

Spinach Salad with Bacon and Yoghurt

450g/1lb fresh young spinach
6 rashers streaky rindless bacon

For the dressing:
2–3 tablespoons plain yoghurt
2 tablespoons oil
2 teaspoons vinegar

1 teaspoon French mustard
½ garlic clove, crushed
Salt, pepper and sugar

1. Heat the grill.
2. Wash the spinach and remove the stalks. Drain well and shred finely.
3. Grill the bacon for about 2 minutes on each side until brown and crispy. Cool, then chop up.

4.   Mix all the ingredients for the dressing together.
5.   Toss the spinach and bacon in the dressing just before serving.

Serves 4

Cauliflower and Ham Salad

1 small cauliflower
2 slices ham, cut into thin strips
3 hardboiled eggs

For the dressing:

1 level tablespoon chopped
  fresh mint
1 level tablespoon chopped
  fresh chives
1 teaspoon chopped fresh
  tarragon

3 tablespoons salad oil
1 tablespoon wine vinegar
1 small garlic clove, crushed
Salt and freshly ground black
  pepper

1.   Break the cauliflower into sprigs and boil in salted water until
     barely cooked. Drain well.
2.   While still hot, put into a bowl and pour over the combined
     dressing ingredients.
3.   When the cauliflower is quite cold arrange on a dish with
     the strips of ham mixed among the sprigs.
4.   Surround with the hardboiled eggs, cut into quarters length-
     wise, and pour any remaining dressing over the eggs.

Serves 4

Salad Niçoise I

3 tomatoes, skinned and
  quartered

225g/½lb cooked French beans
Small can tuna fish

½ mild onion, thinly sliced
1 green pepper, seeded and
   sliced
12 radishes, washed, topped
   and tailed
1 lettuce heart

6 anchovy fillets, split
   lengthwise
2 hardboiled eggs, quartered
   lengthwise
8 black olives

For the dressing:
1 tablespoon wine vinegar
3 tablespoons olive oil
Salt and freshly ground black
   pepper
½ garlic clove, crushed

1 tablespoon finely chopped
   fresh herbs (basil, tarragon,
   marjoram, fennel, chervil,
   chives)

1. Put all the dressing ingredients into a large bowl and whisk well.
2. Reserving a few olives, radishes, tomato quarters and anchovy fillets for the top, put all the rest of the salad ingredients into the bowl. Turn them gently in the dressing. Do not over mix.
3. Tip carefully into a clean salad bowl and put the reserved olives, radishes etc. on the top.

Serves 6 as a starter, 3 as a main course

Salad Niçoise II

½ cucumber
Salt
8 anchovy fillets
Milk
Small can tuna fish
½ mild onion, thinly sliced
Squeeze of lemon

340g/¾lb cooked French beans
4 tomatoes, peeled and sliced
French dressing (page 319)
Stoned black olives
Brown bread and butter to
   serve

1. Slice the cucumber finely, salt it lightly, and leave it to release its juices for 30 minutes.
2. Soak the anchovy fillets in milk to remove some of the salt.

3. Mix the tuna (and its oil) with the onion and a squeeze of lemon juice. Place in the bottom of a glass bowl.
4. Mix the French beans with a tablespoon French dressing and arrange them on top of the tuna fish.
5. Mix the tomatoes with a dessertspoon French dressing and arrange them carefully over the beans, making sure that the top is completely flat.
6. Rinse the cucumber and dry it well. Arrange in very neat overlapping slices on top of the tomatoes.
7. Make a lattice on top of the cucumber with the anchovy fillets and put the black olives in the diagonal spaces. Serve with brown bread and butter.

Serves 6 as a starter, 3 as a main course

Antipasta Salad

1 crisp lettuce
2 heads chicory
1 green pepper
1 red pepper
Small can tuna fish
Salt and pepper

4 anchovy fillets
½ cup milk
6 black olives
4 slices mortadella sausage, skinned
4 slices salami, skinned

For the French dressing:
2 tablespoons oil
2 teaspoons lemon juice
1 small garlic clove, crushed

1 tablespoon chopped fresh parsley
Salt and pepper

1. Wash and drain the lettuce. Wipe the chicory and slice into 4 lengthwise. Wipe and slice the peppers, discarding the seeds.
2. Pour the oil from the tuna and break the flesh up with a fork. Season with salt and plenty of pepper.
3. Soak the anchovy fillets for 30 minutes in the milk to remove excess saltiness. Dry and cut into neat strips.
4. Stone the olives.
5. Roll up the mortadella and salami.

6. Place the lettuce on a large flat serving dish. Arrange the chicory, peppers, tuna, olives, mortadella and salami on the lettuce in groups, taking care with the colour scheme. Garnish with the anchovy fillets.
7. Shake the dressing ingredients together in a screw-top jar, and pour over the salad.

Note: Antipasta, like hors d'oeuvres, means a starter or first course. This is a fairly typical Italian mixed salad starter, but ingredients can be varied to taste.

Serves 4–6

Flageolet and Tuna Salad

85g/3oz shell-shaped pasta
Salt and freshly ground black pepper
1 small can flageolet beans
1 small onion, finely sliced
1 small can tuna fish
1 teaspoon chopped fresh basil
1 teaspoon chopped fresh parsley
French dressing (page 319)
Box of mustard and cress
3 black olives, stoned

1. Cook the pasta in plenty of boiling salted water until just tender (about 10 minutes). Rinse under cold water and drain well. Rinse the starchy liquid off the flageolets and drain.
2. Gently mix the onion, beans, tuna fish (without liquid), pasta and chopped herbs in just enough French dressing to moisten the salad. Add salt and pepper if needed. Care should be taken not to overmix, or an unattractive soggy salad will result.
3. Decorate with snipped cress and the black olives.

Serves 4

Bean and Bean Salad

450g/1lb fresh French beans
450g/1lb cooked haricot beans
  or butter beans (canned are
  fine)
2 tablespoons chopped fresh
  basil *or* spring onion tops

1 tablespoon lemon juice
3 tablespoons salad oil
Salt and freshly ground pepper
1 small garlic clove, crushed

1. Top and tail the French beans and boil them in salted water until just tender. Drain and swish under the cold tap water to prevent further cooking and preserve their colour.
2. Drain the haricot or butter beans if they are canned and rinse away any starchy water. When they are dry mix them with the cooked French beans and put into a dish.
3. Place the basil or spring onions in a jar, add the lemon juice, seasoning, garlic and oil and shake vigorously. Pour over the salad.

Note: All types of beans are good – fresh broad beans (especially if the inner skins are removed after cooking), dried lima, canned flageolets etc.

Serves 4

Watercress Salad with Croutons

Oil for deep frying
4 slices white bread

2 bunches watercress

For the dressing:
3 tablespoons oil
1 tablespoon vinegar
Salt and pepper
½ garlic clove, crushed

½ teaspoon chopped
  fresh parsley
Pinch of sugar (optional)

1. First make the croutons: heat the oil until a crumb will sizzle

298

vigorously in it. Cut off the crusts and cut the bread into small cubes.

2. Fry the bread in the oil until golden brown and crisp. Drain well on absorbent paper. Sprinkle lightly with salt, and leave to cool completely.

3. Combine all the dressing ingredients in a screw-top jar and shake well.

4. Prepare the watercress by washing it, shaking it dry and discarding any thick stalks or yellow leaves.

5. Just before serving toss the watercress in the French dressing, tip into a clean salad bowl and sprinkle the croutons on top.

Serves 4–5

FARINACEOUS SALADS

Rice Salad

Almost any vegetables can be added to cold cooked rice to make a salad, but it is important to have approximately equal quantities of rice and vegetables, or the result may be lifeless and stodgy. The dressing should moisten, not soak, the dish.

225g/½lb long-grain rice
110g/¼lb frozen peas
½ green pepper, seeded and
  chopped
½ red pepper, seeded and
  chopped

Small stick of celery
¼ cucumber peeled
2 tomatoes
Few black olives
Finely chopped fresh parsley,
  mint, chives *or* dill

For the dressing:
4 tablespoons salad oil
1 tablespoon vinegar

1 medium onion, finely
  chopped
Salt and pepper

299

1. Boil the rice in plenty of water until just tender (about 10 minutes).
2. Rinse under the cold tap and leave to drain well.
3. Cook the peas.
4. Chop the peppers (discarding the seeds), celery and cucumber.
5. Plunge the tomatoes into boiling water for 5 seconds so that they will peel easily. Peel them and cut into quarters.
6. Stone the olives.
7. Put the dressing ingredients into a screw-top jar and shake well.
8. Mix everything together and add salt and pepper if necessary.

Note: Rice salad looks pretty when turned out of a ring mould, jelly mould, or even a mixing bowl. Push it down firmly in the oiled mould, then invert it on to a dish. If simply served in a bowl or on a dish keep back a few olives and tomato pieces for the top.

Serves 8

Potato Salad

675g/1½lb potatoes
Sprig of mint
4 tablespoons French dressing
  (page 319)
½ carton soured cream

1 tablespoon mayonnaise
  (page 316)
2 tablespoons fresh chopped
  chives

1. Boil the potatoes with the mint in a pan of boiling salted water until just tender. (If using very small new potatoes they are good left unpeeled. But if they are old or large they should be peeled *after* boiling.) Drain well. Cut up if large.
2. Toss in the French dressing while still hot. Leave to cool.
3. Mix the soured cream and the mayonnaise together. Add half the chives.
4. Turn the potatoes in this creamy dressing and tip into a salad bowl.

5. Sprinkle liberally with the rest of the chopped chives.

Serves 4–6

Barley and Beetroot Salad

1 large beetroot, cooked
1 small onion
½ green apple

French dressing (page 319)
30g/1oz barley
110g/¼lb shredded lettuce *or*
white cabbage

1. Boil the barley in plenty of salted water for about 1 hour, until tender. Drain well.
2. Chop the beetroot, onion and apple (unskinned).
3. Toss these in French dressing with the barley.
4. Serve on a bed of shredded lettuce.

Serves 4

New Potatoes Vinaigrette

675g/1½lb small new potatoes
French dressing (page 319)
Small bunch of fresh mint

1 tablespoon chopped chives
1 shallot, finely chopped

1. Wash the potatoes and scrape them, but do not peel. Cook in boiling salted water with a sprig of mint until tender. Chop 8–10 mint leaves finely.
2. Mix the French dressing with the mint, chives and shallot.
3. Drain the potatoes well and toss immediately in the French dressing. Leave to cool and toss again just before serving. Decorate with a fresh mint leaf or two.

Note: There is always controversy about peeling new potatoes. The best, very new, pale ones need little more than washing. Most need scraping, and some – usually large, dark and patently not very new – need peeling *after* cooking.

Serves 4

4
Stocks and
Savoury Sauces

———◆———

STOCKS

Good strong natural stocks are behind almost every good sauce
or casserole. Stock-cubes are often over-salty and 'packet-
flavoured', so should be used with caution. See page 60 for detailed
notes on stock-making.

White Stock

Onion   Fresh parsley
Celery   Fresh thyme
Carrot   Bay leaf
Chicken *or* veal bones, skin Peppercorns
   or flesh

1.   Peel the onion. Slice it and the celery and carrot roughly.
2.   Put all the ingredients into a saucepan. Cover generously with
     water and bring to the boil slowly. Skim off any fat, and/or
     scum.
3.   Simmer for 2–3 hours, skimming frequently and topping up
     the water level if necessary. The liquid should reduce to half
     the original quantity.
4.   Strain, cool and lift off all the fat.

Aspic

1·14 litres/2 pints white stock (above)
2 egg shells, crushed
2 egg whites

30g/1oz gelatine (use this if the stock is not firmly set when chilled, *or* half if the stock is half-set)

1. Lift or skim any fat from the stock.
2. Put the stock into a large saucepan and sprinkle on the gelatine if you need it. Put over gentle heat.
3. Place the crushed shells in a bowl, add the egg whites and whisk until frothy. Pour into the warming stock and keep whisking steadily with a balloon whisk until the mixture boils and rises. Stop whisking immediately and draw the pan off the heat. Allow the mixture to subside. Take care not to break the crust formed by the egg white.
4. Bring the aspic to the boil again and again allow to subside. Repeat this once more (the egg white will trap the sediment in the stock and clear the aspic). Allow to cool for 10 minutes.
5. Fix a double layer of fine muslin over a clean basin and carefully strain the aspic through it, taking care to hold the egg white crust back. When all the liquid is through (or almost all of it) allow the egg white to slip into the muslin. Then strain the aspic again – this time through both egg white crust and cloth. Do not try to hurry the process by squeezing the cloth, or murky aspic will result.

Brown Stock

Onion
Turnip
Carrot
Celery

Dripping
Fresh parsley stalks
Bay leaf
Pinch of fresh thyme

303

Marrow bones (*or* beef bones,   Black peppercorns
  veal bones, duck carcass,
  bacon – green *or* smoked
  – *or* pieces of raw meat, but
  not mutton, lamb or pork)

1. Peel the onion but keep the skin.
2. Peel the turnip, wash the carrot and the celery.
3. Chop all the vegetables into large dice.
4. Chop the meat or bacon up into small pieces.
5. Heat the fat in a large heavy-bottomed pan and brown the bones, meat and vegetables really well all over, scraping the bottom of the pan frequently.
6. Add the herbs, onion skin and pepper (but not salt).
7. Cover with water and bring very slowly to the boil, skimming off any scum as it rises to the top.
8. When clear of scum, simmer gently for at least 2 hours, preferably all day, skimming off the fat as necessary, and topping up with water if the level gets dangerously low. The longer it simmers, and the more the liquid reduces by evaporation, the stronger the stock will be.
9. Strain, cool and lift off any remaining fat.

Note: Cooked bones are less satisfactory than raw bones as they have lost a good deal of their flavour.

Fish Stock

Onion   Fresh parsley stalks
Carrot   Bay leaf
Celery   Pinch of fresh thyme
Fish bones, skins, fins, heads Pepper
  or tails, crustacean shells
  (e.g. prawn shells, mussel
  shells etc.)

1. Slice the peeled onion, the carrot and the celery.

2. Put everything together in a pan, with water to cover, and bring to the boil. Turn down to simmer and skim off any scum.
3. Simmer for 20 minutes if the fish bones are small, 30 minutes if large. Strain.

Note: Care should be taken not to overcook fish stock, as the flavour is impaired if the bones are cooked too long. Once strained, however, fish stock may be strengthened by further boiling and reducing.

Fond Brun

1·35k/3lb beef and veal bones, bones, broken	3 bay leaves
A little bacon rind	Pinch of fresh thyme
110g/¼lb onion, peeled and chopped roughly	2 fresh parsley stalks
110g/¼lb carrot, chopped roughly	4 peppercorns
	1 litre/2 pints water

1. Set the oven to 200°C/400°F, gas mark 6.
2. Place the broken bones in a large, deep-sided roasting pan.
3. Roast until very brown, about 2 hours, turning the bones occasionally. Add the vegetables and bacon rind and continue roasting for a further 45 minutes.
4. Transfer everything to a heavy saucepan. Add the herbs, peppercorns and water. Simmer slowly, covered, for 2–3 hours.
5. Strain and leave to get cold.
6. Skim off all the fat.

Glace de Viande

570ml/1 pint fond brun as above, absolutely free of fat

1. In a heavy-bottomed saucepan reduce the fond brun by boiling over a steady heat until thick, clear and syrupy.
2. Pour into small pots. When cold cover with polythene or jam covers and tie down.
3. Keep in the refrigerator until ready for use.

Note: Glace de viande keeps for several weeks and is very useful for enriching sauces.

Court Bouillon

1·14 litres/2 pints water
150ml/¼ pint vinegar
1 carrot, sliced
1 onion, sliced

1 stick celery
12 peppercorns
2 bay leaves
2 tablespoons salad oil
Salt

Bring all the ingredients to the boil and simmer for 20 minutes.
  Ideally the liquid should now be allowed to cool and the fish, meat or vegetables should be placed in the cool liquid, and then brought slowly to simmering point.

Beef Bouillon (broth)

1 veal bone
55g/2oz fat bacon pieces
3 carrots
2 turnips
2 leeks
Stick of celery
1 small parsnip
3 onions

900g/2lb shin of beef, cut into
  cubes
3·5 litres/6 pints water
½ teaspoon salt
2 bay leaves
3 cloves
Good handful of parsley stalks
Pinch of thyme

1. Put the bone and fat bacon into a roasting tin and brown in a moderate oven (200°C/400°F, gas mark 6) for 1 hour. Cut the vegetables up roughly (reserving the onion skin, which will

be added later). Put the vegetables and the meat in the pan with the bones. Stir them about to coat them with dripping, then put over direct heat and fry until well browned, stirring occasionally to prevent sticking or burning.

2. Drain off the fat (which is worth keeping as dripping). Put the bones and vegetables with the onion skin, water and salt in a large saucepan. Bring slowly to the boil, skimming off the scum and fat as it rises to the surface. When the water is boiling well, pour in a glass of cold water, and immediately skim off fat and scum again. (This is called to *dépouiller* the liquid. The sudden addition of cold water causes the fat and scum to rise to the surface.) Repeat the process once the liquid is boiling again.

3. Add the flavourings. Turn down the heat and allow the stock to simmer for a good 3 hours. Inspect it occasionally and repeat the skimming process if it is necessary. You should now have about 1·45 litres/2½ pints of stock.

4. Strain and allow to cool, then chill so that any remaining fat sets on the top. Lift off the fat. The bouillon should be jellied, but will of course melt on reheating.

Note: The addition of the veal bone is to ensure a stock that will set to a jelly, but is not always necessary. The addition of poultry giblets (excluding the liver) will give a richer stock, but this will not keep as long as stock made without them.

Pork Jelly

1 pig's trotter
450g/1lb broken pork bones
1·7 litres/3 pints water
1 onion, sliced

Stick of celery
Pinch of thyme
Bunch of parsley
1 bay leaf

1. Put the trotters and bones in a saucepan and cover with the water. Bring to the boil and skim.

2. Add the other ingredients and simmer all day, the longer the better, skimming occasionally.

3. When the liquid is reduced to 570mls/1 pint strain and allow to cool and set.

WHITE SAUCES

White Sauce
(coating consistency)

20g/¾oz butter
20g/¾oz flour
Pinch of dry mustard

290ml/½ pint creamy milk
Salt and white pepper

1. Melt the butter in a thick saucepan.
2. Add the flour and the mustard and stir over the heat for 1 minute. Draw the pan off the heat, pour in the milk and mix well.
3. Return the sauce to the heat and stir continually until boiling.
4. Simmer for 2–3 minutes and season with salt and pepper.

Béchamel Sauce
(coating consistency)

290ml/½ pint creamy milk
Slice of onion
Blade of mace
Few fresh parsley stalks
4 peppercorns

1 bay leaf
20g/¾oz butter
20g/¾oz flour
Salt and white pepper

1. Place the milk with the onion, mace, parsley, peppercorns and bay leaf in a saucepan and slowly bring to simmering point.
2. Lower the temperature and allow the flavour to infuse for about 8–10 minutes.
3. Melt the butter in a thick saucepan, stir in the flour and stir over heat for 1 minute.

4. Remove from the heat. Strain in the infused milk and mix well.
5. Return the sauce to the heat and stir or whisk continuously until boiling.
6. Simmer for 2–3 minutes.
7. Taste and season.

Mornay Sauce (Cheese Sauce)

45g/1½oz butter
45g/1½oz flour
570ml/1 pint milk
85g/3oz grated Gruyère *or* strong Cheddar cheese

30g/1oz grated Parmesan cheese
Salt and pepper

1. Melt the butter and stir in the flour. Cook, stirring, for 1 minute. Draw the pan off the heat. Pour in the milk and mix well.
2. Return the pan to the heat and stir until boiling. Simmer for 2 minutes.
3. Add all the cheese and mix well, but do not re-boil.
4. Season with salt and pepper as necessary.

Parsley Sauce

290ml/½ pint creamy milk
Slice of onion
Good handful of fresh parsley
4 peppercorns

1 bay leaf
20g/¾oz butter
20g/¾oz flour
Salt and pepper

1. Put the milk, onion, parsley stalks (but not leaves), peppercorns and bay leaf in a saucepan and slowly bring to simmering point.

2. Lower the temperature and allow the flavour to infuse for about 10 minutes.
3. Melt the butter in a thick saucepan, stir in the flour and cook, stirring, for 1 minute.
4. Remove from the heat. Strain in the infused milk and mix well.
5. Return the sauce to the heat and stir continuously until boiling, then simmer for 2–3 minutes. Taste and season.
6. Chop the parsley leaves very finely and stir into the hot sauce.

Soubise Sauce

For the béchamel sauce:

20g/¾oz butter   20g/¾oz flour
Bay leaf   .   290ml/½ pint milk

For the soubise:

30g/1oz butter   225g/½lb onions, very finely
4 tablespoons water   chopped
                                   3–4 tablespoons cream

1. To make the soubise, melt the butter in a heavy pan. Add the water and the finely chopped onions and cook very slowly, preferably covered with a lid to create a steamy atmosphere. The onions should become very soft and transparent, but on no account brown. Add the cream.
2. Now prepare the béchamel: melt the butter, add the bay leaf and flour and cook, stirring, for 1 minute. Draw off the heat, and stir in the milk. Return to the heat and bring slowly to the boil, stirring continuously. Simmer for 2 minutes. Remove the bay leaf and mix with the soubise.

Note: This sauce can be liquidized in a blender or pushed through a sieve if a smooth texture is desired.

Green Sauce

(for cauliflower, pasta, fish)

45g/1½oz butter   Salt and pepper
30g/1oz flour   Bunch of watercress
425ml/¾ pint milk

1. Melt the butter and stir in the flour.
2. Cook, stirring, for 1 minute. Stirring briskly as you go, pour in the milk and continue stirring until the sauce boils. Simmer for 2 minutes. Season to taste.
3. Wash the watercress, removing stalks.
4. Cook the leaves briefly (30 seconds) in boiling water. Drain and rinse under the cold tap to stop further cooking and to 'set' the green colour.
5. Press all the moisture out of the watercress and add to the sauce.
6. Liquidize the sauce, or push through a sieve.
7. Reheat briefly – long cooking will spoil the colour.

Note: A handful of spinach may be used instead of watercress.

English Egg Sauce

3 hardboiled eggs   3 tablespoons cream
45g/1½oz butter   4 tablespoons chopped fresh
45g/1½oz flour   parsley
570ml/1 pint fish *or* chicken
    stock

1. Using a stainless steel knife chop the eggs roughly.
2. Melt the butter in a saucepan. Stir in the flour and cook for 30 seconds.
3. Add the liquid and stir until boiling. Add the other ingredients and check for seasoning.

Note: The liquid in which fish or chicken is cooked is suitable as stock. Chicken stock will do for veal, fish or chicken dishes, but fish stock is only good for fish, of course.

BLOND SAUCES

Velouté Sauce

20g/¾oz butter
20g/¾oz flour
290ml/½ pint white stock,
   strained and well skimmed
   (page 302)

Salt, pepper and a few drops of
   lemon juice

1.   Melt the butter, add the flour and cook, stirring, over a gentle heat until pale brown. Remove from the heat.
2.   Add the stock. Bring to the boil, stirring, and simmer until slightly syrupy and semi-clear. Taste and add seasoning and lemon juice.

Crab or Lobster Sauce

About 450g/1lb fish heads *or*
   bones *or* skin
860ml/1½ pints water
Few slices onion
Bunch of parsley
150ml/¼ pint milk
1 small can crab *or* lobster
   meat

30g/1oz butter
2 teaspoons flour
1 teaspoon paprika
1 tablespoon sherry
1 tablespoon thick cream
Salt and pepper

1.   Put the fish heads and/or the bones and skin into a saucepan with the water, onion and parsley. Cover and simmer for

312

30 minutes. Strain and mix the stock with the milk.

2. Break up the crab or lobster meat with a fork, removing any inedible membranes.

3. Melt the butter in a saucepan and stir in the flour. Cook gently for 30 seconds. Add the paprika and cook for a few more seconds. Draw the pan off the heat, blend in the stock and milk and return to the heat. Stir or whisk until the sauce boils.

4. Heat the crab or lobster meat in a separate pan with the sherry and when hot add it to the sauce. Stir in the cream and season with salt and pepper.

Note: If fresh lobster or crab shells are available, add them to the pan when making the stock. They will colour and flavour it excellently.

BROWN SAUCES

Demi-Glace
sauce espagnol
(short method)

2 tablespoons oil
1 small carrot, finely chopped
½ onion, finely chopped
½ stick celery, finely chopped
½ tablespoon flour
290ml/½ pint stock

½ teaspoon tomato purée
A few mushroom stalks
Bouquet garni of 2 parsley
    stalks, bay leaves, blade of
    mace

1. Heat the oil in a heavy saucepan, add the vegetables and fry until brown.

2. Stir in the flour and continue to cook slowly, stirring occasionally with a metal spoon, scraping the bottom of the pan to loosen the sediment. Cook to a good russet brown.

3. Draw aside, add three-quarters of the stock, the tomato purée

313

mushroom peelings and the bouquet garni.

4. Return to the heat, bring to the boil, half cover and simmer for 30 minutes.
5. Depouille twice to remove scum. Strain.

Depouille: To depouiller, add a splash of cold stock to the boiling liquid to help bring scum and fat to the surface. Tilting the pan slightly, skim the surface with a large metal spoon. Repeat as necessary.

Note: This will make about 150ml/¼ pint demi glace sauce.

Demi-Glace
(long method)

290ml/½ pint short-method demi-glace (page 313)

290ml/½ pint fond brun, or good brown stock (page 305)

1. Combine the demi-glace with the fond brun.
2. Simmer over gentle heat, skimming repeatedly until reduced by half.

Note: A good demi-glace looks like a rich syrupy gravy when hot, setting to a jelly when cold.

Sauce Robert

1 tablespoon chopped onion
A little butter
150ml/¼ pint vinegar
290ml/½ pint demi-glace (page 313)

3 gherkins, chopped
1 heaped teaspoon French mustard
1 teaspoon chopped fresh parsley

1. Soften the onion in the butter in a heavy pan over gentle heat. Add the vinegar and boil until the liquid has halved in quantity. Pour in the demi-glace, stir, and simmer for 15 minutes.
2. Immediately before serving add the chopped gherkin, mustard and parsley.

Madeira Sauce

3 tablespoons Madeira
1 teaspoon glace de viande
   (page 305)

290ml/½ pint demi-glace
   (page 314)
Nut of butter

1. Place the Madeira and glace de viande together in a small heavy pan. Boil until halved in quantity.
2. Add the demi-glace and heat up.
3. Beat in the nut of butter.

Sauce Poivrade

1 tablespoon oil
1 small onion, chopped
1 shallot, chopped
1 small carrot, chopped
3 tablespoons red wine
5 tablespoons vinegar
2 parsley stalks

1 bay leaf
15g/½oz butter
15g/½oz flour
150ml/¼ pint beef stock (cold)
4 juniper berries, crushed
Salt and freshly ground black
   pepper

1. Heat the oil and soften the onion, shallot and carrots in it. Add the wine, vinegar, parsley stalks and bay leaf and boil over a moderate heat to reduce by half. Set aside.
2. Melt the butter, stir in the flour and cook until a pale biscuit brown. Pour on three-quarters of the stock. Bring to the boil, stirring well. Add the wine and vegetables and simmer for 30 minutes.
3. Add the juniper berries and seasoning. Simmer for a further 10 minutes. Strain through a very fine sieve, tammy strainer or piece of muslin into a clean pan. Return to the heat and simmer for 20 minutes.
4. Dépouille with the remaining cold stock while the sauce simmers. The sauce should be thick and syrupy. Taste for seasoning.

Sauce Bordelaise

1 shallot
6 peppercorns
Pinch of thyme
1 bay leaf

1 glass claret
290ml/½ pint demi-glace
(page 313)

1. Place the shallot, peppercorns, thyme, bay leaf and claret into a small heavy pan and boil rapidly until reduced by half. Strain into the demi-glace sauce and reheat.
2. Bring to the boil, stirring continuously, and simmer for 2 minutes. Pour into a warmed gravy boat.

Note: Sauce Bordelaise, often served with steaks, should not be confused with Steak Bordelaise, which is topped with chopped, cooked shallot and pieces of beef marrow. A steak served with the above sauce should be described as Steak à la Sauce Bordelaise.

EMULSION SAUCES

Mayonnaise

2 egg yolks
1 teaspoon pale mustard
290ml/½ pint olive oil *or*
  150ml/¼ pint each olive and
  salad oil

Squeeze of lemon juice
1 tablespoon wine vinegar
Salt and pepper

1. Put the yolks into a bowl with the mustard and beat well with a wooden spoon.
2. Add the oil, literally drop by drop, beating all the time. The mixture should be very thick by the time half the oil is added.

3. Beat in the lemon juice.
4. Resume pouring in the oil, going rather more confidently now, but alternating the dribbles of oil with small quantities of vinegar.
5. Add salt and pepper to taste.

Note: If the mixture curdles, another egg yolk should be beaten in a separate bowl, and the curdled mixture beaten drop by drop into it.

Elizabeth Sauce

This sauce was invented by the staff at the Cordon Bleu School for the Coronation in 1953 and has become a classic.

1 small onion, chopped	Salt and pepper
2 teaspoons oil	2 teaspoons apricot jam
2 teaspoons curry powder	1 slice lemon
½ teaspoon tomato purée	1 teaspoon lemon juice
3 tablespoons water	290ml/½ pint mayonnaise
1 small bay leaf	(page 316)
½ wineglass red wine	2 tablespoons double cream

1. Cook the onion gently for 4 minutes in the oil.
2. Add the curry powder and fry gently for 1 minute.
3. Add the tomato purée, water, bay leaf, wine, salt, pepper, jam, lemon slice and juice and simmer for 8 minutes.
4. Strain the mixture, pushing as much as possible through the sieve.
5. Use this sauce to flavour the mayonnaise to the desired strength.
6. Half-whip the cream and stir into the sauce.

Green Mayonnaise

Bunch of watercress
290ml/½ pint mayonnaise

1. Pick over the watercress to remove stalks and yellowed leaves. Wash well.
2. Chop roughly.
3. Add to the mayonnaise and blend in a liquidizer to a smooth sauce.

Note: Cooked and very well drained spinach can be used instead of watercress.

Tartare Sauce

150ml/¼ pint mayonnaise (page 316)
1 tablespoon chopped capers
1 tablespoon chopped gherkins
1 tablespoon chopped fresh parsley
1 shallot, finely chopped
Squeeze of lemon juice

Mix everything together. Taste and add salt or pepper as necessary.

Note: Chopped hardboiled egg makes a delicious addition.

Remoulade Sauce

150ml/¼ pint mayonnaise (page 316)
1 level teaspoon Dijon mustard
½ tablespoon finely chopped capers
½ tablespoon finely chopped gherkin
½ tablespoon finely chopped fresh tarragon *or* chervil
1 anchovy fillet, finely chopped

Mix all the ingredients together.

Note: Remoulade sauce is a mayonnaise with a predominant mustard flavour. The other ingredients, though good, are not always present.

French Dressing (*Vinaigrette*)

3 tablespoons salad oil
1 tablespoon wine vinegar
Salt and pepper

Put all the ingredients into a screw-top jar. Before using shake until well emulsified.

Note I: This dressing can be flavoured with crushed garlic, mustard, a pinch of sugar, chopped fresh herbs etc., as desired.

Note II: If kept refrigerated the dressing will more easily form an emulsion when whisked or shaken, and has a slightly thicker consistency.

Beurre Blanc

225g/½lb butter, unsalted   3 tablespoons water
1 tablespoon shallot, chopped   Salt, white pepper
3 tablespoons wine vinegar   Squeeze of lemon

1. Chill the butter then cut it in three lengthwise, then across into thin slices. Keep cold.
2. Put the shallot, vinegar and water into a thick-bottomed sauté-pan or small shallow saucepan. Boil until the liquid remaining is about 2 tablespoons.
3. Lower the heat under the pan. Using a wire whisk and plenty

of vigorous continuous whisking, gradually add the butter, piece by piece. The process should take about five minutes and the sauce should become thick, creamy and pale – rather like a thin hollandaise. Add salt, pepper and lemon juice.

Easy Hollandaise Sauce

3 tablespoons wine vinegar
6 peppercorns
1 bay leaf
Blade of mace
2 tablespoons water

1 egg
2 egg yolks
110g/$\frac{1}{4}$lb melted butter
Lemon juice
Salt

1. Put the vinegar, peppercorns, bay leaf and mace in a small saucepan and reduce by boiling until only a tablespoon of liquid remains. Remove the solid ingredients and take the pan off the heat. Add the water.
2. Put the yolks and eggs into the pan with the vinegar and water. Whisk, off the heat, until thick and fluffy.
3. Return to a gentle heat and, whisking continuously, slowly add the melted butter. Keep whisking, removing from the heat if the sauce gets more than warm, until the sauce is a thick emulsion. Remove from the heat and add lemon juice and salt to taste.

Hollandaise Sauce

3 tablespoons wine vinegar
6 peppercorns
1 bay leaf
Blade of mace

2 egg yolks
Salt
110g/$\frac{1}{4}$lb softened butter
Lemon juice

1. Place the vinegar, peppercorns, bay leaf and mace in a small heavy saucepan and reduce by boiling to a tablespoon.
2. Cream the egg yolks with a pinch of salt and a nut of butter

TARRAGON CHICKEN

GLAZED BACON JOINT

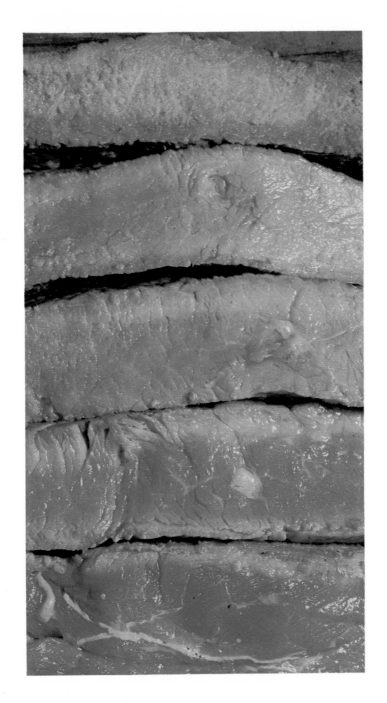

STEAK. From top: well done, medium, medium rare, rare and blue

VEAL AND HAM RAISED PIE. Moulding hot water crust over upturned jar

in a small bowl. Set this in a bain-marie on a gentle heat. With a wooden spoon beat the mixture until slightly thickened, taking care that the water immediately around the bowl does not boil. Mix well.

3. Strain on the reduced vinegar. Mix well. Beat in the softened butter bit by bit, increasing the temperature as the sauce thickens and you add more butter, but take care that the water does not boil.

4. When the sauce has become light and thick take it off the heat and beat or whisk for 1 minute. Taste for seasoning and add lemon juice, and salt if necessary. Keep warm by standing the bowl in hot water. Serve warm.

Note: Hollandaise sauce will set too firmly if allowed to get cold and it will curdle if overheated.

Herby Hollandaise Sauce

1 shallot, finely chopped
2 tablespoons chopped fresh tarragon
2 tablespoons chopped fresh chervil *or* parsley
4 tablespoons wine vinegar
6 peppercorns

1 bay leaf
3 large egg yolks
170g/6oz unsalted butter
Pinch of salt
Pinch of cayenne
Lemon juice

1. Put the shallot, half the tarragon and chervil, the wine vinegar, peppercorns and bay leaf into a small saucepan and boil until the liquid is reduced to about a tablespoon. Cool slightly and strain into a small pudding basin. Add the egg yolks and mix well.

2. Fit the basin over a saucepan of water making sure that the water does not touch the bottom of the basin. (Alternatively set the basin in one end of a roasting tin full of water. Place the empty end of the tin over enough heat to make the water

bubble only in that area, leaving the water immediately around your basin hot but not bubbling.) Get the water under and around the bowl to simmering point, stirring the egg yolk mixture with a wooden spoon all the time. Now gradually add the butter, a teaspoon at a time. The trick is to add the next small blob of butter only when the last one is safely absorbed without curdling. The mixture must stay warm enough for the egg yolk to thicken slightly but must never boil or it will curdle. When all the butter is absorbed you should have a sauce the consistency of soft mayonnaise. Add salt, cayenne and lemon juice (very little) to taste. Stir in the remaining herbs. Serve in a warmed sauce boat.

Béarnaise Sauce

3 tablespoons wine vinegar
6 peppercorns
1 bay leaf
1 small shallot, chopped
Sprig of fresh tarragon
Sprig of fresh chervil
2 egg yolks

Salt and pepper
110g/¼lb softened butter
1 teaspoon chopped fresh
  tarragon
1 teaspoon chopped fresh
  chervil

1. Place the vinegar, peppercorns, bay leaf, shallot, tarragon and chervil in a heavy saucepan and reduce over medium heat to a tablespoon.
2. In a small bowl cream the egg yolks with a pinch of salt and a nut of butter. Set the bowl in a bain-marie over a gentle heat. With a wooden spoon, beat the mixture until slightly thickened.
3. Strain on the reduced vinegar. Mix well. Beat in the softened butter bit by bit, increasing the temperature as the sauce thickens and you add more butter, but take care that the water does not boil immediately round the bowl.
4. When all the butter is added, stir in the chopped tarragon and chervil. Taste for seasoning.

MISCELLANEOUS SAUCES

Apple Sauce

450g/1lb cooking apples
Finely grated rind of $\frac{1}{4}$ lemon
3 tablespoons water

1 teaspoon sugar
15g/$\frac{1}{2}$oz butter
Pinch of cinnamon

1. Peel, quarter, core and slice the apples.
2. Place in a heavy saucepan with the lemon rind, water and sugar. Cover with a lid and cook very slowly until the apples are soft.
3. Beat in the butter and cinnamon. Serve hot or cold.

Horseradish Cream

1–1$\frac{1}{2}$ heaped tablespoons
   grated fresh horseradish
2 teaspoons wine vinegar
$\frac{1}{2}$ teaspoon made English
   mustard

Salt and pepper
Sugar to taste
150ml/$\frac{1}{4}$ pint double cream,
   lightly whipped

Mix all the ingredients together.

Mint Sauce

Large handful of fresh mint
2 tablespoons caster sugar

2 tablespoons hot water
2 tablespoons vinegar

1. Wash the mint and shake it dry.

2. Remove the stalks, and chop the leaves finely. Place in a bowl with the sugar.
3. Pour in the hot water and leave for 5 minutes to dissolve the sugar.
4. Add the vinegar and leave to soak for 1–2 hours.

Note: When mint is plentiful it is a good idea to chop a quantity of it and mix it with golden syrup. This base can then be used for instant mint sauce, vinegar and boiling water being added when the sauce is required.

Bread Sauce

1 large peeled onion
6 cloves
290ml/½ pint milk
1 bay leaf
10 peppercorns *or* 1 pinch of
   white pepper

Pinch of nutmeg
Salt
55g/2oz fresh white
   breadcrumbs
55g/2oz butter
2 tablespoons cream (optional)

1. Cut the onion in half. Stick the cloves into the onion pieces and put with the milk and bay leaf into a saucepan.
2. Add the peppercorns, a pinch of nutmeg, and a good pinch of salt. Leave to stand for 30 minutes or more if you can. If not, bring very slowly to the boil, and then simmer for 10 minutes. If you have had time to let the milk infuse (stand with its flavourings) you will not need to simmer it. But bring it to the boil very slowly just the same.
3. Strain the hot milk on to the breadcrumbs. Add the butter and cream. Mix and return to the saucepan.
4. Reheat the sauce carefully without reboiling.
5. If it has become too thick by the time it is needed, beat in more hot milk. It should be creamy.

Tomato Sauce

396g/14oz tin peeled plum
   tomatoes
1 small onion, chopped
1 carrot, chopped
1 stick celery, chopped
½ garlic clove, crushed
1 bay leaf
Fresh parsley stalks

Salt and pepper
Juice of ½ lemon
Dash of Worcestershire sauce
1 teaspoon sugar
1 teaspoon chopped fresh *or*
   1 pinch of dried basil *or*
   thyme

1. Put all the ingredients together in a thick-bottomed pan and simmer over medium heat for 30 minutes.
2. Sieve the sauce and return it to the pan.
3. If it is too thin reduce by boiling rapidly. Check the seasoning, adding more salt or sugar if necessary.

Lemon Cream Sauce

1 tablespoon lemon juice
1 tablespoon olive oil
Grated rind of ½ lemon

Salt and freshly ground black
   pepper
½ teaspoon sugar
3 tablespoons single cream

Mix all the ingredients together, adding the cream last.

Cumberland Sauce

2 oranges
1 lemon
225g/½lb redcurrant jelly
1 shallot, chopped

150ml/¼ pint port *or* red wine
½ teaspoon pale mustard
Pinch of cayenne pepper
Pinch of ground ginger

1. Peel one orange and the lemon finely, removing only the outer skin, but no pith. Cut the rind into very fine needleshreds.
2. Squeeze all the fruit juice and strain into a pan, add the remaining ingredients with the needleshreds. Simmer for 10 minutes. Leave to cool.

Makes 290ml/½ *pint*

Soured Cream Sauce

½ carton yoghurt   Salt and pepper
½ carton soured cream   ½ garlic clove, crushed

Mix all ingredients together.

Thick Onion and Mint Sauce

1 large Spanish onion   2 tablespoons chopped
55g/2oz butter   fresh mint
3 tablespoons water   Salt and freshly ground black
                                      pepper

1. Chop the onion very finely. Cook slowly in the butter and water until very soft but not coloured. Push through a sieve, or liquidize in a blender.
2. Mix in the finely chopped mint and season with salt and pepper.

Pesto Sauce for Pasta

2 garlic cloves   150ml/¼ pint olive oil
2 large cups basil leaves   Salt
55g/2oz fresh Parmesan cheese, 55g/2oz pinenuts
  finely grated

326

1. In a liquidizer or mortar, grind the garlic and basil together to a paste. Add the cheese, oil and plenty of salt. Keep in a covered jar in a cool place.
2. Add the pinenuts just before serving on freshly boiled pasta.

Note: Pesto is sometimes made with walnuts instead of pinenuts, and the nuts may be pounded with the other ingredients to give a smooth paste.

DIPS AND SPREADS

Soft pâtés, dips and spreads are useful served with raw vegetables (crudités), biscuits, pain grillé or toast, or on cocktail canapés. Tartare dip is good with fried fish or chicken, and cream cheese dip is delicious on iced consommé. Quantities in these recipes would fill two good-sized cups.

Avocado Dip

2 slices fatty bacon
2 avocados, mashed
1 garlic clove, crushed
1 tablespoon chopped fresh
  chives

225g/½lb cream cheese
6 walnuts, chopped
Juice of ½ lemon

Grill the bacon until crisp and chop finely. Combine everything else, beat well, and add the bacon.

Mock Caviar Cream

290ml/½ pint thick cream
1 small jar Danish lump fish roe
Juice of 1 lemon

Salt and freshly ground black
  pepper

Whip the cream stiffly, stir in the lump fish roe and lemon juice.
Season with salt and pepper.

Tartare Dip

2 tablespoons chopped
  gherkins
2 tablespoons chopped capers
1 tablespoon chopped fresh
  parsley
½ small onion, finely chopped

290ml/½ pint mayonnaise
Salt and freshly ground black
  pepper
Squeeze of lemon

Mix the gherkins, parsley, capers and onion with the mayonnaise.
Season with salt, pepper and lemon juice.

Cream Cheese Dip

225g/½lb cream cheese
1 tablespoon soured cream
2 tablespoons chopped fresh
  chives

Salt and freshly ground black
  pepper
A little milk

Mix the cream cheese with the soured cream and chives, season
with salt and pepper and add enough milk to bring the dip to
the required consistency.

Tomato Dip

Handful of fresh parsley
½ onion
290ml/½ pint tomato ketchup
1 teaspoon French mustard

1 garlic clove, crushed
  (optional)
3 tablespoons soured cream

1. Wash the parsley stalks and leaves and chop them finely. Chop the onion.
2. Mix everything together. (Alternatively liquidize all the ingredients except the woody parsley stalks.)

Blue Cheese Dip

225g/½lb blue cheese
1 shallot, minced
1 teaspoon vinegar

Salt and freshly ground black pepper
4 tablespoons soured cream

Beat the cheese with a wooden spoon and mix in the shallot and vinegar. Season with salt and pepper and beat in the soured cream.

Mustard Dip

150ml/¼ pint mayonnaise
150ml/¼ pint soured cream
2 tablespoons Moutarde de Meaux *or* other mustard containing the seeds

Combine all the ingredients.

SAVOURY BUTTERS

Flavoured butters are good served with grilled or fried fish or shellfish, or with plainly grilled chicken or meat dishes. Also excellent with hot toast or bread.

After preparation the butter should be shaped into a cylinder, rolled up in foil or damp greaseproof paper and chilled in the refrigerator. It can then be sliced and used as required. If it is to be kept for more than two days it should be frozen.

329

Almond Butter

55g/2oz butter
30g/1oz ground almonds

Squeeze of lemon
Salt and white pepper

Beat the butter to a light cream. Mix the almonds with the lemon juice and beat this paste into the softened butter. Season to taste.

Anchovy Butter

2 anchovy fillets
½ garlic clove
55g/2oz butter

Freshly ground black pepper
Anchovy essence

Pound the anchovies and garlic and mix well with the butter. Season with pepper and anchovy essence.

Garlic Butter

55g/2oz butter
1 large garlic clove, crushed
  with salt

2 tablespoons lemon juice
Salt and pepper

Beat all the ingredients together.

Green Butter

2 sprigs watercress
Small bunch of fresh tarragon
Sprig of parsley

55g/2oz butter
1 shallot, minced
Salt and pepper

1.   Blanch the watercress, tarragon and parsley for 30 seconds

in boiling salted water. Refresh under running cold water. Drain well and pat dry. Chop very finely.

2. Cream the butter and beat in the shallot, chopped green herbs and spinach. Add salt and pepper. Chill.

Maître d'Hôtel Butter

55g/2oz butter
2 teaspoons lemon juice
1 teaspoon finely chopped
    parsley

Salt and pepper

Cream the butter, stir in the lemon juice and parsley and season to taste. Mix well and chill.

Mint and Mustard Butter

110g/¼lb butter
1 teaspoon Dijon mustard
1 tablespoon finely chopped
    fresh mint

Salt and freshly ground black
pepper

1. Cream the butter until very soft and beat in the mustard and mint. Season with salt and pepper.
2. On a piece of damp greaseproof paper or foil shape the butter into a cylinder and wrap up. Refrigerate until hard. Serve cut in ·5cm/¼in slices.

5
Main Dishes

FISH

Dressed Crab

900g/2lb live crab (weighed
  before cooking)
Salt and freshly ground black
  pepper
Lemon juice
Mustard
Breadcrumbs

Egg yolks, sieved
Fresh parsley
Crisp lettuce
Mayonnaise (page 316)
Tartare sauce (page 318)
Brown bread and butter

1. Place the live crab in a pan of well salted water (about 170g/6oz salt to 2·5 litres/4 pints water), cover and bring to the boil. Simmer, allowing 15 minutes to each pound of crab (weighed in the shell). Remove from the pan and allow to cool.

2. Lay the crab on its back. Twist off the legs and claws. Cracking round the natural line (visible near the edge), remove the pale belly shell and discard it. Remove and throw away the small sac at the top of the crab body and the spongy lungs which line the edge.

3. Have 2 bowls ready, one for white meat, one for brown. Scoop out all the meat from the crab. Wash and dry the shell.

4. Crack the large claws but do not remove the meat.

5. With a larding needle poke out the remaining meat from the legs, and add it to the white meat in the bowl.

6. To dress the crab: cream the brown meat, season with lemon juice, salt, pepper and mustard. Add enough breadcrumbs to bind the mixture. Arrange this down the centre of the shell and pile the white meat up at each side. Decorate with neat lines of sieved egg yolks and chopped parsley.

7. Place on a platter, with the interlocking crab claws on a bed of crisp lettuce. Serve mayonnaise or tartare sauce and brown bread and butter.

Note: This is the usual method of cooking crab. But recently the RSPCA have suggested that live shellfish should be put into *previously* boiled water which has been allowed to cool completely. The theory is that the shellfish become unconscious in the de-oxygenated water before it is slowly brought to the boil.

Serves 3

Serbian Roast Carp

1·5 kilos/3lb carp
1 teaspoon salt
55g/2oz streaky bacon
2 green peppers
2 tomatoes

450g/1lb boiled potatoes, sliced
290ml/½ pint soured cream
85g/3oz melted butter
1 teaspoon paprika
Fresh parsley

1. Set the oven to 180°C/350°F, gas mark 4.

2. Clean the carp and remove the scales. Rub all over with salt. Cut evenly spaced slits in the flesh and stuff slices of bacon, green pepper and tomato in the openings.

3. Grease an ovenproof dish and arrange slices of boiled potato in the bottom. Place the carp on top.

4. Mix the soured cream with the melted butter and paprika and pour it over the fish. Bake, basting frequently, for about 1 hour or until tender.

5. Garnish with plenty of chopped parsley.

Serves 4–6

Eel Pie

340g/¾lb flour-quantity puff
  pastry (pages 649–50)
900g/2lb smoked eel
900g/2lb fresh spinach, well
  washed
Grated nutmeg and freshly
  ground black pepper

For the sauce:
15g/½oz flour
150ml/¼ pint milk
55g/2oz unsalted butter
2 egg yolks

Beaten egg

1. Set the oven to 200°C/400°F, gas mark 6. Wet a baking sheet.
2. Take one-third of the pastry and roll it out to a rectangle, 15cm × 20cm/6in × 8in. Place on a wet baking tray and prick with a fork. Bake to a good brown (about 20 minutes). Do not turn the oven off. Leave the pastry on a wire rack to cool.
3. Meanwhile prepare the fillings. Skin the eel and take it off the bone as neatly as possible.
4. Cook the spinach in a large covered pan with a cupful of water (do not add salt if the eel is very salty). Drain thoroughly, chop roughly, and season with nutmeg and a little freshly ground black pepper.
5. To make the sauce: melt 15g/½oz of the butter, add the flour and cook for 30 seconds. Draw off the heat and stir in the milk. Return to the heat and stir until boiling.
6. Cool slightly, then beat in the rest of the butter and egg yolks. Season with a little freshly ground black pepper.
8. Arrange half the spinach on the cooked pastry base and cover with the eel. Spread the béchamel sauce over the eel and cover with remaining spinach.
9. Roll the remaining 225g/8oz puff pastry on a floured board into a 'blanket' large enough to cover the whole pie. Lay it gently over the spinach. With a sharp knife cut off the corners of the 'blanket', but do not throw away these trimmings.
10. Lift one length of the raw pastry and brush the underside with a little beaten egg. Tuck the 'blanket' neatly underneath

the cooked base. Repeat with the other three sides.

11. Shape the trimmings into leaves. Brush the whole pie with beaten egg. Lay on the pastry leaves and brush again.

12. Bake for 40–45 minutes.

Serve hot or cold.

Note: To counteract the saltiness of the smoked eel, salt is not added to the sauce or to the spinach. But if the smoked eel is mild in flavour, salt may of course be added to spinach and sauce.

Serves 6

Fish Pie

1 kilo/2lb fillet of haddock,
   whiting, cod *or* a mixture of
   any of them
425ml/¾ pint milk
½ onion, sliced
6 peppercorns
1 bay leaf
Salt and pepper
5 hardboiled eggs

1 tablespoon chopped fresh
   parsley
30g/1oz butter
30g/1oz flour
2 tablespoons cream
340g/¾lb mashed potatoes
   made with 675g/1½lb
   potatoes (page 275)
Butter

1. Set the oven to 180°C/350°F, gas mark 4.
2. Lay the fish fillets in a roasting pan.
3. Heat the milk with the sliced onion, the peppercorns, bay leaf and a pinch of salt.
4. Pour over the fish and cook in the oven until the fish is firm and creamy-looking (about 25 minutes).
5. Strain off the milk, reserving it for the sauce.
6. Flake the fish into a pie dish.
7. Halve the hardboiled eggs and add them to the fish.
8. Sprinkle over the chopped parsley.
9. Heat the butter in a saucepan, stir in the flour and cook for 30 seconds. Draw off the heat and add the milk.

10. Return to the heat and stir while bringing slowly to the boil. Taste and add salt and pepper as needed. Stir in the cream and pour over the fish, mixing it with a palette knife or spoon.
11. Spread a layer of mashed potatoes on the top and mark with a fork in a criss-cross pattern. Dot a little butter over the surface.
12. Brown in a hot oven (230°C/450°F, gas mark 8) for about 10 minutes.

Serves 6

Fritto Misto

About 450g/1lb mixture of raw prawns, crayfish tails, crab meat, sole, whiting and whitebait (prepared weight)

Lemon juice
Salt and pepper
Oil *or* fat for deep frying

For the batter:
5g/¼oz fresh yeast
150ml/¼ pint tepid water
110g/¼lb plain flour

Pinch of salt
1 scant tablespoon olive oil
1 egg white

For the garnish:
Deep-fried parsley (page 787)

1. Mix the yeast with the water.
2. Sift the flour and salt into a bowl. Make a well in the centre and pour in the liquid and oil.
3. With a wooden spoon, beat this centre mixture, gradually drawing in the surrounding flour by degrees. Leave in a warm place to rise for 30 minutes.
4. Prepare the fish, shelling them or cutting into strips as appropriate. Sprinkle with lemon juice and pepper and leave for 30 minutes or so.
5. Beat the egg white until stiff and fold it into the batter.

6. Drain the fish. Dip into the batter, coating each piece completely.
7. Heat the fat until a drop of batter will frizzle slowly. Deep fry the pieces, a few at a time, in the hot fat until the batter is golden brown. Drain an absorbent paper, sprinkle with salt and pile on to a serving dish. Garnish with deep-fried parsley.

Serves 4

Grilled Fish Cutlets

This recipe is suitable for brill, cod, halibut, haddock, turbot or salmon cutlets. The pieces of fish should, if possible, be cut to a uniform thickness.

Four 170g/6oz fish cutlets   Freshly ground black pepper
Melted butter   Juice of $\frac{1}{2}$ lemon

For the garnish:
Tender young fresh parsley sprigs *or* watercress
Lemon wedges

1. Heat the grill. Brush the cutlets and the bottom of the grill pan with melted butter. Season the cutlets with pepper and lemon juice. Lay them in the grill tray (not on the wire tray where they might stick).
2. Grill them until pale brown. Turn over and brush with more melted butter. Season again with pepper and lemon juice and grill for a further 3 minutes or until cooked. They will feel firm to the touch, and the flesh will flake easily.
3. Serve on a heated dish with the pan juices poured over, garnished with parsley or watercress and lemon wedges.

Serves 4

Haddock Dugléré

Four 170g/6oz fresh haddock
   fillets
Salt and freshly ground black
   pepper
290ml/$\frac{1}{2}$ pint fish stock
150ml/$\frac{1}{4}$ pint white wine
30g/1oz butter
30g/1oz flour

150ml/$\frac{1}{4}$ pint cream
2 large tomatoes, skinned,
   seeded and cut into
   slivers
1 tablespoon chopped fresh
   parsley
1 tablespoon chopped fresh
   chives

1. Set the oven to 180°C/350°F, gas mark 4. Wash and season the fillets.
2. Lay the fish in an ovenproof dish. Pour over the strained fish stock and the wine. Cover with buttered greaseproof paper or foil and bake in the oven for 15–20 minutes.
3. Melt the butter in a saucepan, add the flour and stir for 30 seconds. Draw off the heat and strain in the liquor from the fish. Whisk out any lumps and reboil, stirring. Add salt and pepper to taste, and the cream. Add the tomatoes, parsley and chives but do not cook any more.
4. Skin the fillets of fish and lay them in a serving dish. Pour over the sauce.

Serves 4

Haddock with English Egg Sauce

1·5 kilos/3lb haddock
570ml/1 pint milk

A bouquet garni of:
   Bunch of parsley
   1 stick celery
   1 bay leaf
   Sprig of thyme

1 onion, sliced

Salt and pepper
570ml/1 pint English egg sauce
   (page 311)

1. Set the oven at 170 C/325 F, gas mark 3.
2. Wash the fish, scrape off any scales and lay in a roasting tin.
3. Pour in the milk and add the onion, bouquet garni and seasoning.
4. Cover the dish with greased paper or a lid and bake in the slowish oven until the fish is tender to the touch of a skewer (40–45 minutes).
5. Take out the fish and dish it on an ovenproof platter.
6. Cover again with the paper and keep warm while you make the sauce.
7. Before serving skin the fish and pour over the sauce.

Serves 4

Halibut au Gratin

4 halibut steaks
For the court bouillon:
570ml/1 pint water
2 tablespoons vinegar
1 carrot, sliced
1 onion, sliced
4 cloves
Salt
6 peppercorns
Parsley stalk, sprig of thyme, bay leaf

For the sauce:
30g/1oz butter
20g/$\frac{3}{4}$oz flour
150ml/$\frac{1}{4}$ pint fish liquor
150ml/$\frac{1}{4}$ pint milk

For the topping:
Dried breadcrumbs
30g/1oz Gruyère *or* strong Cheddar cheese, grated

1. Make up the court bouillon: combine the ingredients, bring to the boil, simmer for 10 minutes and cool.
2. Set the oven to 180°C/350°F, gas mark 4. Place the halibut steaks in a buttered dish. Strain on the court bouillon and cover with a piece of greased paper, foil, or a lid. Poach in the oven or over a gentle heat for 10–15 minutes, until the fish feels firm to the touch.
3. Lift out the fish. Strain the fish liquor into a saucepan and reduce it by rapid boiling to 150ml/$\frac{1}{4}$ pint.

4. Reduce the oven temperature to 70°C/150°F, gas mark ¼.
5. Remove the fish steaks carefully from the dish. Skin them and take out the bone. Drain well. Place them on an ovenproof serving dish and keep warm, covered, in the cool oven.
6. Heat up the grill.
7. Make the sauce: melt the butter in a small pan and stir in the flour. Cook for 1 minute and then remove from the heat. Pour in the fish stock and milk. Return to the heat and bring slowly to the boil, stirring until you have a smooth creamy sauce. Simmer for 2 minutes. Season with salt and pepper as necessary.
8. Spoon the sauce over the fish. Sprinkle with breadcrumbs and grated cheese.
9. Grill until well browned.

Serves 4

Inkfish Stew

Preparation must begin one day in advance

675/1½lb fresh squid (about 3–4 medium-sized squid)
425ml/¾ pint red wine

55g/1½oz butter
2 garlic cloves
1 medium onion, sliced

1. Prepare the squid: pull the intestinal bag gently but firmly from inside the body and discard it and the rib-like piece of transparent cartilege called the pen. Scrape off the purplish-red skin from the body and wash the body well inside and out. Cut into rings – there are two edible fins which should be included. Cut the tentacles from the head and chop them into 2cm/¾in pieces. Add them to the squid rings. In the soft part still attached to the head there will be a long ink sac (in a white skin): remove this and break it into a bowl. Discard the head.
2. Marinate the squid in the ink and red wine overnight.

3. Melt the butter, add the garlic and onions and cook slowly until soft but not coloured.
4. Drain the marinated squid (reserving the liquid) and add it to the frying pan. Sauté for 4 minutes. Add the wine and ink and simmer for about 1½ hours or until the squid is tender.

Serves 4

Boiled Lobster

Two 900g/2lb live lobsters

For the court bouillon:
1 litre/2 pints water
225g/½lb carrots, sliced
1 medium onion, sliced
1 bay leaf
Sprig of thyme

30g/1oz salt
150ml/¼ pint wine vinegar
Bunch of parsley
10 peppercorns

To serve hot:
Hollandaise sauce (page 320)
  or melted butter

To serve cold:
Mayonnaise (page 316)

1. Simmer all the court bouillon ingredients together for 30 minutes. Strain and allow to get completely cold.
2. Weigh the lobsters, then put them into the cold court bouillon and leave them for 30 minutes.
3. Bring to the boil, cover and simmer for 8 minutes per pound weight of the lobsters. Lift out. Allow to cool before splitting if to be served cold.
4. Split the lobsters in half, remove the stomach sac near the head and the dark thread running the length of the body.
5. Serve with hollandaise sauce or melted butter if to be eaten hot, with mayonnaise if cold.

Serves 4

Lobster Thermidor

4 small live lobsters
3 tablespoons oil
30g/1oz butter
1 teaspoon Dijon mustard

1 level tablespoon grated
   Parmesan cheese
Browned crumbs

For the mornay sauce:
20g/¾oz butter
20g/¾oz flour
290ml/½ pint milk

Salt, pepper and cayenne
2 tablespoons grated very fresh
   Parmesan cheese

For the Bercy reduction:
1 tablespoon chopped shallot
110g/¼lb clarified butter
  (page 784)

1 glass white wine

1. First make the mornay sauce: melt the butter, add the flour and cook for 1 minute. Draw the pan off the heat and stir in the milk. Return to the heat and bring slowly to the boil, stirring continuously until you have a creamy white sauce.
2. Season with salt, pepper and cayenne and simmer for 2–3 minutes. Remove from the heat, add the Parmesan and taste for seasoning.
3. Next, the lobsters: set the oven to 180°C/350°F, gas mark 4. Kill each lobster by pushing a sharp knife through its nerve centre (marked by a well-defined cross on the back of the head). When you pierce the middle of the cross the lobster will die instantly, although it will still move alarmingly.
4. Lay the lobster flat out and split it in half lengthwise. Remove the little stomach sac from near the head and the dark thread-like intestine.
5. Heat up the oil and butter and sauté the lobsters, flesh side down, for 5 minutes. Then put the whole pan in the oven for 15 minutes.
6. Make the bercy reduction: soften the shallot in the clarified butter over gentle heat until soft and transparent. Add the wine and boil fast until reduced to 3 tablespoons. Mix this

bercy reduction, and the liquid from the lobster pan, with the mornay sauce. Heat up and add the mustard.

7. Remove all the meat from the lobster shells. Chop up the meat from the claws and the creamy greenish flesh from the head. Cut the tail meat into scallops. Mix the chopped meat with some of the sauce and place this in the bottom of the shell. Place the scalloped meat, rounded side up, on top of this. Coat with the remaining sauce and sprinkle with cheese and crumbs.

8. Place in the oven for 5–10 minutes to reheat and then brown under the grill. Serve 2 half-lobsters to each person.

Serves 4

Lobster and Chicken Salad

Two 340g/¾lb cooked lobsters
225g/½lb cooked chicken meat
A few drops anchovy essence
Juice of ½ lemon
A little Tabasco sauce
290ml/½ pint mayonnaise
  (page 316)

1 tablespoon cream
2 hardboiled eggs
1 level tablespoon chopped
  fresh parsley
1 hearty lettuce
A little French dressing
  (page 319)

1. Place each cold lobster with the head to your left and the tail spread out flat to your right. Hold firmly by the head and with a very sharp knife push the point of the blade into the cross on the top of the head. Carefully cut all the way down the shell to the end of the tail. Turn the lobster around and split the head in two. In the head there is a small bag or stomach sac which must be removed. Remove also the intestine which is a thin grey or black line running down through the tail meat.

2. Take out the remaining lobster meat and chop roughly. Place in a bowl. Crack the claws and remove the meat.

3. Take the chicken off the bone and cut into dice about the same size as the lobster meat. Add the anchovy essence, lemon juice

343

and Tabasco to the mayonnaise and use half of it to mix with all the lobster meat and chicken. Pile this mixture into the lobster shells.

4. Add the cream to the remaining mayonnaise and coat it neatly over each shell. Place on a serving dish.

5. Halve the hardboiled eggs and sieve the yolks. Mix this with the chopped parsley and sprinkle over the lobsters.

6. Remove the outer leaves of the lettuce, wash, dry and shred coarsely. Shred the egg whites and toss with the lettuce and French dressing. Surround the lobsters with the salad.

Serves 4

Stuffed Mullet

900g/2lb grey mullet
1 small can salmon
1 tablespoon fresh chopped
  parsley
Lemon juice
1 level tablespoon fresh white
  crumbs
1 tablespoon cream

1 tablespoon beaten egg
Salt and freshly ground black
  pepper
Oil (preferably olive)
2 bay leaves
Cucumber slices *or* watercress
  to garnish

1. Wash the fish and scrape off the scales. Split down the belly and remove first the entrails and then, opening the fish out more, the backbone and bones: to do this lay the opened fish, skin side up, on a board and press firmly with the heel of your hand. Snip the backbone at tail and head and ease it out, along with its bones.

2. Set the oven to 180°C/350°F, gas mark 4.

3. Skin and bone the salmon and break up the flesh with a fork. Put into a bowl.

4. Add the parsley, lemon juice, breadcrumbs and cream. Add enough beaten egg to hold the stuffing together. Season with salt and pepper.

5. Stuff this mixture into the fish and sew it up with fine string.

6. Brush the fish with oil, season with salt, pepper and lemon juice. Put the bay leaves on top of the fish. Wrap up in oiled foil.
7. Bake until tender – about 35 minutes.
8. Remove the foil and the string. Serve hot or cold, garnished with watercress or cucumber slices.

Note I: Grey mullet is a delicious fish, but not very pretty to look at. Opening the foil at the top to allow the fish to brown while cooking produces a better-looking dish. Alternatively the fish can be coated with sauce just before serving hot, or skinned and coated with creamy mayonnaise when cold. Or a good handful of chopped fresh herbs scattered generously over the fish will greatly improve its appearance.

Note II: A large very fresh mackerel makes a good substitute for grey mullet. Sea bass, though expensive, is the best of all.

Serves 2

Monkfish with Herby Hollandaise

900g/2lb piece of monkfish

For the court bouillon:

570ml/1 pint water	1 bay leaf
5 tablespoons wine vinegar	Stick of celery
1 carrot, sliced	6 peppercorns
1 onion, sliced	½ teaspoon salt
Bunch of parsley	

Herby hollandaise sauce
  (page 321)

1. Put all the court bouillon ingredients into a saucepan and bring to the boil. Simmer for 30 minutes. Strain and cool the liquid.
2. Put the fish into a saucepan that fits it well (the fish should

neither be crammed in nor lost in a huge pan), pour over the cooled court bouillon and put on the heat. Cover with a lid and bring very slowly to simmering point. Now turn down the heat and let the fish poach. The water should barely move; it must *not* boil. Poach for 35 minutes.
3. Lift out the fish carefully, remove the skin and dish on a warmed platter. Hand the sauce separately.

Note: If it is thought the fish looks too plain in its naked and ungarnished state it may be lightly brushed with melted butter and sprinkled with chopped fresh tarragon, or garnished with a few whole fresh tarragon leaves.

Serves 4

Lotte en Gigot

900g/2lb tail piece of monkfish
3 tablespoons olive oil
Salt and pepper

75ml/3 fl.oz hot water
Fresh parsley

For the sauce:
675g/1½lb tomatoes
340g/¾lb mushrooms
2 small garlic cloves
3 tablespoons olive oil
1 tablespoon chopped fresh
parsley

Lemon juice
4 tablespoons double cream
Salt and freshly ground black
pepper

1. Set oven to 190°C/375°F, gas mark 5.
2. Clean the fish and place it in an ovenproof serving dish. Pour over the oil and season with salt and pepper. Bake in the oven for 15 minutes and then reduce the temperature to 170°C/325°F, gas mark 3. Add the water and cook for a further 30 minutes, basting twice during the cooking.
3. Meanwhile prepare the sauce: dip the tomatoes into boiling water for 5 seconds, peel and chop them. Wipe and quarter the mushrooms. Crush the garlic.

4. Gently fry the mushrooms and garlic in half the olive oil. Add the rest of the oil and the tomatoes and cook, stirring occasionally, until the tomatoes are a thick purée (about 1 hour). Add the parsley and lemon juice. Stir in the cream and seasoning. Pour the sauce over the cooked fish and sprinkle with chopped parsley.

Note: This dish gets its name *gigot* (meaning leg of lamb) because its finished appearance is very like a gigot à la provençale.

Serves 4

Poached Fish, Hot or Cold

Use salmon, haddock etc., either whole or in a large piece. If the fish, or piece of fish, weighs over 1·5 kilos/3lb, double the court bouillon quantities.

The fish

For the court bouillon:

About 1·25 litres/2 pints water	Bunch of fresh parsley
1 teaspoon salt	Sprig of fresh thyme
150ml/¼ pint wine vinegar	1 bay leaf
1 medium onion, sliced	6 peppercorns

For hot fish:	*For cold fish:*
Lemon wedges	Watercress
Boiled potatoes	Cucumber slices
Melted butter	Mayonnaise

1. Simmer together all the court bouillon ingredients, except the peppercorns, for 50 minutes.
2. Add the peppercorns and simmer for 10 minutes. Strain and allow to cool.
3. Put the fish in the cold court bouillon and heat gently, bringing up to poaching temperature. Do not allow the water to simmer or boil – it should barely move.

4. If the fish is to be served cold, turn the heat off now and leave the fish to cool. It will finish cooking as it does so. If the fish is to be served hot, poach it for 4 minutes to the pound, then carefully lift it out.
5. If the fish is to be served hot skin it carefully if necessary, garnish with lemon wedges, surround with hot potatoes and pass the melted butter separately.

    If to be served cold garnish the skinned fish with watercress and cucumber and hand the mayonnaise separately.

Note: Starting with a cooled court bouillon is considered to produce moister flesh, but it is not always practicable. If the fish has to be put into a hot court bouillon allow 6 minutes to the pound and remove at once.

Prawn Pilaff

790/1¾lb unshelled raw
  prawns
570ml/1 pint water
115ml/1 small glass white wine
Salt and freshly ground black
  pepper
1 lemon

3–4 parsley stalks
110g/¼lb butter
1 medium onion, finely
  chopped
225g/½lb long-grain rice
2 hardboiled eggs, chopped
1 tablespoon chopped fresh
  parsley

1. Put the whole prawns in a saucepan with the water, wine and a little salt. Bring slowly to the boil and simmer for 2 minutes. Lift out the prawns, leaving the liquid. Shell all but three of the prawns, putting the shells back into the saucepan. Add a slice of lemon and the parsley stalks. Simmer for 15 minutes. Strain and keep the liquid to cook the rice in.
2. Melt 85g/3oz of the butter and in it gently cook the onion until soft. Add the rice and fry slowly until the rice looks opaque. Add the liquid. Bring to the boil, stirring with a fork. Cover and simmer gently until the rice is tender and the water absorbed (about 20–30 minutes).

3. Meanwhile melt the remaining butter, add the prawns and eggs and heat through. Season with salt, pepper and lemon juice. Fork the shelled prawns and eggs into the pilaff rice. Pile into a serving dish, and sprinkle with plenty of chopped parsley. Put the three unshelled prawns on top, and serve.

Note I: If raw whole prawns are unavailable cooked ones will do. But it is important that they should be unshelled – the flavour given to the liquid by the shells is very good.

Note II: If the pilaff is to be kept warm, do not garnish with the parsley and whole prawns until serving. The parsley dries out and the prawns go chalky white.

Serves 4

Easy Fish Quenelles

450g/1lb fish fillet (turbot *or* salmon *or* haddock *or* any lean fish)
225g/½lb whiting fillet
4 slices white bread, crusts off
Milk
2 egg whites
Salt, pepper and cayenne
290ml/½ pint double cream
1 can lobster bisque *or* mussel soup
1 tablespoon sherry

For the poaching liquid:
1·14 litres/2 pints water
3 tablespoons vinegar
Bunch of parsley
1 bay leaf
Slice of onion
Fish heads, skins, bones etc.

1. Simmer the poaching liquid ingredients together for 30 minutes, then strain into a shallow saucepan or large frying pan.
2. Mince the fish flesh twice. Soak the bread in milk, squeeze dryish and beat into the fish. Season with pepper only. Slowly, in a machine or a bowl, work in the egg whites: first beat them with a fork until just frothy, and add bit by bit, mixing well between each addition. When the whites are in, leave the

349

mixture, refrigerated, for at least 1 hour.
3. Heat the poaching liquid. Gradually beat three-quarters of the cream into the fish mixture, and add salt and cayenne to taste. The mixture should be of 'dropping consistency'.
4. Using two wet dessertspoons mould the mixture into egg-shapes and drop them into the hot fish stock. Poach for 8 minutes, or until the quenelles feel firm to the touch. Take care not to overcook.
5. To make the sauce heat the soup, add the rest of the cream and the sherry, and enough of the cooking stock to get it to the right consistency.
6. With a perforated spoon lift the quenelles on to a serving dish and pour over the sauce.

Note: The recipe calls for tasting the raw fish mixture for seasoning. It is important to do this, and anyway it tastes perfectly good. Being squeamish about tasting raw mixtures leads to disappointing flavourless food – a pity after all the trouble of beating and mixing.

Serves 4–6

Salmon Fish Cakes

225g/½lb flaked cooked salmon
  or tinned salmon
225g/½lb cooked mashed
  potato
Salt and freshly ground black
  pepper
25g/1oz melted butter

1 level tablespoon chopped
  fresh parsley
1 egg, beaten
Dry white breadcrumbs
Oil for frying
Parsley sauce (page 309)

1. Mix the fish and potato together. Season well with salt and pepper.
2. Add the melted butter, parsley and enough beaten egg to bind the mixture until soft but not sloppy. Allow to cool.
3. Flour your hands and shape the mixture into 8 flat cakes about 2cm/1in thick. Brush with beaten egg and dip into breadcrumbs.

4. Heat 6 tablespoons of oil in a frying pan and fry until the fish cakes are brown on both sides.
5. Serve with parsley sauce.

Serves 4

Salmon Mayonnaise

1 whole salmon, cleaned

For the court bouillon:
2¼ litres/4 pints water
150ml/¼ pint vinegar
3 bay leaves
1 onion, sliced

Large bunch of parsley
1 carrot, sliced
12 peppercorns

For the garnish:
290ml/½ pint thick mayonnaise
  (page 316)
Lemon wedges

Cucumber
Bunch of watercress

1. To make the court bouillon put the water, vinegar, bay leaves, onion, parsley, carrot and peppercorns in a large pan. Bring to the boil, cover and simmer for 20 minutes. Strain and cool.
2. Prepare the salmon: mitre the tail by cutting a V with a pair of scissors. Place the fish in a fish kettle or large saucepan, curving it into a C or S shape if it will not fit stretched full length.
3. Cover and poach very gently over a low heat for 4 minutes to the 450g/1lb, calculated from the time the liquid reaches poaching temperature (just below simmering).
4. Lift out the fish, cover with a damp cloth or loosely with foil and allow to get completely cold. Then carefully remove the skin but leave head and tail intact.
5. Now garnish the salmon in any way you like. The following suggestion produces a pretty but easily achieved, result.
6. Pile the mayonnaise into a piping bag fitted with a 1cm/½in fluted nozzle. Pipe 'shells' along the backbone. Thin down

the remaining mayonnaise with a little cream, milk or hot water and put in a sauce boat to hand separately.

7. Cut a small piece of cucumber in half horizontally and then slice it finely. Arrange the slices, standing up, between the mayonnaise shells.

8. Arrange the lemon wedges, with more cucumber slices, along one side of the dish and garnish the ends with bunches of watercresss.

Note I: Salmon can be cooked without recourse to careful timing: lay the salmon in a pan into which it just fits nicely and just cover it with cold court bouillon. Bring it to simmering point as slowly as possible. Then remove from the heat. By the time the court bouillon is cold the salmon will be cooked, the theory being that a large salmon, needing a great quantity of liquid, will have longer at cooking temperatures than a small one, with perhaps only 1 litre/2 pints of court bouillon in a small fish kettle.

Note II: A 1·35 kilo/3lb fish will serve 4 people; a 2·4 kilo/8lb fish will serve 10–12 people.

Flat Salmon Pie

450g/1lb flour-quantity pâte à paté (page 655)	225g/½lb smoked salmon
55g/2oz Gruyère or Cheddar cheese, grated	2 tablespoons chopped fresh dill
30g/1oz grated Parmesan	1 large garlic clove, crushed
85g/3oz melted butter	150ml/5 fl.oz soured cream
50g/2oz fresh white breadcrumbs	Freshly ground black pepper
	Juice of ½ lemon
	Beaten egg

1. Make up the pâte à paté and roll out into two rectangles, one to fit a Swiss roll tin, the other slightly larger.

2. Set the oven to 200°C/400°F, gas mark 6.

3. Lightly grease and flour the back of a Swiss roll tin or baking

sheet. Put the smaller rectangle of pastry on it and prick all over with a fork. Bake for 15 minutes and leave to cool.

4. Mix together the Gruyère or Cheddar cheese, the Parmesan, the melted butter and the breadcrumbs. Scatter half of this mixture all over the half-cooked pastry, leaving a good half-inch clear round the edge.

5. Chop the smoked salmon into small pieces and scatter it on top of the cheese mixture. Then scatter over the chopped dill.

6. Mix the crushed garlic with the soured cream and spread all over the salmon. Season well with pepper but no salt.

7. Sprinkle evenly with the lemon juice and top with the rest of the cheese mixture. Wet the edge of the bottom piece of pastry lightly with beaten egg and put the top sheet of pastry in place, pressing the edges to seal it well.

8. Use any pastry trimmings to decorate the pie and brush all over with beaten egg.

9. Bake until the pastry is crisp and pale brown. Serve hot or cold.

Note: Off-cuts and trimmings of smoked salmon can be bought more cheaply than slices, and do well for this dish.

Serves 6

Salmon en Croûte

One 2·3 kilos/5lb salmon

450g/1lb flour-quantity puff
   pastry (pages 649–50)
Few tablespoons fine semolina
Butter
Lemon juice
Tarragon leaves
White pepper and salt
Beaten egg

For the stock:
2 slices onion
1 bay leaf
Small bunch of parsley
6 peppercorns
Salt
Bones, skin and head from the
   salmon
570ml/1 pint water

For the sauce:

55g/2oz butter
20g/¾oz flour
290ml/½ pint fish stock
50ml/½ glass white wine

1 teaspoon chopped fresh
   tarragon *or* parsley
2 tablespoons double cream

1. Fillet the fish keeping the four fillets as intact as possible. Skin the fillets.
2. Use the bones and other trimmings for the stock; put all the ingredients into a saucepan and simmer for 30 minutes. Strain into a measuring jug. Make up to 290ml/½ pint with water if necessary.
3. Heat the oven to 230°C/450°F, gas mark 8.
4. Roll out a third of the pastry into a long thin piece, about the thickness of a penny. Cut it to roughly the size and shape of the original salmon, i.e. fish-shaped.
5. Place on a wet baking sheet, and prick all over. Leave in a cool place for 15 minutes. Bake it in the hot oven until brown and crisp. If, when you turn it over, it is soggy underneath, put it back in the oven, soggy side up, for a few minutes. Cool.
6. Sprinkle the cooked pastry evenly with semolina (this will prevent the fish juices making the pastry soggy).
7. Lay the fillets of fish on the cooked pastry, dotting them with plenty of butter and sprinkling with lemon juice, tarragon, salt and pepper as you go, and assembling them more or less as they were when on the bone.
8. Roll out the rest of the pastry into a large sheet (slightly thinner this time) and lay it over the fish. Cut round the fish, leaving a good border (about 2·5cm/1in) beyond the edge of the bottom layer of the pastry. Carefully tuck the top 'sheet' under the cooked pastry, shaping the tail and pointed head of the fish carefully.
9. Brush with beaten egg. Using the back of a knife, mark the pastry in a criss-cross pattern to represent fish scales (or, if you have the time, mark the scales with the rounded end of a teaspoon). Cut some pastry trimmings into fine strips and use them to emphasize the tail fins and gills and use

a circle of pastry for the eye. Brush again with egg.

10. Bake for 15 minutes in the hot oven to brown and puff up the pastry, then turn down the oven to 150°C/300°F, gas mark 3 for a further 30 minutes to cook the fish. Cover the crust with wet greaseproof paper if the pastry looks in danger of over-browning. To test if the fish is cooked push a skewer through the pastry and fish from the side: it should glide in easily.

11. Melt half the butter in a saucepan, add the flour and cook, stirring, for 1 minute or until the butter and flour are pale biscuit-coloured and foaming. Draw off the heat then add the 300ml/½ pint stock and the wine. Return to the heat and stir until boiling and smooth. Boil rapidly until you have a sauce of coating consistency.

12. Add the chopped tarragon and the cream. Season with salt and pepper as necessary. Beat in the remaining butter, bit by bit. Pour into a warmed sauceboat.

13. Slide the *salmon en croûte* on to a board or salmon dish, and make sure your guests admire it before you cut into it.

14. Hand the sauce separately, or slit the salmon down the middle, lift one side of the pastry case, and pour the sauce inside.

Serves 8

Grilled Sardines

16 small *or* 8 large sardines, fresh *or* frozen, not canned
Oil

Pepper
Lemon juice
Parsley to garnish

1. To clean the sardines: slit along the belly and remove the innards. Rinse the fish under running cold water and with a little salt gently rub away any black matter in the cavity. Cut off the gills.

2. Heat the grill. Score the fish with three or four diagonal cuts on each side, brush with oil, season with pepper and sprinkle with lemon juice.

3. Grill for about 4 minutes on each side, brushing with the hot oil and juices that run from the fish.
4. Lay the sardines on a warmed platter. Pour over the juices from the grill pan and serve at once.

Serves 4

Scallops au Gratin

150ml/¼ pint white wine
1 bay leaf
¼ onion
8 large *or* 12 small scallops
450g/1lb mashed potatoes
30g/1oz butter
30g/1oz flour
To serve:
4 scallop shells

1 tablespoon cream
Lemon juice
Salt and freshly ground black pepper
Dried breadcrumbs
A little extra butter

1. Put the wine with 150ml/¼ pint water, the bay leaf and onion into a saucepan. Bring to the boil. Turn down the heat, add the scallops and poach for 5 minutes very gently.
2. Lift the scallops from the liquid. Pull away the hard muscle (opposite the coral or roe) and cut each scallop into 2 or 3.
3. Divide them between four scallop shells. Pipe or spoon the mashed potato around the edge of the shells.
4. Melt the butter in a pan, add the flour and cook for 30 seconds. Strain over the liquid in which the scallops were cooked and stir until the sauce is thick and smooth. Add the cream and season with lemon juice, salt and pepper.
5. Spoon over the scallops. Sprinkle with the crumbs and melted butter and brown under the grill.

Serves 4

356

Fried Scallops with Garlic

The essence of this dish is quick last-minute cooking. Slow cooking or leaving the scallops after frying will cause them to lose their moisture, making them dry, tough and unappetizing.

16 scallops
55g/2oz butter
1 small garlic clove, crushed
Salt and freshly ground black
   pepper

Juice of ½ lemon
A little chopped fresh parsley

1. Remove the muscle from the scallops (found on the opposite side from the coral or roe).
2. Melt the butter in a frying pan. When the butter begins to foam, add the scallops, garlic and pepper. Toss in the sizzling fat for 5 minutes.
3. Add the lemon juice and parsley and sprinkle with salt. Serve immediately.

Serves 4

Fried Scampi

450g/1lb scampi
Salt and freshly ground black
   pepper
Lemon juice

Oil for deep frying
290ml/½ pint fritter batter
   (page 660)
Fried parsley (page 787)

1. If using frozen scampi sprinkle with pepper and lemon juice and defrost slowly.
2. Heat the deep fat until a crumb dropped into it will sizzle and brown.
3. Dip the scampi in the batter and fry until golden brown. Drain on absorbent paper. Sprinkle with salt.
4. Garnish with fried parsley and serve at once.

Serves 4

Seafood Pancakes with Wine Sauce

8 pancakes (page 659)
110g/¼lb prawns, cooked and peeled
110g/¼lb frozen scampi (raw)
110g/¼lb frozen scallops (raw)
Slice of onion
6 peppercorns

Bay leaf
Parsley stalk
Salt and pepper
15g/½oz butter
15g/½oz flour
5 tablespoons milk
½ teaspoon tomato purée

To finish:
30g/1oz butter, melted

Grated cheese

1. Make the pancakes and set aside. Then tackle the filling.
2. Defrost the prawns slowly.
3. Place the frozen scampi and scallops in a small pan. Cover with cold water, add the onion, peppercorns, bay leaf and parsley stalk. Bring slowly to boiling point. Immediately draw the pan off the heat and leave for 4 minutes, then strain, keeping the liquid.
4. Boil the liquid rapidly until reduced by half.
5. Discard the onion and flavourings from the fish. Remove the tough piece of muscle from the scallops (found on the opposite side of the roe) and cut each scallop into two or three pieces.
6. Melt the butter, add the flour and cook for 30 seconds. Take off the heat. Add 5 tablespoons of the reserved fish stock and mix well. Pour in the milk and return the pan to the heat. Bring slowly to the boil, stirring continuously. Season with salt and pepper and stir in the tomato purée. Simmer for 1 minute, to give a smooth thick mixture.
7. Mix the fish with this. Put a good spoonful of the mixture on each pancake and roll up.
8. Heat the grill.
9. Lay the pancakes side by side in a well-buttered fireproof dish. Brush melted butter over the top of the pancakes and sprinkle them with grated cheese. Grill until lightly browned.

Serves 4

Deep-fried Seafood Envelopes

110g/¼lb cooked prawns
4 scallops
110g/¼lb raw scampi
Slice of onion

6 peppercorns
1 bay leaf
Parsley stalk
Salt

For the sauce:
15g/½oz butter
15g/½oz flour
3 tablespoons milk

Salt and pepper
½ teaspoon tomato purée

For the envelopes:
Oil for deep frying
225g/½lb flour-quantity puff
  pastry (pages 649–50)

Beaten egg
Tomato sauce (page 325)

1. Defrost the prawns. Place the scallops and scampi (fresh or frozen) in a small pan, just cover with cold water and add the onion, peppercorns, bay leaf, parsley stalk and salt. Over a gentle heat bring slowly to simmering point. Take off the heat and leave for 4 minutes. Strain the cooking stock into a saucepan. Boil rapidly until reduced by half.

2. Chop the prawns and scampi. Remove the muscles from the scallops (found on the opposite side to the roe) and cut each scallop into two or three pieces.

3. Melt the butter in a saucepan, add the flour and cook for 30 seconds. Take off the heat. Add 5 tablespoons fish stock and mix well. Pour in the milk and return the pan to the heat. Bring to the boil slowly, stirring continuously. Season, add the tomato purée and simmer for 1 minute. Mix the chopped shellfish with the sauce.

4. Heat the oil until it is hot enough to sizzle when a crumb is dropped into it.

5. Roll and cut the pastry into eight 7cm/3in squares. Brush the edges with a little beaten egg. Place a spoonful of the fish mixture on each square and fold over on the diagonal. Press

the edges well together and brush both sides of the pastry with more beaten egg.

6. Deep fry the envelopes until golden brown. Drain well on crumpled kitchen paper. Serve quickly, handing tomato sauce separately.

Serves 4

Sole Bonne Femme

70g/2½oz butter
3 medium Dover soles, filleted
1 shallot, finely chopped
170g/6oz button mushrooms, sliced
Salt and white pepper
1 glass white wine

290ml/½ pint fish stock made with the bones, head etc. (page 304)
Lemon juice
30g/1oz flour
290ml/½ pint double cream
A little milk if necessary

1. Set the oven to 180°C/350°F, gas mark 4.
2. Use 15g/½oz of the butter to grease an ovenproof dish. Arrange the fillets in the dish, folding the ends underneath. Sprinkle in the shallot and sliced mushroom. Season with salt and pepper, pour over the wine, cold stock and lemon juice. Cover with a lid or greased paper and bake in the oven for 10–15 minutes.
3. Lift the fillets and mushrooms carefully on to a serving dish, taking care not to transfer any of the cooking liquor with the fish. Cover and keep warm.
4. Strain the liquid in which the fish has been poached into a saucepan and boil rapidly until reduced to 75ml/2½ fl.oz.
5. Melt 30g/1oz of the butter, add the flour and cook for 30 seconds. Remove from the heat and add the reduced fish stock. Stir well, return to the heat, and bring slowly to the boil, stirring continuously until very thick.
6. Gradually beat in the double cream – if the sauce looks as though it may curdle beat it vigorously. Take the sauce off

the heat and gradually whisk in the remaining 30g/1oz of butter. The sauce should now be of coating consistency but if it is too thick, a little milk can be added to thin it down. Season to taste with salt, white pepper and lemon juice.

7. Coat this cream sauce over the fillets of sole and serve immediately.

Serves 4

Chaudfroid of Sole

Four 560g/1¼lb soles, skinned
  and filleted

For the stock and aspic jelly:

1 onion	6 peppercorns
1 carrot	1 glass white wine
Stick of celery	55g/2oz gelatine
Bones, head and skins of the soles	2 egg whites and 2 egg shells, crushed
1 bay leaf	

For the farce:

170g/6oz uncooked salmon, minced	2 tablespoons cream
1 egg white	Salt and freshly ground black pepper

For the chaudfroid sauce:

290ml/½ pint milk	20g/¾oz flour
6 peppercorns	7g/¼oz gelatine
Blade of mace	190ml/⅓ pint aspic jelly
Slice of onion	1 tablespoon cream
20g/¾oz butter	Salt and white pepper

For the garnish:
Paper-thin slices of truffle *or*
  mushroom

1. To make the stock cut the onion, carrot and celery into small chunks, put into a pan with the fish heads, bones and skins,

361

and add the bay leaf, peppercorns and wine. Pour over $\frac{3}{4}$ litre/$1\frac{1}{2}$ pints cold water. Bring to the boil, skim and simmer for 30 minutes. Strain and leave to cool.

2. Set the oven to 170°C/325°F, gas mark 3.

3. Next tackle the farce. Put the salmon in a bowl. Whisk the egg white until frothy and beat it slowly into the salmon with the cream. Taste and season with salt and pepper.

4. Wash and dry the sole fillets. Divide the farce equally between them. Spread it on the skinned sides and roll or fold up into neat parcels.

5. Put them into a buttered ovenproof dish with a cup of the fish stock. Cover with buttered foil or greaseproof paper. Bake for 12 minutes or until cooked. Strain off and reserve the liquid; leave the fish to cool, covered.

6. To make the sauce first heat the milk with the peppercorns, blade of mace and slice of onion. Strain and mix with the liquid saved from cooking the fish.

7. Melt the butter and add the flour. Cook, stirring, for 1 minute. Remove from the heat and add the milky liquid. Leave to cool but stir occasionally to prevent a skin forming.

8. To make the aspic put the stock into a large saucepan, sprinkle on 55g/2oz gelatine and put the saucepan over a gentle heat.

9. Place the crushed shells in a bowl, add the egg white and whisk until frothy. Pour into the warming stock and keep whisking steadily with a balloon whisk until the mixture boils and rises. Stop whisking immediately and draw the pan off the heat. Allow the mixture to subside. Take care not to break the crust formed by the egg white.

10. Bring the aspic up to the boil again and again allow to subside. Repeat this once more (the egg white will trap the sediment in the stock and clear the aspic). Allow to cool for 10 minutes.

11. Fix a double layer of fine muslin over a clean basin and carefully strain the aspic through it, taking care to hold the egg white crust back. When all the liquid is through (or almost all of it) allow the egg white to slip into the muslin. Then strain the aspic again – this time through both egg

white crust and cloth. Do not try to hurry the process by squeezing the cloth, or murky aspic will result.

12. In a small pan soak the gelatine for the sauce in about 4 tablespoons of the cleared cool aspic for 5 minutes. Melt over a low heat. Beat into the sauce with the cream. Taste for seasoning, adding salt or white pepper if necessary.

13. Lay the fish 'parcels' on a cake rack with a tray underneath. As the sauce thickens, spoon some over each fillet, covering the top and sides. Refrigerate the coated fillets until the sauce is set.

14. Garnish the fish 'parcels' with truffle or mushroom. When the aspic is cool and on the point of setting, carefully coat each fillet with aspic. Refrigerate to set. Repeat the coating if necessary, the aspic layer should be thin, but very shiny.

15. Set the rest of the aspic in a shallow tray.

16. Arrange the fillets on a serving dish. When the aspic in the tray is set cut it into tiny squares with a sharp knife. Garnish the fish with the chopped aspic. Keep cool.

Note: If the aspic is less than crystal-clear it is wise not to chop it – which seems to emphasize its murkiness.

Serves 4–6

Sole Colbert

Four 340g/¾lb Dover soles
Seasoned flour
Beaten egg
Dry white breadcrumbs

Fat for deep frying
Maître d'hôtel butter (page 331)
Lemon wedges

1. Skin and trim the soles, leaving on the heads. With a small sharp knife make a cut *one side only* down the centre of the backbone, through the flesh to the bone. Raise the side fillets (loosening them with a knife) so that you can snip the bone just below the head and above the tail. Later you will remove the whole backbone so work the fillets away from the bones,

but leaving them still attached at each end and along the edge of the fish – you are working only from the centre out. See drawing. Rinse and dry the fish.

2. Dip in seasoned flour, shaking away any excess. Brush with beaten egg and press on the dry white breadcrumbs. Be sure to egg and crumb the underside of the raised fillets.

3. Heat up the oil so that a crumb will sizzle in it. Fry the whole fish until a good golden brown, holding the fish down with a fish slice to prevent it curling up. Drain well on absorbent paper.

4. Leave for 1–2 minutes. Then carefully pull out the backbone, cutting round the breadcrumb coating to prevent too much of it being pulled off.

5. Fill the space with slices of maitre d'hotel butter. Dish and serve immediately with wedges of lemon.

Note: For a light lunch dish or a starter 'slip' soles are suitable. They weigh 170–225g/6–8oz.

Serves 4

Lemon Sole Doria

Three 675g/1½lb lemon soles   55g/2oz butter
1 large cucumber   Salt and pepper
Seasoned flour   Lemon juice

1. Skin and fillet the soles.
2. Peel the cucumber and, using a melon-baller, scoop the flesh into balls. Place these in a pan of boiling salted water for 4–5 minutes. Drain and dry well.
3. Dip the fillets in seasoned flour. Lay them on a plate but do not allow them to touch each other – they will become soggy and will not fry so well.
4. Heat half the butter in a frying pan. When foaming, put in

the fillets – not too many at a time. Turn them over when a golden brown; allow about 3 minutes on each side. Dish on to a shallow platter and keep warm.

5. Melt the remaining butter in the pan. Add the cucumber balls and fry quite briskly until a delicate brown. Add salt, pepper and lemon juice. Boil up and tip over the fish. Serve at once.

Serves 4

Grilled Sole

| 1 sole per person | Butter |
| Salt and pepper | Lemon juice |

1. Make a cut in the belly (near the head) of each fish and re-move the entrails. Wash the fish thoroughly in cold water.
2. Now skin the fish: place the fish on a piece of greaseproof paper and pour a little pile of salt beside it. Snip off the fins with scissors. Make a cut across the black skin just above the tail with a sharp knife, being careful to cut only the skin and not the flesh. Dip your thumbs and index fingers in the salt and then gently work them under the black skin from the tail upwards until you have raised enough of the skin to be able to take a firm grasp of it. The salt prevents the skin slipping out of your grasp. Using a tea-towel to help get a firm grip, pull the skin off the fish in one sharp tug. Repeat on the other (pale) side. This will prove rather more difficult, and is not strictly necessary.
3. Heat the grill. Melt a little butter and use this to brush both the grill and one side of the fish. Season with pepper and lemon juice and place under the hot grill for about 4 minutes. Turn over and brush the second side with butter. Grill again. Remove and snip a 'V' out of the tail fin. Add salt, pepper and a squeeze of lemon before serving.

Note: Do not add salt before or during grilling as it draws the juices from the fish, making it dry.

Sole Véronique

3 sole, about 450g/1lb each,
   skinned and filleted but
   bones and skin reserved
150ml/¼ pint white wine

1 bay leaf
6 peppercorns
1 onion, sliced
Salt

For the sauce:

20g/¾oz unsalted butter
20g/¾oz flour

290ml/½ pint milk
2 tablespoons single cream

For the garnish:
110g/¼lb white grapes

1.   Set the oven to 180°C/350°F, gas mark 4.
2.   Trim the fillets and fold them up with the skinned side in. Lay them in an ovenproof dish. Pour on the wine and add the bay leaf, peppercorns and onion. Add enough water to cover half the fish. Arrange the skin and fish bones on top and bake for 15–20 minutes.
3.   Dip the grapes into boiling water for 5 seconds, then skin them. Cut in half then discard the pips. Put into a covered dish and heat through in the oven.
4.   When the fish is cooked remove the fillets and keep them warm. Strain the cooking liquor and reduce it by boiling rapidly to 3 tablespoons.
5.   Melt the butter, add the flour and cook for 1 minute. Gradually add the milk, stirring continually as you bring it to the boil. Stir in the reduced fish stock (or *fumet*) and simmer for 1 minute. Taste and adjust the seasoning if necessary. Add the cream and half the hot grapes.
6.   Arrange the fillets of sole on a warmed serving dish. Coat with the Véronique sauce and arrange the remaining grapes at each end of the dish. Serve immediately.

Note I: The perfectionist cook may like to leave the grapes whole:

use the rounded end of a hair grip to extract the pips through the stalk end.

Note II: Canned white grapes are less trouble than fresh ones, and have an excellent flavour and texture for the dish. Do not add the juice, and do not peel them.

Serves 4

Cold Trout with Green Mayonnaise

4 medium-sized trout

For the poaching liquid (court bouillon):

1·14 litres/2 pints water	12 peppercorns
1 teacup vinegar	2 bay leaves
1 sliced carrot	2 tablespoons salad oil
1 sliced onion	Salt
1 stick celery	

Green mayonnaise (page 318)
Watercress

1. Clean the trout (by splitting down the belly and washing out the insides under the cold tap) and snip off the body fins, but leave on the head and tail.
2. Bring the court bouillon ingredients to the boil and simmer for 20 minutes or so. Ideally the liquid should now be allowed to cool and the fish placed in the cool liquid, then brought slowly to simmering point. If this is done the fish will take about 4 minutes (depending on size) from the time the water has reached boiling point. As soon as boiling point is reached, it is vital that the heat is lowered so that the trout *poach* (this means that no bubbles at all rise to the surface, but the water simmers very slightly – it is cooler than simmering). If there is not time to cool the court bouillon before adding the fish, make sure the liquid is below simmering heat and gently drop the trout into it. They will take about 8 minutes if done this way.

367

3. As soon as the fish are cooked (the skin will be easy to remove, and the eyes look very white and prominent), stand the pan in a basin of cold water to cool it. This will prevent further cooking. The fish should cool in the liquid as they will steam dry if exposed to the air while still hot.
4. When the fish are quite cold carefully lift them out, and skin them without removing heads or tails.
5. Arrange them on a serving dish and coat with the green mayonnaise (thinned if necessary with milk), leaving the heads and tails exposed. Garnish with washed watercress.

Serves 4

Sea Trout en Papillote

340g/¾lb fillet of sea trout, skinned
55g/2oz butter
1 tablespoon very finely shredded white of leek
1 tablespoon very finely shredded carrot
55g/2oz mushrooms, thinly sliced

1 teaspoon freshly chopped tarragon *or* fennel leaves
Lemon juice
2 tablespoons white wine
Salt and freshly ground black pepper
Oil for brushing baking sheet and paper

1. Heat the oven to 250°C/500°F, gas mark 9.
2. Fold a large sheet of greaseproof paper in half and cut a semi-circle (20cm/8in radius) from it so that when the double sheet is opened out the cut-out will be a 40cm/16in round. Cut out a second 'papillote'.
3. Melt half the butter and add the leek and carrot to it. Cook slowly without browning for 5 minutes, then add the mushrooms. Cook 1 more minute, then add the tarragon or fennel, and season with salt and pepper.
4. Cut the sea trout fillet into four or six diagonal slices about 1cm/½in thick.

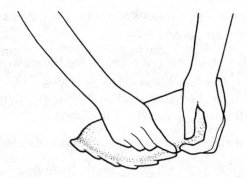

5. Brush the inside of the paper rounds with a little oil taking care to leave a margin without oil. Divide the vegetable mixture between the two papillotes, spooning it on to one side only of the paper round. Lay the fish slices on top of the vegetables, two or three on each. Squeeze a few drops of lemon on each and sprinkle each with a tablespoon of wine. Dot with the remaining butter and add salt and pepper.

6. Fold the free half of the papillote paper over to make a parcel rather like an apple turnover. Fold the edges of the two layers of paper over twice together, twisting and pressing hard to make an air-tight seal. (See diagram.)

7. Lightly brush a baking sheet with oil and put it into the oven for five minutes to heat. Then carefully put the papillotes on the baking sheet, taking care that they do not touch each other. Bake for 5 minutes.

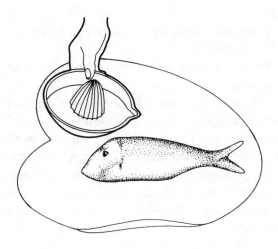

8. Serve immediately on hot flat plates. Each diner unwraps his own puffed-up parcel.

Note I: Halibut, haddock, salmon, indeed almost any fish, can be cooked in this way. Whole trout weighing 340g/¾lb will take 15 minutes to cook. Breast of chicken, boned and skinned, is good too (20 minutes in the piece, 15 if in slices).

Note II: For a richer dish serve with beurre blanc (page 319).

Note III: Papillotes are generally made from circular papers, as in the above recipe, but are better made from heart-shaped pieces if whole small fish or long fillets of fish are to be enwrapped. See previous page.

Serves 2

Trout with Hazelnuts

55g/2oz hazelnuts
4 medium-sized rainbow trout
Seasoned flour
85g/3oz clarified butter (page 784)

Lemon juice
Salt and pepper
Lemon wedges
Chopped fresh parsley

1. Set the oven to 170°C/325°F, gas mark 3. Brown the hazelnuts in the oven. Rub them in a clean cloth to remove the skins. Chop them roughly.
2. Clean the trout very well. Dip them in the flour and shake off any excess.
3. Fry briefly on both sides in all but a tablespoon of the butter. Transfer to an ovenproof dish, pouring over the butter from the pan. Bake for 15 minutes (or until firm to the touch).
4. Fry the chopped hazelnuts in the remaining butter.
5. Arrange the trout on a warm serving dish, pour over the fried hazelnuts and any butter, then sprinkle with lemon juice, and salt and pepper. Garnish with lemon wedges and sprinkle with parsley.

Note I: If trout is not properly cleaned it tastes bitter.

Note II: This is similar to the classic *truites aux amandes.* For this split or flaked almonds instead of hazelnuts should be used. They are simply fried in butter and sprinkled over the fish.

Note III: The fish may be cooked entirely in the frying pan, but they must be fried slowly, for about 7 minutes a side.

Serves 4

Baked Turbot with Cheese and Shrimp Sauce

4 turbot steaks
Salt and freshly ground black
  pepper
150ml/¼ pint white wine
150ml/¼ pint water
1 bay leaf
Slice of onion
1 parsley stalk
2 peppercorns
30g/1oz butter

30g/1oz flour
150ml/¼ pint milk
110g/¼lb cooked, peeled pink
  shrimps *or* prawns
55g/2oz Cheddar cheese, grated
Pinch of cayenne
1 tablespoon Parmesan
1 tablespoon fresh white breadcrumbs
30g/1oz butter

1. Set the oven to 190°C/375°F, gas mark 5. If the shrimps are frozen defrost them slowly sprinkled with lemon juice and pepper.
2. Lay the turbot steaks in an ovenproof dish and season with salt. Cover with the wine and water and add the bay leaf, onion, parsley stalk and peppercorns. Cover and poach in the oven for 20–25 minutes or until the fish is firm and cooked.
3. Lift the steaks from the liquor. Carefully remove skins and bones, and place the steaks in a serving dish. Keep them warm. Boil cooking liquor rapidly to reduce by half.
4. Melt the butter in a saucepan. Stir in the flour and cook, stirring, for 1 minute. Remove from the heat and gradually stir in the poaching liquor. Return to the heat, and stir while the sauce comes to the boil and thickens. Add the milk and reheat.

5. Reduce the heat, add the shrimps and poach gently for 1 minute. Take off the heat and stir in the grated cheese. Season to taste with salt, pepper and cayenne. Pour over the fish.
6. Sprinkle the dish with the Parmesan cheese and breadcrumbs. Dot with butter (or sprinkle with melted butter) and brown under the grill.

Serves 4

Turbot and Scallop Moulds

One 900g/2lb live lobster
16 flat thin slices (about the size of the palm of your hand) turbot *or* brill
4 fillets sole, with skins, bones and heads
Few slices onion
1 bay leaf
Salt, pepper and cayenne
85g/3oz finely chopped shallots
85g/3oz butter
$\frac{1}{4}$ teaspoon crushed garlic

About 30g/1oz flour
85ml/3 fl.oz good white wine
Armagnac
2 teaspoons tomato purée
30g/1oz fresh chopped tarragon *or* chervil
8 fresh scallops in their shells
1 egg white
290ml/$\frac{1}{2}$ pint double cream
3 tablespoons dry Vermouth
450g/1lb fresh spinach

1. With a sharp knife kill the lobster by inserting a knife where the head joins the thorax, and splitting the head. Split the lobster in half lengthwise and remove the stomach sac and intestine. Pull out the flesh from the tail shell, and keep it raw for the mousse.
2. Put the head, claws, leg and shell into a small saucepan and set aside in a cool place while you make the fish stock.
3. Put the sole bones, skin and head, any turbot or brill trimmings or bones, and a sliced onion, a bay leaf, salt and pepper into a saucepan and add a pint of water. Simmer for 15 minutes, then strain and allow to cool.
4. When quite cold, pour over the lobster head, claws etc. and poach gently until the lobster is cooked (about 10 minutes).
5. Take the flesh from the claws and head (including the

372

greenish creamy part), and from the legs, and chop it up. Return the shells (crushed and broken up) to the stock pan and simmer for a further 10 minutes.

6. In a small heavy pan sweat 30g/1oz of the chopped shallot in 30g/1oz of the butter until soft and transparent. Add the crushed garlic. Allow to cook for 1 minute, then add 1 heaped teaspoon of flour, stir well, then add 1 tablespoon of white wine, a dash of Armagnac and the tomato purée. Stir over heat, adding enough fish stock to give a sauce of creamy consistency (about 150ml/¼ pint). Add the cooked lobster meat, the chopped fresh tarragon, and salt and pepper to taste. Set the mixture aside.

7. Lift the scallops from their shells (keeping the shells) and remove the orange/pink corals, which you must set aside for the final sauce.

8. Pound or mince the scallop flesh with the raw lobster and the fillets of sole. Then beat in the egg white, 150ml/¼ pint double cream and season with salt, pepper and a dash of Armagnac.

9. Then make the sauce: gently cook the remaining 55g/2oz chopped shallot in 30g/1oz of the butter until soft. Stir in a heaped tablespoon flour, then add the rest of the white wine and the Vermouth. Add 150ml/¼ pint of the fish stock and bring to the boil, stirring. Simmer for 5 minutes, then strain into a clean saucepan. Stir in the remaining double cream, season with cayenne pepper. Set the sauce aside while you prepare the scallop corals.

10. Strain the remaining fish stock from the lobster shells and boil it rapidly until you are left with a tablespoon or so of thick, clearish liquid. This is concentrated 'glaçe de pois-son'. Add the scallop corals to it, simmer for 1 minute, then pound stock and corals together to make a smooth pink creamy paste. Set aside (you will add it to the sauce at the last minute).

11. Now, having prepared the lobster and tarragon mixture, the lobster and scallop mousse and sauce, you are ready to start on the main construction. Wash the spinach leaves, remove any tough stalks and plunge into boiling salted water for a

few seconds only. Drain very well and immediately dunk into cold water to set the bright green colour.

12. Set the oven to 180°C/350°F, gas mark 4.
13. Take the 8 deeper scallop shells, wash them, and butter them well. Line each shell with a fillet of turbot or brill. Follow this with a layer of the spinach, and then a layer of the mousse. Into the centre of this put a spoonful of the lobster and tarragon mixture. Then another layer of lobster mousse, another of spinach and cover with the remaining fish fillets.
14. Brush the top with melted butter. Put the eight filled scallop dishes into a roasting pan and pour in enough water, round the shells, to cover the pan to the depth of 0·75cm/¼in. Cover the whole dish with foil and bake for 20 minutes.
15. While the fish parcels are baking, reheat the sauce, and add the scallop coral paste.
16. To serve: slide each parcel out of its scallop shell, turn it over on to a warmed serving dish, and coat with the sauce.

Serves 8

CHICKEN

Chicken Elizabeth

The Cordon Bleu School devised this dish for the Coronation celebrations in 1953.

1·35 kilos/3lb roasting chicken, washed and dried
Chicken stock *or* water with:
  1 bay leaf, 6 peppercorns,
  2 parsley stalks, 1 slice lemon
  and 2 teaspoons fresh thyme

225ml/8fl.oz Elizabeth sauce (page 317)

To serve:
Rice salad (page 299)
Bunch of watercress

1. Place the chicken, untrussed, in a saucepan of simmering chicken stock or in a pan of water with flavourings.
2. Cover the pan and cook gently for about $1\frac{1}{4}$–$1\frac{1}{2}$ hours until the chicken is tender and the drumsticks feel loose and wobbly. Remove from the stock and set aside to cool.
3. Take the flesh from the chicken bones, and when it is quite cold mix with the sauce, keeping a little back.
4. Pile the chicken into the middle of a serving dish and coat with the reserved sauce. Surround with the rice salad and garnish with watercress.

Note I: The chicken is removed from the stock to cool, first to prevent further cooking, and secondly to eliminate any possibility of the chicken going bad – a real risk if food is kept at a lukewarm temperature for long periods.

But there is no question that food cooled in the cooking liquid (providing it is not overcooked) is juicier. The best solution perhaps is to cool the chicken in the stock – but as rapidly as possible: stand the saucepan in a plastic washing-up bowl on the drainer or in the sink and fill the bowl with cold water. Allow the cold tap to trickle steadily into the water making it slowly overflow and consequently keeping the water renewed and cool. As soon as the stock in the pan and the chicken are cold remove both to the refrigerator until needed.

Note II: It is easier to strip chicken flesh from the bones if this is done while the bird is still lukewarm. But on no account should the sauce be added to the flesh until the chicken is stone cold.

Serves 4

Poached Chicken with Parsley Sauce

1·8 kilos/4lb chicken, cleaned but not trussed

For the court bouillon:

1 onion, sliced	6 peppercorns
2 carrots	2 sticks celery
2 parsley stalks	2 bay leaves

For the parsley sauce:

30g/1oz butter
30g/1oz flour
150ml/¼ pint milk
About 150 ml/¼ pint chicken
  stock taken from the cooking
  liquid

2 tablespoons single cream
  (optional)
2 tablespoons chopped
  fresh parsley
Salt and freshly ground
  black pepper

1. Put the chicken into a large suacepan with the onion, carrots, parsley stalks, peppercorns, celery and bay leaves. Half-submerge the bird with water and put on a well-fitting lid.
2. Bring to the boil, reduce the heat and simmer gently for 1½ hours or until the chicken is cooked. (The legs will feel loose and wobbly when it is.)
3. Remove the chicken from the pan and strain the stock. Cover the chicken to prevent it drying out.
4. Carefully skim the stock of all the fat: when you have spooned off as much grease as possible, lay successive sheets of absorbent paper on the surface of the liquid to remove the rest.
5. Now start the parsley sauce. Melt the butter, add the flour and cook for 1 minute. Remove from the heat.
6. Gradually add the milk and chicken stock, stirring continuously while bringing to the boil.
7. Simmer for 2 minutes, then add the cream (if using) and set aside, covered tightly.
8. Skin the chicken and remove the bones, leaving the flesh in large pieces.
9. Reheat the sauce and add the parsley. Season if necessary with salt or pepper. Add more stock if the sauce is too thick. Add the chicken to the sauce, turn gently, and tip into a serving dish.

Note: Do not add the parsley to the sauce in advance as it will lose its colour.

Serves 4

Curried Chicken and Ham Pie

45g/1½oz butter
1 onion, chopped
1 teaspoon curry powder
½ teaspoon turmeric
55g/2oz flour
290ml/½ pint stock reserved
after cooking the chicken
150ml/¼ pint creamy milk
1 teaspoon chopped fresh
parsley
1 teaspoon chopped fresh mint
Pinch of crushed cardamon
seeds
Pinch of dry English mustard

Squeeze of lemon juice
Salt and freshly ground black
pepper
2 hardboiled eggs, chopped
110g/¼lb ham, cut into 1cm/
½in dice
1·35 kilos/3lb chicken, poached,
boned and cut into large
chunks
225g/½lb flour-quantity
wholemeal pastry (page 647)
1 beaten egg mixed with 1 pinch
of salt and 1 teaspoon
water (eggwash)

1. Set the oven to 200°C/400°F, gas mark 6.
2. Melt the butter and add the onion. Cook gently until soft but not coloured.
3. Stir in the curry powder and turmeric and cook for 2 minutes.
4. Add the flour and cook over a gentle heat for 2 minutes. Draw the pan off the heat. Add the chicken stock and stir well. Return to the heat. Bring slowly up to the boil, stirring continuously, until you have a thick shiny sauce.
5. Add the milk and stir again until the sauce returns to the boil.
6. Add the parsley, mint, mustard, cardamon seeds and seasoning. Simmer for 2–3 minutes.
7. Taste, adding more salt if necessary, and the lemon juice. Allow to cool.
8. Stir in the hardboiled eggs, the ham and the chicken. Pour the mixture into a pie dish.
9. Roll the pastry on a floured board into a rectangle about ·5cm/¼in thick.

10. Cut a band of pastry slightly wider than the edge of the pie dish. Brush the rim of the dish with water and press on the band of paste. Brush with a little beaten egg or water and lay the pastry lid over the pie. Cut away surplus pastry from the sides with a knife.
11. Press the pie edges together and mark a pattern with a point of a small knife, or pinch with the fingers into a raised border. Shape the pastry trimmings into leaves for decoration.
12. Brush the pastry with beaten egg and decorate with the pastry leaves. Brush again with egg.
13. Bake for 30–35 minutes.

Note: If the pie is not to be baked as soon as it has been assembled it is essential that the curry sauce and the chicken are both completely cold before they are combined. Keep the pie refrigerated or frozen until baking. If frozen thaw in the refrigerator before cooking.

Serves 4

Chicken and Sweetbread Filling for Vol-au-vent or Flan Case

Pair of calves' sweetbreads *or*
  225g/½lb lambs' sweetbreads
45g/1½oz butter
1 small onion, finely chopped
55g/2oz button mushrooms,
  sliced
30g/1oz flour
150ml/¼ pint creamy milk

150ml/¼ pint chicken stock
1 tablespoon sherry
Squeeze of lemon
225g/½lb cooked chicken
Salt and freshly ground black
  pepper
1 large vol-au-vent case
(page 651)

1. Soak the sweetbreads in cold water for 4 hours. Change the water every time it becomes pink (probably four times). There should be no blood at all when the sweetbreads are ready for cooking.

2. Place them in a pan of cold water and bring up to the boil. Simmer for 2 minutes.
3. Drain the sweetbreads and rinse under running cold water. Dry well. Pick them over, removing all the skin and membrane. Chop coarsely.
4. Melt the butter and, when foaming, add the onions and cook slowly until soft but not coloured.
5. Add the sweetbreads and cook for 3 minutes. Stir in the mushrooms and leave over a gentle heat for 1 minute. Remove the sweetbreads and mushrooms with a perforated spoon.
6. Stir the flour into the pan and cook for 1 minute. Draw off the heat and stir in the milk and stock. Bring slowly to the boil, stirring continuously.
7. When the liquid is simmering add the sherry, lemon juice, chicken pieces, sweetbreads, mushrooms and seasoning.
8. Tip the mixture carefully into the pastry case and reheat in the oven for 5 minutes.

Serves 4

Chicken and Yoghurt Cream Curry

1·5 kilos/3lb chicken
Seasoned flour mixed with a
   pinch each of turmeric,
   cayenne, dried English
   mustard and crushed
   coriander
2 tablespoons oil
2 medium onions, chopped
1 garlic clove, crushed
1 teaspoon cumin powder

2 teaspoons turmeric
290ml/½ pint chicken stock
1 bay leaf
2 teaspoons tomato purée
Juice of 1 lemon
2 teaspoons chopped fresh mint
1 tablespoon cream
2 tablespoons plain yoghurt
30g/1oz blanched almonds

To serve:
Boiled rice

1. Joint the chicken into eight and dip the pieces in the very well-seasoned flour. Heat the oil in a sauté pan and brown the chicken all over. With a perforated spoon take up the pieces and place them in a roasting dish or casserole.
2. Heat the oven to 180°C/350°F, gas mark 4.
3. Now fry the onions and garlic until turning brown. Add the cumin and turmeric and cook for 2 minutes. Add the stock, bay leaf, tomato purée, lemon juice and mint. Taste and add salt and pepper as necessary. Bring slowly to the boil, stirring continuously.
4. Pour this over the chicken joints. Cover and cook in the oven for 45–50 minutes or until the chicken is tender. Turn off the oven.
5. Lift the chicken joints out of the sauce on to a serving dish. Cover and keep warm. Meanwhile heat the curry sauce, adding the cream, yoghurt and almonds. Pour over the chicken and serve with boiled rice.

Serves 4

Gougères

105g/3¾oz flour
Pinch of salt
Pepper and cayenne
85g/3oz butter
225ml/7½ fl.oz water

3 eggs, lightly beaten
55g/2oz strong Cheddar cheese
  cut into 5mm/¼in cubes
425ml/¾ pint filling (below)
2 tablespoons browned crumbs

1. Set oven to 200°C/400°F, gas mark 6.
2. Sift the flour with the seasonings.
3. In a large saucepan heat the butter in the water and when completely melted bring up to a rolling boil. When the mixture is bubbling all over, tip in all the flour, take off the heat and beat well with a wooden spoon until the mixture will leave the sides of the pan. Allow to cool for about 10 minutes.
4. Beat in the eggs gradually until the mixture is smooth and

shiny and of 'dropping consistency' – you may not need the last few spoonfuls of egg. Stir in the diced cheese.

5. Spoon the mixture round the edge of a flattish greased ovenproof dish. Pile the filling into the centre, and sprinkle with the crumbs. Bake until the choux is well risen and golden and the filling is hot (about 35–40 minutes).

Makes a gougère for 6

Chicken Filling for Gougère

30g/1oz butter
1 medium onion, finely sliced
½ teaspoon curry powder
85g/3oz large mushrooms, sliced
1 tablespoon flour
2 teaspoons fresh chopped parsley

290ml/½ pint chicken stock
Salt and freshly ground black pepper
85g/3oz ham, chopped
285g/10oz cooked chicken, chopped
Dry breadcrumbs
A little melted butter for the top

1. Melt the butter in a saucepan and in it soften the onion until cooked but not brown. Add the curry powder and the mushrooms and cook for 1 minute.
2. Stir in the flour, cook for 1 minute and add the parsley, stock and freshly ground pepper and salt to taste.
3. Bring to the boil, stirring all the time. Simmer for 2 minutes. Add the ham and chicken.
4. Pile into a gougère case (page 380). Sprinkle with crumbs and melted butter and bake for 35–40 minutes.

Note: This is a good filling for pancakes, vol-au-vents or may be simply served on toast.

Makes filling for a 6-portion gougère

Vinegar Chicken

One 1·8 kilos/4lb chicken,
   jointed into 8 pieces
30g/1oz butter
5 large garlic cloves, unpeeled
5 tablespoons wine vinegar
290ml/½ pint dry white wine
2 tablespoons brandy

2 teaspoons pale French
   mustard
1 heaped teaspoon tomato
   purée
290ml/½ pint very fresh double
   cream
2 tomatoes, peeled and seeded

1. Heat the butter and in it brown the chicken pieces, skin side first. Add the unpeeled garlic and cover the pan. Cook gently for 20 minutes or until the chicken is tender. Pour off all but a tablespoon of the fat.
2. Add the vinegar to the pan, stirring well and scraping any sediment from the bottom. Boil rapidly until the liquid is reduced to about two tablespoons. Lift out the chicken and keep warm.
3. Add the wine, brandy, mustard and tomato purée to the remaining vinegar in the pan, mix well and boil to a thick sauce (about 5 minutes at a fast boil).
4. In a small heavy-bottomed saucepan boil the cream until reduced by half, stirring frequently to prevent burning. Take off the heat and fit a small wire sieve over the saucepan. Push the vinegar sauce through this, pressing the garlic cloves well to extract their pulp.
5. Mix the sauce and add salt and pepper as necessary. Cut the tomato into thin strips and stir into the sauce. Arrange the chicken on a hot serving dish, and spoon over the sauce.

Note I: The deliciousness of this dish – and it *is* delicious – depends on the vigorous reduction of the vinegar and wine. If the acids are not properly boiled down the sauce is too sharp.

Note II: Five cloves of garlic seems a lot. But the resulting smooth sauce does not taste particularly strongly of garlic.

Serves 4

Coq au Vin

55g/2oz butter
110g/¼lb lean bacon, finely
  diced
8 button onions
12 button mushrooms
1·35 kilos/3lb roasting chicken,
  jointed into 8 pieces
290ml/½ pint red wine

Chicken stock
1 small garlic clove, crushed
Bouquet garni (1 bay leaf, 1
  sprig each of thyme and
  parsley and 1 stick of celery,
  tied together with string)
Salt and pepper
20g/¾oz flour

To serve:
Buttered rice (page 262)
12 small triangular
  croutons

1 tablespoon chopped fresh
  parsley

1. Drop the bacon into a pan of boiling water for 30 seconds. Drain and dry well.
2. Put half the butter in a large heavy saucepan and slowly brown the bacon in it.
3. Add the onions, shaking the pan to brown them evenly all over.
4. Add the mushrooms (do not bother to peel them unless the skins are very tough). Fry fast for a further 2 minutes, then lift out all the fried food. Do not wash the pan.
5. Add the remaining butter to the juices in the pan and brown the chicken pieces slowly and well on all sides.
6. Return the vegetables and bacon pieces to the pan, and add the wine and enough stock to nearly cover the chicken pieces.
7. Add the crushed garlic, bouquet of herbs and salt and pepper.
8. With a wooden spoon move the pieces about and stir the sauce until it has come to the boil. Cover with a well-fitting lid and simmer slowly until the onions and chicken are tender (about 1 hour).
9. Remove the bouquet garni. Lift out all the solid ingredients

and put them on to a serving dish. Keep them warm while you make the sauce.

10. Skim all the fat from the cooking liquid, putting a tablespoonful of fat into a cup. Measure the liquid and make it up to 290ml/$\frac{1}{2}$ pint with more chicken stock or water. (If there is more than 290ml/$\frac{1}{2}$ pint boil the liquid rapidly to reduce it.)

11. Mix the flour with the fat in the cup, stir well and add a little of the hot cooking liquid to this paste. Return this mixture to the pan and bring gradually to the boil stirring continuously. Simmer for 2 minutes until the sauce is smooth and shiny.

12. Dish the joints on a deep platter, surround with the rice and spoon the sauce over the chicken. Garnish with the croutons and chopped parsley.

Note I: If there is time, marinade the chicken joints in the wine and bouquet garni for a few hours or overnight – this will improve the taste and colour. Dry the joints well before frying, or browning them will be difficult.

Note II: Coq au vin used to be made with a sauce thickened with the blood of the cockerel – rather like jugged hare. But today a freshly-killed chicken with the blood in a jug is very rare. However, if this method is to be followed, omit the flour from the recipe.

Chicken Sauté Normande

1·8 kilos/4lb roasting chicken
45g/1$\frac{1}{2}$oz butter
1 shallot, chopped
1 tablespoon Calvados
2 teaspoons flour
225ml/8fl.oz dry cider

150ml/$\frac{1}{4}$ pint chicken stock
Bouquet garni (bay leaf,
parsley stalks and 4 sprigs of
thyme, tied together with
string)
2 tablespoons cream

For the garnish:
2 dessert apples
15g/$\frac{1}{2}$oz butter

Chopped fresh parsley

1. Joint the chicken and brown the pieces in the butter.
2. Add the shallot and sauté for 2–3 minutes.
3. Add the Calvados, light it with a match and shake the pan until the flames die down. Remove the chicken joints.
4. Stir in the flour. Add the cider. Blend well and add the stock, bringing slowly to the boil, stirring continuously. Season and add the bouquet of herbs.
5. Replace the chicken, cover and simmer gently for about 40–50 minutes until tender.
6. Meanwhile prepare the garnish by frying slices of peeled apple in the butter until a good brown on each side. Keep warm.
7. When the chicken is tender lift it out and trim the joints neatly. Dish on an ovenproof platter and keep warm.
8. Add the cream to the sauce. Adjust the seasoning and reheat. Spoon over the chicken joints.
9. Garnish with apple slices and sprinkle with chopped parsley.

Serves 4

Chicken Paprika

1·8 kilos /4lb chicken
1 tablespoon oil
1 tablespoon butter
1 onion, finely sliced
2 level tablespoons paprika
225g/7oz can tomatoes
½ glass white wine

570ml/1 pint chicken stock
1 bay leaf
2 slices lemon
1 parsley stalk
Salt and freshly ground black pepper
150ml/¼ pint white sauce (page 308)

For the garnish:
1 tablespoon soured cream

Fresh parsley, chopped

1. Wash and wipe the chicken dry. Set the oven to 200 C/400 F, gas mark 6.
2. Heat the oil in a frying pan and when hot add the butter. When

385

the butter is foaming, add the chicken and brown it well all over. Take it out and put into a casserole.

3. Fry the onion in the oil and butter and when just beginning to brown reduce the heat and add the paprika. Cook for 2–3 minutes. Stir in the tomatoes, wine and stock. Add the bay leaf, lemon slices and parsley stalk. Season well. When boiling pour over the chicken.

4. Cover and bake in the oven for about 1 hour or until the chicken is cooked.

5. When the chicken is tender take it out of the casserole, remove the bay leaf, parsley stalk and lemon slices. Carefully skim off the fat with a spoon, or soak up and lift the fat by laying absorbent paper on the surface of the sauce. Liquidize the sauce or push it through a sieve.

6. Beat the paprika sauce into the white sauce until completely incorporated.

7. Joint the chicken neatly into eight pieces and arrange on a serving dish. Heat up the sauce and spoon it over the chicken. Trickle over the soured cream and sprinkle with chopped parsley.

Serves 4

Jambonneaux de Poulet

55g/2oz cooked ham, minced
55g/2oz cooked chicken livers, mashed
55g/2oz butter, softened
Salt and freshly ground black pepper
2 legs taken from 1 large chicken
45g/1½oz butter for frying

110g/4oz mixed finely chopped onion, celery and carrot (mirepoix)
75ml/4–5 tablespoons Madeira
225ml/8 fl.oz chicken stock
1 bay leaf
Sprig of watercress

1. Beat together the ham, chicken livers and softened butter. Taste and add pepper or salt if needed.

2. Remove the bone from the chicken legs without splitting the skin, working carefully from the thick end. Stuff the ham mixture into the boned-out chicken legs. With a trussing needle and fine string sew up the chicken joints so that they resemble miniature hams.

3. Melt half the butter in a flameproof casserole. When it is foaming and hot add the chicken legs and brown lightly all over, then remove them from the pan. Add the remaining butter to the casserole with the mirepoix of vegetables. Fry until the vegetables are lightly brown.

4. Place the jambonneaux (chicken legs) on top of the vegetables. Heat the Madeira in a small pan or ladle held over the flame. When hot set it alight with a match and pour it, flaming, into the pan. Add the chicken stock, bay leaf, salt and pepper. Bring to the boil, cover and simmer slowly for 1 hour.

5. When the chicken is cooked – when pierced with a skewer the juices that run out should be clear, not pink – remove to a plate and keep warm.

6. Strain the cooking liquor and press the vegetables to extract most of the juice. Reduce to a syrupy consistency, checking the seasoning. Hand the sauce separately in a warmed gravy boat. Garnish the jambonneaux with a sprig of watercress.

Serves 2

Boned Stuffed Chicken

One 1·8 kilos/4lb chicken
A little oil
1 teaspoon butter
1 bay leaf
425ml/$\frac{3}{4}$ pint chicken stock
  (made from the chicken
  bones)

387

For the stuffing:

15g/½oz butter
1 small onion, finely chopped
225g/½lb sausage-meat
2 tablespoons fresh white
   breadcrumbs

1 small apple, chopped
Pinch of fresh sage
1 egg
Salt and freshly ground black
   pepper

For the mirepoix:

1 small onion, finely chopped
1 small carrot, finely chopped

Stick of celery, finely chopped
Bunch of watercress

1. Bone the chicken completely, including the legs and wings (see page 83).
2. Make the stuffing: melt the butter, add the onion and cook until soft but not coloured. Mix together the sausage-meat, onion, breadcrumbs, apple, sage and egg and season well with salt and pepper.
3. Use this stuffing to fill the boned chicken. Draw up the sides and sew together with cotton or fine string.
4. Set the oven to 190°C/375°F, gas mark 5. Heat the oil in a large casserole dish, add the butter. When foaming add the chicken and brown all over. Remove the bird, reduce the heat and then lightly brown the mirepoix of vegetables.
5. Return the chicken to the casserole, add the bay leaf and stock and season well with salt and pepper. Cover and put into the oven for 1½ hours.
6. When the chicken is cooked remove it on to a warmed serving plate and remove the string or cotton.
7. Meanwhile make the sauce. Skim the fat from the top of the cooking juices and liquidize or sieve the remaining liquid and mirepoix. Return this to a rinsed-out saucepan and boil rapidly until a syrupy consistency is reached. Pour into a warmed gravy boat. Garnish the chicken with a small bunch of watercress.

Note: For a thinner, more elegant sauce, simply press the vegetables to extract most of their juices, but discard the vegetables. If necessary, boil the sauce to reduce to a syrupy consistency.

Serves 6

Boned Stuffed Poussin

A very small poussin normally serves one, but if it is boned and stuffed it will be enough for two not over-hungry people.

2 poussins
85g/3oz butter
1 large onion, finely chopped
110g/¼lb button mushrooms, sliced
55g/2oz fresh white breadcrumbs
2 tablespoons finely chopped fresh parsley
Grated rind of ½ lemon
Salt and freshly ground black pepper

About 1 tablespoon beaten egg
170g/6oz mixed chopped onion, carrot, turnip and celery (mirepoix)
290ml/½ pint chicken stock (made from bones of the poussin)
1 bay leaf
Bunch of watercress

1. Bone the poussins without removing the legs or wings (see page 83).
2. Make the stuffing: melt 30g/1oz of the butter, add the onion and cook slowly until soft but not coloured. Add the mushrooms and cook for 1 further minute.
3. Mix the onions and mushrooms with the breadcrumbs, parsley and lemon rind. Season with salt and pepper and add enough egg to just bind the mixture together. (Do not add too much egg or the stuffing will be heavy.)
4. Lay the poussins, skin side down, flat on the table top. Divide the stuffing between them and sew them up using cotton or very fine string. Try to shape them to their original form.
5. Melt half the remaining butter in a flameproof casserole. When it is foaming add the poussins and brown lightly all over, then remove them from the pan.
6. Add the remaining butter to the casserole with the mirepoix of diced vegetables. Fry until the vegetables are lightly brown.
7. Set the poussins on top of the vegetables. Add the chicken stock, bay leaf, salt and pepper. Bring to the boil, cover and simmer slowly for 40–50 minutes.

8. When the poussins are cooked – when pierced with a skewer the juices that run out should be clear, not pink – place them on a plate and remove the cotton or string. Keep warm.

9. Liquidize the cooking liquor and vegetables or press through a sieve to make a sauce. Reheat, checking the seasoning. Spoon a little sauce over the poussins and hand the rest separately in a warmed gravy boat. Garnish with watercress.

Note: For a thinner, more elegant sauce simply press the vegetables to extract most of their juices, but discard the vegetables. If necessary boil the sauce to reduce to a syrupy consistency.

Serves 4

Tarragon Chicken

One 1·8 kilos/4lb roasting chicken
55g/2oz butter
Slice of lemon
4 sprigs fresh tarragon

150ml/¼ pint chicken stock
20g/¾oz flour, sifted
150ml/¼ pint double cream
Salt and pepper

1. Heat the oven to 200°C/400°F, gas mark 6. Wipe inside and outside of chicken. Place inside the cavity a small nut of the butter, the lemon slice and half the tarragon. Season inside and out with salt and freshly milled pepper.

2. Melt the remaining butter in a casserole the size of the chicken and brown all sides of the bird in it. Place the giblets (except the liver) in the casserole, pour over the stock, cover with a lid and place in the oven. Leave to cook for 1½ hours or until the juice runs out clear, rather than pink, when the thigh is pierced with a skewer.

3. Take the chicken out of the casserole, draining the juices back in. Joint the chicken neatly and put the pieces in a covered dish. Keep warm.

4. Skim all the fat from the stock. Mix 1 tablespoon of this fat

with the flour in a teacup. When thoroughly blended pour more of the stock into the cup and mix well. Return this to the casserole and stir over direct heat until boiling.

5. Strain into a clean saucepan and add the remaining leaves of tarragon. Simmer for 1–2 minutes, then stir in the cream. Taste and season if necessary.
6. Pour over the chicken joints and serve.

Serves 4

Chicken Maryland

One 1·8 kilos/4lb chicken
1 tablespoon seasoned flour
1 egg, beaten
1 tablespoon dry white
    breadcrumbs
55g/2oz butter

To garnish:
Sweetcorn fritters (page 284)
8 rashers bacon
4 bananas
30g/1oz butter
Oil for frying
Bunch of watercress

1. Joint the chicken into eight pieces.
2. Dip each piece in seasoned flour, brush with beaten egg and coat with dry white breadcrumbs, pressing them on firmly.
3. Melt 55g/2oz butter in a large sauté pan and when foaming, add the chicken pieces, a few at a time, and fry both sides to a good brown. Reduce the heat and cook uncovered for a further 20–25 minutes.
4. Meanwhile prepare the garnishes: make the sweetcorn fritters and set aside until ready to fry them.
5. Cut the rind off the bacon rashers, stretch the rashers on a board with the back of a knife (this prevents shrinkage), roll up loosely and thread on two skewers. Set aside until ready to grill.
6. Peel the bananas and split them lengthways. Dip in seasoned flour and set aside until ready to fry.
7. When the chicken pieces are cooked and tender, transfer them to a cool oven to keep warm, but do not cover them.
8. Light the grill. You now have to fry the bananas in the

391

butter in one frying pan, the sweetcorn fritters in oil in a second pan and at the same time grill the bacon until crisp. So watch everything carefully, turning the food over as one side cooks. Drain well when cooked.

9. Arrange the chicken on a large serving platter and garnish with the corn fritters, bacon rolls and fried bananas. Arrange a small bunch of watercress on the dish and serve at once.

Serves 4–6

Chicken Croquettes

45g/1½oz butter
1 small onion, chopped
30g/1oz mushrooms, chopped
45g/1½oz flour
290ml/½ pint milk *or* milk and
  chicken stock mixed
Salt and pepper
1 teaspoon chopped fresh
  parsley

Oil for deep frying
1 egg yolk
Lemon juice
285g/10oz cooked chicken,
  diced finely *or* minced
Seasoned flour
1 egg, beaten
Dry white breadcrumbs

1. Melt the butter and add the onion. When the onion is soft but not coloured add the mushrooms and cook for 1 minute.
2. Add the flour and cook, stirring, for 1 minute. Draw the pan off the heat and stir in the milk. Return to the heat and bring slowly up to the boil, stirring continuously. Simmer for 2–3 minutes, season and add the chopped parsley. Remove from the heat and allow to get completely cold.
3. Meanwhile heat the oil until a crumb will sizzle in it.
4. When the sauce is cold beat in the egg yolk, add a squeeze of lemon juice and stir in the chicken flesh.
5. Using floured hands, shape the mixture into cylinders about 3·5cm/1½in long.
6. Coat with beaten egg and dip into breadcrumbs.
7. Deep fry the croquettes until golden brown. Drain well and serve at once.

Serves 4

Deep-Fried Chicken and Gruyère Pancakes

45g/1½oz butter
45g/1½oz flour
150ml/¼ pint chicken stock
150ml/¼ pint creamy milk
3 tablespoons white wine
Pinch of dry English mustard
Pinch of cayenne pepper
Salt and pepper

Oil for deep frying
225g/½lb cooked diced chicken
225g/½lb Gruyère cheese, diced
12 thin French pancakes
  (page 659)
1 egg, beaten

Tomato sauce (page 325)

1. Melt the butter and stir in the flour. Cook for 1 minute. Draw the pan off the heat and stir in the stock and the milk. Return to the heat and bring slowly to the boil, stirring continuously. Add the wine and simmer for 2–3 minutes. Season with mustard, cayenne, salt and pepper.
2. Allow to cool slightly.
3. Heat the oil until a crumb will sizzle gently in it.
4. Stir the chicken and cheese into the sauce and divide the mixture between the pancakes. Roll up the pancakes and brush well with beaten egg.
5. Lower into the deep fat and fry until golden brown.
6. Drain well and serve immediately with a thin tomato sauce handed separately.

Serves 4

Chicken Kiev

110g/¼lb butter
1 tablespoon chopped fresh
  parsley
Squeeze of lemon juice
Salt and freshly ground black
  pepper

The breasts from 2 medium
  chickens
Seasoned flour
Beaten egg
Dried white breadcrumbs
Oil for deep frying

393

1. Mix the butter with the parsely, lemon juice, salt and pepper. Divide the butter into four pieces, shape into rectangles and chill well.
2. Remove the skin and bone from the chicken breasts. You should have four equal-sized pieces of chicken. With a sharp knife split the breasts almost in half horizontally and open them out so that you have a chicken escalope. Put them between sheets of wet greaseproof paper and using a rolling pin carefully bat the chicken pieces to flatten the meat out thinly.
3. Place a piece of the prepared butter in the centre of each chicken piece. Roll up so that the butter is completely wrapped. Dust lightly with seasoned flour. Dip into beaten egg, then roll carefully in the crumbs. Chill for 30 minutes.
4. Brush with more beaten egg and roll again in dried crumbs. Leave to chill for another 30 minutes.
5. Heat the oil until a crumb will sizzle vigorously in it. Fry the chicken pieces in the oil for 8 minutes. Drain well on absorbent paper and serve. (Diners unfamiliar with chicken Kiev should be warned that the 'parcel' contains hot liquid butter and should be pierced carefully – cutting off one end is best – as there is a risk of spurting.)

Note I: Crushed garlic is frequently added to the butter inside the chicken. Though frowned on by classic chefs this is quite delicious. Other flavourings, such as chopped tarragon, smooth liver pâté, mashed anchovies, or a duxelle of mushrooms, can be good too. But the butter is the essential ingredient, providing flavour, moisture and drama all at once.

Note II: If desired, the small wing bone at the shoulder end of the breast can be left in place. When the chicken escalope is rolled up, the bone protrudes from the 'parcel', giving the breast the appearance of a drumstick.

Serves 4

Chicken St Menehould

1 leek
2 tablespoons white wine
1 onion, sliced
1 garlic clove
1 bay leaf
6 peppercorns
Pinch of thyme
570ml/1 pint water
One 1·8 kilos/4lb chicken
150ml/¼ pint milk

140g/5oz butter
85g/3oz flour
Salt and pepper
1 tablespoon fresh chopped
    parsley
Breadcrumbs
Oil for deep frying
Beaten egg
2 parsley stalks

1. Slice the white part of the leek. Put the leek, white wine, onion, garlic, bay leaf, peppercorns, thyme and 570ml/1 pint of water with the chicken into a saucepan. Cover and poach until tender (about 1½ hours). Remove the chicken, set aside and allow to cool. Carefully joint the chicken and remove the bones and skin from the joints. Skim the fat from the stock.
2. Boil the stock rapidly until you have about 150ml/¼ pint left. Strain and add the milk.
3. Melt 85g/3oz of the butter, add the flour and cook for 1 minute. Remove from the heat and beat in the milky stock. Return to the heat and bring slowly up to the boil, stirring continually, until you have a very thick white sauce panade. Check the seasoning and beat in the chopped parsley. Allow to cool.
4. Dry the chicken joints on absorbent paper. Spread them all over with the thick white sauce and roll them in the breadcrumbs. Chill in the refrigerator until firm.
5. Heat the fat in the fryer until a crumb will sizzle gently in it. Mix the egg with a little salt and use to coat the chicken joints well. Press on more breadcrumbs.
6. Fry the chicken until golden brown. To test if the chicken is hot right through, press a skewer into the centre, hold it there for 30 seconds and then lay the skewer on the palm of your hand. It should be hot rather than warm.

7.   Drain well on absorbent paper and serve at once.

Serves 4

French Roast Chicken

Butter
1·8 kilos/4lb roasting chicken
  with giblets
Pepper and salt

Slice of onion
Bay leaf
Few parsley stalks

For the gravy:
About 2 teaspoons flour
200ml/⅓ pint chicken stock *or*
  vegetable water

1.   Set the oven to 200 C/400 F, gas mark 6.
2.   Smear a little butter all over the chicken. Season inside and
     out with pepper only (no salt). Put the bird *breast-side-down* in the roasting tin.
3.   Put all the giblets (except the liver) and the neck into the pan
     with the chicken. Add the onion, bay leaf and parsley stalks.
     Pour in a cup of water. Roast the bird for 30 minutes.
4.   Take out, season all over with salt, turn the bird right side up
     and baste it with the fat and juices from the pan. Return to
     the oven.
5.   Check how the chicken is doing periodically. It will take 60–
     80 minutes. It is done when the leg bones wobble loosely and
     independently from the body. Baste occasionally as it cooks,
     and cover with foil or greaseproof paper if it is browning
     too much. When the chicken is done remove it to a serving
     dish, and keep warm while making the gravy.
6.   Place the pan with its juices on a low heat on top of the
     cooker. Skim off most of the fat.
7.   Whisk in enough flour to absorb the remaining fat.
8.   Add the chicken stock or vegetable water and stir until the
     sauce boils. Strain into a gravy boat.

Note: If liked the chicken liver can be fried in a little butter, chopped and added to the gravy.

Serves 4

English Roast Chicken

1·8 kilos/4lb roasting chicken
Slice of lemon

15g/½oz butter
Freshly ground black pepper

For the stuffing:
30g/1oz butter
1 small onion, finely chopped
55g/2oz fresh breadcrumbs
30g/1oz chopped nuts
1 small cooking apple, grated

2 teaspoons chopped mixed
   fresh herbs
Grated rind ½ lemon
Beaten egg
Salt and pepper

For the garnish:
4 chipolata sausages

4 rashers streaky bacon

For the gravy:
2 teaspoons flour
290ml/½ pint chicken stock
  (made from the neck and
  giblets, see page 302)

To accompany:
Bread sauce (page 324)

1. Set the oven to 200 C/400 F, gas mark 6.
2. Rub the chicken all over with the lemon slice.
3. Start the stuffing by melting the butter and frying the onion until soft but not coloured.
4. Put the breadcrumbs, nuts, cooking apple, herbs and lemon rind together in a mixing bowl.
5. Add the softened onion and enough beaten egg to bind the mixture together. Do not make it too wet. Season to taste.
6. Stuff the chicken from the neck end, making sure the breast is well plumped. Draw the neck skin flap down to cover the stuffing. Secure with a skewer if necessary.
7. Smear a little butter all over the chicken and season with

pepper only – salt draws out the juices and will make the bird less moist. Roast for about 1½ hours or until the juices run clear when the thigh is pierced with a skewer.

8. Meanwhile make each chipolata sausage into two cocktail-sized ones by twisting gently in the middle. Take the rind off the bacon and cut each rasher into two short lengths. Roll them up.

9. When the chicken has had 45 minutes in the oven put the sausages and bacon rolls in the same pan, wedging the bacon rolls so that they cannot come undone.

10. Baste occasionally and check that the sausages and bacon are not sticking to the side of the tin and getting burnt.

11. When the chicken is cooked lift it on to a warm serving dish, surround with the bacon rolls and sausages and keep warm while you make the gravy.

12. Slowly pour off all but a tablespoon of fat from the roasting pan, taking care to keep any juices. Add the flour and stir over heat for 30 seconds. Add the chicken stock and stir until the sauce boils. Simmer for 2 minutes. Taste and add more pepper and salt if necessary. Strain into a gravy boat.

13. Serve the chicken with bread sauce and gravy handed separately.

Note I: English chicken is usually stuffed from the neck end or breast but the stuffing may be put into the body cavity if preferred.

Note II: The chicken looks neater if it is trussed after stuffing, but it is more difficult to get the thighs cooked without the breast drying out if this is done.

Serves 4

Chicken with Prunes

1·8 kilos/4lb chicken
30g/1oz butter
Few slices onion
Slice of lemon

Salt and freshly ground black
  pepper
1 bay leaf
Few slices carrot

For the sauce:
15g/½oz butter
12 shallots, peeled
12 stoned cooked prunes

1 tablespoon sugar
1 tablespoon vinegar

For the garnish:
Bunch of watercress

1. Set the oven to 200 C/400 F, gas mark 6.
2. Wipe the chicken. Place half the butter, half the onion and the lemon in the breast cavity. Put, breast side down, in a roasting dish with 5mm/¼in water. Spread the remaining butter over the chicken and season with salt and pepper. Add the giblets (except the liver), the bay leaf, remaining onion and carrot to the water.
3. Roast for 1–1¼ hours, basting three or four times and turning the bird over at half-time. When the chicken is done clear juices will run from the thigh when pierced with a skewer.
4. Meanwhile prepare the sauce: melt the butter and when foaming add the shallots. Cover and cook slowly, shaking the pan occasionally to prevent them burning but allowing them to brown all over. Add the prunes to the pan and reduce the heat to a minimum.
5. Slowly melt the sugar in a heavy saucepan tilting and turning it as necessary to get an even pale caramel colour. Add the vinegar – stand back as it will hiss and splutter. Add 2 table-spoons of chicken stock from the bottom of the roasting pan. Simmer until the caramel is dissolved. Season if necessary.
6. Arrange the jointed chicken on a serving dish. Spoon over the prunes and shallots and glaze with the caramel sauce. Garnish with watercress.

Serves 4

Lemon Chicken

85g/3oz butter
Juice of 2 lemons
Three 2-portion spring
  chickens *or* two 1·5 kilo/3lb
  roasting chickens

2 teaspoons sugar
Paprika
Salt and freshly ground black
  pepper
Watercress

1. Melt the butter in a large saucepan (or two if necessary) and add the lemon juice.
2. Lay the chickens in whole and cover with the lid.
3. Cook on a gentle heat for 30 minutes, turning the chickens to brown slightly on all sides. They should now be partially cooked, and the butter and lemon juice in the pan should be brown but not burnt.
4. Take out the birds and split them in two or joint them if large.
5. Heat the grill. Lay the portions of chicken cut-side up on the grill tray. Brush them with some of the lemon juice and butter from the saucepan(s). Sprinkle with half the sugar and plenty of paprika and pepper. Grill slowly for about 15 minutes or until a really good brown.
6. Turn the joints over and again brush with lemon juice and butter, and sprinkle with sugar, paprika and pepper. Grill for a further 15 minutes until cooked through and very dark – almost, but not quite, charred. Sprinkle with salt.
7. Arrange on a heated dish, pour over the juices from the grill pan and garnish with sprigs of watercress.

Serves 6

Spatchcock Grilled Chicken

Four 450g/1lb baby chickens
Salt and freshly ground black
  pepper

Lemon juice
55g/2oz butter
15g/½oz Parmesan cheese,
  grated

Pinch of cayenne

For the garnish:

Watercress   Sauce Robert (page 314)
French dressing

1. Split the chickens down one side of the backbone with a pair
    of poultry shears or kitchen scissors. Cut down the other side
    of the backbone to remove it. Open out the chickens and
    flatten well on a board by pressing with the heel of your
    hand. Skewer the birds in position, i.e. flat and open.
2. Season well with salt, pepper and cayenne and sprinkle with
    lemon juice. If possible leave for 1 hour.
3. Heat the grill. Brush the skin side of the chickens with melted
    butter. Place under the grill for about 12 minutes or until
    a good golden brown, brushing with the pan juices frequently.
    Turn over, brush again and grill for a further 7 minutes or
    until the chicken is cooked.
4. Turn the chicken over again, brush once more with the hot
    butter and sprinkle with the Parmesan cheese. Grill until
    golden brown and crisp. Arrange on a serving dish and
    garnish with watercress dipped in French dressing. Serve with
    Sauce Robert.

Serves 4

Chicken and Beanshoot Salad

One 1·8 kilos/4lb cooked   1 tablespoon fresh chopped
  chicken, preferably poached   mint
450g/1lb beanshoots   French dressing (page 319)
1 small onion, finely chopped   Soy sauce

1. Pull the chicken into 2·5cm/1in strips, discarding the skin and
    bones. Mix with the washed but raw beanshoots.
2. Add the onion and mint to the French dressing and mix with
    the chicken and beanshoots.
3. Pile into a serving dish and sprinkle liberally with soy sauce.

Serves 6

Chicken Chaudfroid

One 1·8 kilos/4lb chicken,
  not trussed
1 onion, sliced
¼ carrot

For the aspic jelly:
860ml/1½ pints chicken stock
55g/2oz gelatine
5 tablespoons white wine
5 tablespoons sherry
1 tablespoon wine vinegar
3 egg whites
3 egg shells, crushed

For the garnish:
Fine slices cooked button
  mushroom *or* truffle *or* fresh
  tarragon leaves
1 punnet mustard *or* cress

2 bay leaves
Sprig of parsely
6 peppercorns
½ teaspoon salt

For the chaudfroid sauce:
1 bay leaf
4 peppercorns
Slice of onion
Blade of mace
Sprig of parsley
425ml/¾ pint milk
30g/1oz butter
30g/1oz flour
Salt
150ml/¼ pint chicken aspic
15g/½oz gelatine
5 tablespoons cream

This is cold chicken coated with a white sauce, glazed with aspic jelly, and garnished with slices of truffle or mushroom. The chicken should be cooked the day before serving because the stock in which it is cooked becomes the aspic jelly.

1. On the first day place the chicken in a saucepan, just cover with cold water, add the vegetables, herbs, peppercorns and salt. Bring to the boil, cover and simmer gently until the chicken is tender (about 1¼ hours). When it is cooked a skewer will glide easily into the thigh, and the drumstick should feel loose.
2. Remove the bird from the pan (but see *Note II*), allow it to cool, (loosely covered with foil) and place it in the refrigerator overnight. Strain the stock and leave it to cool. If possible, refrigerate it (this will set the fat and make it easier to remove the next day).

3. The next day remove all the fat from the chicken stock. Put the stock (which should be about 860ml/1½ pints) and gelatine into a clean pan. Add the wine, sherry and vinegar. Put over a gentle heat.

4. Place the crushed shells in a bowl, add the egg white and whisk until frothy. Pour into the warming stock and keep whisking steadily with balloon whisk until the mixture boils and rises. Stop whisking immediately, and draw the pan off the heat. Allow the mixture to subside. Take care not to break the crust formed by the egg white.

5. Bring the aspic up to the boil again and again allow to subside. Repeat this once more (the egg white will trap the sediment in the stock and clear the aspic). Allow to cool for 10 minutes.

6. Fix a double layer of fine muslin over a clean basin and carefully strain the aspic through it, taking care to hold the egg white crust back. When all the liquid is through (or almost all of it) allow the egg white to slip into the muslin. Then strain the aspic again – this time through both egg white crust and cloth. Do not try to hurry the process by squeezing the cloth, or murky aspic will result.

7. Make the chaudfroid sauce: place the bay leaf, peppercorns, onion slice, mace and parsley sprig in a saucepan with the milk. Set over a gentle heat and bring slowly to the boil. Leave to cool for 10 minutes.

8. Melt the butter, add the flour and cook for 1 minute. Draw off the heat and slowly, stirring all the time, strain over the milk. Return the pan to the heat and bring slowly up to the boil, stirring continually until you have a slightly thickened shiny sauce. Season well with salt and simmer gently for 2–3 minutes.

9. In a small pan put 150ml/¼ pint of the aspic, and sprinkle on the gelatine. Allow to soak for 10 minutes then heat gently until clear and warm. Stir this into the white sauce with the cream. Taste and add more salt if necessary. The sauce must be very smooth and shiny: it can be strained through a tammy cloth or strainer or whizzed in a liquidizer to give it a good sheen. Stir the sauce as it cools and begins to

set. When it is the consistency of thick cream it is ready to use for coating.

10. To prepare the chicken, skin and joint it very neatly into four or eight pieces, removing the wing tips and drumstick knuckle. Place the pieces on a wire rack with a tray underneath.

11. Coat each chicken joint very carefully with the nearly set chaudfroid sauce. Allow to set and if necessary give it a second coating, scraping extra sauce (which will need reheating slightly to return it to coating consistency) from the tray underneath the wire rack.

12. When nearly set arrange the slices of mushroom or truffle or the tarragon leaves in a formal simple pattern on each chicken piece. Allow to set.

13. Coat with some of the cool but still liquid aspic. Allow to set. Give a second and perhaps third coating, allowing each coating to set before attempting the next.

14. Pour the remaining aspic on to a shallow tray. Allow to set, then cut it into neat dice. Use it to cover a large flat serving dish and make a slight dome in the centre. Arrange the chicken chaudfroid around this and surround with small clumps of mustard or cress.

Note I: Chaudfroid is classically decorated with sliced truffles. These are delicious if fresh but disappointing and expensive if bought in tins. Mushrooms make an inexpensive and satisfactory substitute. Fresh tarragon leaves are pretty and give the dish a delicious flavour.

Note II: The chicken is undeniably juicier if it is cooled in the cooking stock, rather than out of it. But the cooling must be rapid (prolonged lukewarm temperatures lead to the growth of bacteria). For this reason the recipe suggests cooling stock and bird separately. To get the best of both worlds, however, the whole suacepan, containing chicken and stock, can be stood in a large bowl of cold water in the sink, with the cold tap keeping the water refreshed and cold. In this way cooling will be very quick.

Note III: If the aspic is less than crystal clear it is wise not to chop it – which seems to emphasize its murkiness.

Serves 4

TURKEY

Roast Turkey

A large square of fine muslin (butter-muslin) is needed for this recipe.

5·35 kilos/12lb turkey

For the oatmeal stuffing:
1 large onion, finely chopped
340g/¾lb medium oatmeal
1 teaspoon rubbed dried sage
  or 4 leaves fresh sage, chopped
170g/6oz shredded beef suet
Salt and freshly ground black
  pepper

For the sausage-meat and chestnut stuffing:
450g/1lb sausage-meat
450g/1lb unsweetened
  chestnut purée
110g/¼lb fresh breadcrumbs
1 large egg
Salt and freshly ground black
  pepper

To prepare the turkey for the oven:
170g/6oz butter
Freshly ground black pepper
Giblets
½ onion
2 bay leaves
Few parsley stalks
290ml/½ pint water

For the garnish:
1 chipolata sausage per person
1 streaky bacon rasher per
  person

For the gravy:
1 tablespoon flour
Stock *or* vegetable water

1. Weigh the turkey. Calculate the cooking time with the help of the chart on page 158.

2. Make the oatmeal stuffing: mix together the onion, oatmeal, sage, and shredded suet. Add enough water just to bind the mixture together, taste and season as required. Stuff into the cavity of the turkey.

3. Make the sausage-meat and chestnut stuffing: mix together the sausage-meat, chestnut purée, breadcrumbs and beaten egg. Taste and season as required. Stuff this into the neck end of the turkey, making sure that the breast is well-plumped. Draw the skin flap down to cover the stuffing. Skewer in place.

4. Set the oven to 180 C/350 F, gas mark 4.

5. Melt the butter and in it soak a very large piece of butter-muslin (about four times the size of the turkey) until all the butter has been completely absorbed.

6. Season the turkey well with pepper only – salt draws out the juices and will make the bird less moist. Put it into a large roasting tin with the giblets (except the liver) and neck, add the onion, bay leaf and parsley stalks and pour in the water. Completely cover the bird with the doubled butter-muslin and roast in the prepared oven for the time calculated (a 5·3 kilo/12lb turkey should take 3–3½ hours).

7. Meanwhile prepare the garnishes: make each chipolata sausage into two cocktail-sized ones by twisting gently in the middle. Take the rind off the bacon. Stretch each rasher slightly with the back of a knife, cut into two and roll up. Put the sausages and bacon rolls into a second roasting pan, with the bacon rolls wedged in so that they cannot unravel. Half an hour before the turkey is done put the sausages and bacon in the oven.

8. When the turkey is cooked – the juices that run out of the thigh when pierced with a skewer should be clear – remove the muslin and lift on to a serving dish. Surround with the bacon and sausages and keep warm while making the gravy.

9. Lift the pan with its juices on to the top of the cooker and skim off the fat. Whisk in the flour and add enough chicken stock or vegetable water to make up to about 425ml/¾ pint. Stir until boiling, then simmer for a few minutes. Taste and

add salt and pepper if necessary. Strain into a warm gravy boat.

Serves 12

Christmas Turkey Stuffed with Ham

One 2·3 kilos/5lb piece of boiled bacon *or* ham, skinned
One 6·7 kilos/15lb turkey, boned (page 83)

For roasting:
55g/2oz butter
1 onion, sliced
3 bay leaves
2 parsley stalks
425ml/¾ pint water

For the gravy:
2 tablespoons flour
About 290ml/½ pint turkey stock
Bunch of watercress

For the stuffing:
30g/1oz butter
1 large onion, finely chopped
900g/2lb belly of pork, minced
450g/1lb unsweetened canned chestnut purée *or* mashed cooked fresh chestnuts
225g/½lb fresh white breadcrumbs
2 eggs lightly beaten
1 teaspoon dried sage
2 tablespoons chopped parsley
Salt and freshly ground black pepper

1. Set the oven to 200°C/400°F, gas mark 6.
2. To make the stuffing, melt the butter, add the onion and cook until soft but not coloured.
3. Once cold mix with all the other stuffing ingredients.
4. Open the turkey out flat on a board, skin side down. Spread the stuffing on the turkey and put the ham or bacon on top.
5. Draw up the sides and sew together with needle and fine string. Turn the bird right side up and try to push it into an even, rounded shape.
6. Smear the butter all over the turkey and put it into a roasting tin. Add the giblets (except the liver) and the neck. Add the onion, bay leaves and parsley stalks. Pour in the water. If

the turkey looks too flat, wedge the sides with bread tins to hold it in shape.

7. Roast the bird for 1 hour, lower the temperature to 180°C/350°F, gas mark 4 and roast for a further 3 hours. Baste occasionally as it cooks and cover with foil or grease-proof paper if it is browning too much.

8. When the turkey is cooked (that is when a skewer will glide through the thigh easily) lift it on to a serving dish and keep warm while you make the gravy.

9. Lift the pan with its juices on to the top of the cooker. Pour off as much fat as possible.

10. Stir in (using a wooden spoon or wire whisk) enough flour to absorb the remaining fat. Add 290ml/½ pint stock and stir until the sauce boils. Strain into a warmed gravy boat.

11. Garnish the turkey with the watercress and hand the gravy separately.

Note I: This turkey is delicious served cold with a herby mayonnaise.

Note II: The turkey may be stuffed the day before cooking. If this is done care should be taken that both turkey and stuffing are well chilled before the bird is stuffed. Refrigerate until ready to cook.

Note III: If the turkey is roasted covered in 2 layers of muslin (or J-cloths) completely saturated in melted butter, there is no need for basting during cooking, and when the cloths are removed the bird will be brown and crisp.

Serves 20

DUCK

Stuffed Boned Duck

2·3–2·7 kilos/5–6lb duck, boned
45g/1½oz butter
1 medium onion, finely chopped
85g/3oz mushrooms, sliced
1 small garlic clove, crushed
85g/3oz fresh white breadcrumbs

Four 5cm/¼in slices ham, cut into small cubes
85g/3oz pork belly, minced
1 egg
1 egg yolk
Salt and freshly ground black pepper
Bunch of watercress

1. Carefully remove any extra fat from the duck, especially from the vent end.
2. To make the stuffing melt the butter, add the chopped onion and fry gently until it is soft and transparent. Add the mushrooms and garlic and cook for 2 more minutes.
3. Take the pan off the heat and add the breadcrumbs, diced ham, belly-pork, the egg and the yolk and plenty of salt and pepper. Mix well.
4. Stuff the duck and sew it up with a needle and cotton.
5. Put into a roasting pan on a wire rack. Prick lightly and rub with salt. Roast for 1½ hours at 200°C/400°F, gas mark 6, or until the bird is brown and crisp all over.
6. Drain off the fat and dish the bird on a platter. Serve hot or cold, garnished with the bunch of washed watercress.

Boning: If the butcher will not bone the duck, instructions will be found on pages 45–6.

Serves 6–8

Leith's Roast Duckling

2·3–2·7 kilos/5–6lb duckling
(should have a soft, pliable
backbone, a dry soft skin –
not slimy – and be as plump
as possible)
Salt and pepper
30g/1oz granulated sugar
1 tablespoon vinegar
150ml/¼ pint duck or chicken
stock

2 teaspoons brandy
15g/½oz butter
45g/1½oz flaked almonds
1 celery stick, finely chopped
Juice and grated rind of 1
orange
1 small onion, finely chopped

To garnish:
1 whole orange
Bunch of watercress

1. Set the oven to 200°C/400°F, gas mark 6.
2. Prick the bird all over, dust it with salt, and put it in the roast for 1 hour. It needs no fat, but it is a good idea to lay it legs up for the first 30 minutes and turn it right side up for the next 30 minutes.
3. Take it out, drain well, and joint it. Put the pieces into a clean roasting pan, skin side up. Keep the roasting juices.
4. Put the sugar and vinegar in a thick-bottomed saucepan. Dissolve the sugar over gentle heat, then boil until the sugar caramelizes: it will go dark brown and bubbly, with large slow bubbles. Pour on the stock: it will hiss and splutter so take care. Stir until the caramel lumps disappear. Add the orange rind and juice, any roasting juices from the duck (but no fat) and the brandy. Pour over the duck.
5. Return to the oven and continue cooking until the joints are cooked through (another 20 minutes or so). Do *not* baste. Remove the duck joints on to an ovenproof plate and keep warm. (If the skin is not truly crisp the duck can be returned to the oven for 10 minutes like this without the sauce.)
6. Fry the flaked almonds in the butter until golden brown. Scatter over the duck.

410

7. Skim the sauce to remove any fat, and strain it into a saucepan. Add the finely chopped celery and onion, and boil until the celery is just beginning to soften but is still a little crunchy (about 5 minutes). Taste the sauce and add salt and pepper. You should have a thin, fairly clear liquid with plenty of chopped celery and onion in it. Serve the sauce separately – or poured round, not over, the duck.

8. Cut the orange (with the skin on) in half and slice it. Surround the duck with the orange slices and put a bouquet of watercress at each end of the dish.

Note: This recipe is a speciality of Leith's Restaurant in London.

Serves 3

Pressed Duck

Pressed duck, requiring an expensive duck press, expensive ingredients, skill, timing and showmanship, is seldom made today. But it is a remarkably fine dish, and is the speciality of the famous Tour d'Argent restaurant in Paris. For true pressed duck Rouen duckling is used – its characteristic red flesh and gamey flavour is due to the method of killing: the bird is smothered rather than bled, so loses none of its blood before cooking. Unfortunately dangerous toxins can develop in ducks killed by this method, so they should be eaten very fresh, preferably on the day of killing.

In England, Aylesbury ducks, which have certain similarities to the Rouen breed, although they are killed by the conventional bleeding method, are used. A little demi-glace sauce may be added to the final sauce to make up for the extra juices produced by the Rouen duck but lacking in the Aylesbury.

Two 2·3 kilos/5lb very fresh ducklings
Salt and freshly ground black pepper
Pinch of ground cloves
150ml/¼ pint good red wine

3 tablespoons brandy
150ml/¼ pint demi-glaçe sauce (page 313) if using Aylesbury duck
1 tablespoon butter

411

1. Heat the oven to 450°F/230°C, gas mark 8.
2. Clean the ducks, prick all over and sprinkle with salt. Roast for 15 minutes only. Remove from the oven.
3. In classic pressed duck the legs are not used. But if they are to be used proceed as follows: remove the legs (which will still be raw), make a few cuts on the underside, and season with salt, pepper and ground cloves. Brush with a very little melted butter. Heat the grill, then grill the legs on both sides until cooked. Keep warm.
4. Remove each side of the breast from the carcases in one piece. Set them aside and chop the carcasses up roughly, putting them and any juices into a bowl.
5. The rest of the preparation and cooking should be done in the dining room, using board, knife, duck press, sauté pan, small saucepan and flame lamp or hot plate. You also need to have a napkin, the brandy, wine, butter, duck carcasses, metal serving dish, and of course the duck breasts and legs (if used) close at hand. But the whole dish can be made as well, if less dramatically, in the kitchen.
6. Reduce the wine to 2 tablespoons, by rapid boiling.
7. Cut the breasts across into small pieces and lay them on the serving dish.
8. Put the duck carcasses, the reduced wine and salt, pepper and a pinch of cloves into the press. Put the sauté pan under the spout and press well to extract all the juices. Put the sauté pan over direct heat and add the brandy and demi-glaçe sauce if used; heat carefully without boiling. Taste, add more salt and pepper if necessary, and finally beat in the butter bit by bit.
9. Put the legs (if used) at each end of the serving dish and put over direct heat to warm through. Pour over the hot sauce and serve at once.

Serves 4–6

Roast Duck Apple Sauce

One 3 kilos/6½lb duck
Salt and freshly ground black
  pepper
½ onion
½ orange

30g/1oz flour
290ml/½ pint duck *or* strong
  chicken stock
Apple sauce (page 323)

1. Set the oven to 190°C/375°F, gas mark 5. Wipe the duck clean, inside and out. Season the cavity well with salt and pepper. Place the onion and orange inside the duck. Prick the skin all over and sprinkle with salt.
2. Put the duck upside down, on a rack in a roasting pan and roast for 45 minutes. Then pour off the fat. Turn the duck over and continue roasting until cooked (about 45 minutes). Test by sticking a skewer into the thigh – if the juices come out pink the duck needs further cooking.
3. Tip the juices from the cavity into a bowl and reserve them. Joint the duck into six pieces and arrange the joints on a serving dish; or leave whole for carving at the table. In any event keep it warm, without covering (this would spoil the crisp skin).
4. To make the gravy pour off all the fat in the roasting pan except a tablespoon. Stir the remaining spoon of fat and any juices over a low heat, scraping the bottom of the pan to loosen all the sediment. Whisk in the flour, add the juices from inside the duck and the stock and whisk until smooth. Simmer, stirring, for 1 minute. Taste and season.
5. Pour the gravy into a warmed gravy boat. Fill a second gravy boat with hot or cold apple sauce.

Serves 4

GOOSE

Cold Boned Goose with Aspic

1 medium-sized goose
1 carrot, chopped
1 onion, chopped
2 leeks, chopped
Stick of celery, chopped
6 peppercorns
Bouquet garni (bay leaf,
  parsley stalk, mace and
  thyme)

For the aspic:
150ml/$\frac{1}{4}$ pint dry cider
55g/2oz gelatine
2 egg shells, crushed
2 egg whites

For the garnish:
1 small orange
Bunch of watercress

For the stuffing:
30g/1oz butter
1 onion, finely chopped
4 dates, finely chopped
170g/6oz sausage-meat
2 tablespoons chopped mint
225g/$\frac{1}{2}$lb dessert apples, peeled
  and chopped
225g/$\frac{1}{2}$lb cooking apples,
  peeled and chopped
85g/3oz breadcrumbs
Salt and freshly ground black
  pepper
1 egg, beaten

1. Bone the goose completely, including the legs and wings (see page 83).
2. To make the stock for the aspic place the goose bones and giblets (except the liver) in a large pan with the chopped carrots, onion, leeks, celery, peppercorns and bouquet garni. Bring to the boil, cover and simmer for 1 hour.
3. To make the stuffing melt the butter, add the onion and cook slowly until soft but not coloured. Add the apples and cook for 1 further minute. Allow to cool.
4. Stir the apple and onion mixture into the breadcrumbs, dates and sausage-meat. Add the mint and season well. Add enough beaten egg just to bind the mixture together.
5. Lay the goose, skin side down, on a wooden board. Remove

any excess fat. Pile on the stuffing and roll up the goose into a neat roll, making sure that all the untidy ends are tucked in. Sew up very neatly using a needle and fine string. Wrap the goose in a piece of muslin or a clean tea-towel and tie it securely.

6. Strain the stock and taste for seasoning. Put the goose into a heavy saucepan or fish kettle and pour on the stock. Bring to the boil, cover tightly and simmer slowly for 2 hours. Turn the goose over once during the cooking. Drain, reserving the stock for the aspic.

7. As soon as the goose is cool enough to handle tighten the wrappings, and put on a plate. When cold, refrigerate.

8. Pour the stock into a bowl and leave to cool overnight. If the stock can be transferred to the refrigerator once it is cold so much the better – it will set the fat and make removing it easier. Next day lift or skim off any fat from the goose stock. It must be absolutely fat-free.

9. Put 860ml/1½ pints of the goose stock (make up with water if not enough) into a very large saucepan with the cider and gelatine. Put over a gentle heat.

10. Place the crushed shells in a bowl, add the egg white and whisk until frothy. Pour into the warming stock and keep whisking steadily with a balloon whisk until the mixture boils and rises. Stop whisking immediately, and draw the pan off the heat. Allow the mixture to subside. Take care not to break the crust formed by the egg white.

11. Bring the stock up to the boil again and again allow to subside. Repeat this once more (the egg white will trap the sediment in the stock and clear the aspic). Allow to cool for 10 minutes.

12. Fix a double layer of fine muslin over a clean basin and carefully strain the aspic through it, taking care to hold the egg white crust back. When all the liquid is through (or almost all of it) allow the egg white to slip into the muslin. Then strain the aspic again – this time through both egg white crust and cloth. Do not try to hurry the process by squeezing the cloth or you will get murky jelly. Allow to cool until on the point of setting.

415

13. Unwrap the goose. Wipe away all grease. Place it on a wire rack with a tray underneath.
14. Coat it with the nearly-set aspic. Place in the refrigerator until set.
15. Cut the orange, skin and all, across into very thin even slices. You should end up with seven or eight. Dip the orange slices in a little cool aspic and arrange them in a neat over-lapping row down the centre of the goose. Leave to set. Coat the goose with more aspic. Once this layer has set add further layers until really shiny. Place on a serving dish.
16. Set the remaining aspic in a shallow tray. Cut into neat squares and use to surround the goose. Garnish with water-cress.

Note: If the aspic is less than crystal clear it is wise not to chop it – which seems to emphasize its murkiness.

Serves 10

Confit D'oie
(Preserved goose)

This recipe, still common in France, is for goose flesh preserved in fat. The pieces of goose are lifted from the jar, and wiped clean of fat before being served either cold or reheated, or used in composite dishes. The confit takes 3 days to complete. Use a very fat goose.

One 4·5 kilos/10lb goose   2 bay leaves, pounded
900g/2lb salt   Pinch of thyme
7g/¼oz saltpetre   1·8 kilos/4lb goose fat
4 cloves, crushed   450g/1lb lard

1. Cut the goose into quarters.
2. Mix together the salt, saltpetre, cloves, bay leaves and thyme and rub some of this over the whole surface of the goose.
3. Put the goose into a glazed earthenware pot and add the re-maining spiced salt. Cover and leave for 24 hours.
4. Slowly melt the goose fat in a large saucepan. Remove the

goose pieces from the salt, wipe clean and put into the fat. Place over slow heat and cook very gently for 3 hours. To test if the goose is cooked prick it with a skewer. The juices that run out should be clear, and the flesh feel tender.

5. Drain the pieces of goose and remove the bones. Strain a thick layer of fat in which the goose was cooked into a large glazed earthenware jar.

6. When this fat has completely solidified arrange the pieces of goose on top, being careful to prevent any of them touching the wall of the jar.

7. Cover the pieces of goose with just-liquid cool goose fat. Put into a cool place.

8. Leave to rest for 2 days. Strain some more liquid goosefat into the jar to seal any holes which may have occurred.

9. When this is set melt the lard and pour a layer about 1 cm/½in thick over the surface. When this is set put a circle of grease-proof paper on top, pressing it down to exclude any air. Cover the top of the jar with a double thickness of paper and tie with string.

10. The confit d'oie will keep for months in a cool place. To use it, wipe off all the fat, then treat as fresh-cooked goose. The fat can be simmered, strained and kept for re-use.

Note: Goosefat is seldom available in Britain, but beef dripping, lard (or a mixture of melted duck fat and lard) will do.

Serves 6

GAME

Jugged Hare

1 hare, skinned and jointed, and its blood
Dripping
225g/½lb mirepoix of carrot, onion and celery
Bouquet garni (1 bay leaf, 2 parsley stalks, sprig of thyme)

570ml/1 pint good brown stock
Salt and freshly ground black pepper
1 tablespoon redcurrant jelly
3 tablespoons port

1. Wash and wipe dry the pieces of hare. Heat the dripping in a large saucepan and fry the joints until well browned, adding more dripping if the pan becomes dry. Lift out the joints and brown the mirepoix.
2. Return the hare. Add the bouquet garni, stock, salt and pepper. Cover and simmer for 2½ hours or until the hare is really tender.
3. Arrange the joints in a casserole.
4. Strain the stock into a saucepan. Add the redcurrant jelly and port and simmer for 5 minutes. Draw the pan off the heat.
5. Mix the blood with a cupful of the hot stock. Pour back into the pan without allowing the sauce to boil. The blood will slightly thicken the sauce.
6. Taste the sauce, adding salt and pepper if necessary. Pour over the hare joints in the casserole and serve.

Note: The sauce depends on the blood to thicken it. If very little blood (less than 150ml/¼ pint) comes with the hare, the basic stock must be thickened with a little beurre manié) (flour and butter kneaded together in equal quantities, and whisked in small blobs into the boiling stock). This must be done *before* the addition of the blood, which would curdle if boiled.

Serves 6–8

Partridge Baked with Cabbage

Butter *or* bacon dripping for frying
3 partridges
2 tablespoons each of brandy and Madeira
10 large cabbage leaves
4 rashers rindless streaky bacon
225g/½lb belly of pork, minced
Salt and freshly ground black pepper
Pinch of fresh sage
225g/½lb smoked pork

For the sauce:
1 bay leaf
1–2 slices onion
1 carrot, chopped
Bunch of parsley
15g/½oz flour
15g/½oz butter

1. Melt the fat and fry the partridges fairly fast for 5 minutes on each side, so that they are well browned. Pour in the brandy and the Madeira and set them alight. Leave the birds in the pan(s) to cool so that you can collect any juices that run out.
2. Briefly cook the washed cabbage leaves in boiling water for 2–3 minutes, then lift them out, keeping the water.
3. Butter a large ovenproof pie dish or casserole and lay the rashers of bacon in the bottom. Line the dish with some of the cabbage leaves.
4. Cut the flesh from the partridges and put the breast meat into the dish inside the cabbage lining. Pour on any pan juices.
5. Mince the leg meat and mix it with the minced pork. Flavour with salt, pepper and sage. Roll this mixture (with floured hands) into tiny sausages. Fry these quickly, to brown them only, in butter or bacon fat and add to the partridge meat.
6. Dice the smoked pork and fry it briefly in the pan, then add a little of the cabbage water. Cover and allow to simmer for 10 minutes. Then lift out the smoked pork pieces and add them to the other meats with the pan juices.
7. Put the partridge bones, with the bay leaf, onion, carrot and parsley in a saucepan and cover with water (preferably that in which you cooked the cabbage). Simmer for 45 minutes.
8. Set the oven to 170°C 325°F, gas mark 3.
9. Sprinkle some salt and pepper into the pie dish and cover the meat with a layer of cabbage leaves. Stand the dish in a roasting tin of hot water, cover with buttered foil bake for $2\frac{1}{2}$–3 hours, or until a skewer will glide easily through.
10. Meanwhile make the sauce: reduce the partridge stock to 290ml/$\frac{1}{2}$ pint by rapid boiling. Strain into a clean saucepan. Taste and add salt and pepper if necessary. Work the butter and flour together to a paste. Whisk by degrees into the stock. Stir until boiling. Simmer for 2 minutes.
11. Turn out the partridge and cabbage, upside down, on a serving dish and hand the sauce separately.

Serves 6

Roast Pheasant with Sauerkraut

2 medium pheasants
Salt and pepper
Butter

2 strips of pork fat
6 juniper berries
225g/½lb sauerkraut

For the gravy:
2 teaspoons flour
1 tablespoon ruby port

1 teaspoon redcurrant jelly

1. Wipe the birds and remove any remaining feathers.
2. Set the oven to 220°C/425°F, gas mark 7.
3. Season the birds inside and put a knob of butter in the body cavity.
4. Tie slices of pork fat over the breasts (this is called barding and is to prevent drying out during cooking).
5. Spread a little butter over the rest of the birds and season with salt, pepper and crushed juniper berries.
6. Place in a roasting tin, pour 0·5cm/¼in water into the bottom of the tin and cook for about 50–60 minutes, basting frequently.
7. Drain the sauerkraut. Heat it with a good 30g/1oz of butter over gentle heat.
8. When cooked lift the pheasants out of the tin and keep warm while you make the gravy.
9. Sprinkle the flour into the roasting juices and add the port and the redcurrant jelly.
10. Place the roasting pan over heat and stir and scrape the bottom until the liquid boils.
11. Add a little more water or stock if it is too thick. Boil for 2 minutes, then season well and strain into a warmed gravy boat.
12. Serve the pheasants surrounded with sauerkraut. Hand the gravy separately.

Serves 4–5

Galantine of Pheasant

1 large pheasant, cleaned
225g/½lb raw chicken meat, minced
170g/6oz sausage-meat
2 shallots, chopped
2 tablespoons Madeira
1 tablespoon chopped fresh parsley
Salt and freshly ground black pepper
2 slices cooked tongue, cut into strips
1 flat dark mushroom, sliced

For the decoration:
Slices button mushrooms *or* thin rings of carrot *or* fresh tarragon leaves *or* slices truffle *or* stuffed olives, sliced, *or* pieces tomato *or* diamond-shaped pieces of cucumber skin

For the stock:
1 carrot, sliced
1 onion, sliced
Stick of celery, chopped
6 peppercorns
1 bay leaf
1 parsley stalk
Salt
Pinch of thyme

For the aspic:
2 egg shells, crushed
2 egg whites
15g/½oz gelatine

1. Bone the pheasant completely, including the legs and wings (see page 83). Cut off any excess fat from the vent end.
2. Place the bones in a pan of water with the stock ingredients, bring to the boil, cover and simmer gently for about 1 hour.
3. Meanwhile prepare the farce (stuffing). Mix together the raw chicken meat, sausage-meat, chopped shallot, Madeira and parsley. Season with salt and pepper.
4. Open the bird on a board, skin side down. Spread with half the farce and lay on the tongue and the mushroom slices. Season and cover with the remaining farce. Fold over the sides of the bird and stitch them together with a needle and thread. Wrap the bird in a piece of muslin and tie the ends together.

421

5. Strain the stock. Place the pheasant in a heavy pan and pour over the stock. Bring to the boil, cover tightly with a lid and simmer slowly for 1½ hours, turning the pheasant over once during the cooking.
6. Lift out the bird and keep the stock for the aspic.
7. When cool tighten the muslin cloth round the bird and leave overnight, refrigerated.
8. Pour the stock into a bowl and leave to cool overnight. If the stock can be transferred to the refrigerator once it is cold it will set the fat and make removing it easier. There should be 570ml/1 pint of stock.
9. Lift or skim off any fat from the pheasant stock. If it is well set do not add gelatine. If it is not, put it in a large saucepan and sprinkle on the gelatine. Put over a gentle heat.
10. Place the crushed shells in a bowl, add the egg white and whisk until frothy. Pour into the warming stock and keep whisking steadily with a balloon whisk until the mixture boils and rises. Stop whisking immediately and draw the pan off the heat. Allow the mixture to subside. Take care not to break the crust formed by the egg white.
11. Bring the aspic up to the boil again and again allow to subside. Repeat this once more (the egg white will trap the sediment in the stock and clear the aspic). Allow to cool for 10 minutes.
12. Fix a double layer of fine muslin over a clean basin and carefully strain the aspic through it, taking care to hold the egg white crust back. When all the liquid is through (or almost all of it) allow the egg white to slip into the muslin. Then strain the aspic again – this time through both egg white crust and cloth. Do not try to hurry the process by squeezing the cloth, or murky aspic will result. Allow to cool until on the point of setting.
13. Unwrap the cold pheasant, wipe off all the grease and place it on a wire rack with a plate underneath. Coat it with the nearly set aspic. Place in the refrigerator until set.
14. Decorate with the garnish you have chosen and coat again with aspic. Allow to set and coat again until the pheasant is shiny.

15. Place on a serving dish. Set the remaining aspic in a shallow tray. Cut into dice and use to surround the pheasant.

Note: If the aspic is less than crystal clear it is wise not to chop it because this seems to emphasise its murkiness.

Serves 6

Pigeon Pie

3 plump young pigeons
½ carrot, chopped
½ onion, chopped
Pinch of dried marjoram
Pinch of dried thyme
225g/½lb rump steak
Seasoned flour
1 onion, finely chopped
1 tablespoon chopped fresh
　parsley

A little grated lemon rind
55g/2oz button mushrooms
A little nutmeg
Salt and freshly ground black
　pepper
225g/½lb flour-quantity
　rough-puff pastry (page 647)
A little beaten egg mixed with
　1 pinch of salt and 1
　teaspoon of water (eggwash)

1. Set the oven to 200°C/400°F, gas mark 6.
2. Separate the breasts from pigeons with a small, very sharp knife by running the knife along the length of the breast bone and carefully scraping downwards against the rib cage, removing each breast separately.
3. Treat the legs in the same way, using quick strokes of the knife along the bones. Cube the pigeon flesh.
4. Place the bones and carcass in a small saucepan with the carrot, onion and herbs. Cover with water and bring to the boil. Skim and simmer for 30 minutes to make a good strong stock.
5. Cut the rump steak into very small cubes and toss them in seasoned flour.
6. Slice the mushrooms.
7. Mix the steak, onion, pigeons and mushrooms with the lemon rind and parsley and season with nutmeg, salt and pepper.

8. Turn the mixture into the pie dish and add enough stock to come three-quarters of the way up the dish.
9. Roll out the pastry to about the thickness of a penny. Cover the pie dish with pastry and brush with eggwash.
10. Place the pie in the pre-heated oven and cook for 20–25 minutes (this will cook the pastry).
11. Lower the heat to 140 C/275 F, gas mark 1, to cook the meat very slowly for 1½ hours.
12. After 30 minutes place a piece of wet greaseproof paper over the pastry to prevent burning. Serve hot.

Serves 4

Pigeon Kebabs

Breasts from 4 pigeons
Freshly ground black pepper
16 short rashers rindless
  streaky bacon
16 flat brown mushrooms
Oil
Chopped fresh savory *or* thyme

1. Heat the grill.
2. Skin each pigeon breast and cut into four pieces. Season with pepper. Stretch the bacon on a board with the back of a knife. Completely wrap each breast piece in a strip of bacon.
3. Skewer the wrapped breasts alternately with the mushrooms on four short skewers.
4. Brush well with oil, sprinkle with savory or thyme and season with pepper.
5. Grill the kebabs for about 10 minutes, turning the skewer every 2 minutes. The breasts should be slightly pink inside and the bacon evenly brown. Serve immediately as the meat toughens if kept for any length of time.

Serves 4

Quails with Raisins, Walnuts and Grapes

8 small quails	15g/½oz flour
4 rashers rindless streaky bacon	110g/¼lb green grapes, halved
Salt and freshly ground black	and seeded
pepper	30g/1oz shelled walnuts
1 onion, sliced	30g/1oz raisins
1 bay leaf	2 tablespoons cream
1 parsley stalk	Watercress for garnish
3 tablespoons white wine	

1. Set the oven to 190°C/375°F, gas mark 5.
2. Wash the quails and wipe them dry. Cut each bacon rasher in half.
3. Place the quails in a roasting tin. Season well with pepper and cover each one with half a rasher of bacon. Pour in enough water to cover the bottom of the tin and add the onion, bay leaf, parsley stalk and white wine. Season with salt and pepper.
4. Roast in the oven for 15 minutes. Remove the bacon from the birds but leave it in the tin with the other flavourings. Baste well and return to the oven for a further 10–15 minutes, until the quails are nicely browned and tender.
5. Turn the oven down to 150°C/300°F, gas mark 2 and leave the door open to help it cool down quickly.
6. Take out the quail, place them on a serving dish, cover and put into the warm oven while preparing the sauce.
7. Heat the pan juices and skim off the fat with a metal spoon. Mix a little of the fat to a smooth paste with the flour and put it back into the roasting pan to thicken the sauce. Whisk until the sauce reboils.
8. Strain the sauce into a saucepan. Check the seasoning and add the grapes, walnuts and raisins. Simmer for about 4 minutes.
9. Stir in the cream and spoon the sauce over the quails. Garnish with well-washed watercress.

Serves 4

Mustard Rabbit

Preparation for this dish begins one day in advance.

1 rabbit, skinned and cleaned	85g/3oz bacon *or* salt pork
French mustard	1 onion, finely chopped
1 teaspoon fresh chopped tarragon	1 garlic clove, crushed
	30g/1oz flour
45g/1½oz butter *or* bacon dripping	570ml/1 pint stock

For the garnish:

8 triangular croutes made from 2 slices crustless white bread   Fresh parsley, chopped

1. If the rabbit's head has not been removed, cut it off with a sharp heavy knife. Then cut the rabbit into neat joints: cut off the front of the rabbit at the ribs and divide it into two, cutting along the backbone. Cut off the legs at the thigh.
2. Soak the rabbit in cold salted water for 3 hours. Drain and dry well.
3. Spread 2 tablespoons of mustard mixed with the chopped tarragon over the pieces of rabbit and leave in a cool place overnight.
4. The next day set the oven to 170°C/325°F, gas mark 3.
5. Cut the bacon into dice and place in a pan of boiling water for 2 minutes to remove excess salt. Rinse under cold water.
6. Heat the butter or dripping and in it brown the joints all over. Remove them with a perforated spoon and place in an ovenproof casserole.
7. Add the bacon, onion and garlic to the frying pan. When the onions are soft and just browned stir in the flour and cook for 1 minute.
8. Take the pan off the heat and stir in the stock: return to the heat and bring the sauce slowly to the boil, stirring continuously.

9. Pour this sauce over the rabbit. Put into the heated oven for about 1½ hours or until the rabbit is tender.
10. Lift the rabbit on to a warm serving dish. Add a teaspoon of mustard to the sauce, taste and add salt and pepper if necessary. Boil for 1 minute. (If the sauce is now rather thin, reduce it by boiling rapidly until shiny and rich in appearance.) Pour the sauce carefully over the rabbit pieces.
11. Dip the croutes into finely chopped parsley and use them to garnish the rabbit.

Serves 4–6

Venison Casserole

675g/1½lb venison

For the marinade:

1 onion, sliced	Slice of lemon
1 carrot, sliced	1 bay leaf
Stick of celery, sliced	290ml/½ pint red wine
1 garlic clove	2 tablespoons wine vinegar
6 juniper berries	6 peppercorns

For the casserole:

1 tablespoon oil	1 tablespoon cranberry jam
30g/1oz butter	Salt and freshly ground black
110g/¼lb onions, peeled	pepper
110g/¼lb button mushrooms	110g/¼lb cooked whole
30g/1oz flour	chestnuts
150ml/¼ pint beef stock	Chopped fresh parsley
1 garlic clove, crushed	

1. Cut the venison into 5cm/2in cubes, trimming away any tough membrane or sinew.
2. Mix the ingredients for the marinade together and add the meat. Mix well, cover and leave in a cool place or in the refrigerator overnight.

427

3. Set the oven to 170°C/325°F, gas mark 3.

4. Lift out the venison cubes and pat dry with absorbent paper. Strain the marinade, reserving the liquid for cooking.

5. Heat half the oil in a heavy saucepan and in it brown the cubes of meat well, frying a few at a time. Lay them in a casserole. If the bottom of the pan becomes brown or too dry, pour in a little of the strained marinade, swish it about, scraping off the sediment stuck to the bottom, and pour over the cubes of meat. Then heat a little more oil and continue browning the meat.

6. When all the meat has been browned, repeat the déglaçage (boiling up with a little marinade and scraping the bottom of the pan).

7. Now melt the butter and fry the onions until they are pale brown all over. Add the mushrooms and continue cooking for 2 minutes.

8. Stir in the flour, add the rest of the marinade and the beef stock and stir until boiling, again scraping the bottom of the pan. When boiling, pour over the venison.

9. Add the crushed garlic and the cranberry jam. Season with salt and pepper.

10. Cover the casserole and place in the heated oven for about 1½ hours or until the meat is really tender.

11. Lift the venison pieces, mushrooms and onions with a perforated spoon into a serving dish.

12. Boil the sauce fast until reduced to a shiny, almost syrupy, consistency. Add the chestnuts and simmer gently for 5 minutes.

13. Pour the sauce over the venison and serve garnished with chopped parsley.

Serves 4

Braised Venison

½ saddle of venison	1 bay leaf
30g/1oz butter	Thyme
1 tablespoon oil	Sage
2 onions	150ml/¼ pint red wine
225g/½lb carrots	About 290ml/½ pint beef stock
4 sticks celery	30g/1oz butter
Salt and freshly ground black	30g/1oz flour
pepper	1 tablespoon cranberry jelly

1. Heat the oven to 150°C/300°F, gas mark 2.
2. Prepare the venison by trimming away any tough membrane and sinew.
3. Heat the butter and oil in a large ovenproof casserole and brown the venison well on all sides. Remove from the casserole.
4. Thickly slice the onions, carrots and celery and place them in the bottom of the casserole. Allow to sweat (cook without colouring) for 5–10 minutes.
5. Season with salt and pepper, add the bay leaf and a sprinkling each of thyme and sage. Lay the venison on top of the half-cooked vegetables. Add the wine and enough stock to come about a quarter of the way up the meat.
6. Bring to simmering point, cover tightly and put in the oven for 3–4 hours, or until the meat is tender.
7. When it is cooked lift out the meat, carve neatly and place on a serving dish. Keep warm, covered with a lid or foil.
8. Strain the liquid from the vegetables into a saucepan.
9. Mix the butter and flour together to make a beurre manié. Add this to the liquid bit by bit, stirring, and bring to the boil. Stir in the cranberry jelly and correct the seasoning.
10. Just before serving spoon a thin layer of sauce over the venison to make it look shiny and appetizing; serve the remaining sauce in a sauce boat.

Serves 6

Roast Woodcock

4 woodcock
4 rashers bacon
Salt and freshly ground black
    pepper
4 rounds white bread 13cm/5in
    in diameter, toasted on one
    side (croutes, page 435)

1 teaspoon flour
150ml/$\frac{1}{4}$ pint stock
Squeeze lemon juice
Watercress to garnish

1. Pluck the woodcock. Remove the heads and draw the gizzards through the neck openings, but do not draw entrails. Truss neatly.
2. Set the oven to 180°C/350°F, gas mark 4.
3. Cover the birds with rashers of bacon and season well. Place in a roasting pan and roast for about 25 minutes, removing the bacon after 20 minutes to allow the breasts to brown thoroughly.
4. Spread the entrails on the untoasted side of the bread and place a bird on top of each. Keep warm while you prepare the gravy.
5. Tip off all except a scant tablespoon of the fat from the roasting pan.
6. Add the flour and cook for 1 minute until a russet brown.
7. Pour in the stock and bring up to the boil, stirring continuously with a spoon, scraping the bottom of the pan to loosen the sediment as it comes to the boil.
8. Season with salt, pepper and lemon juice. Strain the gravy into a warmed boat.
9. Place the woodcock on a serving dish and garnish with watercress.

Serves 4

Cold Game Pie (I)

285g/10oz flour-quantity pâte
  à pâté (page 655)
1 grouse
1 partridge
1 pigeon
2 joints of hare
110g/¼lb venison
2 large onions
2 large carrots
2 sticks celery
4 bay leaves

4 tablespoons oil
110g/¼lb butter
290ml/½ pint red wine
1 litre/2 pints good stock
A little fresh thyme
Parsley stalks
Salt and freshly ground black
  pepper
30g/1oz gelatine
Beaten egg

1. Split the birds in half. Cut the venison into small cubes. Chop the carrot, onion and celery roughly.

2. Fry all the vegetables and meats until well browned in the fat. To do this take about a tablespoon each of butter and oil, heat them in a heavy pan and when the butter is foaming add a good handful of the chopped vegetables. Keep the heat at a medium temperature – enough to fry and brown the vegetables without burning the butter. Keep turning the vegetables to get an even colour all over. When they are all done lift them out with a perforated spoon and put in a large deep saucepan. Now add a bit more oil and butter and brown the venison, the hare and finally the birds. If the bottom of the pan becomes sticky and brown, deglaze it with half a glass of the stock or wine: pour in the liquid, boil up, stirring with a metal spoon or fish slice, scraping the bottom of the pan to loosen the sediment. Tip this liquid in with the browned ingredients and continue frying the meats.

3. When all the ingredients are browned and transferred to the deep saucepan deglaze the pan again, pouring the juices in with the meats. Add the rest of the wine, the stock, and if necessary a little water (the ingredients must be just covered). Add the herbs and salt and pepper. Cover with a lid and simmer for 1½ hours or until everything is tender.

431

3. Strain off the liquid and leave until completely cold. Skim very well then transfer to a saucepan and boil to reduce to about ½ litre/1 pint. Add the gelatine to the liquid and leave to soak.

4. When the meat is cool enough to handle remove all the bones from the birds and hare and cut the flesh into small pieces (about the size of the cubes of venison). Discard the cooked vegetables, the bay leaves and parsley stalks (they have finished their job of flavouring the stock). Let the meat cool completely.

5. Set the oven to 190°C/375°F, gas mark 5. Lightly grease a 2 kilos/4lb pie mould or a loose-bottomed cake tin.

6. Roll two-thirds of the pastry into a round big enough to cover the base and sides of the mould or tin. Dust the pastry with a little flour. Now fold it in half, away from you. Place one hand on the fold of the semi-circle and with the other gently push and pull the sides so that you form a 'bag' roughly the shape and size of the pie mould or cake tin. Open out the bag and fit it into the greased mould or tin.

7. Fill the pie with the meat. Roll out the third of the pastry into a round big enough to cover the top of the pie. Dampen the bottom edge then press this 'lid' on to the pastry case pinching the edges together.

8. Decorate with pastry trimmings, shaped into leaves, and make a neat pea-sized hole in the middle of the top. Brush with beaten egg.

9. Bake for 50 minutes. While the pie is in the oven heat up the stock to melt the soaked gelatine. Allow to cool.

10. Remove the pie carefully from the mould or tin and stand on a flat baking sheet. Brush with beaten egg all over and return to the oven for a further 20 minutes. Take out and allow to cool.

11. Using a small funnel pour the cooled, but not quite set, stock into the pie through the hole in the pastry lid. Allow the liquid to seep down into the pie, then pour in some more: this can be a slow process, but the pie should take about ½ litre/1 pint of liquid, and it is important that you get it in as without it the filling will be crumbly and dry.

Note: If buying such small quantities of hare and venison proves difficult, use 225g/½lb lean chuck steak.

Serves 6–8

Cold Game Pie (II)

Preparation for this dish must start two or three days in advance.

For the forcemeat:

1 pheasant, boned (page 83) and skinned
450g/1lb belly of pork, skinless
3 shallots, finely chopped
Piece of pig's caul about 30cm/12ins square
110g/¼lb poultry livers
2 sage leaves, finely chopped

1 teaspoon fresh chopped thyme
1 clove garlic, crushed
2 teaspoons salt
1 teaspoon coarsely ground black pepper
1 tablespoon brandy
3 tablespoons dry white wine

For the jelly:

Stick of celery
1 carrot, sliced
Slice of onion
1 bay leaf
Sprig of parsley
Sprig of marjoram
Bones, giblets (except the liver) and skin of the pheasant
15g/½oz gelatine

For the pastry crust:

285g/12oz flour quantity pâte à paté (page 655)
Beaten egg

1. Trim any discoloured parts, and sinew, from the livers.
2. Reserve one pheasant breast, the pheasant liver and one other poultry liver. Mince the rest of the pheasant meat with the rest of the livers and the pork belly. Add the shallot, sage, thyme, garlic, salt, pepper, brandy and wine. Mix well and put into a deep bowl.
3. Lay the breast meat and livers on top, and cover. Refrigerate for 24 hours.

4. Make up the pâte à paté.
5. Use two-thirds of it to line a raised pie mould or a loose-bottomed cake tin.
6. Line the empty pie shell with the pig's caul, allowing the sides to hang down over the edge.
7. Put half the minced mixture into the mould. Cut the pheasant breast into strips and lay them on top of the forcemeat.
8. Lay the livers on top of the pheasant strips. Cover with the rest of the forcemeat, pressing down well to eliminate any air pockets.
9. Draw the caul up over the forcemeat to envelop it.
10. Set the oven to 190°C/375°F, gas mark 5.
11. Use the remaining pastry to cover and elaborately decorate the top of the pie. Press the edges of the top firmly to the base pastry. Make a hole in the middle of the pastry top to allow steam to escape.
12. Brush with beaten egg.
13. Bake the pie for 15 minutes, then turn the oven down to 150°C/300°F, gas mark 2, for a further $1\frac{3}{4}$ hours. Allow to cool overnight.
14. Make the stock by simmering the jelly ingredients (except the gelatine) in 1·15 litres/2 pints water for 2 hours. Strain through muslin or a double J-cloth and chill overnight.
15. Remove all traces of fat from the stock. Put it into a saucepan and sprinkle on the gelatine. Leave to soak for 10 minutes, then bring slowly to the boil. Boil until there is approximately 290ml/$\frac{1}{2}$ pint of liquid left.
16. Allow to cool until cold but not set. It should be syrupy. Carefully pour, little by little, into the pie, through the hole in the pastry. (A small funnel will make this operation easier.) Continue until the liquid level is visible, and will no longer gradually sink. (If by some mischance the pastry case has a hole in it allowing the liquid to leak out, plug the hole with softened butter.)
17. Chill the pie until the liquid is set (about 2 hours).

Note: If pouring the liquid into the pie proves difficult, carefully make, with the tip of the knife, another hole in the cooked pastry towards the edge, and pour the liquid through this.

Serves 10–12   434

Croutes for Roast Game Birds

When roasting small game birds such as snipe or woodcock, the 'trail' or entrails is left inside and only the gizzard removed. After roasting, the liver, juices etc. are spread on the uncooked side of a slice of bread which has been fried or toasted on one side only. The roasted bird is served on this croute.

Larger birds like pheasant and grouse are drawn before roasting, but the liver may be returned to the body cavity to cook with the bird. This, plus any other scrapings from the inside of the bird, is spread on the uncooked side of the croute, which is then cut diagonally in half and served as a garnish to the whole roast bird.

Fried Crumbs
(for serving with roast game birds)

55g/2oz butter
4 tablespoons dry white
   breadcrumbs

Melt the butter and very slowly fry the crumbs in it until they have absorbed most of the butter, and are golden in colour and crisp. Serve in a warm bowl, handed to the diners with the sauce or sauces.

Note: Fresh white crumbs can be used, but rather more butter will be needed as they are very absorbent, and great care should be taken to fry slowly so that the crumbs become crisp before they turn brown.

BEEF

Steak and Kidney Pudding

675/1½lb chuck steak
225g/½lb ox kidney
Flour
Salt and pepper
340g/¾lb flour-quantity suet
  pastry (page 646)

2 teaspoons chopped onions
2 teaspoons chopped fresh
  parsley

1. Cut the steak into cubes about 1·5cm/¾in square.
2. Chop the kidney, discarding any sinew.
3. Place both steak and kidney in a large sieve. Pour over flour and shake until the meat is lightly coated.
4. On a floured surface, roll out two-thirds of the suet pastry into a round about 1cm/½in thick. Flour the surface lightly to stop it sticking together when folded. Fold the pastry over to form a half-moon shape. Place the pastry with the straight side away from you and roll it lightly so that the straight side becomes curved and the whole rounded again. Now separate the layers, and you should have a bag, roughly the shape of a 1 kilo/2lb pudding basin. Use it to line the basin, easing the pastry where necessary to fit, and trimming off the top so that 1cm/½in sticks up over the edge.
5. Fill the lined basin with the meat, sprinkling plenty of seasoning, chopped onion and parsley in between the layers.
6. Add water to come three-quarters of the way up the meat.
7. Roll the remaining third of suet pastry 0·5cm/¼in thick, and large enough to just cover the pudding filling. Put in place, wet the edges and press them together securely.
8. Cover the pudding with a double piece of greaseproof paper, pleated down the centre (this is to allow room for the pastry to expand), and a similarly pleated piece of foil. Tie down with string.
9. Place in a saucepan of boiling water with tightly closed lid,

or in a steamer, for 4 hours, taking care to top up with boiling water occasionally.

10. Remove the paper and tin foil and serve the pudding from the bowl.

Note I: Traditionally, steak and kidney puddings served from the bowl are presented wrapped in a white linen napkin.

Note II: As the filling of the pudding may, with long cooking, dry out somewhat, it is worth having a gravy boat of hot beef stock handy to moisten the meat when serving.

Serves 4

Steak and Kidney Pie (*I*)
(with pastry and filling cooked together)

675g/1½lb chuck steak
225g/½lb ox kidney
Flour
Salt and pepper
1 onion, finely chopped

Chopped fresh parsley
225g/½lb flour-quantity
   rough-puff pastry (page 647)
Beaten egg
150ml/¼ pint beef stock

1. Preheat the oven to 220°C/425°F, gas mark 7.
2. Trim away the excess fat from the steak and cut the meat into cubes about 2·5cm/1in square.
3. Slice the kidneys very finely, discarding any sinew.
4. Place the meat in a large sieve and pour a small cup of flour over it. Shake thoroughly so that the meat is lightly coated.
5. Pack the meat and onions into a pie dish, adding salt, pepper and parsley as you go. Pour in enough water to come half-way up the pie dish.
6. Roll out the pastry to the thickness of a 50 pence piece. Cut a long strip just wider than the rim of the pie dish, brush the dish with water and press down the strip.
7. Brush the strip with water and lay over the sheet of pastry. Press it down firmly. Cut away any excess pastry.
8. Cut a 1cm/½in hole in the centre of the pie top and cover

437

loosely with a leaf-shaped piece of pastry (the hole is to allow the escape of steam).

9. Decorate the top with more pastry leaves. Brush all over with egg. Leave in the refrigerator to relax for 10 minutes.

10. Bake in the oven for 30 minutes or until the pastry is well risen and golden brown.

11. Lower the heat to 180°C/350°F, gas mark 4. Wrap the whole pie in wet brown or greaseproof paper and continue to cook for a further 2 hours. (The wrapping is to prevent the pastry burning while the meat cooks.)

12. Before serving remove the decoration over the hole in the pastry, test that the meat is tender with a skewer, and carefully fill the pie with the beef stock, heated to boiling point. Return the pastry leaf and serve.

Serves 4

Steak and Kidney Pie (II)
(with pre-cooked filling)

675g/1½ lb chuck steak	Salt and pepper
225g/½lb ox kidney	1 tablespoon chopped fresh
Oil *or* dripping	parsley
1 onion, finely chopped	225g/½lb flour-quantity
30g/1oz flour	rough-puff pastry (page 647)
425ml/¾ pint beef stock	Beaten egg

1. Trim away the excess fat from the steak and cut the meat into cubes about 2·5cm/1in square. Slice the kidneys finely, discarding any sinew.

2. Heat the oil or dripping in a frying pan and brown a few pieces of meat at a time until well browned all over, putting them on to a plate as they are done. Fry the onion in the same fat until soft and brown.

3. Stir in the flour and cook for 1 minute. Gradually add the stock, stirring continuously and scraping any sediment from the bottom of the pan. Bring to the boil and simmer for

1 minute. Return the meat to the pan, season with salt and pepper and simmer slowly until the meat is tender (about 2 hours). Add the chopped parsley.

4. If the sauce is greasy skim off the fat; if it is too thin remove the meat to a pie dish and boil the sauce rapidly until syrupy. Pour the sauce over the meat and leave to get completely cold.
5. Set the oven to 200°C/400°F, gas mark 6.
6. Roll out the pastry to the thickness of a 50 pence piece. Cut a long strip just wider than the rim of the pie dish, brush the lip of the dish with water and press down the strip.
7. Brush the strip with water and lay over the sheet of pastry. Press it down firmly. Cut away any excess pastry.
8. Cut a 1cm/½in hole in the centre of the pie-top and cover loosely with a leaf-shaped piece of pastry (the hole is to allow the escape of steam).
9. Decorate the top with more pastry leaves. Brush all over with egg. Leave in the refrigerator to relax for 10 minutes.
10. Bake in the oven for 30 minutes, or until the pastry is well risen and golden brown.

Serves 4

Pancake Pie

8 French pancakes (page 659)
2 teaspoons beef dripping
450g/1lb minced beef
1 large onion, chopped
Stick of celery, chopped
3 rashers rindless streaky bacon, diced
1 garlic clove, crushed
2 teaspoons flour

150ml/¼ pint stock
1 tablespoon madeira
2 teaspoons tomato purée
Pinch of thyme
1 tablespoon chopped fresh parsley
Salt and freshly ground black pepper
Soured cream sauce (page 326)

1. Make the pancake batter first and allow it to stand while

preparing the meat sauce. (While the sauce simmers fry the pancakes. Keep them warm in the folds of a tea-towel in a low oven while finishing off the sauce.)

2. Melt half the dripping in a pan and when hot add some of the mince and brown thoroughly.
3. Lift out with a perforated spoon and place in a saucepan.
4. Fry the remaining mince, adding more fat if and when necessary, and transfer this to the saucepan too.
5. When all the mince has been fried, fry the onion, celery, bacon and garlic until just turning brown.
6. Add the flour and cook gently, stirring, for 1 minute.
7. Stir in the stock and madeira and bring to the boil, stirring continuously. Pour this into the saucepan.
8. Add the tomato purée, thyme, half the parsley and season with salt and pepper. Simmer gently for about 45 minutes (or until thick and syrupy).
9. When the meat sauce is cooked, reduce by rapid boiling if it is too runny. Season well.
10. Place one pancake on the serving dish, spoon over some meat sauce and cover with a second pancake.
11. Continue to layer the meat sauce and pancakes, finishing with a layer of meat sauce.
12. Sprinkle with the remaining parsley and serve immediately, with soured cream sauce offered separately.

Serves 4

Shepherd's Pie *or* Cottage Pie

1 onion	290ml/½ pint beef stock
1 carrot	1 bay leaf
Stick of celery	1 teaspoon Worcestershire
2 teaspoons beef dripping	sauce (optional)
675/1½lb minced beef	1 teaspoon tomato purée
2 teaspoons flour	Salt and pepper

For the top:

340g/¾lb mashed potato   Butter
  (page 275) made from
  675g/1½lb freshly cooked
  potatoes

1. Finely chop the onion, carrot and celery.
2. Heat the dripping in a large frying pan and when hot add half the mince. Brown well all over.
3. Remove with a draining spoon and place in a saucepan.
4. Add the remaining mince to the frying pan and fry until well browned. Lift out and add to the first batch.
5. Lower the heat and add the onion, carrot and celery.
6. When the vegetables are lightly browned stir in the flour and cook for a further minute.
7. Add the beef stock and slowly bring to the boil, stirring continuously. Add this to the saucepan.
8. Now add the bay leaf, Worcestershire sauce, tomato purée and seasoning.
9. Set the saucepan on a medium heat to simmer. Cover and leave to cook for 45–50 minutes.
10. Heat the oven to 200 C/400 F, gas mark 6.
11. Remove the bay leaf from the mince and tip the meat into a pie dish, reserving some of the liquid if the mixture is very runny.
12. When slightly cooled spread the potato on top.
13. Fork it up to leave the surface rough, or draw the fork over the surface to mark with a pattern.
14. Dot the top with butter. Place in the oven for 20–30 minutes or until the potato is brown and crusty.

Note I: The confusion over Cottage Pie and Shepherd's Pie is complete. Cottage pie used to denote the use of leftover cooked meat, either beef or mutton. 'Shepherd's', naturally enough, meant that mutton was the meat used, usually pre-cooked. But today either name seems to mean either beef or lamb, made with leftover or fresh meat, the only certainty being the mashed potato top.

Note II: To make a cottage pie with leftover meat, simply mince the meat, season well with salt, pepper and Worcestershire sauce, add tomato purée and some fried onions, with any leftover gravy to moisten. Top with mashed potato, brush with butter and reheat.

Serves 4–5

Boiled Silverside

900g/2lb piece of salt silverside
4 pieces of marrow bone
Bouquet garni of 1 bay leaf,
  2 parsley stalks, 6
  peppercorns, 1 small onion,
  tied in muslin

4 medium onions
4 large carrots, quartered
2 turnips, quartered
8 dumplings (page 443)
Chopped fresh parsley

1. Soak the beef in cold unsalted water for about 3 hours.
2. Put the bones and beef in a large pan of fresh unsalted water and bring slowly to the boil, skimming as the scum rises to the surface.
3. When simmering add the bouquet garni and half cover the pan. Simmer for 30 minutes to the pound. Remove the bouquet garni and skim off any fat.
4. Now add the vegetables and simmer for an hour or until the meat and vegetables are tender.
5. Meanwhile cook the dumplings: if there is room in the pot, sink them in the liquid 20 minutes before the end of the cooking time. If not, take some of the stock (topping up with boiling water if necessary) and boil them in a separate saucepan.
6. Place the beef on a large serving dish. Surround it with the vegetables, dumplings, and marrow bones. Cover and keep warm.
7. Taste the stock. If weak-flavoured reduce by rapid boiling. Skim if necessary.
8. Ladle a cupful or so of hot liquid over the meat and

vegetables, sprinkle with chopped parsley and serve at once. Hand more liquid separately in a sauceboat.

Serves 4

Dumplings

225g/½lb self-raising flour
Pinch of salt
110g/¼lb suet

About 5 tablespoons cold water
570ml/1 pint beef stock

1. Sift the flour and salt into a bowl. Mix in the suet.
2. Make a dip or 'well' in the flour. Add a little water to the well and using a palette knife mix in the surrounding flour. Draw the mixture together with your hands and knead gently to a soft dough.
3. With floured hands shape the mixture into dumplings about the size of a ping-pong ball.
4. Drop the dumplings into a pan of simmering beef stock, cover and cook for 20–25 minutes.
5. Remove with a perforated spoon. They should be light, not too doughy.

Serves 4

Family Beef Stew

900g/2lb stewing beef
2 large mild onions, peeled
6 medium carrots, peeled
2 medium turnips, peeled
55g/2oz dripping
570ml/1 pint beef stock

Salt and pepper
1 bay leaf
2 parsley stalks
Pinch of fresh thyme
30g/1oz pearl barley

1. Set the oven to 200 C/400 F, gas mark 6.

2. Remove gristle and excess fat from the meat and cut it into 2·5cm/1in cubes.
3. Thinly slice the onions and carrots and cut the turnip into small cubes.
4. Melt half of the dripping in a sauté pan. Brown the beef cubes well on all sides, a few at a time, and transfer to an ovenproof casserole. If the bottom of the pan becomes too brown and sticky pour in a little stock and swish it about, scraping the sediment from the bottom of the pan. Pour this into the casserole, and then melt a little more fat and continue browning the meat until all is transferred to the casserole.
5. Fry the onion slices until golden brown and add them to the casserole. Lightly fry the carrot and turnip and place them in the casserole.
6. Pour the stock into the pan and bring to the boil, scraping any remaining sediment from the bottom. Stir in the seasoning, bay leaf, parsley stalks, thyme and barley and pour on to the meat.
7. Cover the casserole and place in the oven. After 20 minutes reduce the heat to 170 C/325 F, gas mark 3, and cook for another 2 hours. Skim off any excess fat.

Note: This stew is even better if kept for a day before eating – the barley swells up even more and the flavour improves.

Serves 4

Spaghetti Bolognaise

450g/1lb spaghetti

For the sauce:

55g/2oz chicken livers	1 glass white wine *or* Madeira
85g/3oz unsmoked bacon	290ml/½ pint stock
Oil	One 226g/½lb can tomatoes
170g/6oz minced beef	2 tablespoons tomato purée

15g/½oz butter
110g/¼lb mixed onion and
  celery, finely diced
1 garlic clove, crushed
110g/¼lb mushrooms, diced

Salt and freshly ground black
  pepper
1 teaspoon chopped fresh
  marjoram
Parmesan cheese

1. Trim off and discard the discoloured parts from the chicken livers.
2. Dice the bacon and fry slowly in its own fat, in a large frying pan, until lightly browned. Increase the temperature and fry the chicken livers, adding a little oil if necessary, and then the mince. Fry until well browned all over.
3. With a draining spoon lift the bacon, mince and livers into a saucepan. Melt the butter in the frying pan and add the onion, celery and garlic. Cook slowly, stirring occasionally, until soft and lightly coloured. Add the mushrooms and cook for 30 seconds. Tip into the pan of meat.
4. Pour the wine into the frying pan and bring to the boil, scraping the bottom of the pan with a wooden spoon to loosen all the sediment. Stir in the stock, tomatoes and tomato purée. Season well with salt, pepper and marjoram. Pour on to the meat in the saucepan. Cover and simmer for 45 minutes or until the meat is tender.
5. While the sauce is cooking push the spaghetti into a large pan of boiling salted water and stir until the water reboils. Boil uncovered for about 10–12 minutes or until just tender. Tip into a colander, then rinse under running hot water. Drain well. Return to the rinsed-out pan and heat gently with 1 tablespoon of oil, turning carefully with a wooden spoon.
6. Place the spaghetti in a warmed serving dish and pour over the Bolognese sauce. Serve with grated Parmesan cheese sprinkled on top of the sauce or handed separately.

Serves 6 as a starter or 4 as a main course

Boeuf Bourguignonne

675g/1½lb chuck steak
1 tablespoon beef dripping
12 small button onions *or* shallots
30g/1oz butter
1 garlic clove, crushed
1 tablespoon flour
290ml/½ pint red wine
290ml/½ pint beef stock
Bouquet garni (bay leaf, sprig of thyme, a few parsley stalks and a stick of celery tied up with string)
Salt and freshly ground black pepper
45g/1½oz rindless fatty bacon
110g/¼lb button mushrooms
Fresh parsley for garnish (optional)

1. Set the oven to 150°C/300°F, gas mark 2.
2. Cut the beef into 3cm/1½in cubes, discarding any fat.
3. Melt the dripping in a thick-bottomed casserole pan and brown the beef pieces very well a few at a time. They must be really dark brown on all sides. Put them into a bowl as they are done. If the bottom of the pan becomes very dark or too dry, pour in a little of the wine, swish it about, scraping off the sediment stuck to the bottom, and pour over the meat. Heat up a little more fat and continue to brown the meat. When it is all brown repeat the deglaçage (adding the wine and scraping the pan).
4. Peel the shallots by dunking them in boiling water for 6 seconds and then removing the skins. Dry them and fry in half the butter until well browned.
5. Add the garlic and stir in the flour: Cook, stirring, for 1 minute.
6. Add the wine and stock. Stir until boiling, again scraping the bottom of the pan.
7. Put the meat and sauce together in a casserole and add the bouquet garni. Season. Cover and place in the oven to cook for 2½–3 hours or until the meat is very tender.
8. Meanwhile prepare the bacon and mushrooms: dice the bacon and wipe the mushrooms but do not peel or remove the stalk. Cut into quarters if large. Melt the remaining butter in

a frying pan and when foaming add the bacon and mushrooms and cook fairly fast until delicately browned. Lift them out and add to the stew when it has been in the oven for 2 hours. Continue cooking for a further 30–60 minutes.

9. When the beef is done use a perforated spoon to lift the meat, bacon and vegetables into a clean casserole. Remove the bouquet and boil the sauce fast to reduce to a syrupy consistency. Pour over the beef, and sprinkle with chopped parsley if liked.

Note: This stew can be cooked on top of the cooker, over a low heat, for 1½–2 hours, but slow oven-cooking produces a better result, with the meat as soft as butter but not shredded or falling apart and with no danger of 'catching' on the bottom.

Serves 4

Carbonnade de Boeuf

675g/1½lb chuck steak
1 tablespoon beef dripping
3 onions, finely sliced
1 garlic clove, crushed
2 teaspoons brown sugar
2 teaspoons flour
300–425ml/½–¾ pint Guinness
  or other brown stout
290ml/½ pint brown stock

1 teaspoon wine vinegar
1 bay leaf
Pinch of thyme
Pinch of nutmeg
Salt and freshly ground black
  pepper
4 slices French bread thickly
  spread with French mustard

1. Set the oven to 150°C/300°F, gas mark 2.
2. Cut the meat into small steaks, cutting *across* the grain of the meat. Melt the dripping in a large frying pan and fry the steaks, a few at a time, until well browned all over, putting them into a casserole as they are done.
3. Fry the onions slowly, and when beginning to brown add the garlic and sugar. Cook for a further minute or until nicely brown.

4. Stir in the flour and cook, stirring, over the heat for 1 minute. Take off the heat and pour in the Guinness and the stock.
5. Return to the heat and bring slowly to the boil, stirring continuously. Pour into the casserole and add the vinegar, bay leaf, thyme, nutmeg, salt and pepper.
6. Cover and bring to simmering point over direct heat. Then bake for $2\frac{3}{4}$ hours.
7. Put the slices of bread, mustard side up, on top of the stew (they are there to absorb the fat) and return the casserole, without a lid, to the oven until the bread is brown and crisp (about 15 minutes).

Serves 4

Boeuf à la Mode

140g/5oz larding fat (usually back pork fat)
1·8 kilos/4lb braising beef (boned)
1 veal knuckle
1 calf's foot, chopped
1·14 litres/2 pints good beef stock
2 tablespoons dripping

For the garnish:
450g/1lb button onions
675g/1½lb carrots
45g/1½oz butter
Sugar

For the marinade:
425ml/¾ pint red wine
1 large onion
1 large carrot
3 bay leaves
Sprig of thyme
Parsley stalks
Salt and freshly ground black pepper
3 tablespoons olive oil
2 garlic cloves, crushed
Stick of celery, chopped

1. First prepare the marinade: place the wine in a bowl large enough to hold the piece of beef. Peel and slice the onion and carrot finely and add to the wine with all the other marinade ingredients.
2. Cut the larding fat into very thin strips, like strings. Using

448

CHOPPING ONIONS: leaving root end intact, slice horizontally, then vertically towards root end, then across into dice

CARROT RIBBONS: use peeler to strip into thin slivers

CHOPPING HERBS: Holding knife tip steady on board with one hand, use other to chop up and down

WRAPPING LAMB CUTLETS IN PASTRY

CRIMPING PASTRY

SPARE RIBS

a larding needle, thread them into the beef flesh at regular intervals. Tie the meat neatly but not too firmly with thin string. Lay in the marinade and leave for about 12 hours, turning the meat over after about 6 hours.

3. Put the veal knuckle and calf's foot into a saucepan and cover with the beef stock. Bring to the boil quickly, take off the heat and skim off the scum. Bring back to the boil, remove from heat and skim again.

4. Set the oven to 100°C/200°F, gas mark ½. Take up the meat and wipe dry with absorbent paper or a dry cloth.

5. Melt the dripping in a very heavy casserole and quickly fry all sides of the meat until they are deep brown in colour. Drain off the excess fat. Pour the marinade and the stock over the beef, and add the calf's foot and veal knuckle.

6. Bring to the boil, cover, and then place on the bottom shelf in the oven. Cook for about 4 hours or until the meat is tender, basting and turning frequently.

7. To prepare the garnish: put the onions, still unpeeled, into boiling water and boil for 3 minutes. Take out, tip into cold water, and peel them. Peel the carrots and trim them into baby carrot shapes or thin even strips.

8. Melt half the butter in a sauté pan, add the carrots and put on a lid. Cook over the lowest of heats, shaking the pan occasionally until the carrots are just tender. Take care they do not catch on the pan bottom and burn. Towards the end of the cooking time sprinkle in a little salt, pepper and ¼ teaspoon sugar. Keep warm.

9. Without rinsing the sauté pan, melt the rest of the butter and add half a teaspoon sugar. Put in all the peeled onions and cook as you did the carrots, but this time allowing the onions to colour to an even pale brown all over. Mix with the carrots.

10. When the meat is meltingly tender, lift it out, untie and place on a serving dish. Boil the cooking stock rapidly until you have a thin syrupy sauce. Taste and season as necessary. Place the onions and carrots round the meat and strain over the sauce.

Serves 8–10

Fried Steak

Sirloin steak cut in 2·5cm/1in slices

Freshly ground black pepper
Oil *or* dripping

For the herb butter:
Butter
Lemon juice
Chopped fresh parsley

Chopped fresh tarragon (optional)
Salt and pepper

1. Season the steak with pepper. Leave to warm to room temperature if it has been chilled. Do not be tempted to salt it, as this will draw out the juices.
2. Brush a frying pan out with a little oil or dripping and place over good heat until it is beginning to smoke.
3. Brown the steak quickly on both sides. For a blue or rare steak keep the heat fierce for the whole cooking time. For better done steaks lower the temperature to moderate after the initial good browning. Length of cooking time varies according to the thickness of the meat, the type of steak, the degree of heat, the weight of the frying pan etc. With experience it is possible to tell from the feel of the steak how well cooked it is – it feels very soft when blue, very firm, almost tough, when well done. But, if you want to be certain, there is nothing for it but to cut a tiny slit in the fattest part of the meat, and take a look. Don't do this until you are fairly sure the steak is ready – too many cuts will mean loss of juices. Cooking times, assuming a 2·5cm/1in steak and a good hot pan, would be about:

blue steak	2 minutes per side
rare steak	$2\frac{1}{2}$ minutes per side
medium rare	3 minutes per side
medium steak	$3\frac{1}{2}$ minutes per side
well done steak	$4\frac{1}{2}$ minutes per side

4. For the herb butter: simply cream about 15g/$\frac{1}{2}$oz butter per person and flavour it with lemon juice, chopped herbs, salt

and pepper. Shape into a block or roll and wrap in wet greaseproof paper or foil. Chill well.

5.   Serve the steaks topped with a slice of herb butter.

Note: Steaks are sometimes lightly beaten with a rolling pin or mallet to tenderize them. But as this breaks the flesh, allowing the juices to run out during cooking, it is not advisable unless the steak is likely to be very tough.

Hamburgers

450g/1lb minced lean beef steak
1 small onion, grated
2 tablespoons parsley *or* mixed
    herbs

1 teaspoon Worcestershire
    sauce (optional)
Seasoning

1.   Heat the grill.
2.   Mix all the ingredients together with a fork. Taste for seasoning.
3.   With floured hands shape the meat into flattish rounds, making sure that they are equal in size.
4.   Grill steadily, turning once. Allow 3 minutes each side for rare burgers, 5 for well done.
5.   Serve on a hot dish, or between heated halves of soft buns.

Note: See below for pickles and relishes to serve with the burgers.

Serves 2

RELISHES FOR HAMBURGERS

Hamburgers are usually served with a selection of mustard, chopped raw onion, bottled dill pickles and tomato ketchup. But these alternatives are good too.

Cucumber and Dill Relish

½ cucumber   Sprig of fresh dill
1 small onion   Salt and pepper

1. Finely dice the cucumber and onion.
2. Coarsely chop the dill.
3. Mix together and season with salt and pepper.

Corn and Pepper Relish

2 sweetcorn cobs *or* 1 small   ½ chilli pepper, mashed to a
  packet frozen corn   paste
1 red pepper   Salt and pepper

1. If using fresh corn cook for 10 minutes in boiling water and
   scrape the kernels from the cob. If using frozen corn place
   in boiling water for 5 minutes and drain.
2. Finely chop the red pepper.
3. Mix everything together and add salt and pepper.

Fresh Peach and Ginger Pickle

2 fresh peaches   1 teaspoon cinnamon
2 teaspoons grated fresh ginger 4 cloves
4 tablespoons tarragon vinegar   55g/2oz sugar
2 tablespoons water

1. Dip the peaches into boiling water for 6 seconds.
2. Peel the peaches, cut them in half and remove the stones.
   Chop finely.
3. Place in a pan with the rest of the ingredients and cover.

Slowly bring to the boil and simmer gently for 10 minutes.

4. Remove the lid and continue to cook until the liquid becomes syrupy.
5. Remove the cloves and allow to cool before serving.

Tournedos Chasseur

4 slices white bread
Oil for frying
55g/2oz butter
Four 170g/6oz fillet steaks
1 shallot, finely chopped
110g/¼lb mushrooms

1 tablespoon dry white wine
290ml/½ pint demi-glace sauce
(page 313) *or* good beef
gravy, slightly thickened
1 teaspoon chopped chervil

1. Cut the crusts off the bread, and trim each slice into a round or octagonal croûte. Heat the oil in a frying pan and fry the bread on both sides until crisp and brown. Keep warm on a serving platter.
2. Heat a teaspoon of the oil in a heavy frying pan and cook the steaks on both sides until done to your liking (4–5 minutes a side for well done, 1–2 minutes a side for rare). Lift them out when ready and place on top of the croûte. Keep warm.
3. In the same pan in which you fried the steaks, melt half the butter. Add the chopped shallot and cook over a moderate heat until just turning colour. Add the rest of the butter and fry the mushrooms in this, scraping the bottom of the pan to loosen any of the meat sediment left from the fried steaks (this will help the flavour of the sauce).
4. After about 2 minutes pour in first the white wine, then the demi-glace sauce. Allow to bubble rapidly to reduce and thicken to a coating consistency. Add the chopped chervil and spoon carefully over the steaks.

Serves 4

Filet de Boeuf à la Stroganoff

340g/¾lb fillet of beef
1 medium onion
225g/½lb mushrooms
55g/2oz butter
100ml/1 small glass white wine
150ml/¼ pint good beef stock

1 tablespoon oil
2 tablespoons brandy
2 tablespoons cream
Salt and freshly ground black
   pepper
2 tablespoons soured cream

1. Cut the beef into 5cm/2in strips the thickness of a pencil. Slice the onion finely. Slice the mushrooms.
2. Melt half the butter in a frying pan and in it gently cook the onion until soft and transparent. Add the mushrooms and toss over the heat for 30 seconds. Add the wine and the stock. Boil rapidly to reduce the liquid to about 2 tablespoons. Stir well and tip the lot out into a bowl, scraping the pan carefully.
3. Now heat the oil and the remaining butter in the pan. Get it as hot as you dare. Drop in the beef strips. Shake and toss over fast heat to brown and seal the edges without over-cooking the middle. Then turn the heat down.
4. Pour the brandy into the hot pan. Set it alight.. As soon as the flames have died down, pour in the mushroom and stock mixture. Return the meat to the pan and stir in the cream. Taste the sauce. Add salt and pepper as necessary. (If the sauce is too thin remove the meat and boil the sauce rapidly to reduce it to a syrupy consistency.)
5. Reheat, then tip into a warm serving dish and fork the soured cream in roughly.

Note: The essence of a perfect beef Stroganoff is the speed at which the fine beef strips are cooked. If using tougher meat, there is nothing for it but gently to stew the beef (after adding the mushrooms and stock) until tender. However, that is not a true Stroganoff, though it can be very good.

Serves 4

Grilled Steak

Cooking times for different kinds of grilled steak are given on pages 117–18.

Steaks	Salt
Coarsely ground black pepper	Maître d'hôtel butter (see
Butter	below)

1. Have the steaks at room temperature. Press coarsely ground pepper into the surface.
2. Heat the grill. Do not start cooking until it is at maximum temperature.
3. Brush the grill rack with melted butter, and the steak too if liked (this is not strictly necessary, and it adds calories for the diet-conscious, but improves the flavour).
4. Grill to the required degree, keeping the pan close to the heat.
5. Serve each steak sprinkled with salt and topped with a 15g/½oz pat of maître d'hôtel butter.

Mixed Grill

Grilling times depend on the thickness of the foods, and the temperature of the grill. The suggestions below should be regarded as guidelines only.

110g/¼lb rump *or* sirloin steak	1 whole tomato
55g/2oz lambs' *or* calves' liver	2 large flat mushrooms
1 chipolata sausage	Salt and freshly ground black
1 lamb's kidney	pepper
1 rasher back bacon	Watercress to garnish

When preparing a mixed grill, begin grilling the meat that will take the longest time to cook and then gradually add the other ingredients so that everything is done at the same time.

Steak: Flatten the steak slightly, brush it with oil and season with pepper. Do not use salt as this drains out the juices and makes the meat tough and dry.

Liver: Remove the membrane that surrounds the liver, cut into thin pieces, brush with oil and season with pepper.

Chipolata sausages: Prick with a fork to allow the fat to escape during cooking. Do not add any extra fat.

Kidney: Skin and halve the kidney, snipping out the 'core'. Brush with oil and season with pepper.

Bacon: Cut off the rind. Put the bacon on a board and, using the back of a knife, stretch it. This helps to prevent shrinking and curling during grilling.

Tomato: Cut in half, brush with a little oil and season with salt and pepper.

Mushrooms: Wipe but do not peel the mushrooms, cut the stalk to ·5cm/¼in, brush with oil and season with salt and pepper.

1. Heat the grill.
2. When very hot, place the chipolata sausage under it.
3. After 1 minute add the liver and the kidney.
4. After a further minute add the steak and bacon. Cook for 1 minute.
5. Turn the sausage and steak over and cook for a further minute.
6. Add the tomatoes and mushrooms and grill for a further 2 minutes or so, turning the tomatoes over and turning the sausage if necessary.
7. As the items are ready put them on a heated platter, draining the fat from the sausage and bacon carefully. Just before serving season with salt and garnish with a sprig of watercress.

Note: Mixed grill is traditionally served with potato chips or straw potatoes.

Serves 1

Steak Wellington

Four 170g/6oz fillet steaks *or* tournedos
Salt and freshly ground black pepper
Worcestershire sauce
30g/1oz beef dripping
55g/2oz flat mushrooms, chopped
85g/3oz chicken liver pâté (page 101)

225g/½lb flour-quantity rough puff pastry (page 647)
Beaten egg
⅓ small onion, finely chopped
½ glass red wine
1 scant tablespoon flour
290ml/½ pint beef stock
Watercress

1. Set the oven to 220°C/425°F, gas mark 7. Trim any fat or membrane from the steaks. Season with pepper and a few drops of Worcestershire sauce.
2. Heat the dripping in a pan and brown the steaks quickly on both sides to seal in the juices. The outside should be a good brown, the middle absolutely raw. Reserve the frying pan unwashed. Leave the meat to cool on a wire rack (this is to allow the fat to drip off the steaks rather than cooling and congealing on them).
3. Beat half the mushrooms into the pâté. Taste and add seasoning if necessary. Spread one side of each tournedo with this mixture. Roll out the pastry until it is about the thickness of a large coin. Cut into four equal-sized squares about 18cm/7in square.
4. Place each tournedo, pâté side down, on a piece of pastry. Brush the edges with water and draw them together over the tournedo, making a neat and well-sealed parcel. Place them on a wet baking sheet, pâté side up, and brush with beaten egg. Make a small slit in the top of each parcel so that the steam can escape. Decorate with leaves made from the pastry trimmings. Brush these with egg too. Place in the refrigerator for 10 minutes so that the pastry can relax.
5. Meanwhile make the sauce: fry the onion until soft in the beef dripping left in the frying pan. Add the remaining

457

mushrooms and cook for 30 seconds. Add the wine, and boil rapidly until the liquid is reduced to a tablespoon. Stir in the flour, and then the stock. Stir until boiling. Simmer 1–2 minutes. Season with salt and pepper.

6. Now brush the steak parcels with a little more beaten egg and place in the oven for 15 minutes, by which time the pastry should be golden brown and the meat pink. Dish on a warmed plate. Garnish with watercress and hand the sauce separately.

Serves 4

Fillet of Beef en Croûte

One 1·8 kilos/4lb piece of fillet from the thick end
Freshly ground black pepper
Worcestershire sauce
  (optional)
30g/1oz beef dripping
340g/¾lb flour-quantity puff pastry (pages 649–50)

110g/¼lb flat mushrooms
30g/1oz butter
110g/¼lb chicken liver pâté
  (page 235)
Beaten egg

1. Set oven to 200°C/400°F, gas mark 6. Wet a baking sheet.
2. Skin and trim the fillet, season well with pepper and Worcestershire sauce (if used). Melt the dripping in a roasting pan and when hot add the meat and brown on all sides. Roast it in the oven for 20 minutes.
3. Take one-third of the pastry and roll it on a floured board until it is a little more than the length and breadth of the fillet. Place it on a wet baking sheet, prick with a fork and bake in the oven until a golden brown (about 20 minutes). Do not turn the oven off. Leave the pastry on a wire rack to cool.
4. Remove the fillet from the roasting pan and allow to cool.
5. Chop the mushrooms very finely and quickly fry in the butter. Mix this with the pâté. Spread the pâté to cover the cooked pastry base. Place the cold fillet on top of this and with a

458

sharp knife cut away any pastry which is not covered by the fillet.

6. Roll the remaining pastry on a floured board into a 'blanket' large enough to cover the fillet easily. Lift up the new pastry and lay it gently over the fillet. With a sharp knife cut off the corners of the 'blanket'. (Do not throw away these trimmings.)

7. Lift one length of the raw pastry and brush the underside with egg wash. With a palette knife lift the base and tuck the 'blanket' neatly underneath it. Repeat with the other three sides. Shape the extra pastry into leaves. Brush the pastry-covered fillet with beaten egg. Lay on the pastry leaves and brush again.

8. Place the fillet in the oven for 20 minutes or until the pastry is very dark brown and shiny. (This recipe assumes that rare beef is desired, but longer cooking in the first instance – without the pastry – will ensure a more well-done fillet. For medium beef give it a further 10 minutes and for well-done beef a further 15 minutes.) Serve hot or cold. If served hot it should be carved at the table or the juice will be lost and the meat may have a grey unappetizing look.

Note: The dish may be prepared in advance up to the final baking. It should be left ready for the oven on the baking sheet, loosely covered with plastic film or foil to stop the egg glaze drying. If prepared in advance it is important that the mushrooms and pâté be stone cold before mixing together, and that the meat be cold before covering with the pastry.

Serves 8–10

English Roast Beef

2·5 kilos/5½lb sirloin *or* rib roast of beef
4 tablespoons dripping
A little dry mustard

Salt and freshly ground black pepper
Horseradish cream (page 323)

1. Set the oven to 220°C/425°F, gas mark 7.
2. Place the beef on a rack and smear with the dripping. Sprinkle over a little mustard and plenty of pepper, but no salt.
3. Place the rack and beef over a roasting pan and roast for 20 minutes.
4. Turn the oven down to 165°C/325°F, gas mark 3 and cook slowly for 20 minutes per 0·5 kilo/1lb for medium-rare meat or 15 minutes for very rare.
5. Sprinkle the beef with salt just before serving.

Note I: If allowed to cool for 20 minutes before serving, the meat is easier to carve, but, naturally, not so hot. Serve the horseradish cream separately.

Note II: If thickened gravy is required in addition to 'God's gravy' – the juices that will run from the meat before and during carving – roast the joint directly in the pan, not on a rack over it. Then pour off most of the dripping, taking care not to lose any brown juices. Add enough flour (usually about 2 teaspoons) to the remaining fat and juices and stir over the heat until the flour has browned, and any sediment from the bottom of the pan is loosened. Add up to 290ml/½ pint of stock and stir or whisk until boiling. Add salt and pepper to taste.

Serves 10

Yorkshire Pudding

125g/4½oz plain flour
Good pinch of salt
2 eggs

290ml/½ pint milk *or* milk and
   water mixed
4 tablespoons good beef
   dripping

1. Sift the flour and salt into a bowl. Make a well in the centre and break the eggs into it.
2. With a wooden spoon beat the eggs, gradually drawing in more flour to the centre.

3. Beat in the milk little by little until the batter is smooth. Leave for 30 minutes before use.
4. Heat the oven to 200°C/400°F, gas mark 6.
5. Heat the dripping until smoking hot in a roasting tin, oven-proof dish or Yorkshire-pudding tin.
6. Pour in the batter. Bake for 30 minutes or until the pudding is risen and golden.

Note I: If the pudding is to be served with roast beef it is a good idea to place the pudding between the open rack holding the beef, and the dripping pan below. In this way any dripping juices from the beef will fall on to the pudding and improve its flavour. Alternatively the batter can be poured directly into the hot dripping pan. The oven temperature must be turned up to 200°C/400°F, gas mark 6 when the pudding is put in. The pudding should go in half an hour before the beef will be ready if it is to be cooked in a single tin or dish, and 15 minutes before if individual patty moulds are used.

Note II: If making the pudding as a sweet course use flavourless oil instead of dripping and serve with honey, treacle or maple syrup.

Serves 4

Spiced Beef

This recipe takes 8 days to complete.

1 large garlic clove
One 1·4 kilos/3lb boneless
   sirloin of beef
55g/2oz brown sugar

30g/1oz ground allspice
2–3 bay leaves, chopped
110g/$\frac{1}{4}$lb salt
About 450g/1lb plain flour

1. Peel the garlic and cut it into thin slivers. Stick these into the beef flesh. Rub the surface of the joint with the sugar.
2. Leave in a cool place for 12 hours. Mix together the allspice, chopped bay leaf and salt.

461

3. Take a little of the salt mixture and rub it well into the meat.
4. Keep for a week, turning and rubbing with more salt and spice each day.
5. Set the oven to 190°C/375°F, gas mark 5.
6. Make enough of a fairly thick doughy paste (by mixing flour and water together) to completely envelop the beef.
7. Wrap the meat in the paste.
8. Put it, paste and all, into a roasting tin and pour in a small cup of water. Bake for 2 hours.
9. Remove and allow to cool. Snip off the crust and discard it before serving the beef.

Note: Especially good eaten cold with Cumberland sauce (page 325) or a sweet pickle.

Serves 8

Steak Tartare

450g/1lb lean fillet *or* rump steak

Salt and freshly ground black pepper

About 4 tablespoons salad oil

3 egg yolks

Worcestershire sauce (optional)

About 3 tablespoons chopped onion

About 1 tablespoon chopped green pepper (optional)

About 1 tablespoon chopped capers (optional)

About 1 tablespoon fresh parsley, chopped

Crisp lettuce leaves for garnish

Chop or mince the steak finely and mix with the other ingredients to taste. Shape into four rounds and place on a serving dish garnished with the lettuce leaves.

Note I: Because of the varying tastes of steak tartare eaters, in restaurants this dish is mixed to the customer's requirements at the table. The meat is presented in a hamburger shape on the plate, with the egg yolk in a half shell sitting on the top of it, and surrounded by the prepared chopped vegetables. The waiter then beats the flavourings, oil and yolk into the meat with a fork.

Note II: Steak tartare is sometimes garnished with anchovy fillets or even caviar.

Note III: Steak tartare is surprisingly good with hot potatoes of some kind, rather than a salad. Chips or matchstick potatoes are best.

Serves 3

Boeuf Philippe

560g/1¼lb fillet of beef (ends will do)
Worcestershire sauce
Freshly ground black pepper
1 tablespoon beef dripping
½ cauliflower
170g/6oz French beans

3 tomatoes
½ teaspoon horseradish sauce
1 garlic clove, crushed
3 tablespoons French dressing (page 319)
8 black olives, stoned
Bunch of watercress

1. Set the oven to 200°C/400°F, gas mark 6.
2. Season the meat with Worcestershire sauce and black pepper. Heat the beef dripping in a roasting tin over the cooker ring and add the beef. Brown evenly on all sides. If the beef is in one thick piece put it into the oven for 15 minutes, less if it is thin or in smaller pieces. It should be just pink inside. Allow to cool.
3. Wash the cauliflower and cut into florets. Plunge these into a pan of boiling water for 4–5 minutes. Drain. Rinse under cold water to prevent further cooking. Drain again.
4. Wash and top and tail the beans. Cook in boiling salted water for 5 minutes, then rinse under cold water and drain.
5. Plunge the tomatoes into boiling water for 5 seconds and peel. Cut into quarters.
6. Add the horseradish sauce and crushed garlic to the French dressing. The salad is now ready for assembly but this should not be done until just before serving. The beef will lose its

colour if dressed too soon, and the salad will look tired if left to stand for any length of time.

7. Cut the beef into thin slices and then into thin strips, cutting *across* the grain of the meat. Place in a basin with the other ingredients, reserving 1 tomato and 4 olives for decoration.

8. Using your hands, mix in three-quarters of the French dressing and pile into a serving dish. Place the reserved tomatoes and olives on top of the dish and brush with a little French dressing. Garnish with a bunch of watercress dipped into the remaining dressing.

Serves 6

Boeuf à la Mode en Gelée

Boeuf à la mode (pages 448–9)
2 egg whites
2 crushed egg shells
75ml/2½ fl.oz sherry

For the garnish:
Mustard and cress

1. Allow the meat to cool in the cooking liquid. To speed this up, stand the covered casserole in a large basin of cold water into which the cold tap trickles steadily, so constantly cooling it. When the meat is lukewarm, lift it out on to a wire rack set over a tray. Wipe off all the fat.

2. To make the jellied aspic strain 570ml/1 pint of the cooking stock. Allow to cool and set to a jelly. Then remove any vestige of fat from the surface.

3. Put the stock and sherry into a large clean saucepan over gentle heat.

4. Place the crushed shells in a bowl, add the egg whites and whisk until frothy. Pour into the warming stock and keep whisking steadily with a balloon whisk until the mixture boils and rises. Stop whisking immediately and draw the pan off the heat. Allow the mixture to subside. Take care not to break the crust formed by the egg white.

5. Bring the aspic up to the boil again and again allow to subside.

Repeat this once more (the egg white will trap the sediment in the stock and clear the aspic). Allow to cool for 10 minutes.

6. Fix a double layer of fine muslin over a clean basin and carefully strain the aspic through it, taking care to hold the egg white crust back. When all the liquid is through (or almost all of it) allow the egg white to slip into the muslin. Then strain the aspic again – this time through both egg white crust and cloth. Do not try to hurry the process by squeezing the cloth, or murky aspic will result. Leave to cool.

7. When the jelly is on the point of setting carefully coat the meat with it. Allow to set, then repeat the process until a thin clear layer of aspic is obtained.

8. Set a thin layer of aspic in the bottom of a large serving dish. Set another ½cm/¼in layer in a clean tray or roasting tin. When set carefully cut this last aspic into tiny even dice. Put the meat on the aspic-covered serving dish and decorate with two or three small piles of diced aspic, and the cress.

Note: If the aspic is less than crystal clear it is wise not to chop it – which seems to emphasize its murkiness.

Serves 10

LAMB

Moussaka (I)

340g/¾lb aubergines
225g/½lb can tomatoes
1 onion, finely chopped
1 garlic clove, crushed
Oil for frying
450g/1lb cooked, minced lamb
2 teaspoons chopped fresh marjoram
2 teaspoons chopped fresh parsley
1 bay leaf
Pinch of ground nutmeg
2 teaspoons flour
Salt and freshly ground black pepper
340g/¾lb courgettes

For the topping:

20g/¾oz butter	1 egg yolk
20g/¾oz flour	1 tablespoon cream
290ml/½ pint milk	55g/2oz grated Gruyère *or*
1 bay leaf	strong Cheddar cheese

1. Slice the aubergines into 1cm/½in slices, score the flesh with a sharp knife and sprinkle with salt. Leave for half an hour.
2. Roughly chop or cut up the tinned tomatoes. Keep the juice.
3. Meanwhile, in a heavy saucepan over gentle heat, soften the onions and garlic in one tablespoon of oil.
4. Add the meat, herbs, bay leaf and nutmeg to the onions. Stir in the flour and pour in the tomatoes and their juice. Bring to the boil, stirring, and simmer for 2–3 minutes. Season well.
5. Rinse and wipe the aubergines dry. Slice the courgettes.
6. Heat 2 tablespoons of oil in a frying pan. Fry first the courgettes, then the aubergines on both sides until brown, heating up more oil as necessary. As the courgettes are done put them into the bottom of a shallow casserole.
7. Tip the meat mixture on to the courgettes, then lay the fried aubergine on top of that. See that the top is as flat as possible.
8. Set the oven to 190°C/375°F, gas mark 5.
9. Melt the butter in a saucepan. Stir in the flour. Cook, stirring, for 1 minute, then draw the pan off the heat and add the milk slowly, beating out the lumps as you go. Add the bay leaf.
10. Return the pan to the heat and stir until boiling. Season with salt and pepper and simmer for 2 minutes.
11. Mix the egg yolk with the cream in a large bowl. Pour the sauce on to this mixture, stirring all the time. Add half the cheese and pour over the casserole.
12. Sprinkle the rest of the cheese on top and bake for 30–35 minutes until completely reheated and well browned.

Note: Moussaka can be made with fresh, as opposed to ready-cooked, meat but this *réchauffé* is very good, and is an excellent way of using up leftover roast lamb.

Serves 4

Moussaka (II)

Olive oil
1 large onion, finely chopped
½ garlic clove, crushed
675g/1½lb lean mutton, minced
3 tomatoes
150ml/¼ pint white wine
150ml/¼ pint water
Salt and freshly ground black
   pepper
Handful of fresh parsley, finely
   chopped
Pinch of ground nutmeg

1 medium aubergine
15g/½oz dried breadcrumbs
1 large potato, thinly sliced
15g/½oz butter
15g/½oz flour
1 bay leaf
290ml/½ pint milk
1 egg yolk
1 tablespoon cream
55g/2oz dry Cheddar cheese,
   grated

1. Heat a little olive oil in a large saucepan and brown the onion slowly in it.
2. Add the garlic and meat; cook, stirring, for 5 minutes.
3. Dip the tomatoes in boiling water for 5 seconds, skin, chop and add to the meat.
4. Add wine, water, salt, pepper, parsley and nutmeg and cook over a gentle heat, stirring often, until most of the liquid has evaporated. This will take at least 1 hour.
5. Cut the aubergine in thin slices, salt lightly and leave for about 30 minutes for some of the juice to drain out. Rinse and dry well on a cloth.
6. Heat a little more oil in a frying pan and fry each slice of aubergine on both sides until well browned but not burnt.
7. Put them in the bottom of a large casserole. Sprinkle on the breadcrumbs.
8. Now tip in half the meat mixture. Put half the sliced potatoes

467

in next, seasoning with salt and pepper, then the rest of the meat, and then the rest of the potatoes.

9. Melt the butter in a saucepan. Stir in the flour, add the bay leaf, then the milk and stir constantly while bringing slowly to the boil. Season with salt and pepper and leave simmering while you mix the egg yolks and cream in a bowl.

10. Pour the sauce on to the yolks and cream, stirring all the time. Add half the cheese.

11. Pour the sauce over the dish. Sprinkle the rest of the cheese on top.

12. Put the dish into a slow oven (170°C/325°F, gas mark 3) until the potatoes are tender.

13. Test after 1 hour with a skewer; the whole mass should be soft. The top should be browned too, but if not finish the browning under the grill.

Note: Many great French chefs insist that the custard top and the inclusion of potato make this dish not a true moussaka. But moussaka in its native Greece usually contains both, and the Greeks have as many variations on moussaka as we have on apple pie.

Serves 4

Babotie

1 slice white bread
290ml/½ pint milk
450g/1lb cooked lamb
1 onion
1 small apple
30g/1oz butter
1 tablespoon curry powder

1 tablespoon chutney
15g/½oz almonds, chopped
A few raisins
1 tablespoon vinegar *or* lemon juice
Salt and freshly ground black pepper

For the top:
2 eggs
Salt and pepper

2 lemon leaves

1. Soak the bread in the milk.
2. Grease a fireproof dish and set the oven to 180°C/350°F, gas mark 4.
3. Mince the lamb.
4. Chop the onion and apple and cook slowly in the butter until soft but not coloured. Add the curry powder and cook for a further minute.
5. Mix the apple and onion with the meat, chutney, almonds, raisins and vinegar or lemon juice. Squeeze the milk from the bread (but keep the milk) and fork the bread into the meat. Season with salt and pepper and pile into the dish.
6. Place in a warm oven until a slight crust has formed (about 10 minutes).
7. Meanwhile mix the eggs with the milk in which the bread has been soaked. Season with salt and pepper.
8. Pour this over the meat mixture, place on the lemon leaves and bake until the custard has set and browned (about 30–35 minutes).

Note: Bay leaves will do instead of lemon leaves but the flavour is not the same, though good.

Serves 4

Lancashire Hot-Pot

900g/2lb middle neck of mutton *or* lamb
3 lambs' kidneys (optional)
2 large onions
900g/2lb potatoes
2 carrots
Salt and freshly ground black pepper
Pinch of dried thyme *or* ½ teaspoon chopped fresh thyme
1 bay leaf
290ml/½ pint good stock
55g/2oz butter

1. Set the oven to 180°C/350°F, gas mark 4.
2. Cut the meat into chops, trimming away most of the fat.

3. Skin, split, core and quarter the kidneys.
4. Slice the onions finely.
5. Wash and peel the potatoes, discard any eyes and cut into slices about 0·5cm/¼in thick.
6. Peel the carrots and slice them.
7. Butter a casserole dish and line it with a layer of potatoes. Season well with salt, pepper and thyme.
8. Layer the cutlets, sliced onions, carrots and kidneys on top of the potatoes, seasoning well with salt, pepper and thyme and adding the bay leaf when the pot is half full. Finish with a neat layer of potatoes overlapping each other.
9. Pour in enough stock to come to the bottom of the top layer of potatoes.
10. Brush the top with plenty of melted butter and season well with salt and pepper.
11. Cover the casserole and bake in the oven for about 2 hours.
12. Remove the lid and continue to cook for a further 30–40 minutes until the potatoes are brown and crisp and the meat is completely tender.

Serves 4

Cassoulet

450g/1lb dried white haricot beans
225g/½lb unsmoked bacon (in one piece)
1 onion, thinly sliced
Pinch of thyme
Freshly ground black pepper
1 bay leaf
2 tablespoons tomato purée

Dripping *or* bacon fat
4 tomatoes
450g/1lb breast of lamb
1 garlic clove, crushed
Salt
1 tablespoon white breadcrumbs

1. Soak the beans for 3 hours in water. Drain and place in a deep casserole with the bacon, onion, thyme, pepper, bay leaf and

470

2 tablespoons dripping. Cover with water and bring to the boil. Cover tightly with a lid and simmer for 20 minutes.

2. Skin the tomatoes, quarter them and discard the seeds.
3. Cut the lamb into 2·5cm/1in pieces and fry in dripping until golden.
4. Set the oven to 150°C/300°F, gas mark 2.
5. Place the lamb in the bottom of a fireproof dish. Take the bacon from the beans and cut it into chunks. Place on top of the lamb. Add half the beans and then the tomatoes. Add the remaining beans. Mix the crushed garlic and tomato purée with 290ml/½ pint of the water in which the beans were boiled and pour into the casserole. Taste for seasoning and add salt if necessary. Sprinkle with breadcrumbs.
6. Bake for about 2½ hours removing the cover halfway through to allow a crust to form on the top. At the end of the cooking time the bacon and beans should be very tender, the liquid absorbed and the top crisp and brown.

Note: The ingredients for cassoulet vary from region to region. Preserved goose, or mutton, are frequent additions, but some salt pork or bacon is always included.

Serves 6

Navarin of Lamb

1 kilo/2lb middle neck of lamb
Salt and freshly ground black
  pepper
2 tablespoons dripping
1 tablespoon flour
1·15 litres/2½ pints stock
1 garlic clove, crushed
2 tablespoons tomato purée

Pinch of sugar
Bouquet garni (parsley, bay
  leaf and celery tied together
  with string)
12 button onions, peeled
1 turnip cut into sticks
3 carrots cut into sticks
3 potatoes, in chunks

1. Cut the lamb into neat pieces and season with salt and pepper.
2. Heat 1 tablespoon of dripping in a heavy pan and brown

the meat on all sides. Pour off the fat into a frying pan. Sprinkle the meat with the flour. Cook for 1 minute, then stir in the stock, garlic and tomato purée. Add the bouquet garni. Stir until boiling, then simmer for 1 hour. Skim off any surface fat.

3. Heat a little more fat and in it brown first the onions with the sugar, then the carrots, turnips and potatoes, adding more dripping as needed.

4. Add the browned vegetables to the meat stew, cover tightly and continue cooking over gentle heat, or in a moderate oven, for a further 30–40 minutes or until the meat is tender. Taste for seasoning.

5. Remove the bouquet garni. Allow the navarin to stand for 5 minutes, then skim off the surface fat and spoon the stew into a warmed dish.

Note: Fresh peas or beans are sometimes added to the navarin after the final skimming. The stew must then be cooked until they are just tender.

Serves 4–6

Noisettes of Lamb with Sherry and Mushrooms

2 small lamb best ends of neck, each with 6–7 bones
Salt and freshly ground black pepper
Dripping
1 large onion, finely chopped
225g/½lb large black mushrooms, sliced

1 tablespoon flour
290ml/½ pint brown stock
4 tablespoons sherry
1 bay leaf

Chopped parsley

1. First prepare the noisettes of lamb: see page 39.
2. Set the oven to 170°C/350°F, gas mark 4.
3. Heat the dripping in a frying pan and brown the noisettes well on both sides. Take up with a perforated spoon and shake

472

off any excess fat. Place them in a roasting pan.

4. Heat another spoon of dripping in the frying pan, add the onion, and fry until just turning colour. Add the mushrooms and cook for a further 30 seconds. Stir in the flour. Cook for 1 minute. Pour in the stock and sherry. Bring slowly to the boil, stirring all the time and scraping the bottom of the pan. Pour over the noisettes.

5. Season with salt and pepper. Add the bay leaf and cover with foil or a lid.

6. Bake in the oven until the meat is tender (30 minutes). Remove the bay leaf and lift out the noisettes on to a warmed serving dish. Remove the string.

7. If the sauce is too thin the mushrooms should be removed to the serving dish and the sauce vigorously boiled to reduce it to a syrupy consistency. Spoon the sauce over the noisettes and mushrooms and scatter chopped parsley over the dish.

Serves 4

Lamb Daube

900g/2lb lean lamb (preferably from the leg)
150ml/¼ pint stock
110g/¼lb streaky bacon
1 onion
1 tablespoon oil
55g/2oz flour

For the bouquet garni:
1 bay leaf
Sprig of thyme
Sprig of rosemary
Sprig of parsley
1 strip of orange rind

For the marinade:
290ml/½ pint red wine
1 medium onion, cut in rough slices
Stick of celery, roughly chopped
1 garlic clove
Sprig of parsley
1 bay leaf
Sprig of rosemary
4 whole allspice berries

1. Trim the lamb and cut into large pieces.
2. Prepare the marinade by mixing all the ingredients together. Lay the pieces of meat in it and leave overnight.
3. Set the oven to 150°C/300°F, gas mark 2.
4. Drain the meat from the marinade and pat dry with a cloth.
5. Dice the bacon. Chop the onion. Heat the oil in a heavy pan and in it brown the bacon and the onion. Lift out with a perforated spoon and place in a casserole.
6. Brown the meat (in the same pan) a few pieces at a time. Lay them on top of the bacon and onions.
7. Strain the marinade into the empty pan. Add the stock. Bring to the boil, scraping the bottom of the pan to loosen any sediment. Pour over the meat.
8. Tie the bouquet garni herbs and orange rind together with a piece of string and sink them in the liquid in the casserole.
9. Make a stiff dough by adding water to the flour. Put the lid on the casserole and press a band of dough around the join of lid and dish to seal them completely.
10. Cook in the oven for 3 hours. Remove the lid.
11. Lift the meat out and put it on a serving dish. Keep it warm.
12. Boil the sauce to reduce it to a syrupy consistency and pour over the meat.

Serves 4

Lamb Curry

30g/1oz clarified butter (page 784) *or* ghee

1 small onion, grated *or* chopped

675g/1½lb boneless lamb, preferably shoulder, cut into 4cm/1½in cubes

2 teaspoons turmeric

½ teaspoon ground ginger

1 garlic clove, crushed

1½ tablespoons ground coriander

¼ teaspoon salt

¼ teaspoon cayenne

425ml/¾ pint stock (preferably, but not necessarily, meat stock)

1 tablespoon fresh chopped parsley

½ tablespoon chopped fresh mint

1. Melt the butter in a large saucepan and brown the onions in it. Remove onto a plate.
2. Put the meat into the pan and brown all over. Add the turmeric, ginger, crushed garlic and half the coriander seeds. Return the onions and stir and cook for 1 minute over a low heat.
3. Season with salt and cayenne and add enough stock to come 1cm/½in below the top of the meat. This level should be kept constant. Bring to the boil, cover and simmer gently until the meat is tender (about 1½ hours), adding stock as necessary.
4. Add the remaining coriander, chopped parsley and mint. Stir, cover and simmer for 15 minutes, allowing the liquid to reduce. If at the end of cooking there appears to be too much liquid, remove the meat and reduce the liquid by boiling rapidly. The meat should be moist but not swimming in liquid.

Note I: More (or fewer) spices may be added according to taste.
Note II: Ghee is clarified fat bought in tins in Indian stores.
Serves 4

ACCOMPANIMENTS FOR CURRIES

Banana and Coconut

Chop 2 bananas and squeeze the juice of 1 lemon over them. Mix in 2 tablespoons of desiccated coconut.

Tomato and Onion

Chop 1 large onion and 3 peeled tomatoes finely. Mix them together with salt and pepper, 1 tablespoon of olive oil and a squeeze of lemon.

Chutney and Cucumber

Mix 1 cupful of chopped cucumber into the same amount of sweet chutney (such as mango or apple).

Green Pepper, Apple and Raisin

Chop equal quantities of apple and green pepper finely, or mince them. Add 1 tablespoon of raisins *or* sultanas and salt, pepper, lemon juice, cayenne and sugar to taste.

Poppadums

These are large flat wafers, generally bought in boxes. They are heated in the oven or under the grill, or fried in hot fat until crisp. They can be bought spiced or plain.

Lamb with Dill Sauce

900g/2lb lean leg of lamb, cut into large chunks
1 onion, sliced
1 carrot, sliced
1 tablespoon crushed dill seeds *or* 3–4 sprigs fresh dill
1 bay leaf
12 peppercorns

$\frac{1}{4}$ teaspoon salt
About $\frac{3}{4}$ litre/1$\frac{1}{4}$ pint chicken stock
1 tablespoon flour
30g/1oz butter
1 egg yolk
3 tablespoons cream
2 teaspoons lemon juice

1. Put the meat, onion, carrot, stalks (or seeds) of dill (but not the fresh leaves), bay leaf, peppercorns and salt into a saucepan.
2. Cover with the stock and bring slowly to the boil. Turn down the heat and cook as slowly as possible for 30 minutes, or until the meat is tender.

3. Lift out the cubes of meat, discarding the bay leaf and dill stalks, and put them into a casserole or serving dish. Cover to prevent drying out, and keep warm.

4. Strain the stock, and skim off all the fat: Measure the remaining liquid and make up to 425ml/¾ pint with water if necessary. Return to the saucepan.

5. Mix the butter and flour together to a smooth paste. Whisk this gradually into the hot stock, and whisk steadily until the sauce is smooth. Bring to the boil and simmer for 2 minutes.

6. Mix the egg yolk and cream in a bowl. Mix a little of the hot sauce into the cream mixture, and then stir this back into the sauce. Be careful not to boil the sauce now or the yolk will scramble. Flavour the sauce with the lemon juice and add salt and freshly ground black pepper to taste. Chop the dill leaves if you have them, and stir in. Pour over the meat and serve at once.

Serves 4

Noisettes of Lamb with Onion and Mint Purée

2 best ends lamb each with
   5–7 cutlet bones
Salt and freshly ground black
   pepper
1 scant tablespoon fresh
   chopped mint

Dripping
4 tablespoons thick onion and
   mint sauce, warmed
   (page 326)
Small bunch of watercress

1. First prepare the noisettes of lamb, seasoning the meat with chopped mint, pepper and salt before rolling up. See page 75.

2. Set the oven to 180°C/350°F, gas mark 4.

3. Heat 1 tablespoon of dripping in a heavy roasting pan and over brisk heat brown the noisettes quickly on both sides. Transfer to the oven. Baste once or twice until the meat is cooked but still slightly pink inside (about 15 minutes).

477

Alternatively the noisettes can be fried in the dripping, fast at first to seal them, then more gently for about 3 minutes on each side; or they may be plainly grilled (about 4 minutes per side).

4. Arrange on a warmed serving dish.
5. Spoon a little of the hot onion and mint sauce on top of each noisette and garnish with washed watercress.

Note: Cutlets (trimmed and shortened, but not boned into noisettes) can be used instead of the more elaborate noisettes.

Serves 4

Lamb Cutlets Grilled with Herbs

12 French trimmed lamb cutlets	Fresh herbs: thyme, basil, parsley, marjoram and
30g/1oz butter, melted	rosemary
1 tablespoon oil	Freshly ground black pepper

1. Heat the grill.
2. Brush the cutlets with melted butter and oil, sprinkle over half the herbs and season with pepper.
3. Place the cutlets under the grill, about 8cm/3in away from the heat, and cook for 4–6 minutes.
4. Turn them over, baste with the fat from the bottom of the pan and sprinkle over the remaining herbs.
5. Grill for 4–6 minutes. (4 minutes each side should give a succulent pink cutlet, 6 minutes a well-done cutlet.)
6. Dish the cutlets on a warmed serving dish and pour over the pan juices. Serve at once.

Note: See pages 130–1 for information about French trimmed cutlets.

Serves 4

Lamb Cutlets Soubise

8 French-trimmed cutlets
  (pages 74–5)
Seasoned flour
Beaten egg
Dried breadcrumbs

55ml/2fl.oz oil and 15g/½oz
  butter
Watercress
290ml/½ pint soubise sauce
  (page 310)

1. Dip each cutlet into seasoned flour, shake off the excess, and brush with beaten egg. Press on the dried breadcrumbs.
2. Heat the oil in a frying pan. When hot, add the butter. Fry the cutlets for 3–4 minutes on each side, until golden brown on the outside but not hard to the touch. Drain briefly on absorbent paper to remove any grease. Serve garnished with washed watercress. Hand the soubise sauce separately.

Note: An alternative method is briefly to brown the cutlets to seal them without cooking the meat through; to cool them and then to dip them into a very thick cold soubise sauce, then into beaten egg and finally into breadcrumbs. They are then sprinkled well with melted butter and baked in a moderate oven until done (about 8 minutes for pink meat, 12 for well done).

Serves 4

Lamb Steak à la Catalane

4 lamb steaks, about 1cm/½in
  thick, cut across the upper
  leg, bones removed

Bunch of watercress

For the marinade:
290ml/½ pint olive oil
6 garlic cloves, crushed
1 tablespoon dried *or* a good
  handful of fresh, thyme

1 large onion, finely sliced
24 peppercorns, slightly
  crushed
Salt

1. Lay the lamb steaks in a roasting pan or shallow dish. Pour over the oil and add all the other marinade ingredients. Leave the steaks to marinate for at least 8 hours, preferably 24, turning them over two or three times – unless they are left in the refrigerator, where the oil solidifies and can simply be spread with the slices of onion etc., over the top of the steaks.
2. Get a thick frying pan or griddle really hot. Alternatively pre-heat the grill to maximum.
3. Remove most of the oil from the steaks and immediately put them in the hot pan, or under the grill. Grill or fry, turning once, until both sides are a good brown. Like beef steaks they can be eaten in any state from blue to well done, but if overcooked they become very tough. They are best pink in the middle. Serve immediately with a sprig or two of watercress.

Serves 4

Lamb Cutlets in Pastry

4 double best end lamb cutlets
Dripping *or* oil for frying
2 tablespoons ham, chopped
1 tablespoon tomato purée
55g/2oz mushrooms, chopped
1 tablespoon chopped fresh
  parsley
Salt and freshly ground black
  pepper
225g/½lb flour-quantity puff
  pastry (page 649)
1 egg beaten with salt (egg
  wash)
Tomato sauce (page 325)

1. Set the oven to 200°C/400°F, gas mark 6.
2. Trim off the excess fat from the cutlets and fry briskly in a little dripping or oil to seal the meat. The cutlets must be brown on both sides but raw in the middle. Leave to cool on a wire rack (this prevents the fat from solidifying on the cutlet). Wipe any congealed fat off the cutlets.

CHEESE SOUFFLÉ

FLAMING CHICKEN. Keep a lid to hand in case it flares too high

POTTING MARMALADE through a jam funnel

TREACLE TART. For a traditional edge, cut into pastry at one-inch intervals and fold each section diagonally into a triangle

3. Mix the ham, tomato purée, mushrooms and parsley together. Season with salt and pepper.

4. Roll out the pastry into a square 23 × 23cm/9 × 9in. Cut it diagonally into four triangles.

5. Put a quarter of the filling on to the centre of each triangle and put a cutlet on top of this, so that the meaty part is exactly in the middle of the piece of pastry.

6. Fold over the flaps of pastry on to the top of the cutlet, leaving the bone sticking out. Make sure the pastry 'seams' slightly overlap. Trim away any extra pastry, but keep the trimmings.

7. Turn the cutlets over and place them on a wet baking sheet. Brush the tops with egg wash. Cut 4 leaves out of the pastry trimmings and put one on each cutlet. Brush again with egg.

8. Bake in the oven for 20 minutes or until the pastry is a good brown. The meat inside will be faintly pink. For well-done cutlets cover the pastry with foil to prevent burning, and continue baking for a further 5 minutes.

9. Hand tomato sauce separately.

Note: Double cutlets are thick ones achieved by cutting through the best end so that each piece of meat has two bones to it. One bone is then carefully removed. It is vital that all fat is removed.

Serves 4

Stuffed Breast of Lamb

2 boned breasts of lamb
1 small onion
Stick of celery
30g/1oz butter
1 tablespoon white
   breadcrumbs
110g/¼lb sausage-meat
Grated rind and juice of ½ large
   orange

2 teaspoons chopped fresh mint
1 tablespoon chopped fresh
   parsley
½ beaten egg
Salt and freshly ground black
   pepper
30g/1oz dripping
Watercress to garnish

For the gravy:

2 teaspoons flour
150ml/¼ pint stock

Juice of ½ small orange
1 teaspoon redcurrant jelly
Salt and pepper

1. Set the oven to 200°C/400°F, gas mark 6.
2. Weigh the lamb.
3. Chop the onion and celery very finely. Sweat them in the butter (melt the butter, add the vegetables, cover with a piece of greased paper or a lid and cook very slowly until soft but not coloured).
4. With a fork mix together the breadcrumbs, onion, celery, sausage-meat, orange juice and rind, mint and parsley.
5. Bind together with beaten egg until the mixture just holds its shape (too much egg will result in a heavy, doughy stuffing). Season well with salt and pepper.
6. Lay the breasts on a board, fatty side down. Spread the stuffing on one breast and sandwich the two together. Tie neatly with thin string.
7. Melt the dripping in a roasting pan and when hot add the lamb. Grind over some pepper.
8. Roast in the oven for 20–25 minutes to the pound. Baste every 45 minutes and turn over at half-time. If the lamb begins to brown too much cover with tin foil, but remove it for the last 10 minutes of cooking.
9. Place the lamb on a warmed serving dish and put it in the turned-off oven, leaving the door ajar if it is still very hot.
10. Tip all but a scant tablespoon of fat from the roasting pan, reserving as much of the meat juices as possible.
11. Add the flour and mix over the heat until browned.
12. Draw off the heat, add the stock and mix well with a wire whisk or wooden spoon. Return to the heat. Bring slowly up to the boil, whisking all the time.
13. Add the orange juice and redcurrant jelly, and season well.
14. Simmer for a few minutes until the gravy is shiny, and strain it into a gravy boat.
15. Remove the string from the lamb and garnish with a bunch of watercress.

Note: Breasts of lamb can be rolled up individually rather than sandwiched together but this means rather a lot of fat on the inside. If the meat is sandwiched, the fat, being outside, will be browned and crisp and more appetising.

Serves 4

Arabian Roast Shoulder of Lamb

30g/1oz butter
1 large onion, finely chopped
55g/2oz chicken livers, trimmed and diced
55g/2oz mushrooms, sliced
1 garlic clove, crushed
1 tablespoon mixed fresh chopped herbs (mint, thyme, parsley and rosemary)

Squeeze of orange juice
Salt and freshly ground black pepper
½ cup cooked rice
2 tablespoons sultanas
1 shoulder of lamb, boned

For the gravy:
1 teaspoon tomato purée
2 teaspoons flour

290ml/½ pint stock

1. Set the oven to 190°C/375°F, gas mark 5.
2. Melt half the butter in a frying pan and put in the onion. Fry gently until soft.
3. Add the liver and turn the heat up. Fry fairly fast to brown the liver on all sides.
4. Add the mushrooms, garlic, herbs and orange juice. Cook gently until the mushrooms are soft. Season with salt and pepper.
5. Remove from the heat and mix into the cooked rice. Add the sultanas.
6. Push this stuffing into the shoulder of lamb, sewing up the edges with thin string. Use a darning needle if you do not

have a kitchen larding needle. Spread the remaining butter over the lamb.

7. Roast for about 2 hours, basting occasionally.
8. Lift the meat from the roasting pan and keep warm on a serving platter in the switched-off oven.
9. Pour off most of the fat from the roasting pan, and then stir in first the flour and then the tomato purée.
10. Add the stock, and stir over the heat until the sauce boils, scraping the brown bits from the bottom of the pan as you go. Taste and add salt and pepper if necessary.

Serves 4

Crown Roast of Lamb

1 crown roast *or* 2 matching racks (best ends lamb) with 7 cutlets each, chined

55g/2oz butter
Good sprig of rosemary
Bunch of watercress

To serve hot:
1 tablespoon flour
290ml/½ pint good stock

Salt and freshly ground black pepper

To serve cold:
Redcurrant jelly

1. If the butcher has not trimmed and tied the meat into a crown, follow the instructions on pages 39–40.
2. Set the oven to 200°C/400°F, gas mark 6. Melt the butter in a roasting tin. Add the crumbled rosemary and put in the crown of lamb. Use the excess fat and trimmings to stuff the centre of the crown and help to support it. Wrap up the end of the bones with wet brown paper, then with foil – this is to prevent them from burning. It is easier to cover a few bones at a time than to cover the whole crown. Brush over the melted butter.
3. Roast for 1 hour, basting occasionally. Remove supporting trimmings from the centre and return the crown roast to the

oven for 30 minutes if pink lamb is wanted, or 1 hour for well-done lamb. Lift out the crown.

To serve hot:
4. Pour off all but a tablespoon of fat from the roasting tin, taking care not to pour away any of the meat juices. Stir in the flour, scraping any stuck sediment off the bottom of the pan. Add the stock and stir until boiling. Simmer for 2 minutes. Taste and add salt and pepper if needed.
5. Decorate each bone with a cutlet frill. Garnish with watercress in the centre. Hand the gravy separately.

To serve cold:
6. Slice the meat between the bones to separate the cutlets. Trim off the excess fat from each cutlet, but take care to keep the cutlets in the right order, so you can reassemble the crown. Tie a ham frill round the reassembled crown and decorate each bone with a cutlet frill. Garnish with watercress in the centre. Serve with redcurrant jelly.

Serves 4–6

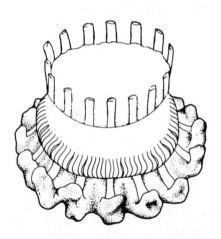

Rack of Lamb with Mustard and Breadcrumbs

2 teaspoons pale French
  mustard
1 tablespoon fresh white
  breadcrumbs
1 tablespoon fresh chopped
  herbs (mint, chives, parsley
  and thyme are good)

¼ teaspoon salt
½ teaspoon freshly ground
  black pepper
2 teaspoons butter
Best end of neck, chined,
  trimmed and skinned

1. Make sure nearly all the fat is removed from the meat.
2. Mix together the French mustard, breadcrumbs, herbs, salt, pepper and butter. Press a thin layer of this mixture over the rounded, skinned side of the best end.
3. Place it, crumbed side up, in a roasting tin and roast at 220°C/425°F, gas mark 7, for 25–30 minutes for a seven-cutlet best end, less for a smaller one. This will give pink, slightly underdone lamb. Serve with the butter and juices from the pan poured over the top.

Serves 2

PORK AND BACON

Pork Puff Pie

225g/½lb flour-quantity rough-
  puff pastry (page 647)
450g/1lb belly of pork, minced
½ teaspoon dried sage

½ teaspoon salt
½ teaspoon freshly ground
  black pepper
2 eggs

1. Roll out the pastry to an oblong 25cm × 10cm (10in × 4in).
2. Mix the minced pork, sage, salt and pepper with one whole

egg and one yolk, reserving one egg white. Taste and add more
seasoning if necessary.

3. Form the mixture into a roll and place down the centre of
    the pastry.
4. Fold one side of the pastry over the meat, brush the edge
    with lightly beaten egg-white and fold the other side over,
    pressing the join lightly to seal it.
5. Put the pastry roll, centre join underneath, on to a baking
    sheet and brush with the rest of the egg white. Make three
    small parallel cuts through the top of the pastry to allow the
    steam to escape.
6. Bake in a moderately hot oven (200 C/400 F, gas mark 6)
    for 40 minutes.

Note I: The pastry may, of course, be decorated with pastry leaves
or shapes, or a fine lattice of pastry strips.

Note II: Tasting raw meat is not as nasty as you may think and
it is vital to get the seasoning right.

Serves 4

Forcemeat Balls

450g/1lb pork sausage-meat
1 medium onion, finely
  chopped
1 tablespoon finely chopped
  fresh parsley
1 tablespoon finely chopped
  fresh sage *or* $\frac{1}{2}$ teaspoon
  dried sage

Grated rind of $\frac{1}{4}$ lemon
30g/1oz fresh breadcrumbs
Salt and pepper
Plain flour for rolling
55g/2oz butter

1. Mix together the sausage-meat, onion, parsley, sage, lemon
    rind and breadcrumbs. Season with salt and pepper. Taste
    and add more seasoning if necessary.
2. Shape into balls the size of a ping-pong ball. Roll in flour.

3. Melt the butter in a frying pan and toss the balls over the heat until cooked and well browned—approximately 8–10 minutes.

Note: Tasting raw meat is not as nasty as you may think and it is vital to get the seasoning right.

Makes 24

Simple Sausages

This sausage meat mixture can be filled into sausage skins or simply made into skinless sausages as described below.

450g/1lb minced fatty pork (e.g. from the belly)	1 egg
1 medium onion (optional)	3 leaves of fresh sage *or* 1 teaspoon rubbed dried sage
4 slices white bread, crusts removed	Salt and pepper
	Fat for frying

1. Mix the belly of pork and onion (if used) together.
2. Make breadcrumbs out of the bread slices, and stir into the meat with the egg and the chopped sage.
3. Add plenty of salt and pepper and mix thoroughly. Taste and season further if necessary.
4. Flour your hands, and form the mixture into sausage shapes. Rolling the mixture on a floured table-top gives good results.
5. Fry the sausages in hot fat, turning them frequently. They should cook slowly, and will take about 12 minutes if 2·5cm/1in diameter. If grilling the sausages, brush them lightly with melted fat before doing so.

Note I: These sausages (especially if the onion is omitted) freeze well uncooked, they can then be slowly fried without prior thawing.

Note II: Tasting raw meat is not as nasty as you may think and it is vital to get the seasoning correct.

Serves 4

Pork Chops with Rosemary

1 small onion, finely chopped
1 teaspoon finely chopped
  fresh parsley
1 teaspoon finely chopped
  fresh rosemary
1 egg
Salt and freshly ground black
  pepper

Four 170g/6oz pork chops,
  neatly trimmed
Dried white crumbs
About 2 tablespoons butter *or*
  dripping

1. Mix the onion, parsley, rosemary and egg together in a bowl. Season well with salt and pepper. Coat each pork chop with the egg mixture and then dip in breadcrumbs, covering them well.
2. Heat the fat in a frying pan. When foaming put in the chops and fry until golden brown on both sides, and tender all the way through (about 12–15 minutes).

Serves 4

Spare Ribs

1¼ kilos/2½lb skinned belly of
  pork pieces (American spare
  ribs)

For the marinade:
2 tablespoons runny honey
2 tablespoons soy sauce
½ garlic clove, crushed

½ teaspoon dried basil
Juice of 1 lemon
Salt and pepper

489

1. Mix together the ingredients for the marinade and soak the spare ribs in it for 5 hours.
2. Heat the grill.
3. When really hot, grill the ribs, basting with the marinade until brown and crisp.
4. Lower the heat and continue grilling and turning the ribs for a further 20 minutes or until tender.

Note: Alternatively the ribs can be roasted in the oven; they are done when *very* dark brown, and tender.

Serves 4

Glazed Bacon Joint

1·35 kilos/3lb forehock of
  bacon
1 onion
1 carrot
1 bay leaf
Fresh parsley stalks

Peppercorns
2 tablespoons demerara sugar
1 teaspoon dry English
  mustard
Handful of cloves

1. Soak the bacon overnight in cold water. This removes excess salt.
2. Place it in a large pan of cold water and add the onion, carrot, bay leaf, parsley stalks and peppercorns. Bring slowly to the boil, cover and simmer for 75 minutes.
3. Leave the joint to cool slightly in the stock. Then lift out and carefully pull off the skin without removing any of the fat.
4. Mix the sugar and mustard together and press it all over the joint to form an even coating.
5. Using a sharp knife, cut a lattice pattern across the bacon through the sugar and fat. Press any sugar that falls off on again. Stick a clove into each diamond segment, or into the cuts where the lines cross.

6.   Heat the oven to 220°C/425°F, gas mark 7 and bake the joint for about 20 minutes, or until brown and slightly caramelized.

Note I: If you haven't time to soak salty bacon overnight, cook it for 30 minutes in plain water and then transfer into a simmering pan ready prepared with the bay leaf, etc.

Note II: The cooking stock is useful for soups (especially pea or lentil soup).

Note III: The bacon joint can be decorated with a ham frill: to make one, cut a piece of greaseproof paper to about 20cm × 44cm/ 8in × 18in. Fold it loosely in half lengthwise, without pressing down the fold. Make 5cm/2in-long cuts, 1cm/½in apart, parallel

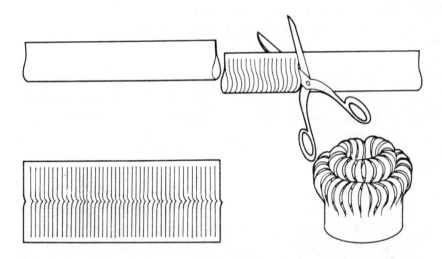

to the end of the paper, cutting through both thicknesses from the folded side towards the open sides. Make the cuts all along the strip. Now open out the paper and re-fold it lengthwise, in the opposite direction from the first time. Wrap the frill round the ham bone and secure with a paper clip.

Serves 4

Roast Pork

1·35 kilos/3lb loin of pork,
   with skin intact
Oil

Salt
Flour

For the gravy:
2 teaspoons flour

290ml/½ pint well flavoured
   stock

To serve:
Small bunch of watercress

Apple sauce (page 323)

1. Set the oven at 200°C/400°F, gas mark 6.
2. Score the rind (crackling skin) with a sharp knife in cuts about ½cm/¼in apart cutting through the skin but not right through the fat.
3. Brush the skin with oil and sprinkle with salt and flour to help give a crisp crackling.
4. Place in roasting pan and roast for 1 hour 40 minutes (25 minutes to the pound, plus 25 minutes extra).
5. Once the pork is cooked turn off the oven, put the pork on a serving dish and put it back into the oven leaving the door ajar if it is still very hot.
6. Tip all but a dessertspoonful of fat from the roasting pan, reserving as much of the meat juices as possible.
7. Add the flour and mix over the heat until well browned.
8. Draw off the heat, add the stock and mix well with a wire whisk or wooden spoon. Return to the heat and bring slowly up to the boil, whisking all the time. Simmer for a few minutes until the gravy is shiny. Season with salt and freshly ground black pepper to taste. Strain into a warmed gravy boat.
9. Garnish the pork with a bunch of watercress and serve with gravy and apple sauce.

Note: Remove the crackling before carving, then cut it with scissors into thin strips.

Serves 4

Spiced Cherry Pork with Tarragon Dressing

This recipe was devised by Caroline Waldegrave for the party to launch Leith's School of Food and Wine.

1·35 kilos/3lb loin of pork with belly flap attached, skinned and boned
1 small can spiced stoned cherries *or* 1 small can stoned black cherries, juice of ½ lemon, pinch of ginger, stick of cinnamon, 4 cloves
1 shallot, finely chopped

15g/½oz butter
1 tablespoon vinegar
6 tablespoons fresh white breadcrumbs
1 tablespoon finely chopped fresh tarragon
Salt and freshly ground black pepper

For the tarragon cream dressing:
1 large egg
3 tablespoons tarragon vinegar
2 tablespoons caster sugar
Pinch of salt
3 tablespoons lightly whipped cream

For the garnish:
6 large tomatoes
Chopped fresh parsley

1. Remove the excess fat from the pork loin, leaving only a thin layer. Set the oven to 150°C/300°F, gas mark 2. If the cherries are not spiced, drain them and infuse them over a very gentle heat with the lemon juice, ginger, cinnamon and cloves for 20 minutes.
2. Cook the shallot gently in the butter until soft but not coloured. Mix together the cherries (with no juice), vinegar, breadcrumbs and tarragon. Season well with salt and freshly ground black pepper.
3. Lay the pork loin skinned side down on the table. Pile the stuffing on to the loin. Roll up from the thick side towards the thin flap and tie neatly, at intervals, with string.
4. Put into a roasting pan. Season with salt and pepper. Roast for 3–3½ hours or until a skewer will glide into the thickest

part of the meat easily, and clear, not pink, juices run out. Lift the pork out of the fat and allow to cool.

5. While the pork is cooling, make the tarragon cream dressing. Beat the egg in a small bowl with a wooden spoon. Add the vinegar and sugar with a pinch of salt. Set the bowl over a pan of simmering water, or place the mixture in a double boiler, over gentle heat. Beat continuously until the mixture thickens slightly. Then whisk until almost doubled in bulk. Then allow to cool. When the mixture is stone-cold, stir in the whipped cream and adjust the seasoning.

6. Slice the pork neatly. Arrange the slices on a large platter and coat with the tarragon dressing.

7. Dip the tomatoes into boiling water for 5 seconds. Peel and quarter them. Remove the seeds. If the tomatoes were very big split each piece in half lengthwise. Dip the tip of each segment into the chopped parsley and arrange down the sides of the dish. Carefully sprinkle a little salt over this garnish.

Note: If using stoned fresh cherries you will need about 225g/1½lb of them plus 2 tablespoons of sugar, and the spicing ingredients.

Serves 6

Pork Chops Vallée d'Auge

Four 170g/6oz pork chops	2 dessert apples
Salt and freshly ground black pepper	Lemon juice
	Caster sugar
1 large onion, chopped	1 tablespoon butter
Stick of celery, chopped	1 egg yolk
2 teaspoons calvados *or* brandy	150ml/¼ pint cream
30g/1oz ham, diced	
150ml/¼ pint *dry* cider	Watercress to garnish

1. Set the oven to 180°C/350°F, gas mark 4.

494

2. Prepare the pork chops by cutting away any excess fat. Dry with absorbent paper and sprinkle with pepper.

3. Put the fat trimmed from the pork chops in a large frying pan and place over moderate heat. When the fat has melted and the pieces are shrivelled and crisp, remove the bits with a perforated spoon.

4. Put the chops in the pan and fry over a fairly high heat for about 4–5 minutes on each side until well browned. Put them into a casserole without any fat, cover and place in the warm oven.

5. Lower the heat under the frying pan and pour off all but a tablespoonful of fat. Add the onion and celery and fry gently until soft but not coloured. Add the calvados and set alight with a match. Add the diced ham and cider. Allow to simmer for 2 minutes.

6. Pour over the pork chops and leave covered in the oven for about 10 minutes or until the chops are completely tender.

7. Meanwhile peel the apples and cut them into rings. Brush each ring with lemon juice and sprinkle with sugar. Melt the butter in the frying pan and fry the apple rings until barely soft, and slightly brown on both sides.

8. Remove the pork chops from the oven, turn it down to 150°C/300°F, gas mark 2 (leave the door open to speed the cooling down process). Take up the chops and place them, surrounded by the fried apple, on a serving dish. Keep warm while you prepare the sauce.

9. Strain the liquor from the casserole and bring it up to simmering point in a clean pan. Mix the egg yolk with the cream in a bowl and add a little of the hot stock to the mixture. Return this to the saucepan and set over a gentle heat until the sauce becomes creamy and slightly thick, but take great care not to curdle it by boiling.

10. Coat the chops, but not the apple rings, with the sauce. Garnish with a bunch of watercress.

Serves 4

Pork Fillets in Cider

1 medium onion, finely
  chopped
1 small cooking apple
1 eating apple
1 tablespoon oil
675g/1½lb pork tenderloin
  (fillet)

15g/½oz butter
290ml/½ pint cider
Seasoning
1 bay leaf

1 tablespoon each flour and
butter for the thickening

To garnish:
Chopped fresh parsley

1. Set the oven to 180°C/350°F, gas mark 4.
2. In a small roasting tin, heat the oil and the butter. Season the fillets and fry them in the fat until lightly browned all over. Add the onion and fry gently for 4 more minutes. Pour over the cider, add the bay leaf and bring to the boil. Cover with foil and bake in the oven for 30 minutes.
3. Peel the apples and dice into cubes. Add to the fillets and continue cooking for a further 10 or 15 minutes, until the pork and apples are tender. Remove from the oven.
4. Take out the fillets and cut them into slices. Place in a serving dish. Spoon over the apple and onion. Knead the butter and flour together to a paste. Heat the cooking liquor over a high heat and whisk in the beurre manié (kneaded butter) until the sauce thickens. Taste for seasoning. Pour over the pork, and sprinkle with parsley.

Serves 4

Jambalaya

450g/1lb pork fillet
2–3 tablespoons oil
1 onion, finely chopped

110g/¼lb shelled prawns,
  preferably raw
Lemon juice

496

2 sticks celery, finely chopped
2 Frankfurters, sliced
55g/2oz garlic sausage, diced
110g/¼lb rice
290ml/½ pint chicken stock

Salt and freshly ground black
  pepper
2 teaspoons ground ginger
½ teaspoon turmeric
½ teaspoon paprika

1. Trim the fillet and cut it into 1cm/½in cubes. Heat half the oil
    in a heavy saucepan and quickly fry the pork until well-
    browned. Lift the pieces out and put them aside. Add the
    onion and celery to the saucepan, reduce the heat and fry
    gently until soft and evenly coloured. Lift them out.
2. Now fry the Frankfurters and garlic sausage, adding more
    oil if necessary and turning them until evenly browned. Lift
    them out. Heat the remaining oil, stir in the rice and fry,
    stirring constantly, until pale brown (about 10 minutes).
3. Add the chicken stock and prawns and put all the fried food
    back. Bring to the boil, season with a dash of lemon juice,
    salt, pepper, ginger, turmeric and paprika. Reduce the heat,
    cover and simmer until all the stock has been absorbed and
    the rice is cooked (about 20 minutes).

Serves 4–6

Sweet and Sour Pork

675g/1½lb lean pork
½ teaspoon salt
1 level tablespoon cornflour

Oil for deep frying
1 green pepper

For the sweet and sour sauce:
1 teaspoon cornflour
4 tablespoons water
2 tablespoons sugar
2 tablespoons vinegar
2 tablespoons tomato purée

2 tablespoons orange juice
2 tablespoons soy sauce
2 tablespoons finely chopped
  pineapple
½ teaspoon oil

1. Start with the sauce: blend the cornflour with the water and

mix it with the sugar, vinegar, tomato purée, orange juice and soy sauce.

2. Fry the chopped pineapple in the oil for 1 minute. Add this to the sauce.
3. Cut the pork into 2cm/¾in cubes. Sprinkle with salt and toss in the cornflour.
4. Heat the oil in the fryer until a crumb will sizzle vigorously in it. Deep fry the pork for 7–8 minutes. Drain on absorbent paper.
5. Heat 1 tablespoon oil in a wide pan. Slice the green pepper and fry it quickly for 30 seconds. Lower the temperature, add the sauce and cook for 1 minute, until it thickens. Add the pork and cook together for 1 further minute.
minute.

Serves 4

Pork Pie

675g/1½lb lean pork
1 pig's kidney
1 small onion, finely chopped
1 teaspoon salt
Pinch of cayenne pepper
Freshly ground black pepper

285g/10oz flour-quantity
   pâte à pâté (page 635)
Beaten egg for glazing pastry
570ml/1 pint pork jelly
   (page 307)

1. Cut the meats into bite-size cubes and mix with the onion and seasonings using plenty of black pepper.
2. Set the oven to 170°C/325°F, gas mark 3. Lightly grease a 2-kilo/4lb pie mould or a 20cm/8in loose-bottomed cake tin.
3. Roll two-thirds of the pâte à pâté into a round big enough to cover the base and sides of the pie mould or cake tin. Dust the surface with a little flour. Fold the pastry in half. Place one hand on the fold and with the other gently push and pull the sides to form a bag roughly the shape and size of the pie mould or cake tin. Open out the bag and fit it in the greased tin or mould. Fill with the meat.

4. Roll out the remaining third of the pastry into a round big enough to cover the top of the pie. Dampen the bottom edge with water. Press this lid on to the pastry case, pinching the edges together well. Decorate with pastry trimmings made into leaves and make a pea-sized hole in the middle .of the top.

5. Brush with egg. Bake in the oven for 1½ hours. After the first hour it may be necessary to cover the pie with a piece of wet paper to prevent it browning too much.

6. Remove the paper and the sides of the tin. Brush the pastry sides with beaten egg, then return to oven and bake until golden (about 15–20 minutes).

7. Take the pie out of the oven and allow it to get quite cold. Warm the jelly enough to make it just liquid but not hot. Using a funnel placed in the hole in the pastry lid, fill up the pie with jelly. After 5 minutes add some more, then more after another few minutes, until you are sure that the pie is completely full. It should take about 570ml/1 pint of liquid. Refrigerate the pie for the jelly to reset.

Note: Sometimes hot watercrust is used instead of the richer pâte à pâté. See pages 656–7

Serves 4–6

Jambon Persillé

One 900g/2lb piece mild gammon *or* unsmoked lean bacon
Slice of onion
1 bay leaf
½ carrot
2 parsley stalks
6 peppercorns
1·14 litres/2 pints veal stock plus 15g/½oz gelatine if the stock is not jellied

2 egg shells
150ml/¼ pint dry white wine
1 scant tablespoon tarragon vinegar
2 egg whites
2 tablespoons finely chopped fresh parsley

1. Soak the bacon in cold water overnight.
2. Simmer it in fresh water (to cover) with the onion, bay leaf, carrot, parsley stalks and peppercorns until tender (about $1\frac{1}{2}$ hours). Leave to cool in the liquid.
3. Put the veal stock into a large clean saucepan. If it is not set to a solid jelly sprinkle in the gelatine. Add the wine and vinegar. Put over gentle heat.
4. Place the crushed shells in a bowl, add the egg white and whisk until frothy. Pour into the warming stock and keep whisking steadily with a balloon whisk until the mixture boils and rises. Stop whisking immediately and draw the pan off the heat. Allow the mixture to subside. Take care not to break the crust formed by the egg white.
5. Bring the aspic up to the boil again and again allow to subside. Repeat this once more (the egg white will trap the sediment in the stock and clear the aspic). Allow to cool for 10 minutes.
6. Fix a double layer of fine muslin over a clean basin and carefully strain the aspic through it, taking care to hold the egg white crust back. When all the liquid is through (or almost all of it) allow the egg white to slip into the muslin. Then strain the aspic again – this time through both egg white crust and cloth. Do not try to hurry the process by squeezing the cloth, or murky aspic will result. Allow to cool.
7. Cut the ham into thick slices and then into neat strips. Arrange a neat layer in the bottom of a mould or soufflé dish which has been rinsed out with cold water.
8. Pour in enough almost-cold jelly to hold the ham in place when the jelly sets. Leave in the refrigerator to set.
9. Mix the chopped parsley into half the just-liquid jelly and pour 1cm/$\frac{1}{2}$in into the soufflé mould. Allow to set. Arrange a second layer of ham on top and set it in place with clear jelly.
10. Continue the layers in this way finishing with clear jelly. Chill well.
11. To turn out: dip the mould into hot water to loosen the jelly. Invert a plate over the mould and turn plate and mould

over together. Give a slight shake to dislodge the jelly and remove the mould.

Note: A good but less elegant jambon persillé is made with uncleared veal jelly, chopped parsley and cubes of cooked ham simply combined in a dish and allowed to set.

Serves 6

VEAL

Veal Escalopes with Rosemary

Four 140g/5oz veal escalopes, preferably from the noix (the best part of the leg) *or* from the loin *or* neck
Salt and freshly ground black pepper

30g/1oz butter
1 teaspoon fresh rosemary *or* ½ teaspoon dried rosemary
2 tablespoons dry white wine
1 tablespoon single cream

1. If the escalopes are not very thin place them between two sheets of greaseproof paper or polythene and gently beat with a mallet or rolling pin. Season with pepper and salt.
2. In a frying pan over a moderate heat melt the butter with the rosemary. When the butter is foaming fry the escalopes (one or two at a time if they won't fit in the pan together) for 3–4 minutes on each side until a very delicate brown. Take out the veal with a perforated spoon or fish slice and keep warm in a very low oven.
3. Pour the wine into the pan and heat, scraping the surface of the pan with a wooden spoon to incorporate any sediment. Boil up well and add the cream. Taste and correct seasoning if necessary. Pour over the veal and serve immediately.

Serves 4

Veal Escalopes with Ragout Fin

110g/¼lb lambs' or calves'
  sweetbreads
20g/¾oz butter
1 small onion, finely chopped
30g/1oz diced bacon
55g/2oz button mushrooms,
  sliced but not peeled
1 level tablespoon chopped
  fresh parsley

7g/¼oz flour
150ml/¼ pint well-flavoured
  chicken stock
Salt and freshly ground black
  pepper
Four 170g/6oz veal escalopes
Extra butter for frying
Squeeze of lemon juice

For the garnish:
Sprig of watercress
Lemon wedges

1. Soak the sweetbreads in cold water for 4 hours, changing the water every time it becomes pink; probably four times. There should be no blood at all when the sweetbreads are ready for cooking.
2. Place them in a pan of cold water and bring up to boiling point, but do not allow to boil. Simmer for 2 minutes. Rinse under running cold water and dry well.
3. Pick over the sweetbreads, removing all the skin and membrane. Chop them coarsely.
4. Melt the butter and add the onion. Cook slowly until soft but not coloured. Add the bacon and sweetbreads and cook for 3 minutes. Stir in the mushrooms and parsley and leave over a gentle heat for 1 minute.
5. Mix in the flour and cook for 30 seconds. Remove from the heat and stir in the stock. Return to the heat and bring slowly to the boil, stirring continuously. Season with salt and pepper. Simmer for 30 seconds and set aside to cool and solidify.
6. Place the veal escalopes between two pieces of greaseproof paper or polythene and with a rolling pin or mallet beat them out until thin.
7. Divide the sweetbread mixture between the escalopes and

wrap each one up so that they look like flat parcels. Tie them up with fine cotton.

8. Melt some butter in a large frying pan and when foaming add the escalopes. Brown lightly on both sides. Reduce the temperature and cook slowly for 4–5 minutes. Lift out the escalopes on to a warmed serving plate.
9. Increase the heat under the frying pan and brown the butter, adding a squeeze of lemon juice. Pour over the escalopes and serve garnished with watercress and lemon wedges.

Serves 4

Veal Marsala

Four 170g/6oz veal escalopes   2 tablespoons Marsala
30g/1oz butter   4 tablespoons single cream
Salt and freshly ground white   Lemon juice
  pepper

1. Put the veal escalopes between two sheets of greaseproof paper and beat out with a mallet or rolling pin.
2. Melt the butter in a frying pan and when it is foaming fry the escalopes briskly to brown them lightly on both sides (2–3 minutes per side). Dish them on a warm plate.
3. Add the Marsala to the pan, swill it about and bring to the boil. Add the cream, season well with salt, pepper and a few drops of lemon juice.
4. Return the veal to the pan to heat through gently.

Serves 4

Hungarian Veal Steaks with Aubergine

1 large aubergine
30g/1oz seasoned flour
675g/1½lb boneless veal (sirloin
  or fillet)
225g/½lb larding pork or
  110g/¼lb thin rindless streaky
  bacon
55g/2oz butter
1 shallot, finely chopped

1 teaspoon paprika
3 tablespoons white wine
150ml/¼ pint cream
290ml/½ pint mornay sauce
  (page 309)
1 tablespoon grated cheese
1 tablespoon dry white
  breadcrumbs

1. Set the oven to 130°C/250°F, gas mark 2.
2. Slice the aubergine in four 1cm/½in thick slices. Sprinkle with salt and leave to release its juices (to dégorge). Rinse well, pat dry and dip in seasoned flour.
3. Roll up and bard the meat (wrap it carefully in the pork fat, cut into thin strips, or in the streaky bacon). Tie the roll at 3cm/1½in intervals with string. Slice through the meat between the strings to give four even-sized steaks, surrounded by fat or bacon and each encircled with string.
4. Melt half the butter and fry the aubergine until golden brown and tender. Remove from the pan and keep warm in the oven.
5. Dust the veal steaks with seasoned flour. Heat the remaining butter in the pan and fry the veal steaks for 6–8 minutes on each side. Remove and keep warm in the oven.
6. Add the shallot to the pan and cook slowly for 2 minutes, then add the paprika and continue cooking a further 2 minutes. Pour on the wine and boil to reduce it by half. Pour in the cream and season with salt and pepper. Reheat without boiling and then keep on one side.
7. Heat the grill. Reheat the mornay sauce.
8. Lay the aubergine slices in an ovenproof dish. Remove the strings from the veal steaks and lay them on top of the aubergines. Coat with the mornay sauce. Sprinkle with

cheese and crumbs and brown under the grill. Reheat the paprika sauce and trickle it around the dish.

Serves 4

Osso Bucco

340g/¾lb ripe tomatoes
3 tablespoons olive oil
1 large *or* 2 small onions, finely chopped
1 large carrot, finely chopped
2 garlic cloves, crushed
4 large meaty pieces knuckle of veal, cut across with the bone and marrow in the centre
2 teaspoons tomato purée
150ml/¼ pint dry white wine

290ml/½ pint good veal stock
Salt and freshly ground black pepper
Bouquet garni (sprig each of parsley and thyme, stick of celery and 1 bay leaf, tied together with string)
1 tablespoon flour
1 tablespoon chopped fresh parsley

1. Dip the tomatoes into boiling water for 5 seconds. Skin and chop them.
2. Put a tablespoon of the oil into a saucepan, add the onion, carrot and garlic and cover with a well-fitting lid. Leave on a gentle heat to cook without browning.
3. Brown the meat on both sides in the rest of the oil in a large pan, one or two pieces at a time. Remove to a plate as they are browned.
4. When all are done sprinkle the flour into the pan and stir well. Add the tomato purée, cooked vegetables, chopped tomatoes, wine, stock, salt and pepper and bring to the boil.
5. Replace the ossi buchi, sink the bouquet garni in the liquid and put on the lid. Simmer for 1½ hours or until the veal is very tender but not quite falling off the bone.
6. Take the veal out and place on a warmed serving platter with a fairly deep lip. Cover with foil and keep warm while you

boil the sauce rapidly until thick. (Stir frequently and watch that it does not catch and burn at the bottom.)

7. Remove the bouquet garni. The sauce should be pushed through a sieve, then poured over the meat, but it is often served without sieving. Osso bucco is, and looks, a substantial peasant dish, made brighter by a last-minute scattering of chopped parsley.

Serves 4

Blanquette de Veau

900g/2lb pie veal
Slice of lemon
Bouquet garni (4 parsley stalks, 2 bay leaves, blade of mace *or* pinch of nutmeg)
Salt and pepper
1 teaspoon cornflour

2 carrots, peeled and cut into sticks
2 onions, peeled and sliced
1 egg yolk *or* 2 for a very rich sauce
150ml/¼ pint double cream

For the garnish:
8 fried bread triangles made from 2 slices crustless white bread

Fresh parsley, chopped

1. Cut the veal into cubes and trim off any skin or gristle. Put in a pan of cold water with a slice of lemon. Bring slowly to the boil, skimming carefully. Add the bouquet garni with a little salt. Remove the lemon slice. Simmer gently for 30 minutes.
2. Add the carrots and onions and continue to simmer until the meat is really tender and the vegetables cooked (probably a further 30 minutes).
3. Strain the liquid into a jug and put the meat and vegetables into an ovenproof serving dish. Remove the bouquet garni. Return the liquid to the pan. Mix the cornflour in a cup with

a few spoons of cold water and add some of the hot liquid from the veal to this. Stir well, then stir the resulting paste into the pan of veal stock. Stir while bringing to the boil. You should now have a sauce that is very slightly thickened – about the consistency of thin cream. If it is still too thin, do not add more cornflour, but boil rapidly until reduced to the correct consistency. Add salt and pepper.

4. Mix the egg yolks and cream together in a bowl. Add some of the sauce, mix well, and return to the pan. *Do not boil* or the eggs will scramble. Reheat gently, stirring until the egg yolks have thickened the sauce to the consistency of double cream, pour over the meat and vegetables.

5. Serve garnished with triangles of fried bread with their corners dipped in chopped parsley.

Note I: Some recipes require the meat to be soaked in water overnight, and then drained before cooking, but unless the veal is very poor quality and more red than pink this is not necessary.

Note II: The inclusion of a teaspoon of cornflour to start the thickening of the sauce would be frowned upon by purists. But it helps greatly, and, as long as the yolks and cream are used too, the flavour is absolutely as it should be.

Serves 4

Veal Florentine

6 tomatoes
1 garlic clove
55g/2oz butter
900g/2lb leaf spinach
Salt and freshly ground black
  pepper
Pinch of nutmeg

Four 140g/5oz veal escalopes
290ml/½ pint cheese sauce
  (page 309)
1 level tablespoon grated cheese
1 level tablespoon dried
  breadcrumbs

1. Set the oven to 180°C/350°F, gas mark 4. Lightly butter an ovenproof dish.
2. Skin the tomatoes and slice them thickly.
3. Crush the garlic and fry it and the tomatoes lightly in a quarter of the butter without allowing the tomatoes to get too soft. Place them in the bottom of the dish.
4. Wash the spinach well and remove the stalks. Put it in a saucepan with a pinch of salt. Cover and cook for 5 minutes, shaking the pan regularly. Drain well, pressing out all the water. Tip on to a board and chop roughly.
5. Return the spinach to the pan and toss in a teaspoon of the butter. Season with salt, pepper and grated nutmeg. Now spread the spinach on top of the tomatoes.
6. Put the veal between two pieces of greaseproof paper and flatten by batting evenly with a rolling pin. Cut across the grain into strips.
7. Heat the remaining butter in a large frying pan. Fry the veal strips in this until lightly browned all over. Put them on top of the spinach and season well with salt and pepper.
8. Heat the cheese sauce and pour evenly over the veal and spinach. Sprinkle with the grated cheese and breadcrumbs.
9. Bake for 15 minutes or until bubbly and hot, then grill to brown the top.

Serves 4

Hungarian Veal Goulash

675g/1½lb veal shoulder *or* leg
450g/1lb onions, sliced
20g/¾oz butter
290ml/½ pint veal stock
Squeeze of lemon juice
1 glass white wine
2 teaspoons tomato purée

1 tablespoon paprika
Salt and freshly ground black pepper
1 teaspoon flour
150ml/5 fl.oz carton soured cream
Fresh parsley for garnish

1. Cut the veal into 5cm/2in cubes.
2. In a large saucepan cook the onions in the butter until soft.
3. Add the veal, stock, lemon juice, wine, tomato purée, salt, pepper and paprika, bring to the boil and simmer until the meat is tender (45–60 minutes).
4. Strain the stock into a jug and place the meat in an oven-proof dish. Return the stock to the pan, mix the flour with a little of the soured cream and add some of the hot veal stock to it. Mix thoroughly and return the paste to the veal stock. Bring slowly to the boil, stirring continuously; cook for 2 minutes.
5. Check the seasoning and pour the sauce over the veal. Streak in the remaining soured cream and scatter chopped parsley on top.

Serves 4

Vitello Tonnato

900/2lb boned loin of veal
1 tablespoon oil
1 glass vermouth
Bouquet garni (1 parsley stalk, 1 bay leaf, sprig of thyme)
Salt and freshly ground black pepper

For the decoration:
570ml/1 pint aspic jelly (page 303)
4 large ripe tomatoes
290ml/½ pint French dressing (page 319)

For the tuna mousse:
1 small can tuna fish
30g/1oz butter
150ml/¼ pint béchamel sauce (page 308)
1 teaspoon tomato purée
3 tablespoons double cream, lightly whipped
Squeeze of lemon juice

1. Set the oven to 190°C/375°F, gas mark 5.
2. Season the veal and tie it up into a neat roll. In a heavy pan

or roasting tin brown it evenly on all sides in the oil over a high heat.

3. Add the vermouth and bouquet garni. Cover and bake in the oven until tender (about 1–1½ hours).

4. Meanwhile prepare the tuna mousse: pound the tuna (without its oil) well with the butter. Beat in the béchamel and stir in the tomato purée and lightly whipped cream. Add a squeeze of lemon juice. Taste and add more salt and pepper if necessary.

5. Remove the veal when cooked and allow it to cool. When cold slice evenly and sandwich the slices together with the tuna mousse in a loaf-like shape, taking care that the tuna mixture is not squeezed out of the top. Leave in the refrigerator until quite firm.

6. Melt the aspic jelly, then allow to cool to the point of setting. Brush or spoon a layer carefully over the vitello. Chill very well and brush again with aspic jelly so that the veal looks very shiny. Carefully lift on to a serving dish.

7. If there is any aspic left over set it in a shallow tray, then cut it into tiny dice. Use to surround the veal.

8. Dip the tomatoes into boiling water for 5 seconds. Peel and slice them. Arrange them around the veal, and spoon the French dressing over.

Note: If the aspic is less than crystal clear it is wise not to chop it – which seems to emphasize its murkiness.

Serves 6

Veal and Ham Raised Pie

675g/1½lb boned shoulder of veal
110g/¼lb ham
Salt and freshly ground black pepper
1 onion, chopped

450g/1lb flour-quantity hot watercrust pastry (pages 656–7)
1 egg, beaten
570ml/1 pint pork jelly (page 307)

2 tablespoons fresh parsley,
  chopped

1. Set the oven to 170°C/325°F, gas mark 3.
2. Cut the veal and ham into small cubes. Season with salt and pepper, chopped onion and chopped parsley. Leave on one side while you make the pastry and mould the pastry case (see page 656).
3. Fill the pie with the seasoned meat and cover with the remaining pastry. Press the edges together. Make a neat hole in the middle of the lid. Brush all over with the beaten egg.
4. Bake for 2 hours. After the first hour it may be necessary to cover the pie with a piece of wet paper to prevent it browning too much. Take the pie out of the oven and allow to get quite cold.
5. Warm the pork jelly enough to make it just liquid but not hot. Using a funnel, fill up the pie with jelly. Allow the liquid to set slightly and then add more liquid until you are sure that the pie is completely full. Leave in the refrigerator for the jelly to reset.

Note: A richer and, frankly, better result is achieved with a pâte à pâté crust, though the classic English pie is made as above. The recipe for pâte à pâté is found on page 655, and the pork pie recipe on pages 498-99 gives instructions for shaping and baking.

Serves 4

OFFAL

Brains with Brown Butter (cervelles beurre noisette)

4 calves' brains	About 10 capers
Court bouillon (page 306)	Chopped fresh parsley
Salt and pepper	55g/2oz butter
About 3 gherkins	3 tablespoons lemon juice

1. Wash the brains well and soak in cold water for 2–3 hours. Drain them.
2. Bring the court bouillon to the boil, add the brains and poach for 15 minutes. Remove and drain thoroughly.
3. Cut the brains into slices, removing any membranes. Lay on a heated serving dish and season with salt and pepper.
4. Chop the gherkins, capers and parsley.
5. Heat the butter in a pan until just turning brown. Immediately add the gherkins, capers, parsley and lemon juice. Boil up, pour over the brains and serve immediately.

Serves 4

Brawn

1 pig's head, split in two
55g/2oz saltpetre
Coarse pure salt
8 lambs' tongues
2 pigs' trotters
2 bay leaves
2 onions, peeled and sliced
2 carrots, peeled and sliced
2 parsley stalks

6 peppercorns
Juice of 1 lemon
2 small turnips, peeled and sliced
12 whole allspice
2 whole cloves
Blade of mace
Pinch of paprika, salt and pepper

1. Prepare the head: cut off the ears, remove the brains and eyes and wash the head thoroughly in plenty of water. Reserve and freeze the ears and brains.
2. Rub plenty of salt over the head and leave it to drain for 24 hours.
3. Mix together the saltpetre with 55g/2oz of salt and rub it all over the head. Leave to stand for 3 days.
4. Place in a pan of cold water and leave in a refrigerator or larder to soak for 2 days.
5. Place the head with the defrosted ears and brains, lambs' tongues and pigs' trotters in a large saucepan and cover with cold water. Bring slowly to the boil, skimming off froth or

fat carefully. Simmer for 2 hours or until the meat will easily leave the bone.

6. Lift out the head, tongues and trotters. Strip off all the flesh from the head.

7. Return the bones to the cooking liquid in the pan with the bay leaves, onions, carrots, parsley stalks, peppercorns, lemon juice, turnips, allspice, cloves and mace. Boil, skimming as necessary, until the stock has reduced to 1·14 litres/2 pints (about 45 minutes). Strain and allow to become completely cold.

8. Skin the ear, remove the membranes from the brain and chop both roughly. Skin the tongues and dice them finely. Put all the meat in a large bowl and mix it together thoroughly by hand, discarding any pieces of gristle.

9. Remove the fat from the stock. Warm the stock until just melted and strain through a J-cloth or muslin. Bring to the boil and stir in the prepared meat.

10. Wet a 1·14 litres/2 pint tin mould and pour in the brawn. Cover with a wooden board, or heavy flat object. (This is to prevent the meat floating above the surface of the liquid.)

11. Allow to cool, then refrigerate until set.

12. To serve, dip the mould briefly in hot water, and turn out on to a serving plate.

Serves 10

Braised Lambs' Hearts

4 lambs' hearts (total weight 675g/1½lb)
1 tablespoon dripping
290ml/½ pint good strong stock
1 bay leaf
1 parsley stalk
Salt and freshly ground black pepper

For the stuffing:
15g/½oz butter
1 onion, finely chopped
110g/¼lb breadcrumbs
125g/4½oz grated carrot
1 teaspoon cumin powder
1½ tablespoons finely chopped fresh mint
1 teaspoon grated root ginger
1 egg

513

For the mirepoix:

1 tablespoon finely diced celery

1 tablespoon finely diced onion

1 tablespoon finely diced carrot

For the gravy:

2 tablespoons port

½ teaspoon redcurrant jelly

1. Wash the hearts, removing the veins and arteries. Leave the hearts to soak in cold water for 1 hour.
2. Put the hearts into a saucepan, cover with cold water and bring slowly to the boil. Drain and pat dry.
3. Prepare the stuffing: melt the butter and add the onion, cook until soft but not coloured. Combine with all the stuffing ingredients except the egg. Season with salt and pepper and add just enough beaten egg to bind. Too much egg will make the stuffing too solid.
4. Set the oven to 150°C/300°F, gas mark 2.
5. Fill the heart cavities with the stuffing.
6. Heat the dripping in a large heavy pan with a lid and brown the hearts all over.
7. Remove the hearts and put in the mirepoix ingredients. Cook slowly in the fat until soft and lightly coloured. Return the hearts and pour on the stock. Add the bay leaf and parsley stalk and season well with salt and pepper. Bring to the boil, cover with a piece of greased paper and the lid and place in the oven.
8. Bake for 2½–3 hours or until tender, basting occasionally and topping up with extra stock as necessary. The mirepoix must not become at all dry.
9. When they are tender remove the hearts and turn off the oven. Put the hearts on a serving dish. Slice them carefully or leave whole, as preferred. Keep warm, well covered.
10. Now make the gravy: strain the cooking juices into a saucepan. If very thin, reduce by boiling rapidly to a syrupy consistency, or thicken by whisking 1–2 teaspoons of beurre manié (flour and butter mixed in equal proportions to a paste) into the simmering liquid.
11. Add the port and boil up well. Stir in the redcurrant jelly. Taste and season with salt and pepper. Spoon the gravy over the meat.

Serves 4

Kidneys Turbigo

9 lambs' kidneys
Butter for frying
225g/½lb small pork sausages
12 baby onions *or* shallots,
 peeled
225g/½lb button mushrooms
2 tablespoons sherry
425ml/¾ pint stock

Bouquet garni (1 stick of celery,
 1 bay leaf, sprigs of parsley
 and thyme, tied together with
 string)
Salt and pepper
30g/1oz butter
30g/1oz flour
1 carton soured cream (about
 150ml/5fl.oz)

1. Skin the kidneys, halve them and remove the core.
2. Heat the butter in a frying pan. Brown the kidneys quickly (a few at a time) on both sides. They should cook fast enough to go brown rather than grey. Remove them into a bowl as you go.
3. Now fry the sausages, then the onions, and finally the mushrooms in the same way. Put them on to a plate – not with the kidneys.
4. Pour off the blood that will have run from the kidneys (it can be very bitter).
5. Put everything back into the pan. Pour over the sherry and stock and sink the bouquet garni in the liquid. Add salt and pepper and cover with the saucepan lid.
6. Cook very gently for about 45 minutes or until the kidneys and onions are tender.
7. Lift the meat and vegetables on to a serving dish and discard the bouquet garni.
8. Work the butter and flour together to a paste (beurre manie). Drop about half of it into the sauce and whisk or stir briskly while bringing slowly to the boil. If the sauce is still on the thin side add the rest of the butter and flour mixture in the same way, whisking out the lumps. Boil for 1 minute.
10. Add the soured cream, stir (but do not boil) and pour over the dish. Alternatively, serve the cream separately.

Note: Classic turbigo does not have the soured cream but the addition is delicious.

Serves 4

Kidneys with Mushrooms in Mustard Sauce

6 lambs' kidneys
30g/1oz butter
110g/¼lb large flat mushrooms, chopped
2 tablespoons single cream
2 teaspoons made English mustard
Salt and freshly ground black pepper
Fresh parsley

1. Skin, split and core the kidneys. Cut into fine slices.
2. Melt the butter and brown the kidneys all over. Add the mushrooms and cook for 1 minute.
3. Reduce the heat and stir in the cream, mustard, salt and pepper. Serve immediately, garnished with chopped parsley.

Serves 2

Vol-au-vent of Veal Kidneys

1 large vol-au-vent case (page 651)
2 veal kidneys
55g/2oz butter
2 level tablespoons flour
1 wineglass Madeira
150ml/¼ pint good brown stock
Salt and freshly ground black pepper
Lemon juice
1 teaspoon chopped fresh parsley

1. Set the oven to 170°C/325°F, gas mark 3, and put the cooked vol-au-vent case on an ovenproof dish.
2. Skin the kidneys and slice them fairly finely, discarding any gristle or membranes.

3. Melt the butter in a frying pan and when foaming add the kidneys and fry rapidly until evenly browned.
4. Add the flour to the frying pan and cook for 1 minute, stirring and scraping the bottom of the pan to loosen any sediment.
5. Draw off the heat and stir in the Madeira and stock. Bring slowly to the boil, stirring well. Simmer for 2–3 minutes to moderate the taste of alcohol and finish cooking the kidneys.
6. Add salt and pepper, lemon juice and chopped parsley.
7. Fill the hot vol-au-vent case with the mixture and serve at once.

Serves 4

Veal Kidneys Robert

150ml/¼ pint dry white wine
450g/1lb veal kidneys
55g/2oz butter
2 teaspoons flour
1 teaspoon made English
   mustard

1 dessertspoon chopped fresh
   parsley
Squeeze of lemon juice
Salt and freshly ground black
   pepper
2 tablespoons cream

1. Put the wine in a saucepan and boil until reduced by half.
2. Remove the membranes and cores from the kidneys, and slice them fairly finely.
3. Fry a handful of kidney slices at a time in hot butter, shaking the pan until the kidneys are brown but still pink inside.
4. Return all the kidneys to the pan and stir in the flour. Cook for 30 seconds and then add the mustard, wine, parsley, lemon juice and seasoning. Bring to the boil, stirring continuously. Stir in the cream. Taste, adding salt and pepper if necessary.
5. Turn into a warm dish and sprinkle with chopped parsley.

Serves 2–3

Calves' Liver Lyonnaise

450g/1lb calves' liver
55g/2oz butter
1 large onion, finely sliced
55g/2oz flour
Salt and freshly ground black
  pepper

290ml/½ pint brown stock
1 tablespoon orange juice
1 heaped teaspoon mixed finely
  chopped fresh herbs
  (rosemary, sage, thyme)
Fresh parsley, chopped

1. Set the oven to 190 C/375 F, gas mark 5.
2. Skin the liver by removing the fine outer membrane. Cut it into slices.
3. Heat half the butter in a frying pan and slowly cook the onion until first soft and transparent and finally evenly pale brown. Set aside.
4. Season the flour well with salt and pepper. Dip the liver slices in the flour shaking off any excess.
5. Heat the rest of the butter until foaming. Fry the liver pieces in it, a few at a time. The liver should be nicely browned on the outside but pale pink in the middle (about 2 minutes on each side). Drain well. Arrange in overlapping slices with the onions, in an ovenproof dish. Keep warm.
6. Sprinkle enough of the seasoned flour (about 1 teaspoon) into the frying pan to absorb the remaining fat. Cook for 1 minute, stirring and scraping any sediment from the bottom of the pan. Gradually stir in the stock and the orange juice. Allow to boil. Season with pepper and salt and add the herbs. Pour this gravy over the liver, garnish with chopped parsley and serve immediately.

Serves 4

Liver and Bacon

450g/1lb calves' *or* lambs' liver
Seasoned flour
6 rashers rindless bacon
55g/2oz butter
1 onion thinly sliced
About 2 teaspoons flour

290ml/½ pint beef stock *or* a
    stock cube and 290ml/½ pint
    water
Small glass sherry (optional)
Watercress to garnish

1. Remove the film of membrane from the liver and cut the meat into 0·5cm/¼in slices. Dip the slices in seasoned flour and keep well separated on a plate.
2. Heat the grill. Cook the bacon under it until crisp and brown but not brittle. Turn off the grill and leave the bacon under it to keep warm.
3. Heat half the butter in a frying pan and fry the onion slowly in it until soft and brown. Tip the onion into a saucer.
4. Heat the rest of the butter in the frying pan and fry the liver slices, a few pieces at a time, adding more butter if necessary. Fry briskly for the first minute or two, and turn over when browned. Fry briskly on the second side at first, then more gently for a further 2 minutes (only about 6 minutes in all: liver is easily spoiled by overcooking). Dish on a shallow platter and keep warm.
5. Put the onion, and any of its fat, back into the pan and add a sprinkling of flour – just enough to absorb the fat. Pour in the stock and stir well as it comes to the boil. Add the sherry if using.
6. Boil the sauce rapidly to reduce in quantity and thicken the gravy. This will also give a richer appearance and concentrate the flavour.
7. Pour the sauce over the liver, top with the bacon and garnish with watercress. Serve at once as liver toughens on standing.

Serves 4

Oxtail Stew

2 oxtails
340g/¾lb carrots
225g/½lb onions
30g/1 oz beef dripping
40g/1¼oz flour
150ml/¼ pint red wine
570ml/1 pint water *or* stock
1 teaspoon chopped fresh
  thyme

Salt and freshly ground black
  pepper
½ teaspoon sugar
1 teaspoon tomato purée
Juice of ½ lemon
2 slices white bread
3 tablespoons oil
2 tablespoons chopped fresh
  parsley

1. Wash and dry the tails. Chop them into 5cm/2in lengths.
2. Peel the carrots and slice them thickly. Slice the onions.
3. Melt the dripping in a heavy saucepan and add the oxtail, browning the sides evenly and well. Remove.
4. Brown the carrots and onions in the same pan.
5. Replace the oxtail. Sprinkle on the flour and blend it in well. Pour over the wine and water or stock, add the thyme, salt and pepper and the sugar. Bring to the boil and simmer for 2 hours.
6. Set the oven to 150 C/300 F, gas mark 2.
7. Take out the pieces of meat and vegetables and place in a casserole.
8. With a small ladle or spoon, skim off the fat which will rise to the top of the remaining liquid. Add the tomato purée and lemon juice and bring quickly to the boil.
9. Pour this over the oxtail, cover with a lid, and place in the pre-heated oven for approximately 3 hours, or until the meat is almost falling off the bone.
10. Remove the crusts from the bread and cut the slices into 4 triangles. Heat the oil in a heavy frying pan and gently fry the triangles in the fat, one side after the other until crisp right through and evenly brown. Drain on absorbent paper.
11. When the oxtail is tender take it out of the oven, place the croutes around the edge of the dish and sprinkle over the chopped parsley. If the sauce is too thin remove the meat

and vegetables to a serving dish and boil the sauce rapidly until reduced to the desired consistency.

Note: When buying oxtail choose short fat tails with a good proportion of meat on them. Long stringy thin tails are poor value – pale in flavour and short on meat.

Serves 4

Pressed Tongue

1 ox tongue, fresh *or* salted
Salt
6 peppercorns
Bouquet garni (stick of celery, bay leaf, sprigs of parsley and thyme, tied together with string)

2 onions
2 carrots
1 stick celery
425ml/¾ pint aspic made from beef stock and gelatine *or* from a packet of aspic mix

1. If the tongue is salted soak it in fresh water for four hours. If the tongue is fresh soak it in brine (salty water) for 1–2 hours.
2. Place it in a saucepan, cover and pour in enough water to cover completely.
3. Add salt if the tongue is fresh. Add the peppercorns, bouquet garni, onions, carrots and celery.
4. Bring gently to the boil, skimming off any scum. Cover tightly and simmer for 2–3 hours, or until tender when pierced with a skewer. Leave to cool for 1 hour in the liquid.
5. Take out and remove the bones from the root of the tongue and peel off the skin.
6. Curl the tongue tightly and fit it into a deep round cake tin or tongue press.
7. Pour a little cool jellied stock or aspic into the tin.
8. Place a plate which just fits inside the tin on top of the tongue. Stand a heavy weight (about 4 kilos/8lb) on the plate and leave overnight in the refrigerator.

To carve: slice thinly across the top of the round.

Note: The stock in which the tongue is cooked is suitable for use in making the jellied stock if it is not too salty.

Serves 4

MISCELLANEOUS

Baked Stuffed Aubergines

2 medium-sized aubergines
15g/½oz beef dripping
285g/10oz minced beef
1 onion, finely chopped
½ green pepper, chopped
55g/2oz mushrooms, chopped
1 garlic clove, crushed
1 teaspoon flour
290ml/½ pint beef stock
1 bay leaf
2 teaspoons tomato purée

1 teaspoon chopped fresh
  parsley
Salt and pepper
Lemon juice
290ml/½ pint tomato sauce
  (page 325)
15g/½oz butter
Grated Gruyère *or*
  strong Cheddar cheese
Dried crumbs.

1. Cut the aubergines in half lengthwise and scoop out the centre leaving the shell with about 0·5cm/¼in of flesh attached. Sprinkle lightly with salt and leave upside down to drain.
2. Chop up the aubergine flesh and sprinkle with salt. Leave to drain on a tilted board or in a sieve for 20 minutes.
3. Melt the beef dripping in a sauté pan. Add the mince and brown thoroughly all over.
4. Rinse and dry the aubergine flesh. Add to the mince with the onion, green pepper, mushroom and garlic and cook for a further 3–4 minutes.
5. Stir in the flour. Cook for 1 minute, then add the beef stock, bay leaf, tomato purée, parsley, pepper and lemon juice.

6. Bring to the boil, stirring continuously, cover and simmer for 20–25 minutes.
7. Remove the bay leaf.
8. While the stuffing is cooking make the tomato sauce.
9. Set the oven to 200 C/400 F, gas mark 6.
10. Wash and dry the aubergine shells, brush with the butter (melted) and fill with the mince mixture.
11. Sprinkle over the grated cheese and crumbs. Bake in the pre-heated oven for 30 minutes, or until the shells are tender and the cheese well browned and crusty.
12. Serve with the tomato sauce.

Serves 4

Bubble and Squeak

450g/1lb mashed potatoes (page 275)   55g/2oz good dripping
450g/1lb cooked vegetables,
  such as cabbage *or* onion *or*
  leek

1. Mix the potato with the other vegetables. Season to taste.
2. Melt the dripping in a heavy-based pan.
3. Put in the vegetable mixture, pressing it down flat on the hot dripping. Cook slowly to heat through and allow a crust to form on the bottom of the mixture.
4. Now flip the cake over on to a plate and return it to the pan to brown the second side.
5. Slide on to a warm serving dish and serve immediately.

Note: Bubble and squeak is really a left-over fry-up and it does not matter if the cake is neat and even or crumbly and broken. But if you prefer it to be round and neat so that you can cut it into slices, a beaten egg added to the mixture will ensure that the ingredients hold together.

Serves 4

Stuffed Green Peppers

4 green peppers
30g/1oz butter
1 medium onion, finely diced
1 garlic clove, crushed
110g/¼lb mushrooms, sliced
30g/1oz split blanched almonds
140g/5oz long-grain rice
290ml/½ pint chicken stock
  (page 302)

1 teaspoon chopped fresh
  rosemary
30g/1oz raisins
1 tablespoon chopped fresh
  parsley
Salt and pepper
290ml/½ pint tomato sauce
  (page 325)

1. Cut off the tops of the peppers and remove core and seeds.
2. Drop the peppers into boiling water for 2 minutes. Plunge immediately into cold water to cool.
3. Set the oven to 190°C/375°F, gas mark 5.
4. Melt the butter and cook the finely diced onion in it until transparent. Add the garlic, mushrooms and almonds.
5. Sauté (fry briskly, while tossing the contents of the pan in the butter) for a further 2 minutes.
6. Stir in the rice and fry for a further minute.
7. Pour on the stock and bring to the boil. Add the rosemary, raisins, parsley and seasoning. Cover and bake in the oven for 20 minutes.
8. When the rice is cooked fill the peppers with it and place them in a deep fireproof dish.
9. Pour on the tomato sauce. Cover and put back into the oven for 40 minutes.

Serves 4

Macaroni Cheese

170g/6oz macaroni
Oil

Salt, pepper and
  English mustard

30g/1oz butter   170g/6oz grated cheese
30g/1oz flour   ½ tablespoon breadcrumbs
425ml/¾ pint milk

Optional additional ingredients:
1–2 fried bacon rashers   1 hardboiled egg
1 small onion   2 tomatoes

1. Lightly butter the sides of a shallow ovenproof dish large enough to hold ½ litre/1 pint.
2. Boil the macaroni in plenty of salted water with a tablespoon of oil. The water must boil steadily to keep the macaroni moving freely and prevent it sticking to the pan; the lid is left off to prevent boiling over. Cook the macaroni for 10–15 minutes or until it is just tender.
3. Meanwhile chop and fry the bacon (if used) and put it in the bottom of the dish; or chop the onion finely and cook it till quite soft in the butter; or chop the hardboiled egg to be added to the sauce later; or scald, skin and slice the tomatoes.
4. Drain the macaroni.
5. Melt the butter (with the cooked onion if used). Add the flour and cook for ½ a minute. Pour on the milk and bring gradually to the boil, stirring continually. Simmer for 1 minute. Add a pinch of mustard.
6. Stir the macaroni into the sauce and reheat if necessary.
7. Season the sauce to taste and add tomatoes or hardboiled egg if using.
8. Stir in all but one level tablespoon of cheese and turn the mixture into the dish.
9. Heat the grill.
10. Mix the reserved cheese with the crumbs and sprinkle evenly over the sauce; make sure that all the sauce is covered or it will form brown blisters under the grill.
11. Grill fairly quickly until the top is browned and crisp.

Serves 4

Pizza Dough

55g/2oz fresh yeast
150ml/¼ pint lukewarm milk
and water mixed
2 teaspoons caster sugar

1 tablespoon olive oil
225g/½lb plain flour
½ teaspoon salt

1. Mix the yeast with 1–2 spoonfuls of the warm liquid. Add the sugar. Stir until smooth then add to the rest of the liquid. Add the oil.
2. Sift the flour with the salt into a warmed bowl. Make a well in the centre and pour in the liquid. Mix to a firm, soft dough (using a knife and then one hand) and knead vigorously for 10 minutes. When you have an elastic, shiny, smooth, non-sticky dough you have kneaded enough.
3. Roll the dough into a ball and with your hand spread a thin layer of oil all over the dough. Put into a bowl, cover with an oiled piece of polythene and allow to rise in a warm place until doubled in bulk (about 2 hours).
4. Punch the dough down again and roll into two really big rounds (about 30cm/12in across, or enough to fill your largest flat tin or baking sheet). Draw the edges up slightly with the fingers to prevent sloppy fillings spilling.
5. Oven to 220°C/425°F, gas mark 7. Spread the dough with the filling and allow to stand (or prove) for 10 minutes before baking.
6. When the pizza looks cooked on top, slide a fish-slice under it and lift it carefully to check that the dough underneath is not soggy. When you are satisfied it is firm, serve the pizza at once. The bread base toughens as it cools.

Yeast: If using dried yeast use half the amount called for, mix it with 3 tablespoons of the liquid (warmed to blood temperature) and 1 teaspoon of sugar. Leave until frothy, about 15 minutes, then proceed. If the yeast does not go frothy it is dead and unusable.

Serves 4 as a starter, 2 as a main course

Pizza Fillings

Pizza Napolitana

450g/1lb ripe tomatoes
10 anchovy fillets
1 tablespoon tomato purée
1 tablespoon chopped spring
  onions
1 tablespoon chopped fresh
  basil *or* marjoram

Salt and freshly ground black
  pepper
85g/3oz mozzarella cheese
2 teaspoons olive oil

Peel the tomatoes and chop roughly. Split the anchovy fillets in half lengthwise. Spread the two rounds of dough with tomato purée and cover with tomatoes. Sprinkle with spring onions, herbs, salt and pepper. Decorate with thin slices of cheese and the anchovy fillets. Moisten with olive oil and bake in the preheated oven.

Pizza al Prosciutto

Follow the Pizza Napolitana recipe but substitute 55g/2oz thinly sliced or finely chopped smoked ham for the anchovy fillets.

Pizza con Funghi e Olivi

Follow the Pizza Napolitana recipe but substitute 55g/2oz finely sliced raw mushrooms and 12 stoned olives, for the spring onions.

Pizza al salami

Follow the Pizza Napolitana recipe but omit the anchovy fillets and substitute 6 or 8 thin slices of rindless salami per pizza.

Chilli con Carne

225g/½lb lean stewing pork
675g/1½lb lean stewing beef
3 tablespoons bacon fat
290ml/½ pint beef stock
1 small onion, finely chopped
2 garlic cloves, crushed
3 tablespoons red wine
2 teaspoons flour
Up to 1 tablespoon
  Mexican chilli powder
1 bay leaf
Pinch of cumin
Pinch of turmeric
Pinch of dried oregano
Salt and freshly ground black
  pepper
225g/½lb dried red kidney
  beans, soaked for 3 hours
  and boiled until soft
Boiled rice to serve

1. Cut the pork and beef into cubes.
2. Melt 1 tablespoon of the fat and when hot brown the meat
   on all sides, frying only a few pieces at a time. If the bottom
   becomes dry deglaze the pan: pour in a few tablespoons of
   the stock and bring it to the boil, scraping the bottom of
   the pan with a spoon to incorporate the sediment into the
   stock. Keep this liquid to add to the stock (it will improve
   the flavour). Place the browned meat in a heavy saucepan with
   all the stock and any deglazing juices.
3. Fry the onion and the garlic in a little more fat and when
   evenly coloured add it to the meat.
4. Add the red wine to the pan, boil up and scrape the bottom
   well with a wooden spoon. Pour over the meat.
5. Cover the saucepan, bring to the boil and simmer for 1 hour.
6. Mix the flour and chilli powder with a little cold water. Then
   add some of the hot juices from the pan. Stir into the saucepan
   with the bay leaf, turmeric, cumin, oregano, salt and pepper.
   Continue to simmer until the meat is tender (about 1–1½
   hours).
7. Add the drained red kidney beans and reheat. Taste and
   correct the seasoning. Serve hot with boiled rice.

Note I: Mexican chilli powder is an aromatic spice mixture
including some mild, and very little hot chilli. Do not confuse

it with powdered chillies or cayenne pepper. Either would make the dish quite uneatable.

Note II: The meat can be minced rather than cut into cubes, when the cooking time will naturally be shorter.

Serves 4–6

Cannelloni with Spinach and Mushroom Filling

900g/2lb fresh spinach, well washed, with stalks removed
55g/2oz butter
225g/½lb flat black mushrooms, sliced
Salt and freshly ground black pepper

12 cooked cannelloni (the bought ones can be very good, and thin French pancakes are an excellent substitute (pages 659–60)
55g/2oz Cheddar cheese, grated
425ml/¾ pint creamy white sauce (page 308)

1. Put the wet spinach in a large saucepan and put on the lid. Cook gently for 5 minutes, stirring occasionally. Drain well, pressing out the moisture. Turn on to a board and chop roughly.
2. Set the oven to 180°C/350°F, gas mark 4.
3. Melt the butter, add the mushrooms and fry for 3 minutes. Stir in the spinach and 150ml/¼ pint of the sauce and season with salt and pepper.
4. Fill the mixture into the cannelloni, or roll up in the pancakes. Lay them in an ovenproof dish, pour over the remaining sauce and sprinkle the cheese on top.
5. Bake in the oven for 20 minutes or until the top is lightly browned.

Serves 4

Prue's Easy Party Pasta

110g/¼lb pasta (tagliatelli *or* shell shapes are best)
2 tablespoons olive oil
110g/¼lb mushrooms, sliced
1 garlic clove, crushed
110g/¼lb cooked ham, cut in thin strips
2 hardboiled eggs, quartered
1 level tablespoon chopped fresh basil
Salt and freshly ground black pepper
55g/2oz Cheddar cheese, grated
1 level tablespoon chopped fresh parsley

1. Boil the pasta in fast-boiling salted water until tender.
2. Take a large heavy frying pan and into it put the oil, mushrooms and garlic. Fry gently for 2 minutes, then add the strips of ham, the eggs and the basil. Cover with a lid or foil and put on to a warming plate or into a coolish oven to warm through.
3. When the pasta is tender but not mushy, drain it well and rinse off any excess starch under the *hot* tap, or by pouring a kettle of fresh boiling water through it. Drain again. Tip the hot pasta into a warm serving bowl and season well with salt and pepper. Tip the frying pan ingredients in on top of the pasta. Mix carefully with a fork, then sprinkle with the grated cheese and chopped parsley.

Note: The dish, as long as it is not overmixed, can be made in advance for a party, and reheated gently in a wide saucepan or, covered, in the oven. But if this is done, the cheese and parsley should be added only before serving. Skinned, seeded and quartered tomatoes are a good addition, and should be added to the frying pan with the eggs. Neither eggs nor tomatoes need real cooking – only heating up – before being tipped on to the pasta.

Serves 4

Cannelloni

Egg pasta (pages 657 using
half quantities)
290ml/½ pint tomato sauce
(page 325)

45g/1½oz strong Cheddar *or*
Gruyère cheese, grated, *or*
30g/1oz Parmesan, grated

For the filling:
2 teaspoons oil *or* dripping
340g/¾lb minced beef
1 onion, chopped
Stick of celery, chopped
1 garlic clove, crushed
2 teaspoons tomato purée
2 teaspoons flour

150ml/¼ pint beef stock
1 bay leaf
1 level tablespoon fresh
chopped parsley
1 tablespoon port *or* Madeira
Salt and freshly ground black
pepper

1. Cut the pasta into 10cm/4in strips about 6cm/2½in wide. Allow to dry for 1 hour.
2. Heat the oil and add the meat. Brown well all over. Add the onion, celery, garlic and tomato purée and cook for 2 minutes.
3. Add the flour and cook for 30 seconds. Draw the pan otf the heat, add the stock, bay leaf and parsley, stir well and return to the heat. Bring slowly to the boil, stirring continuously.
4. Season, cover and simmer for 30 minutes. Then add the port or Madeira and continue to simmer for 15 minutes. Remove the bay leaf.
5. Set the oven to 200°C/400°F, gas mark 6. Heat the grill.
6. Cook the pasta in boiling salted water until just tender (about 5 minutes if home-made, 12 if bought). Drain well, and pat dry with a tea-towel or cloth.
7. Divide the meat mixture between the strips of pasta and roll them up to form the cannelloni. Place them in a greased ovenproof dish.
8. Pour over the tomato sauce and sprinkle with grated cheese. Bake for 15 minutes, then place under the grill until nicely browned.

531

Note I: For a blander version, trickle over a little white sauce or double cream before grilling the finished dish.

Note II: Commercially made cannelloni is usually tube-shaped, and the filling is inserted with a teaspoon.

Serves 4

Ravioli

370g/¾lb flour-quantity egg
   pasta (page 657)

For the meat filling:

85g/3oz cooked beef, minced
85g/3oz cooked veal, minced
15g/½oz butter
2 teaspoons white
  breadcrumbs
2 teaspoons chopped parsley
2 teaspoons beef stock

1 teaspoon tomato purée
Salt and freshly ground black
  pepper
Pinch of nutmeg
Pinch of cinnamon
1 small egg, beaten

To serve:

Parmesan cheese, grated
Melted butter *or* oil *or* tomato
  sauce (page 325)

1. Fry the meats in the butter for 5 minutes. Stir in the breadcrumbs, parsley, stock, tomato purée, salt, pepper, nutmeg and cinnamon. Taste and add more seasonings if required.
2. Add enough egg to bind the mixture together. Allow to cool.
3. Roll the pasta into a very thin rectangle. Cut accurately in half. Keep well covered to prevent drying out.
4. Take one sheet of pasta and place half-teaspoons of filling at 3cm/1½in intervals, in even rows, all over it. Cover loosely with the other sheet of pasta and press together firmly all round each mound of filling. Cut between the rows, making

sure that all the edges are sealed. (See drawing.) Allow to dry on a wire rack for 30 minutes.

5. Simmer the ravioli in near-boiling salted water for 15–20 minutes or until just tender. Drain well. Serve with tomato sauce, oil, or melted butter, and hand grated Parmesan cheese separately.

Serves 4

Lasagne Verde Bolognese

Green pasta (page 658, using half quantities)

Fresh Parmesan cheese, grated

For the meat sauce:

1 tablespoon dripping *or* oil	Salt and freshly ground
340g/¾lb minced beef	black pepper
1 onion, finely diced	1 scant tablespoon chopped
Stick of celery, finely diced	fresh parsley
4 cloves of garlic	1 teaspoon chopped fresh
30g/1oz flour	marjoram
290ml/½ pint stock	Pinch of cinnamon
1 glass white wine	1 tablespoon tomato purée

533

For the cream sauce:

45g/1½oz butter	570ml/1 pint creamy milk
1 bay leaf	Salt and freshly ground black
45g/1½oz flour	pepper and nutmeg

1. Cut the pasta into strips 15cm/6in long and 3cm/1½in wide. Allow to dry for 1 hour.
2. Heat the fat and in it brown the mince well. Add the finely diced vegetables and the garlic and fry, stirring continuously, for 2 minutes.
3. Stir in the flour. Cook for 30 seconds. Pour in the stock and the wine, and add the salt, pepper, parsley, marjoram, cinnamon and tomato purée. Bring to the boil, stirring. Simmer slowly for 45 minutes, then boil rapidly, stirring, until the sauce is very thick and syrupy.
4. To make the cream sauce melt the butter, add the bay leaf and flour and cook, stirring, for 1 minute. Draw off the heat.
5. Add the milk and return to the heat. Bring slowly to the boil, stirring continuously until you have a thick, creamy sauce. Season to taste and remove the bay leaf.
6. To cook the lasagne drop the pasta a few pieces at a time into a large pan of fast-boiling salted water. They will take about 5 minutes if home-made, 12 minutes if out of a packet, to become tender. Rinse under running cold water and pat dry with a tea-towel.
7. Set the oven to 190°C/375°F, gas mark 5. Butter an ovenproof dish and cover the bottom with a layer of pasta, then spoon on a thin layer of meat sauce. Cover with a layer of cream sauce.
8. Arrange a layer of pasta on top of this. Continue the layers in this manner finishing with cream sauce. Sprinkle with cheese.
9. Bake for 20–25 minutes, until bubbling and just brown on top.

Serves 6

6
Puddings
and Sweets

SWEET SAUCES

Creme Chantilly

150ml/¼ pint double cream
2 tablespoons iced water

1 teaspoon icing sugar
2 drops vanilla essence

1. Put all the ingredients into a chilled bowl and whisk with a
   balloon whisk, steadily but not too fast, for about 2 minutes
   or until the cream has thickened and doubled in volume.
2. Whisk faster for 30–40 seconds until the mixture is very fluffy
   and will form soft peaks.

Note: Chilling the ingredients and the bowl gives a lighter, whiter
result.

Crème Pâtissière

290ml/½ pint milk
2 egg yolks
55g/2oz caster sugar

20g/¾oz flour
20g/¾oz cornflour
Vanilla essence

1. Scald the milk.
2. Cream the egg yolks with the sugar and when pale mix in
   the flours. Pour on the milk and mix well.

3. Return the mixture to the pan and bring slowly up to the boil, stirring continuously. (It will go alarmingly lumpy, but don't worry, keep stirring and it will get smooth.) Allow to cool slightly and add the vanilla essence.

Crème Anglaise (English Egg Custard)

290ml/½ pint milk
1 tablespoon sugar

½ vanilla pod *or* few drops of vanilla essence
2 egg yolks

1. Heat the milk with the sugar and vanilla pod (if available) and bring slowly to the boil.
2. Beat the yolks in a bowl. Remove the vanilla pod and pour the milk on to the egg yolks, stirring steadily. Mix well and return to the pan.
3. Stir over gentle heat until the mixture thickens so that it will coat the back of a spoon; do not boil. Pour into a cold bowl.
4. Add the vanilla essence if using.

Sugar Syrup

285g/10oz granulated sugar
570ml/1 pint water

Pared rind of 1 lemon

1. Put the sugar, water and lemon rind in a pan and heat slowly until the sugar has completely dissolved.
2. Bring to the boil and cook until the syrup feels tacky between finger and thumb. Allow to cool.
3. Strain. Keep covered in a cool place until needed.

Note: Sugar syrup will keep unrefrigerated for about five days, and for several weeks if kept cold.

Apricot Sauce with Kernels

85g/3oz granulated sugar 225g/½lb apricots
290ml/½ pint water Juice of ½ lemon

1. Dissolve the sugar in the water over a gentle heat. Do not allow to boil until the sugar has completely dissolved (this will prevent the syrup from crystallizing).
2. Wash and halve the apricots and add to the pan with the stones and lemon juice.
3. Bring to the boil and cook until the apricots are soft (about 15 minutes).
4. Remove the stones, but keep them.
5. Boil the apricots rapidly for a further 5–10 minutes, or until the pulp is reduced to a syrupy consistency. Push the apricot sauce through a nylon or stainless steel sieve. Taste and add extra sugar if necessary.
6. Crack the stones and remove the kernels. Chop the kernels roughly and add to the sauce. Serve hot or cold.

Raspberry Jam Sauce

3 tablespoons raspberry 90g/3oz sugar
  jam 125ml/¼ pint water

1. Put the sugar and water in a saucepan and heat slowly until the sugar has dissolved. Then boil rapidly until the syrup feels tacky between finger and thumb.
2. Add the jam, stir until smooth, then sieve to remove the pips.

Hot Chocolate Sauce

170g/6oz unsweetened
  chocolate
2 tablespoons water

1 teaspoon instant coffee
  powder
15g/½oz butter

1. Melt the chocolate slowly with the water, stirring frequently.
2. Add the coffee and butter, and heat, without boiling, until
   the butter has melted and the sauce is thin and shiny.

Chocolate Sauce

55g/2oz plain chocolate
150ml/¼ pint water
2 tablespoons golden syrup

15g/½oz caster sugar
1 teaspoon brandy

1. Chop the chocolate roughly and put into a small heavy pan
   with the water, syrup and sugar. Allow the chocolate to melt
   and the sugar to dissolve over a gentle heat.
2. When completely dissolved increase the heat and boil the
   sauce rapidly for 30 seconds. Add the brandy. Serve hot or
   cold.

Makes 225ml/8 fl.oz

Apple Purée

450g/1lb cooking apples
110g/¼lb sugar

4 tablespoons water

1. Peel and core the apples. Cut them into chunks. Put them
   with the sugar and water into a heavy saucepan and simmer
   gently until they are a soft pulp. Beat out any lumps with
   a wooden spoon.

2. If the purée is too sloppy boil it rapidly to reduce and thicken it, but leave the lid half on as it splashes dangerously.

Apple Marmalade

3 cooking apples
Strip of lemon rind

A little butter
About 85g/3oz brown sugar

1. Wash the unpeeled apples, quarter and core them. Rub the bottom and sides of a heavy saucepan with butter.
2. Slice the apples thickly into the pan and add the lemon rind. Cover and cook gently, stirring occasionally until completely soft.
3. Push through a sieve. Rinse out the pan and return the purée to it. Add at least 55g/2oz of brown sugar to 570ml/1 pint of purée. Cook rapidly until the mixture is of dropping consistency, about 4 minutes. Allow to cool. Add more sugar if necessary.

Caramel Sauce

170g/6oz granulated sugar
425ml/¾ pint water

1. In a heavy saucepan melt two-thirds of the sugar slowly. When it is bubbly and brown, pour on the water. (It will fizz dangerously, so take care.)
2. Add the rest of the sugar. Reboil, stirring, and then boil the sauce until it is of a syrupy consistency.

Hard Brandy Sauce

Cream equal quantities of unsalted butter and caster sugar together until very light. Add finely grated orange rind and brandy to flavour fairly strongly.

Melba Sauce

225g/½lb fresh *or* frozen raspberries (not canned)

Icing sugar

1. Defrost the raspberries if frozen. Push the raspberries through a nylon or stainless sieve to remove all seeds.
2. Sift in icing sugar to taste. If too thick add a few spoons of water.

Sweet Gooseberry Sauce

225g/½lb ripe gooseberries
150ml/¼ pint water

110g/¼lb sugar
Pinch ground ginger

1. Put all the ingredients in a thick-bottomed saucepan. Bring gradually to the boil and then simmer until the gooseberries pop open and change to a yellowish colour.
2. Push through a sieve and reheat.

CREAM PUDDINGS
AND JELLIES

Fools

Orange Fool

2 small oranges
290ml/½ pint double cream

2 tablespoons icing sugar

1. With a potato peeler, pare about half the rind off 1 orange. The strips should have no white pith on the underside. Using a very sharp fruit knife, cut into tiny thin strips about 2·5cm/ 1in long.
2. Place these needleshreds in a pan of boiling water for 5 minutes. Rinse in cold water until completely cool. Drain.
3. Grate the remaining orange rind and squeeze the juice.
4. Whip the cream. When stiff, stir in the orange juice, grated rind and sugar.
5. Spoon into small glasses or little china pots or coffee cups. Scatter over the needleshreds of orange rind to decorate.

Serves 4

Lemon Syllabub

290ml/½ pint double cream
Finely grated rind of ½ lemon
Juice of 2 lemons

2 tablespoons white wine
Icing sugar to taste, sifted
Thinly pared peel of ½ lemon

1. Place the cream in a bowl with the grated lemon rind. Whip, adding the lemon juice, wine and icing sugar at intervals. Spoon into individual glasses.
2. Cut the lemon peel into very thin needleshreds. Drop them into boiling water and cook for 2 minutes. Drain and dry them. Scatter on top of the syllabub.

Serves 4

Ginger Syllabub

4–5 tablespoons Advocaat
  liqueur
2 heaped tablespoons ginger
  marmalade

290ml/½ pint double cream
1–2 pieces preserved ginger

1. Mix the Advocaat and ginger marmalade together.
2. Whip the cream and stir in the marmalade mixture.
3. Spoon into small glasses, little china pots or coffee cups.
4. Put 2–3 thin slivers of preserved ginger on top of each syllabub. Chill before serving.

Note I: For a smoother texture the ginger marmalade and the Advocaat can be liquidized or sieved together.

Note II: In the absence of ginger marmalade use orange marmalade well flavoured with finely chopped bottled ginger and its syrup.

Serves 6

Layered Chocolate Mousse and Ginger Syllabub

Chocolate mousse (554)   Chopped walnuts
Ginger syllabub (page 541)

1. Prepare the chocolate mousse and ginger syllabub mixtures according to the recipes, but do not dish them up.
2. In the bottom of eight tall glasses place a layer of ginger syllabub. Spoon a layer of chocolate mousse on top. Continue the layers like this until all the mixtures are used finishing with a layer of chocolate mousse. Refrigerate until set (preferably overnight).
3. Decorate the top of each glass with the chopped nuts.

Serves 8

Custards

Crème Brûlée

Crème brûlée is best started a day in advance.

290ml/½ pint double cream	4 egg yolks
1 vanilla pod *or* teaspoon vanilla essence	2 tablespoons caster sugar

For the topping:
Caster sugar

1. Put the cream with the vanilla pod into a pan and heat up to scalding point, making sure it does not boil. Remove the vanilla pod.
2. Set the oven to 170°C/325°F, gas mark 3.
3. Beat the egg yolks with the caster sugar and when light and fluffy stir in the warm cream. Place the mixture in the top of a double saucepan, or in a bowl over a pan of simmering water, on a gentle heat. Stir all the time until the custard coats the back of the spoon. If using vanilla essence add it now.
4. Pour the custard into an ovenproof serving dish and bake for 12 minutes to create a good skin on top. Refrigerate overnight. On no account break the top skin.
5. Next day heat the grill.
6. Sprinkle the top of the custard with a 5mm/¼in even layer of caster sugar: to do this stand the dish on a tray or large sheet of greaseproof paper and sift the sugar over the dish and tray or paper. In this way you will get an even layer. Collect the sugar falling wide for re-use.
7. When the grill is blazing hot put the custard under it, as close as you can get to the heat. The sugar will melt and caramelize before the custard underneath it boils. Watch carefully, turning the custard if the sugar is browning unevenly.
8. Allow to cool completely before serving. The top should be hard and crackly.
   To serve, crack the top with the serving spoon and give each diner some custard (which should be creamy and barely set) and a piece of caramel. Crème brûlée is also good made in individual ramekin dishes. In this event bake the custards for only 5 minutes.

Serves 4–5

Zabaglione

4 egg yolks   4 tablespoons Marsala
110g/4oz caster sugar

1. Put the egg yolks and sugar into a bowl and whisk until frothy and pale.
2. Set the bowl over a saucepan of simmering water and gradually whisk in the Marsala until the mixture is very thick. Take care that the bowl does not touch the simmering water. If it does, the eggs will scramble.
3. Pour into individual glasses and serve at once.

Serves 4

Iced Sabayon

4 egg yolks   2 tablespoons Marsala
4 tablespoons caster sugar   150ml/¼ pint double cream,
150ml/¼ pint white wine   whipped

1. Put the egg yolks, sugar and wine into a bowl. Set over a saucepan of simmering water. Whisk for 10–15 minutes until thick and creamy. Remove from the heat and continue to whisk until cool. Add the Marsala and fold in the cream.
2. Serve well chilled.

Serves 4

Orange Bavarois with Meringues

For the meringues:
1 egg white   55g/2oz caster sugar

For the Bavarois:

3 tablespoons water	425ml/¾ pint milk
2 level teaspoons gelatine	3 egg yolks
5 lumps sugar	1½ tablespoons caster sugar
1 orange	150ml/¼ pint double cream

To serve:
Grated chocolate

1. First prepare the meringues. Whisk the egg white until stiff, add 2 teaspoons of the sugar and continue whisking until stiff again; then fold in the rest. Put this mixture into a forcing bag and pipe into tiny button meringues on baking parchment or greased and floured foil, using a 0·5cm/¼in plain pipe. Dry in a slow oven (130°C/260°F, gas mark ½) for about 40 minutes. Immediately peel off the paper and leave to cool.

2. Put the water into a small saucepan and sprinkle on the gelatine. Leave to soak.

3. Rub the sugar lumps over the orange until the sugar is well coloured by the oils in the rind. Put the lumps into the milk and dissolve over a gentle heat.

4. Cream the egg yolks and caster sugar together until thick and light, then pour the milk on to the mixture. Return to the pan and put over a gentle heat to thicken the custard. Stir constantly and do not allow to boil. When the custard will coat the back of the wooden spoon strain into a bowl and allow to cool.

5. Put the gelatine over gentle heat and when clear and runny add to the custard.

6. Stand the custard in a roasting tin or bowl full of ice and stir gently until the mixture thickens.

7. Half-whip the cream, then fold 2 tablespoons of it into the custard. Pour at once into a lightly oiled plain mould. Refrigerate until set (about 3 hours).

8. Whip the rest of the cream a little stiffer. When the custard is set turn it out on to a plate and mask with the rest of the whipped cream. Cover with the meringues and sprinkle with grated chocolate.

Note: Rubbing the sugar lumps over the orange rind extracts the orange flavour, but is a little tedious. An alternative method is to pare the rind finely from the orange and infuse it in the hot milk, then strain it.

Serves 4

Coffee Cream Bavarois

7g/¼oz gelatine
225ml/8 fl.oz milk
20g/¾oz unsweetened chocolate
3 egg yolks

85g/3oz caster sugar
1 level tablespoon instant
  coffee
150ml/¼ pint double cream

For the decoration:
Grated chocolate   Double cream

1. In a very small saucepan soak the gelatine in 2 tablespoons of water.
2. Place the milk and broken-up chocolate in a saucepan and heat gently until the chocolate has completely melted.
3. Beat the egg yolks and sugar until light and fluffy. Stir in the warm milk and chocolate mixture. Beat well.
4. Dissolve the coffee in 2 tablespoons boiling water and add it to the mixture. Set the bowl over a pan of simmering water and stir continuously with a wooden spoon for 10–20 minutes. It is ready when the custard will coat the back of the spoon. Be careful not to over-heat or the mixture will curdle.
5. Cool by standing the pan in a bowl of cold water.
6. Dissolve the gelatine over a gentle heat; when melted and clear stir it into the cooling custard. Lightly whip the cream and fold it into the coffee mixture.
7. Turn into a large dish or into individual pots and leave in the refrigerator to set. Decorate with grated chocolate and whipped cream.

Serves 4

Milk Puddings

Junket

570ml/1 pint fresh milk   1 teaspoon rennet
2 teaspoons sugar

1. Heat the milk with the sugar to blood temperature (luke-warm).
2. Stir well and pour into a serving bowl.
3. Stir in the rennet and leave to set at room temperature. Once set the dish may be refrigerated.

Variations on plain junket:
Spoon over a little whipped cream and sprinkle with crumbled ratafia biscuits.
Sprinkle the surface with grated nutmeg.
Flavour with coffee essence, orange rind or grated chocolate.

Serves 4

Baked Custard

3 whole eggs plus 1 egg yolk   425ml/¾ pint very creamy milk
3 drops vanilla essence   *or* milk plus single cream
                                                  55g/2oz caster sugar

1. Set the oven to 170°C/325°F, gas mark 3.
2. Lightly mix the eggs, extra yolk and vanilla essence together; don't get them frothy.
3. Heat the milk to boiling point with the sugar, stirring as you do so.
4. Remove from the heat, cool for a second or two, and then pour on to the eggs, stirring all the time with a wooden spoon, not a whisk (you are trying to avoid creating bubbles).

5. Strain the mixture into an ovenproof dish (straining removes any egg 'threads' which would spoil the smooth texture of the finished custard).
6. Stand the custard dish in a roasting tin of hot water and bake in the oven for 40 minutes. It is set when there is a definite skin on the top and when the middle of the custard is no longer liquid (although it will still wobble).
7. Serve hot, warm or chilled.

Note: A good variation of this custard has a thickish layer of real lemon curd (page 743) spread on top when the custard is just warm. Serve with dollops of cream. Or sprinkle ground nutmeg on the surface before baking, or flavour with grated orange rind.

Serves 4

Rice Pudding

A nut of butter   570ml/1 pint milk
1 level tablespoon sugar   Vanilla essence
55g/scant 2oz round (pudding)   Ground nutmeg
  rice

1. Set the oven to 150°C/300°F, gas mark 2.
2. Rub the butter round a pie dish. Put the sugar, rice, milk and vanilla essence into the dish. Sprinkle with nutmeg.
3. Stir, and bake in the oven for 3–4 hours, by which time it should be soft and creamy with an evenly coloured brown skin.

Note: If the milk has not all been absorbed when you are ready to serve the pudding, here is a good trick. Mix a large egg in a teacup, carefully lift the pudding skin and spoon out some of the hot milk. Mix this with the egg in the teacup and then stir this milky egg into the rice. Replace skin and leave for 10 minutes in the oven. The milk should now set as in a custard.

Serves 4

Bread and Butter Pudding

1½ slices of plain bread
30g/1oz butter
2 level tablespoons currants
  and sultanas, mixed
2 teaspoons candied peel

2 eggs and 1 yolk
1 tablespoon sugar
290ml/½ pint creamy milk
Vanilla essence
Ground cinnamon

1. Cut the crusts off the bread and spread with butter. Cut into fingers. Layer in a shallow ovenproof dish, butter side up, and sprinkle with currants, sultanas and candied peel as you proceed.
2. Make the custard: mix the eggs and yolk with the sugar and stir in the milk and vanilla essence.
3. Pour the custard carefully over the bread and leave to soak for 30 minutes. Sprinkle with ground cinnamon.
4. Heat the oven to 180°C/350°F, gas mark 4.
5. Place the pudding in a roasting tin of hot water and cook in the middle of the oven for about 45 minutes or until the custard is set and the top brown and crusty.

Note: The pudding may be baked without the bain-marie (hot water bath) quite successfully, but if used it will ensure a smooth, not bubbly custard.

Serves 4

Crème Caramel

110g/¼lb granulated sugar
2 eggs
2 egg yolks

2 tablespoons caster sugar
570ml/1 pint milk
Vanilla essence

1. Set the oven to 150°C/300°F, gas mark 2. Warm a soufflé dish in it.
2. Place the granulated sugar in a heavy pan with 4 tablespoons

of water and allow it to melt slowly. When melted boil rapidly until it has turned to a good brown toffee. Pour into the hot soufflé dish and coat all over by carefully tipping the dish. Leave until cold.

3. Beat the eggs, egg yolks and caster sugar together.
4. Scald the milk and stir this into the egg mixture. Add the vanilla essence. Strain into the prepared dish.
5. Stand in a bain-marie and cook in the oven for 1½ hours or until the custard has set.
6. Allow to cool until tepid or stone-cold, then turn out on to a dish with a good lip.

Serves 4–5

Queen's Pudding

290ml/½ pint milk
15g/½oz butter
30g/1oz caster sugar for the
   custard
2 tablespoons fresh white
   breadcrumbs

Rind of 1 lemon
2 eggs
2 tablespoons raspberry jam,
   warm
110g/¼lb caster sugar for the
   meringue

1. Butter a fireproof pie dish. Set the oven to 180°C/350°F, gas mark 4.
2. Heat the milk and add the butter and sugar. Stir until the sugar dissolves, then add the breadcrumbs and lemon rind.
3. Separate the eggs. When the breadcrumb mixture has cooled slightly, mix in the egg yolks. Pour into the pie dish and leave to stand for 30 minutes.
4. Bake for 25 minutes or until the custard mixture is set. Remove and allow to cool slightly.
5. Reduce the oven to 170°C/325°F, gas mark 3.
6. Carefully spread the jam over the top of the custard. (This is easier if you melt the jam first.)
7. Whip the egg whites until stiff. Whisk in half the meringue

sugar. Whisk again until very stiff and shiny and fold in all but half a teaspoon of the remaining sugar.

8. Pile the meringue on top of the custard and dust the top with the reserved sugar.

9. Bake until the meringue is set and straw coloured (about 10 minutes).

Note: This is particularly good served hot with cold whipped cream.

Serves 4

Pear Caramel Custard

2 ripe pears
290ml/½ pint sugar syrup
  (page 536)
55g/2oz granulated sugar
2 whole eggs

2 egg yolks
2 tablespoons caster sugar
570ml/1 pint milk
Vanilla essence

1. Set the oven to 170°C/350°F, gas mark 4.

2. Peel, core and quarter the pears. Poach them until tender in the sugar syrup. Drain well.

3. Place the granulated sugar in a heavy saucepan with 4 tablespoons water and allow it to melt slowly. When melted boil rapidly until it has turned a rich brown.

4. Pour the caramel into the bottom of a warmed ovenproof dish.

5. Beat the eggs, yolks and caster sugar together. Scald the milk and stir this into the eggs. Add the vanilla essence. Strain.

6. Liquidize the pears with a little of the custard. Add the rest of the custard and pour the mixture on to the set caramel in the dish.

7. Place the dish in a roasting tin three-quarters full of hot water and bake in the oven for 45 minutes or until the custard is set. Leave to cool until lukewarm.

8. Run a knife around the edge of the dish, and carefully turn out on to a shallow-lipped serving dish.

Serves 4–6

Mousses

Simple Apricot Mousse

For the apricot purée:

425g/15oz can apricots *or* 450g/1lb stoned apricots cooked in 150ml/¼ pint water and 85g/3oz sugar
1 tablespoon caster sugar

2 teaspoons kirsch (optional)
8g/¼oz gelatine
290ml/¼ pint double cream, lightly whipped

For the decoration:
Whipped cream
Apricot pieces
Browned nibbed almonds

1. To make the apricot purée liquidize or sieve the apricots with their syrup.
2. Mix the caster sugar and kirsch with the apricot purée. Taste and add more sugar if necessary to bring out the flavour.
3. Put 3 tablespoons of water in a small saucepan, sprinkle on the gelatine and set aside to 'sponge' for 5 minutes.
3. Dissolve the gelatine over a gentle heat and when clear and warm stir it into the purée. Leave to set slightly, then fold in the lightly whipped cream.
4. Pour the mixture into a dish and leave to set in the refrigerator for 2–3 hours. When set, decorate with rosettes of cream, apricot pieces and browned nuts.

Serves 4

Semolina Cream Mould with Blackcurrant Sauce

Few drops oil
570ml/1 pint milk
85g/3oz semolina
2 eggs

85g/3oz caster sugar
Juice of 1 lemon
Few drops vanilla essence
4–5 tablespoons double cream

For the blackcurrant sauce:
450g/1lb blackcurrants
150ml/¼ pint sugar syrup
  (page 536)

1. Oil a 1½ litre/2½ pint smooth jelly mould or pudding basin.
2. Heat the milk in a heavy saucepan and when boiling gradually stir in the semolina.
3. Reduce the heat and simmer for 10 minutes or until the semolina is cooked. Remove from heat and allow to cool slightly.
4. Separate the eggs. Whisk the yolks and sugar until light and fluffy and stir into the semolina mixture.
5. Beat in the lemon juice, vanilla essence and cream. Cool to lukewarm.
6. Whisk the egg whites until stiff and fold into the semolina mixture with a metal spoon. Pour into the mould and leave in the refrigerator overnight to set.
7. Meanwhile prepare the blackcurrant sauce. Remove the stalks from the blackcurrants. Wash thoroughly and drain.
8. Liquidize the blackcurrants with the sugar syrup and push the purée through a nylon sieve. Taste and if not sweet enough beat in a little sifted icing sugar.
9. To dish, run a knife round the edge of the mould to detach the sides. Put a serving plate over the top of the mould, making sure that it is dead centre, then quickly invert both plate and mould. Give a sharp shake to dislodge the mould.
10. Pour the sauce over the top and serve immediately.

Note I: Semolina is finely ground processed hard wheat.

Note II: If the mould cannot be left overnight to set increase the semolina quantity to 110g/¼lb.

Serves 4–6

Chocolate Mousse

3 eggs
30g/1oz caster sugar

170/6oz dark sweetened (e.g. Bourneville) chocolate

1. Separate the eggs and beat the yolks with the sugar until you have a pale creamy mousse.
2. Put the chocolate in a saucepan with 3 tablespoons of water and melt slowly. (Alternatively, melt the chocolate in a double saucepan or in a saucer over boiling water, but do not melt it on direct heat without any water, as it will go lumpy and hard.)
3. While the chocolate is still warm, add to the yolks and sugar mixture. Whip the whites stiffly and fold them into the chocolate mixture.
4. Turn immediately into a soufflé dish or into individual pots or glasses.
5. Chill until set, preferably overnight, but for at least 4 hours.

Note: Brandy, chopped preserved ginger, rum, grated orange rind and strong coffee flavours are all delicious additions. They should be stirred into the basic mousse mixture before the whites are folded in.

Serves 4

Caramel Mousse

Scant 15g/½oz gelatine
Squeeze of lemon
170g/6oz granulated sugar

55g/2oz caster sugar
3 eggs
150ml/¼ pint double cream

For the decoration:
Double cream, whipped

55g/2oz granulated sugar

1. In a small pan soak the gelatine in the lemon juice with 2 tablespoons water.
2. Melt the granulated sugar in another pan with 1 tablespoon water and boil until it turns to a brown caramel. Pour in 75ml/2½ fl.oz of water very carefully – it will hiss alarmingly. Cook over a gentle heat until the caramel is dissolved. Leave to cool.
3. Whisk the eggs and caster sugar in a bowl over a pan of simmering water until mousse-like and thick. Remove from the heat and whisk until cool.
4. Heat the soaked gelatine very gently until it is quite runny and clear. Do not boil. Stir into the mousse. Stir gently over a bowl of ice until beginning to thicken and set.
5. Lightly whip the cream and add it, with the caramel, to the mixture.
6. Pour into a dish and refrigerate until set.
7. Meanwhile make the caramel chips for the decoration: lightly oil a flat dish or baking sheet. Put the sugar in a heavy-bottomed small saucepan and heat gently (without any water) until it first melts, then turns to caramel. When it is evenly brown pour immediately on to the oiled dish or baking sheet. Allow to cool until hard as glass, then immediately break into small chips with the end of a rolling pin. Keep dry and cool until needed.
8. Decorate the mousse with rosettes of whipped cream and caramel chips.

Serves 4

Prune Mousse

340g/¾lb prunes soaked in
    weak black tea overnight
2 heaped tablespoons caster
    sugar
2–3 strips finely pared lemon
    rind

20g/¾oz gelatine
1 tablespoon lemon juice
150ml/¼ pint double cream,
    lightly whipped
2 egg whites

1. Bring the prunes to the boil in the tea with the sugar and pared lemon rind. Simmer until the prunes are tender.
2. Strain the prunes, removing the lemon rind, and make the liquid up to 570ml/1 pint by adding extra water. Stone the prunes and push the flesh through a sieve.
3. In a small saucepan soak the gelatine in 3 tablespoons of water until spongy. Dissolve over a gentle heat. When clear and liquid stir in the syrup. Taste for sweetness, adding more sugar if necessary. Stir the syrup into the prune purée. Add the lemon juice.
4. When the mixture is on the point of setting fold in 1 tablespoon of the cream. Whisk the egg whites until they form soft peaks and fold into the prune mixture too. Wet a ring mould and pour the mixture into this. Allow to set in the refrigerator.
5. Invert the serving dish over the ring mould and then turn both the mould and dish over together. Give a sharp shake to dislodge the mousse. Remove the mould. If the mousse won't come out, gently separate the sides of the mousse from the bowl with the fingers. If it still won't budge dip the base of the mould into hot water for 2 seconds. But take care not to overdo the dipping or the mousse will be messy.
6. Pile the remaining lightly whipped cream into the centre of the mousse.

Serves 4

Tangerine Mousse in Chocolate Case

For the chocolate case:

170g/6oz best quality plain chocolate

1 large macaroon (optional) (page 701)

2 egg yolks
3 whole eggs
55g/2oz caster sugar
15g/½oz gelatine
Juice of ½ lemon

150ml/¼ pint lightly whipped cream
150ml/¼ pint tangerine juice
Finely grated rind of 4 tangerines

1. First make the chocolate case by breaking up the chocolate and placing it in a pudding basin. Set it over a saucepan of simmering water. Stir until the chocolate is smooth and melted. Do not overheat or the chocolate will lose its gloss.
2. Brush melted chocolate thinly over the inside of an 18cm/7in paper baking case and leave to cool and harden. Repeat the process until you have a fairly thick layer and you have used up all the chocolate. Crush the macaroon and sprinkle on the still soft chocolate. Leave to harden. Carefully peel away the paper.
3. Make the mousse by putting the egg yolks, whole eggs and sugar together in a basin. Set it over a saucepan of simmering water and whisk until thick and mousse-like. Remove from the heat and whisk until cool. (If using an electric whisk, there is no need to whisk over heat.)
4. In a small pan soak the gelatine with the lemon juice and 2 tablespoons of water. Leave for 2 minutes.
5. Stir the tangerine juice and rind into the egg mixture.
6. Dissolve the gelatine over a low heat until warm and clear – do not boil. Stir this into the mousse and when on the point of setting stir in the cream. Pour into the chocolate case. Chill well.

Note: The mousse may be decorated with chocolate shapes. To make these melt plain chocolate and pour it on to greaseproof paper. When just set stamp it into small crescents or rounds or cut it into triangles or squares.

Serves 6

Charlotte Russe

15 sponge fingers (page 702)
150ml/$\frac{1}{4}$ pint clear lemon jelly
   (page 564)

For the custard:

Vanilla pod *or* $\frac{1}{2}$ teaspoon
   essence
425ml/$\frac{3}{4}$ pint milk
45g/1$\frac{1}{2}$oz caster sugar
5 egg yolks

3 tablespoons sherry
15g/$\frac{1}{2}$oz gelatine
4 tablespoons water
325ml/8 fl.oz double cream,
   lightly whipped

For the decoration:

A few pieces angelica

4 glacé cherries cut in half

1. Make the lemon jelly. When it is cool but not set wet a charlotte mould and pour in a thin layer (about 1cm/$\frac{1}{2}$in) of jelly. When it is almost set arrange sponge fingers standing up around the sides of the mould with their ends in the jelly. Decorate the base with cherries and angelica and leave to set. Pour in the rest of the jelly and refrigerate again to set.
2. Make the custard: put the vanilla in the milk and heat gently.
3. In a bowl mix the sugar and egg yolks well together. When the milk is almost boiling, remove the pod and pour on to the yolks, stirring vigorously. If it does not immediately thicken sufficiently to coat the back of a spoon set it over a pan of simmering water and stir until it does. Strain and allow to cool. Add the sherry.
4. In a small pan soak the gelatine in the water, then dissolve over gentle heat. When runny and clear stir into the cooling custard. When the custard begins to set fold in the partially whipped cream and turn the mixture into the mould, spreading it flat. Put in the refrigerator to set.

5. Trim off any biscuits sticking up above the level of the filling. Run a knife between the biscuits and the mould to make sure they are not stuck. Dip the bottom of the mould briefly into hot water to dislodge the jelly. Invert a plate over the mould, turn the two over together and lift off the mould.

Serves 4–6

Soufflés

Cold Lemon Soufflé

7g/¼oz gelatine
3 tablespoons water
3 eggs
140g/5oz caster sugar

Juice and rind of 2 lemons
150ml/¼ pint double cream, lightly whipped

For the decoration:
Double cream, whipped
Lemon slices

Browned nibbed almonds

1. In a small saucepan, soak the gelatine in the water.
2. Separate the eggs. Place the yolks and sugar in a large mixing bowl and whisk together with an electric mixer (or with a balloon whisk or rotary beater with the bowl set over a saucepan of simmering water). Whisk until very thick. Gradually add the lemon juice and rind. If whisking by hand over hot water, remove from the heat and whisk for a few minutes longer (until the mixture is lukewarm).
3. Dissolve the gelatine over a gentle heat and when clear and warm add it to the mousse mixture. Stir gently until the mixture is on the point of setting, then fold in the cream.
4. Whisk the egg whites until stiff but not dry and fold them into the soufflé with a large metal spoon.
5. Pour the mixture into a soufflé dish and leave to set in the refrigerator for 2–3 hours. When set decorate with rosettes of cream, wafer thin lemon slices and browned nuts.

Note: This dish can be given a more soufflé-like appearance by

559

tying a double band of oiled paper round the top of the dish so that it projects about 3cm/1½in above the rim, before pouring in the mixture. (The dish must be of a size that would not quite contain the mixture without the added depth given by the paper band.) Pour it in to come about 2·5cm/1in up the paper (above the top of the dish). When the soufflé is set, carefully remove the paper and press the almonds round the exposed sides.

Serves 4

Cold Raspberry Soufflé

3 eggs
110g/¼lb sugar
3 tablespoons water
15g/½oz gelatine
425ml/¾ pint raspberry purée
150ml/¼ pint double cream

For the decoration:
Browned chopped *or* nibbed
  almonds
150ml/¼ pint double cream
Whole raspberries

1. To prepare a soufflé dish (which should be 15cm/6in diameter), tie a double piece of greaseproof paper around the outside and secure the ends with a paper clip or pin. The paper should stick up about 3cm/1½in above the rim. Brush the inside of the projecting paper with oil.

2. Separate the eggs. Whisk the yolks with the sugar either over a gentle heat (with the bowl set over a pan of simmering water) or in an electric machine, until light and fluffy, and thick enough for the whisk to leave a 'ribbon trail' when lifted.
3. Remove from the heat and whisk again until the mixture is almost cold.
4. Put the water into a small saucepan and sprinkle over the gelatine. Leave to soak.
5. Stir the raspberry purée into the egg yolk mixture.
6. Dissolve the gelatine over a gentle heat – do not allow it to boil – and when warm and clear stir it into the raspberry mixture. Fold in the whipped cream.
7. Whisk the whites until stiff but not dry and fold them into the soufflé mixture. Pile into the dish and flatten the top neatly. The soufflé mixture should come at least 2cm/¾in above the edge of the dish. Refrigerate for at least 4 hours.
8. Remove the oiled paper carefully. Spread the exposed sides thinly with cream. Press browned chopped almonds gently on to the cream. Pipe rosettes of whipped cream round the top and garnish each with a whole raspberry.

Serves 4

Hot Orange Soufflé

45g/1½oz butter
45g/1½oz flour
Grated rind of 1 large orange
290ml/½ pint fresh orange
  juice

55g/2oz caster sugar
4 egg whites

1. Butter a soufflé dish and dust with caster sugar. Set the oven to 200°C/400°F, gas mark 6. Have ready a deep roasting tin and a kettle of very hot water.
2. Melt the butter and add the flour. Cook for 1 minute and

draw off the heat. Add the rind and juice. Return the pan to the heat and bring very gently up to the boil, stirring continuously. Simmer for 2 minutes and add the sugar. Taste and add more if necessary. Cool.

3. When the orange sauce is cool whisk the whites until stiff and fold them into it. Pour into the prepared soufflé dish – do not fill more than two-thirds of the dish. With a knife cut through the mixture several times to ensure that there are no over-large pockets of air. Place in the roasting pan and fill the pan with boiling water.

4. Bake in the hot oven for 25–30 minutes. 5 minutes before the soufflé is due to come out of the oven sprinkle the top with 1 teaspoon caster sugar. This gives the soufflé an attractive glaze.

Serves 4

Hot Chocolate Soufflé

110g/¼lb dark bitter chocolate	4 egg yolks
2 tablespoons brandy	5 egg whites
55g/2oz caster sugar	Icing sugar

1. Set the oven to 200°C/400°F, gas mark 6. Prepare the soufflé dish by greasing the inside with butter and dusting it with caster sugar.

2. Chop the chocolate with a large knife and put it into a saucepan with two tablespoons of water. Heat very gently, stirring, until the chocolate has completely melted.

3. Beat in the sugar and the egg yolks. Add the brandy.

4. Whisk the whites until they will stand in soft peaks when the whisk is withdrawn from the bowl. Gently but thoroughly fold them into the mixture.

5. Turn into the soufflé dish and cook for about 25 minutes.

6. Test by giving the dish a slight shake or push. If it wobbles

alarmingly it needs further cooking, if it is fairly steady, it is ready. Dust with icing sugar and serve at once.

Serves 4

Jellies

These are fruit juices or syrups set with gelatine. Some are clarified in a similar manner to aspic and clear soups.

You will need:
1. Jelly bag – usually made of flannel – or a large double muslin cloth.
2. Balloon whisk.
3. Large saucepan.

Points to remember:
1. All equipment must be spotlessly clean and grease-free. Scalding in boiling water will ensure this.
2. Weigh all ingredients carefully.
3. Follow the whisking and clearing methods very carefully. Short cuts will only lead to murky jelly.
4. When turning out jellies it is a good idea to wet the serving plate. If the unmoulded jelly is not dead centre you can then slide it gently to the correct position. If the plate is dry the jelly will cling to it and be difficult to budge.

Lemon Jelly

4 large lemons
425ml/¾ pint water
30g/1oz gelatine

125g/4½oz sugar
Green *or* yellow colouring
(optional)

1. With a sharp knife or potato peeler carefully remove the rind (without any pith) from the lemons. Squeeze the fruit and measure the juice. You need 225ml/8fl.oz.

563

2. Put 3 tablespoons of the water into a small pan and sprinkle on the gelatine. Do not stir, but set aside to soak and 'sponge'.

3. Put the remaining water, lemon rind and sugar together in a pan, cover and place over gentle heat. Do not boil. Remove from the heat and keep the liquid hot for 15 minutes in order to extract all the flavour from the lemon rind. Make sure that all the sugar has dissolved and then strain it; allow to cool until lukewarm.

4. Slowly dissolve the gelatine over gentle heat, without boiling. When clear add it to the water and sugar.

5. Add the lemon juice. Taste the mixture and add extra sugar, if necessary, stirring until it is dissolved. At this stage a few drops of green or yellow colouring may be added if desired.

6. Wet a jelly mould. Pour in the liquid jelly, and leave refrigerated until set (at least 4 hours), but preferably overnight.

6. Turn out the jelly: loosen the top edge all round with a finger. Dip the mould briefly into hot water. Place a dish over the mould and invert the two together. Give a good sharp shake and remove the mould.

Serves 4

Clear Lemon Jelly

850ml/1½ pints water
55g/2oz gelatine
225g/½lb sugar
Rind of 4 lemons, thinly pared
290ml/½ pint lemon juice

4 small sticks cinnamon
Green colouring (optional)
The white and crushed shell of
  3 eggs
8 tablespoons sherry

1. Make the lemon jelly: put all the ingredients except the egg whites, egg shells and green colouring into a very clean pan and place over a medium heat. Stir until the gelatine and sugar have dissolved. Remove the cinnamon.

2. Place the crushed shells in a bowl, add the egg whites and

whisk until frothy. Pour into the warming jelly and keep whisking steadily with a balloon whisk until the mixture boils and rises. Stop whisking immediately and draw the pan off the heat. Allow the mixture to subside. Take care not to break the crust formed by the egg white.

3. Bring up to the boil again, and allow to subside. Repeat this once more (the egg white will trap the sediment in the liquid and clear the jelly). Allow to cool for 10 minutes.

4. Fix a double layer of fine muslin over a clean basin and carefully strain the jelly through it, taking care to hold the egg white crust back. When all the liquid is through (or almost all of it) allow the egg white to slip into the muslin. Then strain the jelly again – this time through both the egg white crust and cloth. Do not try to hurry the process by squeezing the cloth, or murky jelly will result. If the jelly begins to set before it is completely strained, warm it up again to melt it just enough to filter through the muslin.

5. Colour it delicately with the green colouring, if required.

6. Pour into a wet jelly mould. Leave refrigerated until set (at least 4 hours, but preferably overnight).

7. Turn out the jelly: loosen the top edge all around with a finger. Dip the mould briefly into hot water. Place a dish over the mould and invert the two together. Give a good sharp shake and remove the mould.

Serves 4

Orange Jelly and Caramel Chips

For the orange jelly:
70g/2½oz caster sugar
150ml/¼ pint water
20g/¾oz gelatine

For the caramel:
55g/2oz granulated sugar

570ml/1 pint orange juice, just
tepid
290ml/½ pint double cream,
whipped lightly

1. Start with the jelly: put the caster sugar and water in a small saucepan. Sprinkle on the gelatine and allow to stand for 10 minutes. Dissolve over a very gentle heat without allowing the gelatine to boil. Do not stir.
2. When the gelatine is clear and liquid mix with the orange juice and pour into a wet plain jelly mould or pudding basin.
3. Chill in the refrigerator 2–4 hours, or until set.
4. Meanwhile start the caramel. Put the sugar in a heavy pan and set over a gentle heat.
5. Lightly oil a baking sheet.
6. When the sugar has dissolved boil rapidly to a golden caramel. Immediately pour on to the baking sheet. Leave to harden and cool completely.
7. Break up the caramel into chips.
8. Loosen the jelly round the edges with a finger. Invert a serving plate over the jelly mould, turn the mould and plate over together, give a sharp shake and remove the mould. If the jelly won't budge dip the outside of the mould briefly in hot water to loosen it.
9. Spread over the cream to completely mask the jelly.
10. Just before serving, scatter the caramel over the jelly (do not do this in advance as the caramel softens quickly).

Serves 4

Black Jelly with Port

450g/1lb blackcurrants   20g/¾oz gelatine
225g/½lb sugar   Whipped cream *or* English egg
190ml/⅓ pint ruby port   custard (page 536)

1. Put the currants and sugar into a saucepan and heat slowly. Push through a sieve.
2. Add the port to the purée and enough water to bring the Liquid up to 570ml/1 pint.
3. Put 3 tablespoons of water in a small saucepan and sprinkle the gelatine over it. Allow to soak for 10 minutes. Heat very

gently until the gelatine is clear and liquid, but do not boil. Pour into the blackcurrant mixture and mix well. Pour into a wet jelly mould or dish. Refrigerate until set.

4. To turn out briefly dip the mould into hot water – just enough to loosen it without melting the jelly. Put the serving dish over the mould and invert it so that the jelly falls on to the plate. Serve with whipped cream or English custard.

Note: If the serving plate is wetted, it is easier to shift the jelly to the middle should it end up slightly off-centre.

Serves 4

Claret Jelly

570ml/1 pint claret *or* other red wine
560ml/1 pint water
Rind of 2 lemons
170g/6oz granulated sugar
2 small sticks cinnamon

2 bay leaves
2 tablespoons redcurrant jelly
45g/1½oz gelatine
2 egg whites and the egg shells
Drop of cochineal *or* carmine colouring (optional)

For the filling:
15g/½oz gelatine
2 tablespoons water
15g/½oz glacé cherries

15g/½oz candied peel
3 tablespoons sherry
150ml/¼ pint double cream

1. First make the jelly: put all the ingredients except the egg whites and red colouring into a very clean pan and place over a medium heat. Stir until the gelatine and sugar have dissolved. Remove the bay leaves, cinnamon sticks and lemon rind.

2. Place the crushed shells in a bowl, add the egg whites and whisk until frothy. Pour into the warming jelly and keep whisking steadily with a balloon whisk until the mixture boils and rises. Stop whisking immediately and draw the pan off the heat. Allow the mixture to subside. Take care not to

break the crust formed by the egg white.

3. Bring up to the boil again, and again allow to subside. Repeat this once more (the egg white will trap the sediment in the liquid and clear the jelly). Allow to cool for 10 minutes.

4. Fix a double layer of fine muslin over a clean basin and carefully strain the jelly through it, taking care to hold the egg white crust back. When all the liquid is through (or almost all of it) allow the egg white to slip into the muslin. Then strain the jelly again – this time through both egg white crust and cloth. Do not try to hurry the process by squeezing the cloth, or murky jelly will result.

5. Add a drop of red colouring if necessary. Leave to cool.

6. In a small heavy pan, soak the gelatine for the filling in the water. Chop the fruits and soak them in sherry.

7. Half whip the cream (until thick but not quite solid), and add the fruits.

8. Dissolve the gelatine over a gentle heat. When runny and clear, stir it into the cream mixture.

9. Pour a 2·5cm/1in layer of jelly into a $1\frac{1}{4}$ litre/$1\frac{1}{2}$ pint mould or flat-bottomed fruit bowl. Place in the refrigerator and leave to set.

10. Wet the outside of a tumbler and place it in the centre of the mould on top of the set layer. Fill up around the glass with liquid jelly. To encourage quick setting fill the glass with ice cubes and refrigerate the jelly.

11. When set, turn out the icy water (you can turn the whole jelly over). Fill the glass with warm water to loosen it and remove.

12. Spoon the fruit filling into the centre hole left by the glass. Leave to become completely set.

13. Invert a wet plate over the mould and turn the two over together. Give a sharp shake and remove the mould.

Note: This recipe sounds, and is, rather complicated. The filling is encased in the jelly. For a simpler version set the jelly in a ring mould and once turned out pile the cream mixture (without the gelatine) into the centre.

Serves 4

Banana and Grape Chartreuse

860ml/1½ pints clear lemon jelly 170g/6oz white grapes
 (page 564) 1 banana

1. Prepare the lemon jelly.
2. Rinse a ring mould out with water. Pour a layer of lemon jelly in the bottom of the mould, about 1cm/½in deep. Put into a cold place to set.
3. If using seedless grapes just wash them. If not, cut in half and take out the seeds. (If the skins are tough or spotted the grapes should be peeled: dip them into boiling water for a few seconds to make this easier.)
4. Arrange the grapes and slices of banana in the ring mould. Pour in enough cool but not quite set jelly to come half-way up the grapes and leave in the refrigerator to set. Pour the rest of the cool jelly in so that the fruit is covered and leave to set.
5. To turn out the jelly dip the outside of the mould briefly in hot water. Invert a wet plate over the jelly mould and turn the two over together. Give a sharp shake and remove the mould.

Serves 6

St Clement's Jelly

This jelly consists of a clear lemon lake with a solid orange border.

570ml/1 pint uncleared orange Green colouring
 jelly (page 565)
570ml/1 pint clear lemon jelly *To serve:*
 (page 564) English custard (page 536) *or* cream

1. Set the orange jelly in a 570ml/1 pint ring mould and turn out on to a flat plate. Chill very well.
2. Make the lemon jelly, adding a very little green colouring.
3. When the jelly is cold pour into the centre hollow of the orange jelly. Refrigerate again to set.
4. Serve with English custard or cream.

Note: Angelica, cut into diagonal 'leaves', or fresh mint leaves, look pretty round the orange border.

Serves 5–6

MERINGUE PUDDINGS

Meringues

4 egg whites
225g/½lb caster sugar

For the filling:
Whipped cream

1. Set the oven to 110°C/225°F, gas mark ½.
2. Place greaseproof paper on two baking sheets, brush with oil and dust lightly with sugar.
3. Whisk the egg whites until stiff but not dry.
4. Add 2 tablespoons of the sugar and whisk again until very stiff and shiny.
5. Fold in the rest of the sugar.
6. Put the meringue mixture out on the paper-covered baking sheets in spoonfuls set fairly far apart. Use a teaspoon for tiny meringues, a dessertspoon for large ones.
7. Bake in the oven for about 2 hours until the meringues are dry right through and will lift easily off the paper.
8. When cold sandwich the meringues together in pairs with whipped cream.

Makes 50 miniature or 12 large meringues

Walnut and Lemon Meringue Cake

A little oil *or* melted lard
   for greasing
4 egg whites
255g/9oz caster sugar

140g/5oz walnuts
290ml/½ pint thick cream
4 heaped tablespoons lemon
   curd (page 571)

1. Set the oven to 190°C/375°F, gas mark 5.
2. Line the bottom of two sandwich tins with rounds of grease-proof paper. Brush the paper and sides of the tins with a very little oil or melted lard.
3. Whisk the egg whites until stiff, then add 2 tablespoons of the sugar. Beat again until stiff.
4. Beat in the rest of the sugar and whisk until the meringue holds its shape.
5. Chop the nuts roughly, reserving a handful, and stir into the mixture.
6. Divide the mixture between the two pans, smoothing the tops slightly.
7. Bake the cakes for 40 minutes. Turn them out on a wire rack and peel off the paper.
8. Whip the cream and mix half of it with the lemon curd. Sandwich the cakes with this.
9. Use the rest of the whipped cream and nuts for the top.

Serves 4

Pavlova

2 egg whites
110g/¼lb caster sugar
1 teaspoon cornflour
1 teaspoon vanilla essence
½ teaspoon vinegar

290ml/½ pint double cream
30g/1oz broken walnuts
450g/1lb fresh pineapple, cored
   and cut into cubes, *or* one can
   tinned pineapple pieces

1. Set the oven to 140°C/275°F, gas mark 1.
2. Put a sheet of foil on a baking sheet, brush with oil and dust with caster sugar.
3. Whisk the egg whites until stiff. Add half the sugar and whisk again until thick, shiny, smooth and very stiff.
4. Whisk in the remaining sugar, the cornflour, the vanilla and the vinegar.
5. With a palette knife or spatula spread the meringue mixture on to the baking sheet in a large round or oval shape.
6. Place in the oven for 50 minutes. The meringue should look pale brown and dry but should be soft in the middle.
7. Immediately it is ready, turn it over on to a flat dish or platter, and peel away the paper. (If you allow the meringue to cool it will stick like the devil.) The middle may sink slightly.
8. Whip the cream and incorporate half the nuts and pineapple. Spoon into the hollow.
9. Decorate with the rest of the nuts and pineapple.

Note: Any fruits in season can be substituted for nuts and pineapple.

Serves 4

Meringue Baskets

2 egg whites   110g/¼lb caster sugar
Pinch of salt

For the filling:
Double cream, whipped   (Rice paper *or* oiled foil)
Strawberries *or* raspberries

For the glaze:
Redcurrant jelly

1. Place the rice paper or foil on baking sheets. Set the oven to 100°C/200°F, gas mark ½.
2. Whisk the egg whites with a pinch of salt to a stiff snow. Whisk in 2 tablespoons of the sugar and continue to whisk until

the mixture is shiny, smooth and extremely stiff. Fold in the remaining sugar with a metal spoon.

3. Fill the mixture into a forcing bag fitted with a rose pipe, and pipe on to the rice paper to form little baskets.

4. Leave to dry in the oven for 2 hours. Take out and allow to cool.

5. Place a little cream in each basket and fill with strawberries *or* raspberries.

6. Gently melt the redcurrant jelly and use it to brush neatly over the fruit.

Note: Meringue baskets are often made with 'cooked meringue' mixture (the sugar and egg white mixture is beaten in a bowl standing over a pan of simmering water, and is therefore slightly heated) which is very solid and does not rise out of shape in the oven.

An electric mixer gives a similar result to 'cooked meringue', but the hand-made uncooked kind tastes the best even if it looks less professional.

Makes 6

Banana and Grape Vacherin

4 egg whites	85g/3oz black grapes
225g/½lb caster sugar	85g/3oz green grapes
1 banana	290ml/½ pint double cream,
Lemon juice	lightly whipped

1. Set the oven to 100°C/200°F, gas mark ½. Cover two baking sheets with greaseproof paper, brush with oil and dust with a little caster sugar.

2. Whisk the egg whites until stiff but not dry, then add 2 table-spoons of the sugar. Whisk again until very stiff and shiny. Fold in the remaining sugar.

3. Fill a forcing bag fitted with a large plain nozzle with the meringue. Pipe into two rounds the size of a dessert plate.

4. Place in the oven to dry out slowly for 2–3 hours. The

meringue is done when light and dry, and the paper will peel off the underside easily.

5. Cut the bananas into chunks and toss in the lemon juice. Halve and seed the grapes.

6. Spread three-quarters of the cream on one of the meringue cases and scatter over the banana and all but four each of the black and green grapes. Place the second meringue on top of this. Using the rest of the cream, pipe rosettes around the top. Decorate each alternate rosette with a grape half.

Serves 6

Almond Meringue Cake with Raspberry Sauce

Melted butter *or* lard	½ teaspoon white vinegar
Flour	225g/½lb raspberries
140g/5oz blanched almonds	Icing sugar
4 egg whites	Squeeze of lemon juice
255g/9oz caster sugar	290ml/½ pint double cream
Drop of vanilla essence	

1. Set the oven to 190°C/375°F, gas mark 5. Prepare two 20cm/8in sandwich tins: brush with melted butter or lard and dust with flour. Line the base with greased greaseproof paper or foil, or best of all with rice paper.

2. Place the almonds on a baking sheet and bake until dark brown. Set aside 5 nuts and grind the rest. Do not over-grind or they will become greasy and make the meringue heavy. Weigh the nuts. You will need 100g/3½oz for the meringue.

3. Whisk the egg whites until stiff and then gradually beat in the caster sugar, vanilla and vinegar, beating until very stiff. Fold in the nuts very gently with a large metal spoon. Pile the mixture into the prepared tins, spreading evenly with a spatula.

4. Bake for 35 minutes. Allow to cool in the tin for a few minutes and then turn out on to a wire rack. Remove the foil or paper (unless it is edible rice paper) while the meringue is still warm.

574

5. While the meringue is cooling liquidize the raspberries with icing sugar and lemon juice. Push through a sieve and taste for sweetness. If very thick add a little water.
6. To decorate whip the cream and sandwich the meringue together with two-thirds of it. Dust the top with icing sugar. Pipe five large rosettes of cream round the edge of the top of the meringue and decorate each with a reserved almond. Hand the raspberry sauce separately.

Note: Hazelnuts or walnuts may be substituted for the almonds. If using hazelnuts the skins must be removed (by rubbing in a tea-towel) after browning well in the oven. Walnuts need not be browned.

Serves 6

Meringue Mont Blanc

For the meringue:
3 egg whites
170g/6oz caster sugar
Icing sugar

Chocolate caraque (page 675)
 or coarsely grated chocolate

For the filling:
450g/1lb chestnuts
85g/3oz granulated sugar
150ml/¼ pint water
30g/1oz butter
Vanilla essence
150ml/¼ pint double cream, whipped

1. Set the oven to 100°C/200°F, gas mark ½. Cover a baking sheet with foil, brush lightly with oil and dust with flour.
2. Whisk the egg whites until stiff but not dry, add 1 tablespoon of the sugar and whisk again until very stiff and shiny. Fold in the remaining sugar.
3. Fill the meringue into a forcing bag with a 1cm/½in plain nozzle. Pipe the mixture into an 18cm/7in circle on the prepared baking sheet, starting from the centre and spiralling outwards. Pipe a rim 3cm/1½in deep. Dust lightly with icing sugar.
4. Bake in the oven for at least 2 hours until the meringue is

dry and crisp. When cooked remove carefully, immediately peel off the foil, and allow the meringue to cool on a wire rack.

5. Cut a slit in the skin of each chestnut, place them in a pan of water and bring slowly to the boil. Draw off the heat, then lift out one by one and peel.

6. Dissolve the granulated sugar in the water, add the chestnuts and simmer slowly until soft. Liquidize or sieve the mixture, then return to the pan.

7. Simmer until you have a thick purée, stirring well to prevent the mixture burning. Allow to cool.

8. Beat in the butter and vanilla essence.

9. To assemble the vacherin pile the chestnut filling into the meringue case, spoon over the whipped cream and arrange chocolate caraque on top.

Note: Canned sweetened purée of chestnuts is as good as freshly cooked, and convenient; however it is very expensive.

Serves 6

Floating Islands

For the custard:
425ml/$\frac{3}{4}$ pint milk
280ml/$\frac{1}{2}$ pint cream
2 teaspoons caster sugar
Vanilla pod *or* 3 drops vanilla
  essence
2 level teaspoons cornflour
4 egg yolks

For the meringue:
3 egg whites
Salt
110g/$\frac{1}{4}$lb caster sugar

To serve:
Grated chocolate

1. Place half the milk, the cream and the sugar in a saucepan with the vanilla. Bring gently to the boil, remove from heat and leave to infuse for 30 minutes. Remove the vanilla pod.

2. Mix the cornflour with a little water. Stir a few ounces of the hot milk mixture into it and then pour it back into the

milk. Place over a gentle heat and bring slowly to the boil, stirring continuously. Simmer for 4 minutes to cook the cornflour.

3. Beat the egg yolks then pour the cream mixture on to the yolks in a thin stream, beating well all the time. The custard will probably thicken at once to the consistency which will coat the back of a wooden spoon. If it does not, return to the saucepan and stir steadily over very gentle heat until it does. Take care not to boil or it will curdle. Pour into a shallow wide serving dish, and cover with plastic film to prevent a skin forming.

4. Meanwhile make the islands: put the remaining milk plus 570ml/1 pint of water into a deep frying pan and set over the heat.

5. Whisk the whites with a pinch of salt until stiff but not dry. Whisk in the caster sugar gradually until you have a smooth shiny meringue mixture.

6. The milk and water mixture should now be simmering. Put a tablespoon of meringue mixture into the frying pan and cook gently for only 30 seconds on each side, by which time they will have almost doubled in size. (Do not add more than three or four islands at a time and do not overcook.) Lift out with a perforated spoon and leave on a wire rack or tea-towel to drain completely. Lay the islands carefully on the 'lake' of custard.

7. Sprinkle the islands with the chocolate.

Makes 6–8 islands

Floating Islands with Caramel

Floating islands (page 576)   85g/3oz sugar

Place the sugar in a heavy pan and set over a gentle heat until the sugar has dissolved and cooked to a golden brown. Remove from the heat, and immediately trickle over the islands already in the custard.

Floating Islands with Coffee Custard

Floating islands (page 576)   2 teaspoons boiling water
1 teaspoon coffee

Proceed as for floating islands but dissolve the coffee in boiling water and add it to the custard sauce just before removing it from the heat.

Floating Islands with Orange

Floating islands (page 576   1 orange
    omitting the vanilla)   1 tablespoon Grand Marnier

Proceed as for floating islands but, in addition, pare the rind from the orange, being careful to discard all the pith. Infuse the rind in the cream and milk mixture in place of the vanilla pod. Add the Grand Marnier to the custard before pouring into the serving dish.

Chocolate Meringue Cake

For the meringue:
4 egg whites
255g/9oz caster sugar

For the filling:
100g/3½oz dark chocolate
2 egg whites
110g/¼lb icing sugar
225g/½lb unsalted butter

For the decoration:
Browned chopped *or* nibbled
    almonds
Icing sugar

1. Set the oven to 100°C/200°F, gas mark ½. Line two large (or

four small) baking sheets with greaseproof paper or foil, brush lightly with oil and dust with flour.

2. First make the meringue: whisk the egg whites until stiff but not dry. Add 2 tablespoons of the sugar and keep whisking until very stiff and shiny. Fold in the remaining sugar.

3. Divide the mixture into four and spread thinly into equal-sized circles about 18cm/7in across.

4. Bake until crisp and dry (about $1\frac{1}{2}$ hours). Immediately peel off the paper or foil and leave to cool on a wire rack.

5. Meanwhile prepare the filling: melt the chocolate on a plate over a pan of hot water. Whip the egg whites with the sugar in a bowl set over a pan of simmering water until the mixture is stiff, smooth and shiny.

6. Beat the butter until light and creamy. Gradually beat in the meringue mixture. Stir in the chocolate.

7. Sandwich the meringue discs with chocolate filling and spread the top and sides with the same mixture. Completely cover the sides with browned chopped almonds. Chill.

8. Place three thin strips of greaseproof paper over the gateau in parallel lines. Dust the cake with icing sugar. Carefully remove the greaseproof paper strips, leaving a pretty stripy pattern.

BAKED AND STEAMED PUDDINGS

Apple Charlotte

1·125 kilos/2½lb apples
85g/3oz sugar
2 tablespoons apricot jam

15g/½oz butter
8 slices stale crustless bread
110g/4oz melted butter

Apricot glaze:
3 tablespoons apricot jam
4 tablespoons water

1. Peel, core and slice the apples and put them into a heavy pan. Add the sugar and cook, without water, until very soft. Boil away any extra liquid and push through a sieve. Whisk in the apricot jam.
2. Butter a charlotte mould or deep cake tin.
3. With a pastry cutter stamp one piece of bread into a circle to fit the bottom of your mould or tin and cut it into six equal sized triangles. Cut the remaining bread into strips.
4. Set the oven to 200°C/400°F, gas mark 6.
5. Dip the pieces of bread into the melted butter. Arrange the triangles to fit the bottom of the mould and arrange all but four of the strips in overlapping slices around the sides.
6. Spoon in the apple purée and arrange the four remaining strips of buttery bread on top.
7. Bake for 40 minutes. Allow to cool for 10 minutes.
8. Meanwhile, make the apricot glaze. Put the jam and water into a small heavy pan and heat, stirring occasionally, until warm and completely melted.
9. Turn out the pudding: invert a plate over the mould and turn the mould and plate over together. Give a sharp shake and remove the mould.
10. Brush the charlotte with the apricot glaze and serve with cream or custard.

Serves 5

Chocolate Roulade

5 eggs	1 teaspoon strong instant
140g/5oz caster sugar	coffee
225g/½lb dark sweetened	290ml/½ pint double cream
chocolate	Icing sugar
75ml/3 fl.oz water	

1. Take a large roasting pan and cut a double layer of grease-proof paper slightly bigger than it. Lay this in the tin; don't worry if the edges stick up untidily round the sides. Brush

the paper lightly with oil or melted lard and sprinkle with flour and then caster sugar. Set the oven to 200°C/400°F, gas mark 6.

2. Separate the eggs and beat the yolks and the sugar until pale and mousse-like.

3. Put the chocolate, water and coffee into a thick-bottomed saucepan and melt over a gentle heat. Stir into the yolk mixture.

4. Whisk the whites until stiff but not dry. With a metal spoon stir a small amount thoroughly into the chocolate mixture – this will 'loosen' the mixture and make it easier for the rest of the whites to be folded in gently. Spread the mixture evenly on the paper.

5. Bake for about 12 minutes until the top is slightly browned and firm to touch.

6. Slide the cake and paper out of the roasting tin on to a wire rack. Cover immediately with a damp tea-towel (to prevent the cake from cracking) and leave to cool – preferably overnight.

7. Whip the cream and spread it evenly over the cake. Roll up like a Swiss roll, removing the paper as you go. Put the roll on to a serving dish and, just before serving, sift a little icing sugar over it.

Note I: The cake is very moist, and inclined to break apart. But it doesn't matter. Just stick it together with the cream when rolling up. The last-minute sifted icing sugar will do wonders for the appearance.

Note II: If this cake is used as a Yulelog the tendency to crack is a positive advantage: do not cover with a tea-towel when leaving overnight: Before filling flip the whole flat cake over on to a tea-towel. Carefully peel off the backing paper, then fill with cream and roll up. The firm skin will crack very like the bark of a tree. Bits of holly or marzipan toadstools help to give a festive look. A dusting of icing sugar will look like snow.

Serves 6

Spiced Ginger Roll

For the roll:
110g/¼lb plain flour
1 teaspoon mixed spice
1 teaspoon ground ginger
70g/2½oz butter
2 tablespoons treacle
2 tablespoons syrup
1 egg
150ml/¼ pint water
1 teaspoon bicarbonate of soda
Caster sugar

For the filling:
450g/1lb cooking apples
30g/1oz butter
1 teaspoon cinnamon
55g/2oz sugar

To serve:
Whipped cream

1. First make the filling: peel and core the apples. Slice them roughly.
2. Melt the butter in a saucepan and add the cinnamon, sugar and apples. Cover with a lid and cook very gently, stirring occasionally, until the apples become pulpy. Beat until smooth, adding more sugar if the apples are still tart.
3. Set the oven to 180°C/350°F, gas mark 4. Prepare a Swiss roll tin by greasing the inside, then covering the base with greaseproof paper, and greasing again. Dust with caster sugar.
4. Sift the flour, mixed spice and ginger together. Melt the butter in a pan with the treacle and syrup. Whisk the egg with the water and soda. Draw the syrup mixture off the heat and pour in the egg and water. Mix well.
5. Now pour this into the flour and whisk together for 30 seconds. Pour into the prepared tin and bake for 12–15 minutes or until firm to touch.
6. Turn out on to a sheet of greaseproof paper dusted with caster sugar. Remove the paper now stuck to the back of the cake. Spread the cake with the apple purée, roll up like a Swiss roll and serve, preferably with whipped cream.

Note: The pudding is not pretty, being squashy and dark brown, but the taste is wonderful. A last-minute dusting with icing sugar will help the appearance.

Serves 4

Annabel's Cheesecake

For the crust:
1 packet babies' rusks *or*
  digestive biscuits, crushed
  (about 16 biscuits)
85g/3oz caster sugar
110g/¼lb butter, melted

For the topping:
½ carton soured cream
1 teaspoon caster sugar

For the filling:
225g/½lb best-quality soft
  cream cheese
5 tablespoons double cream
1 whole egg and 1 yolk
1 teaspoon vanilla essence
Sugar to taste (about 1
  tablespoon)

1. Set the oven to 190°C/375°F, gas mark 5.
2. Mix the crust ingredients together and line a shallow pie dish or flan ring with the mixture, pressing firmly against the sides and base. Be careful not to get the corners too thick.
3. Bake for 10 minutes or until hard to the touch.
4. Mix all the filling ingredients together until smooth and pour into the case.
5. Return to the oven until the filling has set (about 20 minutes).
6. Take out and allow to cool.
7. Spread with the soured cream mixed with the sugar.

Note: The top can be decorated with nuts, sultanas or fresh fruit such as redcurrants or halved seeded grapes, but it is very good as it is.

Serves 6

Treacle Sponge

2½ tablespoons golden syrup
2 teaspoons fine white
  breadcrumbs
110g/¼lb butter
Grated rind of 1 lemon
110g/¼lb caster sugar

2 eggs, beaten
110g/¼lb self-raising flour
Pinch of salt
1 teaspoon ground ginger
75ml/3fl.oz milk

To serve:
Custard *or* cream

1. Grease a pudding basin with a knob of butter.
2. Mix together the syrup and breadcrumbs at the bottom of the basin.
3. Cream the butter and when very soft add the lemon rind and sugar. Beat until light and fluffy.
4. Gradually add the eggs, beating well between each addition.
5. Sift and fold in the flour with the salt and ginger.
6. Add enough milk to make the mixture just loose enough to drop from a spoon.
7. Turn into the pudding basin, cover and steam for 2½ hours.
8. Turn out and serve with custard or cream.

Serves 4–6

FRIED PUDDINGS

Sweet Soufflé Omelette

2 eggs
2 tablespoons jam
1 tablespoon lemon juice

30g/1oz caster sugar
15g/½oz butter
Icing sugar to decorate

584

1. Separate the eggs.
2. Set the oven to 180°C/350°F, gas mark 4. Heat the grill set at the highest temperature.
3. Warm the jam with the lemon juice.
4. Beat the yolks with the caster sugar until light and frothy.
5. Whisk the egg whites until stiff but not too dry. (The mixture should form a 'medium' peak when the whisk is lifted from it, not too floppy, not too rigid.)
6. Heat a 15cm/6in frying pan and melt the butter in it.
7. Fold the egg whites into the yolks and when the butter is foaming, but not coloured, pour in the omelette mixture.
8. Lower the heat and cook for 1 minute until the underside has just set.
9. Place in the oven for 10 minutes until the omelette top is just set – do not overcook.
10. Get a long skewer red hot under the grill. Leave it there while dishing the omelette.
11. Spread the warmed jam over half the omelette and fold in two with a spatula.
12. Slip on to a heated flat serving dish. Sprinkle the surface with icing sugar.
13. Brand a criss-cross pattern in the sugar with the red hot skewer. Serve immediately.

Note I: It is not strictly necessary to finish the cooking in the oven, but it avoids the risk of burning the bottom before the top is set.

Note II: The branding with the hot skewer is not essential either, but the omelette should be sprinkled with icing sugar before serving.

Serves 4

Banana Fritters

8 bananas
150ml/¼ pint fritter batter (see below)

Oil for shallow frying
Icing sugar

585

1. Peel the bananas and cut in half lengthwise.
2. Dip immediately into the prepared batter.
3. Heat 6mm/¼in of oil in a frying pan and when hot fry the fritters for about 2 minutes on each side until golden brown. Drain well and dust with icing sugar.

Serves 8

Sweet Fritter Batter

125g/4½oz plain flour
Pinch of salt
2 eggs

1 tablespoon oil
50g/1¾oz sugar
150ml/¼ pint milk

1. Sift the flour with the salt into a bowl.
2. Make a well in the centre, exposing the bottom of the bowl.
3. Put one whole egg and one yolk into the well and mix with a wooden spoon or whisk until smooth, gradually incorporating the surrounding flour and the milk. A thick cream consistency should be reached.
4. Add the oil and sugar. Allow to rest for 30 minutes.
5. Whisk the egg white and fold into the batter with a metal spoon just before using.

Note: This batter can be speedily made in a blender. Simply put all the ingredients, except the egg white, into the machine and whizz briefly.

PASTRY, YEAST AND PANCAKE PUDDINGS

Apple and Orange Crumble

1 kilo/2lb cooking apples
3 tablespoons demerara sugar

Pinch of cinnamon
3 oranges

For the crumble:
110g/¼lb butter
170g/6oz plain flour

Pinch of salt
55g/2oz sugar

1. Peel and core the apples. Cut into chunks and place in a saucepan with the demerara sugar and cinnamon.
2. Add enough water to come 0·5cm/¼in up the pan. Stew gently until the apples are just beginning to soften.
3. Peel the oranges as you would an apple, with a sharp knife, removing all the pith.
4. Cut out the orange segments leaving behind the membranes. Add to the apple mixture.
5. Allow to cool, then tip off any excess juice.
6. Set the oven to 200°C/400°F, gas mark 6.
7. Rub the fat into the flour, add salt and when the mixture resembles coarse breadcrumbs mix in the sugar.
8. Pour the apple and orange mixture into an ovenproof dish and sprinkle over the crumble mixture.
9. Bake for 25–30 minutes or until hot and slightly browned on top.

Note: If using wholemeal flour for the crumble top use 140g/5oz of *melted* butter. Instead of rubbing it into the flour mix briskly with a knife.

Serves 4

Plum Pie

225g/½lb plain flour
Pinch of salt
55g/2oz lard

85g/3oz butter
2–3 tablespoons cold water

For the filling:
675g/1½lb plums
3 tablespoons demerara sugar

½ level teaspoon ground
cinnamon

Caster sugar to dredge

1. Preheat the oven to 220°C/425°F, gas mark 7.
2. Sift the flour with the salt into a bowl. Rub in the fats until the mixture resembles breadcrumbs.
3. Stir in enough water to bind the paste together. Push together into a lump, wrap up and chill in the refrigerator while you prepare the filling.
4. Wash the plums and place them in a pan with just enough water to cover the bottom of the pan. Add the demerara sugar and cinnamon. Stir gently until the sugar dissolves and the plums are half cooked.
5. Put the plums and a cupful of the juice into a 1 litre/1½ pint pie dish. Allow to cool.
6. Roll out the pastry on a floured board. Cut a band of pastry wider than the rim of the dish. Wet the rim and press the band on all the way round. Brush with water and lay over the rolled out pastry. Trim the edges, press them down firmly and mark with a fork or press into a frilly edge with fingers and thumb.
7. Shape the pastry trimmings into leaves. Brush the top of the pie with water and decorate with the leaves. Brush the leaves with water and dredge the whole pie with caster sugar.
8. Cut one or two small slits in the pastry top to allow the steam to escape. Bake for 25–35 minutes.

Note I: Classically, sweet pastry pies are not decorated with leaves etc., but why ever not?

Note II: If the liquid in which the plums have been poached is very thin, reduce it rapidly until slightly thickened.

Serves 6

Treacle Tart

110g/¼lb plain flour
Pinch of salt
70g/2½oz butter

1 level tablespoon caster sugar
1 egg yolk
Very cold water

For the filling:
4 heaped tablespoons fresh
   white breadcrumbs
8 tablespoons golden syrup

Grated rind of ½ lemon and
   2 teaspoons of the juice
Pinch of ginger (optional)

1. Set the oven to 190 C/375 F, gas mark 5.
2. Sift the flour with the salt. Rub in the butter until the mixture looks like breadcrumbs. Add the sugar.
3. Mix the yolk with 2 tablespoons of water, and add to the mixture.
4. Mix to a firm dough – first with a knife, and finally with one hand. It may be necessary to add water but the pastry should not be too wet. (Though crumbly pastry is more difficult to handle, it produces a shorter, less tough result.)
5. Roll the pastry out to 0·5cm/¼in thick, and line a pie plate or flan ring with it. Prick the bottom with a fork.
6. Heat the syrup with the lemon juice and rind to make it a little runny. Add the ginger if using.
7. Pour half the syrup into the pastry case.
8. Sprinkle with crumbs until they are soaked. Pour in the remaining syrup and sprinkle in the remaining crumbs.
9. Bake for about 30 minutes or until the filling is almost set and the edge of the pastry is brown. The filling should be a little on the soft side if the tart is to be eaten cold, because it hardens as it cools. Ideally, serve lukewarm.

Serves 4

Lemon Meringue Pie

170g/6oz plain flour
Pinch of salt
100g/3½oz butter

1 teaspoon caster sugar
1 egg yolk
Very cold water

For the filling:
30g/1oz cornflour
290ml/½ pint milk
30g/1oz sugar

2 egg yolks
Grated rind and juice of 1
   lemon

For the meringue:
2 egg whites
110g/¼lb caster sugar

Little extra caster sugar

1. First make the pastry: sift the flour with the salt. Rub in the butter until the mixture looks like breadcrumbs. Add the sugar.
2. Mix the yolk with 2 tablespoons of water. Add this to the mixture.
3. Mix to a firm dough – first with a knife, and finally with one hand. It may be necessary to add more water, but the pastry should not be too wet. (Though crumbly pastry is more difficult to handle, it produces a shorter, less tough result.)
4. Roll out the pastry and use it to line a 20cm/8in flan ring. Leave it in the refrigerator for about 30 minutes to relax (this prevents shrinkage during cooking).
5. Heat the oven to 190 C/375 C, gas mark 5.
6. Bake the pastry blind.
7. Meanwhile, make the filling: mix the cornflour with a tablespoon of the milk.
8. Heat the remaining milk. Pour this on to the cornflour paste, stir well and return the mixture to the pan. Boil for 3–4 minutes, stirring continuously. Add the sugar.
9. Allow to cool slightly, then beat in the egg yolks, lemon rind and juice.

10. Pour this mixture into the pastry case. Return to the oven for 2 minutes to set. Whisk the egg whites until stiff. Add 1 tablespoon of the caster sugar and whisk again until very stiff and solid.
11. Fold in the remaining sugar. Pile the meringue on to the pie. It is essential to cover the filling completely or the pie will weep. Dust with a little extra caster sugar.
12. Place in the oven for 5 minutes or until the meringue is a pale biscuit colour.

Note: Lemon curd (page 743) makes a good alternative to the lemon custard filling.

Baking blind. See page 245

Serves 4

Custard Tart

140g/6oz flour-quantity rich shortcrust pastry (page 645)

For the filling:

2 eggs	150ml/$\frac{1}{4}$ pint single cream
30g/1oz sugar	Grated nutmeg
150ml/$\frac{1}{4}$ pint milk	

1. Set the oven to 190°C/375°F, gas mark 5. Line a 20cm/8in flan ring or dish with the shortcrust pastry. Bake blind for 15–20 minutes.
2. Lower the oven to 180°C/350°F, gas mark 4.
3. Lightly beat the eggs with the sugar. Pour on the milk and cream. Strain into the prepared flan case and sprinkle a little grated nutmeg over the top.
4. Bake for 40–45 minutes or until the custard has set.

Serves 4

Baking blind. See page 245

Butterscotch Pie

110g/¼lb flour-quantity rich
   shortcrust pastry (page 645)
30g/1oz butter
55g/2oz demarara sugar
290ml/½ pint milk

1 tablespoon cornflour
Pinch of ginger
2 tablespoons double cream,
   lightly whipped
Chopped walnuts to decorate

1. Set the oven to 190°C/375°F, gas mark 5.
2. Line a 15cm/6in flan ring with the pastry and bake blind. Cool on a wire rack.
3. Slowly melt the butter. Add the sugar and cook until dark brown and oily.
4. Carefully pour on three-quarters of the milk (the milk will splutter alarmingly and the butter and sugar will become toffee like). Simmer slowly until the sugar has dissolved.
5. In a cup blend the cornflour with the remaining milk. Pour a little hot milk into the cup and mix well. Pour this back into the butterscotch milk and stir while it boils and thickens. Draw off the heat and stir in the ginger. Allow to cool.
6. Add the cream. Pour the mixture into the pastry case and sprinkle over the chopped nuts.

Baking blind. See page 245

Serves 4

Pumpkin Pie

170g/6oz flour-quantity rich
   shortcrust pastry (page 645)

For the filling:
675g/1½lb pumpkin
55g/2oz soft brown sugar
½ teaspoon cinnamon

½ teaspoon ginger
½ teaspoon salt
2 eggs

$\frac{1}{4}$ teaspoon mace	150ml/$\frac{1}{4}$ pint single cream
$\frac{1}{4}$ teaspoon nutmeg	150ml/$\frac{1}{4}$ pint milk

To serve:

150ml/$\frac{1}{4}$ pint double cream   Caster sugar
Extra cinnamon

1. Set the oven to 180°C/350°F, gas mark 4.
2. Cut the pumpkin in half and scrape out the seeds. Place in a roasting tin shell side up. Bake for 1 hour or until the flesh is tender. Remove the flesh from the shell and pass through a sieve or blender.
3. Set the oven to 200°C/400°F, gas mark 6. Line a 20cm/8in flan ring with the pastry and bake blind until completely cooked.
4. Raise the oven temperature to 230°C/450°F, gas mark 8.
5. Mix the pumpkin with the rest of the filling ingredients and beat well. Put into the top of a double boiler, or in a bowl set over a saucepan of simmering water, and stir until the mixture is thick.
6. Allow the mixture to cool slightly then pour into the cooked flan case. Sprinkle with more brown sugar and a pinch of cinnamon and bake for about 12 minutes or until the top is lightly browned.
7. Whip the cream and flavour with cinnamon and caster sugar. Serve the pie hot or cold, handing the cream separately.

Baking blind. See page 245

Note: If fresh pumpkin is not available a 425ml/15 fl.oz can of pumpkin purée may be used, in which event paragraphs (1) and (2) above are omitted.

Serves 4–6

Mincemeat Flan

170g/6oz flour-quantity rich
    shortcrust pastry (page 645)

For the filling:

1 small cooking apple	45g/1½oz chopped almonds
55g/2oz butter	Grated rind of ½ large lemon
85g/3oz sultanas	½ teaspoon mixed spice
85g/3oz raisins	1 tablespoon brandy
85g/3oz currants	85g/3oz brown sugar
45g/1½oz mixed peel, chopped	1 banana chopped

Caster sugar

1. Heat the oven to 190°C/375°F, gas mark 5.
2. Roll the pastry out to 0·5cm/¼in thick, and line a pie plate or flan ring with it, keeping the pastry trimming for the lattice decoration.
3. Bake blind for 20 minutes.
4. For the mincemeat: grate the apple, skin and all. Melt the butter and add it, with all the other filling ingredients, to the apple. Mix well.
5. Fill the flan with the mincemeat. Cut the pastry trimmings into thin strips and lattice the top of the flan with them, sticking the ends down with a little water. Brush the lattice with water and sprinkle with caster sugar. Return to the oven for 10–12 minutes, removing the flan ring after 5 minutes to allow the sides of the pastry to cook to a pale brown.

Baking blind. See page 245

Serves 8

La Tarte des Demoiselles Tatin

100g/¼lb flour-quantity rich shortcrust pastry (page 645)	55g/2oz butter
55g/2oz caster sugar	55g/2oz granulated sugar
900g/2lb dessert apples	Grated rind of ½ lemon

1. Prepare the pastry and allow to relax in the refrigerator.

2. Heat the oven to 200°C/400°F, gas mark 6. Butter an 18cm/7in flan dish and sprinkle with half the caster sugar.

3. Peel, core and quarter the apples and cut into large chunks. Pack them very tightly in the flan dish, layering with the rest of the caster sugar and pats of butter as you go.

4. Roll out the pastry and lay it on top of the apples. Press the edges down firmly. Bake in the oven for 20–30 minutes.

5. When the pie is cooked slowly melt the granulated sugar in a heavy pan. While it is melting take the dish and invert a plate on top of it. Turn the plate and flan dish over together and remove the flan dish. Allow the sugar to caramelize (go toffee coloured and runny). Sprinkle the top of the apples with the grated lemon rind and pour over the caramelized sugar.

Note I: Classically the caramel top is not made and poured over the apples, but the sugar and butter at the bottom of the flan dish should produce a dark toffee-like mixture. However, the above caramel addition gives a slightly crackly top.

Note II: Occasionally even dessert apples produce too much juice. If this happens (the juice will overflow the flan dish at the edges) tip it off before turning the pie over. The apple should be firm and moist, not wet. The extra juice may be added to the sugar before caramelizing, which will give it extra flavour.

Serves 6

Rhubarb Lattice Flan

170g/6oz flour-quantity
  shortcrust pastry (page
  645)
450g/1lb rhubarb
150ml/¼ pint sugar syrup
  (page 536)
15g/½oz caster sugar

For the glaze:
1 teaspoon arrowroot
1 tablespoon smooth apricot
  jam

1. Make the pastry and line a 15cm/6in flan ring, reserving the trimmings. Chill for 20 minutes.
2. Set the oven to 190°C/375°F, gas mark 5.
3. Prepare the rhubarb: cut it into 4cm/1½in lengths and stew very gently in the sugar syrup until tender. Drain the fruit very well and reserve the juice.
4. Bake the pastry case blind for 20–25 minutes.
5. Arrange the rhubarb neatly in the flan case.
6. Mix the arrowroot with enough of the fruit juice to make it smooth. Put the arrowroot mixture and the juice into a saucepan and bring it to the boil, stirring all the time. Add the jam and boil to a thick syrupy consistency. Cool until warm then pour into the flan, all over the fruit.
7. Roll out the pastry trimmings into long strips 1cm/½in wide. Twist the strips like barley sugar and arrange them in a latticed pattern over the flan, sticking the ends down with a little water. Brush each strip with water and sprinkle with caster sugar.
8. Return the flan to the oven until the pastry becomes a pale golden brown. Leave to cool on a wire rack.

Baking blind. See page 245

Serves 4–5

Raisin and Yoghurt Tartlets

170g/6oz flour-quantity sweet wholemeal pastry (page 647)
1 large egg
55g/2oz caster sugar
1 tablespoon plain flour
Pinch of nutmeg
Pinch of cinnamon
2 teaspoons lemon juice
Rind of ½ lemon
150ml/5 fl. oz yoghurt
55g/2oz raisins

1. Set the oven to 200°C/400°F, gas mark 6.
2. Roll out the pastry thinly and cut into rounds a size larger than the patty tins.

3. Turn the patty tins upside down and press the pastry firmly over the outside of the tin moulds. Prick them lightly. Bake for 10 minutes. Reduce the oven to 180°C/350°F, gas mark 4.
4. Remove the pastry cases from the outside of the tins and turn them right side up on a baking sheet. Return to the oven until the pastry is crisp and cooked.
5. Put the egg and the sugar into a pudding bowl. Stand this over a pan of boiling water. Whisk until the mixture thickens sufficiently to leave a 'ribbon' trail.
6. Fold in the flour, spices, lemon juice, rind, yoghurt and raisins.
7. Fill the mixture into the tartlet cases and bake for 20–25 minutes or until the mixture is firm. Leave to cool on a wire rack.

Makes 18

Apple Florentine

1 kilo/2lb cooking apples
55g/2oz butter
50g/2oz demerara *or* barbados sugar

Spiced cider:
150ml/¼ pint cider
Pinch of ground nutmeg and ginger

To serve:
Icing sugar

1 teaspoon ground cinnamon
Grated rind of 1 lemon
225g/½lb flour-quantity rough-puff pastry (page 647)

1 stick cinnamon
Pared rind of ½ lemon
55g/2oz sugar

Ice cream *or* whipped cream

1. Set the oven to 200°C/400°F, gas mark 6.
2. Peel, core and quarter the apples.
3. Melt the butter in a frying pan and when foaming add the apples. Fry until delicately browned.
4. Tip into a pie dish and mix in the sugar, cinnamon and lemon rind. Allow to cool.

5. Roll out the pastry on a floured board to ½cm/¼in thickness.
6. Cut a strip of pastry very slightly wider than the edge of the dish. Brush the rim with water and press the strip down all round it.
7. Lift the pastry with the aid of the rolling pin and lay it on the pie. Press down the edge and trim the sides.
8. Mark round the edge with the prongs of a folk or the tip of a knife. Brush with cold water and dust with caster sugar.
9. Bake the pie for 25–30 minutes until golden brown.
10. Prepare the spiced cider: heat all the ingredients together in a pan over a gentle heat for 10 minutes without boiling. Strain.
11. Remove the pie from the oven and with a sharp knife lift off the crust in one piece. Pour in the spiced cider.
12. Return the crust on to the pie and dust with icing sugar. Serve hot with ice cream or whipped cream.

Note: 'Florentine' is an obsolete word for pie.

Serves 4

Tarte Française

110g/¼lb flour-quantity rough puff pastry (page 647)
3 tablespoons warm apricot glaze (page 714)
Squeeze of lemon

Fruit as for a fruit salad: say 1 pear, 1 orange, small bunch black grapes, small bunch white grapes, 6 strawberries, 2 bananas etc.

1. Roll out the pastry into as neat a rectangle as you can. It should be the thickness of a penny. Prick it well all over.
2. Bake in a hot oven (230 C/450 F, gas mark 8) for 12 minutes or until crisp and brown.
3. Remove from the oven and turn over on to a flat serving plate. Trim the edges neatly and allow to cool.
4. Use a little of the glaze to brush the surface of the pastry.
5. Cut the fruit up as you would for a fruit salad, and lay the

598

pieces in rows on the pastry as neatly and closely together as possible. Be careful about colour (do not put two rows of white fruit next to each other, or tangerine segments next to orange segments etc.). As each row goes down, paint it carefully with the glaze. This is most important especially with fruit that discolours, like bananas, apples and pears.

6. Serve with crème chantilly (page 539).

Serves 4

Mille Feuilles

225g/½lb flour-quantity rough puff pastry (page 647) *or* puff pastry (page 649)
2 tablespoons strawberry jam

290ml/½ pint double cream, whipped
225g/½lb icing sugar, sifted

1. Set the oven to 220°C/425°F, gas mark 7.
2. On a floured board roll the pastry into a large thin rectangle about 30 × 20cm/12 × 8in. Place on a wet baking sheet. Prick all over with a fork.
3. Leave to relax, covered, for 20 minutes. Bake until brown. Allow to cool.
4. Cut the pastry into three neat strips 10 × 20cm/4 × 8in. (Keep the trimmings for decoration.) Choose the piece of pastry with the smoothest base, and reserve. Spread a layer of jam on the two remaining strips and cover with cream. Place them on top of each other and cover with the third, reserved, piece of pastry, smooth side uppermost. Press down gently but firmly. (See drawing overleaf.)
5. Mix the icing sugar with boiling water until it is thick, smooth and creamy. Be careful not to add too much water. Coat the icing over the top of the pastry and while still warm sprinkle crushed pastry trimmings along the edges of the icing. Allow to cool before serving.

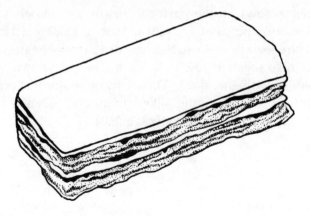

Note: To 'feather' the icing, put a tablespoon of warmed, smooth liquid jam in a piping bag with a 'writing' nozzle. Pipe parallel lines of jam down the length of the newly iced mille feuilles, about 2cm/¾in apart. Before the icing or jam is set drag the back of a knife across the lines of jam. This will pull the lines into points where the knife crosses them. Repeat this every 5cm/2in in the same direction, and then drag the back of the knife in the opposite direction between the drag-lines already made.

Serves 4–6

Jalousie

110g/¼lb flour-quantity rough puff pastry (page 647)	2 tablespoons smooth apricot jam
225g/½lb fresh apple marmalade (page 539)	Milk
	Caster sugar

1. Set the oven to 230°C/450°F, gas mark 8.
2. Roll the pastry into two thin rectangles, one about 2·5cm/1in bigger all round than the other (the smaller one should measure about 13 × 20cm/5 × 8in, the larger 18 × 25cm/7 × 10in). Leave to relax for 20 minutes.
3. Prick the smaller one all over and bake until crisp and brown.

Take it out and turn it over on the baking sheet. Allow to cool.

4. Melt the jam in a small pan, and brush over the top of the cooked pastry.

5. Lay the larger piece of pastry on the board, dust it lightly with flour and fold it, gently so that nothing sticks, in half lengthwise. Using a sharp knife, cut through the folded side of the pastry, at rightangles to the edge, in parallel lines, as though you were cutting between the teeth of a comb. Leave a margin uncut about 1in wide, all round the other edges, so that when you open up the pastry you will have a solid border.

6. Spread the apple all over the cooked piece of pastry, on top of the jam.

7. Now lay the cut pastry on top, and tuck the edges under. Brush the top layer carefully all over with milk (this is a bit messy as the apple keeps coming up between the pastry cuts, but don't worry). Sprinkle well with sugar.

8. Bake in the oven until well browned (about 20 minutes).

Serves 4

Chocolate Profiteroles

For the profiteroles:
3 egg quantity choux pastry
  (page 652)

For the filling and topping:

170g/6oz chocolate	570ml/1 pint whipped cream,
4 tablespoons water	sweetened with 1 tablespoon
15g/½oz butter	icing sugar

1. Set the oven to 200 C/400 F, gas mark 6.

2. Put small teaspoons of the choux mixture on a wet baking sheet, about 8cm/3in apart.

3. Bake for 20–30 minutes. The profiteroles should swell, and

become fairly brown. If they are taken out when only slightly brown they will be soggy when cool.

4. Make a hole the size of a pea in the side of each profiterole and return to the oven for 5 minutes to allow the insides to dry out. Cool on a wire rack.
5. When cold fill each profiterole with cream, using a forcing bag fitted with a small plain nozzle.
6. Melt the chocolate with the water and butter and stir, without boiling, until smooth and shiny.
7. Dip the tops of the profiteroles in the chocolate and allow to cool.

Note: If no piping bag for filling the profiteroles is available they can be split, allowed to dry out, and filled with cream or crème pâtissière when cold, and the icing can be spooned over the top. They are then messier to eat in the fingers, however.

Serves 4

Coffee Éclairs

3 egg quantity choux pastry
  (page 652)

For the filling and topping:

425ml/¾ pint double cream *or* crème pâtissière (page 535)	2 tablespoons very strong hot black coffee
225g/½lb icing sugar	

1. Heat the oven to 200 C/400 F, gas mark 6. Wet two baking sheets.
2. Make up the choux pastry.
3. Using a forcing bag with a 1cm/½in plain nozzle, pipe 5cm/2in lengths of choux pastry on to the baking sheets (keep them well separated as choux pastry swells during cooking). Bake for 25–30 minutes until hard and pale brown.
4. Make a pea-sized hole in each one with a skewer to allow

the steam to escape and return to the oven for 5 minutes to dry the insides out. Place on a wire rack to cool.

5. Whip the cream and put it (or the crème pâtissière) into a forcing bag fitted with a medium nozzle. Pipe cream into the éclairs through the hole made by the skewer, until well filled.
6. Mix the icing sugar and coffee together and beat with a wooden spoon until smooth. The mixture should be just runny.
7. Dip each éclair upside down into the icing so that the top becomes neatly coated.
8. Set aside to dry. Alternatively, the icing can be carefully spooned along the top ridge of each éclair.

Note: The éclairs may be split lengthwise when cooked, allowed to dry out, and filled with cream or crème pâtissière when cold. The tops are then replaced and the icing spooned over. They are then messier to eat in the fingers, however.

Serves 4

Deep-fried Profiteroles
(beignets soufflés)

3-egg-quantity choux pastry   Icing sugar, sifted
Oil for deep frying.
290ml/½ pint crème pâtissière
  (page 535)

1. Heat the oil in a deep fryer until a crumb will sizzle gently in it. Drop small teaspoonfuls of the choux mixture into the fat, one at a time, so that they do not stick together. Cook for about 8 minutes or until the balls are brown and crisp. Drain well.
2. Split open the profiteroles and fill with hot crème pâtissière. Dust with icing sugar and serve immediately.

Note I: A thin apricot glaze (see page 714) is delicious served as a hot sauce. A small teaspoon of not-too-sweet jam under the crème pâtissière is good too. If the apricot sauce is offered the crème pâtissière filling is not essential – the profiteroles may be served simply rolled in caster sugar.

Note II: The profiteroles may be served cold. In this event, cool them first, then filled with the chilled crème pâtissière.

Makes about 30

Gâteau St Honoré

110g/¼lb flour-quantity pâte sucrée (page 654)
3-egg-quantity choux pastry (page 652)

570ml/1 pint crème pâtissière (page 535, double quantity)
110g/¼lb sugar

1. Line an 18cm/7in flan ring with the pâte sucrée and bake it blind at 190°C/370°F, gas mark 5 for 20 minutes until biscuit-coloured.
2. Make the profiteroles: increase the oven temperature to 200°C/400°F, gas mark 6. Wet two baking sheets.
3. Put small teaspoonfuls of the choux mixture on to the baking sheets and bake for 25 minutes until hard and pale brown.
4. Make a pea-sized hole in each one with a skewer and return to the oven for 5 minutes to dry the insides out. Place on a wire rack to cool.
5. Using a forcing bag fitted with a plain nozzle, pipe the créme pâtissière into 17 even-sized profiteroles, piping the mixture through the previously made holes. Spread the remaining crème pâtissière into the bottom of the empty flan case.
6. Slowly heat the sugar in a heavy saucepan until it caramelizes to a pale liquid toffee.
7. Stand the caramel pan in warm water while you proceed: dip six profiteroles in the liquid caramel so that their tops are coated and put them straight into the flan on top of the crème pâtissiere, making sure the cooling caramel sticks them together. Keep dipping the remaining profiteroles in the

caramel, adding them to the original layer to make a pyramid – five in the next layer, three in the next, two in the next, and one on top. Pour any remaining caramel over the top.

Baking blind. See page 245

Note: Vast pyramids of profiteroles filled as here, or with whipped cream, form the traditional French wedding cake. Sometimes icing sugar is sifted over the whole creation.

Serves 6

Apple Strudel

225g/½lb flour-quantity strudel
    pastry (page 653), rolled and
    pulled to at least 40 × 60cm/
    15 × 24in

For the filling:

900g/2lb cooking apples	Pinch of ground cloves
Handful of currants, sultanas and raisins	3 tablespoons browned crumbs
	Rind and juice of ½ lemon
30g/1oz brown sugar	85g/3oz melted butter
½ teaspoon cinnamon	Icing sugar

1.   Heat the oven to 200°C/400°F, gas mark 6. Grease a baking sheet.
2.   Prepare the filling: peel, slice and core the apples and mix together with the dried fruit, sugar, spices, crumbs and lemon rind and juice.
3.   Flour a large tea-towel. Lay the pastry on this. If you have not got a big enough piece of pastry, several smaller ones will do but they must be overlapped well.
4.   Brush with butter. Spread the filling over the pastry evenly. Using the tea-towel to help, roll up as for a Swiss roll, trying to maintain a fairly close roll. Lift the cloth and gently tip the strudel on to the baking sheet. Brush with melted butter.
5.   Bake in the oven until a golden brown (about 40 minutes). Dust with icing sugar while still hot.

Note: In delicatessens strudels are generally sold in one-portion sizes. To make these you will need leaves of pastry about 22cm/ 9in sq. As they are easier to handle they can be lifted without the aid of the cloth – just flour the table-top to prevent sticking. Bake for 20 minutes.

Serves 6

Cherry Strudels

140g/5oz flour-quantity strudel
   paste (page 653)
340g/¾lb cherries, stoned
110g/¼lb sugar
Stick of cinnamon

290ml/½ pint water
55g/2oz butter, melted
2 tablespoons browned crumbs
Icing sugar

1. Make up the strudel paste.
2. Heat the oven to 200°C/400°F, gas mark 6. Grease a baking sheet.
3. Place the cherries with the sugar, cinnamon and water in a thick-bottomed pan and stew until just soft. Drain and allow to cool, removing the cinnamon.
4. Roll and pull the pastry into four paper-thin squares, each about 18 × 18cm/7 × 7in. (Follow the directions in the strudel paste recipe.) Put the squares on floured tea-towels.
5. Trim the edges, brush liberally with half the melted butter and sprinkle with crumbs. Put a quarter of the cherry mixture on each piece of pastry.
6. Fold the sides of the pastry over slightly to prevent the filling escaping during cooking, then, using the tea-towel to help, roll the strudels up.
7. Brush with the remaining melted butter. Bake for about 15 minutes until golden brown. Remove and immediately dust with icing sugar. Serve warm.

Serves 4

Almond Pastry Fruit Flan

110g/¼lb flour-quantity almond pastry (page 655)

For the glaze:
3 tablespoons apricot jam
Squeeze of lemon juice
1 tablespoon water

A selection of: oranges, pears, grapes, cherries, strawberries, bananas, apples, plums etc., depending on the season

1. Set the oven to 200°C/400°F, gas mark 6.
2. On a baking sheet roll or press the pastry into a 15cm/6in circle. Decorate the edges with a fork or the point of a sharp knife (pressed broad side into the pastry) or by pinching between fingers and thumb. Prick lightly all over.
3. Bake for about 15 minutes until a pale biscuit colour. Loosen with a palette knife and allow to cool slightly and harden on the baking sheet. Slip on to a wire rack to cool completely.
4. Meanwhile prepare the apricot glaze: melt the jam with the lemon juice and water. Boil up, sieve and keep warm until ready for use. Do not stir too much or the glaze will be bubbly.
5. Prepare the fruits as you would for a fruit salad, but leaving any that discolour (such as apples or pears) until you are assembling the flan.
6. Brush the pastry with apricot glaze (this helps to stick the fruit in place and prevents the pastry from becoming too soggy).
7. Arrange the fruit in neat overlapping circles, taking care to get contrasting colours next to each other. Brush with apricot glaze as you go, especially on apples, pears or bananas. When all the fruit is in place brush on the rest of the glaze.

Note: This flan should not be put together too far in advance as the pastry will become soggy in about 8 hours.

Serves 6

607

Pear Tart

110g/¼lb flour-quantity pâte
  sucrée (page 654)
290ml/½ pint crème pâtissière
  (page 535)

4 ripe (but not over-ripe) pears
Apricot glaze (page 714)

1. Roll out the pastry and line a flan ring or dish with it. Bake blind for 25 minutes or until pale biscuit-coloured and completely cooked. Allow to cool.
2. Spread the crème pâtissière into the pastry case.
3. Peel, halve and core the pears; arrange them neatly on top of the cream.
4. Brush quickly and thickly with apricot glaze. Avoid stirring the glaze as this makes it bubbly and murky – it should be clear.
5. Serve lukewarm or chilled.

Baking blind. See page 245

Serves 4

Tarte aux Abricots Bourdaloue

110g/¼lb flour-quantity
  pâte sucrée (page 654)

For the bourdaloue cream:
290ml/½ pint milk
2 egg yolks
55g/2oz caster sugar
15g/½oz flour
30g/1oz cornflour

2 tablespoons ground almonds
2 egg whites
2 tablespoons double cream
1 tablespoon kirsch (optional)

For the decoration:
140g/5oz sugar
290ml/10 fl.oz water

450g/1lb apricots

RICE PUDDING and BREAD AND BUTTER PUDDING. For criss-cross effect, overlap fingers of bread

SUMMER PUDDING and PREPARING A PINEAPPLE

COLD RASPBERRY SOUFFLÉ. To pipe evenly, hold bag upright

RHUBARB LATTICE FLAN

1. First prepare the pâte sucrée. Wrap up and leave to relax for at least 30 minutes in the refrigerator.

2. Now prepare the apricots: place the sugar and water together in a heavy pan and set over a gentle heat. Meanwhile halve the apricots and place them in the pan once the sugar has dissolved. Poach in the gently simmering sugar syrup until soft – be careful not to overcook them. Drain well and set the apricots and syrup aside.

3. Set the oven to 190°C/375°F, gas mark 5. Line an 18cm/7in flan ring with the pâte sucrée and bake blind until a pale biscuit colour (about 15 minutes). Remove the paper, blind beans and flan ring and bake for a further 5 minutes until the sides are evenly coloured. Slide on to a rack to cool.

4. To prepare the bourdaloue cream: scald the milk. Cream the egg yolks with half the sugar and when pale mix in the flours. Pour on the milk and mix well. Return the mixture to the pan and bring slowly to the boil, stirring continuously. (It will go alarmingly lumpy, but don't worry, keep stirring and it will get smooth.) Pour into a bowl. Allow to cool. Mix in the ground almonds and, if liked, add the kirsch.

5. Whisk the egg whites and when stiff add the rest of the sugar and whisk again until shiny. Stir in to the cool bourdaloue mixture. Add the lightly whipped cream.

6. To put the flan together: fill the bourdaloue cream into the flan case and spread it flat with a spatula or palette knife. Arrange the well-drained apricots over the cream so that the tart is completely covered. Boil up the sugar syrup in which the apricots were cooked until thick enough to form a thread when tested between finger and thumb. Cool. Brush over the apricots.

Baking blind. See page 245

Apple Flan Ménagère

110g/¼lb plain flour

Pinch of salt

55g/2oz soft butter cut into
little pieces

55g/2oz caster sugar

2 egg yolks

1 teaspoon grated lemon rind

For the filling and topping:

675g/1½lb medium-sized apples

Caster sugar

3 tablespoons warm apricot
glaze (page 714)

1. Make the pastry as follows: sift the flour on to a tabletop and make a hollow or well in the middle of the pile.
2. Place the remaining pastry ingredients in the well and with the fingertips of one hand only, combine the yolks, sugar, butter and rind into a smooth, soft paste. Gradually draw in the surrounding flour.
3. Knead quickly and lightly until you have a smooth paste. Wrap up and place in the refrigerator for 30 minutes.
4. Set the oven to 190°C/375°F, gas mark 5.
5. Roll out the pastry and line a 15cm/6in flan ring. Chill again for 10 minutes.
6. Bake blind for 10 minutes (see page 245).
7. Peel, quarter and core the apples. Using a stainless steel knife, thinly slice them into the flan ring. When the flan is nearly full arrange the apple slices very neatly in overlapping circles.
8. Dust well with caster sugar and bake in the oven for about 20 minutes.
9. Remove the flan ring and return to the oven for a further 7–8 minutes.
10. When the flan is cooked brush with apricot glaze and return to the oven for 5 minutes. Slide on to a wire rack to cool. Brush again with apricot glaze if necessary.

Serves 4

Strawberry Tartlets

170g/6oz flour-quantity
pâté sucrée (page 654)

For the filling:

225g/½lb petit Suisse cheese
55g/2oz caster sugar
450g/1lb strawberries, hulled

4 tablespoons redcurrant jelly,
melted

1. Set the oven to 190°C/375°F, gas mark 5.
2. Roll out the pastry thinly and use it to line the tartlet tins. Bake blind for about 15 minutes or until a pale biscuit colour. Remove the papers and the 'blind' beans. If the pastry is not quite cooked, return to the oven for 5 minutes. Carefully take out the pastry cases and leave to cool on a wire rack.
3. Cream the cheese with the caster sugar and place a teaspoonful of this mixture at the bottom of each case. Arrange the strawberries, cut in half if necessary, on top of the cheese and brush lightly with warm melted redcurrant jelly.

Baking blind. See page 245

Note: Whipped cream may be substituted for the cheese if preferred.

Makes 20

Peach Pastry Cake

70g/2½oz hazelnuts
85g/3oz butter
55g/2oz caster sugar
110g/¼lb plain flour

Pinch of salt
3 fresh peaches *or* 1 small can
290ml/½ pint whipped cream
Icing sugar

611

1. Toast the nuts in a hot oven. When brown rub in a dry cloth to remove the skins. Grind the nuts taking care not to overgrind them or they will be oily.

2. Beat the butter and when soft add the sugar and beat until light and fluffy.

3. Sift the flour with the salt and stir into the mixture with the nuts. Chill for 30 minutes.

4. Set the oven to 190°C/375°F, gas mark 5. Divide the paste into three and press out into thin flat rounds of 15cm/6in diameter. Place on baking sheets and bake for 10–12 minutes. Cut one into six portions before it cools. Allow to cool on a wire rack. They will become crisp as they cool.

5. Skin and slice the peaches or drain off the syrup. Mix the peach slices with the whipped cream. Using half this mixture as a filling, sandwich the two whole rounds of biscuit together. Spread the other half of the filling on the top.

6. Set the cut portions of biscuit into the cream mixture, placing each at a slight angle. Dust with icing sugar before serving.

Note: A more generous, 20cm/8in diameter gateau can be made by doubling all the quantities.

Serves 6

Doughnuts

225g/½lb plain flour	30g/1oz butter
Pinch of salt	150ml/¼ pint warm milk
2 egg yolks	Caster sugar flavoured with
7g/¼oz fresh yeast	cinnamon
45g/1½oz sugar	Fat for deep frying

1. Sift the flour with the salt and warm it in a low oven.
2. Cream the yeast with a teaspoon of the sugar.
3. In a warm bowl, rub the butter into the flour. Make a well in the centre.
4. Mix together the egg yolks, yeast mixture, remaining sugar and warm milk. Pour this into the well in the flour.
5. Using the fingertips of one hand mix the central ingredients together, gradually drawing in the surrounding flour. Mix until smooth.
6. Cover the bowl with a piece of greased polythene and leave to rise in a warm place for 45 minutes.
7. Knead the dough well for at least 10 minutes.
8. Roll out on a floured board to 1cm/½in thick. With a plain cutter press into small rounds.
9. Place on a greased tray and leave to prove until doubled in size.
10. Heat the fat until a crumb will sizzle vigorously in it.
11. Put the doughnuts into the fryer basket and lower into the fat.
12. Fry until golden brown, then drain on absorbent paper.
13. Toss in caster sugar and cinnamon.

Note I: To make a hole in the centre of the doughnuts, stamp out a 2·5cm/1in round from the flattened balls before proving.

Yeast: If using dried yeast see page 616

Makes 10

Rum Baba

For the sugar syrup:
170g/6oz loaf sugar
225ml/8 fl.oz water

2 tablespoons rum

Yeast mixture:
110g/¼lb plain flour
15g/½oz fresh yeast
15g/½oz caster sugar
3 tablespoons warm milk

2 egg yolks
Grated rind of ½ lemon
55g/2oz butter

For the decoration (optional):
Fresh fruit such as grapes and
  raspberries

150ml/¼ pint double *or*
  whipping cream

1. First make the sugar syrup: dissolve the sugar in the water and boil rapidly for 3 minutes. The syrup should be boiled to the 'thread' (when a little syrup is put between finger and thumb and the fingers are opened the syrup should form a short thread). Add the rum.
2. Now make the yeast mixture: sift the flour into a warmed bowl.
3. Mix the yeast with half a teaspoon of the sugar, 1 teaspoon of the flour and enough milk to make a batter-like consistency.
4. Whisk the egg yolks, remaining sugar and lemon rind until fluffy.
5. Clarify the butter: melt it slowly in a saucepan and strain through a folded J-cloth or muslin, leaving the sediment behind.
6. Make a well in the centre of the flour and add the yeast and beaten eggs. With your fingers mix together and gradually draw in the flour from the sides, adding more milk as you take in more flour. When all the flour has been incorporated beat with your hand until smooth.
7. Gradually add the clarified butter, kneading and slapping the dough until it looks like a very thick batter and no

614

longer sticks to the palm of your hand.

8. Cover and leave to rise in a warm place (e.g. the airing cupboard) for about 45 minutes. It should double in size.

9. Set the oven to 190 C/375 F, gas mark 5. Grease a 1 litre/ 1½ pint savarin (ring) mould with plenty of butter.

10. When the dough has risen beat it down again and fill into the mould. It should half fill the tin.

11. Cover and leave to prove (rise again) for 10–15 minutes in a warm place.

12. Bake in the oven for 30–35 minutes until golden brown.

13. Turn out on to a wire rack and while still warm prick with a toothpick and brush with plenty of rum syrup until the baba is really soaked and shiny. Put on a serving dish.

14. Serve plain or surround with fresh fruit and pile the whipped cream into the centre.

Yeast: If using dried yeast see page 616
Serves 4

Savarin aux Fruits

In the absence of a savarin mould use an ordinary cake tin. The fruit will then be piled on top of the cake.

For the savarin:

110g/¼lb plain flour	Grated rind of ½ lemon
7½g/¼oz fresh yeast	55g/2oz butter, softened
15g/½oz caster sugar	3 tablespoons lukewarm milk
2 egg yolks	

For the syrup:

170g/6oz loaf sugar	2 drops vanilla essence
225ml/8 fl.oz water	

For the fruit mixture:

(675–900g/1½–2lb in total)	oranges
bananas	apricots
cherries	apples
plums	pineapple
grapes	

615

To serve:
290ml/½ pint crème Chantilly
  (page 535)

1. Sift the flour into a warmed bowl. Mix the yeast with ½ teaspoon of sugar, add 1 teaspoon flour and enough milk (about 4 tablespoons) to give a batter-like consistency.
2. Whisk the egg yolks, sugar and lemon rind until fluffy.
3. Make a well in the centre of the flour and add the yeast and egg mixtures. Mix them together with the fingers of one hand, and then gradually draw in the flour from the sides, adding milk as you take in more flour. When all the flour has been incorporated beat with your hand until very smooth.
4. Gradually add the butter, kneading and slapping the dough until it looks like a thick batter, and no longer sticks to the palm of your hand.
5. Cover and leave to rise in a warm place for about 45 minutes. It should double in size.
6. Dissolve the sugar in water and boil rapidly for 2 minutes, or until syrupy. When cool add the vanilla essence.
7. Prepare the fruit as for a fruit salad and moisten with 1–2 spoons of the syrup.
8. Heat the oven to 190°C/375°F, gas mark 5. Butter a savarin or large ring mould thickly. When the dough has risen beat it down again and fill into the savarin mould. It should half fill the tin. Cover and leave to prove (rise again) for about 10–15 minutes in a warm place.
9. Bake in the oven for 30–35 minutes until a golden brown. Turn out on to a wire rack and while still hot prick all over with a toothpick and brush with plenty of warm sugar syrup.
10. Allow to cool. Put on a serving dish and again brush with syrup until the cake is completely soaked. Fill the centre with the fruit. Serve with Chantilly cream.

Note: If using dried yeast use half the amount called for, mix it with 3 tablespoons of the liquid (warmed to blood temperature) and a teaspoon of sugar. Leave until frothy, about 15 minutes, then proceed. If the yeast does not go frothy it is dead and unusable.

Serves 4

Orange and Grand Marnier Pancakes

8 French pancakes (page 659)
Grated rind of 1 large orange
290ml/½ pint crème pâtissière
  (page 535)

2 tablespoons Grand Marnier
Icing sugar

1. Heat the grill.
2. Mix the orange rind with the crème pâtissière and the Grand Marnier.
3. Divide the mixture between the pancakes.
4. Fold each pancake in half and dust heavily with icing sugar.
5. Place under a hot grill until the icing sugar begins to caramelize.

Note: May be served with more Grand Marnier poured over and flamed, if liked.

Serves 4

Crêpes Suzette

12 French pancakes
  (page 659)

For the orange butter:
85g/3oz unsalted butter
30g/1oz caster sugar
Grated rind of 1 orange
2 tablespoons orange juice
2 tablespoons orange Curaçao

To flame:
Caster sugar
2 tablespoons orange Curaçao
1 tablespoon brandy

1. Put the butter, sugar, orange rind, juice and Curaçao into a

large frying pan and simmer gently for 2 minutes.

2. Put a pancake into the frying pan and using a spoon and fork fold it in half and then in half again. Add a second pancake and repeat the process until the pan has been filled.

3. Sprinkle the pancakes with caster sugar and pour over the orange Curaçao and brandy. Light a match, stand back, and light the alcohol. Spoon it over the pancakes until the flames have died down. Serve immediately.

Serves 4–6

FRUIT PUDDINGS

Stewed Apples

170g/6oz sugar
570ml/1 pint water
450g/1lb dessert apples

Stick of cinnamon
Squeeze of lemon juice

To serve:
Cream (optional)

1. Dissolve the sugar in the water. When completely dissolved, boil rapidly until you have a thin syrup (3–4 minutes).
2. Peel, core and quarter the apples. Place them in the sugar syrup with the cinnamon.
3. Bring slowly to the boil, then reduce the heat and poach gently until the apples are tender.
4. Remove the apples with a draining spoon and arrange in a shallow dish.
5. Reduce the syrup rapidly by further boiling until it is tacky, then add the lemon juice. Pour over the fruit.
6. Serve hot with cream, or chilled with or without cream.

Serves 4

Blackcurrant Kissel

450g/1lb blackcurrants
Caster sugar to taste (about
170g/6oz)

2 teaspoons arrowroot

1. Wash the blackcurrants and remove the stalks.
2. Barely cover with water and add the sugar. Stew gently for about 20 minutes.
3. Mix a little cold water with the arrowroot and mix to a smooth paste.
4. To the arrowroot add a cupful of the boiling juice and mix thoroughly. Add the arrowroot mixture to the fruit, stirring, and allow to thicken. Simmer for 2–3 minutes.
5. Push the mixture through a nylon or stainless steel sieve. Stir and then pour into a serving bowl. Sprinkle evenly with caster sugar to prevent a skin forming.

Serves 4

Baked Apples

Smallish cooking apples
Brown sugar

Sultanas

1. Wash the apples and remove the cores with an apple corer. With a sharp knife cut a ring just through the apple skin round the fattest part of each apple.
2. Put the apples in a fireproof dish and stuff the centres with a mixture of brown sugar and sultanas.
3. In addition to this scatter a dozen or so sultanas for each apple over the top, and sprinkle 2 teaspoons of brown sugar over each apple. Then pour ½cm/¼in of water into the bottom of the dish.
4. Bake in a moderate oven (200°C/400°F, gas mark 6) for about

1 hour or until the apples are soft right through when tested with a skewer.

Green Fruit Salad

225g/½lb granulated sugar
570ml/1 pint water
Pared rind of 1 lemon
Green-coloured fresh fruit, e.g.:
  1 green dessert apple
  225g/½lb Chinese
    gooseberries

225g/½lb greengages
225g/½lb white grapes
  1 small ripe melon with green
    flesh
Juice of ½ lemon
2 tablespoons kirsch (optional)

1. Put the sugar and water on together to boil and add the lemon rind. Boil until the syrup feels tacky. Remove from the heat and allow to cool.
2. Do not peel the apple, but core it and cut into thin slivers. Put immediately into the syrup.
3. Peel and slice the gooseberries. Stone and quarter the greengages and halve and seed the grapes.
4. Using a melon baller, scoop the melon flesh into balls, or simply cut into even-sized cubes.
5. Put all this into the syrup and add the lemon juice, and kirsch if required. Chill well.

Serves 6–8

Red Fruit Salad

675g/1½lb assorted raspberries, strawberries, redcurrants, watermelon, plums *or* any fresh red fruit

425ml/¾ pint sugar syrup (page 536)
2 tablespoons kirsch (optional)

1. Check over the raspberries, discarding any bad ones.

2. Hull and halve the strawberries.
3. Wash, top and tail the redcurrants.
4. Cut the melon flesh into cubes, discarding the seeds.
5. Halve and stone the plums.
6. Put the fruit into a glass dish and add the syrup, and kirsch if required.

Serves 4

Pineapple in the Shell

1 large pineapple

1. Cut the top and bottom off the pineapple so that you are left with a cylinder of fruit. Do not throw away the leafy top. With a sharp knife cut round inside the skin, working first from one end and then from the other, so that you can push the fruit out in one piece. Try not to pierce or tear the skin.
2. Slice the pineapple very finely. Stand the pineapple skin in a shallow bowl, put the fruit back in it and replace the top. If the fruit is very sour, sprinkle sugar between the slices as you replace them. Kirsch can be sprinkled in too if liked.

Oranges in Caramel

1½ oranges per person
Caramel sauce (page 539)

1. With a potato peeler pare the rind of 1 or 2 oranges very finely, making sure that there is no pith on the back of the strips. Cut into very fine shreds.
2. Simmer these needleshreds in caramel sauce or sugar syrup until soft and almost candied. They should be very sticky and quite dark.

3. Peel the remaining oranges with a knife as you would an apple, making sure that all the pith is removed.
4. Slice each orange.
5. Place the oranges in a glass bowl and pour over the cold caramel sauce. Chill well.
6. Scatter with needleshreds of orange before serving.

Apricot Cheesecake

For the crust:

170g/6oz crushed digestive biscuits

85g/3oz melted butter
Pinch of cinnamon

For the filling:

15g/½oz gelatine
2 tablespoons water
1 small can apricots
225g/½lb soft cheese

150ml/¼ pint whipped cream
Rind and juice of ½ lemon
½ carton soured cream
Sugar to taste (about 45g/1½oz)

For decoration:

150ml/¼ pint whipped cream
3 apricot halves

Browned nibbed almonds

1. Place an oiled flan ring on a flat, lip-less baking sheet. Mix together the crust ingredients and put the mixture into the flan ring, pressing down firmly. Leave in the refrigerator for 20 minutes to harden.
2. Put the gelatine into a small pan with the water and set aside to soak.
3. Liquidize the apricots, reserving three halves for decoration. Beat the cheese until soft, then mix in all the other filling ingredients.
4. Melt the gelatine over a gentle heat until clear and warm. Pour this into the cheese mixture, stirring vigorously. Pile the filling into the flan ring and spread it flat with a palette knife. Leave in the refrigerator to set (about 3–4 hours).
5. To serve: with a sharp knife, loosen the flan ring from the

cheesecake and remove gently, being careful not to knock the edges. With two palette knives, or fish slices, carefully lift or slide the cake on to a serving dish. If this proves difficult, the biscuit base can be loosened by placing the baking sheet above a gentle heat for 30 seconds. Decorate the edges with rosettes of whipped cream and apricot quarters. Sprinkle nibbed almonds over the cream and serve.

Note: In the absence of a lip-less baking sheet use the back of a tray or roasting tin. The cake is easier to slide off a flat surface.

Serves 4

Pineapple and Date Salad

2 small pineapples   12 fresh dates

1. Cut the pineapples in half lengthwise, making sure that each half has an equal amount of green leaves. With a grapefruit knife carefully remove the flesh, leaving the shells intact. Cut the flesh into cubes. Halve and stone the dates.
2. Mix the dates with the pineapple, keeping back four or five for the top. Pile the mixture into the shells and put the reserved date-halves, shiny side up, on top.

Note I: Preserved dates are good too, though not as good as fresh ones.

Note II: If the pineapple is very sharp it may be sweetened with sifted icing sugar.

Serves 4

Bristol Apples

110g/¼lb sugar for the syrup   2 oranges
290ml/½ pint water   55g/2oz sugar for the caramel
4 dessert apples   Oil

1. Place the syrup's sugar and the water in a pan and set over a gentle heat until the sugar dissolves. Boil rapidly for 3 minutes.
2. Peel, quarter and core the apples and place in the sugar syrup. Simmer very gently until just tender. Remove the apples and allow them to cool.
3. With a sharp knife or potato peeler thinly pare the rind from 1 orange, taking care to pare rind only, leaving behind the bitter pith. Cut the rind into very fine even-sized needle-shreds. Put into the syrup and boil until thick and tacky.
4. Peel the oranges with a sharp knife as you would an apple, making sure that all the pith is removed. Cut into neat segments, discarding pips and membrane.
5. Put the caramel's sugar into a thick-bottomed pan and let it dissolve over heat, without stirring.
6. Meanwhile oil a baking sheet.
7. As the sugar bubbles it will become a dark golden colour. Pour this on to the oiled baking sheet and leave it to set into a thin layer like brown glass. When cold break into chips, and put somewhere cool and dry.
8. Arrange the apples and oranges in a glass bowl, pour over the sugar syrup and chill in the refrigerator. When ready to serve scatter over the broken caramel chips.

Serves 4

Yoghurt, Honey and Dates

Unsweetened natural yoghurt, very cold
Runny honey
Best dates, fresh *or* dried

Thick cream
Jordan almonds (shelled but with the inner, brown skin left on, i.e. unblanched)

1. For each person half-fill a pudding bowl or glass with yoghurt.
2. Stone the dates and chop them roughly. Put a few on the top of each helping of yoghurt.

3. Spoon a good dollop of thick cream over the top, then trickle over 1 teaspoon of runny honey.
4. If using the almonds scatter a few on now. (They may be used as well as, or instead of, the dates.)

Raspberry .and Almond Malakoff

170g/6oz caster sugar
170g/6oz unsalted butter
290ml/½ pint double cream
170g/6oz ground almonds

3 tablespoons kirsch
225g/½lb raspberries
1 large packet boudoir biscuits
  (sponge fingers)

1. Beat the sugar and butter until really fluffy, soft and white.
2. Whip the cream. Fold the ground almonds, then the kirsch, then the cream and finally the raspberries into the butter and sugar mixture.
3. Put an oiled circle of greaseproof paper (oiled side up) into the bottom of a 15cm/6in straight-sided cake tin or soufflé dish.
4. Line the sides with the biscuits, standing up round the edge. Spoon the mixture into the middle, pressing down gently and smoothing the top level.
5. Put into the refrigerator for 4 hours.
6. With a bread knife cut the tops of the biscuits to the level of the mixture. Turn the Malakoff out on to a serving plate. Remove the circle of paper.

Note: The top can be decorated with rosettes of whipped cream and a few fresh raspberries, but it looks very pretty without further adornment.

Serves 6

Pêches Cardinales

4 large peaches
570ml/1 pint sugar syrup
  (page 536), for unripe peaches
  only

290ml/½ pint Melba sauce
  (page 540)
About 30g/1oz blanched flaked
  almonds

625

1. Place the peaches in a pan of boiling water for 10 seconds and then remove the skins. If the peaches are unripe put them unskinned into the sugar syrup and allow it to boil up over them – this will prevent discolouring – then poach gently until tender (about 20 minutes), and skin.
2. Put the peaches, cooked or raw, on to a serving dish. Coat with Melba sauce and scatter over a few almonds.

Note: When peaches are out of season Japanese or South African canned whole white peaches can be used. They are not as good as fresh ones but very acceptable.

Serves 4

Greek Iced Fruit Salad

A selection of:
    cantaloupe melon
    red apples
    bananas
    black grapes
    oranges
    strawberries
    cherries
    etc.

Lemon juice
Crushed ice

1. Put all the fruit, unprepared, into the refrigerator for a few hours to chill well.
2. Prepare the fruit for eating with the fingers, i.e. peel the oranges and break into segments, picking off any pith. Wash, quarter and core the apples and slice, using a stainless steel knife. Break the grapes into bunches of three or four grapes each. Peel the bananas and cut into largish pieces. Cut the melon into quarters, remove the peel and cut the flesh into fingers. Leave the strawberries whole and unhulled, washing them only if they are sandy. Wash the cherries leaving the stalks on.

3. Arrange the fruit attractively on a very well chilled dish and sprinkle with lemon juice. Sprinkle with the ice just before serving.

Note I: Apples can of course be peeled. Shiny red ones look good unpeeled.

Note II: Fruit liable to discolour such as bananas, pears or apples should be cut up shortly before serving.

Note III: To crush ice cubes, put them in a stout plastic bag or cloth and beat with a rolling pin.

Summer Pudding

6 slices stale white bread
900g/2lb raspberries, redcurrants, blackcurrants *or* blackberries *or* a mixture of all

2 tablespoons water
170g/6oz sugar
Double cream

1. Lightly grease a pudding basin with butter and line it with pieces of crustless stale bread.
2. Cook the fruit gently in the water and sugar until soft but still bright in colour. Taste and add more sugar if necessary. While the fruit is still just warm pour it into the bread-lined basin, with the juice. Cover with a round piece of bread dipped on both sides in the juice. Stand the basin on a dish.
3. Press a saucer or plate with a 450g/1lb weight on it on top of the pudding. Leave in a cool place overnight. Remove the saucer and the weight and keep any juices that have been pressed out of the pudding.
4. Invert a serving dish over the bowl and turn both over together. Give a sharp shake and remove the bowl. Spoon over the reserved fruit juice. Serve with whipped cream.

Serves 4

Chinese Apple Fritters

450g/1lb sugar
150ml/¼ pint water
3 dessert apples
Lemon juice

85g/3oz cornflour
Oil for frying
2 tablespoons sesame seeds
1 teaspoon wine vinegar

1. Lightly oil a flat serving dish, or have ready a bowl of icy water.
2. Place the sugar and water together in a heavy pan and set over a gentle heat to dissolve without boiling.
3. Peel, core and quarter the apples. Cut into chunks. Sprinkle with lemon juice and roll in cornflour.
4. Put the oil on to heat.
5. Meanwhile toast the sesame seeds in a small heavy dry pan.
6. Deep fry the apples in hot oil for about 8 minutes until golden brown. Drain well on absorbent paper.
7. When the sugar has dissolved boil rapidly until the mixture caramelizes (goes toffee-brown) then add the vinegar, taking care as the mixture will splutter and sizzle.
8. Stir, then add the apples. Mix well and pour in the sesame seeds.
9. Turn on to the oiled serving dish, separating the apple chunks with two spoons – the toffee hardens as it cools and will stick the pieces together unless separated. An alternative method of serving this – and the usual Chinese method – is to dip each fritter into cold water to rapidly cool the caramel and harden it, and then to drain and serve them immediately.

Note: The fritters are easy enough to make but they require organization and timing. It is wise to assemble everything – oiled dish or bowl of icy water, caramel pan, deep-fryer, draining paper, bowl of cornflour, toasted sesame seeds etc. before starting.

Serves 6

ICE CREAMS

Vanilla Ice Cream
(made with a mousse base)

70g/2½oz caster sugar
8 tablespoons water
1 vanilla pod *or* 1 teaspoon
   vanilla essence

425ml/¾ pint double *or* single
   cream
3 egg yolks

1. Put the sugar and water into a saucepan and dissolve over a gentle heat.
2. Beat the egg yolks very well. Half whip the cream.
3. When the sugar has dissolved, bring the syrup up to boiling point and boil 'to the thread'. Allow to cool for 1 minute.
4. Whisk the egg yolks and gradually pour in the sugar syrup. Whisk until the mixture is thick and mousse-like.
5. Cool, whisking occasionally. Fold in the cream and freeze.
6. When the ice cream is half frozen, whisk again and return to the freezer.

To boil to the thread: To test, dip your finger into cold water, then into a teaspoon of the hot syrup, which should form threads between your thumb and forefinger when they are drawn apart.

Serves 4

Rich Vanilla Ice Cream

570ml/1 pint milk
290ml/$\frac{1}{2}$ pint single cream
225g/$\frac{1}{2}$lb caster sugar

8 egg yolks
Few drops vanilla essence

1. Set the freezer or ice compartment to coldest. Put the milk, cream and sugar into a heavy saucepan and bring slowly to the boil. Beat the yolks with the vanilla in a large bowl.
2. Pour the boiling milky mixture on to the yolks, whisking as you do so. Strain into a roasting pan or into two ice trays. Cool.
3. Freeze until solid but still soft enough to give when pressed with a finger.
4. Tip the ice cream into a cold bowl, break it up, then whisk with a rotary beater until smooth, pale and creamy. If you have a Magimix, all the better. Refreeze.

Note: If the ice cream is made more than six hours in advance it will be too hard to scoop. Put it in the refrigerator for 40–60 minutes before serving to allow it to soften.

Serves 6–8

Damson Ice Cream

450g/1lb damsons
340g/$\frac{3}{4}$lb caster sugar
150ml/$\frac{1}{4}$ pint water
2 large egg whites

Juice and finely grated rind of
1 small orange
290ml/$\frac{1}{2}$ pint double cream

1. Wash the damsons and put them, still wet, with 110g/$\frac{1}{4}$lb of the sugar in a thick-bottomed saucepan. Stew gently, covered, over very gentle heat or bake in the oven until soft and pulpy.
2. Push through a sieve removing the stones.
3. Dissolve the remaining 225g/$\frac{1}{2}$lb sugar in the water and bring to the boil.

630

4. Boil steadily for 5 minutes.
5. While the syrup is boiling beat the egg whites in an electric mixer or by hand until stiff. Pour the boiling syrup on to the egg whites, whisking as you do so. The mixture will go rather liquid at this stage but keep whisking until you have a thick meringue.
6. Stir in the orange rind and juice and the purée.
7. Whip the cream until thick but not solid and fold it into the mixture.
8. Freeze. It is not necessary to re-whisk the ice cream during freezing.

Note: The damson purée can be replaced by a purée of cooked plums, greengages, rhubarb, dried apricots or prunes, or a raw purée of soft fruit, apricots or peaches.

Serves 6–8

Coffee Ice Cream
(made with a custard base)

4 egg yolks
85g/3oz caster sugar
Pinch of salt

425ml/¾ pint single cream
5 teaspoons instant coffee

1. Whisk the egg yolks, sugar and salt until light and frothy.
2. Place the cream and coffee essence together in a pan and heat slowly until the coffee dissolves.
3. Add the cream to the egg-yolk mixture whisking all the time.
4. Pour the mixture into the top of a double saucepan or into a bowl set over a pan of simmering water.
5. Stir continuously until thick and creamy.
6. Strain into a bowl and allow to cool, whisking occasionally.
7. Chill, then freeze. (See notes on making ice cream, page 48ff.)
8. When the ice cream is half-frozen, whisk again and return to the freezer

Serves 4–6

Raspberry Ice Cream

(made with a mousse base)

450g/1lb raspberries
85g/3oz icing sugar
Squeeze of lemon
70g/2½oz sugar
110ml/4 fl.oz water

3 egg yolks
¼ litre/½ pint single *or* double cream
A little vanilla essence

1. Liquidize or crush the rasberries and push through a nylon or stainless steel sieve.
2. Sweeten with the icing sugar.
3. Place the 60g/2½oz sugar and the water into a saucepan and dissolve over a gentle heat.
4. When completely dissolved boil 'to the thread' (when a little syrup is put between finger and thumb and the fingers opened, it should form a sticky thread about 2cm/1in long).
5. Cool for 1 minute. Add the vanilla essence.
6. Pour the sugar syrup on to the egg yolks and whisk until the mixture is thick and mousse-like.
7. Cool and add the cream, fruit purée and lemon juice.
8. Taste for sweetness and add more icing sugar if necessary.
9. Chill. Freeze. (See notes on pages 48–51.)
10. If the ice cream is not quite smooth when half-frozen, whisk it once more and return to the freezer.

Serves 4–6

Chocolate Ice Cream

(made with a custard base)

340g/¾lb plain chocolate, cut up
570ml/1 pint milk
1 egg

1 egg yolk
55g/2oz caster sugar
570ml/1 pint double cream
1 teaspoon vanilla essence

1. Dissolve the chocolate in the milk over a gentle heat.
2. Beat the egg and yolk with the sugar until light and fluffy.
3. When the chocolate has melted and the milk nearly boiled pour on to the egg mixture and whisk well. Strain and allow to cool.
4. Whip the cream lightly and fold it into the chocolate mixture with the vanilla essence. Put into a bowl and freeze.
5. When half-frozen re-whisk and re-freeze.

Note: Chocolate mint crisps or mint cracknel, crumbled up and added to the mixture at the time of the final whisking, gives a delicious flavour and crunchy texture.

Serves 4

Pistachio Ice Cream in Biscuit Cups

For the biscuit mixture:
85g/3oz butter
85g/3oz caster sugar
3 egg whites
85g/3oz plain flour

For the ice cream:
570ml/1 pint milk
225g/½lb caster sugar
1 vanilla pod
290ml/½ pint single cream
8 egg yolks, beaten
110g/¼lb chopped pistachio
   nuts

For the sauce:
3 whole eggs
3 egg yolks
140g/5oz sugar
3 tablespoons Framboise
   liqueur
340g/¾lb fresh raspberries,
   sieved

1. Set the oven to 220°C/425°F, gas mark 7.
2. To make the biscuit cups melt the butter, add the sugar, stir until dissolved and allow to cool.
3. Gradually beat in the unwhisked egg whites, using a wire whisk. Fold in the sifted flour. Spread the mixture out in eight very large paper-thin rounds on a greased and floured

baking sheet. (Warm the sheet for easier spreading.)

4. Bake for 4 minutes. The biscuits should be just brown at the edges and pale in the middle.

5. While still hot and pliable shape the discs of biscuit over greased upturned jam jars. Remove the jam jars when the paste has set. (If the cups are not quite crisp when cold, return them to the oven on the jam jars.)

6. Make the ice cream: bring the milk, sugar, vanilla pod and cream very slowly to the boil. Pour on to the beaten yolks, stirring well. Remove the vanilla pod.

7. If the mixture is still very thin and runny return it to a gentle heat and stir continuously until it will coat the back of the spoon. Immediately pour into a cold bowl and allow to cool. Add the nuts.

8. Freeze, either in an ice cream maker, or in ice trays in the freezer, taking it out and beating two or three times during the freezing process to prevent large ice crystals forming.

9. When ready to serve fill each biscuit cup with ice cream, stand on a platter and put back into the coldest part of the refrigerator or into the freezer while making the sauce.

10. Whisk the whole eggs, yolks, sugar and liqueur together in a bowl. Then stand over a saucepan of simmering water and keep whisking. It will thicken like zabaglione. Stir in the sieved berries and serve, lukewarm, with the biscuit cups.

Serves 8

Redcurrant Water Ice

450g/1lb sugar
425ml/$\frac{3}{4}$ pint water

7g/$\frac{1}{4}$oz gelatine
425ml/$\frac{3}{4}$ pint redcurrant juice

1. Dissolve the sugar in the water over a low heat and when completely dissolved boil to the thread (i.e. when a little syrup is put between finger and thumb and the fingers opened, it should form a sticky thread 2·5cm/1in long).

2. In a small saucepan soak the gelatine in 2 tablespoons of redcurrant juice.

3. Add the rest of the juice to the sugar syrup.
4. Dissolve the gelatine over a low heat and when clear stir into the redcurrant mixture.
5. Allow to get quite cold.
6. Chill, then freeze. (See freezing notes.)

Serves 4

Lemon Sorbet

Pared rind and juice of 3 lemons
170g/6oz granulated sugar

570ml/1 pint water
½ egg white

1. Place the lemon rind, sugar and water together in a thick-bottomed saucepan. Dissolve the sugar over a gentle heat and when completely clear boil rapidly until you have a thick syrup (i.e. sufficiently thick for a thread to form between finger and thumb when the fingers are dipped in the syrup and then moved apart).
2. Allow to cool. When the syrup is cold add the lemon juice and strain.
3. Freeze for 30 minutes or until the syrup is beginning to solidify.
4. Whisk the egg white until stiff and fold into the lemon syrup mixture.
5. Freeze until solid.

Serves 4

Strawberry Sorbet

170g/6oz caster sugar
560ml/½ pint water
Juice of ½ lemon *or* ½ small orange.

340g/¾lb fresh or frozen strawberries
2 egg whites

1. Place the sugar and water together in a thick-bottomed saucepan. Dissolve over a gentle heat and when clear boil gently for 5 minutes. Add the lemon or orange juice and cool.
2. Liquidize or mash the strawberries to a pulp and add the syrup. Put in a bowl in the freezer for 30 minutes or until the syrup is beginning to solidify.
3. Whisk the egg whites until stiff and fold into the half frozen mixture. Return to the freezer until solid.

Serves 4

Passion Fruit Sorbet

170g/6oz granulated sugar
425ml/¾ pint water
Pared rind and juice of 1 lemon

450g/1lb passion fruit pulp
½ egg white

1. Dissolve the sugar in the water. Add the lemon rind. Boil rapidly for 5 minutes, or until the syrup is tacky.
2. Sieve the passion fruit and add to the syrup with the lemon juice. Cool.
3. Place in the deep freeze and leave until icy and half frozen.
4. Tip into a chilled bowl and whisk well. Refreeze until almost solid.
5. Whisk the egg white until very stiff.
6. Tip the sorbet into a chilled bowl again and break up. Whisk until smooth and fold in the egg white.
7. Freeze again until firm.
8. If the ice is not absolutely creamy and smooth give it one more freezing and whisking.

Serves 6

Black Cherry Frozen Dessert

1 can morello cherries
1 can raspberries

1 tablespoon brandy *or* kirsch
(optional)

110g/¼lb meringues (page 570)
570ml/1 pint double cream *or*
   675g/1½lbs vanilla ice cream
   (page 630)

Icing sugar to taste

For the sauce:
2 teaspoons arrowroot
1 tablespoon brandy *or* kirsch

1. Drain the cherries and raspberries well, reserving the juice. Chop them into small pieces. Break up the meringues roughly.
2. Whip the cream until stiff, add the liqueur and sweeten to taste. (If using ice cream allow it to soften but not to melt.) Mix in the chopped fruit, and meringues.
3. Spoon the mixture into a bombe mould or bowl and put immediately into the freezer. It will take at least 2 hours, and probably 4, to harden. It can then be turned out on to a plate and put back in the freezer until needed.
4. Mix the arrowroot with a little water. Heat the reserved cherry and raspberry juices together in a saucepan, pour some of the hot juice on to the arrowroot, stirring, and then pour the arrowroot and juice into the saucepan. Bring to the boil, stirring. Allow to simmer 1 minute after boiling. Add the brandy or kirsch and serve hot with the bombe.

Note: This dessert can be made with fresh or frozen strawberries, pineapple or peaches, but the fruit should be chopped rather than left whole or in large pieces.

Serves 8

Basic Bombe Filling

140g/5oz granulated sugar   5 egg yolks

1. Dissolve the sugar in 150ml/¼ pint water and when completely clear, boil to the thread. Allow to cool.
2. In a double saucepan or in a bowl over a pan of gently simmering water, beat the egg yolks until light. Gradually pour in the sugar syrup, whisking all the time until the mixture is thick and has doubled in bulk.

3. Remove from the heat and cool immediately by standing in a bowl of cold water while whisking until the mixture is cold.
4. Pour into the bombe and freeze for at least 12 hours.

To the thread: see page 629, *note.*

Makes about ½ litre/1 pint

Chocolate and Praline Bombe

Chocolate ice cream (page   Vanilla ice cream (page 630)
  632)   Praline (page 786.)

1. Read the instructions for making bombes on pages 88–9.
2. Pack the chocolate ice cream round the sides and bottom of the bombe mould or basin. Freeze.
3. Flavour the vanilla ice cream with praline and pack it into the middle of the bombe. Freeze.
4. Unmould and return to the freezer until needed.

Note I: A tablespoon or two of mincemeat, plus a tablespoon of brandy beaten into vanilla ice cream makes a good bombe filling. The outer layer of ice cream can be coffee, apricot or peach.

Note II: If you are not using a bombe mould but a pudding basin you may find that a vacuum is formed between the outer layer of ice cream and the bowl, which makes removing the bowl very difficult even if you dip it in hot water to ·melt the ice cream. The best thing to do is to prick the outer layer of ice cream with a hot fork before piling in the filling. A proper bombe mould has a screw at the top which when undone releases the vacuum and enables the bombe to slide out easily.

Serves 6

Chocolate and Vanilla Bombe

For this recipe a 860ml/1½ pint bombe mould is essential.

170g/6oz plain chocolate   450g/1lb vanilla ice cream
                                  (page 630)

1. Break up the chocolate and put it in a pudding basin. Set it over a saucepan of simmering water. Stir until the chocolate is smooth and melted. Do not overheat or the chocolate will lose its gloss.
2. Brush melted chocolate over the inside of the bombe mould. Leave to cool and harden. Repeat the process until you have a fairly thick layer and you have used up all the chocolate. Again leave to harden.
3. Pack the vanilla ice cream into the middle of the bombe and spread flat. Close the mould and freeze.
4. 30 minutes before serving put the bombe into the refrigerator, to soften slightly.
5. To serve, remove the base of the mould and unscrew the top (this releases a vacuum). Invert a plate over the mould and turn the mould and plate over together. Give a sharp shake and remove the mould.

Flaming Baked Alaska

1 round of whisked sponge   3 egg whites
  cake (page 671)   170g/6oz caster sugar
425ml/¾ pint vanilla ice cream   2 tablespoons rum
  (page 630)

1. Put the sponge cake on an ovenproof serving dish. Place the block of ice cream on it. Freeze at coldest temperature for at least 1 hour. Set the oven to 230°C/450°F, gas mark 8.
2. Whisk the egg whites and when they are very stiff, whisk in 2 tablespoons of the sugar. Continue to whisk until again

stiff and shiny. When the whisk is lifted the meringue mixture should stand in solid peaks – not moving at all. Fold in the remaining sugar.

3. Spoon into a forcing bag fitted with a fluted pipe. Pipe the meringue mixture over the entire surface of the cake, completely covering it and the ice cream.

4. Bake in the oven for 3 minutes until the meringue is browned. Just before the Alaska is to come out of the oven heat up the rum in a small pan. Remove the Alaska. Set the rum alight, pour around the pudding and serve while flaming.

Note I: This dish is sometimes called Norwegian Omelette. The above is the simplest recipe, but variations are legion. The cake may be sprinkled with liqueur, or replaced by shortcake or almond pastry. The ice cream can be any flavour, and jam or fresh fruit are sometimes included. The meringue can be flavoured with coffee or almond essence, it may have ground hazelnuts in it, or be sprinkled with almonds before baking.

Note II: The Alaska can be kept in the freezer, with the meringue covering, until the last minute – then baked from frozen.

Serves 6

COMPOSITE PUDDINGS

Coffee Rum Tipsy Cake

2 plain sponge cakes *or* 2 boxes small bought sponge cakes
150ml/¼ pint boiling water
3 heaped tablespoons instant coffee
4 tablespoons sugar
1 tablespoon rum

140g/5oz icing sugar
85g/3oz butter
290ml/½ pint double cream
55g/2oz whole blanched almonds

STRAWBERRY TARTLETS

STRETCHING STRUDEL PASTRY

PREPARING BRIOCHES

PLAITED BREAD

1. Break up the cakes roughly and put them in a large bowl.
2. Boil the water, pour on to the coffee and sugar, and stir until the sugar has dissolved.
3. Add the rum and pour over the cake. Do not mix it in too much (the cake should retain a 'marbled' look, half white, half brown) but turn with a metal spoon.
4. Press the cake into a mixing bowl, and leave it with a weight on top (a 1 kilo/2lb can of fruit standing on a side plate will do) while you make the icing.
5. Beat the icing sugar and butter together until very light and creamy.
6. Whip the cream until just firm enough to hold its shape.
7. Brown the nuts under the grill.
8. Unmould the cake on to a plate. Using a palette knife dipped in hot water, spread the butter icing over the cake.
9. Then spread a layer of whipped cream over the icing and stud with the almonds.

Serves 4

Chocolate Crumble Cake

85g/3oz dark chocolate
85g/3oz butter
45g/1½oz caster sugar
2 tablespoons golden syrup

340g/¾lb broken biscuits
85g/3oz glacé cherries
85g/3oz flaked almonds

1. Chop the chocolate and melt it slowly with the butter, sugar and syrup, stirring all the time.
2. Add the crushed biscuits, cherries and almonds.
3. Grease a sheet of greaseproof paper and the inside of a 20cm/8in flan ring.
4. Press the mixture on to the paper and flatten it, using the flan ring to get a round shape.
5. Allow to cool until set hard.
6. Cut into small slices.

Serves 4

Cannon-Ball Christmas Pudding

1 dessert apple
110g/¼lb self-raising flour
Pinch of salt
1 level teaspoon mixed spice
½ level teaspoon ground
  cinnamon
¼ level teaspoon ground
  nutmeg
225g/½lb shredded beef suet
225g/½lb fresh white
  breadcrumbs
340g/¾lb soft brown sugar
55g/2oz flaked almonds

225g/½lb seedless raisins
225g/½lb currants
225g/½lb sultanas
110g/¼lb chopped mixed peel
110g/¼lb prunes, soaked
2 tablespoons black treacle
3 eggs
290ml/½ pint stout *or* brown ale
  or milk
2 tablespoons rum (optional)
Grated rind and juice of 1
  lemon

To serve:
1 sprig of holly
Brandy *or* rum

Hard brandy sauce

1. Grate the apple, skin and all.
2. Sieve the flour, salt and spices into a large bowl. Add the suet, apple, and the other dry ingredients.
3. Heat the treacle until warm and runny. Mix all the liquids together (treacle, eggs, beer or milk, rum and lemon juice). Then add to the dry ingredients. Mix well – the mixture should fall off the spoon in large blobs.
4. Fill the mixture into a buttered 'freezing quality' polythene bag and tie the top. Put into a muslin cloth. Using strong string, tie up like Dick Whittington's bag.
5. Suspend this bag in a large pan of boiling water so that the whole pudding is submerged but not touching the bottom. (Use a really large saucepan with a wooden spoon laid across the top to tie the pudding strings to.)
6. Boil gently but steadily for 10 hours, topping the pan up with more boiling water as necessary.
7. Cool the pudding in the suspended position, with the water

poured away (cooling it on a plate would spoil its cannon-ball shape).

8. Hang in a cool place until needed.
9. To reheat: replace the buttered polythene bag with a fresh one, wrap in a cloth again, suspend in the saucepan as before and repeat the boiling process for 3 hours.
10. Unwrap with care. Dish the pudding, best and smoothest side up. Stick in a sprig of fresh holly.
11. Slightly warm a small ladle of brandy or rum, set it alight and pour it flaming over the pudding. The holly will crackle and splutter, drawing the attention of the diners to the burning pudding.

Note: This pudding may be steamed or boiled in the usual way in two 1 litre/2 pint basins or one 2 litre/4 pint. Two smaller basins will require 6 hours' cooking and 2 hours' reheating, the larger one 10 hours' cooking and 3 hours' reheating.

Serves 12

Trifle

1 sponge cake, preferably stale
Raspberry jam
4 tablespoons sherry
2 tablespoons brandy
425ml/$\frac{3}{4}$ pint milk
2 tablespoons sugar
5 egg yolks
2 drops vanilla essence

290ml/$\frac{1}{2}$ pint double cream
30g/1oz split blanched almonds
6 glacé cherries
Angelica (optional)
A few ratafia biscuits (optional)

1. Cut the sponge cake into thick pieces. Spread each piece sparingly with jam. Pile them into a glass dish.
2. Pour over the sherry and brandy and leave to soak while you prepare the custard.
3. Put the milk and sugar into a saucepan and bring to the point of boiling.
4. In a large bowl, lightly beat the yolks with a fork. Pour the

scalding milk on to them, stirring with a wooden spoon.

5. Return the mixture to the saucepan and reheat carefully, stirring all the time, until it thickens enough to coat the back of the spoon. Care must be taken not to boil the custard, lest it curdle. Add the vanilla.

6. Strain on to the cake and leave to get quite cold.

7. Whip the cream until fairly stiff and spread or pipe over the trifle.

8. Decorate with the almonds, glacé cherries, angelica cut into diamond-shapes, and ratafia biscuits.

Note I: A perfectly acceptable quick custard can be made more simply by first making a very thin custard with custard powder, and then pouring this boiling custard from a height on to the egg yolks, stirring continuously. Alternatively the milk can be thickened with a level tablespoon of cornflour, and then poured on to the egg yolks. The inclusion of the egg yolks is desirable, however.

Note II: A fruit trifle is made by adding cooked or raw fruits before pouring on the custard. The use of jelly is abominable.

Serves 4

7
Pastry, Pasta
and Batters

Shortcrust Pastry

170g/6oz plain flour
Pinch of salt
30g/1oz lard

55g/2oz butter
Very cold water

1. Sift the flour with the salt.
2. Rub in the fats until the mixture looks like breadcrumbs.
3. Add 2 tablespoons of water to the mixture. Mix to a firm dough – first with a knife, and finally with one hand. It may be necessary to add more water, but the pastry should not be too damp. (Though crumbly pastry is more difficult to handle, it produces a shorter, less tough result.)
4. Chill, wrapped, for 30 minutes before using. Or allow to relax after rolling out but before baking.

Rich Shortcrust Pastry

170g/6oz plain flour
Pinch of salt
100g/3½oz butter

1 egg yolk
Very cold water

1. Sift the flour with the salt.

2. Rub in the butter until the mixture looks like breadcrumbs.
3. Mix the yolk with 2 tablespoons of water and add to the mixture.
4. Mix to a firm dough – first with a knife, and finally with one hand. It may be necessary to add more water, but the pastry should not be too damp. (Though crumbly pastry is more difficult to handle, it produces a shorter, less tough result.)
5. Chill, wrapped, for 30 minutes before using, or allow to relax after rolling out but before baking.

Suet Pastry

(And how to line a pudding basin)

Butter for greasing
340g/¾lb self-raising flour
Salt

170g/6oz shredded beef suet
Water to mix

1. Grease a pudding basin.
2. Sift the flour with a good pinch of salt into a bowl. Rub in the shredded suet and add enough water to mix, first with a knife, and then with one hand, to a soft dough.
3. On a floured surface roll out two-thirds of the pastry into a round about 1cm/½in thick. Sprinkle the pastry evenly with flour.
4. Fold the round in half and place the open curved sides towards you.
5. Shape the pastry by rolling the straight edge away from you and gently pushing the middle and pulling the sides to form a bag that, when spread out, will fit the pudding basin.
6. With a dry pastry brush remove all excess flour and place the bag in the well-greased basin.
7. Fill the pastry bag with the desired mixture.
8. Roll out the remaining piece of pastry and use it as a lid, damping the edges and pressing them firmly together.

9. Cover the basin with buttered greaseproof paper, pleated in the centre and a layer of pleated tin foil. (Pleating the paper and foil allows the pastry to expand slightly without bursting the wrappings.) Tie down firmly to prevent water or steam getting in during cooking.

Note: Occasionally suet pastry is used for other purposes than steamed puddings, in which case it should be mixed as above and then handled like any other pastry, except that it does not need to relax before cooking.

Wholemeal Pastry

140g/5oz butter
110g/¼lb wholemeal flour
110g/¼lb plain flour
Pinch of salt
1 egg yolk
Water

1. Rub the butter into the flours and salt until the mixture looks like coarse breadcrumbs.
2. Mix the yolk with 2 tablespoons of water and add to the mixture.
3. Mix to a firm dough – first with a knife and then with one hand. It may be necessary to add more water, but the pastry should not be too damp. (Although crumbly pastry is more difficult to handle, it produces a shorter, less tough result.)
4. Chill in the refrigerator for at least 30 minutes before using, or allow the rolled-out pastry to relax before baking.

Note I: To make sweet wholemeal pastry mix in two level tablespoons of sugar once the fat has been rubbed into the flour.

Note II: All wholemeal flour may be used if preferred.

Rough-Puff Pastry

225g/½lb plain flour
Pinch of salt
140g/5oz butter
Very cold water

1. Sift the flour and salt into a cold bowl. Cut the butter into knobs about the size of a sugar lump and add to the flour. Do not rub in but add enough water to just bind the paste together. Mix first with a knife, then with one hand.

2. Wrap the pastry up and leave to relax for 10 minutes in the refrigerator.

3. On a floured board, roll the pastry into a strip about 15cm × 10cm (6in × 4in). This must be done carefully: with a heavy rolling pin press firmly on the pastry and give short sharp rolls until the pastry has reached the required size. The surface of the pastry should not be over-stretched and broken.

4. Fold the strip into three and turn so that the folded edge is to your left, like a closed book.

5. Again roll out into a strip 1cm/$\frac{1}{2}$in thick. Fold in three again and leave, wrapped, in the refrigerator for 15 minutes.

6. Roll and fold the pastry as before then chill again for 15 minutes.

7. Roll and fold again, by which time the pastry should be ready for use, with no signs of streakiness.

8. Roll into the required shape.

9. Chill again before baking.

Flaky Pastry

225g/$\frac{1}{2}$lb plain flour   85g/3oz lard
Pinch of salt   150ml/$\frac{1}{4}$ pint cold water
85g/3oz butter

1. Sift the flour with a pinch of salt. Rub in half the butter. Add enough cold water to mix with a knife to a doughy consistency. Turn out on to a floured board and knead until smooth.

2. Roll into an oblong about 12 × 25cm/5 × 10in. Cut half the lard into tiny pieces and dot them evenly all over the top two-thirds of the pastry, leaving a good margin.

3. Fold the pastry in three, folding first the unlarded third

up, then the larded top third down and pressing the edges to seal them. Give a 90 anti-clockwise turn so that the folded closed edge is to your left.

4. Repeat the rolling and folding process (without adding any fat) once more so that the folded, closed edge is on your left.
5. Roll out again, dot with butter as before, fold and seal as before.
6. Roll out again, dot with the rest of the lard, fold, seal and roll once more.
7. Fold, wrap the pastry and 'relax' (or chill) for 10–15 minutes.
8. Roll and fold once again (without adding any fat) and then use as required.

Note I: As a general rule flaky pastry is rolled out thinly, and baked at about 220 C/425 F, gas mark 7.

Note II: If the pastry becomes too warm or sticky and difficult to handle, wrap it up and chill it for 15 minutes before proceeding.

Puff Pastry

225g/½lb plain flour   150ml/¼ pint icy water
Pinch of salt   140–200g/5–7oz butter
30g/1oz lard

1. If you have never made puff pastry before use the smaller amount of butter: this will give a normal pastry. If you have some experience more butter will produce a lighter, very rich pastry.
2. Sift the flour with a pinch of salt. Rub in the lard. Add the icy water and mix with a knife to a doughy consistency. Turn on to the table and knead quickly until smooth. Wrap in polythene or a cloth and leave in the refrigerator for 30 minutes to relax.
3. Lightly flour the table-top or board and roll the dough into a rectangle about 13 × 25cm/5 × 10in.
4. Tap the butter lightly with a floured rolling pin to get it into

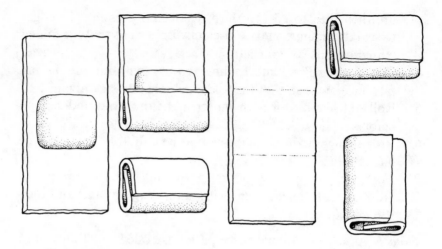

a flattened block about 10 × 8cm/4 × 3in. Put the butter on the rectangle of pastry and fold both ends over to enclose it. Press the sides together to prevent the butter escaping.

5. Now tap the pastry parcel with the rolling pin to flatten the butter a little; then roll out, quickly and lightly, until the pastry is three times as long as it is wide. Fold it very evenly in three, first folding the third closest to you over, then bringing the top third down. Give it a 90° anti-clockwise turn so that the folded, closed edge is on your left. Again press the edges firmly with the rolling pin. Then roll out again to form a rectangle as before.

6. Now the pastry has had two rolls and folds, or 'turns' as they are called. It should be put to rest in a cool place for 30 minutes or so. The rolling and folding must be repeated twice more, the pastry again rested, and then again given two more 'turns'. This makes a total of six. If the butter is still very streaky, roll and fold it once more.

Bouchée Cases

225g/½lb flour-quantity puff Beaten egg
 pastry (page 649)

1. Set the oven to 220 C/425 F, gas mark 7.
2. Roll out the pastry to 0·5cm/¼in. With a round pastry cutter stamp it out in rounds. With a slightly smaller cutter cut a circle in the centre of each round, but be careful not to stamp the pastry more than half-way through.
3. Brush the tops with beaten egg, taking care not to get egg on the sides, which would prevent the pastry layers separating and rising.
4. Bake on a wet baking sheet until brown and crisp; about 12 minutes.
5. Take off the pastry 'lids' and scrape out any raw pastry left inside. Return the bouchée cases to the oven for 4 minutes to dry out. Cool on a wire rack.

Note: Bouchée cases, if they are to be eaten hot, should either be filled while they are still very hot with a cooked hot filling, or (if they are cooked and cold) with a cooked cold filling. Hot fillings will tend to make the pastry soggy during the re-heating process. If both filling and pastry go into the oven cold the pastry will have time to become crisp again before the filling is hot.

Makes about 20 cocktail-size bouchées

Vol-au-vent

225g/½lb flour-quantity   Beaten egg
  puff pastry (page 649)   Salt

1. Set the oven to 220 C/425 F, gas mark 7.
2. Roll the pastry to 1cm/½in thickness and cut into a round about the size of a dessert plate. Place on a wet baking sheet. Using a cutter half the size of the pastry round cut into the centre of the pastry, but taking care not to cut right through to the baking sheet.
3. Flour the blade of a knife and use this to 'knock up' the sides of the pastry: try to slightly separate the leaves of the pastry horizontally; this means that the edge will flake readily when

cooking. (It counteracts the squashing effect of the cutter used to cut out the round, which may have pressed the edges together, making it more difficult for the pastry to rise in even layers.)

4. With the back of the knife-blade make a star pattern on the borders of the vol-au-vent case and mark a lattice pattern on the inner circle. (The back rather than the sharp edge of the blade is used as this will not cut into the pastry – the idea is to make a pattern without cutting through the surface of the pastry.)

5. Mix a pinch of salt into the beaten egg. Brush the pastry carefully with this eggwash avoiding the knocked up sides – if they are covered with egg the pastry will be prevented from rising.

6. Bake in a hot oven for 30 minutes, and carefully lift off the top of the inner circle. Keep this for the lid of the case when filled. Pull out and discard any partially cooked pastry from the centre of the case.

7. Return the case to the oven for 2 minutes to dry out. The vol-au-vent is now ready for filling. Ideally the heated pastry case is filled with hot filling, and then served.

Note I: The above quantity of pastry will make two smaller (saucer-size) vol-au-vents.

Note II: Flaky or rough-puff pastry are also suitable. But the method of cutting is different: cut the pastry into two rounds the size of a side-plate. Stamp a circle right out of the centre of one of them. Brush the uncut round with egg and place the ring of pastry on top. Bake the middle small round of pastry too, and use it as a lid.

Choux Pastry

85g/3oz butter
220ml/7½fl.oz water
105g/3¾oz plain flour, well
   sifted

Pinch of salt
3 eggs

1. Put the butter and water together in a heavy saucepan. Bring slowly to the boil so that by the time the water boils the butter is completely melted.
2. *Immediately* the mixture is really boiling fast, tip in all the flour and draw the pan off the heat.
3. Working as fast as you can, beat the mixture hard with a wooden spoon: it will soon become thick and smooth and leave the sides of the pan. Beat in the salt.
4. Stand the bottom of the saucepan in a basin or sink of cold water to speed up the cooling process.
5. When the mixture is cool, beat in the eggs a little at a time until it is soft, shiny and smooth. If the eggs are large it may not be necessary to add all of them. The mixture should be of dropping consistency – not too runny. ('Dropping consistency' means that the mixture will fall off a spoon rather reluctantly and all in a blob – if it runs off it is too wet, if it will not fall off even when the spoon is slightly jerked, it is too thick.)
6. Use as required.

Strudel Pastry (or Filo Pastry)

285g/10oz plain flour   150ml/$\frac{1}{4}$ pint water
Pinch of salt   1 teaspoon oil
1 egg

1. Sift the flour and salt into a bowl.
2. Beat the egg and add the water and oil. First with a knife and then with one hand mix the water and egg into the flour, adding more water if necessary to make a soft dough.
3. The paste now has to be beaten: lift the whole mixture up in one hand and then with a flick of the wrist throw it on to a lightly floured board. Continue doing this until the paste no longer sticks to your fingers and the whole mixture is smooth and very elastic. Put it into a clean floured bowl. Cover and leave in a warm place for 15 minutes.

4. The pastry is now ready for rolling and pulling. To do this, flour a tea towel or large cloth on a table-top and roll out the pastry as thinly as you can. Now put your hand (well floured) under the pastry and, keeping your hand fairly flat, gently stretch and pull the pastry, gradually and carefully working your way round until the paste is paper thin. (You should be able to see through it easily.) Trim off the thick edges.

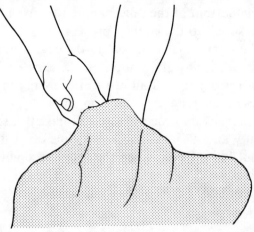

5. Use immediately – strudel pastry dries out and cracks very quickly. Brushing with melted butter or oil helps to prevent this. Or the pastry sheets may be kept covered with a damp cloth.

Note: If the paste is not for immediate use wrap it well and keep refrigerated (for up to three days) or frozen. Flour the pastry surfaces before folding up. This will prevent sticking.

Makes 450g/1lb pastry

Pâte Sucrée

170g/6oz plain flour
A pinch of salt
85g/3oz butter, softened

3 egg yolks
85g/3oz sugar
2 drops vanilla essence

1. Sift the flour on to a board with a pinch of salt. Make a large

well in the centre and put the butter in it. Place the egg yolks and sugar on the butter with the vanilla essence.

2. Using the fingertips of one hand mix the butter, yolks and sugar together. When mixed to a soft paste draw in the flour and knead until the pastry is just smooth.

3. If the pastry is very soft chill before rolling or pressing out to the required shape. In any event the pastry must be allowed to relax for 30 minutes either before or after rolling out, but before baking.

Almond Pastry (*Pâte Frolle*)

Care must be taken when making this because if it is overkneaded the oil will run from the almonds resulting in an oily paste.

110g/¼lb plain flour
Pinch of salt
45g/1½oz ground almonds
45g/1½oz caster sugar

1 egg yolk *or* ½ beaten egg
2 drops vanilla essence
85g/3oz butter, softened

1. Sift the flour with the salt on to a board or table-top. Scatter over the ground almonds. Make a large well in the centre and put in the sugar, beaten egg or yolk and vanilla essence.

2. Using one hand only mix the egg and sugar with your fingertips. When creamy add the softened butter and continue to mix, gradually drawing in the flour and almonds.

3. Knead gently to a paste and chill. Allow to relax for 30 minutes before baking.

Pâte à Pâté

285g/10oz plain flour
½ teaspoon salt
200g/7oz butter

2 egg yolks
Up to 3 tablespoons water

1. Sift the flour on to the table-top. Make a large well in the centre and put the butter and yolks in it. Work the yolks and butter together with the fingers of one hand and gradually draw in the surrounding flour, adding the water only if required to give a soft malleable, but not sticky paste.
2. Wrap and leave to rest in the refrigerator for 30 minutes. Use as required.

Hot Watercrust Pastry
(and how to mould)

225g/½lb plain flour
½ teaspoon salt
1 beaten egg

100ml/3½ fl.oz water
38g/1¼oz butter
38g/1¼oz lard

1. Wrap a piece of greaseproof paper around the outside of a wide jar or small straight-sided saucepan. The paper can be held in position by tucking it in the opening of the jar or saucepan. Leave it upside down while you make the pastry.
2. Sift the flour and salt into a bowl. Make a dip in the middle of it, break the egg into it and toss a liberal covering of flour over the egg.
3. Put the water, butter and lard into a saucepan and bring slowly to the boil.
4. Once the liquid is boiling pour it on to the flour, mixing with a knife as you do so. Knead until all the egg streaks have gone and pastry is smooth.
5. Wrap in a piece of polythene and leave at room temperature for 30 minutes.
6. Reserve about a third of the paste for the lid, keeping it covered or wrapped and in a warm place. Roll out the remaining paste to a round and drape it over the jar or saucepan. Working fast, shape the pastry to cover the jar or saucepan to a depth of about 7cm/2¾in. Leave to chill in the refrigerator.

7. As the pastry cools it will harden. When hard turn the jar or saucepan over and remove it carefully, leaving the grease-proof paper inside the pastry case. Carefully draw the paper away from the pastry and when it is all loosened take it out. Stand the pastry case on a baking sheet and fill as required. Use the reserved third of the pastry to make the lid, wetting the rim of the pie case to make it stick down well. Bake as required.

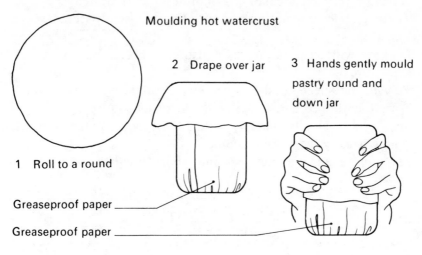

Moulding hot watercrust

1 Roll to a round

2 Drape over jar

3 Hands gently mould pastry round and down jar

Greaseproof paper

Greaseproof paper

Egg Pasta

450g/1lb strong flour	1 tablespoon oil
Pinch of salt	3–4 tablespoons water
4 eggs	

1. Sift the flour and salt on to a wooden board. Make a well in the centre and drop in the eggs, oil and water.
2. Using the fingers of one hand mix together the eggs, oil and water and gradually draw in the flour. The mixture should be a very stiff dough.
3. Knead until smooth and elastic (about 15 minutes). Wrap in polythene and leave to relax in a cool place for 1 hour.
4. Roll one small piece of dough out at a time until paper

thin. Cut into the required sized noodles.

5. Allow to dry (except ravioli) hanging over a chair back if long noodles, lying on a wire rack or dry tea-towel if small ones, for at least 30 minutes before boiling. Ravioli is dried after stuffing.

The commonest noodle shapes are:

Cannelloni: rectangles about the size of a side-plate. Generally stuffed (like a pancake) after boiling, then reheated.

Tagliatelle (fettucine): thin ribbons of pasta, usually served with a sauce.

Lasagne: wide strips usually used in alternate layers with a savoury mixture.

Ravioli: flat sheets used to form small stuffed envelopes, which are then boiled and served with or without sauce.

Spaghetti: originally made by pulling the dough into thin strands, now usually made by machine.

Macaroni: made commercially into short tube-like pieces.

Green Pasta

225g/$\frac{1}{2}$lb fresh spinach   2 eggs
340g/$\frac{3}{4}$lb strong flour   1 tablespoon cream
Pinch of salt

1. Wash the spinach well, remove the stalks and put into a pan without water. Add a sprinkling of salt. Cover and cook, shaking the pan, until tender (5–7 minutes). Drain well, pressing out all the water. Chop or liquidize it and push through a sieve to get a fairly dry paste.

2. Sift the flour and salt on to a wooden board. Make a well in the centre and in it put the eggs, spinach and cream. Using the fingers of one hand mix together the eggs, spinach and cream, gradually drawing in the flour. The mixture should be a stiff dough.

3. Knead until smooth and elastic (about 15 minutes). Wrap in polythene and leave to relax in a cool place for 1 hour.

4. Roll one small piece of the dough out at a time until paper

thin. Cut into the required size. Allow to dry (hanging over a chair back if long noodles, or lying on a wire rack or clean tea-towel if small) for at least 30 minutes before cooking.

French Pancakes (Crêpes)

110g/¼lb plain flour
Pinch of salt
1 egg
1 egg yolk

290ml/½ pint milk *or* milk and
  water mixed
1 tablespoon oil
Oil for frying

1. Sift the flour and salt into a bowl and make a well in the centre exposing the bottom of the bowl.
2. Into this well place the egg and egg yolk with a little of the milk.
3. Using a wooden spoon or whisk mix the egg and milk and then gradually draw in the flour from the sides as you mix.
4. When the mixture reaches the consistency of thick cream beat well and stir in the oil.
5. Add the rest of the milk—the consistency should now be that of thin cream. (Batter can also be made by placing all the ingredients together in a liquidizer for a few seconds, but take care not to over-whizz or the mixture will be bubbly.)
6. Cover the bowl and refrigerate for about 30 minutes. This is done so that the starch cells will swell, giving a lighter result.
7. Prepare a pancake pan or frying pan by heating well and wiping out with oil. Pancakes are not fried in fat like most foods – the purpose of the oil is simply to prevent sticking.
8. When the pan is ready, pour in about 1 tablespoon of batter and swirl about the pan until evenly spread across the bottom.
9. Place over heat and, after 1 minute, using a palette knife and your fingers, turn the pancake over and cook again until brown. (Pancakes should be extremely thin, so if the first one is too thick, add a little extra milk to the batter. The

first pancake is unlikely to be perfect, and is often discarded.)
10. Make up all the pancakes, turning them out on to a tea-towel or plate.

Note I: Pancakes can be kept warm in a folded tea-towel, on a plate over a saucepan of simmering water, in the oven, or in a warmer. If allowed to cool, they may be reheated by being briefly returned to the frying pan or by warming in an oven.

Note II: Pancakes freeze well, but should be separated by pieces of greaseproof paper. They may also be refrigerated for a day or two.

Makes about 12

Fritter Batter

125g/4½oz plain flour   1 tablespoon oil
Pinch of salt   280ml/8–10 fl.oz milk
2 eggs

1. Sift the flour with the salt into a bowl.
2. Make a well in the centre, exposing the bottom of the bowl.
3. Put 1 whole egg and 1 yolk into the well and mix with a wooden spoon or whisk until smooth, gradually incorporating the surrounding flour and the milk. A thick creamy consistency should be reached.
4. Add the oil. Allow to rest for 30 minutes.
5. When ready to use the batter whisk the egg white until stiff but not dry. Fold it into the batter with a metal spoon. Use the batter to coat the food and fry immediately.

Note: If the batter is wanted for sweet fritters (say apple or pineapple) add 2 teaspoons of caster sugar.

Waffles

2 eggs
170g/6oz plain flour
Pinch of salt
3 level teaspoons baking
  powder

30g/1oz caster sugar
290ml/½ pint milk
55g/2oz butter, melted
Vanilla essence
Extra melted butter

To serve:
Butter
Honey, maple syrup *or* jam

1. Separate the eggs.
2. Sift the flour, salt, baking powder and sugar together. Make a well in the centre and drop in the egg yolks.
3. Stir the yolks, gradually drawing in the flour from the edges and adding the milk and melted butter until you have a thin batter. Add the vanilla essence.
4. Grease a waffle iron and heat it up.
5. Whisk the egg whites until stiff but not dry and fold into the batter.
6. Add a little melted butter to the hot waffle iron, pour in about 4 tablespoons of the mixture, close and cook for 1 minute per side.
7. Serve hot with butter and honey, maple syrup or jam.

Note: The first waffle always sticks to the iron.

Makes 10

Scotch Pancakes or Drop Scones

225g/½lb plain flour
½ teaspoon salt
½ teaspoon bicarbonate of soda
½ teaspoon cream of tartar

2 tablespoons golden syrup
½ a beaten egg
290ml/½ pint milk

To serve:
Butter
Jam

1. Sift together the flour, salt, bicarbonate of soda and cream of tartar.
2. Make a well in the centre of the mixture and into it pour the syrup and half the milk.
3. Beat the syrup and milk, gradually drawing in the flour from the sides of the bowl.
4. Add the egg and beat well.
5. Stir in more milk until the batter is the consistency of thick cream and will just run from a spoon. Cover and leave to stand for 10 minutes.
6. Meanwhile grease a heavy frying pan or girdle iron and heat it. When really hot, drop 2 or 3 spoonfuls of batter on to the surface, keeping them well separated.
7. Cook for 2–3 minutes. When the undersides of the pancakes are brown, bubbles have risen to the surface and the pancakes can be lifted with a fish-slice, turn over and brown the other side.
8. Serve hot or cold with butter and jam.

Makes 20

8
Baking

CAKES

Lemon Victoria Sponge

Oil *or* melted lard for preparing
  the cake tins
170g/6oz butter
170g/6oz sugar

Grated rind and juice of 1
  lemon
3 large eggs
170g/6oz self-raising flour

For the filling and topping:
Lemon curd (page 743)
Feather icing (page 716)

1. Set the oven to 190°C/375°F, gas mark 5.
2. Prepare two 18cm/7in cake tins (see page 42, creaming method).
3. Cream the butter and sugar together and add the lemon rind. Beat until light and fluffy.
4. Beat in one egg at a time, each time with a tablespoon of flour.
5. Beat very well, adding the lemon juice gradually. Then fold in the remaining flour.
6. Divide the mixture between the tins and bake for 20–25 minutes or until the cakes are well risen, golden and feel spongy to the finger tips.
7. Allow the cakes to cool for a few minutes in the tins, then turn out on to a wire rack to cool completely.

8. Sandwich the cakes with lemon curd.
9. Ice the top and 'feather' it as described in the recipe.

Madeira Cake

Melted lard for greasing
170g/6oz unsalted butter
Grated rind of 1 lemon
Pinch of ground cinnamon
225g/½lb caster sugar

4 eggs
285g/10oz plain flour
1 teaspoon baking powder
75ml/2½fl.oz milk
4 slices candied citron peel

1. Prepare a 20cm/8in cake tin (see page 42, creaming method).
2. Set the oven to 180°C/350°F, gas mark 4.
3. Cream the butter and gradually beat in the lemon, cinnamon and sugar until light and fluffy.
4. Beat in the eggs one at a time, adding a little flour as you beat, to prevent the mixture from curdling.
5. Sift the remaining flour with the baking powder. Fold it in with a metal spoon.
6. Add enough milk to bring the mixture to dropping consistency (it will drop rather than run off a spoon).
7. Spoon the mixture into the cake tin and spread with a palette knife or spatula. Decorate with peel.
8. Bake for 1½ hours, turning the temperature down to 165°C/325°F, gas mark 3 after 45 minutes.
9. Cool the cake for 10 minutes in the tin before gently easing out on to a wire rack.

Christmas Cake
(With rough icing)

This cake is for a 20cm/8in cake tin, 8cm/3in deep.

170g/6oz butter
170g/6oz soft dark brown sugar

110g/¼lb chopped almonds
3 tablespoons brandy *or* stout

4 eggs
225g/½lb plain flour
Pinch of salt
¼ teaspoon mixed spice
2 tablespoons black treacle
225g/½lb currants, washed and
  dried
225g/½lb sultanas
55g/2oz chopped candied peel
110g/¼lb glacé cherries, cut in
  half

1 small apple grated

For the covering and icing:
450g/1lb marzipan (page 725)
450g/1lb icing sugar
1–2 egg whites
½ teaspoon glycerine
Few drops blue colouring

For the decoration:
Red ribbon
2 sprigs holly

1. Set the oven to 180°C/350°F, gas mark 4. Grease and line the cake tin as instructed on page 42.
2. Cream the butter and sugar until light and fluffy.
3. Beat the eggs in one by one, then fold in the flour, salt and spice.
4. Stir in the remaining ingredients in the order in which they are listed. Beat very well.
5. Put the mixture into the greased and lined tin and bake for 1 hour. Turn the oven down to 170°C/325°F, gas mark 3 and bake for a further 1½ hours, covering the top of the cake with thick brown paper for the last hour if it seems to be browning too fast.
6. The cake is cooked when a skewer will emerge dry after being stuck into the middle.
7. Cool the cake before turning it out. Remove the paper.
8. When the cake is quite cold wrap it up in greaseproof paper and put into an air-tight container.
9. If the cake is to be iced it should be covered in marzipan at least two weeks before Christmas: follow the instructions on pages 726–7.
10. About a week before Christmas ice the cake. Sift the icing sugar.
11. Whisk the egg whites until frothy and beat enough of the icing sugar into them to get the icing absolutely smooth but stiff enough to stand up in peaks.
12. Beat in half a teaspoon of glycerine (to prevent the icing

665

setting like concrete) and a drop or two of colouring (to make it look less yellow and more pure-white).

13. Using a large knife or spatula spread the icing all over the cake: dip the knife in hot water to get the sides smooth, and use a fork to lift the top into spiky peaks all over.

14. Next day, when the icing is dry, wrap the ribbon round it and cover the join with one of the holly sprigs, secured with a long pin. Put the other holly sprig on top.

Simnel Cake

A festive Easter cake. The eleven balls of marzipan are said to represent the apostles (without Judas). Sometimes they are made into egg-shapes, the symbol of Spring and rebirth.

Large pinch each of salt and baking powder
225g/$\frac{1}{2}$lb plain flour
55g/2oz rice flour
225g/$\frac{1}{2}$lb sultanas
110g/$\frac{1}{4}$lb currants
110g/$\frac{1}{4}$lb glacé cherries
30g/1oz candied peel, chopped

225g/$\frac{1}{2}$lb butter
Grated rind of 1 lemon
225g/$\frac{1}{2}$lb caster sugar
4 eggs, separated
110g/$\frac{1}{4}$lb marzipan (page 725)
Beaten egg
110g/$\frac{1}{4}$lb glacé icing (page 716)

1. Set the oven to 180°C/350°F, gas mark 4. Prepare a 20cm/8in cake tin with a double lining of greased and floured greaseproof paper. Wrap the outside of the cake tin with a double thickness of brown paper to insulate the cake from direct heat.
2. Sift the salt, baking powder and flours. Cut the cherries in half.
3. Cream the butter with the lemon rind. Add the sugar gradually and beat until light and fluffy.
4. Beat in the egg yolks. Whisk the whites until stiff.
5. Fold one-third of the sifted flour into the mixture. Fold in the egg whites by degrees, alternating with the remaining flour and the fruit.
6. Put half the mixture into the prepared tin, spreading a little up the sides of the tin.
7. Take just over one-third of the marzipan paste. Roll it into a smooth round. Place in the cake tin. Cover with the remaining mixture.
8. With a palette knife make a dip in the centre of the cake to counteract any tendency to rise in the middle.
9. Bake for 2 hours, then reduce the oven heat to 150°C/300°F, gas mark 2. Bake for a further 30 minutes.
10. Roll the remaining marzipan into a circle the same size as the top of the cake. Cut a piece from the centre about 12·5cm/5in in diameter and shape into eleven small even-sized balls.
11. Heat the grill. Lay the ring of marzipan on top of the cake and brush with egg wash. Arrange the marzipan balls on top of the ring and brush again with beaten egg. Grill until golden brown.
12. When cold pour a little glacé icing into the centre of the cake. Tie a ribbon around the side.

Rice Cake

110g/¼lb butter	4 eggs
225g/½lb caster sugar	225g/½lb ground rice
Finely grated rind of ½ lemon	

1. Set the oven to 180 C/350 F, gas mark 4. Line a 18cm/7in cake tin with a double layer of greased and floured grease-proof paper.
2. Cream the butter in a mixing bowl. Beat in the sugar until light and fluffy. Add the lemon rind and mix well.
3. Separate the eggs. Add the yolks to the mixture one at a time, beating hard all the time.
4. Whisk the egg whites until fairly stiff but not dry. Take a spoonful of egg white and mix it in. Stir in half the rice. Add half the remaining egg white. Add the rest of the rice, then the rest of the egg white.
5. Pour into the tin. Make a slight hollow in the centre of the mixture to counteract any tendency to rise in the middle.
6. Bake for 45 minutes or until firm to the touch and slightly shrunken at the edges.
7. Cool in the tin for 5 minutes, then turn out on to a wire rack to cool completely.

Squashy Rhubarb Cake

For the cake:
85g/3oz butter
85g/3oz sugar
2 small eggs
85g/3oz self-raising flour, sifted
   with a pinch of salt
Milk

Icing sugar to finish

For the filling:
675g/1½lb rhubarb, cut into
   2·5cm/1in pieces
1 tablespoon sugar

For the crumble top:
85g/3oz plain flour
55g/2oz butter
30g/1oz sugar

1. Prepare a deep 20cm/8in cake tin (see page 42, creaming method). Set the oven to 190°C/375°F, gas mark 5.
2. First make the crumble mixture: rub the butter into the flour and add the sugar. Set aside.
3. Now make the cake: cream the butter until soft and well-beaten. Add the sugar and beat until very pale, light and fluffy.

4. Lightly beat the eggs and add them to the sugar mixture, beating in a little at a time, and folding in a spoon of flour if the mixture curdles.
5. Fold in the rest of the flour and add a few dribbles of milk if the mixture is now too stiff. It should be of 'dropping' consistency – it will fall off a spoon rather reluctantly.
6. Turn the cake mixture into the prepared cake tin and spread it flat.
7. Cover carefully with the raw rhubarb pieces and sugar. Sprinkle with the crumble mixture.
8. Bake for about 45 minutes or until the cake feels firm on top. Leave to cool in the tin.
9. Just before serving remove from the tin and sift over a thin layer of icing sugar.

Note: If using canned rhubarb you will need a 450g/1lb can.

Pain de Gênes (*rich almond cake*)

110g/¼lb blanched almonds
3 eggs
140g/5oz caster sugar
55g/2oz potato starch *or* plain flour
½ teaspoon baking powder
Good pinch of salt
85g/3oz butter
1 tablespoon Amaretto *or* kirsch
Icing sugar

1. Set the oven at 180°C/350°F, gas mark 4. Brush a moule-à-manqué or 20cm/8in cake tin with butter, line the bottom with a circle of greaseproof paper and brush it again.
2. Grind the almonds finely and put them into a bowl with the sugar. Add the eggs one at a time, beating thoroughly between each addition until the mixture is pale and thick.
3. Sift the potato starch or flour, baking powder and salt into the mixture, folding as lightly as possible with a large metal spoon.
4. Melt the butter and carefully fold it in with the minimum

of stirring. Add the kirsch or Amaretto. Pour the mixture into the cake tin.

5. Bake for 30–35 minutes or until the cake is brown on top and springs back when lightly pressed with a finger.

6. Allow the cake to cool for 5 minutes in the tin, then loosen the sides with a knife and turn out on to a wire rack to cool. When cold sift a thin layer of icing sugar over the top.

Sticky Ginger Cake

110g/¼lb preserved ginger
110g/¼lb butter
110g/¼lb treacle
110g/¼lb soft brown sugar
½ teaspoon bicarbonate of soda

4 tablespoons milk
225g/½lb plain flour
Pinch of salt
1 teaspoon ground ginger
1 egg

1. Prepare a shallow rectangular cake tin (see page 42, melting method). Set the oven to 170°C/325°F, gas mark 3.

2. Chop the preserved ginger finely.

3. Melt the butter, treacle and sugar together without boiling.

4. When the sugar has dissolved add the chopped ginger and allow to cool.

5. Mix the bicarbonate of soda with a tablespoon of the milk.

6. Sift the flour into a bowl with the salt and the ground ginger and make a well in the centre.

7. Add the milk and the slightly beaten egg to the treacle mixture.

8. Slowly beat the treacle mixture into the flour, pouring a little at a time into the well, and drawing the flour in from the sides as you mix.

9. When all the flour is incorporated in the treacle mixture stir in the bicarbonate of soda.

10. Turn the mixture into the prepared tin and bake for about 1 hour. The gingerbread should feel moist and slightly tacky, but firm.

11. Let it cool before turning it out. It will keep for about 2 weeks in an airtight container, and freezes perfectly.

Whisked Sponge

3 eggs
85g/3oz caster sugar

85g/3oz plain flour
Pinch of salt

1. Set the oven to 180 C/350 F, gas mark 4. Prepare a cake tin (see page 42, whisking method).
2. Place the eggs and sugar in a bowl and fit it over (not in) a saucepan of simmering water. Whisk the mixture until light, thick and fluffy. (If using an electric mixer no heat is required.)
3. Remove the bowl from the heat and continue whisking until cool.
4. Sift the flour and salt and, with a large metal spoon, fold into the mixture, being careful not to beat out any of the air.
5. Turn the mixture into the prepared tin and bake in the middle of the oven for about 30 minutes.
6. Test to see if it is cooked. (When the cake is done it will shrink slightly and the edges will look crinkled. When pressed gently it will feel firm but spongy and will sound 'creaky'.)
7. Turn out on to a wire rack to cool.

Swiss Roll

55g/2oz plain flour
Pinch of salt
2 eggs
55g/2oz caster sugar

1 tablespoon warm water
2–3 drops vanilla essence
3 tablespoons warmed jam
Caster sugar

1. Heat the oven to 190 C/375 F, gas mark 5. Prepare a Swiss roll tin by brushing a little melted lard or oil on the bottom and sides. Place in it a piece of greaseproof paper cut to fit the bottom of the tin exactly and brush again with melted fat. Dust with flour and sugar. (If no Swiss roll tin

671

is available a baking sheet fitted with a tray of doubled greaseproof paper will do.

2. Sift the flour with the salt.
3. Put the eggs and sugar in a bowl and fit it over (not in) a saucepan of simmering water. Whisk the mixture until light, thick and fluffy. (If using an electric mixer no heat is required.) Continue beating until the mixture is cool again.
4. Using a large metal spoon fold the water, essence and flour into the egg mixture.
5. Pour the mixture into the tin.
6. Bake for 12–15 minutes. It is cooked when, if touched with a finger gently, no impression remains. The edges will also look very slightly shrunk.
7. Lay a piece of greaseproof paper on the work top and sprinkle it evenly with caster sugar. Using a knife, loosen the the edges of the cooked cake, then turn it over on to the sugared greaseproof paper. Remove the rectangle of grease-proof paper from the bottom of the cake.
8. While the cake is still warm spread it with the jam.
9. Using the paper under the cake to help you, roll the cake up firmly from one end.
10. Dredge the cake with caster sugar. To serve, cut in slices.

Note: If the cake is to be filled with cream this cannot be done while it is hot. Roll the cake up, unfilled, and keep it wrapped in greaseproof paper until cool. Unravel carefully, spread with whipped cream, and roll up again.

Angel Food Cake

110g/¼lb flour
340g/¾lb caster sugar
12 egg whites

1¼ teaspoons cream of tartar
¼ teaspoon salt
1 teaspoon vanilla essence

To serve:
85g/3oz chocolate, melted

1. Set the oven to 170 C/325 F, gas mark 3.
2. Sift the flour with 110g/¼lb of the sugar three times.
3. Whisk the egg whites in a clean, dry bowl until frothy. Add the cream of tartar and salt and continue to whisk until the mixture forms soft peaks. Gradually whisk in the remaining sugar. Stir in the vanilla essence.
4. Carefully fold in the sugar and flour mixture using a large metal spoon.
5. Spoon the cake mixture into an ungreased 25cm/10in angel cake tin. Bake for 45 minutes or until firm. Put the tin, cake side down, on to a wire rack and leave to cool for 1½ hours before removing the tin. Spoon over the melted chocolate.

Note I: Do not try to cut angel cake with a knife. Being very light it is easily compressed and the shape and texture is spoilt. Use a cake cutter or two forks to pull the cake apart.

Note II: This basic recipe can be varied:
(a) Add chocolate, coffee or orange flavouring or chopped nuts, mixed peel or chocolate chips.
(b) Divide the mixture into two, flavour and colour one half and swirl in the other half, so you have a 'marbled' mixture.

Genoise Commune (Butter Sponge Cake)

4 eggs
125g/4½oz caster sugar

125g/4½oz plain flour
55g/2oz butter, very soft

1. Set the oven to 190 C/375 F, gas mark 5. Prepare a moule à manqué or deep sandwich tin (see page 26, whisking method).
2. Break the eggs into a bowl. Add the sugar. Place the bowl over a saucepan of simmering water and whisk until the mixture has doubled in bulk, and will leave a ribbon trail on the surface when the whisk is lifted. Lift the bowl off the heat and continue to whisk until the mixture has cooled slightly (about 5 minutes). (If using an electric beater whisking need not be done over heat.)
3. Sift in about half the flour and fold it in gently but thoroughly with a metal spoon.

4. Pour and fold in the very soft, but not melted, butter and sift and fold in the remaining flour.
5. Pour the mixture into the prepared tin. Bake for 30–35 mins. Allow to cool slightly before turning out on to a wire rack.

Note: Classic cooks would not call a Genoise (which contains fat) a sponge cake (which should be made from eggs, flour and sugar only). But in everyday English the word sponge is used for both types of cake.

Genoise Fine

4 eggs
125g/4½oz caster sugar
100g/3½oz plain flour

100g/3½oz butter, runny but not melted

1. Prepare a moule-à-manqué or deep sandwich tin with flour, greaseproof paper and sugar. Set the oven to 190°C/375°F, gas mark 5.
2. Break the eggs into a large bowl and add the sugar. Set the bowl over (not in) a pan of simmering water and whisk until light, fluffy and doubled in bulk. Take off the heat and whisk until cool.
3. Fold in the sifted flour – be very careful not to stir at all vigorously, or this will push out all the air that has been laboriously whisked in.
4. Pour in the butter and mix it in with a large metal spoon. Do not stir for a second longer than is necessary or the light consistency will be spoiled.
5. Turn into the prepared tin and bake for 30–35 minutes. Leave to cool in the tin for a few minutes then turn on to a wire rack to cool.

Note: This is sometimes called a 'butter sponge'. However, this description is not culinarily correct, as a true sponge contains no fat.

Coffee Genoise with Chocolate Caraque

For the cake:
4 eggs
125g/4½oz caster sugar
100g/3½oz plain flour

55g/2oz butter, very soft but
   not melted
2 teaspoons coffee powder

For the coffee butter cream
  filling and icing:
110g/¼lb sugar
150ml/¼ pint milk
2 egg yolks
225g/½lb unsalted butter
Coffee essence

For the chocolate caraque:
30g/1oz dark chocolate
Icing sugar
Browned chopped almonds for
  decoration

1. Prepare a moule à manqué or deep sandwich tin (see page 26, whisking method). Set the oven to 190°C/375°F, gas mark 5.
2. Break the eggs into a bowl, add the sugar and set the bowl over a saucepan of simmering water. Whisk until the mixture has doubled in bulk. Whisk for 3–4 minutes off the heat until the mixture has cooled slightly (if using an electric mixer beating need not be done over heat).
3. Sift in about half the flour and fold it in gently but thoroughly with a metal spoon. Pour in the butter and sift and fold in the remaining flour. Flavour the mixture with coffee powder. Pour into the prepared tin.
4. Bake for about 35 minutes or until cooked – the edges should look slightly shrivelled. Allow to cool slightly in the tin and then turn out on to a wire rack. Peel off the paper and allow to cool completely.
5. To make the butter cream: add the sugar to the milk and bring to the boil. Beat the egg yolks, pour on the milk, mix well and return all the mixture to the saucepan. Stir over a gentle heat without boiling until slightly thickened. Strain and cool.
6. Beat the butter until creamy and gradually whisk in the custard mixture. Flavour with coffee essence.
7. To make the chocolate caraque: melt the chocolate on a plate over a pan of boiling water. Spread thinly on a marble slab

or other hard cold surface. When just set use a long knife to shave off curls of chocolate: hold the knife with one hand on the handle, and one hand on the tip of the blade. Hold it horizontally and scrape the chocolate surface by pulling the knife towards you. Chill the curls to harden them.

8. To decorate: split the cake in half and sandwich with one third of the butter cream. Spread the tops and sides with the remainder. Press browned chopped almonds on to the sides of the cake. Cover the top with a pile of caraque chocolate and sift over a very fine dusting of icing sugar.

Note: If you do not want to make caraque the cake can be very simply and attractively decorated in this way. Melt the chocolate meant for the caraque and stir it into the coffee butter cream. Spread the icing as smoothly as possible on the top of the cake. Lightly place a lacy paper doily over it. Sift icing sugar over cake and doily. Carefully remove the doily, taking pains to prevent the icing sugar on it from falling on to the cake.

Black Cherry Cake

Chocolate Genoise, the cake
only (page 677)
225g/½lb black cherries
Kirsch
290ml/½ pint double cream

3 tablespoons water
85g/3oz dark chocolate, grated
110g/¼lb icing sugar
About 55g/2oz browned split
almonds

1. Remove the stones from the cherries and sprinkle the fruit with a little kirsch.
2. Whip the cream until it will just hold its shape.
3. Split the cake into three thin rounds. On the bottom layer spread about one third of the cream and sprinkle with half the cherries. Place the next layer of cake on top. Spread on another third of cream and the rest of the cherries. Place the top round on and flatten gently with your hands.
4. Place the chocolate in a pan with 3 tablespoons of water and stir over gentle heat until smooth, taking care not to boil.

5. Sift the icing sugar into a bowl and blend in the chocolate, adding a little extra water if necessary. Do this drop by drop to make a thick pouring consistency. Pour over the top of the cake and allow to set.

6. Spread the remaining cream around the side of the cake and press the browned split almonds against it.

7. Cut three strips of paper about 25cm/10in long and about 2·5cm/1in wide. Place them over the cake about 2·5cm/1in apart and sift over a heavy dusting of icing sugar.

8. Remove the paper strips carefully to reveal a striped brown and white top.

Chocolate Genoise

For the cake:

55g/2oz dark chocolate	62g/2¼oz plain flour
3 eggs	Pinch of salt
85g/3oz caster sugar	

For the chocolate butter cream:

170g/6oz dark chocolate, grated	110g/¼lb icing sugar
2 egg whites	225g/½lb unsalted butter

For the chocolate caraque:
30g/1oz dark chocolate
Icing sugar

1. Set the oven to 190 C/375 F, gas mark 5. Prepare a 20cm/8in moule à manqué cake tin (see page 26).

2. Now make the cake: break the chocolate up and put it on a saucer over gentle heat. Stir until melted.

3. Break the eggs into a bowl, add the sugar and set the bowl over a simmering saucepan of water. Whisk over heat until the mixture has doubled in bulk. It should be pale and mousse-like. Whisk for 3–4 minutes off the heat while the mixture cools slightly. (If using an electric mixer the whisking need not be done over heat.)

4. Sift the flour with the salt. Fold the flour and the melted chocolate into the egg mixture. Pour into the prepared tin.
5. Bake for 35–40 minutes or until cooked: the edges should look a little shrivelled. Allow to cool slightly in the tin and then turn out on to a wire rack. Peel off the paper and allow the cake to cool completely.
6. To make the butter cream: melt the chocolate as before over gentle heat.
7. Whisk the whites with the sugar in a bowl set over a saucepan of simmering water until thick and firm.
8. Cream the butter and gently beat in the meringue mixture. Stir in the almost cool melted chocolate.
9. To make the chocolate caraque: melt the chocolate as before over a pan of boiling water. Spread thinly on a marble slab or other hard cold surface. When just set use a large straight knife to drag off curls of chocolate: hold the knife in both hands (one on the handle, one on the tip) and pull it towards you, scraping the surface of the chocolate with a slight side-to-side sawing motion. Chill the curls to harden them.
10. To decorate: split the cake in half and sandwich together with one third of the butter cream. Spread the remainder on the top and sides of the cake and pile the chocolate caraque on top of the cake. Dust with a little icing sugar.

Dobez Torte

This is a cake with five layers. The mixture will not deteriorate if all layers cannot be baked at the same time because of a lack of baking sheets or space in the oven.

For the cake:
4 eggs
170g/6oz caster sugar
140g/5oz plain flour
Pinch of salt

For the decoration:
140g/5oz sugar
2 tablespoons browned
  chopped almonds *or* ground
  browned hazelnuts
6 whole hazelnuts

For the butter cream:
85g/3oz sugar
4–5 tablespoons water
3 egg yolks
225g/½lb butter
Coffee essence
55g/2oz skinned, toasted and
  ground hazelnuts

1. Set the oven to 190°C/375°F, gas mark 5. Grease and flour five baking sheets and mark a 20cm/8in circle on each sheet (use a flan ring or saucepan lid in the floured surface).
2. Start with the cake: whisk the eggs, adding the sugar gradually. Set the bowl over (not in) a pan of simmering water and whisk until the mixture is thick and mousse-like. Remove from the heat and whisk until cold. Sift the flour and salt and fold into the egg mixture with a metal spoon. Divide the mixture between the five baking sheets and spread into circles as marked.
3. Bake for 8 minutes. Trim the edges and leave to cool on a wire rack.
4. Prepare the butter cream: dissolve the sugar in the water and when clear boil rapidly to the thread (to test, put a little sugar syrup on to a wooden spoon, dip your index finger and thumb into cold water and then into the syrup in the spoon. When you pull your finger and thumb apart there should be a thread of syrup between them). Allow to cool slightly.
5. Separate the eggs. Whisk the yolks in a bowl and then pour the syrup slowly on to them, whisking all the time. Keep whisking until you have a thick, mousse-like mixture. Cream the butter well and beat in the egg and sugar mixture. Flavour 2 tablespoons of the butter cream with coffee essence and keep for decoration. Mix the ground hazelnuts and coffee essence into the remaining mixture.
6. Lay one piece of cake on a wire rack over an oiled tray. Melt the sugar for the caramel in a little water and when dissolved boil fiercely until a good caramel colour and pour immediately over the piece of cake, covering it completely.

7. Allow to harden *slightly* and mark into six portions with an oiled knife. (The idea is to cut through the setting caramel but not through the cake.) Trim the edges of excess caramel.
8. Sandwich the cake layers together with the coffee and hazelnut butter cream, placing the one with caramel on top. Spread the coffee and hazelnut butter cream thinly around the sides and press on the nuts.
9. Using a forcing bag with a large fluted nozzle pipe a rosette with the remaining plain butter cream on top of each portion of cake. Decorate each rosette with a whole hazelnut.

Serves 6

Carrot Cake

This is one of those cranky-sounding cakes which is surprisingly good, though pretty solid.

225g/½lb wholemeal flour
Pinch of salt
¼ teaspoon bicarbonate of soda
225g/½lb carrots, grated
55g/2oz butter, melted

55g/2oz runny honey
55g/2oz brown sugar
¼ teaspoon nutmeg
2 teaspoons cinnamon
1 egg, beaten

1. Set the oven to 190°C/375°F, gas mark 5. Lightly grease a small loaf tin.
2. Sift the flour with the salt and soda. Stir in all the remaining ingredients.
3. Spoon the mixture into the loaf tin and bake for about 50 minutes. The top should be well browned and firm to touch. Leave to cool for a few minutes, then turn out of the tin on to a wire rack to cool completely.

BREADS

White Bread

You will need a 1 kilo/2lb bread tin. If it is old and used you may not need to grease or flour it, but if it is new and not non-stick brush it out very lightly with flavourless oil and dust with flour.

15g/½oz fresh yeast
290ml/½ pint lukewarm milk
1 teaspoon caster sugar
30g/1oz butter

450g/1lb plain flour
1 teaspoon salt
1 egg, lightly beaten

1. Dissolve the yeast with a little of the milk and the sugar in a teacup.
2. Rub the butter into the sifted flour and salt as you would for pastry.
3. Pour in the yeast mixture, the milk and the beaten egg and mix to a stiffish dough.
4. Add a small amount of flour if the dough is too sticky. When the dough will leave the sides of the bowl press it into a ball and tip it out on to a floured board.
5. Knead until it is elastic, smooth and shiny (about 15 minutes).
6. Put the dough back in the bowl and cover it with a piece of lightly greased polythene.
7. Put it somewhere warm and draught-free and leave it to rise until it has doubled in size. This should take at least 1 hour. Bread that rises too quickly has a yeasty, unpleasant taste; the slower the rising the better – overnight in a cool larder is better than half an hour over the boiler!
8. Knead for a further 10 minutes or so.
9. Shape the dough into an oblong and put it into the loaf tin.
10. Cover with the polythene again and allow to rise again until it is the size and shape of a loaf.
11. Set the oven to 220 C/425 F, gas mark 7. Bake the loaf for

681

10 minutes, then turn the oven down to 190 C/375 F, gas mark 5 and bake for a further 25 minutes or until it is golden and firm.

12. Turn the loaf out on to a wire rack to cool. It should sound hollow when tapped on the underside. If it does not, or feels squashy and heavy, return it to the oven, without the tin, for a further 10 minutes.

Yeast: If using dried yeast see page 616

Plaited White Loaf

450g/1lb warmed plain flour (preferably 'strong')
1 teaspoon salt
290ml/½ pint tepid milk
15g/½oz butter

15g/½oz fresh yeast
1 teaspoon caster sugar
1 egg, beaten
Milk and poppy seeds for glazing

1. Sift the flour and salt into a warm mixing bowl. Make a well in the centre.
2. Heat the milk, melt the butter in it and allow to cool until tepid. Cream the yeast and sugar together. Mix the milk, egg and creamed yeast together and pour into the well.
3. Mix and knead until smooth and elastic (this should take 10–15 minutes). The dough should be soft.
4. Cover the bowl with a piece of oiled polythene and put to rise in a warm place for about an hour. It should double in bulk.
5. Heat the oven to 200°C/400°F, gas mark 6.
6. Divide the dough into three equal pieces and knead on a floured board. Form a long sausage with each piece and plait them together. Place on a greased baking sheet.
7. Cover again with the oiled polythene and prove (allow to rise) in a warm place for 15 minutes.
8. Brush with milk, sprinkle with poppy seeds and bake for about 25 minutes or until the loaf is golden and sounds hollow when tapped on the underside.

Yeast: If using dried yeast see page 616

Wholemeal Baps

20g/¾oz fresh yeast
290ml/½ pint lukewarm milk
1 teaspoon caster sugar
225g/½lb wholemeal flour

225g/½lb plain white flour
1 teaspoon salt
55g/2oz butter
1 egg, lightly beaten

1. Dissolve the yeast with a little of the milk and the sugar in a teacup.
2. Warm a large mixing bowl and sift the flours and salt into it. Rub in the butter as you would for pastry.
3. Pour in the yeast mixture, the milk and the beaten egg and mix to a fairly slack dough.
4. When the dough will leave the sides of the bowl press it into a ball and tip it out on to a floured board. Knead it until it is elastic, smooth and shiny (about 15 minutes).
5. Put the dough back in the bowl and cover it with a piece of lightly greased polythene. Put it somewhere warm (on a shelf above a radiator, on the grill rack over a pan of very gently simmering water on the cooker, in the airing cupboard or just a draught-proof corner of the kitchen). Leave it there until the dough has doubled in size. This should take at least 1 hour, the longer the better.
6. Take the dough out of the bowl, punch it down and knead it again for 10 minutes.
7. Set the oven to 200°C/400°F, gas mark 6.
8. Divide the dough into eight pieces and shape them into flattish ovals (using a rolling pin if you like). Put on a floured baking sheet and prove (allow to rise again) for 15 minutes.
9. Bake for 20 minutes or until firm.

Yeast: If using dried yeast see page 616

Brown Soda Bread

900g/2lb wholemeal flour *or*
675g/1½lb wholemeal flour
and 225g/½lb plain white
flour
2 teaspoons salt
2 teaspoons bicarbonate of
soda
4 level teaspoons cream of
tartar

2 level teaspoons sugar
45g/1½oz butter
570–860ml/1–1½ pints milk
(if using all wholemeal flour
the recipe will need more
liquid than with a mixture of
two flours)

1. Set the oven to 190°C/375°F, gas mark 5.
2. Sift the dry ingredients into a warm dry bowl.
3. Rub in the butter and mix to a soft dough with the milk.
4. Shape into a large round about 5cm/2in thick. With the handle of a wooden spoon make a cross on the top of the loaf. The dent should be 1·5cm/¾in deep.
5. Bake on a greased baking sheet for 25–30 minutes. Allow to cool on a wire rack.

Chelsea Buns

15g/½oz fresh yeast
85g/3oz caster sugar
450g/1lb plain flour
1 teaspoon salt
85g/3oz butter

1 egg
225ml/7½fl.oz tepid milk
½ teaspoon mixed spice
55g/2oz sultanas
55g/2oz currants

1. Cream the yeast with a teaspoon of the sugar.
2. Sift the flour into a warm dry bowl with the salt. Rub in half the butter and stir in half the sugar.
3. Beat the egg and add to the yeast mixture with the tepid milk.
4. Make a well in the centre of the flour and pour in the liquid.

684

Using first a knife and then your hand gradually draw the flour in from the sides of the bowl and knead until smooth.

5. Cover the bowl and leave to rise in a warm place until doubled in bulk (about 1 hour).
6. Punch the dough down again and knead again on a floured board. Roll into a square about 23cm/9in across.
7. Mix the remaining butter with half the remaining sugar and dot it over the bun mixture.
8. Fold the dough in half and roll it out again to form a second square.
9. Set the oven to 220°C/425°F, gas mark 7. Grease a baking sheet.
10. Sprinkle the remaining sugar, the spice, sultanas and currants over the yeast mixture.
11. Roll it up like a Swiss roll and cut into 3·5cm/1½in slices.
12. Arrange the buns cut side up on the baking sheet and leave to prove for 15 minutes.
13. Sprinkle with sugar. Bake for 20–25 minutes.
14. Leave the buns to cool on a wire rack before separating.

Makes 8

Yeast: If using dried yeast see page 616

Cornish Splits

15g/½oz fresh yeast
1 teaspoon sugar
2 level teaspoons salt
450g/1lb plain flour
45g/1½oz lard
290ml/½ pint milk
15g/½oz margarine *or* butter

For the filling:
290ml/½ pint whipped cream
Fresh raspberries *or* raspberry jam

To finish:
Icing sugar

1. Set the oven to 220°C/425°F, gas mark 7. Grease two baking sheets and dredge them lightly with flour.

2. Cream the yeast with the sugar and salt and leave for 10 minutes.
3. Sift the flour into a warmed bowl and rub in the lard until the mixture resembles breadcrumbs.
4. Heat the milk to blood temperature and add it to the yeast mixture.
5. Make a well in the centre of the flour and pour in the yeast mixture. Mix the liquid and gradually draw in the surrounding flour. Mix to a soft dough.
6. Knead until the mixture is smooth and shiny and leaves the fingers.
7. Put the dough in a greased mixing bowl, cover with a greased piece of polythene and leave to rise in a warm place until it has doubled in bulk (about 1 hour).
8. Turn the risen dough on to a floured surface and knead for 10 minutes. Shape into 18–20 balls, flattening them slightly. Leave to prove on the greased baking sheets for 15–20 minutes.
9. Bake for 20–25 minutes. Then brush with a little melted butter or margarine and leave on a wire rack to cool.
10. Cut the Cornish splits diagonally across from the top. Fill with whipped cream and raspberries or raspberry jam and dust with icing sugar.

Makes 18

Yeast: If using dried yeast see page 616

Flower Pot Loaf

An attractive loaf of bread can be baked in an old-fashioned earthenware flower pot.

Bread dough (page 681–2)

1. Wash and dry the flower pot. Oil it inside and out.
2. Leave it in the oven whenever you cook anything else until it has had four or five bakings.

3. Oil it again.
4. Fill two-thirds full with bread dough that has been kneaded, allowed to rise and knocked back.
5. Prove in a warm place until the dough is well risen.
6. Bake as you would a loaf in a bread tin, removing the loaf when it is firm and brown and sounds hollow when rapped on the underside. *Yeast: If using dried yeast see page 616*

Beer Bread

55g/2oz butter
1 heaped tablespoon soft
  brown sugar
290ml/½ pint brown ale
30g/1oz fresh yeast

1 level teaspoon salt
1 egg
225g/½lb wholewheat flour
225g/½lb plain white flour

1. Use a little of the butter to brush out a 1 kilo/2lb loaf tin.
2. Bring the sugar, beer and the rest of the butter to boiling point then allow to cool until lukewarm.
3. Use 1–2 spoons of this liquid to cream the yeast. Add creamed yeast, salt and lightly beaten egg to the beer mixture.
4. Warm a large mixing bowl and sift the flours into it. Make a well in the centre and pour in the liquid. Mix, first with a knife, and then with your fingers, to a soft but not sloppy dough. Knead for 10 minutes or until smooth and a little shiny. The dough should be very elastic.
5. Put the dough back in the bowl and cover it with a piece of greased polythene. Put in a warm place until it has doubled in bulk.
6. Take out, punch down and knead until smooth again. Shape the dough into a loaf shape and put into the tin. Cover with the greased polythene again and put back in the warm place to prove (rise again to double its bulk). It should now look the shape of the finished loaf.
7. While it is proving heat the oven to 190°C/375°F, gas mark 5. Bake the loaf in the middle of the oven for 35 minutes or until it is brown on top and the bread (out of its tin)

sounds hollow when tapped on the underside. Cool tipped out on a wire rack.

Yeast: If using dried yeast see page 616

Cheese Gannet

15g/½oz fresh yeast
⅓ teaspoon sugar
225g/½lb wholemeal flour
1 teaspoon salt
55g/2oz butter
105ml/3½ fl.oz milk
2 eggs, beaten

110g/¼lb cheese, grated,
    preferably strong Cheddar
    or Gruyère
Pinch of cayenne
Pinch of English mustard
Freshly ground black pepper
A little milk for glazing

1. Cream the yeast with the sugar and leave for 10 minutes.
2. Sift the flour with the salt into a warmed bowl.
3. Melt the butter in the milk and when at blood heat mix with the eggs and the creamed yeast. Pour this liquid into the flour and mix to a soft dough.
4. Cover and leave to rise in warm place (do not worry if it does not rise very much: it will when cooking).
5. Set the oven to 200°C/425°F, gas mark 7.
6. Mix three-quarters of the cheese into the dough and season well with cayenne, mustard and pepper.
7. Pile into a well greased 20cm/8in sandwich tin and flatten so that the mixture is about 2·5cm/1in deep. Put back in the warm place to prove (rise again) for 10–15 minutes.
8. Bake in a hot oven for 35–40 minutes.
9. 5 minutes before the end of cooking brush lightly with the milk and sprinkle with the remaining cheese.

Note I: The mixture can be divided into six round rolls: put five round the edge of a Victoria sandwich tin and one in the middle. Leave to prove and then bake. It will look like a crown loaf.

Yeast: If using dried yeast see page 616

Hot Cross Buns

20g/¾oz fresh yeast
85g/3oz caster sugar
220ml/7½ fl.oz scant milk
2 eggs, beaten
450g/1lb plain flour
½ teaspoon salt

½ tablespoon mixed spice
85g/3oz butter
170g/6oz currants
30g/1oz finely chopped peel
A little sweetened milk for glazing

1. Cream the yeast with the sugar.
2. Warm the milk to blood heat. Mix about two-thirds of the milk, the beaten eggs and the yeast together.
3. Sift the flour, salt and spice into a mixing bowl. Rub in the butter. Make a well in the centre of the flour. Tip in the warm milk mixture and beat until smooth, adding more milk if necessary to produce a soft, just sticky, dough.
4. Turn the dough on to a floured board. Knead until the dough is very elastic. Work in the currants and the peel.
5. Place in a lightly oiled bowl. Sprinkle with flour. Cover with a damp tea-towel or an oiled sheet of polythene. Leave to rise in a warm place for about 1½ hours until doubled in bulk.
6. Set the oven to 220°C/425°F, gas mark 7.
7. Turn out on to the floured board again and knock down. Knead again for a few minutes, making sure the fruit is evenly distributed.
8. Shape into small round buns. Mark a cross on top of each bun with a knife. Place on baking trays and leave to prove for approximately 15 minutes or until doubled in bulk. Brush the tops with sweetened milk.
9. Bake for about 15 minutes. Brush again with sweetened milk, bake for 2 minutes more, then cool on a wire rack.

Note I: The crosses can be made by laying strips of shortcrust pastry on top of the buns just before baking.

Yeast: If using dried yeast see page 616

Makes 8

French Bread

30g/1oz fresh yeast
1 teaspoon sugar
55ml/2 fl.oz warm water
345ml/12 fl.oz warm milk
110ml/4 fl.oz warm water

2 teaspoons salt
900g/2lb plain flour
1 teaspoon salt (for brushing)
110ml/4 fl.oz warm water (for
    brushing)

1. Cream the yeast and sugar with the 55ml/2 fl.oz warm water.
2. Pour the warm milk, 110ml/4 fl.oz warm water and salt into a bowl.
3. Stir in the yeast mixture and slowly add the flour, a little at a time. Mix with a wooden spoon until the mixture becomes a medium firm dough.
4. Knead well on a lightly floured surface, for at least 10 minutes. Sprinkle the surface with more flour if the dough becomes sticky.
5. Place the dough in a bowl, cover with a damp cloth and leave to rise in a warm place until doubled in size (at least 1 hour). Knock back, knead for 2 minutes, then leave to rise, covered with the cloth, for about 40 minutes.
6. Knock back again, then divide the dough into 3 equal portions. Shape into 3 loaves, as long as your baking tray. This is best achieved by rolling the dough into 3 flat rectangles and then rolling them up like tight Swiss rolls. With a sharp knife cut diagonal slashes about $\frac{1}{2}$cm/$\frac{1}{4}$in deep at 5cm/2in intervals on top of the loaves.
7. Dissolve the salt in the warm water and use to lightly brush the loaves. Cover again and let the loaves rise until doubled in bulk.
8. Set the oven to 220°C/425°F, gas mark 7. Put a roasting tin of hot water on the oven floor. (The steam will help to make the crust crisp.)
9. Bake the loaves for 15 minutes. Reduce the heat to 190°C/375°F, gas mark 5 and brush the loaves with more salt water. Bake for a further 25–30 minutes, brushing once or twice more

with salt water. When the loaves feel rigid and light in weight, and sound hollow when tapped on the underside, they are done. Cool on a wire rack.

Yeast: If using dried yeast see page 616

Brioche

225g/½lb flour
Pinch of salt
5 level teaspoons caster sugar
2 eggs, beaten

2 tablespoons warm water
55g/2oz melted butter
7g/¼oz fresh yeast

For the glaze:
1 egg mixed with 1 tablespoon
water and ¼ teaspoon sugar

1. Grease a large brioche mould or 12 small brioche tins.
2. Mix the yeast with 1 teaspoon of the sugar and the water. Leave to dissolve.
3. Sift the flour with a pinch of salt into a bowl. Sprinkle over the sugar. Make a well in the centre. Drop in the eggs, yeast mixture and melted butter and mix with the fingers of one hand to a soft but not sloppy paste. Knead on an unfloured board for 5 minutes or until smooth. Put into a clean bowl, cover with a damp cloth or greased polythene and leave to rise in a warm place until doubled in bulk (about 1 hour).
4. Turn out and knead again on an unfloured board for 2 minutes.
5. Place the dough in the brioche mould (it should not come more than half way up the mould). If making individual brioches divide the dough into 12 pieces. Using three-quarters of each piece roll them into small balls and put them in the brioche tins. Make a dip on top of each brioche. Roll the remaining paste into 12 tiny balls and press them into the prepared holes. Push a pencil, or thin spoon handle, right

through each small ball into the brioche base as this will anchor the balls in place when baking.

6. Cover with greased polythene and leave in a warm place until risen to the top of the tin(s). The individual ones will take 15 minutes, the large one about 30 minutes.
7. Set the oven to 230°C/450°F, gas mark 8.
8. Brush the egg glaze over the brioche. Bake the large one for 20–25 minutes, or small ones for 10 minutes.

Yeast: If using dried yeast see page 616

BUNS AND SCONES

Rock Buns

225g/½lb self-raising flour
Pinch of salt
110g/¼lb butter
85g/3oz caster sugar
110g/¼lb sultanas and currants, mixed

30g/1oz chopped candied peel
2 eggs, lightly beaten
A little milk if necessary

1. Set the oven to 190°C/375°F, gas mark 5. Grease a large baking sheet.
2. Sift the flour into a bowl with the salt. Rub in the butter until the mixture resembles breadcrumbs.
3. Stir in the sugar, fruit and peel.
4. Mix in the eggs, adding a little milk if necessary, but the mixture should be very stiff.
5. Using two forks put the mixture out on the baking sheet, each rocky-looking bun being the size of a small egg.
6. Bake for 15–20 minutes until pale brown. Leave to cool on a wire rack.

Makes 10

Scones

225g/½lb plain flour
3 level teaspoons baking
   powder
½ level teaspoon salt

55g/2oz butter
55g/2oz sugar (optional)
150ml/¼ pint milk

For glazing:
1 egg, beaten

1. Set the oven to 220°C/425°F, gas mark 7. Lightly grease a baking sheet.
2. Sift the flour with the other powder ingredients.
3. Rub in the butter until the mixture resembles breadcrumbs. Stir in the sugar if required.
4. Make a deep well in the flour, pour in all the liquid and mix to a soft, spongy dough with a palette knife.
5. On a floured surface, knead the dough very lightly until it is smooth. Roll or press out to about 2½cm/1 in thick and stamp into small rounds.
6. Brush the scones with beaten egg for a glossy crust or sprinkle with flour for a soft one.
7. Bake the scones at the top of the hot oven until well risen and

brown. Leave to cool on a wire rack, or serve hot from the oven.

Note: 30g/1oz sultanas or other dried fruit may be added to the dried ingredients.

For cheese scones substitute 30g/1oz grated strong cheese for half the butter, and omit the sugar.

Makes 12

Coffee Buns

110g/¼lb butter
110g/¼lb caster sugar
2 eggs
110g/¼lb self-raising flour
2 teaspoons instant coffee
   powder

¼ teaspoon vanilla essence
55g/2oz chopped walnuts
55g/2oz chocolate

1.   Set the oven to 180°C/350°F, gas mark 4. Grease and flour 12 bun tins or paper moulds.
2.   Cream the butter and sugar until light and fluffy.
3.   Beat in the eggs a little at a time.
4.   Fold in the flour, coffee, vanilla essence and chopped nuts. Add a little water if necessary to make a soft dropping consistency.
5.   Fill the tins or paper moulds two-thirds full and bake for 15–20 minutes. Leave to cool on a wire rack.
6.   Grate the chocolate. Melt it on a plate over a pan of boiling water.
7.   Spread each bun with a little melted chocolate and leave to cool and harden.

Makes 12

English Madeleines

110g/¼lb butter	110g/¼lb self-raising flour
110g/¼lb caster sugar	2 tablespoons redcurrant jelly
2 eggs	55g/2oz desiccated coconut

1. Set the oven to 180°C/350°F, gas mark 4. Grease and flour about 12 dariole moulds.
2. Cream the butter and sugar until light and fluffy.
3. Beat in the eggs a little at a time.
4. Fold in the flour. Add a little water, if necessary, to make a soft dropping consistency.
5. Fill the tins half full and bake for 15–20 minutes.
6. Cool upside down on a wire rack.
7. Brush with warm redcurrant jelly and roll in desiccated coconut.

Makes 12

Eccles Cakes

225g/½lb flour-quantity rough-puff pastry (page 647)

For the filling:

15g/½oz butter	¼ teaspoon nutmeg
55g/2oz brown sugar	¼ teaspoon ground ginger
110g/¼lb currants	Grated rind of ½ lemon
30g/1oz chopped mixed peel	1 teaspoon lemon juice
½ teaspoon cinnamon	

For the glazing:

1 egg white	Caster sugar

1. Set the oven to 220°C/425°F, gas mark 7.
2. Roll the pastry to 0·5cm/¼in thick. Cut out rounds 7·5cm/3in across. Put aside to relax.

2. Melt the butter in a pan and stir in all the other filling ingredients.
3. Place a good teaspoon of filling in the centre of each pastry round.
4. Damp the edge of the pastry and press together in the centre, forming a small ball. Turn the balls over and lightly roll them until the fruit begins to show through the pastry.
5. With a sharp knife make 3 small parallel cuts on the top.
6. Lightly beat the egg white with a fork. Brush the top of the Eccles cakes with this and sprinkle with caster sugar.
7. Place on a wet baking sheet and bake for 20 minutes or until lightly browned.

Makes 12

BISCUITS

Easter Biscuits

55g/2oz butter
55g/2oz caster sugar
Grated rind of $\frac{1}{2}$ lemon
$\frac{1}{2}$ an egg *or* 1 yolk
110g/$\frac{1}{4}$lb plain flour

$\frac{1}{2}$ teaspoon caraway seed
55g/2oz currants
30g/1oz granulated sugar

1. Set the oven to 180 C/350 F, gas mark 4. Cover a baking sheet with a piece of greaseproof paper.
2. Cream together the butter, caster sugar and lemon rind. Beat in the egg.
3. Fold in the flour, caraway and currants.
4. Roll out the dough on a floured board to 5mm/$\frac{1}{4}$in thick. Cut into large rounds and carefully lift them on to the baking sheet. Prick with fork and sprinkle with granulated sugar.
5. Bake for 10–15 minutes until set and pale golden.
6. Remove from the oven and leave on a wire rack to crisp and cool.

Note: If the dough becomes soft and difficult to handle, wrap it up and chill for 15 minutes before proceeding.

Makes 8

Digestive Biscuits

85g/3oz butter
170g/6oz wholemeal flour
30g/1oz oatmeal
½ teaspoon salt

30g/1oz flour
30g/1oz sugar
½ teaspoon baking powder
3 tablespoons golden syrup

1. Set the oven to 190°C/375°F, gas mark 5. Lightly grease a baking sheet.
2. Rub the butter into the dry ingredients until the mixture resembles breadcrumbs. Add the golden syrup and mix well.
3. Roll the paste out thinly and stamp into rounds with a cutter. Place on a baking sheet.
4. Bake for 5–8 minutes. Leave to cool on a wire rack.

Makes 20

Almond and Apricot Cookies

85g/3oz butter
85g/3oz granulated sugar
110g/¼lb ground almonds

Small paper cake cases

For the decoration:
Apricot jam
Flaked almonds

1. Set the oven to 180°C/350°F, gas mark 4.
2. Cream the butter and when soft add the sugar and beat until light and fluffy. Stir in the ground almonds and roll the paste into balls the size of a ping-pong ball.
3. Place each ball into a paper case and put the cases into patty moulds. Bake in the oven for about 20 minutes. Allow to cool in their cases.

697

4. Remove from the cases, spread with a little apricot jam and decorate with a flaked almond.

Makes 18

Shortbread Fingers

110g/¼lb butter   170g/6oz plain flour
55g/2oz caster sugar   30g/1oz split almonds

1. Set the oven to 190°C/375°F, gas mark 5.
2. Beat the butter and sugar together until soft and creamy.
3. Work in the flour by degrees, with a minimum of beating.
4. Pat the paste into a smooth ball, then into a square about 1cm/½in thick.
5. Slide a floured baking sheet under the paste.
6. Prick with a fork and cut into fingers. Sprinkle with caster sugar. Decorate with split almonds, pressing them in gently.
7. Bake to a pale biscuit colour (about 20 minutes).

Makes about 18

Gingernuts

30g/1oz brown sugar   ½ teaspoon bicarbonate
55g/2oz butter   soda
85g/3oz golden syrup   1 heaped teaspoon ground
110g/¼lb flour   ginger

1. Set the oven to 170 C/325 F, gas mark 3. Grease a baking sheet.
2. Melt the brown sugar, butter and syrup together slowly, without boiling. Make sure the sugar has dissolved. Allow to cool.
3. Sift the flour, bicarbonate of soda and ground ginger into a mixing bowl. Make a well in the centre.

4. Pour the melted mixture into the well, beat it with a wooden spoon, gradually drawing in the flour from the sides as you mix.
5. Place the mixture in teaspoonfuls 8cm/3in apart on the prepared baking sheet. Bake for 15–20 minutes. The ginger-nuts will not be crisp until they cool and set.

Makes 16

Brandy Snap Cups

110g/¼lb sugar
110g/¼lb butter
110g/¼lb *or* 4 tablespoons golden syrup

Juice of ½ a lemon
110g/¼lb flour
Large pinch of ground ginger

To serve:
Whipped cream *or* ice cream

1. Set the oven to 190°C/375°F, gas mark 5. Grease a baking sheet, palette knife and one end of a wide rolling pin or a narrow jam jar or bottle.
2. Melt the sugar, butter and syrup together. Remove from heat.
3. Sift in the flour, stirring well. Add the lemon juice and ginger.
4. Put the mixture on the baking sheet in small teaspoonfuls about 15cm/6in apart. Bake for 5–7 minutes. They should go golden brown but still be soft. Watch carefully – they burn easily. Remove from the oven.
5. When cool enough to handle, lever each biscuit off the baking sheet with a greased palette knife.
6. Working quickly, shape them around the end of the rolling pin or greased jam jar to form a cup-shaped mould.
7. When the biscuits have taken shape remove them and leave to cool on a wire rack.
8. Serve filled with whipped cream or ice cream.

Note I: If the brandy snaps are not to be served immediately they must, once cool, be put into an airtight container for storage. They become soggy if left out.

Similarly, brandy snaps should not be filled with wettish mixtures like whipped cream or ice cream until shortly before serving, or the biscuit will quickly lose its crispness.

Note II: Do not bake too many snaps at a time as once they are cold they will be too brittle to shape – though they can be made pliable again if briefly returned to the oven.

Makes 8

Brandy Snaps

The mixture for these is exactly the same as for brandy snap cups (above) but the biscuits are shaped round a thick wooden spoon handle and not over the end of a rolling pin or jam jar. They are filled with whipped cream. This is done with a piping bag fitted with a medium nozzle.

Miniature brandy snaps (served as petits fours after dinner) are shaped over a skewer. These are not generally filled.

Langues de Chat

100g/3½oz butter   3 egg whites
100g/3½oz caster sugar   100g/3½oz plain flour

1. Set the oven to 200°C/400°F, gas mark 6. Grease and flour a baking sheet.
2. Soften the butter with a wooden spoon and add the sugar gradually. Beat until pale and fluffy.
3. Whisk the egg whites slightly and add gradually to the mixture, beating thoroughly between each addition.

4. Sift the flour and fold into the mixture with a metal spoon. Put into a forcing bag fitted with a medium-sized plain nozzle. Pipe into fingers the thickness of a pencil and about 5cm/2in long.
5. Tap the baking sheet on the table to release any over large air bubbles from the fingers. Bake for 5–7 minutes or until biscuit-coloured in the middle and brown at the edges. Cool slightly, then lift off the baking sheet with a palette knife. Cool completely before putting into an airtight container.

Makes 30

Macaroons

110g/¼lb ground almonds
170g/6oz caster sugar
1 teaspoon plain flour
2 egg whites

2 drops vanilla essence
Rice paper for baking
Split almonds for decoration

1. Set the oven to 180°C/350°F, gas mark 4.
2. Mix the almonds, sugar and flour together.
3. Add the egg whites and vanilla. Beat very well.
4. Lay a sheet of rice paper or vegetable parchment on a baking sheet and with a teaspoon put on small heaps of the mixture, well apart.
5. Place a split almond on each macaroon and bake for 20 minutes. Allow to cool.

Note I: To use this recipe for petits fours the mixture must be put out in very tiny blobs on the rice paper. Two macaroons can then be sandwiched together with a little stiff apricot jam and served in petits fours paper cases.

Note II: Ratafia biscuits are tiny macaroons with added almond essence.

Makes 25

Sponge Fingers

3 eggs
85g/3oz caster sugar
Vanilla essence

85g/3oz plain flour sifted with a
pinch of salt
Extra caster sugar for glazing

1. Set the oven to 190°C/375°F, gas mark 5. Grease and flour a baking sheet and have ready a piping bag fitted with a medium-sized plain nozzle.
2. Whisk the egg yolks with the sugar until light and fluffy.
3. Add a few drops of vanilla essence.
4. Whisk the whites until stiff and fold a third of them into the yolk mixture.
5. Fold in the flour. Fold in the remaining whites very lightly with a large metal spoon.
6. Pile the mixture into a piping bag and pipe on to the baking sheet in 5cm/2in lengths.
7. Dust each finger with plenty of caster sugar. Bake for 5–6 minutes and cool on a wire rack.

Makes 12

Tuiles à l'Orange

2 egg whites
110g/¼lb caster sugar
55g/2oz butter

55g/2oz plain flour
Grated rind of 1 orange

1. Set the oven to 190°C/375°F, gas mark 5. Grease a baking sheet.
2. Whisk the egg whites until stiff. Add the sugar and beat thoroughly.
3. Melt the butter. Add it to the meringue mixture by degrees with the sifted flour. Fold in the orange rind.
4. Spread out teaspoonfuls very thinly on the prepared baking

sheet, keeping them well apart to allow for spreading during cooking. Bake until golden brown (5–6 minutes).

5. Oil a rolling pin or the handle of a large wooden spoon. Loosen the tuiles from the baking sheet while still hot. While they are still warm and pliable curl them over the rolling pin or round the wooden spoon handle. When they are quite firm slip them off. When cold, store in an airtight container.

Makes 16

Amandine Tuiles

30g/1oz blanched almonds	55g/2oz plain flour
2 egg whites	$\frac{1}{2}$ teaspoon vanilla essence
110g/$\frac{1}{4}$lb caster sugar	55g/2oz melted butter

1. Set the oven to 180 C/350 F, gas mark 4. Lightly grease at least three baking sheets and a rolling pin.
2. Cut the almonds into fine slivers or shreds.
3. Place the egg whites in a bowl. Beat in the sugar with a fork. The egg white should be frothy but by no means snowy. Sift in the flour and add the vanilla and almonds. Mix with the fork.
4. Cool the butter (it should be melted but not hot) and add it to the mixture. Stir well.
5. Place the mixture in teaspoonfuls at least 13cm/5in apart on the baking sheets and flatten well.
6. Bake in the oven until a good brown at the edges and pale biscuit-coloured in the middle (about 6 minutes). Remove from the oven and cool for a few seconds.
7. Lift the biscuits off carefully with a palette knife. Lay them, while still warm and pliable, over the rolling pin to form them into a slightly curved shape. As soon as they are stone cold put them into an airtight can or plastic bag to keep them crisp.

Makes 16

PASTRIES

Danish Pastries

Most Danish pastries require almond filling and icing as well as the basic dough. Instructions for these are given first, with the individual instructions for Pinwheels, Almond Squares etc., following. But the icing should not be made until the pastries are baked.

Danish pastries are frequently scattered with flaked browned almonds while the icing is still wet. Sometimes sultanas or small pieces of canned pineapple, or apple purée, are included in the filling.

For the pastry:
15g/½oz fresh yeast
1 tablespoon caster sugar
5 tablespoons milk, warmed
225g/½lb plain flour
Pinch of salt
1 egg, lightly beaten
110g/¼lb unsalted butter,
  softened

For the glacé icing:
110g/¼lb icing sugar
Boiling water to mix

For the almond paste filling:
45g/1½oz butter
45g/1½oz icing sugar
30g/1oz ground almonds
2 drops vanilla essence

For the glaze:
1 egg, beaten

When rolling out Danish pastry, care should be taken to prevent the butter breaking through the paste and making the resulting pastry heavy. Use a heavy rolling pin, bring it firmly down on to the pastry and roll with short, quick, firm rolls. Do not 'push' it. Avoid using too much flour. If the paste is becoming warm and unmanageable, wrap it up and chill it well before proceeding.

1. Dissolve the yeast with 1 teaspoon of the sugar and the milk.

2. Sift the flour with a pinch of salt into a warmed bowl. Add the remaining sugar. Make a well in the centre and drop into it the egg and the yeast mixture.

3. Using a round-bladed knife mix the liquids, gradually drawing in the surrounding flour to make a soft dough. If extra liquid is required add a little more water.

4. When the dough leaves the sides of the bowl turn it on to a floured surface and beat and knead until smooth. Roll into a longish rectangle ½cm/¼in thick.

5. Divide the butter into hazelnut-sized pieces and dot it over the top two-thirds of the dough leaving a 1cm/½in clear margin round the edge. Fold the pastry in three, folding the unbuttered third up over the centre section first, and then the buttered top third down over it. You now have a thick 'parcel' of pastry. Give it a 90° turn so that the former top edge is on your right. Press the edges together.

6. Dust lightly with flour and roll into a long rectangle again. Fold in three as before. Chill for 15 minutes.

7. Roll and fold the pastry once or twice again until the butter is well worked in and the paste does not look streaky. Chill for at least 30 minutes or overnight.

8. To make the almond paste, cream the butter, add the sugar and beat well until light and soft. Mix in the ground almonds and flavour with vanilla essence. Mix well but do not overbeat or the oil will run from the almonds making the paste greasy.

9. When ready to use the glacé icing mix enough boiling water into the sugar to give an icing that will run fairly easily – about the consistency of cream.

Yeast: If using dried yeast see page 616

Almond Squares

1. Follow the instructions on pages 704–5, then:
2. Set the oven to 200°C/400°F, gas mark 6.

3. Roll the pastry into a rectangle 25 × 20cm/10 × 7½in. Cut into 5cm/2½in squares. Put on to a floured baking sheet.
4. Put a spoonful of the filling into the centre of each piece of pastry. Fold each corner into the middle and press it down lightly into the almond paste to stick it in position.
5. Prove for 15 minutes (put into a warm draught-free place to allow the dough to rise). Press down the middle of the squares.
6. Brush with beaten egg and bake for 15–20 minutes.
7. When cool spoon over the freshly made glacé icing.

Crosses

1. Follow the instructions on pages 704–5, then:
2. Set the oven to 200°C/400°F, gas mark 6.
3. Roll the pastry out thinly and cut it into 13cm/5in squares. Place on a floured baking sheet.
4. Cut through each square as indicated in the drawing, stage 1, and then overlap the two opposite corners as shown in stages 2 and 3.

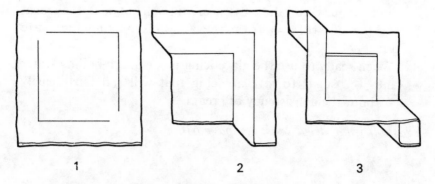

1   2   3

5. Fill the centre hole with almond paste filling or apple purée.
6. Prove for 15 minutes in a warm draught-free place.
7. Brush with beaten egg and bake for 15–20 minutes.
8. When cool dust with icing sugar or spoon over freshly-made glacé icing.

Pinwheels

1. Follow the instructions on pages 704–5 then:
2. Set the oven to 200°C/400°F, gas mark 6.
3. Roll the pastry out thinly and cut it into 13cm/5in squares. Place on a floured baking sheet.
4. From each corner towards the centre of each square, make a cut about 3cm/1½in long. Put a blob of almond filling in the uncut centre of each square.
5. Fold alternate points of pastry (one from each corner) into the middle and press on to the filling to secure. This leaves one unfolded point at each corner, and the pastry should now resemble a child's pinwheel (see drawing).
6. Prove in a warm place for 15 minutes (allow to rise and puff up). Press down the corners.
7. Brush with beaten egg and bake for 15–20 minutes.
8. When cool spoon on the freshly made glacé icing.

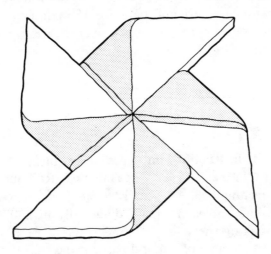

Cinnamon Wheels

In this recipe the almond paste is replaced with a cinnamon filling

55g/2oz butter
55g/2oz sugar
2 teaspoons cinnamon

Small handful of dried fruit and
chopped mixed peel

1. Follow the instructions on pages 704–5, omitting the almond filling, then:
2. Cream the butter with the sugar. Add the cinnamon and mix well.
3. Set the oven to 200°C/400°F, gas mark 6.
4. Roll the pastry to a rectangle 25 × 20cm/12 × 8in. Place on a floured baking sheet.
5. Spread the butter mixture over the dough, leaving a narrow margin all round. Scatter over the dried fruit and chopped peel.
6. Roll the pastry, from one end, into a thick roll. Cut into 2·5cm/1in slices. With a lightly floured hand, flatten each slice to the size of the palm of your hand. Put somewhere warm and draught-free to rise (prove) for 15 minutes.
7. Brush with egg glaze and bake for 15 minutes.
8. Allow to cool slightly and spoon over the freshly made glacé icing.

Crescents

1. Follow the instructions on pages 704–5, then:
2. Set the oven to 200°C/400°F, gas mark 6. Roll out the pastry into a rectangle 30 × 15cm/12 × 6in. Cut into 7·5cm/3in squares and cut each square diagonally in half. Put on a floured baking sheet.
3. Place a small piece of almond paste at the base (long side) of each triangle. Roll it up from the base to the tip and curve into a crescent shape.
4. Put into a warm, draught-free place to rise (prove) for 15 minutes.
5. Bake for 15–20 minutes or until a good brown. When cool spoon over the freshly made glacé icing.

Croissants

370g/12oz flour,
Pinch of salt
15g/½oz fresh yeast
225ml/8 fl.oz lukewarm water
and milk mixed

225g/8oz butter at room
temperature
Beaten egg for glazing

1. Sift the flour with the salt into a clean bowl. Rub in 55g/2oz of the butter. Cut remaining butter into small pieces.
2. Cream the yeast in a small bowl with two tablespoons of the liquid. Add the remaining liquid.
3. Make a well in the centre of the flour and pour in the yeast mixture. Mix quickly with a knife, then with your hand to a soft but firm dough.
4. Turn onto a lightly floured table top and knead for 10 minutes.
5. Roll out the dough into a rectangle three times as long as it is wide. Dot the top 2/3 of the dough with half the butter. Fold and turn as for flaky pastry pages 291–2. Roll out again into a rectangle. Dot the top 2/3 with the remaining butter. Fold, turn and roll again. Fold, then wrap loosely in a large plastic bag and refrigerate for 1 hour.
6. Roll and fold twice more. Relax for as long as possible, preferably overnight in the refrigerator.
7. Set the oven to 190°C/375°F, gas mark 5.
8. Divide the dough into two. Roll each one into a circle approximately 25cm/10in diameter. Turn over. With a sharp knife, cut each circle into six wedges. Roll up each piece from the broad end to the point. Curve slightly to form a crescent. Place on a floured tray and cover loosely with polythene.
9. Prove at room temperature till doubled in size. Brush with beaten egg and place in the oven for approximately 25 minutes until well risen and golden.

Yeast: If using dried yeast see page 616

Makes 12

Scotch Crescents (*Aberdeen rowies*)

225g/½lb butter
110g/¼lb lard
30g/1oz fresh yeast
1 tablespoon caster sugar

290ml/½ pint lukewarm water
450g/1lb plain flour
Salt

1. Cream the fats together.
2. Put the yeast and sugar into a jug and mix well. Add half the lukewarm water.
3. Sift the flour with a good pinch of salt into a basin and pour in the yeasty liquid. Add more water if required and mix to a soft dough. Cover the bowl and leave in a warm place until doubled in bulk. This should take about 40 minutes depending on the temperature.
4. With floured hands knead the dough briefly, then roll it out into a long rectangle. Put a third of the butter/lard mixture, in tiny blobs or dots, over the top two-thirds of the pastry strip. Fold the bottom (unbuttered) piece up over the buttered middle section, and bring the top (buttered) third down to form a parcel. Give the block of pastry a 90° turn so that the folded closed side previously furthest from you is now on your right.
5. With a rolling pin press the edges together to prevent the fats escaping. Then roll out to a rectangle again. Again butter the top two-thirds, fold as before, turn and roll as before. Repeat the whole process once more, by which time the fat will all be used up.
6. Now divide the dough into three and roll each one into a 25cm/10in square. Cut each square into four smaller ones. Cut each square into two triangles.
7. Roll each triangle up from the broadest side to the tip. Pinch the ends together tightly, and pull gently into crescent shapes. Put on greased baking sheets, well apart. Cover with greased polythene and allow to prove in a warm place until croissant-sized (doubled in bulk).
8. While this is going on heat the oven to 220°C/425°F, gas mark 7.

9. Brush the crescents gently with beaten egg. Bake for 15 minutes or until crisp and a good brown. Cool slightly on a wire rack and serve warm.

Yeast: If using dried yeast, see page 616.

Makes 24

Palmiers

Palmiers are usually made from leftover pieces of puff pastry.

1. Set the oven to 200°C/400°F, gas mark 6.
2. Do not push the trimmings up into a ball as you would short-crust pastry – this would spoil the carefully created layers in the paste. Lay the strips or pieces flat on top of each other, folding them if necessary.
3. Using caster sugar instead of flour, roll the pastry out into an oblong ½cm/¼in thick. Sprinkle well with caster sugar. Fold each end of the pastry to the centre, and then fold the pastry in half. Cut the roll across into slices 1¼cm/½in wide.
4. Lay the slices flat on a wet baking sheet, far apart, and flatten well with a sugared rolling pin or your hand. Bake for 10 minutes or until pale brown, with the underside caramelized. Turn over and bake for a further 10 minutes. Cool on a wire rack.

Gaufrettes Viennoise

170g/6oz butter
225g/½lb plain flour
Pinch of salt
1 egg
85g/3oz caster sugar

85g/3oz ground almonds
Royal icing (page 719)
Redcurrant jelly *or* raspberry jam

1. Heat the oven to 190°C/375°F, gas mark 5. Take the butter from the refrigerator and allow it to warm to room temperature.

711

2. Sift the flour and salt on to a pastry board or marble slab. Make a large well in the centre. Drop the egg and sugar into the well. Sprinkle the almonds on the flour. Using the thumb and fingertips of one hand only, 'peck' sugar and egg until light and creamy. Work in the butter, then gradually absorb the flour and almonds.
3. Knead until smooth, then chill for about 30 minutes. Roll the pastry into an oblong. Place on an ungreased baking sheet. Trim the edges with a floured knife and cut into squares.
4. Add a good pinch of flour to the royal icing. Fill into a paper cornet fitted with a fine plain nozzle and decorate half the squares with a lattice pattern.
5. Bake for about 7–8 minutes until just golden. When cool spread each undecorated square thinly with jelly or jam and place a decorated square on the top.

Note: Gaufrettes are waffles. These are so named because their square shape and latticed icing makes them look like waffles.

Makes 12

Honey Boats

110g/¼lb pâté sucrée (page 654)

For the filling:

85g/3oz unsalted butter	1 tablespoon honey
85g/3oz caster sugar	Coffee essence
85g/3oz ground almonds	Coffee fondant icing (page 718)

1. Line boat moulds thinly with the pâte sucrée. Bake blind.
2. Cream the butter and sugar together until light. Stir in the almonds and honey and flavour with coffee essence. Fill the cooked cases with this coffee almond cream, shaping it to give a slightly domed surface. Leave in a cool place to set.
3. Melt the fondant icing and spoon over the boats.

Baking blind: See page 245.

Makes 9

Almond Cakes

125g/4½oz caster sugar
125g/4½oz ground almonds
25g/scant 1oz flour
2 small egg whites

55g/2oz pounded praline
  (page 786)
Icing sugar
Rice paper

1. Set the oven to 180°C/350°F, gas mark 4.
2. Sift together the caster sugar, almonds and flour. Add enough egg white to just bind the mixture together and stir in the praline.
3. Roll into balls the size of a walnut, brush with egg white and coat with icing sugar. Bake on rice paper for 15 minutes.

Makes 24

Printaniers

4 egg-quantity Genoise
  commune mixture (page 673)
170g/6oz butter-quantity crème
  au beurre mousseline
  (page 715) with the lemon
  rind omitted

Vanilla essence
Coffee essence
Sieved strawberry jam
White fondant icing (page 718),
  warmed

1. Set the oven to 190°C/375°F, gas mark 5.
2. Brush a Swiss roll tin, lined with paper, with melted lard. Dust with caster sugar. Pile in the Genoise mixture, making sure that it is evenly distributed throughout the tin. Bake for 25 minutes, allow to cool and turn out on to a wire rack.
3. Split the cake and sandwich it with a little of the crème au beurre. Cut it into strips 3·75cm/1½in wide.
4. Divide the remaining crème au beurre into three and flavour one-third with vanilla essence, one-third with coffee essence and one-third with sieved strawberry jam.

5. Using a forcing bag fitted with a 1·75cm/⅜in plain pipe, pipe one row of coffee- and one of vanilla-flavoured crème au beurre side by side along the top of each strip of cake. Then pipe a row of strawberry crème au beurre on top of the first two strips and refrigerate to harden.
6. Using a large spoon carefully coat each strip with the warm fondant icing. Leave to set.
7. Cut each cake strip on the diagonal, into pieces about 2cm/¾in wide. Keep cool until ready to serve.

Makes 24

ICINGS AND MARZIPAN

Apricot Glaze

3 tablespoons apricot jam   Juice of ½ lemon
2 tablespoons water

1. Place all the ingredients together in a thick-bottomed pan.
2. Bring slowly up to the boil, stirring gently (avoid beating in bubbles) until syrupy in consistency. Strain.

Note: When using this to glaze food, use when still warm, as it becomes too stiff to manage when cold. It will keep warm standing over a saucepan of very hot water.

Chocolate Butter Icing

110g/¼lb plain chocolate,   110g/¼lb icing sugar, sifted
  chopped   1 egg yolk
55g/2oz unsalted butter

1. Melt the chocolate in a heavy saucepan with a tablespoon of water, stirring continuously.
2. Beat the butter and sugar until light and fluffy.
3. Beat in the egg yolk followed by the melted chocolate.

Crème au Beurre Meringue

A light soft frosting for cakes.

For the meringue:
2 egg whites
110g/¼lb icing sugar
170g/6oz unsalted butter

Suggested flavourings:
Grated lemon *or* orange rind
Melted chocolate
Coffee essence

1. Put the egg whites with the sugar into a mixing bowl and set it over a pan of simmering water. Whisk until the meringue is thick and will hold its shape. Remove from the heat and continue to whisk until slightly cooled.
2. Beat the butter until soft and gradually beat in the meringue mixture.
3. Flavour to taste as required.

Crème au Beurre Mousseline

A rich creamy cake filling.

55g/2oz granulated sugar
4 tablespoons water
2 egg yolks

Grated rind of ½ lemon
110g/¼lb butter

1. Dissolve the sugar in the water and when completely dissolved boil rapidly to about 105 C/215 F. At this point the syrup, if tested between finger and thumb, will form short threads. Take off the heat immediately.

2. Whisk the yolks and lemon rind and pour on the syrup. Keep whisking until thick.
3. Soften the butter and whisk into the mixture slowly. Allow to cool.

Glacé Icing

225g/½lb icing sugar
Boiling water

1. Sift the icing sugar into a bowl.
2. Add enough boiling water to mix to a fairly stiff coating consistency. The icing should hold a trail when dropped from a spoon but gradually find its own level.

Note: Hot water produces a shinier result than cold. Also the icing, on drying, is less likely to craze, crack or become watery if made with boiling water.

Feather Icing

Icing sugar   Colouring *or* chocolate
Boiling water

1. Sift the icing sugar into a bowl (225g/½lb will be sufficient for an 18cm/7in sponge).
2. Add enough boiling water to mix to a fairly stiff coating consistency. The icing should hold a trail when dropped from a spoon but gradually find its own level.
3. Take 2 tablespoons of the icing and colour it with food colouring or chocolate.
4. Place in a piping bag fitted with a fine writing nozzle.
5. Spread the remaining icing smoothly and evenly over the top of the cake, using a warm palette knife.

6. While it is still wet quickly pipe lines, about 2·5cm/1in apart, across the top of the cake.
7. Now draw lines at right angles to the coloured lines with a pin or a sharp knife, dragging the tip through the coloured lines which will be pulled into points.

If the pin is dragged in one direction through the coloured icing lines this pattern will result:

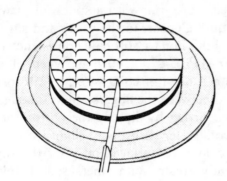

If the pin is dragged alternately in opposite directions through the coloured icing lines this pattern will result:

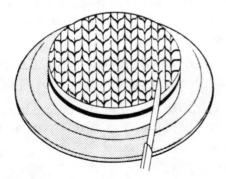

Note: Smooth melted jam can be used instead of coloured icing for the feathering.

717

Fondant Icing

220g/½lb loaf sugar   ½ teaspoon liquid glucose *or*
115ml/4 fl.oz water   pinch of cream of tartar

1. Dissolve the sugar in the water over a low heat without boiling.
2. Mix the cream of tartar with a spoonful of water and add it, or the liquid glucose, to the water and sugar. Cover and bring to the boil. Boil to 'soft ball' consistency (to a temperature of 110°–115°C/230°–240°F or when, if a spoonful is dropped into a bowl of cold water, it will form a soft ball when rubbed between the fingers). Stop the sugar syrup from cooking any further by dipping the bottom of the pan into a bowl of cold water. Let it cool slightly.
3. Moisten a cold hard surface and pour the sugar syrup on to it in a steady stream. With a metal spatula fold the outsides of the mixture into the centre.
4. Continue to turn with a spatula and work until the fondant becomes fairly stiff. Knead into balls. Place in a bowl and cover with a damp cloth for 1–2 hours.
5. If the fondant is to be stored place in a screw-top jar. When ready to use put it in a bowl and stand over a pan of simmering water to melt.

Note I: A sugar thermometer is almost essential. It is vital to get the syrup exactly the right consistency, not too liquid or hard.

Note II: To make coffee fondant icing proceed as above but add 2 teaspoons of coffee essence to the syrup before pouring on to the work surface.

Royal Icing

Royal icing is a hard icing, traditionally used (over a layer of marzipan) for the coating and decoration of special-occasion cakes, which keeps very well. There are some important points to remember:

1. More than with any other cooking it is vital to clean up as you go along. It is almost impossible to produce delicate and neat work from a cluttered work surface. Get all the nozzles and bags lined up before you begin icing.
2. Never overfill the piping bag. This leads to the sticky icing squeezing out of the top.
3. Keep all full piping bags under a damp cloth to prevent the icing in the nozzle drying out.
4. Always keep the icing covered with a damp cloth when not in use to prevent it drying out.
5. Always clean the nozzles immediately after use using a pin to ensure that no icing is left in the tip.
6. Practise the required pattern on the table top before tackling the cake. Don't try complicated things like roses and scrolls before you have thoroughly mastered the easier decorations like trellis, shells, stars and dots.
7. Follow the instructions slavishly.

Note I: Never lick your fingers or equipment. Even a little wet icing can make you feel very sick.

Note II:
>   450g/1lb sugar makes enough for a 20cm/8in cake.
>   900g/2lb sugar makes enough for a 30cm/12in cake.

For the first coat of icing for a 20cm/8in cake:
2 egg whites
450g/1lb icing sugar

(Make up more icing for the second and third coats and for the decoration as you need it.)

719

Additions (*optional*)

A few drops blue food colouring (makes white icing very bright white)

1 teaspoon lemon juice to each 225g/½lb sugar (makes the icing a little sharper and less sickly)

½ teaspoon glycerine to each 225g/½lb sugar (produces a softer icing which will not splinter when cut. Without glycerine royal icing eventually hardens to an unbreakable cement. More glycerine can be added, but this will give a softer icing unsuitable for a tiered cake. None need be used if the cake is to be eaten within 24 hours of icing)

Mix the egg white with 3 tablespoons of the sugar, add lemon juice or glycerine if required and beat well. Gradually add the remaining sugar and beat for about 15 minutes in all until the icing is soft, very white, fluffy and will hold its shape. More sugar can be added if the mixture is too sloppy. The blue colouring, if used, is added last.

Consistency   A cake is normally covered with 2–3 coats of icing and decorated with either piping or 'run in' work. The consistency varies for each coat.

First coating: Very thick; the icing should stand up in points if the beating spoon is lifted from the bowl.

Second coating: A little thinner (the points should flop over at the tips, like rabbit ears).

Third coating: The icing should be of pouring consistency.

For piping: Consistency as for first coating.

For run-in-work: As for the third coating.

Beating   The icing should be smooth and glossy. It is difficult to beat properly if the icing is too solid or too thin, so first get the consistency to that described above for the first coating. It can be thinned once beaten absolutely smooth.

Beating with an electric whisk   The machine must be robust. Use the heaviest beater rather than a wire whisk. Icing made with an electric beater will have air bubbles if beaten too quickly at the beginning, or for too long. Beat for 5 minutes at the lowest speed, then gradually turn up the speed until, after 10 minutes, the machine is at full speed. Once smooth and glossy, stop. If there are any bubbles, leave the icing, covered with a damp cloth, in the refrigerator overnight.

First coating

Make sure that the marzipan is smooth. Brush away any excess sugar or crumbly paste with a dry pastry brush. Put all the icing on top of the cake and work it across the top and down the sides with a spatula or large knife. Completely cover the cake and spread the icing smooth and free from air bubbles. Do not 'pat' the cake as this will cause air bubbles. Make sure that all the almond paste is covered.

To smooth the top   You will need a long-bladed straight ham knife, palette knife or metal ruler, longer if possible than the diameter of the cake to be iced. It is used either wet and hot, or dry:

> *Wet:*   If you dip the knife in hot water it helps to smooth the surface, especially if the icing is beginning to set; the water, however, dilutes some of the icing and may cause a streaked effect.

> *Hot:* If you heat the knife it helps to smooth the surface, especially if the icing is beginning to set, but it tends to dry out the icing and form a crust.

> *Dry:*   This is the best method for a fine finished result, but the hardest to accomplish.

Hold the knife blade or ruler at both ends and draw it in one long steady slow movement across the cake top, tilting the top edge of the ruler slightly towards you. An even pressure should be maintained. Alternatively, place the cake on an icing turntable. Hold the palette knife or ruler so that the tip or end is at the centre of the cake and the blade is just touching the surface of the icing. Keep the blade or ruler still and rotate the cake under it. Always wipe the knife clean after each attempt at smoothing.

To trim and neaten the sides of the cake   If the cake is square, hold the ruler or blade upright and with an even pressure draw it along the sides of the cake. If the cake is round, place it on an icing turntable. Put the left arm as far round the cake as possible

721

and hold the turntable. Hold the ruler or knife upright in your right hand and rotate the cake slowly anti-clockwise. An attractive pattern can be achieved by using a serrated knife.

To store Store the cake for at least 24 hours in a clean, cool, dry place. If the storage place is damp it will prevent the icing from drying and it will slowly slip down the sides of the cake. If it is too warm the cake will 'sweat' and oil from the marzipan will be drawn into the icing.

Second coating

When the icing is dry pare away any projecting edges with a sharp knife and smooth flat with sandpaper. Brush away all the dust.

Ice the cake following the rules for the first coating but using a slightly thinner icing. When dry place on a cake board 5cm/2in larger in diameter or width than the cake. Leave to dry for at least 24 hours.

Third coating (or float)

The third coating may not be necessary if the second is perfect and the cake is not to be kept for more than a few weeks before eating. If it is necessary, proceed when the second coating is dry. Prepare the surface as previously instructed. Before converting the icing into the desired pouring consistency, pile a little thick icing into an icing bag fitted with a no. 1 or 2 writing nozzle and cover it with a damp cloth.

Add a little egg white to the remaining icing and beat until smooth and of pouring consistency. Leave in a tightly covered container for 30 minutes. (Stretching a piece of polythene wrap over the bowl will do.) This is to make the air bubbles rise to the surface. If you do not do this air bubbles will break all over the surface of the cake, making little holes in the icing.

With the writing tube pipe an *unbroken* line around the top edge of the cake. Pour the runny icing into a piping bag without a nozzle and guide it over the top of the cake, flooding the surface and carefully avoiding the piped line. With the handle of a teaspoon work the flooding to the edge of the cake. The piped line will prevent the icing running off.

Decorating

You must have a clear idea of the design before you begin. If it is a geometric pattern, draw it on a piece of tracing paper and place this on the cake. Using a large pin, prick where the lines meet. Remove the paper and you will be left with guidelines made by the pin points. Join these up with a fine pencil or with more pricked holes so that the design is visible.

Half-fill the piping bags, fitted with the chosen nozzles, with the icing mixed to the correct consistency (see above). Put them under a wet cloth until needed. Get everything you will need ready on or near your work surface (e.g. more bags and extra nozzles, a large spoon, a palette knife, a small basin of hot water to wash the nozzles in).

Direct piping

Star piping: Hold the pipe upright, immediately above and almost touching the top of the cake and squeeze gently from the top of the bag. Stop pressing and lift the bag away. Always stop pressing *before* lifting the bag away.

Dot or pearl piping: Pipe as for stars. If the dots are too small, do not try to increase their size by squeezing out more icing; use a larger nozzle.

Straight lines: Press the bag as for making a dot but leave the icing attached to the cake surface – do not draw away by lifting the bag. Hold the point of the nozzle about 4cm/1½in above the surface of the cake and, pressing gently as you go, guide rather than drag the icing into place. The icing can be more easily directed into place if it is allowed to hang from the tube.

Trellis work: Pipe parallel lines ·5cm/¼in apart. Pipe a second layer over the top at right angles or at an angle of 45° to the first. Then pipe another layer as closely as possible over the first set of lines, then another set over the second layer, and so on until you have the desired height of trellis. Six layers (three in each direction) is usual for an elaborate cake.

Shells: Use a star nozzle. Hold the bag at an angle of about 45°. Pipe a shell, release the pressure on the bag and begin a new shell one-eighth of the way up the first shell, so that each new shell overlaps its predecessor.

Scrolls: Use a star nozzle. Hold the bag at an angle of about 45°. Pipe a scroll first from left to right and the second from right to left.

Run in work: Using a writing nozzle pipe the outline of a design (e.g. leaf, Father Christmas etc.) on to oiled foil or greaseproof paper. 'Float' runny icing in the centre, and leave to set. Lift off and stick on to the cake with wet icing.

Note: Variations of pressure when piping both shells and scrolls make the icing emerge in the required thicknesses. Shells and scrolls can be made into very attractive borders when combined with trellis work and edged with pearls.

Causes of failure

Broken lines	(a)	icing too stiff
	(b)	pulling rather than easing into place
	(c)	making the icing with a mixer set at too high a speed, causing air bubbles
Wobbly lines	(a)	squeezing the icing out too quickly
	(b)	icing too liquid
Flattened lines	(a)	icing too liquid
	(b)	bag held too near the surface

Indirect piping

This piping is done on to oiled moulds or waxed paper and when dry the piped shapes are stuck to the cake with a little wet icing.

Trellised shapes: Pipe as for direct piping on to waxed paper or oiled moulds (the backs of teaspoons, patty tins, cups or glasses). Leave for 24 hours then warm over a very gentle heat to dislodge them. Slide off the mould and fix to the cake with a little wet icing.

Flowers: You need confectioners' 'flower nails' and petal nozzles. The icing should be thick. The petals are piped individually on to the oiled surface of the 'flower nail', the biggest petals first and then the smaller ones. If the flower nails are covered with oiled foil, this can be removed carefully after piping so that the nail can be used for the next flower. When dry green icing leaves (piped and dried separately) can be attached to the back of the flowers with a little wet icing.

When making coloured flowers it is helpful to tint the icing to a *pale* colour first. After they have dried they can be touched up with a paint brush to give the flowers a more natural appearance. By varying the angle at which the piping bags are held, flatter petals (for daisies, violets and primroses) or thicker, more rounded petals (for roses) can be made. Sweet peas are made with 2–3 flat petals slightly overlapping each other with a smaller upright rounded petal piped on top of each flat one.

Marzipan or Almond Paste

225g/½lb caster sugar
225g/½lb icing sugar
450g/1lb ground almonds
2 egg yolks

2 whole eggs
2 teaspoons lemon juice
6 drops vanilla essence

1. Sift the sugars together into a bowl and mix with the ground almonds.
2. Mix together the egg yolks, whole eggs, lemon juice and vanilla essence. Add this to the sugar mixture and beat briefly with a wooden spoon.
3. Lightly dust the working surface with icing sugar. Knead the paste until just smooth (overworking will draw the oil out of the almonds, giving a too greasy paste).
4. Wrap well and store in a cool place.

Cooked Marzipan

This recipe gives a softer, easier-to-handle paste than the more usual, uncooked marzipan.

2 eggs
170g/6oz caster sugar
170g/6oz icing sugar

340g/¾lb ground almonds
4 drops vanilla essence
1 teaspoon lemon juice

1. Lightly beat the eggs.
2. Sift the sugars together and mix with the eggs.
3. Place the bowl over a pan of boiling water and whisk until light and creamy. Remove from the heat.
4. Add the ground almonds, vanilla and lemon juice, and beat briefly with a wooden spoon. The marzipan should be a soft paste.
5. Lightly dust the working surface with icing sugar. Carefully knead the paste until just smooth. (Overworking will draw out the oil from the almonds giving a too greasy paste.) Wrap well and store in a cool place.

To Cover a Cake with Marzipan

675g/1½lb marzipan (this will amply cover a 23cm/9in diameter cake)

Icing sugar
Apricot jam

If using uncooked marzipan or almond paste:
1. Take one-third of the marzipan and roll it into a circle a little larger than the cake top, using a rolling pin and board dusted with icing sugar to prevent the paste sticking.
2. Roll the remaining two-thirds to a strip as long as the circumference of the cake and just a little wider than the height of the cake.
3. Melt and sieve the jam. Bring to the boil and use it to paint the sides of the cake.

726

4. Turn the cake on its side and roll it on to the long strip of marzipan, keeping the top edge of the cake level with the edge of the marzipan, and sticking the marzipan to the cake as you go.
5. Turn the cake right side up again and brush the top with boiling jam.
6. Place the cake upside down on top of the circle of marzipan.
7. Using a palette knife and your fingers work the joins together, making sure that the edge meets the table-top (i.e. it is square, not rounded).
8. Turn the cake right side up and brush off any excess icing sugar.
9. Leave the cake to stand uncovered to dry for at least 2 days before icing.

If using cooked marzipan:
1. Melt and sieve the jam. Bring to the boil and brush over the top and sides of the cake.
2. Lightly dust the table-top with icing sugar and roll the marzipan to a large circle, about 10cm/4in bigger than the diameter of the cake.
3. Turn the cake upside down on to the marzipan.
4. Using the side of your hand work the marzipan evenly up the sides of the cake.
5. Take a jam jar and roll it around the sides of the cake to make sure that the sides are quite straight, and the edges square.

PETITS FOURS

Marzipan Dates

About 20 dates (fresh *or* dried)
225g/½lb marzipan (page 727)
Green colouring (optional)

1. Split the dates lengthwise almost in half. Take out the stones carefully, making sure that the dates stay whole.
2. Form the marzipan into a long sausage about 0·5cm/¼in diameter. Cut it into lengths about the size of the dates.
3. Place a piece of marzipan in each date and half-close the opening. Place in tiny paper cases.

Note: The marzipan can be coloured pale green by the addition of a few drops of green colouring. Work the colour into the marzipan by kneading with one hand.

Makes 20

Tommies

70g/2½oz caster sugar
110g/¼lb butter
85g/3oz ground hazelnuts

140g/5oz plain flour
Honey
225g/½lb dark chocolate

1. Set the oven to 180°C/350°F, gas mark 4.
2. Cream the sugar and butter together until white.
3. Stir in the hazelnuts and flour.
4. As soon as the mixture becomes a paste wrap and leave it in the refrigerator for 30 minutes.
5. Roll out thinly and cut into 2·5cm/1in rounds with a biscuit cutter or an upturned glass.
6. Place on a baking sheet and bake for 12 minutes. Put on a wire rack to cool.
7. Spread honey on half the biscuits, then sandwich them with the others. Return to the cooling rack.
8. Warm the chocolate on a plate over a pan of hot water until it has melted and there are no lumps.
9. Spoon over the chocolate to cover the biscuits completely.
10. When set (and if there is enough chocolate) fill a small piping bag fitted with a writing nozzle with melted chocolate and pipe a design over the set chocolate. Store in an airtight container.

Makes 20

Marzipan Logs

110g/¼lb caster sugar
110g/¼lb icing sugar
225g/½lb ground almonds
1 egg

1 egg yolk
2 drops peppermint essence
Few drops green colouring
170g/6oz plain chocolate

1. First make the marzipan: sift the icing sugar and caster sugar together in a bowl. Mix with the ground almonds.
2. Mix together the egg, egg yolk, peppermint essence and green colouring.
3. Add the sugar mixture and beat briefly with a wooden spoon. Knead with the hands just enough to give smoothness (over-working will draw the oil out of the almonds, giving too greasy a paste).
4. Shape the paste into thin sausages 1cm/½in in diameter and leave to dry slightly on a wire rack. Meanwhile break the chocolate into a pudding basin, put the basin in a pan of simmering water and melt the chocolate, stirring occasionally. Remove the basin and allow the chocolate to cool until runny but fairly thick.
5. Put the wire rack over a tray to catch any drips of chocolate, then spoon the melted chocolate over the top and sides of the marzipan and leave to set.
6. When the chocolate has set turn the log over and spoon chocolate (you may have to melt it again slightly) on to the other side.
7. When the chocolate is on the point of setting take a fork and mark lines on the chocolate with the prongs to represent the bark of a log. Cut into 2½cm/1in pieces.

Makes about 30

Coconut Ice

450g/1lb granulated sugar
190ml/⅓ pint milk
170g/6oz desiccated coconut
Peppermint *or* vanilla
  flavouring

2 tablespoons sweetened
  condensed milk
Pink colouring

1. Put the sugar and milk into a pan and place over a low heat until the sugar has melted.
2. Let it boil for about 10 minutes (or until it reaches 125 C/ 240 F) when the mixture will form a soft ball if dropped into cold water.
3. Remove from the heat, add the coconut and a few drops of peppermint or vanilla flavouring. Mix well and pour half of the mixture into a greased tin.
4. Add a few drops of pink colouring to the other half of the mixture and stir well. Pour this over the white half of the mixture in the tin. Leave until it is cold and firm. Cut into small oblong pieces.

Makes 24

Chocolate Fudge

450g/1lb caster sugar
290ml/½ pint water
1 large can condensed milk

30g/1oz butter
110g/¼lb chocolate
Vanilla essence

1. Lightly oil two shallow baking tins.
2. Dissolve the sugar slowly in the water, bring to the boil and add the condensed milk and butter.
3. Boil for a further 30 minutes, stirring occasionally to prevent sticking, or until the mixture leaves the side of the pan.

4. Melt the chocolate and add it to the mixture with a few drops of vanilla essence.
5. Pour into the oiled tins, cut into small squares and leave to set.
6. Cut again and put into an airtight tin or jar for storage.

Makes 16

Truffles

110g/¼lb cake crumbs
55g/2oz caster sugar
55g/2oz cocoa powder
55g/2oz unsalted butter, melted

2 tablespoons rum
225g/½lb plain chocolate
2 tablespoons water
Extra cocoa to finish

1. Place the crumbs, caster sugar and cocoa and stir well together in a mixing bowl.
2. Stir in the butter and rum and mix to a soft but firm paste, shape into balls and leave in the refrigerator until firm.
3. Meanwhile melt the chocolate with the water. Dip the truffles in the melted chocolate and leave on a piece of greaseproof paper.
4. When the truffles are nearly dry, roll them in cocoa powder.

Note: These are best made a few days in advance.

Makes 20

9
Preserving

───────◆───────

The word 'preserves' should cover all food that has been treated to keep for longer than it would if fresh. Frozen food, dried food, salted food and smoked food are all preserves. But the word in household language means jams, jellies, marmalades, pickles, and sometimes bottled food; in short, the sort of preserves found on a good countrywoman's larder shelf.

To be precise: *Jellies* are clear preserves, made from strained fruit juice. They should be neither runny nor too solid. *Jams* are made from crushed fruit. They should almost hold their shape, but be runnier than jelly. *Conserves* are jams containing a mixture of fruits, generally including citrus fruit, and sometimes raisins or nuts. *Marmalade* is jam made exclusively from citrus fruit. *Fruit butters* are made from smooth fruit purées, cooked with sugar until the consistency of thick cream. *Fruit cheeses* are made in the same way but cooked until very thick. Butters and cheeses, because they are not set solidly and generally contain less sugar than jams, should be potted in sterilized jars. *Curds* generally contain butter and eggs, are best kept refrigerated, and will not keep more than a month or two.

To add to the confusion the word 'preserve' is sometimes used to mean whole fruit jams, or whole fruits suspended in thick syrup.

732

JAMS, JELLIES AND MARMALADES

These preserves depend on four main factors to make them keep:

a. The presence of pectin. This is a substance, converted from the gum-like pectose found to some degree in all fruit, which acts with the acids of the fruit and with the sugar to form a jelly-like set. Slightly under-ripe fruit is higher in pectin than over-ripe fruit, and some fruit, notably apples, quinces, damsons, sour plums, lemons and redcurrants are high in pectin so that jam from them will set easily. Jam from low-pectin fruit such as strawberries, rhubarb, mulberries and pears may need added commercial pectin or lemon juice (or a little high-pectin fruit) to obtain a set.

To test for pectin: take a teaspoon of the simmered fruit juice (before adding the sugar) and put it into a glass. When it is cold add three tablespoons of methylated spirit. After a minute a jelly will have formed. If it is in one or more firm clots there is adequate pectin in the fruit. If the jelly clots are numerous and soft the jam will not set without the addition of more pectin.

b. A high concentration of sugar, which is itself a preservative. Without sufficient sugar the pectin will not act to form the set.

c. The presence of acid which, like sugar, acts with the pectin to form a gel or set. Acid also prevents the growth of bacteria, and it helps to prevent the crystallization of the sugar in the jam during storage. If the fruit is low in acid, tartaric acid, citric acid or lemon juice may be added.

d. The elimination and exclusion of micro-organisms. The jam itself is sterilized by rapid boiling. Jam jars need not normally be sterilized since the heat of the jam should be sufficient to sterilize them. However, harmless moulds do sometimes form round the

733

rim and on the surface of jams potted in this way, and sterilizing the jars does help to prevent this. Jam jars to be sterilized should be put, clean, into a large saucepan, covered with hot but not boiling water and brought to the boil. 20 minutes' boiling will sterilize jars in an open saucepan, 2 minutes' in a pressure cooker. Alternatively they may be soaked in solutions bought at chemists for sterilizing babies' bottles etc. Ordinary household bleach will do too, but the bottles should be rinsed in boiling water afterwards. The jam funnel should be sterilized with the jars. It is not necessary to sterilize ladles or spoons except by leaving them in the bubbling jam for a minute or two. Jelly cloths or bags need not be sterilized as the juice is dripped through them before being boiled.

The jam, once put into the clean jars, is sealed to prevent the infiltration of mildew spores etc. Melted paraffin wax (melted white candles will do) poured over the surface of the jam, or used to stick down the edges of the paper covers, makes a good old-fashioned and most effective seal, but most cooks rely on ordinary paper jam covers and a bit of luck.

Ideally sealing should be done while the jam is boiling hot – i.e. before any fresh mildew spores can enter. However, if liquid wax is used on hot jam it may disturb the flat surface. So the slightly cooled but still clear wax is poured on once the jam is set. Two applications of wax are necessary if the first covering shrinks away from the sides of the jar, leaving a gap.

Perhaps the best method of sealing is to use screw-tops. They should be sterilized and checked for a tight fit. The jam should be poured up to the shoulder of the jars, leaving a good 1cm/$\frac{1}{2}$in. The caps are screwed on tightly as soon as the jars are filled. The cooling air in the neck will form a partial vacuum, tightly sealing the jar. (A word of warning: if the screw-tops are rusty or are of metal not coated in plastic they should not be used.)

If, in spite of all precautions, mould appears on the top of the jams, it can be scraped off and the jam beneath will be perfectly good. But it should be eaten fairly soon as mould spores in the air of the larder could affect other preserves. Scraping off visible mould will not prevent the invisible spores from multiplying.

YIELD

The amount of finished jam obtained varies according to type, jellies giving comparatively little, marmalades and whole fruit jams much more. But, as a general rule, the mixture will yield between $1\frac{1}{2}$ times and double the weight of sugar used. It is wise to over-estimate the amount of jars needed, rather than have to prepare more at the last minute.

EQUIPMENT

Making jam is easy enough, but it requires a little organization. First the equipment should be assembled:

Accurate scales
Preserving pan *or* a large heavy pan with a solid base
Sharp knives
Grater
Mincer
Long-handled wooden spoons
Perforated spoon
Metal jug with a large lip *or* a jam funnel
Jam jars
Jam covers, labels and rubber bands (available from chemists and stationers) *or* screw-top lids with enamelled *or* plasticized inner rims
Sugar thermometer (not essential but useful)
Perforated skimmer (not essential but useful)

POINTS TO REMEMBER

a. Make sure all equipment is absolutely clean.
b. Use dry, unblemished, barely ripe fruit.
c. Use preserving, lump, granulated or caster sugar. Modern white sugars are highly refined and therefore suitable. They need little skimming and give a clear preserve. Using preserving sugar has a slight advantage, because the crystals are larger and

the boiling liquid circulates freely round them, dissolving them rapidly. Caster sugar is inclined to set in a solid mass at the bottom of the pan and take longer to dissolve. Brown sugar gives an unattractive colour to preserves.

d. Covering lukewarm jam could lead to mildew. If the jam is covered immediately any bacteria or mildew spores present in the atmosphere are trapped between jam and seal and will be killed by the heat. If the atmosphere is lukewarm and steamy, perfect incubating conditions are created.

BASIC PROCEDURE

1. Wash and dry the jam jars and warm them in the oven.
2. Pick over the fruit and wash or wipe if necessary.
3. Put the fruit and water in the pan and set to simmer.
4. Warm the sugar in a cool oven. (When it is added to the fruit it will then not lower the temperature too much, and cause prolonged cooking which could impair the colour of the jam.)
5. Bring the fruit to a good boil. Tip in the sugar and stir, without reboiling, until the sugar has dissolved.
6. Once the sugar has dissolved boil rapidly, stirring gently but frequently.
7. When the mixture begins to look like jam (usually about 10 minutes) test for setting. It is important not to overboil since this can make the colour too dark and the texture too solid. It will also ruin the flavour. Overboiling can sometimes even prevent a set by destroying the pectin. If using a thermometer, setting point is 105°C/220°F for jam and 106°C/222°F for marmalade. *To test for setting* put a teaspoon of the jam on to an ice-cold saucer and return it to the ice compartment or freezer to cool rapidly. When cold, push it gently with a finger. The jam will have a slight skin, which will wrinkle if setting point is reached. If a finger is drawn through the jam, it should remain separated, not run together. Also, clear jam or jelly should fall from a spatula, not in a single stream but forming a wavy curtain or 'sheet'. (See the drawings.)

736

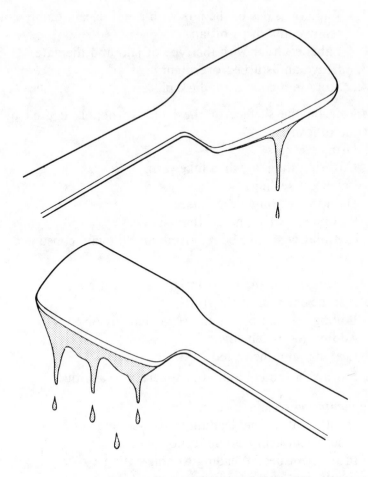

8. As soon as a setting test proves positive draw the jam off the heat. Skim carefully then, if the jam contains whole fruit or large pieces of fruit, allow to cool for 15 minutes. This will prevent the fruit rising to the top of the jam jars.

9. Put the hot jars close together on a wooden board or tray. Fill them with hot jam with the aid of a jug or jam funnel.

10. Seal at once with screw-tops or put waxed paper-discs, waxed-side down, on the surface of the jam, and cover the tops of the jars with cellophane covers, securing them with a rubber band. Brush the cellophane tops with water which will slightly stretch them. Carefully pull them tight. As they dry they will shrink tightly around the jars.

737

11. Wipe the sides of the jars with a hot, clean, damp cloth to remove any drips of jam.
12. Label each jar with the type of jam and the date.
13. Leave undisturbed overnight.
14. Store in a cool, airy, dark place.

Mildew on the surface of the jam is probably caused by one of the following:
a. Using wet jars
b. Covering the jam when lukewarm
c. Imperfect sealing
d. Damp or warm storage place
e. Equipment which is less-than-spotless
  The mildew should be removed, and the jam consumed fairly quickly.

Crystallization of the sugar in jam is caused by:
a. Insufficient acid in the fruit
b. Boiling the jam before the sugar has dissolved
c. Adding too much sugar
d. Leaving jam uncovered
e. Storing in too cold an atmosphere, e.g. a fridge

Fermentation of jam is caused by:
a. Insufficient boiling leading to non-setting
b. Insufficient acid leading to non-setting
c. Insufficient pectin leading to non-setting
d. Insufficient sugar leading to non-setting
e. A storage place which is too warm
f. Jars which are less than spotless

Gooseberry and Orange Jam

450g/1lb gooseberries
Grated rind and juice of 2
  oranges

900g/2lb warm sugar
150ml/¼ pint water

1. Top and tail the gooseberries.
2. Put them with the rind and juice of the oranges and the water into the pan. Simmer until soft and yellowish.

3. Add the warmed sugar, allow it to dissove, then boil rapidly until setting point is reached.
4. Pour into dry, warm jars.
5. Cover and label the jars.
6. Leave undisturbed overnight. Store in a cool, dark, airy place.

Blackcurrant and Rhubarb Jam

450g/1lb blackcurrants   150ml/¼ pint water
55g/2oz rhubarb   450g/1lb sugar

1. Wash the blackcurrants and remove the stalks.
2. Cut the rhubarb into 0·5cm/¼in chunks.
3. Put the rhubarb, blackcurrants and water together in a pan and boil for 30 minutes.
4. Warm the sugar and add it to the pan.
5. When the sugar has dissolved boil rapidly until the jam reaches setting point (about 10–15 minutes).
6. Pour into dry, warm jars.
7. Cover and label the jars.
8. Leave undisturbed overnight. Store in a cool, dark, airy place.

Plum Jam

900g/2lb barely ripe plums   900g/2lb sugar

1. Halve and stone the plums. Crack half the stones and remove the kernels.
2. Put the fruit and sugar together in a bowl and leave to stand overnight. (Do not use a metal container.)
3. Next day transfer to a large saucepan or preserving pan and heat slowly until the sugar has dissolved. Then boil fast until the jam reaches setting point (about 7–10 minutes). Add the kernels while the jam is still bubbling.

4.   Pour into dry, warm, clean jars.
5.   Cover and label the jars.
6.   Leave undisturbed overnight. Store in a cool dark, airy place.

Note I: If the plums are difficult to stone, or damsons or greengages are used, simply slit the flesh of each fruit before mixing with the sugar. During boiling the stones will float to the top and can be removed with a perforated spoon.

Note II: As no water is added to this recipe the flavour is very concentrated. But the basic method described on pages 736–7 works well too.

Strawberry Jam

900g/2lb barely ripe
   strawberries
675g/1½lb sugar, warmed

Juice of 2 lemons
15g/½oz unsalted butter

1.   Hull the strawberries.
2.   Crush a handful in the bottom of a preserving pan with 2 tablespoons of the sugar. Add the lemon juice and stir over a gentle heat until the sugar dissolves.
3.   Add the remaining fruit and bring to the boil.
4.   Add the warmed sugar and when dissolved boil rapidly for 10–12 minutes until the jam reaches setting point.
5.   Stir in the butter and allow to cool for 15 minutes. This will help prevent the berries rising in the jars.
6.   Pour into warm, dry, clean jars.
7.   Cover, and label the jars. Leave undisturbed overnight.
8.   Store in a cool, dark, airy place.

Note: The making of a little syrup with fruit, sugar and lemon juice before adding the bulk of the fruit is done to provide some liquid in which to cook the fruit. Stirring it in a dry pan would lead to crushing and mashing. If possible the fruit should remain whole, suspended in the jam.

740

Orange Marmalade

900g/2lb Seville oranges   2·85 litres/5 pints water
2 lemons   1·8 kilos/4lb sugar

1. Cut the oranges and lemons in half and roughly squeeze them into a large bowl. (Do not bother to extract all the juice: squeezing is simply done to make removing the pips easier.)
2. Remove the pips and tie them up in a piece of muslin or a clean J-cloth.
3. Slice the fruit skins, finely or in chunks as required, and add them to the juice with the bag of pips and the water. Leave to soak for 24 hours.
4. Transfer to a preserving pan or large saucepan and simmer gently until the orange rind is soft and transparent looking – about 2 hours.
5. Warm the sugar in a slow oven for 20 minutes or so, then tip into the orange pulp. Stir while bringing the mixture slowly to the boil.
6. Once the sugar has dissolved boil rapidly until setting point is reached (106°C/222°F). This may take as much as 20 minutes, but is usually less. Test after 5 minutes and then again at 3-minute intervals.
7. Allow to cool for 10 minutes then fill into warm dry jars. Cover with jam covers and leave for 24 hours.
8. Label and store in a cool, dark, airy place.

Clear Grapefruit Marmalade

2 grapefruit   2·28 litres/4 pints water
4 lemons   1·5 kilos/3lb sugar

1. Wash the grapefruit and lemons. Cut in half and squeeze out the juice.
2. Strain the juice into a bowl with the water.

3. Shred or chop the peel and pith of both lemons and grapefruit. Put them in a loose muslin bag with the pips of the lemons only.
4. Put the bag in the pan of juice and water. Allow to soak overnight.
5. Transfer the juice and muslin bag to a preserving pan or saucepan and boil until the skins in the bag are tender ($1\frac{1}{2}$–2 hours) and the liquid in the pan has reduced by half.
6. Warm the sugar.
7. Remove the muslin bag, squeezing it to extract all the juice before discarding.
8. Add the warmed sugar, stir and bring to the boil.
9. Boil rapidly for 8–10 minutes and test for setting.
10. Pour the marmalade into warm, dry jars and cover. Leave undisturbed for 24 hours. Store in a dark, dry place.

Note: If shreds of rind are wanted in the jelly pare the rind from the pith and shred it separately. Add to the boiling liquid.

Redcurrant Jelly

Redcurrants   450g/1lb sugar to each 570ml/
                                      1 pint of juice extracted

1. Place the washed fruit in a stone or earthenware pot, cover and place in a moderate oven, 180°C/350°F, gas mark 4. If your jar or pot is glass rather than pottery stand it in a bain-marie before placing in the oven.
2. Cook until the fruit is tender and the juice has run from it (about 1 hour). Mash the fruit with a fork 3 or 4 times during the cooking process.
3. Turn into a scalded muslin or jelly bag and allow to drain overnight.
4. Measure the juice and mix with 450g/1lb sugar to each 570ml/1 pint of juice.

5. Dissolve over a gentle heat and then boil rapidly until setting point is reached (about 5 minutes).
6. Pour into warm, dry jars.
7. Cover and tie down. Label and store.

Note: This jelly, made without the addition of water, gives a strong concentrated fruit flavour, but yields comparatively little jelly. It is not worth doing with less than 1·35 kilos/3lb fruit. The more usual method is to simmer the fruit in water, then proceed from 3.

Lemon Curd

2 large lemons
85g/3oz butter

225g/½lb granulated sugar
3 eggs

1. Grate the rind of the lemons on the finest gauge on the grater, taking care to grate rind only, not pith.
2. Squeeze the juice from the lemons.
3. Put the rind, juice, butter, sugar and lightly beaten eggs into a heavy saucepan or double-boiler and heat gently, stirring all the time until the mixture is thick.
4. Strain into a bowl and allow to cool.

Note: This curd will keep in the refrigerator for about three weeks.

BOTTLING FRUIT

The preservation of food by bottling works on the principle of destruction (by heat) of all micro-organisms present in the fruit or syrup. Because a partial vacuum is created in the jar (by expelling air during processing) a tight seal is formed between lid and jar, keeping the sterilized contents uncontaminated.

The principle of canning is similar. But cans need a special machine to seal them.

The procedure described here applies to the bottling of fruit only. Vegetables and meat (because they contain little or no acid, and therefore are likely to harbour bacteria) need considerably longer processing at higher temperatures to become safe. This lengthy heating tends to spoil the texture and flavour of the vegetables or meat. In general, bottling meat and vegetables is not worth the effort, time and risks involved. But fruit and tomatoes, because they are fairly acid, will not contain bacteria; and the relatively harmless yeasts and moulds are more easily destroyed.

PREPARING THE FRUIT

Fruit can be bottled raw or cooked. If the fruit is cooked the processing time need only be long enough for sterilization, not for tenderizing the fruit. If raw, the fruit is cooked and sterilized at the same time, and may need longer processing. Some fruits, which cook to a pulp easily, such as berries and cooking apples, are generally processed from raw as the minimum time at great heat is the objective. Other fruits such as pears and peaches, which require an uncertain time to soften, are frequently pre-cooked as it is then possible to tell if they are tender. Pre-cooking has a further advantage. Once the fruit is cooked and softened, more of it can be packed into the jars. Also, it will not rise up in the jar when sterilized. Fruit bottled from raw frequently rises. This does not matter but means the expensive jars contain more syrup and less fruit. The only certain way to prevent fruit rising is to bottle it in a very light syrup, which is not always desirable. Once the jars are sealed testing is of course impossible. A few points are worth remembering:

a. Make sure the bottling jars are not cracked and the tops are in good condition. Kilner jars must have new lids each year, and Parfait jars new washers. Screw bands or metal clips should work properly and jars should be clean.
b. Make the sugar syrup before peeling the fruit.

c. Choose perfect, not over-ripe fruit.

d. If fruit needs cutting or peeling use a stainless steel knife.

e. If it is likely to discolour (apples or pears) drop the pieces into cold water containing a teaspoon of ascorbic acid (vitamin C powder or a fizzy Redoxon tablet will do) until you are ready to process them.

f. Pack the fruit (cooked or raw) up to the necks of the jars.

JARS

Kilner jars come with a metal lid with a rubber band incorporated in it. The lid is kept in place by a metal screw-band. The lid must not be re-used as it will not give a good seal twice, and the rubber is perishable. Kilner jars are closed loosely before processing, and only tightened fully when they come *out* of the sterilizer or saucepan, while still hot. As the hot air inside cools it will contract, pulling the lid on tightly as it does so. The pressure of the partial vacuum will cause the lid (which starts off convex in shape) to 'pop' into a concave position. The sound of this can be alarming but it simply means that a vacuum seal has been achieved.

Parfait jars are similar to Kilner jars but have glass lids with rubber washers round them. The lid is held in place by a metal gimp or clip. It is clipped shut *before* processing. There is sufficient spring in the gimp to allow the escape of steam during heating. The lid tightens automatically as the jar cools after processing.

PROCESSING THE FRUIT

Processing (or sterilizing) of the fruit can be done in the following ways:

a. In a sterilizer (sometimes called a pressure canner). This is a purpose-made machine like a large pressure cooker. It is reliable and easy to use, but by no means essential. Follow the manufacturer's instructions.

b. *In a pressure cooker*, which works like a sterilizer but holds fewer jars and will not hold tall ones. About 2·5cm/1in of water in the bottom is sufficient as no evaporation will take place: the process is very quick, and the jars and fruit sterilize in the steam. Wedge the jars with cloths to stop them rattling. Allow the pressure to fall before opening the cooker. Consult the maker's manual.

c. *In a deep saucepan or bath of boiling water*. Stand the jars in the container and wedge them with cloths to stop them rattling or cracking. Fill with hot water right over the tops of the jars, or at least up to their necks. Cover as best you can with lid or foil and tea-towels to keep in the steam. (See table on pages 747–51.)

Note I: Processing in the oven is not recommended. The temperatures cannot be reliably checked and the jars sometimes crack or explode, or boil over.

Note II: If the fruit has been cooked in an open pan with its syrup, it is possible to get a good seal by closing the jar as soon as the hot fruit and boiling syrup are in it, without further sterilization, but the method is less reliable.

TESTING FOR SEALING

After processing, the jars should be lifted on to a board. Kilner jars should be screwed up tight. Jars should be left undisturbed for 24 hours. They must then be tested for sealing. Remove the metal bands on the Kilner jars, or loosen the clips on the Parfait jars. It should be possible to lift the jars by the lids, without breaking the seal. If the lid of a jar comes off the jar must be reprocessed with a new washer (Parfait jars) or lid (Kilner jars) or the contents must be eaten within a day or two.

STORING

Wipe the jars with a damp clean cloth, label them with the date of bottling, and store in a dark place. They will keep for at least 18 months, probably for many years.

BOTTLING FRUITS AND TOMATOES

Fruits are usually bottled in sugar syrup, made by dissolving sugar in water. The more sugar the heavier the syrup. Equal measures (using a cup, a jug, or any container) of sugar and water heated together will give a very thick syrup suitable for peaches or sour plums, half as much sugar as water will give a light thin syrup. Use whatever kind of syrup you like, or you think the fruit calls for. The sugar is not necessary as a preservative but for flavour. Tomatoes are bottled in salted water.

PROCESSING

Fruit	Preparation	Pre-cook or pack raw?	Syrup	Length of time in deep saucepan or boiling water bath (at rolling boil)	Length of time in pressure cooker or canner (at 5lb pressure)
Whole dessert apples	Peel, core, quarter. Keep in water containing a teaspoon of vitamin C powder to prevent discoloration until ready.	Poach in thin syrup until tender.	Pack in hot jars with hot syrup.	1 kilo/2lb jars for 10 minutes. 2 kilos/4lb jars for 15 minutes.	1 kilo/2lb jars for 1 minute. 2 kilos/4lb jars for 2 minutes. Leave undisturbed until pressure is reduced to normal.

Fruit	Preparation	Pre-cook or pack raw?	Syrup	Length of time in deep saucepan or boiling water bath (at rolling boil)	Length of time in pressure cooker or canner (at 5lb pressure)
Slices of cooking apple	Peel and slice. Keep in water containing a teaspoon of vitamin C powder to prevent discoloration until ready.	Pack raw slices tightly in jars. Fill up to neck of jars.	Cover with hot thin syrup.	1 kilo/2lb jars for 20 minutes. 2 kilos/4lb jars for 30 minutes.	1 kilo/2lb jars for 1 minute. 2 kilos/4lb jars for 2 minutes. Leave undisturbed until pressure is reduced to normal.
Soft berries and currants	Wash only if sandy or muddy. Pick over carefully.	Pack raw, to neck of jars, liberally sprinkle with sugar and leave to stand overnight.	Do not add any more liquid. The juice will be enough.	1 kilo/2lb jars for 10 minutes. 2 kilos/4lb jars for 15 minutes.	1 kilo/2lb jars for 1 minute. 2 kilos/4lb jars for 2 minutes. Leave undisturbed until pressure is reduced to normal.

Cherries	Wash, de-stalk and prick each cherry with a needle (to prevent bursting).	Pack raw, shaking down firmly, to neck of jars.	Cover with hot heavy syrup for sour cherries; hot medium syrup for sweet ones.	1 kilo/2lb jars for 20 minutes. 2 kilos/4lb jars for 30 minutes.	1 kilo/2lb jars for 1 minute. 2 kilos/4lb jars for 2 minutes. Leave undisturbed until pressure is reduced to normal.
Gooseberries Rhubarb	Wash and prepare as for stewing.	Pack raw, filling jars to neck.	Cover with hot thick syrup.	1 kilo/2lb jars for 10 minutes. 2 kilos/4lb jars for 15 minutes.	1 kilo/2lb jars for 1 minute. 2 kilos/4lb jars for 2 minutes. Leave undisturbed until pressure is reduced to normal.
Peaches (halved)	Boil in water for 10 seconds, or until the skin will come off easily. Peel, halve and stone.	Pack raw, filling jars to neck.	Cover with hot medium or heavy syrup.	1 kilo/2lb jars for 25 minutes. 2 kilos/4lb jars for 30 minutes.	1 kilo/2lb jars for 2 minutes. 2 kilos/4lb jars for 3 minutes. Leave undisturbed until pressure is reduced to normal.

Fruit	Preparation	Pre-cook or pack raw?	Syrup	Length of time in deep saucepan or boiling water bath (at rolling boil)	Length of time in pressure cooker or canner (at 5lb pressure)
Peaches (sliced)	Peel as above and slice.			1 kilo/2lb jars for 20 minutes. 2 kilos/4lb jars for 25 minutes.	1 kilo/2lb jars for 1 minute. 2 kilos/4lb jars for 2 minutes. Leave undisturbed until pressure is reduced to normal.
Ripe pears	Peel, half and core.	Pack raw, filling jars to neck.	Cover with hot medium syrup.	1 kilo/2lb jars for 30 minutes. 2 kilos/4lb jars for 40 minutes.	1 kilo/2lb jars for 3 minutes. 2 kilos/4lb jars for 4 minutes. Leave undisturbed until pressure is reduced to normal.

	Preparation	Pack	Processing	Leave undisturbed
Whole hard pears	Peel. Keep in water containing a teaspoon of vitamin C powder to prevent discoloration until ready. Poach in medium syrup until tender.	Pack in hot jars with hot syrup.	1 kilo/2lb jars for 10 minutes. 2 kilos/4lb jars for 15 minutes.	1 kilo/2lb jars for 1 minute. 2 kilos/4lb jars for 2 minutes. Leave undisturbed until pressure is reduced to normal.
Plums	Wash, de-stalk and prick with large needle. Halve and remove stones if of the 'free stone' type.	Pack raw, filling jars to neck. Cover with hot medium syrup.	1 kilo/2lb jars for 20 minutes. 2 kilos/4lb jars for 25 minutes.	1 kilo/2lb jars for 1 minute. 2 kilos/4lb jars for 2 minutes. Leave undisturbed until pressure is reduced to normal.
Tomatoes	Dip into boiling water for 5 seconds. Skin and quarter or slice.	Pack raw, with a sprinkling of salt and sugar between layers, filling jars to neck. Do not add any more liquid. The juice will be enough.	1 kilo/2lb jars for 35 minutes. 2 kilos/4lb jars for 40 minutes.	1 kilo/2lb jars for 3 minutes. 2 kilos/4lb jars for 4 minutes. Leave undisturbed until pressure is reduced to normal.

Bottled Apples

340g/¾lb sugar   12 apples
1 litre/2 pints water

1. Prepare the sugar syrup: dissolve the sugar in 1 litre/2 pints of water over a gentle heat and when completely dissolved boil rapidly for 2–3 minutes.
2. Peel and slice the apples.
3. Pack tightly into 1 kilo/2lb jars.
4. Pour over the hot syrup.
5. Cover with the lids (not screwed too tight if Kilner jars) and place in the hot water bath. Cover with boiling water.
6. Boil steadily for 20 minutes.
7. Remove the jars and (if Kilner jars) seal firmly.
8. Leave for 24 hours and test for sealing.

Spiced Pears

560g/1¼lb sugar   15g/½oz stick cinnamon
0·5 litre/¾ pint white malt   5 cloves
  vinegar or white wine   2 dried chillies (optional)
6 small whole pears, peeled   2 pieces stem ginger, diced

1. Heat the sugar with the vinegar over gentle heat and when completely dissolved, bring to the boil.
2. Add the prepared pears, the spices and the ginger.
3. Simmer gently until the pears are tender but not broken (about 35 minutes).
4. Remove the pears with a draining spoon and pack into a preserving jar.
5. If the syrup is rather thin boil it rapidly until fairly thick and tacky.
6. Pour over the pears, and add the spices and ginger.
7. Put on the lid (if using a Kilner jar do not tighten). Process in a boiling water bath for 10 minutes.

752

8. Lift out and (if using a Kilner jar) tighten the lid.
9. Leave for 24 hours, then test for sealing.

Bottled Raspberries

900g/2lb raspberries 340g/¾lb granulated sugar

1. Pick over the fruit but do not wash it.
2. Pack into 1 kilo/2lb jars, sprinkling with dry sugar between the layers. Shake the jars to settle the fruit. Leave overnight.
3. Top up to absolutely full with more fruit and sugar.
4. Cover with the lids (not screwed too tightly if Kilner jars). Process in a boiling water bath for 10 minutes.
5. Lift out of the water and tighten the lids if using Kilner jars.
6. Leave for 24 hours, then test for sealing.

PICKLES

Note: Brass, old-fashioned iron or copper preserving pans or saucepans should not be used in the preparation of foods containing vinegar. The acid reacts with the metal, spoiling both colour and flavour of the food, and sometimes rendering it mildly poisonous.

Pickles are foods, usually vegetables or fruit, preserved in vinegar. Fruit for pickles is generally cooked in sugared vinegar, and stored in this sweetened vinegar syrup. Vegetables are usually, but not always, pickled raw, and are generally salted in dry salt, or steeped in brine before being immersed in the vinegar. This salting is done to draw moisture out of the food. If the salting is omitted the juices from the vegetables would leak into the vinegar during storage and so dilute it and impair its keeping quality.

Salt also has preservative powers, and its penetration into the food must help to prevent it 'going bad', but the main preservative in pickles is vinegar, which prevents the growth of bacteria.

The best salt is pure rock salt or crushed block salt. Pure sea salt is good too, but very expensive. Table salt has additives which make it conveniently free-flowing, but which may cause the pickle to go cloudy.

Brining

Brine is a solution of salt in water, and is suitable for the steeping of vegetables for pickling. Firm vegetables such as shallots should be pierced with a needle to allow the brine to penetrate.

450g/½lb pure salt (not table salt)   3 litres/4 pints water

1. Heat the salt and water slowly together until the salt has dissolved.
2. Allow to cool.
3. Prepare (peel, cut up, prick etc.) the vegetables to be pickled, put them into a bowl and pour over the cold brine. Put a plate on top to keep the food submerged.
4. After 24 hours (usually, but check individual recipes) drain well, pat dry and pack into clean jars ready for pickling.

Dry-Salting

This is particularly suitable for 'wet' vegetables such as marrow and cucumber.

110g/¼lb dry pure salt (not table salt) is needed for each 1 kilo/2lb prepared vegetables

1. Prepare (peel, cut up etc.) the vegetables. If they are tough (like onions or shallots) pierce them deeply with a needle.
2. Put them in a bowl, sprinkling each layer liberally with salt. Cover and keep cool for 24 hours.

3. Tip off all the liquid, rinse the vegetables in cold water and pat dry in a clean cloth.
4. Pack into clean jars ready for pickling.

THE VINEGAR

Pickling vinegar should be strong, containing at least 5 per cent acetic acid. Most brand vinegars contain sufficient acid, but home-made vinegars or draught vinegars will not do. Brown malt vinegar is the best vinegar for flavour, especially if the pickle is to be highly spiced, or is made from strong-tasting foods. White vinegar has less flavour, but obviously gives a clearer pickle. Wine vinegar is suitable for delicate mild-tasting foods. Commercial cider vinegar is good too. The vinegar may be spiced and flavoured according to taste by the addition of hot spices such as cayenne, ginger or chillies, or aromatic spices such as cardamon seeds, cloves or nutmeg. Whole spices are best as they can be easily removed, and will not leave the vinegar murky. Ready-spiced pickling vinegar may also be bought.

Basic Spiced Vinegar for Pickles

1·14 litres/2 pints malt vinegar
8g/¼oz blades of mace
8g/¼oz cinnamon stick
8g/¼oz allspice berries
8g/¼oz black peppercorns

8g/¼oz mustard seed
4 whole cloves
1 chilli
15g/½oz sliced root ginger

1. Put everything into a large saucepan (not an unlined copper or brass or iron one) and heat gently, covered tightly, until on the point of simmering. Remove from heat.
2. Leave for 3 hours, then strain through muslin, a jelly bag or J-cloth. The vinegar is now ready for use.

THE JARS AND LIDS

Any wide-necked jar is suitable for pickles provided it has a good air-tight lid. This is not so much to keep bacteria out (the vinegar will see to that) but to prevent the vinegar evaporating. Cork stoppers, glass stoppers, or stone lids are suitable. Raw metal corrodes if allowed in contact with vinegar, so metal screw-tops must be protected by waxed cardboard, plastic film, or thick greaseproof paper. Many jars from commercial products are suitable as their lids are sprayed with a coat of paint or a thin film of plastic. Preserving jars with sealing lids are suitable but not necessary. Paper jam covers do not make sturdy enough seals. They are unsuitable for liquids and anyway might allow the evaporation of the vinegar.

Stoppers that do not fit perfectly can be sealed tight with a little melted paraffin wax.

Sterilization of the jars for pickles is not normally considered necessary as the vinegar will prevent the growth of micro-organisms.

PACKING THE JARS

1. Pack the vegetables or fruit, tightly but without bruising, in the clean jars.
2. Top up with the vinegar (hot or cold according to the recipe). Cover the food by at least 1cm/½in to allow for evaporation. If the jars have metal lids (even protected as described above) leave a little headroom. Otherwise fill to the brim.
3. Cover the jar (and seal it with paraffin wax if necessary) at once.
4. Store for six months, if possible, before using.

Pickled Shallots or Small Onions

An example of a raw pickle, salted in brine.

Small, even-sized onions, *or*   Brine (page 754)
   shallots   Pickling vinegar (page 755)

1. Scald the onions to make peeling them easier. Peel them. Prick deeply all over with a needle or skewer.
2. Put the onions or shallots in a bowl and cover with brine. Leave for 48 hours.
3. Drain thoroughly and pat dry with a clean cloth.
4. Pack tightly, but without bruising, into clean jars.
5. Cover well with the cold pickling vinegar.
6. Seal and store for six months before eating.

Pickled Beetroot

An example of a cooked pickle, not given preliminary salting.

Small, even-sized beetroots   Pickling vinegar (page 755)
Pure salt

1. Cook the beetroots, unpeeled, in boiling, heavily salted water (1 tablespoon to 1·1 litres/2 pints) until tender ($1\frac{1}{2}$–2 hours).
2. Drain and allow to cool. Skin them.
3. Pack, without bruising, into jars.
4. Cover well with cold pickling vinegar.
5. Add a level teaspoon pure salt to each 1 kilo/2lb jar.
6. Seal and store.

Note: If a milder pickle is wanted the vinegar may be diluted by an equal amount of water. But if this is done the beetroot must be packed in a preserving (Kilner or Parfait) jar, and must be given a sterilization treatment in a boiling water bath for 30 minutes, or in a pressure cooker or canner for 2 minutes (see page 745).

Dill Cucumber Pickle

An example of a pickle dry-salted and packed in sweet spiced vinegar.

900g/2lb cucumbers
Pure salt
Pickling vinegar (page 755)
1 fresh dill head, *or* 1 tablespoon
  dill seeds

2 teaspoons mustard seed
2 garlic cloves, sliced
170g/6oz granulated *or*
  preserving sugar

1. If the cucumbers are small enough to leave whole, prick them all over with a needle. If large cut them into chunks, without peeling, and put into a bowl, sprinkling each layer liberally with salt. Leave for 24 hours.
2. Put the spiced vinegar (about 1 litre/1¾ pints) into a saucepan and add the dill, mustard seed, garlic and sugar. Bring slowly to the boil, then cool.
3. Rinse the cucumber and pat dry with a clean cloth.
4. Pack the cucumber into jars. Cover with the cooled vinegar, adding the flavourings if liked.
5. Seal and store.

CHUTNEYS

Chutneys are the easiest preserves to make. They are mixtures, always sweet and sour, somewhere between a pickle and a jam. They are generally made of fruit (or sometimes soft vegetables such as tomato or marrow), with vinegar, onion and spices.

Both sugar and salt, themselves preservatives, are present in chutneys, but they are there for flavour more than for their keeping powers. As with jams, the boiling of the ingredients destroys micro-organisms, but with chutneys obtaining a set is

758

not necessary – like pickles, they depend on vinegar for their keeping qualities.

Fruit and vegetables for chutneys should be sliced or cut small enough to be lifted with a teaspoon, but not so small as to be unidentifiable in the chutney.

As the ingredients are seldom used whole, damaged or bruised fruit, with the imperfect bits removed, can be used.

Chutneys improve with keeping. They can generally be eaten after two months (before this their taste is harsh) but are at their best between six months and two years.

If the chutney is to be kept for more than six months a more certain seal than a jam cover is advisable. See the notes for jars and lids for pickles on page 756.

BASIC PROCEDURE FOR CHUTNEY

1. Prepare the ingredients: wash fruit and vegetables, peel where necessary, cut up etc. Wash dried fruit if bought loose. Chop or mince onions. Use a stainless steel fruit knife for fruit or vegetables liable to discolour.
2. Put all ingredients, except sugar and vinegar, into a saucepan (*not an unlined copper, brass or old-fashioned iron one:* see note on page 753). The spices should be tied in a muslin bag if they are to be removed later.
3. Add enough to the vinegar to easily cover the other ingredients.
4. Cook slowly, covered or not, until the fruit or vegetables are soft, and most of the liquid has evaporated.
5. Add the sugar and the rest of the vinegar and stir until the sugar has dissolved.
6. Boil to the consistency of jam, thick and syrupy.
7. Put into clean, hot jars. Cover as for jam if to be eaten within six months. Use non-metal lids or stoppers if to be kept longer.

Note: In recipes for chutneys that do not require prolonged cooking to soften the ingredients (e.g. apricot and orange chutney, page 760) the sugar and vinegar may be added with the other ingredients – the whole being boiled together.

Green Tomato and Apple Chutney

1·35 kilos/3lb green tomatoes
900g/2lb apples (any kind)
2 large onions, chopped
110g/¼lb sultanas
1 teaspoon salt
1 teaspoon ground ginger
½ teaspoon ground nutmeg
½ teaspoon white pepper
Pinch of allspice
860ml/1½ pints vinegar
340g/¾lb granulated *or* preserving sugar

1. Chop the tomatoes. Peel and chop the apples.
2. Put everything except the sugar and a cup of the vinegar into a saucepan and simmer gently, giving an occasional stir, for 1½ hours or until the ingredients are soft and the liquid almost gone.
3. Add the rest of the vinegar and the sugar, and stir slowly until the sugar has dissolved.
4. Boil fast, stirring, until thick.
5. Pour into hot, dry jars. If to be eaten within six months, cover as for jam. If to be kept longer use non-metal lids or stoppers.

Apricot and Orange Chutney

4 oranges
900g/2lb apricots (weight when stoned)
1 onion, thinly sliced
225g/½lb sultanas
450g/1lb demerara sugar
170g/6oz preserving sugar, chopped
2 teaspoons rock salt
570ml/1 pint cider vinegar
1 tablespoon mustard seed
1 teaspoon turmeric

1. Boil the oranges whole for 5 minutes. Pare the skin with a sharp knife, removing all pith left on the back.
2. Shred the rind into thin needleshreds.
3. Peel the oranges and discard all the pith. Chop up the flesh.
4. Place the orange rind and flesh together with all the other

ingredients in a large pan and simmer until the fruit is soft
and pulpy and the mixture thick and syrupy.

5. Pour immediately into warm, dry jars and cover with jam
    covers if to be eaten within a few months, or more securely
    with non-metal lids or stoppers if to be kept longer.

10
Breakfast

Framed Eggs

4 large slices of white bread   Butter
Oil for frying   2 large tomatoes
4 large flat mushrooms   4 eggs

1. With a large round biscuit cutter remove the middle from the bread slices. Do not throw away the rest of the bread.
2. Fry the rounds in oil until brown on both sides.
3. Dot the mushrooms with butter and grill them.
4. Cut the tomatoes in half; grill them until just cooked.
5. Set each mushroom on a round of fried bread and put half a tomato on top. Keep warm.
6. Now fry the bread frames (the pieces left after the middle was removed from the bread slices) on one side.
7. Turn them over and break an egg into the middle of each.
8. Fry until the whites are set, spooning over some of the hot fat to help the process.
9. Serve each framed egg with the mushroom and tomato on fried bread.

Serves 4

Poached Eggs on Toast

Salt and vinegar   4 very fresh cold eggs
4 slices fresh toast, buttered

1. Fill a large saucepan with water until 7·5cm/3in deep. Add salt and 1 tablespoon vinegar and bring to simmering point.
2. Crack an egg on the side of the pan and, holding the shell as near to the water as possible, drop the egg in.
3. Raise the temperature so that the water bubbles gently.
4. With a perforated spoon, draw the egg white close to the yolk.
5. Poach each egg for 2 or 3 minutes.
6. Lift out with the perforated spoon, drain on absorbent paper and, if the egg whites are very ragged at the edges, trim them.
7. Place each egg on a piece of toast and sprinkle with salt and pepper. Serve immediately.

Serves 4

Jugged Kippers

4 kippers   Freshly ground black pepper
Butter

1. Place the kippers, tail up, in a tall stoneware jug. Pour over enough boiling water to cover the kippers and leave to stand for 5–10 minutes.
2. Serve immediately on a warm dish with a knob of butter and plenty of pepper.

Note: This is a simple labour-saving method of cooking kippers.

Serves 4

Kedgeree

55g/2oz butter
140g/5oz long-grain rice, boiled
  (weighed before cooking)
340g/¾lb smoked haddock
  fillet, cooked, skinned and
  boned *or* cooked fresh
  salmon if preferred

3 hardboiled eggs, coarsely
  chopped
Salt, pepper and cayenne

1. Melt the butter in a large shallow pan and add everything else.
2. Stir gently until very hot.

Note: If making large quantities, heat in the oven instead of on the top. Kedgeree will not spoil in a low oven (130°C/250°F, gas mark 1). Stir occasionally to prevent the sides getting hot before the middle.

Serves 4

Muesli

Named after Bircher Muesli, a Swiss doctor and health fanatic, this should contain nothing but natural ingredients, and no refined cereals. It usually consists of flaked oats, crushed or flaked wheat (including the bran and wheatgerm) and can include other cereals too. If cracked wheat or maize is included it needs to be soaked overnight before eating. Instant porridge oats or flaked oats can be eaten without soaking. Almost any fresh fruit can be added to muesli and it is served with yoghurt, milk or cream (or mixture of any or all of these). If muesli is sweetened this should be done with raw unrefined brown sugar or honey.

To make a family supply of Muesli mix together:

450g/1lb instant porridge oats
55g/2oz dried apricots,
  chopped
55g/2oz sultanas
110g/¼lb dried apple flakes
55g/2oz hazelnuts, chopped
55g/2oz bran

30g/1oz flaked almonds
110g/¼lb 'honey crunch' *or*
  'granola' *or* other toasted
  cereal (optional, but
  improves the texture)
30g/1oz unrefined brown sugar

Porridge

1·14 litres/2 pints water
110g/¼lb medium oatmeal

1 good teaspoon salt

1. Boil the water in a saucepan and add the salt.
2. Sprinkle in the oatmeal, keeping the water on the boil and stirring all the time.
3. Simmer for 30 minutes, stirring occasionally. If necessary add a little more water.

Note: Porridge keeps for an hour or so in a cool oven if covered with a lid, but should not be made too far in advance. Traditionall it is served with salt in Scotland, but in the south milk and sugar are added. Brown sugar and cream are wonderful.

Serves 4

11
Cocktail bits,
Snacks and Savouries

COCKTAIL BITS

Pumpernickel with Salami

450g/1lb salami, skinned and
  thinly sliced
About 30 slices of pumpernickel
  bread

Butter

1. Get the delicatessen to skin and slice the salami on their machine as thinly as they can.
2. Cut each slice of pumpernickel into two, or cut two rounds out of it with a pastry cutter.
3. Butter and cover with slices of salami.

Makes 60 *canapés*

Curried Eggs

10 hardboiled eggs
1 tablespoon butter
1 teaspoon mild curry powder

1 tablespoon thick mayonnaise
  (page 316)
Sliced gherkin *or* sultanas for
  garnish

1. Trim the pointed end from each egg and cut in half across the middle parallel to the trimmed end.
2. Remove and sieve the yolks.
3. Melt the butter and add the curry powder; cook for 1 minute and add to the egg yolks. Stir in the mayonnaise.
4. Stand the egg whites on the flat ends and fill the egg mixture into them using a forcing bag or spoon.
5. Decorate with a piece of sliced gherkin or a sultana.

Note: Each egg will yield three curried eggs if the instructions for cutting and filling them, given in the next recipe, are followed.

Makes 20

Caviar Eggs

10 hardboiled eggs   1 tablespoon mock caviar
1 tablespoon soured cream   (Danish lumpfish roe)
Pepper

1. Trim the pointed end from each egg. Cut the eggs across in three (see diagram).

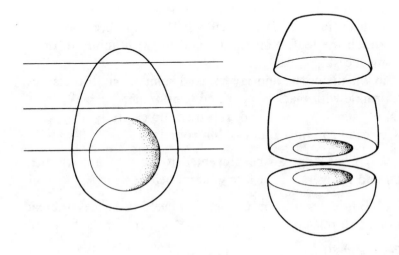

2. Remove the yolks and mash or sieve them until smooth. Add enough sour cream to make a soft but not sloppy paste. Season with pepper.
3. Fill the egg white 'cups' with the mixture, using a forcing bag or spoon, and, treating the slices of egg white as a base, simply pipe a small round of mixture on to them.
4. Decorate the top of the stuffed eggs with the caviar.

Makes 30

Smoked Salmon Catherine Wheels

1 very large square-edged loaf of brown bread	450g/1lb thinly sliced smoked salmon
Butter, well softened	Freshly ground black pepper
	Lemon juice

1. Put the loaf of bread on a board and carefully cut off the top crust all along the length of the loaf.
2. Butter the top of the bread, being careful not to crumble it.
3. Now cut as thin a horizontal slice as you can.
4. Again butter the loaf and cut off the next slice and so on through the loaf. You should end up with about 10 or 12 long slices.
5. Cut off the crusts and lay smoked salmon on all the slices. Sprinkle with black pepper and lemon juice.
6. Now, starting at one end, roll them up carefully.
7. Cut each roll into about 8 thin rounds.

Note I: Unravelling can be prevented if the rolls are wrapped in foil and refrigerated for a few hours before slicing.

Note II: For larger rolls or 'Catherine wheels' two slices of bread may be used: roll up one, then roll the next round the first roll.

Makes about 80

Smoked Salmon Triangles

Butter   Pepper
20 slices brown bread   450g/1lb smoked salmon

1. Butter the bread, sprinkle with pepper and lay the smoked salmon slices carefully on top.
2. Cut off the crusts and cut each slice into four triangles.

Makes 80

Stuffed Dates

110g/¼lb nibbed almonds   340g/¾lb cream cheese
60 dates (about 2 boxes)

1. Brown the almonds under the grill or in a hot oven and allow to cool.
2. Cut the dates open lengthwise. Replace each stone with a teaspoon of cream cheese.
3. Slightly close the dates, leaving the cream cheese showing. Dip the cheese into the nuts.

Note: Dried dates are good. Fresh ones are wonderful.

Makes 60

Prawn Ritz

450g/1lb frozen peeled prawns   4 tablespoons very thick
Butter   mayonnaise (page 316)
60 Ritz crackers (about 1   Paprika
    packet) *or* small savoury
    biscuits

1. Thaw the prawns.
2. Butter the crackers well.
3. Squeeze out any moisture from the prawns – they should be quite dry.
4. Mix the prawns with the mayonnaise and spoon a blob on to each biscuit. Sprinkle with paprika.

Makes 60

Celery and Cream Cheese

10 sticks celery
340g/¾lb cream cheese

Chives, finely chopped
Pepper and salt

1. Wash and scrub the celery, and cut into 5cm/2in lengths. If the sticks are very wide they should be split into two.
2. Cream the cheese and add the chives, pepper and salt.
3. Using a forcing bag fitted with a fluted nozzle pipe the cheese into the hollow of the celery sticks. It may be necessary to trim the underside of each celery stick to prevent it rolling over when on a plate.

Makes about 50

Pâté on Baked Bread

15 large slices white bread
Butter
450g/1lb smooth pâté (fish *or* meat) beaten until soft

Slices of black olive for decoration

1. With a small round cutter cut four rounds out of each slice of bread.
2. Bake these in a cool oven until crisp and dry like rusks.

3. When cool spread well with butter and pipe a swirl of pâté on to each.
4. Decorate with a slice of olive.

Makes about 60

Chicken Livers Wrapped in Bacon

450g/1lb chicken livers   (Wooden cocktail sticks)
60 small slices streaky bacon

1. Set the oven to 220°C/425°F, gas mark 7.
2. Trim and discard the discoloured part from the livers.
3. Roll small pieces of liver in bacon and lay them side by side in a roasting pan, fairly tightly packed to prevent unravelling.
4. Bake for about 15 minutes or until they are just beginning to go brown on top. Drain well.
5. Stick a cocktail stick into each roll. They are now ready to serve, but if they are to be reheated, remove them from the roasting pan and keep in a cool place until needed. If the cocktail sticks are stuck in before reheating, make sure they are wood and not plastic. Reheat for 10 minutes.

Makes about 60

Prawn Bouchées

60 bouchée cases, cooked *or*   Beaten egg
    450g/1lb flour-quantity puff
    pastry (frozen is fine)

For the filling:
55g/2oz butter
$\frac{1}{2}$ onion, finely chopped   560ml/1 pint creamy milk
55g/2oz flour   Salt and pepper
340g/$\frac{3}{4}$lb frozen peeled prawns,
    thawed and well drained

771

1. Set the oven to 200°C/400°F, gas mark 6.
2. Roll out the pastry to about the thickness of a penny.
3. With a small round pastry cutter stamp it out in rounds.
4. With a slightly smaller cutter or the end of a large piping nozzle mark a circle in the centre of each round, but be careful not to stamp the pastry through.
5. With the beaten egg brush the top of the outer rings only.
6. Bake until very brown and crisp (about 12 minutes). Cool.
7. Melt the butter, add the onion and cook slowly until pale and transparent.
8. Add the flour and cook for a further minute.
9. Stir the milk to make a thick paste. Season with salt and pepper. Simmer for 2 minutes.
10. Add the prawns and bring to the boil, stirring.
11. Fill the hot bouchées with the mixture.

Makes 60

Cocktail Sausages with Mustard Dip

60 chipolata *or* 120 cocktail   (Cocktail sticks)
  sausages (450g/1lb)

For the dip:
Mustard mayonnaise
  (page 773)

1. Set the oven to 200°C/400°F, gas mark 6.
2. Make the chipolata sausages into cocktail size by twisting each sausage into two. After twisting, cut them apart.
3. Put them into a greased roasting pan and bake for 20 minutes or until beginning to brown. The roasting pan should be shaken at intervals to prevent the sausages sticking. They should be stirred around to prevent those in the edge getting browner than those in the middle.

4. Drain well and stick in the cocktail sticks. Serve the dip separately.

Makes 120

Mustard Mayonnaise

French mustard
Mayonnaise (page 316)
Finely chopped onion

Crushed garlic
Chopped mint

Mix together French mustard and mayonnaise in equal quantities and add finely chopped onion, crushed garlic and freshly chopped mint to taste.

Stuffed Artichokes

50 artichoke bottoms (about 6 cans)
450g/1lb crab meat (frozen *or* canned)

290ml/½ pint thick mayonnaise (page 316)
2 teaspoons lemon juice
Salt, pepper and cayenne

1. Drain the artichoke bottoms and lay them hollow-side-up on a tray.
2. Pick over the crab meat, removing any pieces of hard cartilage. Drain well and mix with the mayonnaise, lemon juice, salt, pepper and cayenne to taste.
3. Fill each artichoke bottom with a spoonful of crab mixture.

Note: Canned artichoke hearts may be more easily available than bottoms. Drain very well and remove a few inside leaves to make room for the filling.

Makes 50

Anchovy Puff Pastry Fingers

225g/½lb flour-quantity rough-
    puff pastry (page 647)
40 anchovy fillets (about 1
    can)

6 tablespoons milk
Beaten egg

1. Divide the pastry into two and roll each piece thinly to a rectangle 30cm × 10cm/12in × 4in. Slide on to baking sheets and put in the refrigerator to relax.
2. Soak the anchovies in milk for 15 minutes to remove oil and and excess salt. Drain and trim the fillets neatly.
3. Heat the oven to 200°C/400°F, gas mark 6.
4. Brush one piece of pastry with beaten egg, prick with a fork and place the anchovy fillets neatly on it. You should be able to lay out two neat rows of twenty fillets in each row.
5. Cover with the second piece of pastry and brush again with egg wash. Press well together and prick all over with a fork.
6. Bake in the oven for 10–12 minutes until a golden brown. Leave to cool on a wire rack.
7. When cold cut the pastry into neat fingers of 5cm × 1cm/ 2in × ½in in such a way that each finger has an anchovy fillet sandwiched between it.
8. Warm through before serving.

Makes 40

Asparagus Rolls

15 pieces canned asparagus
Butter

15 slices very fresh brown bread
Pepper and salt

1. Drain the asparagus well on absorbent paper. It should be as dry as possible.

2. Butter the bread, season and cut off the crusts.
3. Lay a piece of asparagus along the edge of a slice of bread and roll up.
4. Trim the edges neatly and cut in half. If the slice of bread is very large it will have to be trimmed or the roll will be too thick.

Note: If the bread is not fresh enough to roll easily without cracking, the slices (crusts cut off) can be lightly rolled with a rolling pin before buttering: this makes them easier to roll up. If the rolls are inclined to unravel lay them tightly packed in a covered box in the refrigerator for a few hours (or overnight).

Makes 30

Twisted Cheese Straws

170g/6oz plain flour
Pinch of salt
100g/3½oz butter
45g/1½oz grated Parmesan *or*
  mixed Parmesan and
  Gruyère *or* Cheddar cheese

Pinch of pepper
Pinch of cayenne pepper
Pinch of dry English mustard
Beaten egg

1. Set the oven to 190°C/375°F, gas mark 5.
2. Sift the flour into a basin with a pinch of salt. Rub the butter into the flour with your fingertips until the mixture resembles breadcrumbs. Add the grated cheese and seasonings.
3. Bind the mixture together with enough egg to make a stiff dough. Refrigerate for 10 minutes.
4. Line a baking sheet with greaseproof paper. Roll the paste into a rectangle and cut into strips 9cm × 2cm/3½in × ¾in. Twist each strip two to three times like a barley sugar stick. Bake for 8–10 minutes. They should be a biscuit brown.

Makes 50

Cheese Sablés

225g/¼lb plain flour
Salt and freshly ground black
  pepper
225g/¼lb butter
225g/¼lb Gruyère *or* strong

Cheddar cheese, grated
Pinch of dry mustard
Pinch of cayenne pepper
Beaten egg

1. Set the oven to 190°C/375°F, gas mark 5. Line two baking sheets with greaseproof paper. This will prevent the sablés burning at the edges.
2. Sift the flour with a pinch of salt into a bowl. Rub in the butter until the mixture resembles breadcrumbs.
3. Add the cheese, salt, pepper, mustard and cayenne. Work into a paste but do not over-handle or the pastry will become greasy and be tough.
4. Roll out on a floured board until 5mm/¼in thick. Cut into rounds or triangles and brush with beaten egg.
5. Bake until golden brown (about 10 minutes). Leave to cool on a wire rack.

Makes 24

SNACKS AND SAVOURIES

Welsh Rarebit

55g/2oz Gruyere cheese
55g/2oz Cheddar cheese
Salt, pepper and cayenne
1 egg, beaten

1 tablespoon beer
2 slices bread
Butter for spreading

1. Heat the grill.
2. Grate the cheese and mix all but one level tablespoonful with the mustard, seasoning, beaten egg and beer.
3. Toast the bread and spread with butter.
4. Spoon the cheese mixture on to the toast and spread it neatly, making sure that all the edges are covered.
5. Sprinkle over the remaining cheese and grill until nicely browned.

Serves 2

Roquefort Toasts

2 slices streaky rindless
  bacon
110g/¼lb Roquefort cheese
1 level tablespoon tomato
  chutney

1 teaspoon Worcestershire
  sauce
1 teaspoon grated onion
4 slices bread, cut into 4
  squares

1. Set the oven to 200°C/400°F, gas mark 6.
2. Dice the bacon finely. Fry in a heavy pan until crisp but not brittle. Drain well on absorbent paper and break up into small pieces.
3. Mix the Roquefort, tomato chutney, Worcestershire sauce and onion into a smooth paste.
4. Divide the mixture between the squares of bread and spread it evenly, being sure to cover all the edges.
5. Bake for 5 minutes until crisp and brown.
6. Sprinkle with the fried bacon and serve immediately.

Makes 16

Croque Monsieur

85g/3oz butter
8 slices thin white bread
4 slices ham
4 slices Edam *or* Gruyère
  cheese

Freshly ground black pepper
Fat *or* oil for frying

1. Butter the bread.
2. Make four sandwiches, each with a slice of ham and a slice of cheese inside, seasoned with pepper but not salt. Press well together.
3. Fry in 0·5cm/¼in hot fat until golden brown on both sides, turning the sandwiches over as necessary. Drain well, cut in half, and serve immediately.

Serves 4

Mozzarella in Carozza

Oil for deep frying
Butter
8 slices soft white bread
4 large slices Mozzarella cheese

Salt and pepper
Milk
Beaten egg
Breadcrumbs

1. Heat the deep fat until a crumb will sizzle vigorously in it.
2. Butter the bread and make four rounds of cheese sandwiches, seasoning well with salt and pepper, and making sure that there is plenty of filling, mostly in the centre of the sandwich.
3. Trim off the crusts and press the edges together firmly. Lay each sandwich for 1–2 minutes each side in a dish of milk. They should be wet but not thoroughly soggy.
4. Pat the bread dry with a piece of absorbent paper or a cloth, then dip each sandwich in beaten egg, covering them well. Dip the edges in the breadcrumbs, then again in more egg, to seal them well.

5. Fry until crisp and brown and serve at once.

Note: The carozzas ('carriages' for the cheese) can also be shallow-fried, turning once to brown the second side.

Sausage Rolls

400g/14oz sausage-meat
30g/1oz chopped parsley
30g/1oz chopped onion
Salt and pepper

225g/½lb flour-quantity
   shortcrust pastry (page 645)
1 egg, beaten

1. Set the oven to 200 C/400 F, gas mark 6.
2. Mix together sausage-meat, parsley, onion and seasonings.
3. Roll out the pastry to a large rectangle about 0·25cm/⅛in thick and cut in half lengthwise.
4. With floured hands roll the meat mixture into two long sausages the same length as the pastry and place one down the centre of each piece.
5. Damp one edge of each strip and bring the pastry over the sausage-meat, pressing the edges together and making sure that the join is underneath the roll.
6. Brush with beaten egg. Cut into 5cm/2in lengths. Using a pair of scissors snip a small V in the top of each sausage roll. (This is to allow steam to escape during cooking. A couple of small diagonal slashes made with a sharp knife will do as well.)
7. Place on a baking sheet and bake for 25–30 minutes.

Makes 12

Cheese Aigrettes

105g/3¾oz plain flour
Salt and pepper
½ teaspoon mustard
Cayenne pepper
85g/3oz butter
225ml/7½ fl.oz water

3 eggs, lightly beaten
55g/2oz strong Cheddar cheese,
  finely diced
Oil *or* fat for deep frying
Grated Parmesan cheese

1. Sift the flour with the seasonings.
2. Slowly heat the butter and water together in a large pan. Immediately the butter is completely melted bring to a full rolling boil and tip in the flour. Take off the heat at once and beat with a wooden spoon until the mixture leaves the side of the pan. Allow to cool for 10 minutes.
3. Gradually beat in the eggs until the mixture is smooth and shiny and of a 'dropping' consistency. (You may not need all the egg.) Add the Cheddar cheese.
4. Heat the deep fat until a crumb will sizzle vigorously in it.
5. Shape the mixture to even-sized balls (using 2 teaspoons) and drop them into the hot fat. Fry only a few at a time, leaving plenty of room for them to rise. Cook for about 7 minutes or until they are puffed and golden.
6. Lift them out and drain on absorbent paper. Dust with grated Parmesan cheese and serve without delay.

Makes about 30

Angels on Horseback

12 oysters
6 rashers rindless streaky bacon
6 small slices bread

Butter
Watercress

1. Set the oven to 200°C/400°F, gas mark 6. Heat the grill.
2. Prepare the oysters: wrap a tea-towel round your left hand. Place an oyster on your left palm with the flat side upwards. Slip a short, wide-bladed kitchen or oyster knife under the hinge and push it into the oyster. Press the middle fingers of your left hand on to the shell and with your right hand jerk up the knife and prize the two shells apart. Free the oyster from its base.
3. On a board, stretch the bacon with the back of a knife (this helps to prevent shrinking during cooking). Wrap half a rasher around each oyster. Place the rolls on a baking sheet, tightly packed side by side to prevent them unravelling. Bake for about 8 minutes.
4. Meanwhile cut the bread into rounds and toast them. Butter the toast and set two 'angels' on each round. Arrange on a serving dish and garnish with watercress.

Serves 3

Devils on Horseback

12 prunes   6 small slices bread
6 rashers rindless streaky bacon   Butter
Mango chutney   Watercress

1. Pour boiling water over the prunes and leave to soak for 30 minutes. Set the oven to 200°C/400°F, gas mark 6. Heat the grill.
2. Remove the stones from the prunes and stuff the cavity with half a teaspoon of mango chutney.
3. On a board stretch the bacon with the back of a knife (this helps to prevent shrinking during cooking). Wrap half a rasher around each prune.
4. Place on a baking sheet, packed tightly side by side to prevent them unravelling. Bake for about 8 minutes.
5. Meanwhile cut the bread into rounds and toast them. Butter

the toast and set two 'devils' on each round. Arrange on a serving dish and garnish with watercress.

Serves 3

Scotch Woodcock

8 anchovy fillets
30g/1oz butter
Freshly ground black pepper
4 slices bread, crustless
4 egg yolks

290ml/¼ pint single cream
1 tablespoon chopped fresh
  parsley
Pinch of cayenne pepper

1. Heat the grill.
2. Pound the anchovy fillets into the butter and add pepper to taste.
3. Toast the bread and spread thinly with the anchovy paste. Put on to a heated plate and keep warm.
4. Put the egg yolks, cream, parsley and cayenne pepper together in a saucepan. Stir or whisk over moderate heat until thick and creamy.
5. Pour over the toasts and serve immediately.

Serves 4

Camembert Fritters

1 Camembert cheese, chilled
1 beaten egg
Dried white breadcrumbs

Oil for frying
Deep-fried parsley (page 787)

1. Cut the chilled Camembert into small wedges and roll each first in beaten egg, then in breadcrumbs. Chill again for 30 minutes.
2. Heat the oil in a deep fryer until smoking hot. Test for heat by putting in a crumb: if it starts to sizzle immediately the fat is ready.

3. Fry until very pale brown. Drain well.
4. Serve the fritters at once, garnished with the parsley.

Note: These are delicious served with gooseberry sauce.

Serves 3

Mushroom Strudel

225g/½lb streaky bacon rashers
30g/1oz butter
2 small onions, finely chopped
450g/1lb button mushrooms, sliced
150ml/¼ pint stock
Salt and freshly ground black pepper
1 tablespoon chopped fresh parsley
225g/½lb flour-quantity strudel paste, rolled and pulled out (page 653)
Melted butter
Beaten egg

1. Set the oven to 200°C/400°F, gas mark 6.
2. Cut the rind off the bacon and dice the meat. Fry the bacon pieces in their own fat until cooked and slightly browned. Add the 30g/1oz of butter.
3. Reduce the heat, add the onion and cook until soft but not coloured. Add the mushrooms and cook briskly for 30 seconds. Add the stock.
4. Season with salt and pepper and add the chopped parsley. Boil rapidly to reduce the liquid by half. Allow to cool.
5. Cut the strudel leaves into 13cm/5in squares. Brush each square with melted butter.
6. With a draining spoon lift the mushroom mixture on to the centre of each square.
7. Using both hands, draw the edges of the pastry together so that the strudel looks like a Dick Whittington sack. Pinch the 'neck' of the sack with your fingers to secure it tightly. Alternatively, roll each strudel up into a sausage shape. Brush the pastry bag with beaten egg. Bake on a greased baking sheet for 25 minutes or until the pastry is a golden brown.

Note: When working with strudel paste, it is vital to prevent the thin leaves drying out and cracking. Keep paste covered with polythene or a damp cloth, and when the leaves are exposed to the air, work fast. Brush the strudels with butter as quickly as you can.

Serves 4

MISCELLANEOUS

Clarified Butter

Method 1: Put butter in a pan with a cupful of water and heat until the butter is melted and frothy. Allow to cool and set solid, then lift the butter, now clarified, off the top of the liquid.

Method 2: Heat the butter until foaming without allowing it to burn. Pour it through a fine muslin or a double layer of J-cloth

Method 3: Melt butter in a heavy pan and skim off the froth with a perforated spoon.

Note: Clarified butter will act as a 'seal' on pâtés or potted meats, and is useful for frying as it will stand great heat before burning.

Croutons

2 slices bread from an unsliced slightly stale white loaf

Oil for frying
Salt

1. Cut the crusts off the bread and cut into small 0·5cm/¼in cubes.
2. Heat the oil until a crumb will sizzle vigorously in it. Fry the bread for about 1 minute or until golden brown.
3. Drain on absorbent paper and sprinkle with salt.

Walnut Bread

1½ slices brown bread per person

Butter
Chopped walnuts

1. Place a whole loaf in the deep freeze for half an hour. This will stiffen the loaf and make it easier to cut accurately.
2. Using a sharp knife cut off the crust and spread the exposed bread with softened butter.
3. Cut a thin slice and repeat until you have enough slices.
4. Place each slice, butter side down, in a flat dish containing the walnuts, and press down slightly so that the walnuts stick to the butter.
5. Cut each slice in half diagonally.

Melba Toast

6 slices white bread

1. Light the grill and set the oven to 150°C/300°F, gas mark 2.
2. Grill the bread on both sides until well browned.
3. While still hot, quickly cut off the crusts and split the bread in half horizontally.
4. Put the toast in the oven and leave until dry and brittle.

Note: Melba toast can be kept for a day or two in an airtight tin but it will lose its flavour if kept longer, and is undoubtedly best straight from the oven.

French Toast

4 slices white bread
2 eggs
150ml/¼ pint milk

Good pinch of nutmeg
55g/2oz butter
Oil

1. Cut the crusts from the bread. Cut each slice into four fingers.
2. Beat the eggs, milk and nutmeg together in a pie dish or soup plate.
3. Dip the pieces of bread in this mixture, coating them well.
4. Melt half the butter with a tablespoon of oil in a heavy-bottomed frying pan. When the butter is foaming fry the bread in it until golden brown on both sides. Drain on absorbent paper. Add the rest of the butter and more oil as needed, until all the bread fingers are done.

Note: French toast is sometimes served with crisp bacon, or with marmalade, maple syrup or a mixture of sugar and cinnamon.

Makes 16

Praline

Few drops oil
55g/2oz unblanched (with the skins on) almonds

55g/2oz caster sugar

1. Oil a baking sheet.
2. Put the almonds and sugar in a heavy pan, and set over a gentle heat. Stir with a metal spoon as the sugar begins to melt and brown. When thoroughly caramelized (browned) tip onto the oiled sheet.
3. Allow to cool completely, then pound to a coarse powder in a mortar or blender.
4. Store in an air-tight jar.

Note: Whole praline almonds, as sold in the streets of Paris, are made in the same way, but are not crushed to a powder. They are sometimes used for cake decoration.

Deep-fried Parsley

Pick sprigs of fresh but dry parsley and place in a frying basket. Heat the oil until a crumb will sizzle in it, then lower the basket into the fat. It will hiss furiously. When the noise stops the parsley is cooked. It should be bright green and brittle, with a very good concentrated flavour.

Note: To avoid splashing hot fat, tie parsley on the end of a piece of string and lower into the fat from a height.

INDEX